MANAGEMENT

McGRAW-HILL SERIES IN MANAGEMENT

Fred Luthans and Keith Davis, *Consulting Editors*

Allen: The Management Profession
Arnold and Feldman: Organizational Behavior
Benton: Supervision and Mangement
Buchele: The Management of Business and Public Organizations
Cascio: Managing Human Resources: Productivity, Quality of Work Life, Profits
Cleland and King: Management: A Systems Approach
Cleland and King: Systems Analysis and Project Management
Dale: Management: Theory and Practice
Davis and Newstrom: Human Behavior at Work: Organizational Behavior
Davis and Newstrom: Organizational Behavior: Readings and Exercises
Del Mar: Operations and Industrial Management: Designing and Managing for Productivity
Dobler, Lee, and Burt: Purchasing and Materials Management: Text and Cases
Dunn and Rachel: Wage and Salary Administration: Total Compensation Systems
Feldman and Arnold: Managing Individual and Group Behavior in Organizations
Finch, Jones, and Litterer: Managing for Organizational Effectiveness: An Experimental
    Approach
Flippo: Personnel Management
Frederick, Davis, Post: Business and Society: Management, Public Policy, Ethics
Gerloff: Organizational Theory and Design: A Strategic Approach for Management
Hampton: Management
Hampton: Inside Management: Readings from *Business Week*
Hicks and Gullett: Management
Hicks and Gullett: Modern Business Management: A Systems and Environmental
    Approach
Hicks and Gullett: Organizations: Theory and Behavior
Hodgetts: Effective Supervision: A Practical Approach
Jauch and Glueck: Business Policy and Strategic Management
Jauch and Glueck: Strategic Management and Business Policy
Jauch and Townsend: Cases in Strategic Management and Business Policy
Johnson, Kast, and Rosenzweig: The Theory and Management of Systems
Karlins: The Human Use of Human Resources
Kast and Rosenzweig: Experiential Exercises and Cases in Management
Knudson, Woodworth, and Bell: Management: An Experiential Approach
Koontz, O'Donnell, and Weihrich: Essentials of Management
Koontz and Weihrich: Management
Kopelman: Managing Productivity in Organizations: A Practical, People-Oriented
    Perspective
Levin, McLaughlin, Lamone, and Kottas: Production/Operations Management:
    Contemporary Policy for Managing Operating Systems
Luthans: Organizational Behavior

Luthans and Thompson: Contemporary Readings in Organizational Behavior

McNichols: Executive Policy and Strategic Planning

McNichols: Policymaking and Executive Actions

Maier: Problem-Solving Discussions and Conferences: Leadership Methods and Skills

Margulies and Raia: Conceptual Foundations of Organizational Development

Mayer: Production and Operations Management

Miles: Theories of Management: Implications for Organizational Behavior and Development

Miles and Snow: Organizational Strategy, Structure, and Process

Mills: Labor-Management Relations

Mitchell and Larson: People in Organizations: An Introduction to Organizational Behavior

Molander: Responsive Capitalism: Case Studies in Corporate Social Conduct

Monks: Operations Mangement: Theory and Problems

Newstrom, Reif, and Monczka: A Contingency Approach to Management: Readings

Parker: The Dynamics of Supervision

Pearce and Robinson: Corporate Strategies: Readings from Business Week

Porter, Lawler, and Hackman: Behavior in Organizations

Prasow and Peters: Arbitration and Collective Bargaining: Conflict Resolution in Labor Relations

Quick and Quick: Organizational Stress and Preventive Management

Reddin: Managerial Effectiveness

Rue and Holland: Strategic Management: Concepts and Experiences

Rugman, Lecraw, and Booth: International Business: Firm and Environment

Sartain and Baker: The Supervisor and the Job

Sayles: Leadership: What Effective Managers Really Do . . . and How They Do It

Schlesinger, Eccles, and Gabarro: Managing Behavior in Organizations: Text, Cases and Readings

Schroeder: Operations Management: Decision Making in the Operations Function

Sharplin: Strategic Management

Shore: Operations Management

Steers and Porter: Motivation and Work Behavior

Steinhoff and Burgess: Small Business Management Fundamentals

Sutermeister: People and Productivity

Vance: Corporate Leadership: Boards, Directors, and Strategy

Walker: Human Resource Planning

Weihrich: Management Excellence: Productivity through MBO

Werther and Davis: Personnel Management and Human Resources

Wofford, Gerloff, and Cummins: Organizational Communications: The Keystone to Managerial Effectiveness

NINTH EDITION

MANAGEMENT

Harold Koontz
(Deceased)
University of California, Los Angeles

Heinz Weihrich
University of San Francisco

McGraw-Hill Book Company

New York   St. Louis   San Francisco   Auckland   Bogotá   Caracas
Colorado Springs   Hamburg   Lisbon   London   Madrid   Mexico   Milan
Montreal   New Delhi   Oklahoma City   Panama   Paris   San Juan
São Paulo   Singapore   Sydney   Tokyo   Toronto

MANAGEMENT

1234567890   VNHVNH   89210987

ISBN 0-07-035552-5

This book was set in Baskerville by the College Composition Unit
in cooperation with Better Graphics, Inc.
The editor was Kathleen L. Loy;
the designer was Charles Carson;
the cover designer was Rafael Hernandez;
the production supervisor was Leroy A. Young.
Von Hoffmann Press Inc., was printer and binder.

Cover Photo Credits

Stockholm—© 1985 Donald Johnson/The Stock Market
Manhattan skyline—© 1982 Louis Goldman/Photo Researchers, Inc.
Hong Kong—© 1985 Andrew Holbrooke/Black Star

Library of Congress Cataloging-in-Publication Data

Koontz, Harold (date).
    Management.

    (McGraw-Hill series in management)
    Includes bibliographies and indexes.
    1. Management   2. Industrial management.
I. Weihrich, Heinz.   II. Title.   III. Series.
HD31.K6   1988   658.4   87-21519
ISBN 0-07-035552-5

About the Authors

HEINZ WEIHRICH is Professor of Management at the University of San Francisco. He received his doctorate degree from the University of California, Los Angeles (UCLA), where he conducted the first research study on management by objectives as a comprehensive, integrated management system. Weihrich taught at Arizona State University, the University of California at Los Angeles, and in Europe, and was a visiting scholar at the University of California at Berkeley. He has published several books, including *Management Excellence: Productivity through MBO; Essentials of Management*, fourth edition, with Professors Harold Koontz and Cyril O'Donnell; and *Executives Skills: A Management by Objectives Approach*, with Professors George S. Odiorne and Jack Mendleson. Three of his books have been translated into several other languages. Over eighty of his articles have been published in the United States and abroad. Weihrich is a member of the core faculty at Eastman Kodak Company, and his business and consulting experience in the United States and abroad includes work with firms such as Volkswagen and Hughes Aircraft Company. He is listed in *International Businessmen's Who's Who, Men of Achievement*, and *Who's Who in the West*.

The late HAROLD KOONTZ was active as a business and government executive, university professor, company board chairman and director, management consultant, worldwide lecturer to top management groups, and author of many books and articles. From 1950 he was Professor of Management and from 1962 Mead Johnson Professor of Management at the University of California, Los Angeles; from 1978 to 1982 he was World Chancellor at The International Academy of Management. He was author or coauthor of nineteen books and ninety journal articles, and his *Principles of Management* (now in its ninth edition as *Management*) has been translated into sixteen languages. His *Board of Directors and Effective Management* was given the Academy of Management Book Award in 1968. After taking his doctorate at Yale, Professor Koontz served as Assistant to the Trustees of the New Haven Railroad, Chief of the Traffic Branch of the War Production Board, Assistant to the Vice President of the Association of American Railroads, Assistant to the President of Trans World Airlines, and Director of Sales for Convair. He acted as management consultant for, among others, Hughes Tool Company, Hughes Aircraft Company, Purex Corporation, KLM Royal Dutch Airlines, Metropolitan Life Insurance Company, Occidental Petroleum Corporation, and General Telephone Company. Professor Koontz's honors included election as a Fellow of the American and the International Academies of Management, and a term of service as President of the American Academy of Management. He received the Mead Johnson Award in 1962 and the Society for Advancement of Management Taylor Key Award in 1974 and is listed in *Who's Who in America, Who's Who in Finance and Industry*, and *Who's Who in the World*. Harold Koontz passed away in 1984.

TO MARY
AND URSULA

Contents in Brief

PREFACE   xxv

PART 1. THE BASIS OF MANAGEMENT THEORY AND SCIENCE
CHAPTER 1. MANAGEMENT: SCIENCE, THEORY, AND PRACTICE   3
CHAPTER 2. THE EVOLUTION OF MANAGEMENT THOUGHT AND THE PATTERNS OF
MANAGEMENT ANALYSIS   24

PART 2. PLANNING
CHAPTER 3. THE NATURE AND PURPOSE OF PLANNING   57
CHAPTER 4. OBJECTIVES   80
CHAPTER 5. STRATEGIES, POLICIES, AND PLANNING PREMISES   103
CHAPTER 6. DECISION MAKING   134

PART 3. ORGANIZING
CHAPTER 7. THE NATURE AND PURPOSE OF ORGANIZING   161
CHAPTER 8. BASIC DEPARTMENTATION   181
CHAPTER 9. LINE STAFF AUTHORITY AND DECENTRALIZATION   207
CHAPTER 10. COMMITTEES AND GROUP DECISION MAKING   241
CHAPTER 11. EFFECTIVE ORGANIZING AND ORGANIZATIONAL CULTURE   265

PART 4. STAFFING
CHAPTER 12. THE NATURE AND PURPOSE OF STAFFING   295
CHAPTER 13. SELECTION: MATCHING THE PERSON WITH THE JOB   317
CHAPTER 14. PERFORMANCE APPRAISAL AND CAREER STRATEGY   338
CHAPTER 15. MANAGER AND ORGANIZATION DEVELOPMENT   362

PART 5. LEADING
CHAPTER 16. MANAGING AND THE HUMAN FACTOR   391
CHAPTER 17. MOTIVATION   410
CHAPTER 18. LEADERSHIP   436
CHAPTER 19. COMMUNICATION   460

PART 6. CONTROLLING
CHAPTER 20. THE SYSTEM AND PROCESS OF CONTROLLING   489
CHAPTER 21. CONTROL TECHNIQUES AND INFORMATION TECHNOLOGY   509
CHAPTER 22. PRODUCTIVITY AND OPERATIONS MANAGEMENT   539
CHAPTER 23. OVERALL AND PREVENTIVE CONTROL   565

PART 7. CHALLENGES IN THE DOMESTIC AND INTERNATIONAL ENVIRONMENT
CHAPTER 24. MANAGEMENT AND SOCIETY: THE EXTERNAL ENVIRONMENT,
SOCIAL RESPONSIBILITY, AND ETHICS   599
CHAPTER 25. COMPARATIVE AND INTERNATIONAL MANAGEMENT   622

GLOSSARY   653

INDEXES   665

Contents

Preface   xxv

PART 1. THE BASIS OF MANAGEMENT THEORY AND SCIENCE

CHAPTER 1. MANAGEMENT: SCIENCE, THEORY, AND PRACTICE   3
Definition of Management: Its Nature and Purpose   4
The functions of management / Management as an essential for any organization / Management at different organizational levels / Women in the organizational hierarchy / The aim of all managers / *Perspective: Which Are the Excellent Companies?* / Productivity, effectiveness, and efficiency
Managing: Science or Art?   8
The Elements of Science   9
The scientific approach / The role of management theory / Management techniques / *Perspective: Management Techniques or Fads?*
The Systems Approach to Operational Management   12
Inputs and claimants / The managerial transformation process / The communication system / External variables / Outputs / Reenergizing the system
The Functions of Managers   15
Planning / Organizing / Staffing Leading / Controlling / Coordination, the essence of managership
The Systems Model of Management and the Organization of This Book   18
For Discussion / Exercises / Action Steps   19
Case 1-1. The Paragon Radar Corporation   20
Case 1-2. People Express   21
References / For Further Information   22

CHAPTER 2   THE EVOLUTION OF MANAGEMENT THOUGHT AND THE PATTERNS OF MANAGEMENT ANALYSIS   24
Frederick Taylor and Scientific Management   25
Taylor's major concern / Taylor's principles / *Perspective: Taylor's Principles*
Followers of Taylor   28
Henry L. Gantt / Frank and Lillian Gilbreth
Fayol: Father of Modern Operational-Management Theory   30
Industrial activities / General principles of management / *Perspective: Fayol's Principles* / Elements of management
Emergence of the Behavioral Sciences   33
The emergence of industrial psychology / Development of the sociological approach to management / The Hawthorne studies / Chester Barnard and social systems theory
Recent Contributors to Management Thought   37
Patterns of Management Analysis: A Management Theory Jungle?   37
The empirical, or case, approach / The interpersonal behavior approach / The group behavior approach / The cooperative social systems approach / The sociotechnical systems approach / The decision theory approach / The systems approach / The mathematical, or management science, approach / The contingency, or situational, approach / The managerial roles approach / *Perspective: The Ten Managerial Roles Identified by Mintzberg* / McKinsey's 7-S approach / The operational approach
For Discussion / Exercises/Action Steps   50
Case 2-1. Fred Denny   51
Case 2-2. LMT, Incorporated   52
References / For Further Information   52

PART 2 PLANNING

CHAPTER 3   THE NATURE AND PURPOSE OF PLANNING   57
The Nature of Planning   58
The contribution of planning to purpose and objectives / The primacy of planning / The pervasiveness of
planning / The efficiency of plans
Types of Plans   61
Purposes or missions / Objectives / Strategies / *Perspective: International Dimension: GM's
Strategy* / Policies / *Perspective: A Company's Policy Manual* / Procedures Rules *Perspective: Procedures
and Rules Imposed by the Outside* / Programs / Budgets
Steps in Planning   70
Being aware of opportunities / Establishing objectives / Developing premises / Determining alternative
courses / Evaluating alternative courses / Selecting a course / Formulating derivative plans / Numberizing
plans by budgeting
The Planning Process: A Rational Approach to Goal Achievement   73
The planning period / The commitment principle / What the commitment principle implies / Application of
the commitment principle / Coordination of short- and long-range plans
For Discussion / Exercises/Action Steps   77
Case 3-1. International Machine Corporation   78
Case 3-2. Eastern Electric Corporation   78
References / For Further Information   79

CHAPTER 4.   OBJECTIVES   80
The Nature of Objectives   81
A hierarchy of objectives / *Perspective: Key Result Areas According to Drucker* / The process of setting
objectives and the organizational hierarchy / A network of objectives / Multiplicity of objectives /
Perspective: Some Overall Objectives, or Aims, of a Business / *Perspective: Overall Objectives of a
University*
Evolving Concepts in Management by Objectives   87
Early impetus to MBO / Emphasis on performance appraisal / Emphasis on short-term objectives and
motivation / Inclusion of long-range planning in the MBO process / The systems approach to MBO
The Process of Managing by Objectives   89
Preliminary setting of objectives at the top / Clarification of organizational roles / Setting subordinates
objectives / Recycling objectives
How to Set Objectives   92
Quantitative and qualitative objectives / Setting objectives in government / Guidelines for setting
objectives
Benefits and Weaknesses of Management by Objectives and Some Recommendations   94
Benefits of management by objectives / Weaknesses in managing by objectives
For Discussion / Exercises/Action Steps   98
Case 4-1. Developing Verifiable Goals   99
Case 4-2. The Municipal Water District   100
References / For Further Information   101

CHAPTER 5.   STRATEGIES, POLICIES, AND PLANNING PREMISES   103
The Nature and Purpose of Strategies and Policies   104
Strategy and policy / Giving direction to plans / Furnishing the framework of plans / *Perspective: IBM's
Tactics* / The need for operational planning: Tactics / The effect on all areas of managing
The Strategic Planning Process   106
Perspective: Top Management Choices / *Perspective: Strategies in Declining Industries*
The TOWS Matrix: A Modern Tool for Analysis of the Situation   111
Four alternative strategies / Time dimension and the TOWS Matrix
The Portfolio Matrix: A Tool for Allocating Resources   112
Major Kinds of Strategies and Policies   114
Growth / Finance / Organization / Personnel / Public relations / Products or services / Marketing

Three Generic Competitive Strategies by Porter 116
Overall cost leadership strategy / Differentiation strategy / Focused strategy
Effective Implementation of Strategies 117
Strategic planning failures and some recommendations / Successful implementation of strategies
Premising and Forecasting 120
Environmental Forecasting 121
Values and areas of forecasting / Forecasting with the Delphi technique
The Sales Forecast: Key Plan and Premise 122
The nature and use of the sales forecast / Methods of sales forecasting / Combination of methods / Sales forecasting in practice
Effective Premising 128
For Discussion / Exercises/Action Steps 128
Case 5-1. Semiconductors, Inc. 129
Case 5-2. McDonald's: Serving Fast Food around the World 130
References / For Further Information 131

CHAPTER 6. DECISION MAKING 134
The Importance and Limitations of Rational Decision Making 135
Rationality in decision making / *Perspective: Compaq vs. IBM* / Limited or "bounded" rationality
Development of Alternatives 136
Perspective: Generating Alternatives in an Adverse Situation / The principle of the limiting factor / Discovering the limiting factor
Evaluation of Alternatives 138
Quantitative and qualitative factors / Marginal analysis / Cost effectiveness analysis
Selecting an Alternative: Three Approaches 140
Experience / Experimentation / Research and analysis
Programmed and Nonprogrammed Decisions 143
Decision Making under Certainty, Uncertainty, and Risk 143
Modern Approaches to Decision Making under Uncertainty 144
Risk analysis / Decision trees / *Perspective: Investment in a New Product* / Preference theory
Evaluating the Importance of a Decision 148
Other Factors in Decision Making 149
Decision Support Systems 149
The Systems Approach and Decision Making 152
Perspective: Investment Decisions in a Hospital
For Discussion / Exercises/Action Steps 152
Case 6-1. Olympic Toy Company 153
Case 6-2. King's Supermarkets 153
References / For Further Information 154

SUMMARY OF MAJOR PRINCIPLES OF PLANNING 156

PART 3. ORGANIZING
CHAPTER 7. THE NATURE AND PURPOSE OF ORGANIZING 161
Formal and Informal Organization 162
Formal organization / Informal organization
Organizational Division: The Department 164
Organization Levels and the Span of Management 164
Choosing the span / *Perspective: Moses and the Span of Management* / Problems with organization levels / Operational-management position: A situational approach
Factors Determining an Effective Span 168
Subordinate training / Clarity of delegation of authority / Clarity of plans / Use of objective standards / Rate of change / Communication techniques / Amount of personal contact needed / Variation by organization level / Other factors / The need for balance

Organizational Environment for Entrepreneuring and Intrapreneuring ... 172
The Structure and Process of Organizing ... 173
Perspective: Post-it Notes
The logic of organizing / Some misconceptions
Basic Questions for Effective Organizing ... 176
For Discussion / Exercises/Action Steps ... 176
Case 7-1. Measurement Instruments Corporation ... 177
Case 7-2. American Aircraft Company ... 178
References / For Further Information ... 179

CHAPTER 8. BASIC DEPARTMENTATION ... 181
Departmentation by Simple Numbers ... 182
Departmentation by Time ... 183
Advantages / Disadvantages
Departmentation by Enterprise Function ... 183
Advantages / Disadvantages
Departmentation by Territory or Geography ... 186
Extent of use / Advantages / Disadvantages
Customer Departmentation ... 188
Advantages / Disadvantages
Process or Equipment Departmentation ... 189
Departmentation by Product ... 190
Advantages / Some notes of caution / Disadvantages
Matrix Organization ... 193
Why matrix management is used / Variations in practice / Solutions in engineering and research and development / Solutions in product management / Problems with matrix management / Guidelines for making matrix management effective
Strategic Business Units (SBU) ... 199
Choosing the Pattern of Departmentation ... 199
The aim: Achieving objectives / Mixing types of departmentation
For Discussion / Exercises/Action Steps ... 202
Case 8-1. Agricultural Fertilizer Division of the Northern Chemical Corporation ... 203
Case 8-2. Univeral Food Products Company ... 204
References / For Further Information ... 204

CHAPTER 9. LINE/STAFF AUTHORITY AND DECENTRALIZATION ... 207
Authority and Power ... 208
Line and Staff Concepts ... 209
The nature of line and staff relationships / Line and staff relationships or departmentation? / *Perspective: Line or Staff? What Is Your Career Goal?*
Functional Authority ... 212
Delegation of functional authority / Functional authority as exercised by operating managers / Restricting the area of functional authority / Complications in exercising functional authority
Benefits of Staff ... 215
Limitations of Staff ... 217
The danger of undermining line authority / Lack of staff responsibility / *Perspective: The Role of the Personnel Manager* / Thinking in a vacuum / Managerial problems
Decentralization of Authority ... 218
The nature of decentralization / Different kinds of centralization / *Perspective: Degrees of Decentralization* / Decentralization as a philosophy and policy
Delegation of Authority ... 220
How authority is delegated / Clarity of delegation / Splintered authority / *Perspective: Splintered Authority at the Railroad* / Recovery of delegated authority
The Art of Delegation ... 222
Personal attitudes toward delegation / Guides for overcoming weak delegation

Factors Determining the Degree of Decentralization of Authority   225
Costliness of the decision / Desire for uniformity of policy / Size and character of the organization / History and culture of the enterprise / Management philosophy / Desire for independence / Availability of managers / Control techniques / Decentralized performance / Business dynamics: The pace of change / Environmental influences
Recentralization of Authority   231
Obtaining the Desired Degree of Decentralization   231
Clarifying Decentralization: Chart of Approval Authorization   232
Balance: The Key to Decentralization   233
For Discussion / Exercises/Action Steps   237
Case 9-1. ABC Airlines   237
Case 9-2. Decentralization at American Business Computers and Equipment Company   238
References / For Further Information   239

CHAPTER 10. COMMITTEES AND GROUP DECISION MAKING   241
The Nature of Committees   242
Group processes in committees / Functions and formality of committees / The use of committees in different organizations
Reasons for Using Committees   244
Group deliberation and judgment / Fear of too much authority in a single person / Representation of interested groups / Coordination of departments, plans, and policies / Transmission and sharing of information / Consolidation of authority / Motivation through participation / Avoidance of action
Disadvantages of Committees   248
High cost in time and money / *Perspective: What People Say about Committees* / Compromise at the least common denominator / Indecision / Tendency to be self-destructive / Splitting of responsibility / Tyranny of the minority
The Plural Executive and the Board of Directors   251
Origin / Authority / Role in policy making / Role in policy execution / *Perspective: Trends in the Composition of Boards*
Plural versus Individual Executive   253
American Management Association Survey / Evaluation
Misuse of Committees   255
As replacement for a manager / For research or study / For unimportant decisions / For decisions beyond participants authority / To consolidate divided authority
Successful Operation of Committees   256
Authority / Size / Membership / Subject matter / Chairperson / Minutes / Cost effectiveness
Other Groups in Managing   258
Characteristics of groups / *Perspective: Pressure toward Conformity: How Would You Respond?* / Functions and advantages of groups / Disadvantages of groups
For Discussion / Exercises/Action Steps   261
Case 10-1. The Humbold Retail Chain   262
Case 10-2. Committee Management at the University of California   263
References / For Further Information   263

CHAPTER 11. EFFECTIVE ORGANIZING AND ORGANIZATIONAL CULTURE   265
Some Mistakes in Organizing   266
Failure to plan properly / Failure to clarify relationships / Failure to delegate authority / Failure to balance delegation / Confusion of lines of authority with lines of information / Granting authority without exacting responsibility / Holding people responsible who do not have authority / Careless application of the staff device / Misuse of functional authority / Multiple subordination / Misunderstanding of the function of service departments / Overorganization and underorganization
Avoiding Mistakes by Planning   271
Planning for the ideal / Modification for the human factor / Advantages of organization planning
Avoiding Organizational Inflexibility   272
Signs of inflexibility / Avoiding inflexibility through reorganization / The need for readjustment and change

Making Staff Work Effectively   273
Understanding authority relationships / Making line listen to staff / Keeping staff informed / Requiring completed staff work / Making staff work as a way of organizational life
Avoiding Conflict by Clarification   275
Organization charts / Position descriptions and charts of approval authorizations
Ensuring Understanding of Organizing   278
Teaching the nature of organizing / Recognizing the importance of informal organization
Promoting an Appropriate Organization Culture   280
Defining organization culture / Influence of the leader on organization culture / *Perspective: Merging Corporate Cultures at General Motors*
Contingencies in Organizing   282
Studies by Burns and Stalker / Studies by Woodward / Studies by Lawrence and Lorsch
For Discussion / Exercises/Action Steps   284
Case 11-1. The VGI Company   284
Case 11-2. Organization Culture at IBM   285
References / For Further Information   287

SUMMARY OF MAJOR PRINCIPLES, OR GUIDES, FOR ORGANIZING   289

PART 4. STAFFING
CHAPTER 12. THE NATURE AND PURPOSE OF STAFFING   295
Definition of Staffing   296
Defining the Managerial Job   296
Rewards and Stress of Managing   297
Rewards of managing / *Perspective: Financial Rewards of CEOs* / Stress in managing / Fitting the needs of the individual to the demands of the job
The Systems Approach to Human Resource Management: An Overview of the Staffing Function   299
Factors affecting the number and kinds of managers required / Determination of available managerial resources: The management inventory / Advantages and limitations of the manager inventory chart / Analysis of the need for managers: External and internal information sources / Recruitment, selection, placement, and promotion / Managerial appraisal and career planning / Training and development / Leading and controlling
Situational Factors Affecting Staffing   306
The external environment / *Perspective: Career Opportunities for Women* / The internal environment / *Perspective: Companies with Policies of Promotion from Within*
For Discussion / Exercises/Action Steps   313
Case 12-1. Belden Electronics Company   313
Case 12-2. Texas Oil Company   314
References / For Further Information   314

CHAPTER 13. SELECTION: MATCHING THE PERSON WITH THE JOB   317
Systems Approach to the Selection of Managers: An Overview   317
Position Requirements and Job Design   318
Identifying job requirements / Job design / *Perspective: Job Design at Volvo in Sweden*
Skills and Personal Characteristics Needed by Managers   322
Managerial skills and the organizational hierarchy / Analytical and problem-solving abilities / Personal characteristics needed by managers
Matching Manager Qualifications with Position Requirements   325
Recruitment of managers / Information exchange contributing to successful selection / Selection, placement, and promotion Balancing skills and the age factor / *Perspective: Meet the Young Work Force* / Dual-career couples / The Peter Principle / Responsibility for selection
The Selection Process, Techniques, and Instruments   329
The selection process / Interviews / Tests / Assessment centers / Limitations of the selection process
Orienting and Socializing New Employees   334

For Discussion / Exercises/Action Steps   335
Case 13-1. Carl Wendover   335
Case 13-2. The Denied Promotion   336
References / For Further Information   336

CHAPTER 14. PERFORMANCE APPRAISAL AND CAREER STRATEGY   338
The Purposes and Uses of Appraisal   339
The Conference Board study / The General Electric studies
The Problem of Management Appraisal   340
Choosing the Appraisal Criteria   341
Performance in accomplishing goals / Performance as managers
Traditional Trait Appraisals   342
Weaknesses of trait appraisal / Attempts to strengthen trait rating
Appraising Managers against Verifiable Objectives   344
The appraisal process / Frequency of performance reviews / Three kinds of reviews / Strengths of
appraisal against verifiable objectives / Weaknesses of appraisal against verifiable objectives
A Suggested Program: Appraising Managers as Managers   347
Sample questions for appraising managers as managers / Advantages of the new program / *Perspective:
Performance Appraisal: An Illustration* / Weaknesses of the new program
A Team Evaluation Approach   352
Formulating the Career Strategy   353
Preparation of a personal profile / Development of long-range personal and professional goals / Analysis
of the environment: Threats and opportunities / Analysis of personal strengths and
weaknesses / Development of strategic career alternatives / Consistency testing and strategic
choices / Development of short-range career objectives and action plans / Development of contingency
plans / Implementation of the career plan / Monitoring progress
For Discussion / Exercises/Action Steps   357
Case 14-1. Hardstone Corporation   358
Case 14-2. Foresite Incorporated   358
References / For Further Information   360

CHAPTER 15. MANAGER AND ORGANIZATION DEVELOPMENT   362
The Need for Effective Manager Development   363
Management development failures / Operational management premises / *Perspective: Making
Management Education Relevant*
The Manager Development Process and Training   366
Present job / Next job / Future needs
Approaches to Manager Development: On-the-Job Training   368
Planned progression / Job rotation / Creation of "assistant-to" positions / Temporary
promotions / Committees and junior boards / Coaching
Approaches to Manager Development: Internal and External Training   370
Sensitivity training, T-groups, and encounter groups / *Perspective: The Variety of Conference
Programs* / Conference programs / University management programs / *Perspective: University Executive
Programs* / Readings / Special training programs / Evaluation and transfer
Managing Change   374
Changes that affect manager and organization development / Techniques for initiating
change / Resistance to change
Organizational Conflict   376
Sources of conflict / Managing conflict
Organization Development   377
The organization development process / Grid organization development and other methods / OD in action
For Discussion / Exercises/Action Steps   382
Case 15-1. Aerospace, Inc.   382
Case 15-2. Management Development at the Pendleton Department Stores Corporation   383
References / For Further Information   383

SUMMARY OF MAJOR PRINCIPLES, OR GUIDES, OF STAFFING   386

PART 5. LEADING

CHAPTER 16. MANAGING AND THE HUMAN FACTOR — 391

Human Factors in Managing — 392
Multiplicity of roles / No average person / The importance of personal dignity / Considering the whole person

Behavioral Models — 393
From the rational-economic view to the complex person / Contrasting views and models of people / McGregor's Theory X and Theory Y / Behavioral models in a historical perspective / A dual-model theory / Toward an eclectic view of behavioral models / *Perspective: Some Experiences Supporting the Dual-Model Theory*

Creativity and Innovation — 401
The creative process / Techniques to enhance creativity / Limitations of traditional group discussion / The creative manager / Innovation and entrepreneurship / *Perspective: Creative Thinking at Bell Telephone Laboratory*

Harmonizing Objectives: The Key to Leading — 405
For Discussion / Exercises/Action Steps — 406
Case 16-1. What Do We Know for Sure? — 407
Case 16-2. Customer's Electric Appliance Company — 407
References / For Further Information — 408

CHAPTER 17. MOTIVATION — 410

Motivation and Motivators — 411
Motivation / The need-want-satisfaction chain / *Perspective: Self-Motivation* / The complexity of motivation

Motivation: The Carrot and the Stick — 414
The Hierarchy of Needs Theory — 415
The need hierarchy / Questioning the need hierarchy

The Motivation-Hygiene Approach to Motivation — 417
The Expectancy Theory of Motivation — 418
The Vroom theory and practice / The Porter and Lawler model / Implications for practice

Equity Theory — 421
Reinforcement Theory — 422
McClelland's Needs Theory of Motivation — 422
The need for power / The need for affiliation / The need for achievement / How McClelland's approach applies to managers

Special Motivational Techniques — 424
Money / *Perspective: The Other Side of the Coin* / Participation / Quality of working life (QWL) / *Perspective: QWL in Action*

Job Enrichment — 427
The claims of job enrichment / Limitations of job enrichment / Problems with job enrichment / Making job enrichment effective

A Systems and Contingency Approach to Motivation — 430
Dependence of motivation on organizational climate / Motivation, leadership, and managership

For Discussion / Exercises/Action Steps — 430
Case 17-1. Motivation at the Bradley Clothing Company — 431
Case 17-2. Consolidated Motors Corporation — 432
References / For Further Information — 433

CHAPTER 18. LEADERSHIP — 436

Defining Leadership — 437
Perspective: Leader-Followership at McDonald's
Perspective: Leadership at Southwest Airlines

Ingredients of Leadership — 438
Trait Approaches to Leadership — 439

Leadership Behavior and Styles 440

Styles based on use of authority/ Likert's four systems of management/ _Perspective: Management by Walking Around (MBWA)_/ The managerial grid/ Leadership as a continuum/ _Perspective: Leadership at ITALTEL_

Situational, or Contingency, Approaches to Leadership 449

Fiedler's contingency approach to leadership/ The path-goal approach to leadership effectiveness

For Discussion/ Exercises/Action Steps 455
Case 18-1. Leaders in Government Departments and Agencies 456
Case 18-2. Palmer Machinery Company 456
References/ For Further Information 457

CHAPTER 19. COMMUNICATION 460
The Communication Function in Organizations 461

The importance of communication/ The purpose of communication

The Communication Process 462

The sender of the message/ Use of a channel to transmit the message/ The receiver of the message/ Noise and feedback in communication/ Situational and organizational factors in communication

Communication in the Enterprise 465

The manager's need to know/ The communication flow in the organization/ Perspective: Lack of Upward Communication/ Written, oral, and nonverbal communication

Barriers and Breakdowns in Communication 470

Lack of planning/ Unclarified assumptions/ Semantic distortion/ Poorly expressed messages/ Communication in the international environment/ Loss by transmission and poor retention/ Poor listening and premature evaluation/ Impersonal communication/ Distrust, threat, and fear/ _Perspective: The Closed-Circuit Television Failure_/ Insufficient period for adjustment to change/ Information overload/ Other communication barriers

Toward Effective Communication 474

The Communication audit/ Guidelines for improving communication/ Listening: The key to understanding/ Some tips for improving written communication

Double-Loop Learning 478
Electronic Media in Communication 478

Telecommunication/ Teleconferencing/ The use of computers for information handling

For Discussion/ Exercises/Action Steps 480
Case 19-1. Haynes Fashion Stores, Incorporated 481
Case 19-2. Home Radio and Television Company 482
References/ For Further Information 483

SUMMARY OF MAJOR PRINCIPLES, OR GUIDES, OF LEADING 485

PART 6. CONTROLLING

CHAPTER 20. THE SYSTEM AND PROCESS OF CONTROLLING 489
The Basic Control Process 490

Establishment of standards/ Measurement of performance/ Correction of deviations

Critical Control Points and Standards 492

Questions for selecting critical points of control/ Types of critical-point standards

Control as a Feedback System 494

Perspective: Examples of Feedback Systems

Real-Time Information and Control 496
Feedforward Control 497

Techniques of future-directed control/ Feedforward in engineering/ Feedforward in human systems/ Feedforward versus feedback systems/ Feedforward in management/ Requirements for feedforward control

Requirements for Effective Controls   **502**
Tailoring controls to plans and positions / Tailoring controls to individual managers / Controls pointing up exceptions at critical points / Objectivity of controls / Flexibility of controls / Fitting the control system to the organizational climate / Economy of controls / Controls leading to corrective action
For Discussion / **Exercises/Action Steps**   **506**
Case 20-1. The Kappa Corporation   **506**
Case 20-2. Hanover Space and Electronics Corporation   **507**
References / **For Further Information**   **507**

CHAPTER 21. CONTROL TECHNIQUES AND INFORMATION TECHNOLOGY   **509**
Control Techniques: The Budget   **510**
The concept of budgeting / The purpose of budgeting / Types of budgets / Dangers in budgeting / Variable budgets *Perspective: Example of a Variable Budget* / Alternative and supplementary budgets / Zero-base budgeting / Effective budgetary control
Traditional Nonbudgetary Control Devices   **518**
Statistical data / Special reports and analyses / The operational audit / Personal observation
Time-Event Network Analyses   **520**
Gantt charts / Milestone budgeting / Program evaluation and review technique / *Perspective: Planning and Control in Engineering (PERT)*
Program Budgeting   **525**
What program budgeting is / Problems in applying program budgeting in government
Procedures Planning and Control   **526**
How procedures get out of control / Guidelines for effective procedures / Procedures analysis and electronic data processing
Information Technology   **528**
Perspective: Planning and Control at Volkswagen / Expanding basic data / Information indigestion / Intelligence services
The Use of Computers in Handling Information   **531**
The impact of computers on managers at different organizational levels / The application and impacts of microcomputers
Challenges Created by Information Technology   **532**
Resistence to computer application / Speech recognition devices / Telecommuting / Computer networks
For Discussion / **Exercises/Action Steps**   **535**
Case 21-1. The Electrical Construction Company   **536**
Case 21-2. The Wholesale Drug Company   **536**
References / **For Further Information**   **537**

CHAPTER 22. PRODUCTIVITY AND OPERATIONS MANAGEMENT   **539**
Productivity Problems and Measurement   **540**
Productivity problems / Measuring productivity of knowledge workers / Several approaches to productivity improvement
Production and Operations Management   **541**
Operations Management Systems   **542**
Planning operations / Operating the system / Controlling operations with emphasis on information systems / *Perspective: How an Information System Works*
Operations Research for Planning, Controlling, and Improving Productivity   **547**
The concept of operations research / The essentials of operations research / Operations research procedure / Linear programming / Inventory planning and control / The just-in-time inventory system / Distribution logistics / Limitations of operations research
Other Tools and Techniques for Improving Productivity   **555**
Time-event networks / Value engineering / Work simplification / Quality circles / *Perspective: Quality Circles in Japan* / CAD/CAM and MAP / *Perspective: IBM's PC Convertible*
The Future of Operations Management   **558**
For Discussion / **Exercises/Action Steps**   **559**
Case 22-1. Lampert & Sons Company   **560**

Case 22-2. Manufacturing Requirements Planning (MRP)   561
References / For Further Information   562

CHAPTER 23. OVERALL AND PREVENTIVE CONTROL   565
Control of Overall Performance   566
Budget Summaries and Reports   567
Profit and Loss Control   568
The nature and purpose of profit and loss controls / *Perspective: Kodak's Profit Picture in Full Color Again* / Limitations
Control through Return on Investment (ROI)   570
The return-on-investment system in action / Application to product lines / Advantages / Limitations
Direct Control versus Preventive Control   575
Direct Control   575
Perspective: Control at Apple Computer
Causes of negative deviations from standards / Questionable assumptions underlying direct control
The Principle of Preventive Control   578
Assumptions of the principle of preventive control / Advantages
The Management Audit and the Enterprise Self-Audit   580
The management audit / The enterprise self-audit
Developing Excellent Managers   584
A willingness to learn / Acceleration of management development / The importance of planning for innovation / Measuring and rewarding management / Tailoring information / The need for research and development in tools and techniques / The need for managerial inventions / The need for strong intellectual leadership
For Discussion / Exercises/Action Steps   587
Case 23-1. Hospital Services, Inc.   588
Case 23-2. BankAmerica Corporation   589
References / For Further Information   589

A SUMMARY OF MAJOR PRINCIPLES, OR GUIDES, OF CONTROLLING   592

PART 7. CHALLENGES IN THE DOMESTIC AND INTERNATIONAL ENVIRONMENT
CHAPTER 24. MANAGEMENT AND SOCIETY: THE EXTERNAL ENVIRONMENT,
SOCIAL RESPONSIBILITY, AND ETHICS   599
Operating in a Pluralistic Society   600
The External Environment: Economic   600
Capital / Labor / Price Levels / Government fiscal and tax policy / Customers
The External Environment: Technological   603
The impact of technology: Benefits and problems / Categories of technological change
The External Environment: Social   604
The complexity of environmental forces / Social attitudes, beliefs, and values
The External Environment: Political and Legal   606
The political environment / The legal environment
The Social Responsibility of Managers   607
Social responsibility and social responsiveness / Arguments for and against business involvement in social actions / The mission of the enterprise / Reaction or proaction? / The role of the government / The influence of values and performance criteria on behavior / The social audit
Ethics in Managing   611
Ethical theories and a model for political behavior decisions / *Perspective: A Code of Ethics for Government Service* / Institutionalizing ethics / Code of ethics and its implementation through formal committees / Factors that raise ethical standards / Differing ethical standards of various societies
For Discussion / Exercises/Action Steps   617
Case 24-1. To Stay or Not to Stay in South Africa   618
Case 24-2. Bishops' Pastoral   618
References / For Further Information   619

CHAPTER 25. COMPARATIVE AND INTERNATIONAL MANAGEMENT 622

Comparative Management 623
Management as a critical element in economic growth / *Perspective: Is Management Catching On in the Soviet Union?* / A new management frontier? / Is management culture-bound? / The Koontz model of comparative management

Differences in Managing in Selected Countries 628
France: Le plan / Germany: Authority and codetermination / Selected factors influencing managing in other countries / Preparing foreign managers for work in the United States

Japanese Management and Theory Z 630
Lifetime employment / Decision making / Japanese versus U.S. management practices and Theory Z / Japanese companies operating in the United States / *Perspective: Bridgestone Tire Company*

International Management and Multinational Corporations 634
The nature and purpose of international business / Multinational corporations / *Perspective: Women CEO Manages by the Textbook*

The Managerial Functions in International Business 638
Planning in the multinational corporation / Organizing the multinational corporation / Staffing in the multinational corporation / Leading in the multinational corporation / *Perspective: Leadership at Lufthansa* / Controlling in the multinational corporation

Toward a Unified Global Theory of Management 642
The need for untangling the management theory jungle / The empirical approach: Distilling basics / Systems thinking—not a separate approach / Situational and contingency approaches—not new or separate / The confluence of motivation and leadership theory / The new, managerially oriented "organization development" / The impact of technology: Researching an old problem / The merger of theory and practice / *Perspective: Recent Research Supporting the Operational Approach* / Clarification of semantics: Some hopeful signs / The internationalization of management

For Discussion / Exercises/Action Steps 646
Case 25-1. Consolidated Computers, Inc. 646
Case 25-2. Honda Moves to the United States 647
References / For Further Information 648

GLOSSARY 653

INDEXES
Name Index 667
Organization and Product Index 671
Subject Index 674

PREFACE

*T*his is an invitation to the reader of this book to become more effective as a person and as a managerial leader by applying the principles, concepts, and theories discussed in these pages. The book prepares men and women for an exciting, challenging, and rewarding career in managing.

The ninth edition of *Management*, whose prior editions and translations into sixteen languages have been well received by readers and educators around the world, is an up-to-date and comprehensive introduction to managing.

Who Will Benefit from This Book?

All persons who work in enterprises will benefit from learning about managing. They include, for example, aspiring managers, those who already possess managerial skills and who want to become more effective, and other professionals who want to understand the organization in which they work. This book is relevant not just to business firms but to nonbusiness organizations as well: government, health care, and educational institutions, and other not-for-profit enterprises.

The functions of managers, as managers, are essentially the same whether they are first-line supervisors, middle managers, or top executives. To be sure, there may be considerable variation in environment, scope of authority, and types of problems dealt with. But all managers undertake the same basic functions to obtain results by establishing an environment for effective and efficient performance of individuals operating in groups.

Organization of the Book

Managerial knowledge is classified according to the functions of planning, organizing, staffing, leading, and controlling. A systems model, shown on the inside cover, integrates these functions into a system and links the enterprise with its environment.

Part 1 covers the basis of management theory and practice, main contributions to management thought, and the patterns of management analysis. Parts 2 through 6 focus on the managerial functions of planning, organizing, staffing, leading, and controlling. Part 7 discusses challenges in the domestic and international environment, including social responsibility and ethics, as well as comparative and international management. These topics are placed in the last part because they are the basis of the courses on business and society, as well as international business management, that are taught at many colleges and universities after students have learned about the principles of management.

Revision Work in This Edition

This is one of the most comprehensive revisions since the book was first published in 1955. We have retained material that was well received over the years and have added much new information. For example, we have built on the strong characteristics of the eighth edition—its breadth and depth, its use of examples and cases—identified in the textbook survey published in the *Academy of Management Review* (July 1986), while at the same time adding modern features, ideas, and techniques. Some structural changes have also been made.

In this and earlier editions, we have responded to two major influences. One is the valuable feedback from teachers, scholars, and students who have used past editions at various levels of academic and practical management education in a wide variety of universities and operating enterprises. The other is the great volume of research, new ideas, and advanced techniques, especially those being applied to management from the behavioral, social, and physical sciences. The emphasis is on managerial practice based on sound theory.

Although not all changes can be mentioned here, certain revision work should be pointed out. All chapters have been updated, and their number has been reduced (from twenty-nine) to twenty-five in this edition. For example, the old chapters "The Emergence of Management Thought" and "Patterns of Management Analysis" have now been combined as Chapter 2. A great deal of material from the chapter "Premising: Essential Step in Planning" in the previous edition is now included in Chapter 5, "Strategies, Policies, and Planning Premises." Similar changes, indicated in the titles, have been made in chapters dealing with organizing and controlling.

While some material has been condensed, other topics have been expanded. For example, a separate chapter is now devoted to the topic of management and society, discussing the external environment, social responsibility, and ethics. Similarly, a new chapter on comparative and international management covers managerial practices in both Asian and European countries.

New topics.   These are some of the new topics in this edition:

- Identification of characteristics of excellent companies (Chapter 1)
- The importance of the role of women in managing (see, for example, Chapters 1, 12, and 25)

- McKinsey's 7–S framework, which was the conceptual framework for the book *In Search of Excellence* by Peters and Waterman (Chapter 2)

- Porter's generic competitive strategies (Chapter 5)

- Decision support systems (Chapter 6)

- Entrepreneuring and intrapreneuring (Chapter 7)

- Organization culture (Chapter 11)

- Strategic career management (Chapter 14)

- Self-motivation (Chapter 17)

- Equity theory (Chapter 17)

- Argyris's double-loop learning (Chapter 19)

- The role of microcomputers, computer networks, telecommuting, and the office of the future (see especially Chapter 21)

- Productivity of knowledge workers for gaining a competitive advantage (Chapter 22)

- Computer-aided design (CAD), computer-aided manufacturing (CAM), and manufacturing automation protocol (MAP) (Chapter 22)

- A model for ethical decision making (Chapter 24)

- A code of ethics for government service (Chapter 24)

- Managing in various countries (Chapter 25)

New or expanded features.　Here are some other new or expanded features:

- Many examples are given from companies such as Compaq, Eastman Kodak, General Electric, General Motors, IBM, Lufthansa, McDonald's, 3M Company (Post-It Notes), and Volkswagen.

- Two cases are presented at the end of each chapter. Almost all cases describe real situations, many of them based on our consulting experience. Sometimes company names are disguised to protect confidentiality, but other cases reveal the names of such firms as People Express, Honda, IBM, and McDonald's, as well as the University of California and the country of South Africa.

- Many real-life situations illustrate managerial concepts and theories thoughout the book.

- Boxed inserts called "Perspectives" provide additional insights.

- Each chapter has two recommendations for "Exercises/Action Steps" to encourage student involvement in the subject.

- Many new figures and tables have been added. For example, Table 2–2 compares McKinsey's 7–S framework with the chapters in this book.

- There are frequent references to nonbusiness organizations.

- An organization and product index has been added to the comprehensive name and subject indexes.

- New terms have been added to the already comprehensive glossary.

Learning Aids

Each chapter begins with learning objectives and concludes with discussion questions and the new "Exercises/Action Steps" section. Then, as mentioned above, there are two cases for each chapter, giving a total of 50 cases. "For Further Information" suggests sources for additional study and/or preparation of term papers.

Parts 2 through 6, dealing with the five managerial functions—planning, organizing, staffing, leading, and controlling—are each summarized by a list of principles, or guides.

Instructional Aids

Because this text has been successfully used for over 30 years and has been updated with each revision, several teaching aids have been developed and tested in the classroom.

- *Study Guide* by John Halff.

- *Instructor's Resource Manual* prepared by John Halff.

- *Transparency Masters.*

- *Test Bank* by Thomas Quirk.

Acknowledgments

It is noted with very deep regret that Dr. Harold Koontz passed away in 1984. He is sorely missed by those who knew him. At the memorial session at the Academy of Management meeting in 1984, Professor Ronald Greenwood stated that Howdy Koontz was many years ahead of his time. Indeed, his inspiration and guidance popularized the classification of management knowledge according to the managerial functions, a framework now used around the world. He will always be remembered for his contributions to management and for his many books, especially the first edition of this book, with Cyril O'Donnell, originally published as *Principles of Management* in 1955 and continuously updated ever since.

As might be expected in a book of this kind, we are indebted to so many persons that a complete acknowledgment would be encyclopedic. When appropriate, scholars, writers, and managers are acknowledged through references in the text. Managers with whom we have served in business, government, education, and other enterprises have contributed by word and precept. Thousands of managers in all kinds of enterprises in various countries have honored us over the years by allowing us to test our ideas in executive training classes and lectures. Especially helpful were the Eastman Kodak managers around the world who generously shared their international experiences. To the executives of all these companies with whom we have been privileged to work as directors or consultants, we express special appreciation for the opportunity to gain the clinical practice of managing.

Many colleagues, scholars, managers, and students have contributed their ideas and suggestions to this book. My good friend Professor Keith Davis, at Arizona State University, was particularly helpful with his advice. One of my mentors at UCLA, Professor George S. Steiner, has done much to stimulate my interest in the area of planning. Professors Peter F. Drucker, George S. Odiorne, and Gene Seyna, to whom my book *Management Excellence: Productivity through MBO* has been dedicated, have sharpened my thinking about goal-driven management systems and managerial productivity.

We are indebted to those who reviewed this edition and offered valuable suggestions. They include Matt A. Amano, Oregon State University; Richard D. Babcock, University of San Francisco; Allen Bluedorn, University of Missouri—Columbia; James C. Carver, Iowa State University; Doug Elvers, University of North Carolina—Chapel Hill; G. B. Giglioni, Mississippi State University; Dr. Nell Hartley, Robert Morris College; Timothy Hinkin, University of Virginia—Charlottesville; Pravin C. Kamdar, Cardinal Stritch College; James C. McElroy, Iowa State University; Dr. Alfred J. Modica, Mercy College; Andrew J. Papageorge, California State College; Thomas Quirk, Principia College; Dr. Mary Thibodeaux, North Texas State University; and John Villarreal, California State University—Hayward.

We wish to thank the many people at McGraw-Hill who contributed to this edition, especially Kathleen L. Loy and Laura D. Warner. We also appreciate the conscientious and diligent work of Robin Scroggins and Elizabeth Demesa in typing the manuscript.

Finally, my wife, Ursula, has helped greatly with her patience and critique. To her and Mary Koontz this book is dedicated.

Heinz Weihrich

PART 1

The Basis of Management Theory and Science

Management: Science, Theory, and Practice

CHAPTER OBJECTIVES

After completing this chapter, you should be able to:

1. Define and describe the nature and purpose of management.

2. Understand that management, as used in this book, applies to all kinds of organizations and to managers at all organizational levels.

3. Identify excellent companies and their characteristics.

4. Recognize that the aim of all managers is to be productive, that is, to carry out their activities effectively and efficiently and to create a "surplus."

5. Explain that management as practice is an art, applying the underlying theory and science in light of situations.

6. Realize that managing requires a systems approach and that practice must always take into account situations and contingencies.

7. Define the managerial functions of planning, organizing, staffing, leading, and controlling.

8. Understand how this book is organized.

*O*ne of the most important human activities is managing. Ever since people began forming groups to accomplish aims they could not achieve as individuals, managing has been essential to ensure the coordination of individual efforts. As society has come to rely increasingly on group effort, and as many organized groups have become large, the task of managers has been rising in importance. The purpose of this book is to promote excellence of all persons in organizations, but especially managers, aspiring managers, and other professionals.[1]

DEFINITION OF MANAGEMENT: ITS NATURE AND PURPOSE

We define **management** as *the process of designing and maintaining an environment in which individuals, working together in groups, accomplish efficiently selected aims.* This basic definition needs to be expanded:

1. As managers, people carry out the managerial functions of planning, organizing, staffing, leading, and controlling.

2. Management applies to any kind of organization.

3. It applies to managers at all organizational levels.

4. The aim of all managers is the same: to create a surplus.

5. Managing is concerned with productivity; that implies effectiveness and efficiency.

The Functions of Management

Many scholars and managers have found that the analysis of management is facilitated by a useful and clear organization of knowledge. As a first order of classification of knowledge, we have used the five functions of managers: planning, organizing, staffing, leading, and controlling. Thus, the concepts, principles, theory, and techniques are organized around these functions and become the basis of this book.

We have used and tested this framework since the first edition of this book in 1955. Although there are different ways of organizing managerial knowledge, most textbook authors today have adopted this or a similar framework even after experimenting at times with alternative ways of structuring knowledge.

Some scholars have organized managerial knowledge around roles of managers. Indeed, some valuable contributions have been made since this approach also focuses on what managers do and are evidence of planning, organizing, staffing, leading, and controlling. However, this roles approach has some limitations, as you will learn in Chapter 2 of this book.

Although we emphasize managers' tasks in designing an internal environment for performance, it must never be overlooked that managers must operate in the external environment of an enterprise as well as in the internal environment of the various departments within an organization.[2] Clearly, managers cannot perform their tasks well unless they have an understanding of, and are responsive to, the many elements of the external environment—economic, technological, social, political, and ethical factors that affect their areas of operations.

Management as an Essential for Any Organization

Managers are charged with the responsibility of taking actions that will make it possible for individuals to make their best contributions to group objectives. Management thus applies to small and large organizations, to profit and not-for-profit enterprises, to manufacturing as well as service industries. The term "enterprise" refers to business, government agencies, hospitals, universities, and other organizations since almost everything said in this book refers to business as well as nonbusiness organizations. Effective managing is the concern of the corporation president, the hospital administrator, the government first-line supervisor, the Boy Scout leader, the bishop in the church, the baseball manager, and the university president.

Management at Different Organizational Levels

You will find that we make no basic distinction between managers, executives, administrators, and supervisors. To be sure, a given situation may differ considerably among various levels in an organization or various types of enterprises. Similarly, the scope of authority held may vary and the types of problems dealt with may be considerably different. Furthermore, the person in a managerial role may be directing people in the sales, engineering, or finance department. But the fact remains that, as managers, all obtain results by establishing an environment for effective group endeavor.

All managers carry out managerial functions. However, the time spent for each function may differ. Figure 1-1 shows an approximation of the relative time

FIGURE 1-1

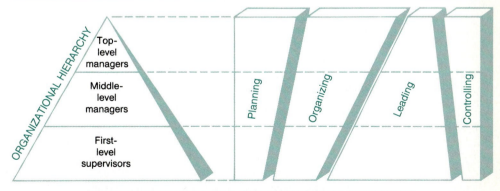

TIME SPENT IN CARRYING OUT MANAGERIAL FUNCTIONS.

Partly based on and adapted from Thomas A. Mahoney, Thomas H. Jerdee, and Stephen J. Carroll, "The Job(s) of Management," *Industrial Relations* (February 1965), pp. 97–110.

spent for each function. Thus, top-level managers spend more time on planning and organizing than lower-level managers. Leading, on the other hand, takes a great deal of time for first-line supervisors. The difference in time spent on controlling varies only slightly for managers at various levels.

Women in the Organizational Hierarchy

In the last decade or so, women have made significant progress in obtaining responsible positions in organizations. Among the reasons for this development are laws governing fair employment practices, changing societal attitudes toward women in the workplace, and the desire of companies to project a favorable image by placing qualified women in managerial positions.

In 1965, readers of the *Harvard Business Review* were surveyed to determine their attitudes toward women in business organizations.[3] About half of the men and women (and there was not much difference between them) responding felt that women seldom expect to achieve or even desire positions of authority.

Twenty years later, in 1985, the results showed that the attitudes toward women in business had changed significantly. Only 9 percent of the men and 4 percent of the women in the survey thought that women do not aspire to top positions. Moreover, it was found that men saw women much more as competent, equal colleagues. However, over 50 percent of those answering in the survey thought that women would never be completely accepted in business. This may indeed be discouraging to those women who aspire to top management positions. Yet, twenty years ago, few people would have expected the progress toward equality that has been made since 1965.

Some evidence suggests that women do have difficulties making it to the top. For example, there are no women on the way to the chief executive officer's job in the *Fortune 500* corporations. Discrimination has been given as one reason, according to a *Fortune* article.[4] On the other hand, Marisa Bellisario, as we will discuss in greater detail in the chapter on comparative and international management, is one of the most successful executives in Italy, with the press calling her "Lady Computer" and the "manager in jeans" (she occasionally wears jeans at work). In fact, companies such as IBM, AT&T, and GTE Corporation have unsuccessfully tried to recruit her.

The Aim of All Managers

Nonbusiness executives sometimes say that the aim of business managers is simple—to make a profit. But profit is really only a measure of a surplus of sales dollars (or in any other currency) over expense dollars. In a very real sense, in all kinds of organizations, whether business or nonbusiness, the logical and publicly desirable aim of all managers should be a surplus—managers must establish an environment in which people can accomplish group goals with the least amount of time, money, materials, and personal dissatisfaction, or where they can achieve as much as possible of a desired goal with available resources. In a nonbusiness enterprise such as a police department, as well as in units of a business (such as an accounting department) that are not responsible for total business profits, managers still have goals and should strive to accomplish them

PERSPECTIVE:
WHICH ARE THE EXCELLENT COMPANIES?

In a society such as that in the United States, profitability is an important measure for company excellence. At times, other criteria are also used, which, however, frequently coincide with financial performance. In their book *In Search of Excellence,* Peters and Waterman identified 43 companies that they considered excellent.[5] In choosing some of the firms, the authors considered measures such as growth of assets and equity, average return on total capital, and similar measures. They also asked industry experts about the innovativeness of the companies.

The authors identified eight characteristics of excellent enterprises. Specifically, these firms:

- Were oriented toward action

- Learned about the needs of their customers

- Promoted managerial autonomy and entrepreneurship

- Achieved productivity by paying close attention to the needs of their people

- Were driven by a company philosophy often based on the values of their leaders

- Focused on the business they knew best

- Had a simple organization structure with a lean staff

- Were centralized as well as decentralized, depending on appropriateness

Two years after the book *In Search of Excellence* was published, *Business Week* took a second look at those companies that were considered excellent.[6] This survey showed that at least 14 of the 43 companies did not measure up very well to several of the eight characteristics of excellence. Nine companies showed a great decline in earnings. While the authors have been criticized in several respects, including the method of collecting and interpreting the data (they extensively used anecdotes and quotations of leaders in the field rather than more scientific research methods),[7] the performance review of the firms indicated that success may be only transitory and that it demands continuing hard work to adapt to the changes in the environment.

A more recent survey by *Fortune* magazine of 31 industrial groups showed the following ranking of the ten most admired companies:[8] (1) International Business Machines (IBM), (2) 3M, (3) Dow Jones (printing and publishing), (4) Coca-Cola, (5) Merck (pharmaceuticals), (6) Boeing, (7) Rubbermaid, (8) Procter & Gamble, (9) Exxon, and (10) J. P. Morgan (banking).

In addition, companies were rated on eight attributes of reputation. IBM ranked first in the following five categories: quality of management; long-term investment value; financial soundness; the ability to attract, develop, and retain talented people; and the use of the assets of the corporation.

In the other three categories these companies ranked first: Dow Jones in quality of products and services, Citicorp in innovativeness, and Eastman Kodak in community and environmental responsibility.

with the minimum of resources or to accomplish as much as possible with available resources.

Productivity, Effectiveness, and Efficiency

Another way to view the aim of all managers is to say that they must be productive. After World War II the United States was the world leader in productivity. But in the late 1960s the deceleration of productivity growth began. Today the urgent need for productivity improvement is recognized by government, private industry, and universities. Often we look to Japan to find answers to our productivity problem, and indeed we will do so in Chapter 25 of this book, but what we often overlook is the importance of performing effectively the basic managerial and nonmanagerial activities.

Definition of productivity.   Successful companies create a surplus through productive operations. Although there is not complete agreement on the true meaning of productivity, we will define it as *the output-input ratio within a time period with due consideration for quality.* It can be expressed as follows:

$$\text{Productivity} = \frac{\text{outputs}}{\text{inputs}} \quad \text{within a time period, quality considered}$$

Thus, productivity can be improved by increasing outputs with the same inputs, by decreasing inputs but maintaining the same outputs, or by changing the ratio favorably by increasing output and decreasing inputs. In the past, productivity improvement programs were mostly aimed at the worker level.[9] Yet, as Peter F. Drucker, one of the most prolific writers in management, observed, "The greatest opportunity for increasing productivity is surely to be found in knowledge, work itself, and especially in management."[10]

Definitions of effectiveness and efficiency.   Productivity implies effectiveness and efficiency in individual and organizational performance. **Effectiveness** is the achievement of objectives. **Efficiency** is the achievement of the ends with the least amount of resources. To know whether they are productive, managers must know their goals and those of the organization, a topic that will be discussed in Chapter 4.

MANAGING: SCIENCE OR ART?

Managing, like all other practices—whether of medicine, music composition, engineering, accountancy, or even baseball—is an art. It is know-how. It is doing things in the light of the realities of a situation. Yet managers can work better by using the organized knowledge about management, and it is this knowledge, whether crude or advanced, whether exact or inexact, that, to the extent it is well organized, clear, and pertinent, constitutes a science. Thus, managing as practice is an art; the organized knowledge underlying the practice may be referred to as a science. In this context science and art are not mutually exclusive but are complementary.

As science improves so should art, as has happened in the physical and biological sciences. To be sure, the science underlying managing is fairly crude and inexact. This is true because the many variables with which managers deal are extremely complex. But such management knowledge as is available can certainly improve managerial practice. Physicians without the advantage of science would be little more than witch doctors. Executives who attempt to manage without such management science must trust to luck, intuition, or what they did in the past.

In managing, as in any other field, unless practitioners are to learn by trial and error (and it has been said that managers' errors are their subordinates' trials), there is no place they can turn for meaningful guidance other than the accumulated knowledge underlying their practice.

THE ELEMENTS OF SCIENCE

Science is organized knowledge. The essential feature of any science is the application of the scientific method to the development of knowledge. Thus, we speak of a science as having clear concepts, theory, and other accumulated knowledge developed from hypotheses (assumptions that something is true), experimentation, and analysis.

The Scientific Approach

The scientific approach first requires clear **concepts**—mental images of anything formed by generalization from particulars. These words and terms should be exact, relevant to the things being analyzed, and informative to the scientist and practitioner alike. From this base, the **scientific method** involves determining facts through observation. After classifying and analyzing these facts, scientists look for causal relationships. When these generalizations or hypotheses are tested for accuracy and appear to be true, that is, to reflect or explain reality, and therefore to have value in predicting what will happen in similar circumstances. they are called **principles.** This designation does not always imply that they are unquestionably or invariably true, but that they are believed to be valid enough to be used for prediction.

Theory is a systematic grouping of interdependent concepts and principles which give a framework to, or tie together, significant knowledge. Scattered data, such as what we may find on a blackboard after a group of engineers has been discussing a problem, are not information unless the observer has knowledge of the theory which will explain relationships. Theory is, as Homans has said, "in its lowest form a classification, a set of pigeon holes, a filing cabinet in which fact can accumulate. Nothing is more lost than a loose fact."[11]

The Role of Management Theory

In the field of management, then, the role of theory is to provide a means of classifying significant and pertinent management knowledge. In the area of designing an effective organization structure, for example, there are a number of principles that are interrelated and that have a predictive value for managers. Some principles give guidelines for delegating authority; these include the principle of delegating by results expected, the principle of equality of authority and responsibility, and the principle of unity of command.

Principles in management, are fundamental truths (or what are thought to be truths at a given time), explaining relationships between two or more sets of variables, usually an independent variable and a dependent variable. Principles may be *descriptive* or *predictive*, and not prescriptive. That is, they describe how one variable relates to another—what will happen when these variables interact. They do not prescribe what we should do. For example, in physics, if gravity is the only force acting on a falling body, the body will fall at an increasing speed; this principle does not tell us whether anyone should jump off the roof of a high building. Or take the example of Parkinson's Law: Work tends to expand to fill the time available. Even if Parkinson's somewhat frivolous principle is correct (as it probably is), it does not mean that a manager should lengthen the time available for people to do a job. To take another example, in management, the principle of unity of command states that the more often an individual reports to a single superior, the more that individual is likely to feel a sense of loyalty and obligation and the less likely it is that there will be confusion about instruction. The principle merely predicts. It in no sense implies that individuals should never report to more than one person. Rather, it implies that if they do so, their managers must be aware of the possible dangers and should take these risks into account in balancing the advantages and disadvantages of multiple command.

Like engineers who apply physical principles to the design of an instrument, managers who apply theory to managing must usually blend principles with realities. An engineer is often faced with the necessity of combining considerations of weight, size, conductivity, and other factors in designing an instrument. Likewise, a manager may find that the advantages of giving a controller authority to prescribe accounting procedures throughout an organization outweigh the possible costs of multiple authority. But if they know theory, these managers will know that such costs as conflicting instructions and confusion may exist, and they will take steps (such as making the controller's special authority crystal clear to everyone involved) to minimize disadvantages.

Management Techniques

Techniques are essentially ways of doing things, methods of accomplishing a given result. In all fields of practice they are important. They certainly are in managing, even though few really important managerial techniques have been invented. Among them are budgeting, cost accounting, network planning and control techniques like the Program Evaluation and Review Technique (PERT) or the Critical Path Method (CPM), rate-of-return-on-investment control, various devices of organizational development, and managing by objectives, all of

PERSPECTIVE:
MANAGEMENT TECHNIQUES OR FADS?

A **management fad** can be defined as a managerial interest or practice followed for a period of time with exaggerated zeal or craze. But fads come and go—some slowly, others fast; some survive and others fall by the wayside. These managerial fads can be found in all managerial functions. *Business Week* identified some that are out and some that are currently in vogue.[12] Let us look at some of those that are "in" in the various managerial functions.

Fads in planning?   One of the fashionable buzzwords is **strategic alliance,** which essentially means that companies cooperate, as in forming a joint venture. These alliances even cut across national boundaries: American Telephone and Telegraph joins forces with Olivetti in Italy; General Motors builds cars with the Japanese car manufacturer Toyota; American Motors links up with the French firm Renault.[13]

Fads in organizing?   **Corporate culture** is also "in." It pertains to the values and beliefs shared by employees and the general patterns of their behavior.

Fads in staffing?   Organizations have to be staffed by people who are not only competent but also healthy. This requires **wellness** or **fitness** programs and the management of **stress. Paying for performance** is also currently fashionable. This simply means measuring the contributions of individuals and rewarding them accordingly. Another term you may hear at times is **demassing.** It is a euphemism for laying off employees or demoting managers.

Fads in leading?   Then there is the **intrapreneur,** a person who acts like an entrepreneur, but within the organizational environment. Gifford Pinchot, who coined the term, describes the intrapreneur as "any of the 'dreamers who do.' Those who take hands-on responsibility for creating innovation of any kind within an organization. The intrapreneur may be the creator or inventor but he or she is always the dreamer who figures out how to turn an idea into a profitable reality."[14]

Fads in controlling?   People admire success. Managers, rightly or wrongly, look to Japan to solve their productivity or quality problems. Thus, **quality circles,** widely used in Japan, are seen as a way to improve quality and to make U.S. products more competitive.

Fads can become techniques and they may contribute to the functioning of the organization. Indeed, we will discuss some of them later in this book. But if they are considered short-term solutions to deep-seated problems, or when they are considered a quick fix, then their value may be questioned. On the other hand, if some techniques get integrated into a comprehensive system of management with a real commitment to managerial excellence, then these fads can become useful techniques.

which will be discussed in later chapters. Techniques normally reflect theory and are a means of helping managers undertake activities most effectively.

THE SYSTEMS APPROACH TO OPERATIONAL MANAGEMENT

An organized enterprise does not, of course, exist in a vacuum. Rather, it is dependent on its external environment; it is a part of larger systems such as the industry to which it belongs, the economic system, and society. Thus, the enterprise receives inputs, transforms them, and exports the outputs to the environment, as shown by the very basic model in Figure 1-2. However, this simple model needs to be expanded and developed into a model of operational management that indicates how the various inputs are transformed through the managerial functions of planning, organizing, staffing, leading, and controlling. Clearly, any business or other organization must be described by an open-system model that includes interactions between the enterprise and its external environment.

Inputs and Claimants

The inputs from the external environment (see Figure 1-3) may include people, capital, and managerial skills, as well as technical knowledge and skills. In addition, various groups of people make demands on the enterprise. For example, employees want higher pay, more benefits, and job security. On the other hand, consumers demand safe and reliable products at a reasonable price. Suppliers want assurance that their products will be bought. Stockholders want not only a high return on their investment but also security for their money. Federal, state, and local governments depend on taxes paid by the enterprise, but they also expect the enterprise to comply with their laws. Similarly, the

FIGURE 1-2

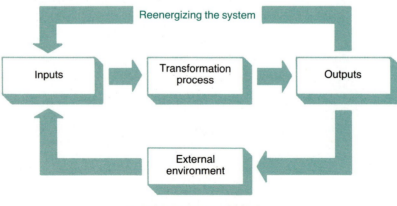

INPUT-OUTPUT MODEL.

FIGURE 1-3

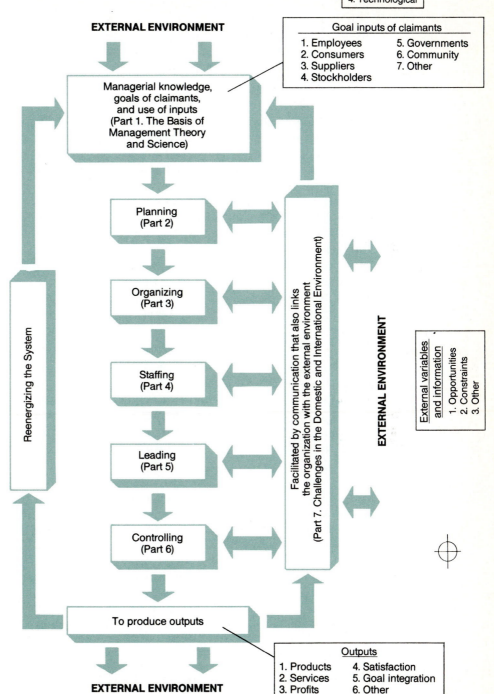

SYSTEMS APPROACH TO MANAGEMENT

community demands that enterprises be "good citizens," providing the maximum number of jobs with a minimum of pollution. Other claimants to the enterprise may include financial institutions and labor unions; even competitors have a legitimate claim for fair play. It is clear that many of these claims are incongruent, and it is the managers' job to integrate the legitimate objectives of the claimants.

The Managerial Transformation Process

It is the task of managers to transform the inputs in an effective and efficient manner into outputs. Of course, the transformation process can be viewed from different perspectives. Thus, one can focus on such diverse enterprise functions as finance, production, personnel, and marketing. Writers on management, as you will see in Chapter 2, look on the transformation process in terms of their particular approaches to management. Specifically, as you will see, writers belonging to the human behavior school focus on interpersonal relationships, social systems theorists analyze the transformation by concentrating on social interactions, and those advocating decision theory see the transformation as sets of decisions. We will suggest later in this chapter that the most comprehensive and useful approach for discussing the job of managers is to use the managerial functions of planning, organizing, staffing, leading, and controlling as a framework for organizing managerial knowledge (see Figure 1-3).

The Communication System

Communication is essential to all phases of the managerial process: It integrates the managerial functions and it links the enterprise with its environment. For example, the objectives set in planning are communicated so that the appropriate organization structure can be devised. Communication is essential in the selection, appraisal, and training of managers to fill the roles in this structure. Similarly, effective leadership and the creation of an environment conducive to motivation depend on communication. Moreover, it is through communication that one determines whether events and performance conform to plans. Thus, it is communication which makes managing possible.

The second function of the communication system is to link the enterprise with its external environment, where many of the claimants are. For example, one should never forget that the customer, who is the reason for the existence of virtually all businesses, is outside a company. It is through the communication system that the needs of customers are identified; this knowledge enables the firm to provide products and services at a profit. Similarly, it is through an effective communication system that the organization becomes aware of competition and other potential threats and constraining factors.

External Variables

Effective managers will regularly scan the external environment. While it is true that managers may have little or no power to change the external environment, they have no alternative but to respond to it. The forces acting in the external environment are discussed in Chapters 24 and 25.

Outputs

It is the task of managers to secure and utilize inputs to the enterprise, to transform them through the managerial functions—with due consideration for external variables—to produce outputs.

Although the kinds of outputs will vary with the enterprise, they usually include many of the following: products, services, profits, satisfaction, and integration of the goals of various claimants to the enterprise. Most of these outputs require no elaboration, and only the last two will be discussed.

The organization must indeed provide many "satisfactions" if it hopes to retain and elicit contributions from its members. It must contribute to the satisfaction not only of basic material needs (for example, earning money to buy food and shelter or having job security) but also of needs for affiliation, acceptance, esteem, and perhaps even self-actualization.

Another output is goal integration. As noted above, the different claimants to the enterprise have very divergent—and often directly opposing—objectives. It is the task of managers to resolve conflicts and integrate these aims. This is not easy, as one former Volkswagen executive discovered. Economics dictated the construction of a Volkswagen assembly plant in the United States. However, this plan was opposed by an important claimant, German labor, because of fear of the elimination of some jobs. The conflict was so deep that it contributed to the executive's resignation and a change in leadership. After a costly delay, the Volkswagen assembly plant was eventually built in the United States. This illustrates the importance of the integration of the goals of the various claimants to the enterprise, which is indeed an essential task of any manager.

Reenergizing the System

Finally, we should notice that in the systems model of operational management, some of the outputs become inputs again. Thus, the satisfaction of employees becomes an important human input. Similarly, profits, the surplus of income over costs, are reinvested in cash and capital goods, such as machinery, equipment, buildings, and inventory. You will see shortly that the model shown in Figure 1-3 will serve as a framework in this book for organizing managerial knowledge. But let us first look closer at the managerial functions.

THE FUNCTIONS OF MANAGERS

The functions of managers provide a useful framework for organizing management knowledge. There have been no new ideas, research findings, or techniques that cannot readily be placed in the classifications of planning, organizing, staffing, leading, and controlling.

Planning

Planning involves selecting missions and objectives and the actions to achieve them; it requires decision making, that is, choosing future courses of action from among alternatives. As you will see in Chapter 3, there are various types of plans, ranging from overall purposes and objectives to the most detailed actions to be taken, such as to order a special stainless steel bolt for an instrument or to hire and train workers for an assembly line. No real plan exists until a decision—a commitment of human or material resources or reputation—has been made. Before a decision is made, all we have is a planning study, an analysis, or a proposal, but not a real plan.

Planning bridges the gap from where we are to where we want to be in a desired future. It strongly implies not only the introduction of new things but also sensible and workable implementation. It makes it possible for things to occur that would not otherwise happen. Although the future can seldom be predicted with accuracy and unforeseen events may interfere with the best-laid plans, unless there is planning, actions tend to be aimless and left to chance. There is no more important and basic element in establishing an environment for performance than enabling people to know their purposes and objectives, the tasks to be performed, and the guidelines to be followed in performing them. If group effort is to be effective, people must know what they are expected to accomplish. The various aspects of planning are discussed in Part 2 of this book.

Organizing

People working together in groups to achieve some goal must have roles to play, much like the parts actors fill in a drama, whether these roles are ones they develop themselves, are accidental or haphazard, or are defined and structured by someone who wants to make sure that people contribute in a specific way to group effort. The concept of a "role" implies that what people do has a definite purpose or objective; they know how their job objective fits into group effort, and they have the necessary authority, tools, and information to accomplish the task.

This can be seen in as simple a group effort as setting up camp on a fishing expedition. Everyone could do anything he or she wanted to do, but activity would almost certainly be more effective and certain tasks would be less likely to be left undone if one or two persons were given the task of gathering firewood, others the assignment of getting water, others the task of making a fireplace and starting a fire, others the job of cooking, and so on.

Organizing, then, is that part of managing that involves establishing an intentional structure of roles for people to fill in an organization. It is intentional in the sense of making sure that all the tasks necessary to accomplish goals are assigned and, it is hoped, assigned to people who can do them best. Imagine what would have happened if such assignments had not been made in the program of flying the special aircraft *Voyager* around the globe without stopping or refueling.

The purpose of an organization structure is to help in creating an environment for human performance. It is, then, a management tool and not an end in and of itself. Although the structure must define the tasks to be done, the roles so established must also be designed in the light of the abilities and motivations of people available.

To design an effective organization structure is not an easy managerial task. Many problems are encountered in making structures fit situations, including both defining the kind of jobs that must be done and finding the people to do them. These problems and the essential theory, principles, and techniques of handling them are the subjects of Part 3 of this book.

Staffing

Staffing involves filling, and keeping filled, the positions in the organization structure. This is done by identifying work-force requirements, inventorying the people available, recruiting, selecting, placing, promoting, planning the career, compensating, and training or otherwise developing both candidates and current job holders to accomplish their tasks effectively and efficiently. This subject is dealt with in Part 4 of this book.

Leading

Leading is influencing people so that they will contribute to organization and group goals; it has to do predominantly with the interpersonal aspect of managing. All managers would agree that their most important problems arise from people—their desires and attitudes, their behavior as individuals and in groups—and that effective managers also need to be effective leaders. Since leadership implies followership and people tend to follow those who offer a means of satisfying their own needs, wishes, and desires, it is understandable that leading involves motivation, leadership styles and approaches, and communication. The essentials of these subjects are dealt with in Part 5 of this book.

Controlling

Controlling is the measuring and correcting of activities of subordinates, to ensure that events conform to plans. It measures performance against goals and plans, shows where negative deviations exist, and, by putting in motion actions to correct deviations, helps ensure accomplishment of plans. Although planning must precede controlling, plans are not self-achieving. The plan guides managers in the use of resources to accomplish specific goals. Then activities are checked to determine whether they conform to plans.

Control activities generally relate to the measurement of achievement. Some means of controlling, like the budget for expense, inspection records, and the record of labor-hours lost, are generally familiar. Each measures and each shows whether plans are working out. If deviations persist, correction is indicated. But what is corrected? Activities, through persons. Nothing can be done about reducing scrap, for example, or buying according to specifications, or handling sales returns unless one knows who is responsible for these functions. Compelling events to conform to plans means locating the persons who are responsible for results that differ from planned action and then taking the necessary steps to improve performance. Thus, outcomes are controlled by controlling what people do. This subject is treated in Part 6.

Coordination, the Essence of Managership

Some authorities consider coordination to be a separate function of the manager. It seems more accurate, however, to regard it as the essence of managership, for the achievement of harmony of individual efforts toward the accomplishment of group goals is the purpose of managing. Each of the managerial functions is an exercise contribuing to coordination.

Even in the case of a church or a fraternal organization, individuals often interpret similar interests in different ways, and their efforts toward mutual goals do not automatically mesh with the efforts of others. It thus becomes the central task of the manager to reconcile differences in approach, timing, effort, or interest, and to harmonize individual goals to contribute to organization goals.

The best coordination occurs when individuals see how their jobs contribute to the goals of an enterprise. They are able to see this only when they know what those goals are. If, for example, managers are not sure whether the goal of their firm is sales volume, quality, advanced techniques, or customer service, they cannot coordinate their efforts to achieve any objective. Each would be guided by his or her own ideas of what is in the interest of the firm or, without any such conviction, might work for self-enrichment. To avoid such splintering of efforts, the dominant goal of the enterprise should be clearly defined and communicated to everyone concerned. And, naturally, goals of subordinate departments should be designed to contribute to the goals of the enterprise.

THE SYSTEMS MODEL OF MANAGEMENT AND THE ORGANIZATION OF THIS BOOK

The model of the Systems Approach to Management is also the basis for organizing managerial knowledge. In Part 1 you learn about the basis of management, that is, the various theories, the emergence of management thought, and some general patterns of management. This part cuts across all managerial functions.

But when you look at the model in Figure 1-3, you will see that the various aspects of **planning** (Part 2) are discussed in Chapters 3 through 6. Note that the numbers shown in the model correspond to the parts of this book. Thus, **organizing** (Part 3) consists of Chapters 7 through 11. Similarly, Part 4 deals with **staffing** (Chapters 12 to 15), Part 5 with **leading** (Chapters 16 to 19), and Part 6 with **controlling** (Chapters 20 to 23).

Environmental topics, domestic and international, are discussed in Part 7 (Chapters 24 and 25). These aspects relate to the inputs, to the claimants of the organization, to external variables and information, and to the outputs in the model. However, some of the factors external to the organization such as strategic planning, are also discussed in other chapters. This is as it should be because the organization is viewed in this book as an open system that interacts with the external environment.

You will see the model shown in Figure 1-3 again at the beginning of Parts 2 to 7, with the chapters discussed in the respective parts being highlighted. Our aim is to provide you with an integrative model that shows the relationships of the topics you will learn in this book.

FOR DISCUSSION

1. Is managing a science or an art? Could the same explanation apply to engineering or accounting?

2. In what fundamental way are the basic goals of all managers at all levels and in all kinds of enterprises the same?

3. Look up the terms "science," "theory," and "principle" in a dictionary and determine how they are used. Compare these definitions with the usage of these terms as applied to management in this book. What advantages are there in attempting to identify science, theory, and principles in a book on management?

4. Why do management analysis and practice require a systems approach? Do managers operate in an open or a closed system? Explain.

5. What is the systems approach to management as suggested in this book? Could a manager operate in any other way?

EXERCISES/ACTION STEPS

1. Interview two local business managers and ask them how they learned about managing. Ask what kind of books they might have read on management (e.g., textbooks or popular books such as *In Search of Excellence* by Thomas J. Peters and Robert H. Waterman, Jr., *The One Minute Manager* by Kenneth H. Blanchard, *Theory Z* by William Ouchi, *The Art of Japanese Management* by Richard Tanner Pascale and Anthony G. Athos, *Reinventing the Corporation: Transforming Your Job and Your Company for the New Information Society*). Probe to what extent these books have helped them to manage. You may also find it interesting to buy one of the best-selling books on management (most are available in paperback) and mention them in the class discussion.

2. Interview two public administrators and ask them how their job differs from that of business managers. How do they know how well their department, agency, or organization is performing since profit is probably not one of the criteria for measuring effectiveness and efficiency?

CASES

CASE 1-1
THE PARAGON RADAR CORPORATION

The Paragon Radar Corporation was organized and managed by three engineers who had formerly worked for the McDonnell Aircraft Company. They were instrumental in developing a radar capable of handling transmissions over distances far greater than those formerly permitted by the curvature of the earth. The Paragon people were adequately financed and decided upon a market policy of dealing only with government agencies, especially the air force, navy, army, and National Aeronautics and Space Administration (NASA). The budgets of these agencies grew steadily as the years passed, and business was very good.

The Paragon people did not have a marketing department in the usual sense. The heads of each department were expected to develop their own business. Consequently, the engineers would keep in close touch with their counterparts in the several agencies, help them identify their needs, help them "sell" these needs to relevant policy-making executives and contracting officers, and write the proposals as soon as the requests came through.

Then the federal government drastically cut back the budget for the Department of Defense and NASA. Business was scarce and hard to get. The Paragon people bid more and more contracts with less and less success. This state of affairs became the subject of a staff meeting at the corporate level.

"Ladies and gentlemen," said the president, "you all know the causes for the decline in our business. The corporation is gradually approaching a precarious posture. We do have excellent technical abilities, and there is still some $100 billion being spent on national defense; so our potential is still there. I have pointed out to the department heads that you must get new business if you are to remain part of the organization. It seems that my words have fallen on deaf ears. But

I assure you that I am really serious. The time has come when we must either get well or be acquired by another firm."

James Simpson, one of the department heads, spoke up, saying, "You may think that there is something lacking in my loyalty, but I really believe that we are not organized in an effective way to do what we must do. In the good years we did very well. Business was good, our bids were highly successful, indeed so much so that department managers would turn down business if the technical content did not interest them. Now that we need business we don't have the contacts. The way we have approached the problem, no one is responsible for getting business: We all are, but no one can say how much. Authority is widely diffused. We all share the blame and yet no one accepts it."

The members of the staff were shocked. The president had the good sense to remain silent for a time while each examined his or her position. One member eventually reached for his alibis. "I don't view the matter in that light. Here we have been successful for going on two decades, we get business like other aerospace companies do, and you can't expect a department head to accept and work on a contract that he is not interested in. You know, the defense business is not like selling soap."

"I know," said Simpson. "I used to believe that too. Recently I have been looking at the management literature to see if there is some principle we have overlooked. These chaps seem to be saying that the best results occur when a man has a definite objective to achieve, when he is personally held responsible for achieving it, when he has the authority to make the decisions that must be made in order to achieve it. We operate this way in everything except marketing. Why is this an exception?"

The meeting adjourned at this point. The

president said he would reexamine the matter and try to bring a proposal to the next meeting. Two weeks later, after many hours of study and consultation, he opened the regular staff meeting with an announcement.

"Ladies and gentlemen," he said, "I think it is time we stop fighting management principles; let's use them for our own benefit. I think we should have a 'business-getting' activity centralized in the hands of one person and reporting to me. We might call it 'advanced program development.' I visualize this activity comprising three functions. One would be staffed by engineers with marketing ability, another with engineers who will write the proposals, and another with market research capability. The head of this whole group would be responsible for bringing in new business and would have the necessary decision-making authority. The head would be expected to run a tight ship. I do not want an expanding bureaucracy. We will borrow technical people as needed from the operat-ing departments, in order that the technical people in the new department will not grow stale and useless. I feel that whoever is head of a proposal committee should be made program manager when and if the contract is secured. Thus, I can see a great deal of lateral movement among the engineers in all our activities."

The proposal was so revolutionary that no one could be expected to take a position on its feasibility. The staff was dismissed with the injunction to study it and bring back suggestions that would make it more viable.

1. Do you believe that the president's proposal for an "advanced program development" department would work at Paragon? What do you see to be the strengths and weaknesses of this proposal?

2. Can you suggest anything else that could be done to solve Paragon's problem?

CASE 1-2
PEOPLE EXPRESS[15]

Donald Burr, the founder and chairperson of People Express, has been hailed in his attempt to build a more humane organization. But his leadership style was changing as the organization grew. Managers at People Express had a distinct managerial style: hard-driving, but giving employees a great deal of freedom. All employees are expected to carry out a great variety of tasks. Thus, pilots help out in handling the baggage. Even top executives rotate from job to job to learn the major aspects of the business. Full-time employees must buy stock in the company, although with a large discount.

But the company's emphasis on participative management seemed to change when the company experienced its first losses and the airline grew. With the acquisition of Frontier Airlines Inc., it became the fifth largest airline in a very short time from its beginning in 1980 to 1985. With its growth, however, the firm also changed its character from a family-style organization to the more traditional one. Critics maintain that it is even risky to ask unpopular questions. One of the original managing directors, Lori Dubose, who was one of the architects of lifetime employment at People Express, was unexpectedly fired. She thinks now that asking Burr challenging questions was risky and probably was a mistake. Another director, Harold Parety, who did not like being told that he had to be at work from 6:00 a.m. to 9:00 p.m. regardless of the work load, quit and formed his own airline (Presidential Airways, Inc.), applying many of People Express's managerial practices.

1. What do you think of Burr's way of firing an officer, although the company has an implied policy of great job security?

2. Should a company be managed the same way regardless of its size or its profitability?

REFERENCES

1. At times we use the term "nonmanagers," which refers to persons who have no subordinates. Thus, nonmanagers include professionals who may have a high status in organizations.

2. William H. Peace, "I Thought I Knew What Good Management Was," *Harvard Business Review* (March–April 1986), pp. 59–65.

3. Charlotte Decker Sutton and Kris K. Moore, "Executive Women—20 Years Later," *Harvard Business Review* (September–October 1985), pp. 42–66.

4. Susan Fraker, "Why Women Aren't Getting to the Top, *Fortune* (Apr. 16, 1984), pp. 40–45. In certain firms, such as Federal Express and Hewlett-Packard, and in some industries, such as banking and retailing, chances for promotion to upper-level management are better for women. See Irene Pave, "A Woman's Place Is at GE, Federal Express, P&G . . . ," *Business Week* (June 23, 1986), pp. 75–76. But some women are also leaving the work force, as discussed by Alex Taylor III, "Why Women Managers Are Bailing Out," *Fortune* (Aug. 18, 1986), pp. 16–23.

5. Thomas J. Peters and Robert H. Waterman, Jr., *In Search of Excellence* (New York: Harper & Row, 1982).

6. "Who's Excellent Now?" *Business Week* (Nov. 5, 1984), pp. 76–88.

7. Daniel T. Carroll, "A Disappointing Search for Excellence," *Harvard Business Review* (November–December 1983), pp. 78–88. See also Terence R. Mitchell, "In Search of Excellence versus The 100 Best Companies to Work for in America: A Question of Perspectives and Values," *Academy of Management Review* (April 1985), pp. 350–355.

8. Cynthia Hutton, "America's Most Admired Corporations," *Fortune* (Jan. 6, 1986), pp. 16–27. But a year later, IBM slipped to number 7, indicating that success is transitory. See Edward C. Baig, "America's Most Admired Corporations," *Fortune* (Jan. 19, 1987), pp. 18–31.

9. Heinz Weihrich, *Management Excellence—Productivity Through MBO* (New York: McGraw-Hill Book Company, 1985).

10. Peter F. Drucker, *Management: Tasks, Responsibilities, Practices* (New York: Harper & Row, 1973), p. 69.

11. G. C. Homans, *The Human Group* (New York: Harcourt, Brace & World, 1958), p. 5.

12. John A. Byrne, "Business Fads: What's In—and Out," *Business Week* (Jan. 20, 1986), pp. 52–61.

13. Howard V. Perlmutter and David A. Heenan, "Cooperate to Compete Globally," *Harvard Business Review* (March–April 1986), pp. 136–152.

14. Gifford Pinchot III, *Intrapreneuring* (New York: Harper & Row, 1985), p. ix. For a review of books on entrepreneurship, see David E. Gumpert, "Stalking the Entrepreneur," *Harvard Business Review* (May–June 1986), pp. 32–36.

15. Case References: "Up, Up and Away?—Expansion is Threatening the 'Humane' Culture at People Express," *Business Week* (Nov. 25, 1985), pp. 80–94; James R. Norman, "People Is Plunging, but Burr Is Staying Cool," *Business Week* (July 7, 1986), pp. 31–32. Note that in 1986, Texas Air Corporation acquired People Express. See James R. Norman, "Nice Going, Frank, but Will It Fly?" *Business Week* (Sept. 29, 1986), pp. 34–35.

FOR FURTHER INFORMATION

Barnard, Chester I. *The Functions of the Executive* (Cambridge, Mass.: Harvard University Press, 1938).

Buehler, Vernon M., and Y. Krishna Shetty (eds.), *Productivity Improvement* (New York: AMACOM, 1981).

Donnelly, James H., Jr., James L. Gibson, and John M. Ivancevich (eds.). *Perspectives on Management,* 5th ed. (Plano, Tex.: Business Publications, 1984).

Dublin, Robert. "Management: Meanings, Methods, and Moxie," *Academy of Management Review* (July 1982), pp. 372–379.

Global Competition: The New Reality, Report of the President's Commission on Industrial Competitiveness, vol. I (January 1985).

Hurst, David K. "Of Boxes, Bubbles, and Effective Management," *Harvard Business Review* (May–June 1984), pp. 78–88.

Lorsch, Jay W., and Paul R. Lawrence. *Studies in Organization Design* (Homewood, Ill.: The Dorsey Press and Richard D. Irwin, 1970).

March, James. G., and Herbert A. Simon. *Organizations* (New York: John Wiley & Sons, 1958).

Matteson, Michael T., and John M. Ivancevich (eds.). *Management Classics,* 3d ed. (Santa Monica, Calif.: Goodyear Publishing Company, 1986).

CHAPTER 2

The Evolution of Management Thought and the Patterns of Management Analysis

CHAPTER OBJECTIVES

After studying this chapter you should be able to:

1. Discuss the "scientific management" thinking of Frederick Taylor and his major followers.

2. Give special attention to the ideas of Henri Fayol and his pioneering theory that managing is a universal activity to be identified and analyzed.

3. Understand the emergence of the behavioral sciences, especially the "social man" concepts of Mayo and his colleagues, and the "social system" theory of Chester Barnard.

4. Recognize some recent contributions to management thought.

5. Explain the nature of the "management theory jungle."

6. Describe the various approaches to management, their contributions as well as their limitations.

7. Show how the operational approach to management theory and science has a basic core of its own and also draws eclectically from the other approaches.

*D*espite the inexactness and relative crudity of management theory and science, the development of thought on management dates back to the days when people first attempted to accomplish goals by working together in groups. Although modern operational-management theory dates primarily from the early twentieth century, there was serious thinking and theorizing about managing many years before.

While this chapter can do little more than sketch some of the high spots in the emergence of management thought,[1] it is worthwhile for persons interested in management to know something of the background of the evolution of management thought. Even limited knowledge can help one appreciate the many insights, ideas, and scientific underpinnings which preceded the upsurge of management writing during recent years. Familiarity with the history of management thought may help you avoid rediscovering previously known ideas.

You will see that the many different contributions of writers and practitioners have resulted in different approaches to management, resulting in a kind of management theory jungle. Later in this chapter you will learn about the different patterns of management analysis and what can be done to untangle the jungle. But let us first focus on the emergence of management thought summarized in Table 2-1. While it would be too complex and voluminous to include in such a table all the persons who have made significant contributions in the evolution of management thought, major contributors are noted.

FREDERICK TAYLOR AND SCIENTIFIC MANAGEMENT

Frederick Winslow Taylor gave up going to college and started out as an apprentice patternmaker and machinist in 1875, joined the Midvale Steel Works in Philadelphia as a machinist in 1878, and rose to the position of chief engineer after earning a degree in engineering through evening study. He invented high-speed steel-cutting tools and spent most of his life as a consulting engineer. Taylor is generally acknowledged as "the father of scientific management." Probably no other person has had a greater impact on the early development of management. His experiences as an apprentice, a common laborer, a foreman, a master mechanic, and then the chief engineer of a steel company gave Taylor ample opportunity to know at first hand the problems and attitudes of workers and to see the great opportunities for improving the quality of management.

Taylor's patents for high-speed steel-cutting tools and other inventions, as well as his early engineering consulting work, made him so well off that he retired from working for payment in 1901, at the age of 45, and spent the remaining 14 years of his life as an unpaid consultant and lecturer to promote his ideas on scientific management.

Taylor's Major Concern

Taylor's major concern throughout most of his life was that of increasing efficiency in production, not only to lower costs and raise profits but also to make possible increased pay for workers through their higher productivity. As a

TABLE 2-1 The Emergence of Management Thought

Name and year (approx.)	Major contribution to management
Scientific management	
Frederick W. Taylor *Shop Management* (1903) *Principles of Scientific Management* (1911) *Testimony before the Special House Committee* (1912)	Acknowledged as "the father of scientific management." His primary concern was to increase productivity through greater efficiency in production and increased pay for workers through the application of the scientific method. His principles emphasized using science, creating group harmony and cooperation, achieving maximum output, and developing workers.
Henry L. Gantt (1901)	Called for scientific selection of workers and "harmonious cooperation" between labor and management. Developed the Gantt chart (Chapter 21). Stressed the need for training.
Frank and Lillian Gilbreth (1900)	Frank is known primarily for his time and motion studies. Lillian, an industrial psychologist, focused on the human aspects of work and the understanding of workers' personalities and needs.
Modern operational-management theory	
Henri Fayol *Administration Industrielle et Générale* (1916)	Referred to as "the father of modern management theory." Divided industrial activities into six groups: technical, commercial, financial, security, accounting, and managerial. Recognized the need for teaching management. Formulated fourteen principles of management, such as authority and responsibility, unity of command, scalar chain, and esprit de corps.
Behavioral sciences	
Hugo Münsterberg (1912)	Application of psychology to industry and management.
Walter Dill Scott (1911)	Application of psychology to advertising, marketing, and personnel.
Max Weber (translations 1946, 1947)	Theory of bureaucracy.
Vilfredo Pareto (books 1896–1917)	Referred to as "the father of the social systems approach" to organization and management.
Elton Mayo and F. J. Roethlisberger (1933)	Famous studies at the Hawthorne plant of the Western Electric Company. Influence of social attitudes and relationships of work groups on performance.
Systems theory	
Chester Barnard *The Functions of the Executive* (1938)	The task of managers is to maintain a system of cooperative effort in a formal organization. He suggested a comprehensive social systems approach to managing.
Emergence of modern management thought and recent contributors to management	

Many authors are discussed in the book. Major contributors include Chris Argyris, Robert R. Blake, C. West Churchman, Ernest Dale, Keith Davis, Peter Drucker, Mary Parker Follett, Frederick Herzberg, G. C. Homans, Harold Koontz, Rensis Likert, Douglas McGregor, Abraham H. Maslow, Lyman W. Porter, George A. Steiner, Lyndall Urwick, Norbert Wiener, and Joan Woodward.

Laurence Peter (1969)	Observed that eventually people get promoted to a level where they are incompetent.
William Ouchi (1981)	Discussed selected Japanese managerial practices adapted in the U.S. environment.
Thomas Peters and Robert Waterman (1982)	Identified characteristics of companies they considered excellent.

Source: Some information in this table is based on Claude S. George, Jr., *The History of Management Thought* (Englewood Cliffs, N.J.: Prentice-Hall, 1972).

FREDERICK W. TAYLOR
1856–1912

Historical Pictures Service, Chicago

young man working in machine shops, he was impressed with the degree of "soldiering" on the job, of making work, and of producing less rather than more, due primarily to the workers' fear that they might work themselves out of a job if they produced more. He saw "soldiering" as a system. From his own experience, he knew that much higher productivity was possible without unreasonable effort on the part of the workers.

Taylor decided that the problem of productivity was a matter of ignorance on the part of both management and labor. Part of this ignorance arose from the fact that neither managers nor workers knew what constituted a "fair day's work" and a "fair day's pay." Moreover, he believed that both managers and workers were concerned too much with how they should divide the surplus that arose from productivity—the split in thinking between pay and profits—and not enough with increasing the surplus so that *both* owners and laborers could get more compensation. In brief, Taylor saw productivity as the answer to both higher wages and higher profits. He believed that the application of scientific methods, instead of custom and rule of thumb, could yield productivity without the expenditure of more human energy or effort.

Taylor's Principles

Taylor's famous work entitled *The Principles of Scientific Management* was published in 1911. But one of the best expositions of his philosophy of management is found in his testimony before a committee of the House of Representatives, where he was forced to defend his ideas before a group of congressmen, most of whom were hostile because they believed, along with labor leaders, that Taylor's ideas would lead to overworking and displacing workers.[2]

The fundamental principles that Taylor saw underlying the scientific approach to management are summarized in the Perspective on the next page. You will notice that these basic precepts of Taylor's are not far from the fundamental beliefs of the modern manager. It is true that some of the techniques Taylor and his colleagues and followers developed in order to put his philosophy and principles into practice had certain mechanistic aspects. To

> **PERSPECTIVE:**
> **TAYLOR'S PRINCIPLES**
>
> **1.** Replacing rules of thumb with science (organized knowledge)
>
> **2.** Obtaining harmony in group action, rather than discord
>
> **3.** Achieving cooperation of human beings, rather than chaotic individualism
>
> **4.** Working for maximum output, rather than restricted output
>
> **5.** Developing all workers to the fullest extent possible for their own and their company's highest prosperity

determine what a fair day's work was and to help in finding the one best way of doing any *given* job, the careful study of time and motion was widely applied. Likewise, various pay plans based on output were used in an attempt to increase the "surplus" (as Taylor referred to "productivity"), to make sure that workers who produced were paid according to their productivity, and to give workers an incentive for performance. As can be seen, techniques such as these were necessary to make Taylor's philosophy work, based as it was on improving productivity, on giving people their best opportunity to be productive, and on rewarding workers for individual productivity. It is likewise true that these techniques could be used, as they often were by many factory owners over the world, to increase labor productivity without providing ample reward, adequate training, or managerial help. But this was certainly not what Frederick Taylor had in mind.

On the contrary, throughout Taylor's written work, even though it does seem to be unduly preoccupied with productivity at the shop level, runs a strongly humanistic theme. He believed that people should be carefully selected and trained and that they should be given the work they could do best. He had perhaps an idealist's notion that the interests of workers, managers, and owners could and should be harmonized. Moreover, Taylor emphasized the importance of careful advanced planning by managers and the responsibility of managers to design work systems so that workers would be helped to do their best. But, as he spoke of management, he never overlooked the fact that "the relations between employers and men form without question the most important part of this art."[3]

FOLLOWERS OF TAYLOR

Among the immediate disciples of Taylor were such outstanding pioneers as Henry L. Gantt and Frank and Lillian Gilbreth, to mention only a few.

Henry L. Gantt

Gantt—like Taylor, a mechanical engineer—joined Taylor at the Midvale Steel Company in 1887. He stayed with Taylor in his various assignments until 1901,

HENRY L. GANTT
1861–1919

Historical Pictures Service, Chicago

when he formed his own consulting engineering firm. Although he strongly espoused Taylor's ideas and did much consulting work on the scientific selection of workers and the development of incentive bonus systems, he was far more cautious than Taylor in selling and installing his scientific-management methods. Like Taylor, he emphasized the need for developing a mutuality of interests between management and labor, a "harmonious cooperation." In doing this, he stressed the importance of teaching, of developing an understanding of systems on the part of both labor and management, and of appreciating that "in all problems of management the human element is the most important one."

Gantt is perhaps the best known for his development of graphic methods of depicting plans and making possible better managerial control. He emphasized the importance of time, as well as cost, in planning and controlling work. This led eventually to the famous Gantt chart, which, as we shall see in Chapter 21, is in wide use today and was the forerunner of such modern techniques as PERT (Program Evaluation and Review Technique), as well as being regarded by some social historians as the most important social invention of the twentieth century.

Frank and Lillian Gilbreth

The ideas of Taylor were also strongly supported and developed by the famous husband-and-wife team of Frank and Lillian Gilbreth. Frank Gilbreth gave up going to the university to become a bricklayer at the age of 17 in 1885; he rose to the position of chief superintendent of a building contracting firm 10 years later and became a building contractor on his own shortly thereafter. During this period, and quite independently of Taylor's work, he became interested in wasted motions in work; by reducing the number of bricklaying motions from eighteen to five, he made possible the doubling of a bricklayer's productivity with no greater expenditure of effort. His contracting-firm work soon gave way largely to consulting on the improvement of human productivity. After meeting Taylor in 1907, he combined his ideas with Taylor's to put scientific management into effect.

In undertaking his work, Frank Gilbreth was greatly aided and supported by his wife, Lillian. She was one of the earliest industrial psychologists and received her doctor's degree in this field in 1915, 9 years after her marriage and during the period when she was involved in having and raising her celebrated dozen children (later made famous by the book and movie *Cheaper by the Dozen*). After her husband's untimely death in 1924, she carried on his consulting business and was widely acclaimed as the "first lady of management" throughout her long life, which ended in 1972 when she was 93.

Lillian Gilbreth's interest in the human aspects of work and her husband's interest in efficiency—the search for the one best way of doing a given task—led to a rare combination of talents.[4] It is therefore not surprising that Frank Gilbreth long emphasized that in applying scientific-management principles, we must look at workers first and understand their personalities and needs. It is interesting, too, that the Gilbreths came to the conclusion that it is not the monotony of work that causes so much worker dissatisfaction, but rather management's lack of interest in workers.

There were, of course, many other management pioneers who built some of their thinking and practice on the ideas and findings of Frederick Taylor. But the three mentioned here will give you some idea of Taylor's influence and the nature of the thinking developed by his disciples.

FAYOL: FATHER OF MODERN OPERATIONAL-MANAGEMENT THEORY

Perhaps the real father of modern management theory is the French industrialist Henri Fayol. Although there is little evidence that management scholars, either in England or in the United States, paid much heed to Fayol's work or knew much about it until the 1920s or even years later, his acute observations on the principles of general management first appeared in 1916 in French, under the title *Administration Industrielle et Générale*. This monograph, reprinted in French several times, was not translated into English until 1929; even then, it was printed by the International Institute of Management at Geneva, and only a few copies were made available for sale outside Great Britain. No English translation was published in the United States until 1949, although the work of Fayol was brought to the attention of American management scholars in 1923 by Sarah Greer's translation of one of Fayol's papers, later incorporated in a collection of papers by Gulick and Urwick.[5] In this same collection, the more general aspects of Fayol's work were referred to in a paper by the British management consultant and scholar Lyndall Urwick.[6]

Industrial Activities

Fayol found that activities of an industrial undertaking could be divided into six groups, as shown in Figure 2-1: (1) technical (production), (2) commercial (buying, selling, and exchange), (3) financial (search for, and optimum use of, capital), (4) security (protection of property and persons), (5) accounting (includ-

FIGURE 2-1

FAYOL'S ACTIVITIES IN INDUSTRIAL UNDERTAKING.

ing statistics), and (6) managerial (planning, organization, command, coordination, and control). Pointing out that these activities exist in businesses of every size, Fayol observed that the first five were well known, and consequently he devoted most of his book to an analysis of the sixth.

General Principles of Management

Noting that principles of management are flexible, not absolute, and must be usable regardless of changing and special conditions, Fayol listed fourteen, based on his experience. They are summarized in the Perspective.

PERSPECTIVE:
FAYOL'S PRINCIPLES

1. Division of work. This is the specialization which economists consider necessary to efficiency in the use of labor. Fayol applies the principle to all kinds of work, managerial as well as technical.

2. Authority and responsibility. Here Fayol finds authority and responsibility to be related, with the latter the corollary of the former and arising from it. He sees authority as a combination of official, deriving from the manager's position, and personal, "compounded of intelligence, experience, moral worth, past service, etc.," factors.

3. Discipline. Seeing discipline as "respect for agreements which are directed at achieving obedience, application, energy, and the outward marks of respect," Fayol declares that discipline requires good superiors at all levels.

4. Unity of command. This means that employees should receive orders from one superior only.

5. Unity of direction. According to this principle, each group of activities with the same objective must have one head and one plan. As distinguished from the fourth principle, it relates to the organization of the "body corporate," rather than to personnel. (Fayol did not in any sense mean that all decisions should be made at the top.)

6. Subordination of individual to general interest. This is self-explanatory; when the two are found to differ, management must reconcile them.

7. Remuneration. Remuneration and methods of payment should be fair and afford the maximum possible satisfaction to employees and employer.

8. Centralization. Without using the term "centralization of authority," Fayol refers to the extent to which authority is concentrated or dispersed. Individual circumstances will determine the degree that will "give the best overall yield."

9. Scalar chain. Fayol thinks of this as a "chain of superiors" from the highest to the lowest ranks, which, while not to be departed from needlessly, should be short-circuited when to follow it scrupulously would be detrimental.

10. Order. Breaking this into "material" and "social" order, Fayol follows the simple adage of "a place for everything [everyone], and everything [everyone] in its [his or her] place." This is essentially a principle of organization in the arrangement of things and people.

11. Equity. Loyalty and devotion should be elicited from personnel by a combination of kindliness and justice on the part of managers when dealing with subordinates.

12. Stability of tenure. Finding unnecessary turnover to be both the cause and the effect of bad management, Fayol points out its dangers and costs.

13. Initiative. Initiative is conceived of as the thinking out and execution of a plan. Since it is one of the "keenest satisfactions for an intelligent man to experience," Fayol exhorts managers to "sacrifice personal vanity" in order to permit subordinates to exercise it.

14. Esprit de corps. This is the principle that "in union there is strength," as well as an extension of the principle of unity of command, emphasizing the need for teamwork and the importance of communication in obtaining it.

In concluding his discussion of these principles, Fayol observed that he had made no attempt to be exhaustive but had tried only to describe those he had had the most occasion to use, since some kind of codification of principles appeared to be indispensable in every undertaking.

Elements of Management

Fayol regarded the elements of management as its functions—planning, organizing, commanding, coordinating, and controlling.[7] A large part of his treatise is given to an examination of these functions, and his observations are, on the whole, still valid after more than seven decades of study and experience of others in the field. Throughout Fayol's treatise there exists an understanding of the universality of principles. Again and again, he points out that these apply not only to business but also to political, religious, philanthropic, military, and other undertakings. Since all enterprises require managing, the formulation of a theory of management is necessary to its effective teaching.

EMERGENCE OF THE BEHAVIORAL SCIENCES

During practically the same period that Taylor, Fayol, and others were concentrating on scientific management and the manager's tasks, many scholars and practitioners were thinking about, experimenting with, and writing on industrial psychology and on social theory, both of which, in many instances, were stimulated by the scientific-management movement. We can get the flavor of these developments by looking briefly at the emergence of industrial psychology, the growth of personnel management, the development of a sociological approach to human relations and management, and Chester Barnard's social systems approach.

The Emergence of Industrial Psychology

Acknowledged to be "the father of industrial psychology," Hugo Münsterberg was trained as a psychologist, receiving his Ph.D. at the University of Leipzig in 1885. He also was trained as a medical doctor, receiving the M.D. degree at the University of Heidelberg in 1887. At the age of 29, in 1892, Münsterberg went to

Brown Brothers

HUGO MÜNSTERBERG
1836–1916

Harvard at the invitation of psychologist William James to take charge of the psychological laboratory and to act as professor of experimental psychology. In 1910 his interest turned to the application of psychology to industry, where he saw the importance of applying behavioral science to the new scientific-management movement. In his landmark book entitled *Psychology and Industrial Efficiency,* first published in 1912,[8] Münsterberg made it clear that his objectives were to discover (1) how to find people whose mental qualities best fit them for the work they are to do, (2) under what psychological conditions the greatest and most satisfactory output can be obtained from the work of every person, and (3) how a business can influence workers in such a way as to obtain the best possible results from them. Like Taylor, he was interested in the mutuality of interests between managers and workers. He stressed that his approach was even more strongly aimed at workers and that through it he hoped to reduce their working time, increase their wages, and raise their "level of life."

Münsterberg's work was supplemented by the pioneering thinking of Lillian Gilbreth, who attempted in her *Psychology of Management,* published in 1914,[9] to apply early psychological concepts to the practice of scientific management. Another important early behavioral scientist who applied psychology to management was Walter Dill Scott. He received his doctorate in psychology in 1900, wrote many books on the application of psychological concepts to advertising and marketing and on the development of such personnel-management practices as effective selection, and later became president of Northwestern University.[10]

Development of the Sociological Approach to Management

In part preceding and in large part concurrent with the development of scientific management by Taylor and administrative management by Fayol, a considerable amount of thinking and research were being devoted to observing people as products of group behavior. This is sometimes called the "social man" approach to management. Generally regarded as "fathers of organization theory," or the "social systems approach to management," were three outstanding scholars who wrote books and essays at the close of the nineteenth century and during the early years of the twentieth century.

One of these was the German intellectual Max Weber, whose empirical analyses of church, government, the military, and business led him to the belief that hierarchy, authority, and bureaucracy (including clear rules, definition of tasks, and discipline) lie at the foundation of all social organizations. Another was the French scholar Emile Durkheim, whose doctoral dissertation, published in 1893,[11] and subsequent writings emphasized the idea that groups, by establishing their values and norms, control human conduct in any social organization.

The third was the French-Italian Vilfredo Pareto, who, in a series of lectures and books between 1896 and 1917, earned the right to be called "the father of the social systems approach" to organization and management.[12] Pareto viewed society as an intricate cluster of interdependent units, or elements—that is, as a social system with many subsystems. Among his many ideas was the tendency of social systems to seek equilibrium upon being disturbed by outside or inside influence. His thesis was that social attitudes, or sentiments, function to cause the system to seek an equilibrium when disturbed by these forces. He saw also that it was the task of the elite (the "ruling class") in any society to provide the leadership to maintain the social system.

The Hawthorne Studies

Although these few words give inadequate expression of the views of the social man or social system pioneers (and space does not permit even the mention of many others), there is no question that they did have considerable influence on Elton Mayo, F. J. Roethlisberger, and others who undertook the famous experiments at the Hawthorne plant of the Western Electric Company between 1927 and 1932.[13] Earlier, from 1924 to 1927, the National Research Council made a study in collaboration with Western Electric to determine the effect of illumination and other conditions upon workers and their productivity. Finding that, when illumination was either increased or decreased for a test group, productivity improved, the researchers were about to declare the whole experiment a failure until Elton Mayo (see photo), of Harvard, saw in it something unusual and, with Roethlisberger and others, continued the research.

What Mayo and his colleagues found, partly on the basis of the earlier thinking of Pareto, was to have a dramatic effect on management thought. Changing illumination for the test group, modifying rest periods, shortening workdays, and varying incentive pay systems did not seem to explain changes in productivity. Mayo and his researchers then came to the conclusion that other factors were responsible. They found, in general, that the improvement in productivity was due to such social factors as morale, satisfactory interrelationships between members of a work group (a "sense of belonging"), and effective management—a kind of managing that would understand human behavior, especially group behavior, and serve it through such interpersonal skills as motivating, counseling, leading, and communicating. This phenomenon, arising basically from people's being "noticed," has been known as the **Hawthorne effect.**

GEORGE E. MAYO
1880–1949

Baker Library, Harvard University
Graduate School of Business Administration

What the Hawthorne studies dramatized was that humans are social—that business operations are a matter not merely of machinery and methods but also of gearing these with the social system to develop a complete sociotechnical system. These experiments led to increased emphasis on the behavioral sciences as applied to management and to the recognition that managers operate in a social system. It should not be inferred from this that prior to the Hawthorne experiments successful managers did not recognize the importance of the human factor, or that management theorists overlooked it. As the brief discussions earlier in this chapter clearly indicate, this is simply not true. But what the work of Mayo and his associates did underscore was the need for a greater and deeper understanding of the social and behavioral aspects of management.

Chester Barnard and Social Systems Theory

One of the most influential books published in the entire field of management is the classic treatise entitled *The Functions of the Executive,* written by Chester I. Barnard in 1938.[14] A lifelong executive himself and president of the New Jersey Bell Telephone Company from 1927 to 1948, Barnard was a first-rate scholar and intellectual who was greatly influenced by Pareto, Mayo, and other faculty members at Harvard, where he occasionally lectured. His analysis of the manager is truly a social systems approach since, in order to comprehend and analyze the functions of executives, Barnard looked for their major tasks in the system where they operate.

In determining that the task of executives (by which he meant all kinds of managers) was one of maintaining a system of cooperative effort in a formal organization, Barnard addressed himself to the reasons for, and the nature of, cooperative systems. The book is a social systems approach, concentrating on major elements of the managerial job, containing extraordinary insights on decision making and leadership, and bearing the authority of an intellectual with exceptional executive experience.

New Jersey Bell

CHESTER I. BARNARD
1886–1961

RECENT CONTRIBUTORS TO MANAGEMENT THOUGHT

Among the several contributors to management are public administrators, business managers, and behavioral scientists whose important works are discussed throughout this book. We will mention only a few here.

Laurence Peter suggested that eventually people get promoted to a level where they are incompetent and no further promotion is possible. Unfortunately, this may result in organizations with incompetent people.[15] William Ouchi, who wrote the best-selling book *Theory Z,* shows how selected management practices may be adapted in the United States.[16] Finally, Thomas Peters and Robert Waterman, as well as Peters and Nancy Austin, discuss characteristics of excellent companies.[17] Most of these works are discussed in greater detail in other parts of this book.

PATTERNS OF MANAGEMENT ANALYSIS: A MANAGEMENT THEORY JUNGLE?

Although academic writers and theorists contributed notably little to the study of management until the early 1950s, previous writing having come largely from practitioners, the past three to four decades have seen a veritable deluge of writing from the academic halls. The variety of approaches to management analysis, the welter of research, and the number of differing views have resulted in much confusion as to what management is, what management theory and science are, and how managerial events should be analyzed. As a matter of fact, the senior author some years ago called this situation "the management theory jungle."[18] Since that time, the vegetation in this jungle has changed somewhat, new approaches have developed, and older approaches have taken on some new meanings with some new words attached, but the developments of management science and theory still have the characteristics of a jungle.

The various approaches to management analysis—summarized in Figure 2-2—are grouped here into the following categories: (1) the empirical, or case, approach, (2) the interpersonal behavior approach, (3) the group behavior approach, (4) the cooperative social systems approach, (5) the sociotechnical systems approach, (6) the decision theory approach, (7) the systems approach, (8) the mathematical or "management science" approach, (9) the contingency, or situational, approach, (10) the managerial roles approach, (11) McKinsey's 7-S approach, and (12) the operational approach.

Although we cannot treat the approaches here in much detail, we can sketch the nature of each so that you can at least identify the point of view from which any book or article on management has probably been written. As we shall note later in this chapter, there are a number of currently popular approaches with attractive new names like "organizational behavior" and "organization development"; they are really not new, basic approaches to management analysis but are, rather, special areas of knowledge or techniques attempting to improve managerial practice.

FIGURE 2-2   APPROACHES TO MANAGEMENT

CHARACTERISTICS/ CONTRIBUTIONS	LIMITATIONS	ILLUSTRATION
EMPIRICAL, OR CASE, APPROACH		
Studies experience through cases. Identifies successes and failures.	Situations are all different. No attempt to identify principles. Limited value for developing management theory.	
INTERPERSONAL BEHAVIOR APPROACH		
Focus on interpersonal behavior, human relations, leadership, and motivation. Based on individual psychology.	Ignores planning, organizing, and controlling. Psychological training is not enough to become an effective manager.	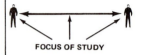
GROUP BEHAVIOR APPROACH		
Emphasis on behavior of people in groups. Based on sociology and social psychology. Primarily study of group behavior patterns. The study of large groups is often called "organization behavior."	Often not integrated with management concepts, principles, theory, and techniques. Need for closer integration with organization structure design, staffing, planning, and controlling.	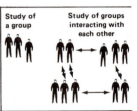
COOPERATIVE SOCIAL SYSTEMS APPROACH		
Concerned with both interpersonal and group behavioral aspects leading to a system of cooperation. Expanded concept includes any cooperative group with a clear purpose.	Too broad a field for the study of management. At the same time, it overlooks many managerial concepts, principles, and techniques.	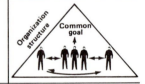
SOCIOTECHNICAL SYSTEMS APPROACH		
Technical system has great effect on social system (personal attitudes, group behavior). Focus on production, office operations, and other areas with close relationships between the technical system and people.	Emphasis only on blue-collar and lower-level office work. Ignores much of other managerial knowledge.	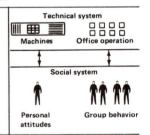
DECISION THEORY APPROACH		
Focus on the making of decisions, persons or groups making decisions, and the decision-making process. Some theorists use decision making as a springboard to study all enterprise activities. The boundaries of study are no longer clearly defined.	There is more to managing than making decisions. The focus is at the same time too narrow and too wide.	

CHARACTERISTICS/ CONTRIBUTIONS	LIMITATIONS	ILLUSTRATION

SYSTEMS APPROACH

Systems concepts have broad applicability. Systems have boundaries, but they also interact with the external environment; i.e., organizations are open systems. Recognizes importance of studying interrelatedness of planning, organizing, and controlling in an organization as well as the many subsystems.	Analyses of the interrelatedness of systems and subsystems as well as the interactions of organizations with their external environment. Can hardly be considered a new approach to management.	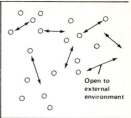

MATHEMATICAL OR "MANAGEMENT SCIENCE" APPROACH

Managing is seen as mathematical processes, concepts, symbols, and models. Looks at management as a purely logical process, expressed in mathematical symbols and relationships.	Preoccupation with mathematical models. Many aspects in managing cannot be modeled. Mathematics is a useful tool, but hardly a school or an approach to management.	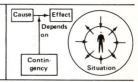

CONTINGENCY OR SITUATIONAL APPROACH

Managerial practice depends on circumstances (i.e., a contingency or a situation). Contingency theory recognizes the influence of given solutions on organizational behavior patterns.	Managers have long realized that there is *no* one best way to do things. Difficulty in determining all relevant contingency factors and showing their relationships. Can be very complex.	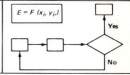

MANAGERIAL ROLES APPROACH

Original study consisted of observations of five chief executives. On the basis of this study, ten managerial roles were identified and grouped into (1) interpersonal, (2) informational, and (3) decision roles.	Original sample was very small. Some activities are not managerial. Activities are evidence of planning, organizing, staffing, leading, and controlling. But some important managerial activities were left out (e.g., appraising managers).	

MCKINSEY'S 7-S FRAMEWORK

The seven S's are (1) strategy, (2) structure, (3) systems, (4) style, (5) staff, (6) shared values, (7) skills.	Although this experienced consulting firm now uses a framework similar to the one found useful by Koontz et al. since 1955 (see Table 2-2) and confirms its practicality, the terms used are not precise and topics are not discussed in depth.	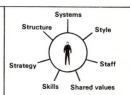

OPERATIONAL APPROACH

Draws together concepts, principles, techniques, and knowledge from other fields and managerial approaches. The attempt is to develop science and theory with practical application. Distinguishes between managerial and non-managerial knowledge. Develops classification system built around the managerial functions of plannng, organizing, staffing, leading, and controlling.	Does not, as some authors do, identify "representing" or "coordination" as a separate function. Coordination, for example, is the essence of managership and is the purpose of managing.	

The Empirical, or Case, Approach

The empirical, or case, approach analyzes management by studying experience, usually through cases. It is based on the belief that, through the study of managers' successes and mistakes in individual cases and of their attempts to solve specific problems, students and practitioners will somehow come to know how to manage effectively in similar situations.

However, unless a study of experience is aimed at determining why something happened or did not happen, in many cases it is likely to be a useless and even a dangerous approach to understanding management. What happened or did not happen in the past is not likely to offer a solution for the problems of what will almost certainly be a different future. Experience may be a helpful guide if it is distilled to reveal the basic reasons why an action succeeded or failed and if the differing circumstances of the past are taken into account.

If this distillation of experience takes place with a view to generalizations, the empirical, or case, approach can be a useful way to develop principles of management. Also, there can be no doubt that cases can provide a laboratory situation for introducing, explaining, and testing management knowledge. But this approach has serious limitations in developing management theory and techniques simply because experience has definite limitations in a subject as complex and broad as management.

The Interpersonal Behavior Approach

The interpersonal behavior approach is based on the idea that managing involves getting things done through people, and therefore, its study should be centered on interpersonal relationships. Variously called the human relations, leadership, or behavioral science approach, this school concentrates on the human aspect of management. Its proponents believe that when people work together to accomplish objectives, "people should understand people."

The writers and scholars using this approach are heavily influenced by psychological theory. Their focus is the individual and his or her motivations and relationships with others. In this school are those who emphasize human relations as an art which a manager, perhaps even acting as an amateur psychiatrist, should understand and practice. There are those who focus attention on the manager as a leader and who sometimes equate managership with leadership, thus, in effect, treating all "led" activities as "managed" situations. Linked to these are specialists who see leadership as largely a matter of understanding and developing means of obtaining response to human motivations.

No one can deny that managing involves human behavior or dispute that the study of human interactions, whether in the context of managing or elsewhere, is useful and important. It would likewise be a mistake not to regard leadership and the ability to motivate others as important for effective managing. On the contrary, effective managers do tend to become good leaders. In creating and maintaining an environment for performance, managers will almost surely develop situations where people will find it advantageous to follow them.

The field of interpersonal behavior scarcely encompasses all there is to management. It is entirely possible for all the managers of a company to understand psychology and yet not be effective in managing. As a matter of fact, a fairly large company undertook extensive psychological training of managers at all levels only to find that this training did not guarantee effective managing. The company quickly found that managers need to know something of planning, control and control techniques, and devising a suitable organization structure, as well as other matters, in order to accomplish the entire managerial task.

Moreover, many members of the interpersonal behavior school are finding that they must extend their views far beyond psychological matters. For example, in the area of leadership, research has shown that the entire organizational climate has much to do with effective leading. And in understanding human motivations, psychologically oriented specialists are finding that such operational-management techniques as setting meaningful and verifiable objectives, designing organization structures showing clearly who is responsible for what, and giving accurate and prompt feedback on how well a person is doing are among the most important arousers of human interest and effort.

The Group Behavior Approach

The group behavior approach is closely related to the interpersonal behavior approach and is often confused or combined with it. But it is concerned primarily with behavior of people in groups rather than behavior of individuals. It thus tends to be based on sociology and social psychology rather than on individual psychology. Its supporters include those writers and scholars who look on the study of management as primarily a study of group behavior patterns.

The group behavior approach varies all the way from the study of small groups with their cultural and behavioral patterns to the study of the behavioral composition of large groups. This latter is often called the organization behavior approach, and an "organization" may mean the system, or pattern, of any set of group relationships in a company, a government agency, a hospital, or any other kind of undertaking.

Proponents of this approach have made many worthwhile contributions to management. The recognition that any organized enterprise is a social arrangement, made up in turn of many social units within it, with a complex of interacting attitudes, pressures, and conflicts arising from people's cultural backgrounds, has been helpful to both theorists and practicing managers. Many of our problems in managing stem from group behavior patterns, attitudes, and desires, some arising within a company or some other enterprise, but many coming from people's backgrounds.

Some group behaviorists have drawn a line between "organization behavior" and "management." In organizing management knowledge, all behavioral sciences related to managing should be interwoven logically with management concepts, principles, theory, and techniques. Other authors understand that the study of behavioral elements in group operations must be more closely integrated with study of organizational structure design, staffing, planning, and control. As important as the analysis of group behavior is, it is not all there is to management.

The Cooperative Social Systems Approach

The interpersonal and group behavior approaches have instigated an increased focus on the study of human relationships as cooperative social systems. This change has been due in part to the vogue of looking at everything from a systems point of view. It is also the result of a desire to refine the group behavior approach by giving emphasis to well-organized cooperation.

About 50 years ago, seeking to explain the work of executives in his notable book, *The Functions of the Executive,* Chester Barnard saw executives as operating in, and maintaining, cooperative social systems which he referred to as "organizations."[19] In other words, Barnard saw social systems as the cooperative interaction of the ideas, forces, desires, and thinking of two or more people. He therefore was concerned with both interpersonal and group behavior elements, and he saw their interaction as leading to systems of cooperation.

The Barnard concept of cooperative social systems pervades the work of many social scientists concerned with management. For example, Herbert Simon at one time defined organizations as "systems of interdependent activity, encompassing at least several primary groups and usually characterized at the level of consciousness of participants by a high degree of rational direction of behavior towards ends that are objects of common knowledge."[20] Simon and an increasing number of writers in recent years have expanded this concept to apply to any system of cooperative group interrelationships or behavior where a clear purpose exists, and they have given the field the rather general title of "organization theory."

The cooperative social systems approach is pertinent to the study of management. All managers do, of course, operate in a cooperative social system. But we do not find people who are generally referred to as managers in all kinds of cooperative social systems. We would hardly think of a group of motorists sharing a main highway as being managed. We would not regard the leaders of a mob as managers. Nor would we think of a family group gathering to celebrate a birthday as being managed. Therefore, we can conclude that this approach is broader than the field of management but that, at the same time, it also tends to overlook many concepts, principles, and techniques that are important to managers.

The Sociotechnical Systems Approach

One of the schools of management identifies itself as the sociotechnical systems approach. Its development is generally credited to E. L. Trist and his associates at the Tavistock Institute in England. In studies of production problems in coal mining, this group found that merely to study social problems was not enough. Instead, it found, in dealing with problems of productivity, that the technical system (machines and methods) had a strong effect on the social system. In other words, personal attitudes and group behavior are influenced by the technical system in which people work.

It is, therefore, the position of this school that social systems and technical systems must be made harmonious. If they are found not to be, changes should be made, usually in the technical systems. Most of the work of this school has consequently been concentrated on production, office operations, and other areas where the technical systems have a close relationship to people. It therefore tends to be heavily oriented to industrial engineering.

This relatively new school has made some interesting contributions to management practice. However, technology in such fields as transportation, products assembly, and chemical processing has long been known to influence the ways in which managers organize and manage their operations.

At the same time, particularly where technology has a great effect on group behavior patterns, as it does in so much blue-collar and lower-level white-collar work, the orderly analysis and coordination of social and technical systems can have great managerial benefits. But as promising as this approach is in such areas, there is much pertinent management knowledge not encompassed in this approach.

The Decision Theory Approach

The decision theory approach to management is based on the idea that, since managers make decisions, those studying management must concentrate on decision making—the selection from among possible alternatives of a course of action. Decision theorists concentrate primarily on the making of decisions, on the persons or organized groups making decisions, and on an analysis of the decision process. Study of the process of evaluating alternatives has become, for some decision theorists, a springboard for examining the entire area of enterprise activity, including the psychological and social reactions of individuals and groups, the nature of organization structure, the need for and development of information for decisions, and the analysis of values.

The result has been that decision theory no longer concentrates narrowly on decisions but, rather, has tended to take a broader view of companies or other enterprises and social systems. As one prominent decision theorist informed the authors when accused of looking at management through a narrow keyhole, his school of thought is concerned not only with the making of decisions but also with everything that precedes a decision and everything that follows one. Thus, nothing is left out.

It is not surprising that many theorists believe that, since managing is characterized by decision making, the central focus of management theory can be decision making and the rest of management thought can be built around it. This argument has a degree of reasonableness. But it does seem to overlook the fact that there is much more to managing than making decisions and that, for most managers, the actual making of a decision is a fairly easy thing—if goals are clear, if adequate information is available, if the organization structure provides a clear understanding of responsibility for decisions, and if many of the other requirements of the managerial task are present.

Important as it is in managing, decision making appears to be too narrow a focus for a total theory of management or, if its implications are considerably extended, too wide a focus. For, as most decision theorists recognize, decision theory could be applied to the thinking and problems of a Robinson Crusoe as well as of the United States Steel Corporation.

The Systems Approach

During recent years, many management scholars and writers have emphasized the systems approach to the study and analysis of management.

A **system** is essentially a set or assemblage of things interconnected, interdependent, things that form a complex unity. These things may be physical, such as the parts of an automobile engine; or they may be biological, like components of the human body; or they may be theoretical, as is a set of concepts, principles, theory, and techniques in an area such as managing. All systems, except perhaps that of the universe, interact with, and are influenced by, their environments, although we define boundaries for them so that we can see them more clearly and analyze them.

The use of systems theory and analysis in the physical and biological sciences has given rise to a considerable body of systems knowledge. Systems theory has been found applicable to management. Although management theory, as a system, does have boundaries in order to make it convenient to study, it is a system open to the environment. Thus, when managers plan, they have no choice but to take into account such external variables as markets, technology, social forces, laws, and regulations. When they design an organizational system to provide an environment for performance, they cannot help but be influenced by the behavior patterns people bring to their jobs from the environment external to an enterprise.

Systems also play an important part within the area of managing itself. There are planning systems, organizational systems, and control systems. And within these we can perceive many subsystems, such as systems of delegation, network planning, and budgeting.

Intelligent and experienced practicing managers see their problems and operations as a network of interrelated elements with daily interaction between environments inside or outside their companies. The conscious study of, and emphasis on, systems have forced many managers and scholars to consider more perceptively the various interacting elements affecting management theory and practice. But this can hardly be regarded as a new approach to management thought.

The Mathematical, or Management Science, Approach

There are theorists who see managing primarily as mathematical processes, concepts, symbols, and models. Perhaps the most widely known of these theorists are the operations researchers, many of whom have called themselves "management scientists." This group believes that if managing or organizing or planning or decision making is a logical process, it can be expressed in mathematical symbols and relationships. The primary focus of this school is the mathematical model. Through this device, problems can be expressed in terms of basic relationships, and where a given goal is sought, the model can often be constructed so as to suggest a decision as to the best thing to do. An example of a mathematical model will be given in Chapter 21, in which we discuss operations research. There is often an almost complete absorption with mathematics, and some members of this school have even taken the extreme position that "if you cannot express it mathematically, it is not worth expressing."

No one interested in any scientific field can overlook the great usefulness of mathematical analyses. Mathematical analysis makes us define problems first and allows us to use symbols for unknown quantities. Mathematics also provides a powerful logical tool for simplifying and solving complex problems. But it is as difficult to see mathematics as a separate approach to management as it is to see it as a separate approach to physics, chemistry, or engineering.

The Contingency, or Situational, Approach

One approach to management thought and practice which was quite popular a decade or so ago is the contingency, or situational, approach. Proponents of this approach emphasized that what managers do in practice depends upon a given set of circumstances (a contingency or a situation). According to some scholars, contingency theory takes into account not only situations but also the influence of given solutions on behavior patterns of an enterprise. For example, an organization structured around operating functions, such as finance, engineering, production, and marketing, might be most suitable for a given situation; however, managers using this approach should consider that it may foster patterns of group loyalty to the function rather than to the company.

By its very nature, managerial practice requires that managers take into account the realities of a given situation when they apply theory or techniques. It is not the task of science and theory to prescribe what should be done in a given situation. Management science and theory does not advocate a best way to do things in every situation, any more than the science of astrophysics or mechanics tells an engineer how to design a single best instrument for all kinds of applications. How theory and science are applied in practice naturally depends upon the situation.

This is to say that there is science and there is art, that there is knowledge and there is practice. You can clearly understand that a corner grocery store could hardly be organized like General Motors, or that the technical realities of petroleum exploration, production, and refining make impracticable autonomously organized product divisions for gasoline, jet fuel, and lubricating oils.

The Managerial Roles Approach

One of the newer approaches to management theory is the managerial roles approach, popularized by Professor Henry Mintzberg of McGill University.[21] Essentially, his approach is to observe what managers actually do and from such observations come to conclusions as to what managerial activities (or roles) are.

Although many researchers have studied the actual work of managers from chief executives to line supervisors, Mintzberg has given this approach higher visibility.

After systematically studying the activities of five chief executives in a variety of organizations, Mintzberg came to the conclusion that executives do not act out the classical classification of managerial functions—planning, organizing, coordinating, and controlling. Instead, they engage in a variety of other activities.

From his research and the research of others who have studied what managers actually do, Mintzberg has come to the conclusion that managers really fill a series of ten roles, as shown in the Perspective.

Mintzberg refers to the usual way of classifying managerial functions as "folklore," although most modern management textbooks use this framework. As you will see in the following discussion on the operational-management approach, operational theorists have used such managerial functions as planning, organizing, staffing, leading, and controlling as the means of classifying the growing body of managerial knowledge. While the functions are believed to be real, they are not intended to describe all activities of managers.

Mintzberg's approach has also been criticized. In the first place, the sample of five executives used in his research is far too small to support so sweeping a conclusion. In the second place, in analyzing the actual activities of managers—

PERSPECTIVE:
THE TEN MANAGERIAL ROLES IDENTIFIED BY MINTZBERG

Interpersonal roles
1. The figurehead role (performing ceremonial and social duties as the organization's representative)
2. The leader role
3. The liaison role (particularly with outsiders)

Informational roles
1. The recipient role (receiving information about the operation of an enterprise)
2. The disseminator role (passing information to subordinates)
3. The spokesperson role (transmitting information to those outside the organization)

Decision roles
1. The entrepreneurial role
2. The disturbance-handler role
3. The resource-allocator role
4. The negotiator role (dealing with various persons and groups of persons)

agers do some work that is not purely managerial; one would expect even presidents of large companies to spend some of their time in public and stockholder relations, in raising money, perhaps in dealer relations, marketing, and so on.

In the third place, many of the activities Mintzberg found are, in fact, evidences of planning, organizing, staffing, leading, and controlling. For example, what is resource allocation but planning? The entrepreneurial role is certainly an element of planning. And the interpersonal roles are mainly instances of leading. In addition, the informational roles can be fitted into a number of the functional areas.

Nevertheless, looking at what managers really do can have considerable value. In analyzing activities, an effective manager might wish to ascertain how activities and techniques fall into the various fields of knowledge reflected by the basic functions of managers. However, the roles Mintzberg identified appear to be incomplete. Where does one find such unquestionably important managerial activities as structuring organization, selecting and appraising managers, and determining major strategies? Omissions such as these make one wonder whether the executives in his sample were really effective managers. It certainly raises a serious question as to whether the managerial roles approach, at least as put forth here, is an adequate one on which to base a practical, operational theory of management.

McKinsey's 7-S Approach

In recent years, the 7-S framework for management analysis developed by the respected consulting firm of McKinsey & Company has gained in popularity, partly because it became the basis for the research of two best-selling books, *The Art of Japanese Management*,[22] and *In Search of Excellence*.[23] The seven S's are strategy, structure, systems, style, staff, shared values, and skills, as summarized in Table 2-2. However, the author of one of the above-mentioned books admitted that in the attempt to make the key aspects of the model begin with an "s" (to serve as a memory hook), the meaning of some of the terms had to be stretched. For example, in traditional management literature the term "skills" is generally applied to personal skills (e.g., technical, human, conceptual) while in the 7-S framework "skills" means the capabilities of the organization as a whole. Organizational capabilities, or the lack of them, are generally referred to in management literature as strengths and weaknesses of the firm.

The outstanding feature of the 7-S model is that it has been tested extensively by McKinsey consultants in their studies of many companies. At the same time, this framework has been used by respected business schools, such as Harvard and Stanford. Thus, theory and practice seem to support each other in the study of management. Perhaps the most surprising fact about the 7-S framework is that it supports, and is similar to, the framework of the managerial functions (planning, organizing, staffing, leading, and controlling) used in this and in previous editions of this book. Table 2-2 shows the relationships of the seven S's and the chapter references of this textbook edition.

By using the term "shared values," also sometimes called "superordinate

TABLE 2-2   Comparison of 7-S Framework and the Operational-Management Approach

McKinsey's 7-S framework for management analysis	Textbook reference
Strategy: Systematic action and allocation of resources to achieve company aims	Strategies, Policies (Chap. 5)
Structure: Organization structure and authority/responsibility relationships	Part 3: Organizing, especially: Basic Departmentation (Chap. 8) Line/Staff Authority and Decentralization (Chap. 9)
Systems: Procedures and processes such as information systems, manufacturing processes, budgeting and control processes	Part 6: Controlling, especially: The System and Process of Controlling (Chap. 20) Control Techniques and Information Technology (Chap. 21) Productivity and Operations Management (Chap. 22)
Style: The way management behaves and collectively spends its time to achieve organizational goals	Part 5: Leading (Chaps. 16–19)
Staff: The people in the enterprise and their socialization into the organizational culture	Part 4: Staffing (Chaps. 12–15)
Shared values (superordinate goals): The values shared by the members of an organization	Various parts of the book, especially: Effective Organizing and Organizational Culture (Chap. 11) Leadership (Chap. 18)
Skills: Distinctive capabilities of an enterprise	Strategies, Policies (Chap. 5)

Source: R. T. Pascale and A. G. Athos, *The Art of Japanese Management* (New York: Warner Books, Inc., 1981); R. H. Waterman, Jr., "The Seven Elements of Strategic Fit," in A. A. Thomson, Jr., A. J. Strickland III, and W. E. Fulmer (eds.), *Readings in Strategic Management* (Plano, Tex.: Business Publications, Inc., 1984), pp. 333–339.

goals," 7-S theorists emphasize that goal statements are very important in determining the destiny of the enterprise, as emphasized in Chapter 4; they also point out that values must be shared by organization members. Therefore, special attention is given to personal and organizational values in Chapter 11, where we discuss organizational effectiveness.

Identifying key aspects of the management system and showing the interrelatedness of the variables is a positive contribution to management theory. A simple, easy-to-remember framework, such as that suggested by McKinsey, is certainly an effort to be welcomed by practitioners and academicians. Although the terminology it employs is, at times, not quite clear, and may have somewhat increased the semantic jungle, the positive contributions of this framework must be recognized.

The Operational Approach

The operational approach to management theory and science attempts to draw together the pertinent knowledge of management by relating it to the managerial job—what managers do. Like other operational sciences, it tries to put together the concepts, principles, and techniques that underlie the task of managing.

The operational approach recognizes that there is a central core of knowledge about managing pertinent only to the field of management. Such matters as line and staff, departmentation, managerial appraisal, and various managerial control techniques involve concepts and theory found only where managers are involved. But, in addition, this approach draws on and absorbs knowledge from other fields, including systems theory, decision theory, theories of motivation and leadership, individual and group behavior, social systems, and cooperation and communications, and the application of mathematical analyses and concepts.

The nature of the operational approach can be seen in Figure 2-3. As this diagram shows, the operational management school recognizes the existence of a central core of science and theory peculiar to managing and also draws important contributions from various other schools and approaches. As the circle

FIGURE 2-3

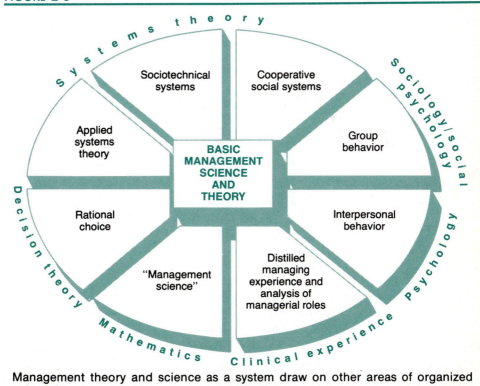

Management theory and science as a system draw on other areas of organized knowledge. The figure shows how operational-management theory and science, here enclosed in the circle, have a core of basic science and theory and draw from other fields of knowledge pertinent to understanding management. Basic management is thus, in part, an eclectic science and theory.

shows, the operational theorist is not interested in all the important knowledge in these various fields, but only that which is deemed most useful and relevant to managing.

Those who subscribe to the operational approach do so with the hope of developing science and theory which have practical application to managing and yet are not so broad as to apply to everything that might have any relationship to the managerial task. They recognize that managing is a difficult task with an immense number of variables affecting it. They realize that any field as complex as managing, which deals with the production and marketing of anything from bread to money, with religion, and with government services, can never be isolated from the physical, biological, or social environment. But they also recognize that some partitioning of knowledge is necessary and that some boundaries must be set if meaningful progress is to be made there or in any other field.

Because the functions of managers are emphasized in the operational approach, it is often called the "management process" school. Because the great French industrialist and management pioneer Henri Fayol first attempted to organize management knowledge around managerial functions, the school is also often referred to as the "classical" or the "traditional" school. But it is really merely an approach that has been found useful to, and understandable by, practicing managers and that also furnishes a means of distinguishing between managerial knowledge and the special knowledge and expertise of such non-managerial fields as marketing or production. In addition, it is a way of integrating into management useful and pertinent knowledge from all schools and approaches.

Although the operationalists generally believe that the fundamentals of management are universal, theorists of this school would readily admit that the problems managers face and the situations in which they operate vary among managerial levels in an enterprise and among different enterprises, and that the application of concepts, theories, and techniques will naturally vary. But, as indicated in Chapter 1, this diversity is characteristic of the difference between theory and practice in any field.

FOR DISCUSSION

1. "The systems approach is new, having been used or recognized in management only in the past few years." Analyze and comment on this statement.

2. Why has Frederick Taylor been called "the father of scientific management," and why is Henri Fayol known as "the father of modern operational management theory"?

3. To what extent and how has the development of behavioral thought tended to parallel and supplement the evolution of management thought?

4. Taylor, Fayol, and other management pioneers have been accused of seeking and recommending a one best way to do things in managing. To what extent, if at all, is this accusation correct?

5. Chester Barnard has been referred to as the "originator of the social systems approach" to management. Why might he be so regarded?

6. Do the various approaches to the analysis of management represent a management theory jungle, or do they represent simply an intellectual division of labor?

7. To what extent is the "management science" approach truly management science?

8. As you read the following chapters of this book, watch for signs of convergence of the various approaches to management theory and science. Is it reasonable to refer to the various approaches as the "management theory jungle"?

EXERCISES/ACTION STEPS

1. Take any four books or articles on management that you like and ascertain what approach to management each author takes and the extent of the semantic differences among them.

2. Divide the class into groups. Each group should take a management approach, except the operational one, and identify its major elements and its contributions, as well as the limitations of the approach. Each group should select a spokesperson to present the findings of each group.

CASES

CASE 2-1
FRED DENNY

"The trouble with management as a field of study and practice," Fred Denny, a space physicist, said to his laboratory head, Claude Greenwood, "is that it has no scientific base. I feel I know what I am doing when I design a guidance system for a missile because I have the space, propulsion, and other sciences available to tell me what to do. But, when you ask me if I am doing a good job as a supervisor of my engineering and technical team, there is nothing, no science of management, to guide me. In my reading of the books on management, I get the idea that managers must operate on a closed-system basis, that the best things managers can do are to be friendly, consult with their subordinates on every little thing, and develop strict rules and procedures so that no subordinate can make a mistake.

"As I think about it, Claude, I cannot see much science in management. And I wonder what good management books, articles, and management development courses are ever going to do any of us. Do we have to wait for centuries when a science of management, as an exact science like physics, is developed?"

Claude Greenwood, having been exposed to a number of management development seminars which had emphasized the usefulness and importance of management knowledge, was taken aback by Fred's outburst. But he was impressed that what his subordinate had said did make a lot of sense. He was, however, at a loss as to how to respond to Fred.

1. If you were Claude Greenwood, how would you respond to Fred Denny's statement?

2. What would you suggest be done to make management more scientific?

CASE 2-2
LMT, INCORPORATED

Frank W. Bates was president of LMT, Incorporated, a large company making wheels, brakes, springs, radios, and other components for the automobile manufacturing companies. The firm also had a division developing and manufacturing components for the space program. LMT's space program activities were in a division headed by a general manager, Julia Sanders. Her personnel manager, Lewis Lemke, recommended that the way to develop managers at all levels in the division was to give them courses and exercises in psychology and human relations. He made the point that, after all, managing is a "people" problem, and the only way people can be good managers is to thoroughly understand themselves and their fellow managers and employees.

Ms. Sanders, impressed with this idea, told Mr. Lemke to go ahead with the program. The personnel manager did so with great energy and thoroughness. After a few years, all the managers from top to bottom of the division had gone through a number of courses and exercises to make them understand themselves and other people as well as the entire area of human relations.

But then Ms. Sanders found that the quality of management in the division had not improved, even though it was clear that people did better understand people. In fact, it became apparent that the other divisions of LMT were performing far better than the space division. President Bates had also noted this and asked Ms. Sanders to explain how her division developed managers. After hearing about the program, Mr. Bates said, "I wonder if you have been on the right track."

1. What do you think of the space division's approach to training managers in the essentials of management?

2. If you were Mr. Bates, what would you suggest that Ms. Sanders should have done?

REFERENCES

1. For one of the most comprehensive histories of management thought, see Daniel A. Wren, *The Evolution of Management Thought* (New York: The Ronald Press Company, 1972; 2d ed., New York: John Wiley & Sons, 1979). See also Claude S. George, Jr., *The History of Management Thought* (Englewood Cliffs, N.J.: Prentice-Hall, 1968).

2. Taylor's principal works, *Shop Management* (originally published in 1903), *Principles of Scientific Management* (published in 1911), and *Testimony before the Special House Committee* (given in 1912), are combined in one book entitled *Scientific Management* (New York: Harper & Brother, 1947). For a review of classic books on management, see Allen C. Bluedorn, ed., "Special Review Section on the Classics of Management," *Academy of Management Review* (April 1986), pp. 442–464.

3. *Shop Management*, p. 25. For a more recent discussion of Taylor's contributions see Edwin A. Locke, "The Ideas of Frederick W. Taylor: An Evaluation," *Academy of Management Review* (January 1982), pp. 14–24.

4. Although the Gilbreths were known for their search for the "best way," it should be noted that they really were interested in the "best way" to do something under a given set of realities, not in every possible situation.

5. L. Gulick and L. Urwick (eds.), *Papers on the Science of Administration* (New York: Institute of Public Administration, 1937). Fayol's paper was translated by Greer as "The Administrative Theory of the State."

6. "The Function of Administration," in Gulick and Urwick, *Papers* (1937).

7. Gulick and Urwick, *Papers* (1937), chap. 5.

8. Published in German in 1912 and in English in 1913 (Boston: Houghton Mifflin Company).

9. (New York: Sturgis and Walton Company.) This book was also Dr. Gilbreth's Ph.D. dissertation.

10. Among his books were *Influencing Men in Business* (New York: The Ronald Press Company, 1911); *Increasing Human Efficiency* (New York: The Macmillan Company, 1911); and (with R. C. Clothier) *Personnel Management: Principles, Practices and Point of View* (New York: McGraw-Hill Book Company, 1923).

11. *De la Division du Travail Social* (The Division of Labor) (Paris: F. Alcan, 1893).

12. The most famous of which was his *Trattato di Sociologia Generale,* published in Florence in 1916, with a second edition in 1923; it may be found in English translation as *The Mind and Society: A Treatise on General Sociology* (New York: Harcourt, Brace and Company, 1935; also New York: Dover Publications, 1963).

13. For a full description of these experiments, see Elton Mayo, *The Human Problems of an Industrial Civilization* (New York: The Macmillan Company, 1933), chaps. 3–5; and F. J. Roethlisberger and W. J. Dickson, *Management and the Worker* (Cambridge, Mass.: Harvard University Press, 1939).

14. (Cambridge, Mass.: Harvard University Press, 1938).

15. Laurence J. Peter and Raymond Hall, *The Peter Principle* (New York: Bantam Books, 1969).

16. William G. Ouchi, *Theory Z: How American Business Can Meet the Japanese Challenge* (Reading, Mass.: Addison-Wesley Publishing Company, 1981).

17. Thomas J. Peters and Robert H. Waterman, Jr., *In Search of Excellence* (New York: Harper & Row, 1982); and Thomas J. Peters and Nancy Austin, *A Passion for Excellence* (New York: Random House, 1985).

18. See Harold Koontz, "The Management Theory Jungle," *Journal of the Academy of Management* (December 1961), pp. 174–188. See also Harold Koontz, "Making Sense of Management Theory," *Harvard Business Review* (July–August 1962), pp. 24ff. and "The Management Theory Jungle Revisited," *Academy of Management Review* (April 1980), pp. 175–187. Much of this material has been drawn from these articles.

19. Chester I. Barnard, *The Functions of the Executive* (Cambridge, Mass.: Harvard University Press, 1938).

20. "Comments on the Theory of Organizations," *American Political Science Review,* vol. 46, no. 4 (1952), p. 1130.

21. Especially his article "The Manager's Job: Folklore and Fact," *Harvard Business Review* (July–August 1975), pp. 49–61, and his book *The Nature of Managerial Work* (New York: Harper & Row, 1973).

22. Richard Tanner Pascale and Anthony G. Athos, *The Art of Japanese Management* (New York: Warner Books, 1981).

23. Peters and Waterman, *In Search of Excellence* (1982).

FOR FURTHER INFORMATION

Austin, Larry M., and James R. Burns. *Management Science* (New York: The Macmillan Company, 1985).

Baker, Kenneth R., and Dean H. Kroop. *Management Science: An Introduction to Decision Models* (New York: John Wiley & Sons, 1985).

Fayol, Henri. *General and Industrial Management* (New York: Pitman Publishing Corporation, 1949).

Koontz, Harold, Cyril O'Donnell, and Heinz Weihrich (eds.). *Management—A Book of Readings,* 5th ed. (New York: McGraw-Hill Book Company, 1980).

Matteson, Michael T., and John M. Ivancevich (eds.). *Management Classics,* 3d. ed. (Plano, Texas: Business Publications, 1986).

Nussbaum, Bruce, and Alex Beam. "Remaking the Harvard B-School," *Business Week,* March 24, 1986, pp. 54–58.

Richards, Max D. (ed). *Readings in Management,* 7th ed. (Cincinnati: South-Western Publishing Company, 1986).

Scott, William G. "Organization Theory: An Overview and an Appraisal," *Academy of Management Journal* (April 1961), pp. 7–26.

Shafritz, Jay M., and Philip H. Whitbeck (eds.). *Classics of Organization Theory* (Oak Park, Ill.: Moore Publishing Company, 1978).

Thierauf, Robert J. *Management Science: A Model Formulation Approach with Computer Applications* (Columbus, Ohio: Merrill, 1985).

Planning

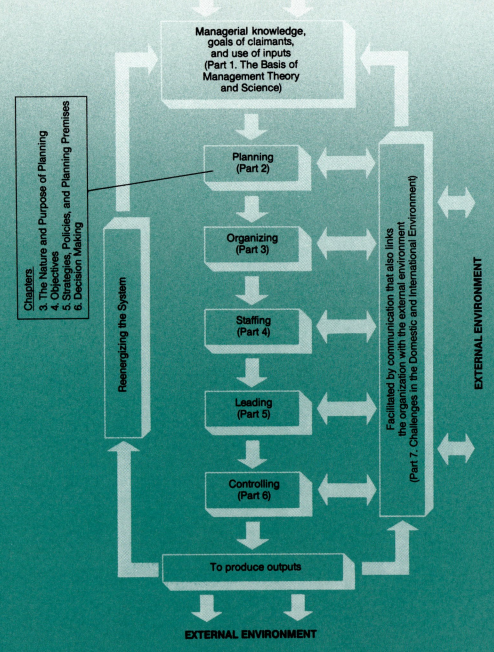

EXTERNAL ENVIRONMENT

Managerial knowledge,
goals of claimants,
and use of inputs
(Part 1. The Basis of
Management Theory
and Science)

Chapters
3. The Nature and Purpose of Planning
4. Objectives
5. Strategies, Policies, and Planning Premises
6. Decision Making

Planning
(Part 2)

Organizing
(Part 3)

Staffing
(Part 4)

Leading
(Part 5)

Controlling
(Part 6)

Reenergizing the System

Facilitated by communication that also links
the organization with the external environment
(Part 7. Challenges in the Domestic and International Environment)

EXTERNAL ENVIRONMENT

To produce outputs

EXTERNAL ENVIRONMENT

SYSTEMS APPROACH TO MANAGEMENT.

The Nature and Purpose of Planning

CHAPTER OBJECTIVES

After reading this chapter you should be able to:

1. Understand what managerial planning is and why it is important.

2. Identify and analyze the various types of plans and show how they relate to one another.

3. Outline and discuss the logical steps in planning and see how these steps are essentially a rational approach to setting objectives and selecting the means of reaching them.

4. Gain appreciation for basic principles underlying determination of how far in the future to plan and of how to build desirable flexibility into plans to meet future uncertainties at the least cost.

5. Learn the importance of reviewing plans periodically to make as sure as possible that they are up to date in the light of any new developments.

*Y*ou are now familiar with basic management theory and have been introduced to the five essential managerial functions: planning, organizing, staffing, leading, and controlling. The following four chapters on planning form Part 2 of the book.

In designing an environment for the effective performance of individuals working together in groups, a manager's most essential task is to see that everyone understands the group's purposes and objectives and its methods of attaining them. If group effort is to be effective, people must know what they are expected to accomplish. This is the function of planning. It is the most basic of all the managerial functions. **Planning** involves selecting missions and objectives and the actions to achieve them; it requires decision making, that is, choosing from among alternative future courses of action. Plans thus provide a rational approach to preselected objectives. Planning also strongly implies managerial innovation, as will be discussed in Chapter 16.

Planning bridges the gap from where we are to where we want to go. It makes it possible for things to occur which would not otherwise happen. Although we can seldom predict the exact future and although factors beyond our control may interfere with the best-laid plans, unless we plan, we are leaving events to chance. Planning is an intellectually demanding process; it requires that we consciously determine courses of action and base our decisions on purpose, knowledge, and considered estimates.

THE NATURE OF PLANNING

We can highlight the essential nature of planning by examining its four major aspects: (1) its contribution to purpose and objectives, (2) its primacy among the manager's tasks, (3) its pervasiveness, and (4) the efficiency of resulting plans.

The Contribution of Planning to Purpose and Objectives

Every plan and all its supporting plans should contribute to the accomplishment of enterprise purpose and objectives. This principle derives from the nature of organized enterprise, which exists for the accomplishment of group purpose through deliberate cooperation.

The Primacy of Planning

As you can see in Figure 3-1, since managerial operations in organizing, staffing, leading, and controlling are designed to support the accomplishment of enterprise objectives, planning logically precedes the execution of all other managerial functions. Although in practice all the functions mesh as a system of action, planning is unique in that it involves establishing the objectives necessary for all group effort. Besides, a manager must plan in order to know what kind of organization relationships and personal qualifications are needed, along which course subordinates are to be led, and what kind of control is to be applied. And,

FIGURE 3-1

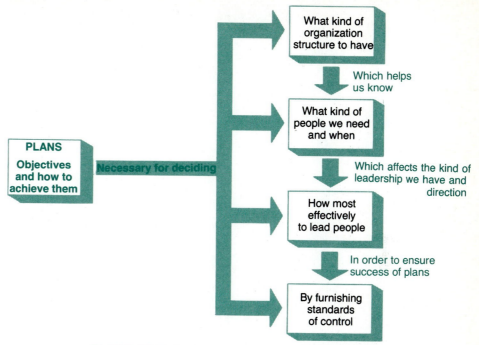

PLANS AS THE FOUNDATION OF MANAGEMENT.

of course, all the other managerial functions must be planned if they are to be effective.

Planning and **control** are inseparable—the Siamese twins of management (see Figure 3-2). Any attempt to control without plans is meaningless, since there is no way for people to tell whether they are going where they want to go (the result of the task of control) unless they first know where they want to go (part of the task of planning). Plans thus furnish the standards of control.

The Pervasiveness of Planning

Planning is a function of all managers, although the character and breadth of planning will vary with each manager's authority and with the nature of policies and plans outlined by superiors. If managers are not allowed a certain degree of discretion and planning responsibility, they are not truly managers.

If we recognize the pervasiveness of planning, we can more easily understand why some people distinguish between policy making (the setting of guidelines for decision making) and administration, or between the "manager" and the "administrator" or "supervisor." One manager, because of his or her authority or position in the organization, may do more—or more important—planning than another, or the planning of one may be more basic and applicable to a larger portion of the enterprise than that of another. However, all managers—

FIGURE 3-2

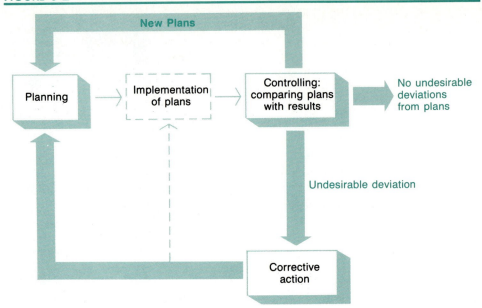

CLOSE RELATIONSHIP OF PLANNING AND CONTROLLING.

from presidents to first-level supervisors—plan. Even the head of a road gang or a factory crew plans in a limited area under fairly strict rules and procedures. Interestingly, in studies of work satisfactions, a principal factor in the success of supervisors at the lowest organization level was found to be the extent of their ability to plan.

Although all managers plan, the work schedule of the first-line supervisor differs from the strategic plan developed by top managers. Roger Smith, the chief executive officer at General Motors, planned the grand strategy of producing small cars in Japan and Korea. Chairman Fauber of K Mart, a retailer known for its no-frills discount stores, planned to "upscale" the operation by offering a wider selection and higher-margin apparel. Thornton Bradshaw of the RCA Corporation redirected strategy, moving the company away from videodiscs and selling businesses not directly related to the company's main purpose. He focused instead on the company's strengths in communication satellites and radar display systems produced for the navy. While top executives plan the general direction of the firm, managers at all levels must prepare their plans so that they contribute to the overall aims of the organization.

The Efficiency of Plans

We measure the **efficiency** of a plan by its contribution to our purpose and objectives, offset by the costs and other factors required to formulate and operate it. A plan may enhance the attainment of objectives, but at unnecessarily high cost. Plans are efficient if they achieve their purpose at a reasonable cost, when cost is measured not only in terms of time or money or production but also in the degree of individual and group satisfaction.

Many managers have followed plans whose costs were greater than the revenue that could be obtained. For example, one airline acquired certain aircraft with costs exceeding revenues. Companies have also tried to sell products that were unacceptable to the market; an example is an auto manufacturer that tried to capture a market by emphasizing engineering without making competitive advances in style. Plans can even make it impossible to achieve objectives if they make enough people in an organization dissatisfied or unhappy. The new president of a company that was losing money attempted to reorganize and cut expenses quickly by wholesale and unplanned layoffs of key personnel. The resulting fear, resentment, and loss of morale led to productivity so much lower as to defeat the new executive's objective of eliminating losses and making profits. And some attempts to install management appraisal and development programs have failed because of group resentment of the methods used, regardless of the basic soundness of the programs.

TYPES OF PLANS

The failure of some managers to recognize that there are a number of different types of plans has often caused difficulty in making planning effective. It is easy to see that a major program, such as one to build and equip a new factory, is a plan. But a number of other courses of future action are also plans. Keeping in mind that a plan encompasses any course of future action, we can see that plans are varied. They are classified here as (1) purposes or missions, (2) objectives, (3) strategies, (4) policies, (5) procedures, (6) rules, (7) programs, and (8) budgets. To some extent, they are a hierarchy, as illustrated in Figure 3-3.

Purposes or Missions

Every kind of organized operation has—or at least should have, if it is to be meaningful—purposes or missions. In every social system, enterprises have a basic function or task which is assigned to them by society. The purpose of a business generally is the production and distribution of goods and services. The purpose of a state highway department is the design, building, and operation of a system of state highways. The purpose of the courts is the interpretation of laws and their application. The purpose of a university is teaching and research. And so on.

Although we do not do so, some writers distinguish between purposes and missions. While a business, for example, may have a social purpose of producing and distributing goods and services, it can accomplish this by fulfilling a mission of producing certain lines of products. The missions of an oil company, like Exxon, are to search for oil and to produce, refine, and market petroleum and a wide variety of petroleum products, from diesel fuel to chemicals. The mission of the Du Pont Company has been expressed as "better things through chemistry," and Kimberly-Clark (noted for its Kleenex trademark) regards its business

FIGURE 3-3

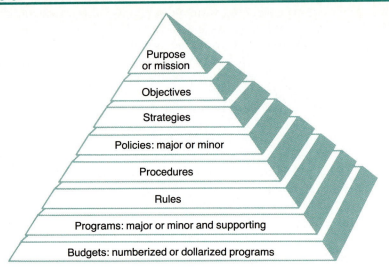

THE HIERARCHY OF PLANS.

mission as the production and sale of paper and paper products. In the 1960s, the mission of NASA was to get a person to the moon before the Russians. Hallmark, which has expanded its business beyond greeting cards, defines its mission as "the social expression business."[1] It is true that in some businesses and other enterprises, the purpose or mission often becomes fuzzy. For example, many of the conglomerates have regarded their mission as **synergy**,[2] which is accomplished through the combination of a variety of companies.

People sometimes think that the mission of a business, as well as its objective, is to make a profit. It is true that every kind of enterprise must have, as we pointed out in Chapter 1, a "surplus"—in business, a "profit"—goal or objective if it is to survive and do the task society has entrusted to it. But this basic objective is accomplished by undertaking activities, going in clearly defined directions, achieving goals, and accomplishing a mission.

Objectives

Objectives or **goals**—terms we use interchangeably in this book—are the ends toward which activity is aimed. They represent not only the end point of planning but the end toward which organizing, staffing, leading, and controlling are aimed. While enterprise objectives are the basic plan of the firm, a department may also have its own objectives. Its goals naturally contribute to the attainment of enterprise objectives, but the two sets of goals may be entirely different. For example, the objective of a business might be to make a certain profit by producing a given line of home entertainment equipment, while the goal of the manufacturing department might be to produce the required number of television sets of given design and quality at a given cost. These objectives are consistent, but they differ in that the manufacturing department alone cannot ensure accomplishing the company's objective.

Strategies

For years the military used the word "strategies" to mean grand plans made in the light of what is believed an adversary might or might not do. While the term "strategies" still usually has a competitive implication, managers increasingly use it to reflect broad areas of an enterprise operation.

Three definitions are indicative of the most common usages of the term **strategies:** (1) general programs of action and deployment of resources to attain comprehensive objectives; (2) the program of objectives of an organization and their changes, resources used to attain these objectives, and policies governing the acquisition, use, and disposition of these resources; and (3) the determination of the basic long-term objectives of an enterprise and the adoption of courses of action and allocation of resources necessary to achieve these goals.

Thus, a company has to decide what kind of business it is going to be in. Is it a transportation or a railroad company? Is it a container or a paper box manufacturer? The firm also has to decide on its growth goal and its desired profitability. A strategy might include such major policies as to market directly rather than through distributors, or to concentrate on proprietary products, or to have a full line of autos, as General Motors decided to have many years ago.

The purpose of strategies, then, is to determine and communicate, through a system of major objectives and policies, a picture of what kind of enterprise is envisioned. Strategies do not attempt to outline exactly how the enterprise is to accomplish its objectives, since this is the task of countless major and minor supporting programs. But they furnish a framework for guiding thinking and action. Their usefulness in practice and their importance in guiding planning do, however, justify the separation of strategies as a type of plan for purpose of analysis.

**PERSPECTIVE:
INTERNATIONAL DIMENSION: GM'S STRATEGY**

Strategies have become increasingly complex and internationally oriented.[3] Take General Motors, which has been threatened by foreign competitors, especially the Japanese. For decades, GM had a "do-it-yourself" strategy. But now some GM cars are made by rival Asian companies such as Suzuki Motors Company and Isuzu Motors Ltd. of Japan. In addition, GM engaged in a joint venture with Toyota Motor Corporation to produce subcompacts in California. Equally surprising is GM's strategic move into nonautomotive businesses such as information processing and robotics. To implement this strategy, GM bought Electronic Data Systems Corporation and engaged in a joint venture with the Japanese robot maker Fanuc Ltd. But a change in strategy usually requires a reorganization, and GM is currently in the process of changing the organization structure that served the company well for over 60 years.

Policies

Policies also are plans in that they are general statements or understandings which guide or channel thinking in decision making. Not all policies are "statements"; they are often merely implied from the actions of managers. The president of a company, for example, may strictly follow—perhaps for convenience rather than as policy—the practice of promoting from within; the practice may then be interpreted as policy and carefully followed by subordinates. In fact, one of the problems of managers is to make sure that subordinates do not interpret as policy minor managerial decisions that are not intended to serve as patterns.

Policies define an area within which a decision is to be made and ensure that the decision will be consistent with, and contribute to, an objective. Policies help decide issues before they become problems, make it unnecessary to analyze the same situation every time it comes up, and unify other plans, thus permitting managers to delegate authority and still maintain control over what their subordinates do. For example, a certain railroad has the policy of acquiring industrial land to replace all company acreage sold along its right-of-way. This policy permits the manager of the land department to develop acquisition plans without continual reference to top management, while at the same time furnishing a standard of control.

Policies ordinarily exist on all levels of the organization and range from major company policies through major department policies to minor policies applicable to the smallest segment of the organization. They may be related to functions such as sales and finance, or merely to a project such as the design of a new product to meet a specified competition.

There are many types of policies. Examples include policies to hire only university-trained engineers or to encourage employee suggestions for improved cooperation, to promote from within, to conform strictly to a high standard of business ethics, to set competitive prices, or to insist on fixed, rather than cost-plus, pricing.

Since policies are guides to decision making, it follows that they must allow for some discretion. Otherwise, they would be rules. Too often, policies are interpreted as a kind of "ten commandments" that leave no room for discretion. Although discretion, in some instances, is quite broad, it can be exceedingly narrow. For example, a policy to buy from the lowest of three qualified bidders leaves to discretion only the question of which bidders are qualified; a requirement to buy from a certain supplier, regardless of price or service, would, however, be a rule.

Policy is a means of encouraging discretion and initiative, but within limits. The amount of freedom will naturally depend upon the policy and in turn will reflect position and authority in the organization. The president of a company with a policy of aggressive price competition has a broad area of discretion and initiative in which to interpret and apply this policy. The district sales manager (who reports to the regional sales manager) abides by the same basic policy, but the interpretations made by the president, the vice-president for sales, and the

> ## PERSPECTIVE:
> ## A COMPANY'S POLICY MANUAL
>
> To see how policies are often misunderstood, let us look at examples from a company's policy manual. In each case, there is room for a person in a decision-making capacity to use discretion.
>
> *Gifts from suppliers.*   Except for token gifts of purely nominal or advertising value, no employee shall accept any gift or gratuity from any supplier at any time. (What is "token" or "nominal"?)
>
> *Entertainment.*   No officer or employee shall accept favors or entertainment from an outside organization or agency which are substantial enough to cause undue influence in the selection of goods or services for the company. (What is "substantial" or "undue"?)
>
> *Outside employment.*   It is improper for any employee to work for any company customers, or for any competitors, or for any vendors or suppliers of goods or services to the company (this is actually more like a rule because it allows no discretion); outside employment is further prohibited if it (1) results in a division of loyalty to the company or in a conflict of interest, or (2) interferes with or adversely affects the employee's work or opportunity for advancement in the company. (What is meant by "division of loyalty," "conflict of interest," and "adversely"?)
>
> *Pricing.*   Territorial division managers may each establish such prices for the products under their individual control as they deem to be in the division's interest, so long as (1) these prices result in gross profit margins for any line of products which are consistent with the approved profit plan, (2) price reductions will not result in detrimental effects on prices of similar products of another company division in another state or country, and (3) prices meet the legal requirements of the state or country in which the prices are effective. (What are "consistent profit margins," "detrimental effects," and "legal requirements"?)

regional sales manager become derivative policies that might narrow the district manager's scope to the point of being, for example, only wide enough to approve a special sale price not exceeding a 10 percent reduction to meet competition (see Figure 3-4).

Making policies consistent and integrated enough to realize enterprise objectives is difficult for many reasons. First, policies are too seldom defined in writing and their exact interpretations are too little known. Second, the very delegation of authority that policies are intended to implement leads, through its decentralizing influence, to widespread participation in policy making and interpretation, with almost certain variations among individuals. Third, it is not always easy to control policy because actual policy may be difficult to ascertain and intended policy may not always be clear.

FIGURE 3-4

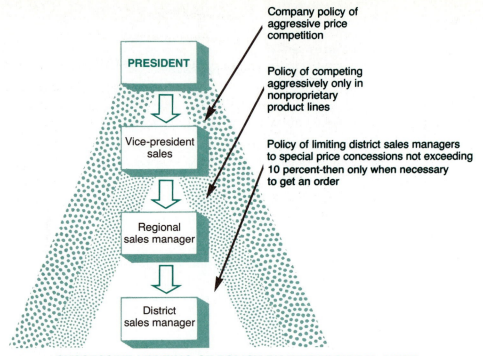

SUCCESSIVE LIMITING OF POLICY BY HIERARCHICAL LEVEL.

Procedures

Procedures are plans that establish a required method of handling future activities. They are guides to action, rather than to thinking, and they detail the exact manner in which certain activities must be accomplished. They are chronological sequences of required actions.

Procedures are found in every part of an organization. The board of directors follows many procedures quite different from those of the supervisor; the expense account of the vice-president may go through quite different approval procedures than that of the salesperson; the procedures for carrying out vacation and sick leave provisions may differ considerably at various levels of the organization. But the important fact is that procedures exist throughout an organization, even though, as we might expect, they become more exacting and more numerous at the lower levels, largely because of the necessity for more careful control, the economic advantages of spelling out actions in detail, the lower-level managers' lesser need for leeway, and the fact that many routine jobs can be performed most efficiently when management prescribes the best way to carry them out.

Like other types of plans, procedures exist in a hierarchy. Thus, in a typical corporation, we may find a manual called "Corporation Standard Practice," outlining procedures for the corporation as a whole; a manual called "Division

Standard"; and special sets of procedures for a department, a branch, a section, or a unit.

Procedures often cut across department lines. For example, in a manufacturing company, the procedure for handling orders will almost certainly involve the sales department (for the original order), the finance department (for acknowledgment of receipt of funds and for customer credit approval), the accounting department (for recording the transaction), the production department (for the order to produce goods or authority to release them from stock), and the traffic department (for determination of shipping means and route).

Let us look at a few examples of the relationship between procedures and policies. Company policy may grant employees vacations; procedures established to implement this policy will provide for scheduling vacations to avoid disruption of work, setting methods and rates of vacation pay, maintaining records to assure each employee of a vacation, and spelling out the means for applying for a vacation. A company may have a policy of shipping orders quickly; particularly in a large company, careful procedures will be necessary to ensure that orders are handled in a specific way. Company policy may require the public relations department to clear its employees' public utterances; to implement this policy, managers must establish procedures for obtaining clearance with minimum inconvenience and delay.

Rules

Rules spell out specific required action or nonaction, allowing no discretion. They are usually the simplest type of plan.

People frequently confuse rules with policies or procedures. Rules are unlike procedures in that they guide action without specifying a time sequence. In fact, a procedure might be looked upon as a sequence of rules. A rule, however, may or may not be part of a procedure. For example, "No smoking" is a rule quite unrelated to any procedure, but a procedure governing the handling of orders may incorporate the rule that all orders must be confirmed the day they are received. This rule allows no deviation from a stated course of action and in no way interferes with the rest of the procedure for handling orders. It is comparable to a rule that all fractions of weight of over half an ounce are to be counted as a full ounce or that receiving inspection must count or weigh all materials against the purchase order. The essence of a rule is that it reflects a managerial decision that some certain action must—or must not—be taken.

Be sure you can distinguish rules from policies. The purpose of policies is to guide decision making by marking off areas in which managers can use their discretion. Although rules also serve as guides, they allow no discretion in their application. Many companies and other organizations think they have policies when they really have spelled-out rules. The result is confusion as to when people may use their own judgment, if at all. This can be dangerous. Rules and procedures, by their very nature, are designed to repress thinking; we should use them only when we do not want people in an organization to use their discretion.

PERSPECTIVE:
PROCEDURES AND RULES IMPOSED BY THE OUTSIDE

At times, rules and procedures are implemented because of unfavorable publicity. General Dynamics, one of the largest defense contractors, has been accused of some improprieties.[4] In order not to be suspended from bidding on defense contracts, the company had to agree to a list of rules and procedures imposed by the Defense Department.

These new requirements are designed to prevent the shifting of costs from one contract to another. For example, workers have to prepare and sign their own time cards. The supervisor has to check this card, and, if it is incorrectly filled out, the worker has to make the correction, which then has to be initialed by the worker and the boss. The original entry must not be erased so that it can be checked later. Also, General Dynamics was required to establish tight rules for charging overhead expenses. Employees are not allowed to accept gifts—not even a pen or a calendar.

Thus, rules and procedures can be imposed by an important customer and are examples not only of planning but also of controlling, showing the close relationship between the two functions.

Programs

Programs are a complex of goals, policies, procedures, rules, task assignments, steps to be taken, resources to be employed, and other elements necessary to carry out a given course of action; they are ordinarily supported by budgets. They may be as major as an airline's program to acquire a $400 million fleet of jets or the five-year program embarked upon by the Ford Motor Company several years ago to improve the status and quality of its thousands of foremen. Or they may be as minor as a program formulated by a single supervisor to improve the morale of workers in a parts-manufacturing department of a farm machinery company.

A primary program may call for many supporting programs. To cite an airline again, its program to invest in new jets, costing many millions of dollars for the aircraft and the necessary spare parts, requires many supporting programs if the investment is to be properly used. A program for providing the maintenance and operating bases with spare parts and components must be developed in detail. Special maintenance facilities must be prepared and maintenance personnel trained. Pilots and flight engineers must also be trained and, if the new jets mean a net addition to flying hours, flight personnel recruited. Flight schedules must be revised and ground station personnel trained to handle the new airplanes and their schedules as service is expanded to new cities in the airline's system. Advertising programs must give adequate publicity to the new service. Plans to finance the aircraft and provide for insurance coverage must be developed.

These and other programs must be devised and implemented before any new aircraft are received and placed in service. Furthermore, all these programs call for coordination and timing, since the failure of any part of this network of supporting plans means delay for the major program as well as unnecessary costs and loss of profits. Some programs, particularly those involving hiring and training of personnel, can be accomplished too soon as well as too late, and needless expense results from employees' being available and trained before their services are required.

Budgets

A **budget** is a statement of expected results expressed in numerical terms. It may be referred to as a "numberized" program. In fact, the financial operating budget is often called a "profit plan." It may be expressed either in financial terms or in terms of labor-hours, units of product, machine-hours, or any other numerically measurable term. It may deal with operations, as the expense budget does; it may reflect capital outlays, as the capital expenditures budget does; or it may show cash flow, as the cash budget does.

Since budgets are also control devices, we reserve our principal discussion of them for Chapter 21 on control techniques. However, making a budget is clearly planning. The budget is the fundamental planning instrument in many companies. A budget forces a company to make in advance—whether for a week or five years—a numerical compilation of expected cash flow, expenses and revenues, capital outlays, or labor- or machine-hour utilization. The budget is necessary for control, but it cannot serve as a sensible standard of control unless it reflects plans.

Although a budget usually implements a program, it may in itself be a program. One company in difficult financial straits installed an elaborate budgetary control program designed not only to control expenditures but also to instill cost consciousness in management. In fact, one of the major advantages of budgeting is that it makes people plan; because a budget is in the form of numbers, it forces precision in planning. Moreover, since budgets are usually developed for an entire company, budgeting is an important device for consolidating plans of an enterprise.

Budgets vary considerably in accuracy, detail, and purpose. Some budgets vary according to the organization's level of output; these are called **variable** or **flexible budgets.** Government agencies often develop **program budgets** in which the agency (and each department within the agency) identifies goals, develops detailed programs to meet the goals, and estimates the cost of each program. To plan an effective program budget, a manager must do some fairly detailed and thorough planning.

Still another type, really a combination of the variable and the program budget, is the **zero-base budget.** A manager using this approach thinks of the goals and the programs needed to achieve them as a "work package," as though the programs were started from scratch, or "base zero."

STEPS IN PLANNING

Although we present the steps in planning here in connection with major programs such as the acquisition of a plant or a fleet of jets or the development of a product, managers would follow essentially the same steps in any thorough planning. Since minor plans are usually simpler, certain of the steps are more easily accomplished, but the practical steps which we list below, and which are diagrammed in Figure 3-5, are of general application. In practice, however, we must study the feasibility of possible courses of action at each stage. For example, in establishing objectives we must have some idea about the premises underlying

FIGURE 3-5

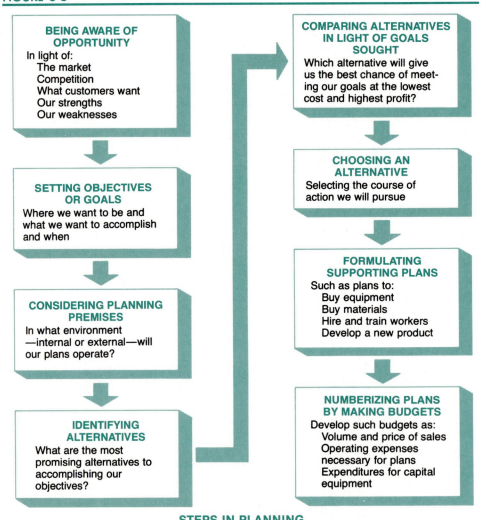

BEING AWARE OF OPPORTUNITY
In light of:
 The market
 Competition
 What customers want
 Our strengths
 Our weaknesses

SETTING OBJECTIVES OR GOALS
Where we want to be and what we want to accomplish and when

CONSIDERING PLANNING PREMISES
In what environment —internal or external—will our plans operate?

IDENTIFYING ALTERNATIVES
What are the most promising alternatives to accomplishing our objectives?

COMPARING ALTERNATIVES IN LIGHT OF GOALS SOUGHT
Which alternative will give us the best chance of meeting our goals at the lowest cost and highest profit?

CHOOSING AN ALTERNATIVE
Selecting the course of action we will pursue

FORMULATING SUPPORTING PLANS
Such as plans to:
 Buy equipment
 Buy materials
 Hire and train workers
 Develop a new product

NUMBERIZING PLANS BY MAKING BUDGETS
Develop such budgets as:
 Volume and price of sales
 Operating expenses necessary for plans
 Expenditures for capital equipment

STEPS IN PLANNING.

the plans. An ambitious objective of increasing sales by 200 percent may be unrealistic in an environment with a projected economic recession. Similarly, feedback is also essential. In formulating supportive plans we may have to reevaluate and change the overall objectives set earlier. Also, a discriminating manager obviously would not use $100 worth of time to make a decision worth 50 cents, but it is shocking to see 50 cents worth of time used to make a planning decision involving millions of dollars.

1. Being Aware of Opportunities

Although it precedes actual planning and is therefore not strictly a part of the planning process, an awareness of opportunities in the external environment as well as within the organization[5] is the real starting point for planning. We should take a preliminary look at possible future opportunities and see them clearly and completely, know where we stand in the light of our strengths and weaknesses, understand what problems we wish to solve and why, and know what we expect to gain. Our setting of realistic objectives depends on this awareness. Planning requires realistic diagnosis of the opportunity situation.

2. Establishing Objectives

In planning a major program, the second step is to establish objectives for the entire enterprise and then for each subordinate work unit, for the long term as well as for the short range. Objectives specify the expected results and indicate the end points of what is to be done, where the primary emphasis is to be placed, and what is to be accomplished by the network of strategies, policies, procedures, rules, budgets, and programs.

Enterprise objectives give direction to the major plans which, by reflecting these objectives, define the objective of every major department. Major department objectives, in turn, control the objectives of subordinate departments, and so on down the line. The objectives of lesser departments will be better framed, however, if subdivision managers understand the overall enterprise objectives and the implied derivative goals, and if they are given an opportunity to contribute their ideas to setting their own goals and those of the enterprise.

3. Developing Premises

A third logical step in planning is to establish, circulate, and obtain agreement to utilize critical planning premises such as forecasts, applicable basic policies, and existing company plans. They are *assumptions* about the environment in which the plan is to be carried out. It is important for all the managers involved in planning to agree on the premises. In fact, the major **principle of planning premises** is this: *The more thoroughly individuals charged with planning understand and agree to utilize consistent planning premises, the more coordinated enterprise planning will be.*

Forecasting is important in premising: What kind of markets will there be? What volume of sales? What prices? What products? What technical developments? What costs? What wage rates? What tax rates and policies? What new plants? What policies with respect to dividends? What political or social environment? How will expansion be financed? What are the long-term trends?

Managers have a number of sources to draw from when preparing a forecast for their enterprise. The government publishes a wealth of information that can be useful. Here are just a few examples: Business Cycle Developments, Survey of Current Business, and Economic Indicators. Most large banks publish newsletters on current economic conditions, often on a monthly basis. *Business Week* magazine prepares outlooks for specific industries, such as basic manufacturing (autos, chemicals, machinery, steel), natural resources (agriculture, energy, forest products, communications), services and consumer products (entertainment, food processing, health care, personal care). Many universities, such as UCLA, make national and regional economic forecasts. Managers interested in long-term trends will find John Naisbitt's book *Megatrends* useful.[6]

Because the future is so complex, it would not be profitable or realistic to make assumptions about every detail of the future environment of a plan. Therefore, premises are, as a practical matter, limited to assumptions that are critical, or strategic, to a plan, that is, those which most influence its operation.

4. Determining Alternative Courses

The fourth step in planning is to search for and examine alternative courses of action, especially those not immediately apparent. There is seldom a plan for which reasonable alternatives do not exist, and quite often an alternative that is not obvious proves to be the best.

The more common problem is not finding alternatives but reducing the number of alternatives so that the most promising may be analyzed. Even with mathematical techniques and the computer, there is a limit to the number of alternatives that can be thoroughly examined. The planner must usually make a preliminary examination to discover the most fruitful possibilities.

5. Evaluating Alternative Courses

Having sought out alternative courses and examined their strong and weak points, we must next evaluate them by weighing them in the light of premises and goals. One course may appear to be the most profitable but require a large cash outlay with a slow payback; another may look less profitable but involve less risk; still another may better suit the company's long-range objectives.

If the only objective were to maximize immediate profits in a certain business, if the future were not uncertain, if cash position and capital availability were not worrisome, and if most factors could be reduced to definite data, this evaluation would be relatively easy. But since planners typically encounter many uncertainties, problems of capital shortage, and various intangible factors, evaluation is usually very difficult, even with relatively simple problems. A company may wish to enter a new product line primarily for purposes of prestige; the forecast may show a financial loss; but the question is still open as to whether the loss is worth the gain in prestige.

Because there are so many alternative courses in most situations and there are numerous variables and limitations to be considered, evaluation can be exceedingly difficult. Because of these complexities, the newer methodologies and applications of operations research and analysis discussed in Chapter 22 are helpful. Indeed, it is at this step in the planning process that operations research and mathematical as well as computing techniques have their primary application to the field of management.

6. Selecting a Course

This is the point at which the plan is adopted—the real point of decision making. Occasionally an analysis and evaluation of alternative courses will disclose that two or more are advisable, and the manager may decide to follow several courses rather than the one best course.

7. Formulating Derivative Plans

At the point when a decision is made, planning is seldom complete, and a seventh step is indicated. Derivative plans are almost invariably required to support the basic plan. When an airline decided to acquire a fleet of new planes, this decision was the signal for the development of a host of derivative plans, for the hiring and training of various types of personnel, for the acquisition and positioning of spare parts, for the development of maintenance facilities, for scheduling, and for advertising, financing, and insurance.

8. Numberizing Plans by Budgeting

After decisions are made and plans are set, the final step to give them meaning, as was indicated in the discussion of types of plans, is to numberize them by converting them to budgets. The overall budgets of an enterprise represent the sum total of income and expenses, with resultant profit or surplus, and budgets of major balance sheet items such as cash and capital expenditures. Each department or program of a business or other enterprise can have its own budgets, usually of expenses and capital expenditures, which tie into the overall budget.

   If done well, budgets become a means of adding together the various plans and also set important standards against which planning progress can be measured. We will discuss budgets in connection with managerial control in Chapter 21.

THE PLANNING PROCESS: A RATIONAL APPROACH TO GOAL ACHIEVEMENT

As we saw in the planning steps above, planning is a rational approach to accomplishing objectives. The process can be illustrated as shown in Figure 3-6. In this diagram, progress (toward more sales, more profits, lower costs, and so forth) is on the vertical axis, and time is on the horizontal axis. Here x indicates where we are (at t_0 or "time zero") and y where we want to be, at a future time (at

FIGURE 3-6

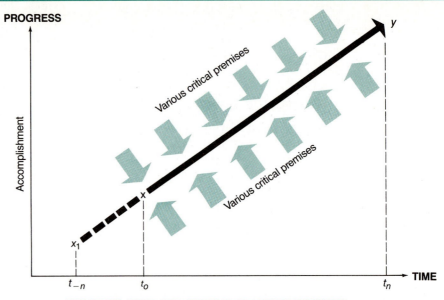

PROGRESS, TIME, AND CRITICAL PLANNING PREMISES.

t_n). In short, we are at x and want to go to y. Often we do not have all the data, but we start planning anyway. We may even have to start our planning study at x_1 (at t_{-n}). The line xy is the decision path.

If the future were completely certain, the line xy would be relatively easy to draw. However, in actuality, a myriad of factors may push us away from or toward the desired goal. These are the planning premises. Again, because we cannot forecast or consider everything. we try to develop our path from x to y in the light of the most critical premises.

The essential logic of planning applies regardless of the time interval between t_0 and t_n, whether it is 5 minutes or 20 years. However, the clarity of premises, the attainability of goals, and the simplification of planning are almost certain to be inversely related to the time span. That is, if the time span is long, premises may be unclear, goals may be more difficult to set, and other planning complexities may be great.

Decision making may be the easiest part of planning, although it involves techniques of evaluation and considerable skill in applying them. The real difficulties arise primarily in sharpening and giving meaning to objectives and critical premises, seeing the nature and relationships of the strengths and weaknesses of alternatives, and communicating goals and premises to those throughout the enterprise who must plan.

The Planning Period

Shall plans be for a short period or a long one? How shall short-range plans be coordinated with long-range plans? These questions suggest multiple horizons of planning—in some cases, planning a week in advance may be ample, and in others, the desirable period may be a number of years. Even within the same firm at the same time, various planning periods may exist for various matters.

The Commitment Principle

Some criteria must be used in selecting the time range for company planning. The key to choosing the right planning period seems to lie in the **commitment principle:** *Logical planning encompasses a future period of time necessary to fulfill, through a series of actions, the commitments involved in decisions made today.*

Perhaps the most obvious application of this principle is the setting of a planning period long enough to anticipate, as well as we can, the recovery of costs sunk into a project. But, since other things than costs can be committed for various lengths of time and because a commitment to spend often precedes an expenditure and may be as unchangeable as sunk costs, it seems inadequate to refer to recovery of costs alone. Thus a company may commit itself for varying lengths of time to a personnel policy, such as promotion from within, or to other policies or programs involving commitments of direction not immediately measurable in terms of dollars (or any other currency).

We can readily grasp the logic of planning far enough in the future to foresee, as well as possible, the recovery of capital sunk in a building or a machine. Since capital is the lifeblood of an enterprise and is normally limited in relation to the firm's needs, its expenditure must be accompanied by a reasonable possibility of recovering it, plus a return on investment, through operations. For example, when Lever Brothers sank $35 million into a new factory on the West Coast, it decided, in effect, that the detergent business would permit the recovery of this investment over a period of time. If this period was 20 years, then logically the plans should have been based on a 20-year projection of business. Of course, the company might have introduced some flexibility and reduced its risk (as it did) by spending extra funds to make the plant modifiable for other purposes.

What the Commitment Principle Implies

The commitment principle implies that long-range planning is not really planning for future decisions but, rather, planning for the future impact of today's decisions. In other words, a decision is a commitment, normally of funds, direction of action, or reputation. And decisions lie at the core of planning. While studies and analyses preceded decisions, any type of plan implies that some decision has been made. Indeed, a plan does not really exist as such until a decision has been made. Knowing this, the astute manager will recognize the validity of gearing longer-term considerations to present decisions. To do otherwise is to overlook the basic nature of both planning and decision making.

Application of the Commitment Principle

There is no uniform or arbitrary length of time for which a company should plan or for which a given program or any of its parts should be planned. An airplane company embarking on a new commercial jet aircraft project should probably plan this program for at least 12 years ahead, with 5 or 6 years for engineering and development and at least as many more years for production and sales, in order to recoup total costs and make a reasonable profit. An instrument manufacturer with a product already developed might need to plan revenues and expenses only 6 months ahead, since this period may represent the cycle of raw-materials purchasing, production, inventorying, and sales. But the same company might wish to see much further into the future before assuming a lease for specialized manufacturing facilities, undertaking a program of management training, or developing and promoting a new product. Other examples showing that different planning areas require different time periods are illustrated in Figure 3-7.

Coordination of Short- and Long-Range Plans

Often short-range plans are made without reference to long-range plans. This is plainly a serious error. The importance of integrating the two types can hardly be overemphasized, and no short-run plan should be made unless it contributes

FIGURE 3-7

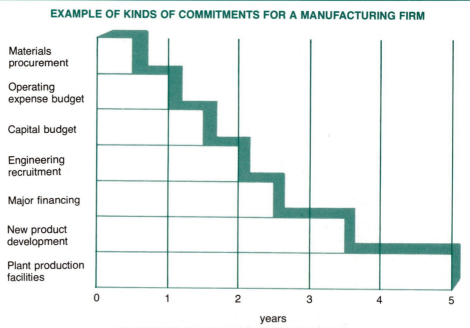

EXAMPLE OF KINDS OF COMMITMENTS FOR A MANUFACTURING FIRM

PLANNING AREAS AND TIME PERIODS.

Various management decision areas typically involve planning ahead for differing periods of time. These periods also vary according to the kind of business. For example, a large public utility may plan new power-production plants twenty-five or thirty years into the future, whereas a small garment manufacturer may plan new production facilities only one year ahead.

to the achievement of the relevant long-range plan. Much waste arises from decisions about immediate situations that fail to consider their effect on more remote objectives.

Sometimes short-range decisions not only fail to contribute to a long-range plan but actually impede, or require changes in, the long-range plan. For example, if a small company accepts a large order without reckoning the effect of the order on its capacity to produce or its supply of cash, it may hamper its future ability to finance a systematic expansion enough to require changes in its long-range program. Or, in another company, small additions to the plant (which may be urgently needed) may utilize vacant property so haphazardly as to thwart the land's longer-range use as the site for a large new plant. In other instances, the decision of a plant superintendent to discharge workers without adequate cause may interfere with the company's long-range objective of developing a fair and successful personnel program. The short-range decision of Sewell Avery, chairman of Montgomery Ward, to curtail expansion of the business after World War II because he believed that a serious recession was at hand interfered with the long-range program of enhancing the profitability of the company.

Responsible managers should continually review and revise immediate decisions to determine whether they contribute to long-range programs, and subordinate managers should be regularly briefed on long-range plans so that they will make decisions consistent with the company's long-range goals. It is far easier to do this than to correct inconsistencies, especially since short-term commitments tend to lead to further commitments along the same line.

FOR DISCUSSION

1. "Planning is looking ahead, and control is looking back." Comment.

2. If planning involves a rational approach to selected goals, how can goals or objectives be a type of plan?

3. Draw up a statement of policy and devise a brief procedure that might be useful in implementing it. Are you sure your policy is not a rule?

4. If all decisions involve commitments and if the future is always uncertain, how can a manager guard against costly mistakes?

5. Using as an example a planning decision with which you are familiar, show to what extent, and how, the commitment principle applies to it.

6. "Planning theory illustrates the open-system approach to management." Comment.

EXERCISES/ACTION STEPS

1. Taking a planning problem which is now facing you, proceed to deal with it in accordance with the planning steps outlined in this chapter.

2. Interview a manager in your area and ask about the planning process (i.e., the steps in planning).

CASES

CASE 3-1
INTERNATIONAL MACHINE CORPORATION

Gilbert Brown, the president of International Machine Corporation (IMC), leaned back in his chair and reflected with well-deserved satisfaction on the success of his company, which produces and distributes a line of farm machinery. That afternoon, at a meeting of distributors from various parts of the world, Mr. Brown had been urged to introduce new models to satisfy the changing demands of customers.

The president, who had an engineering background, recognized the implications of the distributors' suggestion. It would require greater investments in research and development. Furthermore, the changes in the highly automated production line would be very costly indeed. Also, having a greater variety of models would require stocking many more spare parts. Depending on the kinds of changes, mechanics also might need to be retrained.

Reflecting on previous staff meetings, the president realized that sales and marketing people always wanted a greater variety of models but never acknowledged the costs involved in changing models. After all, the company had been extremely successful with just a few models. Consequently, the president decided against the introduction of new models. Instead, he considered improving the current models and reducing the cost and price. He felt that what the customer really wants is value. Nevertheless, to test his judgment, the president asked a consultant for an opinion.

1. How would you state the mission of the enterprise?

2. What do you think are the opportunities and threats in the external environment?

3. How would you go about evaluating the strengths and weaknesses of the firm? What factors are critical for success or failure?

4. It is often said that to be successful, an organization must be an open system. What does this mean, and how does it apply to this case?

CASE 3-2
EASTERN ELECTRIC CORPORATION

Margaret Quinn, the president of Eastern Electric Corporation, one of the large electric utilities operating in the Eastern United States, had long been convinced that effective planning in the company was absolutely essential to success. For more than 10 years she had tried to get a company planning program installed without seeing much result. Over this time she had consecutively appointed three vice-presidents in charge of planning and, although each had seemed to work hard at the job, she noticed that individual department heads kept going their own ways. They made decisions on problems as they came up, and they prided themselves on doing an effective job of "fighting fires."

But the company seemed to be drifting, and individual decisions of department heads did not always jibe with each other. The executive in charge of regulatory matters was always pressing state commissions to allow higher electric rates without having very much luck, since the commissions felt that costs, although rising, were not justified. The head of public relations was constantly appealing to the public to understand the problems of electric utilities, but electric users in the various communities felt that the utility was making enough money and that the company should solve its problems without raising rates. The vice-president in charge of operations, pressed by many communities to expand electric lines, to put all lines underground to get rid of unsightly poles and lines, and to give customers better service, felt that costs were secondary to keeping customers off his back.

When a consultant called in at the request of Ms. Quinn looked over the situation, he found that the company really was not planning very well. The vice-president—planning and his staff were working hard making studies and forecasts and submitting them to the president. There they stopped, since all the department heads looked on them as impractical paperwork that had no importance for their day-to-day operations.

1. If you were the consultant, what steps would you suggest to get the company to plan effectively?

2. What advice would you give the company as to how far in the future to plan?

3. How would you suggest to the president that your recommendations be put into effect?

REFERENCES

1. William L. Glueck and Lawrence R. Jauch, *Business Policy and Strategic Management* (New York: McGraw-Hill Book Company, 1984), chap. 2.

2. The concepts of synergy can be expressed simply as a situation where 2 plus 2 becomes equal to 5, or where the whole is greater than the sum of the parts.

3. Based on a variety of sources, including U.C. Lehner, "With His Bid for EDS, GM's Smith Continues to Make Bold Changes," *The Wall Street Journal* (July 2, 1984); "GM Moves into a New Era," *Business Week* (July 16, 1984), pp. 48–54; "Roger Smith Takes on GM's Critics," *Fortune* (Aug. 18, 1986), pp. 26–27.

4. Ford S. Worthy, "Mr. Clean Charts a New Course at General Dynamics," *Fortune* (Apr. 28, 1986), pp. 70–76.

5. The word "problem" might be used instead of "opportunity." A state of disorder or confusion and a need for a solution to gain a given goal can more constructively be regarded as an opportunity. In fact, one very successful and astute company president does not permit his colleagues to speak of problems, but only of opportunities.

6. John Naisbitt, *Megatrends* (New York: Warner Books, 1982).

FOR FURTHER INFORMATION

Chaffee, Ellen E. "Three Models of Strategy," *Academy of Management Review* (January 1985), pp. 89–98.

Dowd, Ann Reilly. "What Managers Can Learn from Manager Reagan," *Fortune* (Sept. 15, 1986), pp. 33–41.

Hamermesh, Richard G. "Making Planning Strategic," *Harvard Business Review* (July–August 1986), pp. 115–120.

Lorange, Peter. *Corporate Planning* (Englewood Cliffs, N.J.: Prentice-Hall, 1980).

Pearce II, John A., and Richard B. Robinson, Jr. *Strategic Management*, 2d ed. (Homewood, Ill.: Richard D. Irwin, 1985).

Shim, Jae K., and Randy McGlade. "Current Trends in the Use of Corporate Planning Models," *Journal of Systems Management* (September 1984), pp. 24–31.

Steiner, George A., John B. Miner, and Edmund R. Gray. *Management Policy and Strategy*, 3d ed. (New York: The Macmillan Publishing Company, 1986).

4

Objectives

CHAPTER OBJECTIVES

After reading this chapter, you should be able to:

1. Explain the nature of objectives.

2. Outline the evolving concepts in management by objectives (MBO) and explain the systems approach to MBO.

3. Analyze the process of managing and appraising by objectives.

4. Show how verifiable objectives can be set for different situations.

5. Describe the benefits of MBO.

6. Recognize the weaknesses of MBO and offer ways to overcome them.

*I*n Chapter 3 we stated that objectives are the important ends toward which organizational and individual activities are directed. Since writers and practitioners make no clear distinction between the terms "goals" and "objectives" we will use them interchangeably. Within the context of our discussion it will become clear whether they are long-term or short-term, broad or specific. The emphasis in this chapter is on verifiable objectives; that is, at the end of the period one should be able to determine whether or not the objective has been achieved. The goal of every manager is to create a surplus, and clear and verifiable objectives facilitate measurement of the effectiveness and efficiency of managerial actions.

THE NATURE OF OBJECTIVES

Objectives state end results and overall objectives need to be supported by subobjectives. Thus, objectives form a hierarchy as well as a network. Moreover, organizations and managers have multiple goals which are sometimes incompatible and may lead to conflicts within the organization, within the group, and even within individuals. A manager may have to choose between short-term and long-term performance, and personal interests may have to be subordinated to organizational objectives.

A Hierarchy of Objectives

As you can see in Figure 4-1, objectives form a hierarchy, ranging from the broad aim to specific individual objectives.[1] The zenith of the hierarchy is the purpose, which has two dimensions. First, there is the purpose of society, such as requiring the organization to contribute to the welfare of the people by providing goods and services at a reasonable cost. Second, there is the purpose of the business, which might be to furnish convenient, low-cost transportation for the average person. The stated mission might be to produce, market, and service automobiles. As you will notice, the distinction between purpose and mission is a fine one and therefore many writers and practitioners do not differentiate between the two terms. At any rate, these aims are, in turn, translated into general objectives and strategies (discussed in Chapter 5), such as designing, producing, and marketing reliable, low-cost, fuel-efficient automobiles. At the next level of the hierarchy, we find more specific objectives, such as those in the **key result areas.** These are the areas in which performance is essential for the success of the enterprise.

> **PERSPECTIVE:**
> **KEY RESULT AREAS ACCORDING TO DRUCKER**
>
> Although there is no complete agreement on what the key result areas of a business should be—and they may differ for various enterprises—Peter F. Drucker suggests the following: market standing, innovation, productivity, physical and financial resources, profitability, manager performance and development, worker performance and attitude, and public responsibility.[2]

FIGURE 4-1

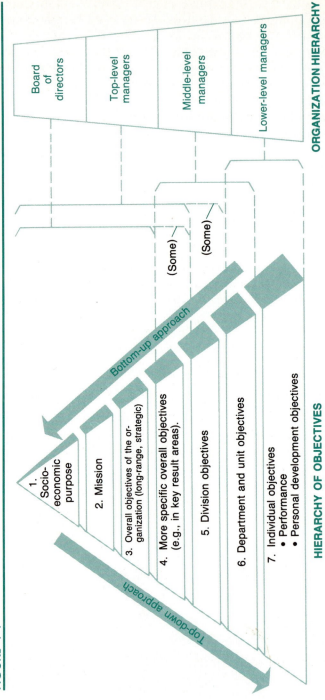

HIERARCHY OF OBJECTIVES

ORGANIZATION HIERARCHY

Board of directors

Top-level managers

Middle-level managers

Lower-level managers

(Some)

(Some)

Bottom-up approach

Top-down approach

1. Socio-economic purpose

2. Mission

3. Overall objectives of the organization (long-range, strategic).

4. More specific overall objectives (e.g., in key result areas).

5. Division objectives

6. Department and unit objectives

7. Individual objectives
   • Performance
   • Personal development objectives

RELATIONSHIP OF OBJECTIVES AND THE ORGANIZATIONAL HIERARCHY.

Adapted from H. Weihrich and J. Mendleson, *Management: An MBO Approach* (Dubuque, Iowa: Wm. C. Brown Co., 1978), p. xi. Used with permission.

Some examples of objectives for key result areas are the following: to obtain 10 percent return on investment by the end of calendar year 1990 (profitability); to increase the number of units of product X by 7 percent without an increase in cost or a reduction of current quality level by June 30, 1991 (productivity).

The objectives have to be further translated into division, department, and unit objectives down to the lowest level of the organization.

The Process of Setting Objectives and the Organizational Hierarchy[3]

As you can see in Figure 4-1, managers at different levels in the organizational hierarchy are concerned with different kinds of objectives. The board of directors and top managers are very much involved in determining the purpose, the mission, and the overall objectives of the firm, and also the more specific overall objectives in the key result areas. Middle-level managers, such as the vice-president or manager of marketing, or the production manager, are involved in the setting of key-result-area objectives, division as well as department objectives. The primary concern of lower-level managers is the setting of objectives on the department and unit level as well as the objectives of their subordinates. Although we show individual objectives, consisting of performance and development goals, at the bottom of the hierarchy, managers at higher levels also should set objectives for their own performance and development.

There is some controversy about whether an organization should use the top-down or the bottom-up approach in setting objectives, as indicated by the arrows in Figure 4-1. In the top-down approach, upper-level managers determine the objectives for subordinates, while in the bottom-up approach subordinates initiate the setting of objectives for their position and present them to the superior.

Proponents of the top-down approach suggest that the total organization needs direction through corporate objectives provided by the chief executive officer (in conjunction with the board of directors). Proponents of the bottom-up approach, on the other hand, argue that top management needs to have information from lower levels in the form of objectives. In addition, subordinates are likely to be highly motivated by, and committed to, goals which they initiate. Our experience has been that the bottom-up approach is underutilized, but also that either approach alone is insufficient. Both are essential but the emphasis should depend on the situation, including such factors as the size of the organization, the organizational culture, the preferred leadership style of the executive, and the urgency of the plan.

A Network of Objectives

Both objectives and planning programs normally form a network of desired results and events. If goals are not interconnected, and if they do not support one another, people very often pursue paths that may seem good for their own department but may be detrimental to the company as a whole.

Goals and plans are seldom linear; that is, when one objective is accomplished, it is not neatly followed by another, and so on. Goals and programs form

FIGURE 4-2

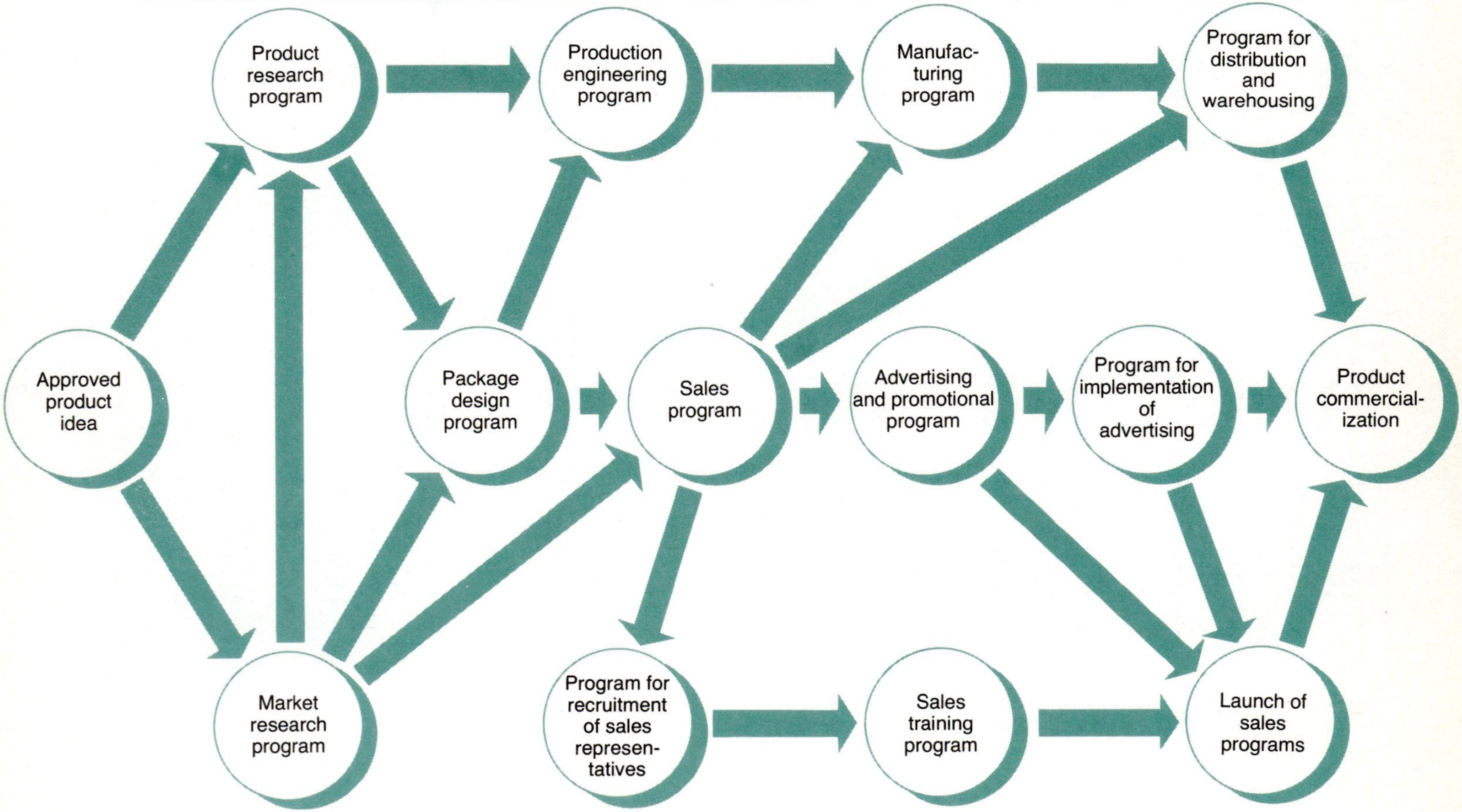

NETWORK OF PROGRAMS CONSTITUTING A TYPICAL NEW-PRODUCT PROGRAM.

an interlocking network. Figure 4-2 depicts the network of contributing programs (each of which has appropriate objectives) that constitute a typical new-product program. Each of the programs could itself be broken down into an interlocking network. Thus, the "product research program" shown in Figure 4-2 as a single event might involve within it a network of such goals and programs as development of preliminary schematic design, development of a breadboard model (such as a design that focuses on the product's function but disregards its appearance), simplification of electronic and mechanical elements, packaging design, and other events.

Managers must make sure that the components of the network "fit" one another. Fitting is a matter not only of having the various programs carried out but also of timing their completion, since undertaking one program often depends upon first completing another.

It is easy for one department of a company to set goals that may seem entirely appropriate for it, only to be operating at cross-purposes with another department. The manufacturing department may find its goals best served by long production runs, but this might interfere with the marketing department's desire to have all products in the line readily available, or the finance department's goal of maintaining investment in inventory at a certain low level.

Organizational studies by Gordon Donaldson showed that companies too often set goals that are unrealistic without recognizing the many constraining factors such as the economic condition or the moves by competitors.[4] Moreover, setting the company's financial goals is a continuing process in which conflicting priorities must be balanced. In fact, managers too often see the objectives from their own perspective—based on their self-interest—without understanding the total network of aims.

PERSPECTIVE:
SOME OVERALL OBJECTIVES, OR AIMS, OF A BUSINESS

A business might include the following among its overall objectives:

- Obtaining a certain rate of profit and return on investment

- Emphasizing research to develop a continuing flow of proprietary products

- Developing publicly held stock ownership

- Financing primarily by earnings plowback and bank debt

- Distributing products in foreign markets

- Ensuring competitive prices for superior products

- Achieving a dominant position in an industry

- Adhering to the values of the society in which it operates

It is bad enough when goals do not support and interlock with one another. It may be catastrophic when they interfere with one another. What is needed is what one executive described as a matrix of mutually supportive goals.

Multiplicity of Objectives

Aims are, of course, many. Even the mission and broad major enterprise objectives are normally multiple, as shown in the Perspective on page 85.

Similarly, to say that a university's mission is education and research is not enough. It would be much more accurate (but still not verifiable) to list the overall objectives, as shown in the Perspective.

PERSPECTIVE:
OVERALL OBJECTIVES OF A UNIVERSITY

The overall objectives of a university might be the following:

- Attracting highly qualified students

- Offering basic training in the liberal arts and sciences as well as in certain professional fields

- Granting the Ph.D. degree to qualified candidates

- Attracting a highly regarded faculty

- Discovering and organizing new knowledge through research

- Operating as a private school supported principally through tuition and gifts of alumni and friends

---

Likewise, at every level in the hierarchy of objectives, goals are likely to be multiple. Some think that a manager cannot pursue effectively more than a few objectives, perhaps two to five. The argument is that too many objectives tend to dilute the drive needed for their accomplishment and may unduly highlight minor objectives to the detriment of major ones.

There is something to that position, but two to five objectives seem too arbitrary and too few. It is true that minor goals should not be given the status of important objectives unless we are dealing with a lower-level job. It would hardly be useful for an upper-level manager to occupy his or her time with such lesser objectives as greeting callers, attending meetings, or answering correspondence. There are certain things that any manager is expected to do, and they need not be made into specific and special objectives. Goals are not conceived of as dealing with every facet of a person's job; they should not be confused with activities.

Even if routine matters are excluded, it seems that there is no definite number of objectives. To be sure, if there are so many that none receives adequate attention, planning will be ineffective. At the same time, managers might pursue simultaneously as many as ten or fifteen significant objectives. However, it would be wise to state the relative importance of each objective. At any rate, the number depends on how much the managers will do themselves and how much they can assign to subordinates, thereby limiting their role to one of assigning, supervising, and controlling.

EVOLVING CONCEPTS IN MANAGEMENT BY OBJECTIVES

Management by objectives (MBO) is now practiced around the world. Yet, despite its wide applications, it is not always clear what is meant by MBO. Some still think of it as an appraisal tool; others see it as a motivational technique; still others consider MBO a planning and control device. In other words, definitions and applications of MBO differ widely, and it is therefore important to highlight the evolving concepts.[5] Before we do that, however, we will define **management by objectives** as: *A comprehensive managerial system that integrates many key managerial activities in a systematic manner, and is consciously directed toward the effective and efficient achievement of organizational and individual objectives.* Our view of MBO as a system of managing is not shared by all. Some still define MBO in a very narrow, limited way.

Early Impetus to MBO

No one person can be called the originator of an approach that emphasizes objectives. Common sense has told people for many centuries that groups and individuals expect to accomplish some end results. However, certain individuals have long placed emphasis on management by objectives and, by doing so, have speeded its development as a systematic process.

One of these is Peter F. Drucker.[6] In 1954 he acted as a catalyst by emphasizing that objectives must be set in all areas where performance affects the health of the enterprise. He laid down a philosophy that emphasizes self-control and self-direction. About the same time, if not earlier, the General Electric Company was using elements of MBO in its reorganization efforts to decentralize managerial decision making. The company implemented this philosophy of appraisal by identifying key result areas and undertaking considerable research on the measurement of performance.

Emphasis on Performance Appraisal

In 1957, in his classic article in the *Harvard Business Review,* Douglas McGregor, a major contributor to the behavioral sciences, criticized traditional appraisal programs that focused on personality trait criteria for evaluating subordinates.[7] In the traditional approach, managers are required to pass judgment on the personal worth of subordinates. Consequently, McGregor suggested a new approach to appraisal based on Drucker's concept of management by objectives. Specifically, subordinates assume the responsibility of setting short-term objectives for themselves and review them with their superior. Of course, the superior has veto power over those objectives, but in the appropriate environment it will hardly need to be used.

Performance is then evaluated against the preset objectives, primarily by subordinates themselves. In this new approach, which encourages self-appraisal and self-development, the emphasis is where it ought to be, on performance rather than on personality. The active involvement of subordinates in the appraisal process leads to commitment and creates an environment for motivation.

Emphasis on Short-Term Objectives and Motivation

Researchers, consultants, and practitioners have long recognized the importance of individual goal setting. Early studies at the University of Maryland found that specific objectives were related to higher performance than when people were asked to do their best.[8] Furthermore, high levels of intentions were associated with high levels of performance.[9] One of the early field studies on an MBO program, as well as a follow-up study, found "a significant upward movement in the overall average level of goals."[10] Also, an improvement in the attainment of goals and a continuing increase in productivity was noted in this firm. However, productivity had tapered off when the follow-up study was made. Although goal setting is not the only factor in motivating employees, it is an important one (other factors are incentives, participation, and autonomy).[11] Certainly the importance of goal setting as a motivational technique is not restricted to business but is also useful in public organizations.[12] The general vagueness of objectives in many public organizations is a challenge for managers, but there is evidence that this challenge can be met.[13]

Inclusion of Long-Range Planning in the MBO Process

In MBO programs that emphasize performance appraisal and motivation, the focus tends to be on short-term objectives. This orientation, unfortunately, may result in undesirable managerial behavior. For example, a production manager, in an effort to reduce maintenance costs, may neglect the necessary expenses for keeping the machines in good working order. The breakdown of machinery may not be evident at first but can result in costly repairs much later. In an effort to show a good return on investment in a given year, the nurturing of good customer relations may be neglected. Similarly, a manager may not invest in new products that would take several years before contributing to profit. Recognizing these shortcomings, many organizations now include long-range and strategic planning in MBO programs.

The Systems Approach to MBO

Management by objectives has undergone many changes; it has been used in performance appraisal, as an instrument for motivating individuals, and, more recently, in strategic planning. But there are still other managerial subsystems that can be integrated into the MBO process; they include design of organizational structures,[14] portfolio management,[15] management development, career development, compensation programs, and budgeting.[16] These various managerial activities need to be integrated into a system. For example, George Odiorne, the most vocal spokesperson for MBO today, considers it to be a system of managerial leadership. Others discuss the systematic relationships of MBO and many other key managerial activities in different environments.[17]

One of the early research studies that investigated MBO as a comprehensive system of managing indicates that most key managerial activities can and should be integrated with the MBO process. The degree of integration, however, differs for individual activities. It was found, for example, that the highest degree of integration of MBO with managerial functions was in controlling, planning, and directing. But several key managerial activities in staffing and organizing also were well integrated into the MBO process. These findings suggest that MBO, to be effective, has to be viewed as a comprehensive system. In short, it must be considered a way of managing, and not an addition to the managerial job.[18]

THE PROCESS OF MANAGING BY OBJECTIVES

We can best see the practical importance of objectives in management by summarizing how successful managing by objectives works in practice.[19] Figure 4-3 graphically portrays this process. Ideally, the process starts at the top of an organization and has the active support of the chief executive, who gives direction to the organization. It is not essential that objective setting start at the top, however. It can start at division level, at marketing-manager level, or even lower. For example, in one company the system was first started in a division where it was carried down to the lowest level of supervision with an interlocking network of goals. Under the personal leadership and tutelage of the division general manager, it succeeded in areas of profitability, cost reduction, and improved operations. Soon, some other division managers and the chief executive became interested in, and attempted to implement, similar programs. In another case, the head of an accounting section developed a system for his group; his success not only earned him recognition (and promotion) but served as the starting point for a company-wide program.

As in all planning, one of the critical needs in MBO is the development and dissemination of consistent planning premises. No manager can be expected to set goals or establish plans and budgets without guidelines.

Preliminary Setting of Objectives at the Top

Given appropriate planning premises, the first step in setting objectives is for the top manager to determine what he or she perceives to be the purpose or mission and the more important goals of the enterprise for a given period ahead. These goals can be set for any period—a quarter, a year, 5 years, or whatever is appropriate in given circumstances. In most instances, objectives are set to coincide with the annual budget or the completion of a major project. But this is not necessary and often not desirable. Certain goals should be scheduled for accomplishment in a much shorter period and others for a much longer period. Also, typically, as one proceeds down the organizational hierarchy, the length of time set for accomplishing goals tends to get shorter. It is seldom feasible or wise for first-level supervisors, for example, to set many annual goals since their goal span on most operating matters, such as cost or scrap reduction, rearrangement

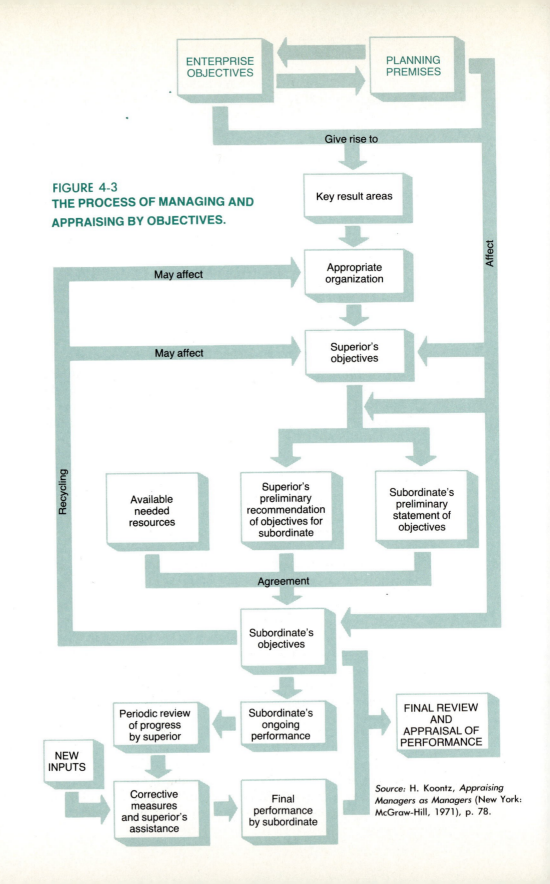

ENTERPRISE OBJECTIVES

PLANNING PREMISES

Give rise to

FIGURE 4-3
THE PROCESS OF MANAGING AND
APPRAISING BY OBJECTIVES.

Key result areas

Appropriate organization

May affect

Superior's objectives

May affect

Affect

Recycling

Available needed resources

Superior's preliminary recommendation of objectives for subordinate

Subordinate's preliminary statement of objectives

Agreement

Subordinate's objectives

Subordinate's ongoing performance

Periodic review of progress by superior

FINAL REVIEW AND APPRAISAL OF PERFORMANCE

NEW INPUTS

Corrective measures and superior's assistance

Final performance by subordinate

Source: H. Koontz, *Appraising Managers as Managers* (New York: McGraw-Hill, 1971), p. 78.

of facilities, or instituting of special personnel programs, is short (most of these goals may be accomplished in weeks or months).

The goals set by the superior are preliminary, based on an analysis and judgment as to what can and should be accomplished by the organization within a certain period. This requires taking into account the company's strengths and weaknesses in the light of available opportunities and threats. These goals must be regarded as tentative and subject to modification while the entire chain of verifiable objectives is worked out by subordinates. It is usually not advisable to force objectives on subordinates since force can scarcely give rise to a sense of commitment. Most managers also find that the process of working out goals with subordinates reveals both problems to be dealt with and opportunities they were not previously aware of.

When setting objectives, the manager also establishes measures of goal accomplishment. If verifiable objectives are developed, these measures, whether in sales dollars, profits, percentages, cost levels, or program execution, will normally be built into the objectives.

Clarification of Organizational Roles

The relationship between expected results and the responsibility for attaining them is often overlooked. Ideally, each goal and subgoal should be some one person's clear responsibility. By analyzing an organization's structure, however, we often find that the responsibility is vague and that clarification or reorganization is needed. Sometimes it is impossible to structure an organization so that a given objective is someone's personal responsibility. In setting goals for launching a new product, for example, the managers of research, marketing, and production must carefully coordinate their activities. Their separate functions can be centralized by putting a product manager in charge. But, if this is not desirable, at least the specific parts of each coordinating manager's contribution to the program goal can and should be clearly identified.

Setting Subordinates' Objectives

After making sure that subordinate managers have been informed of pertinent general objectives, strategies, and planning premises, the superior can then proceed to work with subordinates in setting their objectives. The superior asks what goals the subordinates believe they can accomplish, in what time period, and with what resources. They will then discuss some preliminary thoughts about what goals seem feasible for the company or department.

The superior's role at this point is extremely important. Questions that she or he should ask include: What can you contribute? How can we improve your operation to help me improve mine? What stands in the way; what obstructions keep you from a higher level of performance? What changes can we make? How can I help? It is amazing how many things can be identified that might obstruct performance and how many constructive ideas can be dredged up from the experience and knowledge of subordinates.

Superiors must also be patient counselors, helping their subordinates develop consistent and supportive objectives and being careful not to set goals that are impossible to achieve. It is human nature to believe that anything can be accomplished a year hence, but that much less can be done next week. And one of the things that can weaken a program of managing by objectives is to allow managers to set unrealistic objectives.

At the same time, when subordinates set goals, it does not mean that people can do whatever they want to do. Superiors must listen to, and work with, their subordinates, but in the end they must take responsibility for approving subordinates' goals. The superior's judgment and final approval must be based upon what is reasonably attainable with "stretch" and "pull," what is fully supportive of upper-level objectives, what is consistent with goals of other managers in other functions, and what is consistent with the longer-run objectives and interests of the department and the company.

One of the major advantages of carefully setting up a network of verifiable goals and a requirement for doing so effectively is tying in the need of capital, material, and human resources at the same time. All managers at all levels require these resources to accomplish their goals. By relating these resources to the goals themselves, superiors can better see the most effective and most economical way of allocating them. It helps to avoid the bane of any upper-level manager's existence—"nickel and diming" by subordinates who need "one more" technician or engineer or "one more" piece of equipment, requests that are easy for them to "sell" to their boss and difficult for the superior to refuse.

Recycling Objectives

Objectives can hardly be set by starting at the top and dividing them up among subordinates. Nor should they be started from the bottom. A degree of recycling is required. Recycling is indicated by the arrows in Figures 4-1 and 4-3. Top managers may have an idea as to what their subordinates' objectives should be— but they will almost certainly change these preconceived goals as the contributions of the subordinates come into focus. Thus, setting of objectives is not only a joint process but also one of interaction. For example, a sales manager may realistically set a goal to achieve much higher sales of a product than what top management has believed possible. In this event, the goals of the manufacturing and finance departments will surely be affected.

HOW TO SET OBJECTIVES

Without clear objectives, managing is haphazard. No individual and no group can expect to perform effectively and efficiently unless there is a clear aim. Table 4-1 lists some objectives, with restatements that allow measurement.

Quantitative and Qualitative Objectives

To be measurable, objectives must be verifiable. This means one must be able to answer the question: At the end of the period, how do I know if the objective has been accomplished? For example, the objective of making a reasonable profit

TABLE 4-1   Examples of Nonverifiable and Verifiable Objectives

Nonverifiable objectives	Verifiable objectives
1. To make a reasonable profit	1. To achieve a return on investment of 12% at the end of the current fiscal year
2. To improve communication	2. To issue a two-page monthly newsletter beginning July 1, 1988, involving not more than 40 working hours of preparation time (after the first issue)
3. To improve productivity of the production department	3. To increase production output by 5% by December 31, 1988, without additional costs and while maintaining the current quality level
4. To develop better managers	4. To design and conduct a 40-hour in-house program on the "fundamentals of management," to be completed by October 1, 1989, involving not more than 200 working hours of the management development staff and with at least 90% of the 100 managers passing the exam (specified)
5. To install a computer system	5. To install a computerized control system in the production department by December 31, 1988, requiring not more than 500 working hours of systems analysis and operating with not more than 10% downtime during the first 3 months

can at best indicate whether the company made a profit or had a loss (see Table 4-1), but it does not state how much profit is to be made. Also, what is reasonable to the subordinate may not be at all acceptable to the superior. In case of such a disagreement it is, of course, the subordinate who loses the argument. In contrast, a return of investment of 12 percent at the end of the fiscal year can be measured; it gives answers to the questions: How much or what? and When?

At times it is more difficult to state results in verifiable terms. This is especially true for staff personnel and also in government. For example, installing a computer system is an important task, but "to install a computer system" is not a verifiable goal. But suppose we say "to install a computerized control system (with certain specifications) in the production department by December 31, 1989, with an expenditure of not more than 500 working hours"? Then, goal accomplishment can be measured. Moreover, quality can also be specified (in terms of computer downtime).

Setting Objectives in Government

The need of managing by objectives in government has been recognized by Frederic V. Malek, a former special assistant to the President and one of the driving forces in the implementation of MBO in the federal government.[20] He stated: "If the executive branch of government is to be managed effectively, it clearly needs a system for setting priorities, pinpointing responsibility for their achievement, requiring follow-through, and generating enough feedback that programs can be monitored and evaluated from the top." The MBO program initiated in the federal government in the early 1970s indeed had some success.

For example, the Department of Health, Education, and Welfare set an objective for training and placing 35,000 welfare recipients in meaningful jobs, an objective that seemed almost impossible to achieve. The goal was not only achieved but was exceeded; 40,000 welfare recipients were trained and on payrolls.

To be sure, the management of government has some special problems. Many expenditures are uncontrollable because they are mandated by law. There is also the tendency to perpetuate ineffective programs for political reasons, and congressional members have a political rather than a managerial orientation. Finally, the traditional budgeting process is not conducive to managerial productivity.

Improving the operation of the federal government, and other governments as well, requires

1. Identifying ineffective programs by comparing performance against pre-established objectives

2. Using zero-base budgeting (discussed in Chapter 21)

3. Applying MBO concepts for measuring individual performance

4. Preparing short- and long-range objectives and plans

5. Installing effective controls

6. Designing sound organization structures with clear responsibilities and decision-making authority at appropriate levels

7. Developing and preparing government officials for managerial responsibilities

We can conclude that the setting of objectives, as in MBO programs, not only is essential in making line managers in business organizations more effective but is equally important for improving the performance of staff personnel and public administrators.

Guidelines for Setting Objectives

Setting objectives is indeed a difficult task. It requires intelligent coaching by the superior and extensive practice by the subordinate. We have prepared some guidelines, shown in Table 4-2, that will help managers in setting their objectives.

The list of objectives should not be too long, yet it should cover the main features of the job. We have emphasized that objectives should be verifiable and should state what is to be accomplished and when. If possible, the quality desired and the projected cost of achieving the objectives should be indicated. Furthermore, objectives should present a challenge, indicate priorities, and promote personal and professional growth and development. These and other criteria for good objectives are summarized in Table 4-2. Testing objectives against the criteria shown in the checklist is a good exercise for managers and aspiring managers.

TABLE 4-2   Checklist for Manager Objectives

If the objectives meet the criteria, write "+" in the box at the right of the statement. If they do not, mark "−" in the box.

1. Do the objectives cover the main features of my job? ☐

2. Is the list of objectives too long? If so, can I combine some objectives? ☐

3. Are the objectives verifiable; i.e., will I know at the end of the period whether or not they have been achieved? ☐

4. Do the objectives indicate
   (a) Quantity (how much)? ☐
   (b) Quality (how well, or specific characteristics)? ☐
   (c) Time (when)? ☐
   (d) Cost (at what cost)? ☐

5. Are the objectives challenging, yet reasonable? ☐

6. Are priorities assigned to the objectives (ranking, weighing, etc.)? ☐

7. Does the set of objectives also include
   (a) Improvement objectives? ☐
   (b) Personal development objectives? ☐

8. Are the objectives coordinated with those of other managers and organizational units? ☐
   Are they consistent with the objectives of my superior, my department, the company? ☐

9. Have I communicated the objectives to all who need to be informed? ☐

10. Are the short-term objectives consistent with long-term aims? ☐

11. Are the assumptions underlying the objectives clearly identified? ☐

12. Are the objectives expressed clearly, and in writing? ☐

13. Do the objectives provide for timely feedback so that I can take any necessary corrective steps? ☐

14. Are my resources and authority sufficient for achieving the objectives? ☐

15. Have I given the individuals who are expected to accomplish objectives a chance to suggest their objectives? ☐

16. Do my subordinates have control over aspects for which they are assigned responsibility? ☐

BENEFITS AND WEAKNESSES OF MANAGEMENT BY OBJECTIVES AND SOME RECOMMENDATIONS

Although goal-oriented management is now one of the most widely practiced managerial approaches, its effectiveness is sometimes questioned. Often faulty implementation is blamed, but another reason is that MBO may be applied as a mechanistic technique focusing on selected aspects of the managerial process without integrating them into a system.

A review of 185 studies showed that it is rather difficult to evaluate the true effectiveness of MBO.[21] For one, MBO is defined and practiced differently by various organizations. For some it means simply goal setting while others see it as a comprehensive system of managing. Also, effectiveness is not easy to define and an increase or a decrease in performance may be due to factors other than MBO. It may take 2 to 5 years to implement an MBO program, and during that time many factors other than the program can influence the operation of the firm. As pointed out several years ago—and it is still true today—if a goal-oriented management approach is to produce results, it has to be adapted to the specific situation.[22]

Nevertheless, one can learn from experience and research by taking a realistic view and analyzing some of the benefits and weaknesses of MBO.

Benefits of Management by Objectives

As pointed out earlier, there is considerable evidence, much of it from laboratory studies, that shows the motivational aspects of clear goals. But there are other benefits.

Better managing. We could summarize all the advantages of management by objectives by saying that it results in much-improved management. Objectives cannot be established without planning, and results-oriented planning is the only kind that makes sense. Management by objectives forces managers to think about planning for results, rather than merely planning activities or work. To ensure that objectives are realistic, it also requires managers to think of the way they will accomplish results, the organization and personnel they will need to do so, and the resources and assistance they will require. Also, there is no better incentive for control and no better way to know the standards for control than a set of clear goals.

Clarified organization. Another major benefit of managing by objectives is that it forces managers to clarify organizational roles and structures. To the extent possible, positions should be built around the key results expected of people occupying them.

Companies that have effectively embarked on MBO programs have often discovered deficiencies in their organization. Managers often forget that to get results, they must delegate authority according to the results they expect. As an executive of Honeywell is reported to have said: "There are two things that might also be considered fundamental creed at Honeywell: decentralized management is needed to make Honeywell work and management by objectives is needed to make decentralization work."

Personal commitment. One advantage of management by objectives is that it encourages people to commit themselves to their goals. No longer are people just doing work, following instructions, and waiting for guidance and decisions; they are now individuals with clearly defined purposes. They have had a part in actually setting their objectives; they have had an opportunity to put their ideas into planning programs; they understand their area of discretion—their authority—and they have been able to get help from their superiors to ensure that they can accomplish their goals. These are elements that make for a feeling of commitment. People become enthusiastic when they control their own fate.

Development of effective controls.   In the same way that management by objectives sparks more effective planning, it also aids in developing effective controls. Recall that control involves measuring results and taking action to correct deviations from plans in order to ensure that goals are reached. As you will see in Chapter 20, on the system and process of management control, a major problem is knowing what to watch; a clear set of verifiable goals is the best guide.

Weaknesses in Managing by Objectives

With all its advantages, a system of management by objectives has a number of weaknesses. Most are due to shortcomings in applying the MBO concepts.

Failure to teach the philosophy of MBO.   As simple as management by objectives may seem, managers who would put it into practice must understand and appreciate a good deal about it. They in turn must explain to subordinates what it is, how it works, why it is being done, what part it will play in appraising performance, and, above all, how participants can benefit. The philosophy is built on concepts of self-control and self-direction aimed at making managers professionals.

Failure to give guidelines to goal setters.   Management by objectives, like any other kind of planning, cannot work if those who are expected to set goals are not given needed guidelines. Managers must know what the corporate goals are and how their own activity fits in with them. If corporation goals are vague, unreal, or inconsistent, it is virtually impossible for managers to tune in with them.

Managers also need planning premises and a knowledge of major company policies. People must have some assumptions as to the future, some understanding of policies affecting their areas of operation, and an awareness of the objectives and programs with which their goals interlock in order to plan effectively. Failure to fill these needs can result in a fatal vacuum in planning.

Difficulty of setting goals.   Truly verifiable goals are difficult to set, particularly if they are to have the right degree of stretch or pull, quarter in and quarter out, year in and year out. Goal setting may not be much more difficult than any other kind of effective planning, although it will probably take more study and work to establish verifiable objectives that are formidable but attainable than to develop many plans, which tend only to lay out work to be done. Participants in MBO programs report at times that the excessive concern with economic results puts pressure on individuals that may encourage questionable behavior.[23] To reduce the probability of selecting unethical means for achieving results, top management must agree to reasonable objectives, clearly state behavioral expectations, and give a high priority to ethical behavior, rewarding it as well as punishing unethical activities.

Emphasis on short-run goals.   In most management-by-objectives programs, managers set goals for the short term, seldom for more than a year, and often for a quarter or less. There is clearly a danger of emphasizing the short run, perhaps at the expense of the longer range. This means, of course, that superiors must always assure themselves that current objectives, like any other short-run plan, are designed to serve longer-range goals.

Danger of inflexibility.   Managers often hesitate to change objectives. Although goals may cease to be meaningful if they are changed too often and do not represent a well-thought-out and well-planned result, it is nonetheless foolish to expect a manager to strive for a goal that has been made obsolete by revised corporate objectives, changed premises, or modified policies.

Other dangers.   There are some other dangers and difficulties in management by objectives. In their desire to make goals verifiable, people may overuse quantitative goals and attempt to use numbers in areas where they are not applicable, or they may downgrade important goals that are difficult to state in terms of end results. A favorable company image may be the key strength of an enterprise, yet it is difficult to state this in quantitative terms. Sometimes managers fail to use objectives as a constructive force even with the full participation and assistance of their superiors. There is also the danger of forgetting that there is more to managing than goal setting.

There may also be difficulties in applying goal-oriented planning in a very dynamic and complex environment. In human services delivery systems it was noted that MBO was rejected because of difficulties in (1) converting broad organizational objectives into more detailed organizational unit objectives, (2) measuring performance and to provide feedback, (3) determining what is meritorious performance and rewarding individuals accordingly, (4) stating long-term objectives congruent with short-term goals, and (5) adjusting to the fast-changing environment.[24]

But even with the difficulties and dangers of managing by objectives in certain situations, this system emphasizes in practice the setting of goals, long known to be an essential part of planning and managing.

FOR DISCUSSION

1. To what extent do you believe that managers you have known in business or elsewhere have a clear understanding of their objectives? If, in your opinion, they do not, how would you suggest that they go about setting them?

2. Some people object to defining long-term goals because they think it is impossible to know what will happen over a long period. Is this an intelligent position to take?

3. Take any program of any kind that you would like to see accomplished and draw a network of contributing programs and goals necessary for its accomplishment.

4. "The only planning tool we need in this company is the budget. If everyone meets his or her budget, we need nothing else, and management by objectives would be an unnecessary frill." Comment.

5. Why do you suspect that, although so many business enterprises talk about and introduce programs of management by objectives, the actual record of performance under these programs has been so poor?

6. Do you believe that managing by objectives could be introduced in a government agency? A university? A college fraternity or sorority?

7. What are your five most important personal objectives? Are they long- or short-range? Are the objectives verifiable?

8. In your organization, what does your superior expect from you in respect to the level of performance? Is it stated in writing? If you wrote your job objective on a sheet of paper and your boss wrote down what he or she expects of you, would the two be consistent?

EXERCISES/ACTION STEPS

1. Make a list of goals you wish to achieve in the next 5 years. Are they verifiable? Are they attainable?

2. Interview two managers in the local community, one in a business enterprise, the other of a government agency. Ask them what the long- and short-term overall objectives of their organizations are. Are they clear, in writing, and understood? Also ask the managers about their objectives. If these organizations have a systematic approach to goal setting, ask about the process and try to diagram it. Present and explain the diagram to the class.

CASES

CASE 4-1
DEVELOPING VERIFIABLE GOALS

The division manager had recently heard a lecture on management by objectives. His enthusiasm, kindled at that time, tended to grow the more he thought about it. He finally decided to introduce the concept and see what headway he could make at his next staff meeting.

He recounted the theoretical developments in this technique, cited the advantages to the division of its application, and asked his subordinates to think about adopting it.

It was not as easy as everyone had thought. At the next meeting, several questions were raised. "Do you have division goals assigned by the president to you for next year?" the finance manager wanted to know.

"No, I do not," the division manager replied. "I have been waiting for the president's office to tell me what is expected, but they act as if they will do nothing about the matter."

"What is the division to do, then?" the manager of production asked, rather hoping that no action would be indicated.

"I intend to list my expectations for the division," the division manager said. "There is not much mystery about them. I expect $30 million in sales, a profit on sales before taxes of 8 percent, a return on investment of 15 percent, an ongoing program in effect by June 30, with specific characteristics I will list later, development of our own future managers, completion of development work on our XZ model by the end of the year, and stabilization of employee turnover at 5 percent."

The staff was somewhat stunned that their superior had thought through to these verifiable objectives and stated them with such clarity and assurance. They were also surprised about his sincerity in wanting to achieve them.

"During the next month I want each of you to

translate these objectives into verifiable goals for your own functions. Naturally they will be different for finance, marketing, production, engineering, and administration. However you state them, I will expect them to add up to the realization of the division goals."

1. Can a division manager develop verifiable goals, or objectives, when they have not been assigned to him or her by the president? How? What kind of information or help do you believe is important for the division manager to have from headquarters?

2. Was the division manager setting goals in the best way? What would you have done?

CASE 4-2
THE MUNICIPAL WATER DISTRICT

The district proposed an incentive program for its higher-level managers to be tried for 1 year. The program, based on MBO concepts, was a response to criticism from citizens in the community. Here is a summary of the proposed program:

The objectives are to be set to represent higher-than-normal performance. Furthermore, the emphasis will be on verifiable objectives against which performance can be measured. One of the objectives, for example, will be to keep the average water bill increase at 75 percent or less of the inflation rate. The participating managers will receive only half of the cost-of-living increases granted to other employees. To be eligible for the other half they will have to achieve *some* of the objectives. If, on the other hand, *most* of the above-normal objectives are achieved, their pay increases will be above the inflation rate. No lump-sum bonuses will be granted, but the performance of the managers will be reflected in their wages.

It was figured that the program would result in $15,000 to $25,000 savings for the district if none of the objectives were met. On the other hand, if all objectives were met the cost to the company would be between $25,000 and $35,000 in salary increases. But the indirect savings were estimated at $1 million or more. This incentive program was submitted to the public through a poll with arguments for and against the plan.

The arguments *for* the incentive program were as follows:

1. It would stop the rise in water rates.

2. Rewards would be based on performance.

3. Turnover of management personnel would be reduced.

4. The cost for outstanding performance would be low compared with the potential savings.

The arguments *against* the incentive program were as follows:

1. The program would raise the current objectives only to what would normally be expected of the managers.

2. The company has one of the highest water costs in the state.

3. If the general manager were to meet all the objectives, he would get paid more than a United States senator. If three other high-level managers were to achieve all of their objectives, they would get paid more than the governor of the state.

4. Since the budget is prepared by the same person who would be the beneficiary of the incentives, there would be the temptation to "pad" the budget.

5. The past performance was considered substandard; no bonus should be offered to managers for improving their substandard performance and doing what they are supposed to in the first place.

6. The policy of the company states that it should supply adequate water at the lowest possible cost. If the managers are not capable of performing their job, they should seek employment elsewhere.

1. What do you think about the incentive program?

2. Do you think that the public should be polled on such a program? Why, or why not?

3. As a consultant, what would you recommend?

REFERENCES

1. George A. Steiner, John B. Miner, and Edmund R. Gray, *Management Policy and Strategy,* 3d ed. (New York: The Macmillan Company, 1986), pp. 86–87.

2. Peter F. Drucker, *The Practice of Management* (New York: Harper & Brothers, 1954), p. 63.

3. Parts of this discussion are based on Heinz Weihrich, "A Hierarchy and Network of Aims," *Management Review* (January 1982), pp. 47–54.

4. Gordon Donaldson, "Financial Goals and Strategic Consequences, *Harvard Business Review* (May–June 1985), pp. 57–66.

5. For a detailed discussion of the history of MBO see George S. Odiorne, "MBO: A Backward Glance," *Business Horizons* (October 1978), pp. 14–24. An excellent discussion of the early history of MBO is by Ronald G. Greenwood, "Management by Objectives: As Developed by Peter Drucker, Assisted by Harold Smiddy," *Academy of Management Review* (April 1981), pp. 225–230.

6. For his original discussion of managing by objectives, see Peter F. Drucker, *The Practice of Management* (New York: Harper & Brothers, 1954), pp. 121–136. In conversation with Harold Koontz, Drucker gave credit for the concept to the late Harold E. Smiddy, then of General Electric. See also Ronald G. Greenwood, "Management by Objectives: As Developed by Peter Drucker, Assisted by Harold Smiddy," *Academy of Management Review* (April 1981), pp. 225–230.

7. "An Uneasy Look at Performance Appraisal," *Harvard Business Review* (May–June 1957), pp. 89–94. In even more recent writings the emphasis in MBO is still on goal setting and appraisal, as shown by Mark L. McConkie, "A Clarification of the Goal Setting and Appraisal Process in MBO," *Academy of Management Review* (January 1979), pp. 29–40.

8. Edwin A. Locke and Judith F. Bryan, "Performance Goals as Determinants of Level of Performance and Boredom," *Journal of Applied Psychology* (April 1967), pp. 120–130.

9. Edwin A. Locke, "The Relationship of Intentions to Level of Performance," *Journal of Applied Psychology* (February 1966), pp. 60–66.

10. Anthony P. Raia, "A Second Look at Management Goals and Controls," *California Management Review* (Summer 1966), pp. 49–58.

11. Edwin A. Locke, "The Ubiquity of the Technique of Goal Setting in Theories of and Approaches to Employee Motivation," *Academy of Management Review* (July 1978), pp. 594–601.

12. James L. Perry and Lyman W. Porter, "Factors Affecting the Context for Motivation in Public Organizations," *Academy of Management Review* (January 1982), pp. 89–98.

13. Heinz Weihrich, "The Application of Management by Objectives in Government," *Faculty Working Paper MG 76-3* (Tempe, Arizona: Arizona State University, 1976).

14. Richard D. Babcock, "Summary of Five Key Elements for Adapting MBO to Different Organizational Designs," *1981. Proceedings, IX Annual Management by Objectives State of the Art Conference* (Washington, D.C., 1981), pp. 14–18.

15. George S. Odiorne, "Portfolio Management and MBO," *1981 Proceedings, IX Annual Management by Objectives State of the Art Conference* (Washington, D.C., 1981), pp. 119–124.

16. M.A. Quereshi and Richard Babcock, "A Proposal for Integrating Budgeting and MBO," in Richard D. Babcock and Peter F. Sorensen, Jr. (eds.), *Strategies and Tactics in Management by Objectives* (Champaign, Ill.: Stripes Publishing Company, 1980), pp. 96–112.

17. Anthony P. Raia, *Managing by Objectives* (Glenview, Ill.: Scott, Foresman and Company, 1974); Dale D. McConkey, *MBO for Nonprofit Organizations* (New York: AMACOM, American Management Association, 1975); George L. Morrisey, *Management by Objectives and Results in the Public Sector* (Reading, Mass.: Addison-Wesley Publishing Company, 1976, 1983).

18. Heinz Weihrich, "A Study of the Integration of Management by Objectives with Key Managerial Activities and the Relationship to Selected Effectiveness Measures," doctoral dissertation, University of California, Los Angeles, 1973.

19. Some of the material in this section is drawn from Harold Koontz, *Appraising Managers as Managers* (New York: McGraw-Hill Book Company, 1971), chaps. 3–4.

20. This discussion is based on Malek's book *Washington's Hidden Tragedy* (New York: The Free Press, 1978), chaps. 7–9. It provides one of the best insights into the operation of MBO in the federal government.

21. Jack N. Kondrasuk, "Studies in MBO Effectiveness," *Academy of Management Review* (July 1981), pp. 419–430.

22. Heinz Weihrich, "An Uneasy Look at the MBO Jungle—Toward a Contingency Approach to MBO," *Management International Review*, Vol. 16, No. 4 (1976), pp. 103–109.

23. Charles D. Pringle and Justin G. Longenecker, "The Ethics of MBO," *Academy of Management Review* (April 1982), pp. 305–312.

24. Mark A. Covaleski and Mark W. Dirsmith, "MBO and Goal Directedness in a Hospital Context," *Academy of Management Review* (July 1981), pp. 409–418.

FOR FURTHER INFORMATION

Humble, John W. *Improving Business Results* (Maidenhead, England: McGraw-Hill Book Company (U.K.), 1968).

Koontz, Harold. *Appraising Managers as Managers* (New York: McGraw-Hill Book Company, 1971).

Mark, M. A. "Productivity Measurement of Government Services—Federal, State, and Local," *White House Conference on Productivity,* Panel Background Papers, 1983.

Odiorne, George S. *MBO II* (Belmont, Calif.: Fearon Pitman, 1979).

Odiorne, George S., Heinz Weihrich, and Jack Mendleson (eds.). *Executive Skills—A Management by Objectives Approach* (Dubuque, Iowa: Wm. C. Brown Company, 1980).

Odiorne, George S. *The Change Resisters* (Englewood Cliffs, N.J.: Prentice-Hall, 1981).

Raia, Anthony P. *Managing by Objectives* (Glenview, Ill.: Scott, Foresman and Company, 1974).

Weihrich, Heinz. *Management Excellence—Productivity Through MBO* (New York: McGraw-Hill Book Company, 1985).

Strategies, Policies, and Planning Premises

CHAPTER OBJECTIVES

After reading this chapter, you should be able to:

1. Explain the nature and purpose of strategy and policy.

2. Describe the strategic planning process.

3. Understand the TOWS Matrix and the Product Portfolio Matrix.

4. Describe the major kinds of strategies and policies.

5. Identify Porter's generic strategies.

6. Make recommendation for effective implementation of strategies.

7. Discuss the nature and types of premises and forecasts.

8. Make premising effective.

*T*oday most business enterprises engage in strategic planning, although the degrees of sophistication and formality vary considerably. Conceptually, strategic planning is deceptively simple: Analyze the current and expected future situation, determine the direction of the firm, and develop means for achieving the mission. In reality, this is an extremely complex process which demands a systematic approach for identifying and analyzing factors external to the organization and matching them with the firm's capabilities.

Planning is done in an environment of uncertainty. No one can be sure what the external as well as the internal environment will be, not even next week, much less several years from now. Therefore we make assumptions or forecasts about the anticipated environment. Some of the forecasts become assumptions for other plans. For example, the gross national product forecast becomes the assumption for sales planning, which, in turn, becomes the basis for production planning, and so on.

In this chapter you will learn about (1) the nature and purpose of strategies and policies, (2) the strategic planning process which identifies the critical aspects of formulating a strategy, (3) a tool for systematically integrating external and internal factors (called the "TOWS Matrix"), (4) another tool for allocating resources (called the "Portfolio Matrix"), (5) major kinds of strategies, (6) descriptions of three generic strategies, and (7) means for effectively implementing strategies. Since plans are made in an environment of uncertainty, you will learn to appreciate (8) the various aspects of premising and forecasting, (9) environmental forecasting, showing how the Delphi technique may be used, (10) various kinds of sales forecasting, and (11) how to make premising effective.

THE NATURE AND PURPOSE OF STRATEGIES AND POLICIES

Strategies and policies are closely related. Both give direction, both are the framework for plans, both are the basis of operational plans, and both affect all areas of managing.

Strategy and Policy

The term "strategy" (which is derived from the Greek word *strategos,* meaning "general") has been used in different ways. Authors differ in at least one major aspect about **strategies.** Some writers focus on both the end points (purpose, mission, goals, objectives) and the means of achieving them (policies and plans). But others emphasize the means to the ends in the strategic process rather than the ends per se. The great variety of meanings of the word "strategies" were listed in Chapter 3.

Since ends have already been discussed (Chapter 4), we will turn our attention now to situation analysis. It is assumed that the purpose of the enterprise has already been established yet is subject to change after an evaluation of the situation.

Policies are general statements or understandings which guide our thinking in decision making. They ensure that decisions fall within certain boundaries. They usually do not require action but are intended to guide managers in their commitment to the decisions they ultimately make.

The essence of policy is discretion. Strategy, on the other hand, concerns the direction in which human and material resources will be applied in order to increase the chance of achieving selected objectives.

Certain major policies and strategies may be essentially the same. A policy to develop only those new products that fit into a company's marketing plan, or one to distribute only through retailers, may be an essential element of a company's strategy for new product development or marketing. One company may have a policy of growth through acquisition of other companies, while another may have a policy of growing only by expanding present markets and products. While these are policies, they are also essential elements of major strategies. Perhaps one way to draw a meaningful distinction is to say that policies will guide our thinking in decision making—if a decision is to be made—while strategies imply that an enterprise has made the decision to commit resources in a given direction.

Giving Direction to Plans

The key function of strategies and policies is to unify and give direction to plans. In other words, they influence the course in which an enterprise is trying to go. But, standing alone, they do not ensure that an organization will, in fact, go where it wants to go.

Furnishing the Framework of Plans

Strategies and policies help managers plan by guiding operating decisions and often premaking them. The underlying **principle** is, then, that *the more carefully developed and clearly understood strategies and policies are, the more consistent and effective the ensuing plans will be.* For example, if a company has a major policy of

---

**PERSPECTIVE:
IBM'S TACTICS**

When IBM ventured into the retail market, setting up IBM product centers to sell personal computers (PCs) and typewriters, it decorated the sales offices in red.[1] However, the bright colors alarmed customers and irritated salespeople. Also, these centers were staffed by IBM personnel who often did not have retail experience. Their thorough product knowledge—reflected in their sales discussions—intimidated many customers with little computer knowledge. But IBM corrected both tactical mistakes by switching to subdued colors for decor and giving formal sales training to their personnel. Nevertheless, in 1986 IBM sold its product centers to Nynex Business Information. This case illustrates that a strategy, to be successful, must be supported by carefully developed tactics.

developing only new products that fit its marketing organization, it will avoid wasting energy and resources on new products that do not meet this test.

The Need for Operational Planning: Tactics

To be effective, strategies and policies must be put into practice by means of plans, increasing in detail until they get down to the nuts and bolts of operations. **Tactics,** then, are the action plans through which strategies are executed. Strategies must be supported by effective tactics (see Perspective on page 105).

The Effect on All Areas of Managing

Since strategies and policies affect planning, they also greatly affect other areas of managing. For example, major strategies and policies will naturally influence organization structure and, through this, other functions of the manager. In his extraordinary analysis of the history of some of the nation's largest companies, Alfred Chandler, Jr., depicts in detail how strategy affected organization structure.[2] In the Du Pont Company, the organization around product lines, with centralized control, followed the strategy of product diversification. General Motors had essentially the same situation. In Du Pont, the strategy of diversification was dictated by the need to use resources made surplus by the post-World War I decline in the explosives business. In General Motors, on the other hand, the strategy was one of integration and expansion of a large, disparate group of companies acquired by W. C. Durant in his formation of the company during the two decades before 1920. While the strategies of these two companies were based on different premises and situations, they led to essentially the same organization structures.

THE STRATEGIC PLANNING PROCESS

Although specific steps in the formulation of the strategy may vary, the process can be built, at least conceptually, around the key elements shown in Figure 5-1.

   1. The various organizational *inputs*, including the goal inputs of the claimants, were discussed in Chapter 1 and need no elaboration.

   2. The *enterprise profile* is usually the starting point for determining where the company is and where it should go. Thus, top managers determine the basic purpose of the enterprise and clarify the firm's geographic orientation, such as whether it should operate in selected regions, in all states in the United States, or even in different countries. In addition, managers assess the competitive situation of their firm (see Perspective on page 108).

   3. The enterprise profile is shaped by people, especially *top managers*, and their *orientation* is important for formulating the strategy. They set the organizational climate, and they determine the direction of the firm. Consequently, their values, their preferences, and their attitudes toward risks have to be carefully examined because they have an impact on the strategy.

FIGURE 5-1

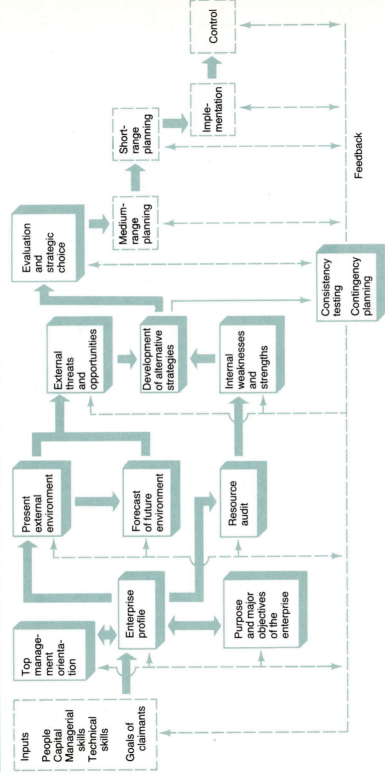

STRATEGIC PLANNING PROCESS.

Adapted from Heinz Weihrich, "The TOWS Matrix: A Tool for Situational Analysis," *Long-Range Planning*, vol. 15, no. 2 (1982), pp. 54–66.

PERSPECTIVE:
TOP MANAGEMENT CHOICES

Top managers get paid for making tough decisions. Many of them are strategic for the future of the company. Let us look at some examples of decisions that altered the course of the company.[3]

General Motors.   Roger Smith of General Motors saw the opportunities in the high-tech field and their importance for GM. Consequently, he decided on acquiring Electronic Data Systems Corporation, a large data processing company. But the resistance to the merger of these two companies (with very different organizational cultures) by GM's staff was substantial. Long established organizations do not change easily, and Roger Smith learned a great deal about the difficulty of making dramatic changes.

Gould Inc.   William Ylvisaker, the CEO at Gould Inc., changed the firm from a manufacturer of car batteries and electrical equipment to a high-tech electronics firm. This new direction required a change in personnel; half of its management committee left the company. To make such drastic decisions requires a strong-willed person; Ylvisaker was named one of the ten toughest corporate managers by *Fortune* magazine.

Warner-Lambert.   When Ward Hagan wanted to restructure Warner-Lambert, he had to streamline the drug company. This required selling the eyeglass manufacturer American Optical (a loser) as well as Entenmann, a profitable bakery firm. To give a new direction to the firm, he employed the consulting services of McKinsey & Co. to teach its managers strategic planning. To be sure, nobody can predict the long-term future with great accuracy, but strategic planning forces managers to think critically and analytically about the future. The company sent 500 of its managers to a program to train them in critical thinking. To demonstrate the importance of strategic thinking, the company rewarded such activities with promotions.

Rolm Corporation.   Rolm Corporation was concerned about its dependence on military customers, which led to a search for related product lines. Despite a thorough search, the results were at first disappointing. Persistence and continuing search led to the development of digital switching equipment that was more advanced than that of its competitors. Some risk-taking decisions turned out to be right and made the company a giant in its field before the firm was acquired by IBM.

    4. The *purpose* and the major *objectives* are the end points toward which the activities of the enterprise are directed. Since we dealt with these topics at lengths in the previous chapter, we will continue with the next key aspect in the strategic planning process shown in Figure 5-1.

    5. The present and future *external environment* must be assessed in terms of threats and opportunities. The evaluation focuses on economic, social, political, legal, demographic, and geographic factors. In addition, the environment is scanned for technological developments, for products and services on the market, and for other factors necessary in determining the competitive situation of the enterprise.

6. Similarly, the firm's *internal environment* should be audited and evaluated in respect to its resources and its weaknesses and strengths in research and development, production, operations, procurement, marketing, and products and services. Other internal factors important for formulating a strategy include the assessment of human resources, financial resources, and other factors such as the company image, the organization structure and climate, the planning and control system, and relations with customers.

7. Strategic *alternatives* are *developed* on the basis of analysis of the external and internal environment. An organization may pursue many different kinds of strategies. It may specialize or concentrate, as American Motors did by producing lower-priced cars (in contrast to General Motors, which has a complete product line ranging from inexpensive to luxury cars).

Another strategy is diversification, by extending the operation into new and profitable markets. Sears not only is in retailing but also provides many financial services.

Still another strategy is to go international and to expand the operation into other countries. Multinational firms, discussed in Chapter 25, provide many examples. In the same chapter you will also see that joint ventures may be appropriate, especially for big undertakings in which firms have to pool their resources, as illustrated by the joint venture of General Motors and Toyota to produce small cars in California.

Under certain circumstances, a company may have to adopt a liquidation strategy by terminating an unprofitable product line or even dissolving the firm. But in some cases liquidation may not be necessary and a retrenchment strategy may be appropriate. In such a situation the company may curtail its operation temporarily (see also Perspective on page 110).

These are just a few examples of possible strategies. In practice, companies, especially large ones, pursue a combination of strategies.

8. The various strategies have to be carefully *evaluated* before the *choice* is made. Strategic choices must be considered in light of the risks involved in a particular decision. Some profitable opportunities may not be pursued because a failure in a risky venture could result in bankruptcy of the firm. Another critical element in choosing a strategy is timing. Even the best product may fail if it is introduced to the market at an inappropriate time. Moreover, the reaction of competitors must be taken into consideration. When IBM reduced its price of the PC computer in reaction to the sales success of Apple's Macintosh computer, other IBM-compatible computer firms had little choice but to reduce their prices as well. This illustrates the interconnections of the strategies of several firms in the same industry.

9. Although not a part of the strategic planning process (and therefore shown by broken lines in Figure 5-1), *medium-* and *short-range planning* as well as the *implementation* of the plans must be considered during all phases of the process. *Control* must also be provided for monitoring performance against plans.[4] The importance of *feedback* is shown by the loops in the model.

PERSPECTIVE:
STRATEGIES IN DECLINING INDUSTRIES

The traditional wisdom in managing a declining industry was to milk the company for cash and use it for diversification, then divest the firm operating in the declining industry.

But when firms leave the industry, this opens opportunities for the remaining ones. Indeed, money may be made in declining industries. However, the strategic and tactical approaches have to be different. For example, the strategy may be not to gain market share but to do other things—and do them well.[5]

Fortune magazine studied seven successful companies which sell rather mundane products, such as commercial pumps, retreaded tires, steel products, and valves for industrial use.

The companies that were successful in the declining industries are quite different and they employ different strategies and tactics. Here are some:

- Emphasis is on profit margins (not market share).

- Executives know their business well, many of them having grown up in them.

- Companies and managers are intensely involved in the business they are in.

- The family spirit pervades the company.

- It is hands-on management, using an informal style.

- Companies are quick to innovate.

These companies also do the following:

- Provide good service.

- Focus on cost control.

- Have a lean staff.

- Are persistent in their efforts on gradual improvement of the operation.

- Elicit suggestions and ideas from their employees.

- Keep the inventory low.

- Offer a share in the success of the company.

- Have an incentive system that encourages productivity.

The lesson to be learned is that problems can become opportunities. Indeed, when competitors follow conventional wisdom and leave the declining industry, opportunities for profit open up for the remaining ones.

10. The last key aspect of the strategic planning process is the testing for *consistency* and the preparation for *contingency plans*. Both topics will be discussed later in this chapter.

THE TOWS MATRIX©:
A MODERN TOOL FOR ANALYSIS OF THE SITUATION

Today, strategy designers have been aided by a number of matrixes showing the relationships of critical variables. For example, the Boston Consulting Group developed the Business Portfolio Matrix, which will be discussed later. More recently, the TOWS Matrix has been introduced for analyzing the situation.[6]

The TOWS Matrix has a wider scope and has different emphases from those of the Business Portfolio Matrix. The former does not replace the latter. The TOWS Matrix is a conceptual framework for a systematic analysis that facilitates matching the external threats and opportunities with the internal weaknesses and strengths of the organization.

It has been common to suggest that companies identify their strengths and weaknesses, and the opportunities and threats in the external environment. But what is often overlooked is that combining these factors may require distinct strategic choices. To systematize these choices, the TOWS Matrix is proposed in which "T" stands for threats, "O" for opportunities, "W" for weaknesses, and "S" for strengths. The TOWS model starts with the threats because in many situations a company undertakes strategic planning because of a perceived crisis, problem, or threat.

Four Alternative Strategies

As you can see in Figure 5-2, there are four alternative strategies[7] based on the analysis of the external environment (threats and opportunities) and the internal environment (weaknesses and strengths).

1. The WT strategy (see the lower right-hand quadrant) is to minimize both weaknesses and threats and may require the company, for example, to form a joint venture, retrench, or even liquidate.

2. The WO strategy attempts to minimize the weaknesses and maximize opportunities. Thus, a firm with certain weaknesses in some areas may either develop those areas within the enterprise or acquire those needed competencies from the outside (such as technology or persons with needed skills), making it possible to take advantage of opportunities in the external environment.

3. The ST strategy is based on the organization's strengths to deal with threats in the environment. The aim is to maximize the former while minimizing the latter. Thus, a company may use its technological, financial, managerial, or marketing strengths to cope with the threats of a new product introduced by its competitor.

FIGURE 5-2

External factors / Internal factors	Internal strengths (S) e.g., strengths in management, operations, finance, marketing, R&D, engineering	Internal weaknesses (W) e.g., weaknesses in areas shown in the box of "strengths"
External opportunities (O) (Consider risks also) e.g., current and future economic conditions; political and social changes, new products, services, and technology	SO Strategy: Maxi-Maxi Potentially the most successful strategy, utilizing the organization's strengths to take advantage of opportunities	WO Strategy: Mini-Maxi e.g., developmental strategy to overcome weaknesses in order to take advantage of opportunities
External threats (T): e.g., lack of energy, competition, and areas similar to those shown in the "opportunities" box above	ST Strategy: Maxi-Mini e.g., use of strengths to cope with threats or to avoid threats	WT Strategy: Mini-Mini e.g., retrenchment, liquidation or joint venture

THE TOWS MATRIX FOR STRATEGY FORMULATION.

4. The most desirable position is when a company can use its strengths to take advantage of opportunities (SO strategy). Indeed, it is the aim of enterprises to move from other positions in the matrix to this situation. If they have weaknesses, they will strive to overcome them, making them strengths. If they face threats, they will cope with them so that they can focus on opportunities.

Time Dimension and the TOWS Matrix

So far, the factors displayed in the TOWS Matrix pertain to analysis at a particular point in time. External and internal environments are dynamic: Some factors change over time while others change very little. Because of the dynamics in the environment, the strategy designer must prepare several TOWS Matrixes at different points in time, as shown in Figure 5-3. Thus, one may start with a TOWS analysis of the past, continue with an analysis of the present, and, perhaps most important, focus on different time periods (T_1, T_2, etc.) in the future.

THE PORTFOLIO MATRIX: A TOOL FOR ALLOCATING RESOURCES

The Business Portfolio Matrix was developed by the Boston Consulting Group (BCG).[8] Figure 5-4, a simplified version of the matrix, shows the linkages between the growth rate of the business and the relative competitive position of

FIGURE 5-3

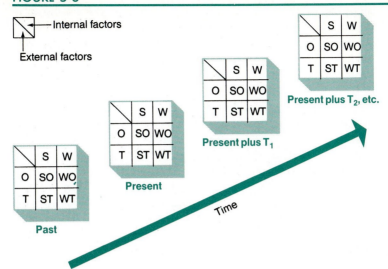

DYNAMICS OF TOWS ANALYSIS.

FIGURE 5-4

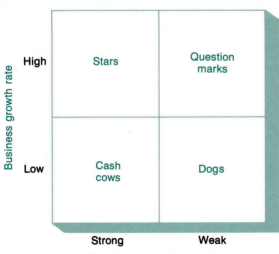

BUSINESS PORTFOLIO MATRIX.

Adapted from *The Product Portfolio Matrix*, copyright © 1970, The Boston Consulting Group, Inc.

the firm, identified by the market share. Businesses in the "question mark" quadrant, with a weak market share and a high growth rate, usually require cash investment so that they can become "stars," the businesses in the high-growth, strongly competitive position. These kinds of businesses have opportunities for growth and profit. The "cash cows," with a strong competitive position and a low growth rate, are usually well established in the market, and such enterprises are in the position of making the products at low cost. Therefore, the products of such enterprises provide the cash needed for their operation. The "dogs" are businesses with a low growth rate and a weak market share position. These businesses are usually not profitable and generally should be disposed of.

The Portfolio Matrix was developed for large corporations with several divisions often organized around strategic business units (SBUs).[9] While portfolio analysis was popular in the 1970s, it is not without its critics, who contend that it is too simplistic. Also, the growth rate criterion has been considered insufficient for the evaluation of an industry's attractiveness. Similarly, the market share as a yardstick for estimating the competitive position may be inadequate.[10]

MAJOR KINDS OF STRATEGIES AND POLICIES

For a business enterprise (and, with some modification, for other kinds of organizations as well), the major strategies and policies that give an overall direction to operations are likely to be in the following areas.[11]

Growth

Growth strategies give answers to such questions as how much growth should occur, and how fast, where, and how it should occur.

Finance

Every business enterprise and, for that matter, any nonbusiness enterprise must have a clear strategy for financing its operations. There are various ways of doing this and usually many serious limitations.

Organization

Organizational strategy has to do with the type of organizational pattern an enterprise will use. It answers such practical questions as how centralized or decentralized decision-making authority should be, what kinds of departmental patterns are most suitable, and how to design staff positions. Naturally, organization structures furnish the system of roles and role relationships that help people to accomplish objectives.

Personnel

There can be many major strategies in the area of human resources and relationships. They deal with such topics as union relations, compensation, selection, hiring, training, and appraisal, as well as with special areas such as job enrichment.

Public Relations

Strategies in this area can hardly be independent but must support other major strategies and efforts. They must also be designed in the light of the company's type of business, its closeness to the public, and its susceptibility to regulation by government agencies. To develop strategies in any area, we must ask the right questions. While no set of strategies can be formulated that will fit all organizations and situations, certain key questions will help any company to discover what its strategies should be.

To show how the right questions can lead to answers, we will raise some key questions in only two major strategic areas: products and services, and marketing. With a little thought, you can devise key questions for other major strategic areas.

Products or Services

A business exists to furnish products or services. In a very real sense, profits are merely a measure—although an important one—of how well a company serves its customers.

New products or services, more than any other single factor, determine what an enterprise is or will be. The key questions in this area can be summarized as follows:

What is our business?

Who are our customers?

What do our customers want?

How much will our customers buy and at what price?

Do we wish to be a product leader?

Do we wish to develop our own new products?

What advantages do we have in serving customer needs?

How should we respond to existing and potential competition?

How far can we go in serving customer needs?

What profits can we expect?

What basic form should our strategy take?

Marketing

Marketing strategies are designed to guide managers in getting products or services to customers and encouraging customers to buy. Marketing strategies are closely related to product strategies; they must be interrelated and mutually supportive. As a matter of fact, Peter Drucker regards the two basic business functions as innovation (for example, the creation of new goods or services) and marketing. A business can scarcely survive without at least one of these functions and preferably both.

These key questions serve as guides for establishing a marketing strategy:

Where are our customers and why do they buy?

How do our customers buy?

How is it best for us to sell?

Do we have something to offer that competitors do not?

Do we wish to take legal steps to discourage competition?

Do we need, and can we supply, supporting services?

What is the best pricing strategy and policy for our operation?

THREE GENERIC COMPETITIVE STRATEGIES BY PORTER

Michael Porter at Harvard identified three generic strategies a firm may adopt.[12] These strategies are generic because they may be suitable on a broad level to different kinds of organizations. Any enterprise, however, may use more than one strategy.

Overall Cost Leadership Strategy

This strategic approach aims at reductions in cost, based to a great extent on experience. Thus, the emphasis may be on keeping a close watch on costs in areas such as research and development, sales, service, and others. The objective is for a company to have a low cost structure compared with its competitors. This strategy often requires a large relative market share and cost-efficient facilities, as illustrated by the well-publicized Lincoln Electric company, which produces arc welding and supplies.

Differentiation Strategy

A company following a differentiation strategy attempts to offer something unique in the industry in respect to products or services. Porsche sports cars are indeed special, and so is the Caterpillar company that is known for its prompt service and availability of spare parts.

Focused Strategy

A company adopting a focused strategy concentrates on special groups of customers, a particular product line, a specific geographic region, or other aspects that become the focal point of the firm's efforts. Rather than serving the total industry with its products or services, an enterprise may emphasize a specific segment of the market. This may be accomplished by a low-cost strategy, differentiation, or both.

EFFECTIVE IMPLEMENTATION OF STRATEGIES

Strategic planning, to be effective, must go beyond the allocation of resources to achieve organizational objectives. It must be accompanied by strategic thinking that also includes designing an appropriate organization structure, an effective management information system, a budgeting system to facilitate the accomplishments of strategic objectives, and a reward system that supports the strategy.

Strategic Planning Failures and Some Recommendations

Let us look first at some of the reasons why strategic planning may fail and what can be done about it.

A recent study attributed strategic planning failures to the following factors:[13]

1. Managers are inadequately prepared for strategic planning.

2. The information for preparing the plans is insufficient for planning for action.

3. The goals of the organization are too vague to be of value.

4. The business units (a distinct form of organization discussed in Chapter 8) are not clearly identified.

5. The reviews of the strategic plans of the business units are not done effectively.

6. The link between strategic planning and control is insufficient.

Strategic planning is the job of line managers who, especially in large companies, may be assisted by staff planners. But in order to do an effective job, line managers must be coached in strategic planning.

The overall strategic plan needs to be supplemented by specific action plans. This, in general, requires the contributions of line managers from different functional departments, such as research and development, engineering, production, marketing, financing, and personnel, to plan for the people required to carry out the plan. But integrating the various functional groups is not easy. Thus, companies have set up a task force, with heavy presentation of middle managers, to cut across the functional barriers.

Goals and objectives, to be meaningful, have to be more than platitudes such as "achieving excellence." The degree of specificity depends on the level in the hierarchy of objectives, as pointed out in Chapter 4.

When organizations become too large, they are frequently broken down into strategic business units (SBUs). These units are expected to operate as if they were relatively independent businesses. But it is important that the boundaries of the different SBUs are correctly drawn. Otherwise, strategic planning may be difficult.

Let us consider a large organization with many SBUs, each with its strategic plan, each competing with the others for scarce resources, each making overly optimistic projections for its own strategic plan. Conflicts are bound to arise at the corporate level. It is indeed an art of the top executive to integrate these strategic plans into a meaningful whole that serves the interest of the total organization. More about SBUs when we discuss departmentation.

Plans are the basis for control. Without plans no control is possible. Too often strategic plans and budgets are in conflict. Too often budgets are based on last year's budgets rather than on the strategic plan. Too often budgets are prepared without a specific action plan to implement the strategy. Strategic plans can also be thwarted by a compensation system that rewards short-term results at the expense of the long-term health of the organization.

From this discussion it is clear that strategic planning needs to be integrated with the total managerial process, such as the organization structure, the appraisal, reward, and motivational system, and the controls used to measure performance against objectives. This is just another illustration that effective management requires a systems approach that recognizes the interdependence of the managerial activities.

Successful Implementation of Strategies

It is one thing to develop clear and meaningful strategies. It is another matter, and one of very great practical importance, to implement strategies effectively.[14] If strategic planning is to be successful, we must take certain steps to implement it. Following are eight recommendations that should be considered by managers who wish to put their strategies to work.

1. Communication of strategies to all key decision-making managers. It does little good to formulate meaningful strategies unless we communicate them to all those managers who are in a position to make decisions on programs and plans designed to implement them. Nothing has been communicated unless it is clear to the receiver. Strategies may be clear to the executive committee members and the chief executive who participate in developing them. Strategies should be in writing, and top executives and their subordinates must make sure that everyone involved in implementing strategies understands them.

2. Developing and communicating planning premises. We will stress later the importance of planning premises. Managers must develop premises critical to plans and decisions, explain them to all those in the decision-making chain, and give instructions to develop programs and make decisions in line with them. Too few organizations do this. But if premises do not include key assumptions about the environment in which plans will operate, decisions are likely to be based on personal assumptions and predilections. This will almost certainly lead to a collection of uncoordinated plans.

3. Action plans contributing to and reflecting major objectives and strategies.   Action plans are tactical or operational programs and decisions, major or minor, that take place in various parts of an organization. If they do not reflect desired objectives and strategies, the result will be vague hopes or useless intentions. If care is not taken in this area, strategic planning is not likely to have a bottom-line impact, that is, to have an important effect on company profits.

There are various ways of making sure that action plans contribute to major goals. If every manager understands strategies, all managers can certainly review the recommendations of staff advisers and line subordinates to see that they contribute something and are consistent. It might even be a good idea for major decisions to be reviewed by an appropriate small committee, such as one including a manager's superior, the superior's superior, and a staff specialist. This would lend an atmosphere of formality to the program decision, and important influences on implementation of strategies might become clear. Budgets likewise should be reviewed with objectives and strategies in mind.

4. Regular review of strategies.   Even carefully developed strategies may cease to be suitable if conditions change. Therefore, they should be reviewed from time to time, certainly not less than once a year for major strategies, and perhaps more often.

5. Development of contingency strategies and programs.   Where considerable change in competitive factors or other elements in the environment may occur, strategies for such contingencies should be formulated. No one, of course, can wait to make plans until a future is certain. Even where there is considerable uncertainty and events may occur that make a given set of objectives, strategies, or programs obsolete, one has no choice but to proceed on the most credible set of premises we can come up with at a given time. But even then, one need not be totally unprepared if certain possible contingencies do occur. Contingency plans can give us this degree of preparation.

6. Making organization structure fit planning needs.   The organization structure with its system of delegations should be designed to help managers accomplish goals and make the decisions necessary to put plans into effect. If possible, one person should be responsible for the accomplishment of each goal and for implementing strategies to achieve this goal. In other words, end-result areas and key tasks should be identified and assigned to a single position as far down the organization structure as is feasible. Since this assignment sometimes cannot be made, there may be no alternative but to utilize a form of matrix organization, a type of organization structure discussed in Chapter 8. But, where this is done, the responsibilities of the various positions in the matrix should be clearly defined.

The role of staff analyst in an organization structure should be so defined as to make it clear that the job of people in a staff position is to advise. Staff studies and recommendations then enter the decision system at the various points where decisions are actually made. Unless they do so, we end up with independent staff work of no value for planning.

7. Continuing emphasis on planning and implementing strategy.   Even where we may have a workable system of objectives and strategies and their implementation, it can easily fail unless responsible managers continue to stress the nature and importance of these elements. This process may seem tedious and unnecessarily repetitious, but it is the best way to make sure that members of an organization learn about them. Teaching does not necessarily mean attending seminars; rather, much of the teaching can take place in the day-to-day interaction between superiors and subordinates.

8. Creating a company climate that forces planning.   People tend to allow problems and crises that arise today to interfere with effective planning for tomorrow. The only way to ensure that planning of all kinds will be done is to develop strategies carefully and to take pains to implement them. In fact, if a company or any other kind of organization is to be successful over a period of time, it really has no other alternative.

PREMISING AND FORECASTING

One of the essential and often overlooked steps in effective and coordinate planning is premising, which is the establishment of, and the agreement by managers and planners to utilize, consistent assumptions critical to plans under consideration. **Planning premises** are defined as *the anticipated environment in which plans are expected to operate. They include assumptions or forecasts of the future and known conditions that will affect the operation of plans.* Examples are prevailing policies and existing company plans that control the basic nature of supporting plans.

A distinction should be drawn between forecasts that are planning premises and forecasts that are translated into future expectancies, usually in financial terms, from actual plans developed. For example, a forecast to determine future business conditions, sales volume, or political environment furnishes premises on which to develop plans. However, a forecast of the costs or revenues from a new capital investment translates a planning program into future expectations. In the first case, the forecast is a prerequisite of planning; in the second case, the forecast is a result of planning.

At the same time, plans themselves and forecasts of their future effects often become premises for other plans. The decision by an electric utility company to construct a nuclear generating plant, for example, creates conditions that give rise to premises for transmission line plans, and other plans necessarily dependent upon the generating plant being built.

ENVIRONMENTAL FORECASTING[15]

If the future could be forecast with accuracy, planning would be relatively simple. Managers would need only to take into account their human and material resources and their opportunities and threats, compute the optimum method of reaching their objective, and proceed with a relatively high degree of certainty toward it. In practice, however, forecasting is much more complicated than that.

Values and Areas of Forecasting

Forecasting has values aside from its use. First, the making of forecasts and their review by managers compel thinking ahead, looking to the future, and providing for it. Second, preparation of the forecast may disclose areas where necessary control is lacking. Third, forecasting, especially when there is participation throughout the organization, helps to unify and coordinate plans. By focusing attention on the future, it assists in bringing a singleness of purpose to planning.

The environmental areas that are frequently chosen for making forecasts usually include the (1) economic, (2) social, (3) political/legal, and (4) technological environment. You will learn more about these areas in Chapters 24 and 25, when we examine the domestic and international environments and their impacts on managing. Here we will restrict the discussion to a technique that is used for technological forecasting.

Forecasting with the Delphi Technique

One of the attempts to make technological forecasting more accurate and meaningful is the use of the Delphi technique.[16] While it smacks somewhat of hunch and judgment, or brainstorming, it is much more. This technique, developed by Olaf Helmer and his colleagues at the RAND Corporation, has a degree of scientific respectability and acceptance. A typical process of the Delphi technique is as follows:

1. A panel of experts on a particular problem area is selected—usually from both inside and outside the organization.

2. The experts are asked (anonymously, so that they will not be influenced by others) to make a forecast as to what they think will happen, and when, in various areas of new discoveries or developments.

3. The answers are compiled, and the composite results are fed back to the panel members.

4. With this information at hand (but still with individual anonymity), further estimates of the future are made.

5. This process may be repeated several times.

6. When a convergence of opinion begins to evolve, the results are then used as an acceptable forecast.

Note that the purpose of the successive opinions and feedback is not to force the experts to compromise but rather, by bringing additional informational inputs to bear, to make opinions more informed. It is thus hoped, and experience has verified this hope, that an informed consensus among experts will be arrived at.

THE SALES FORECAST: KEY PLAN AND PREMISE[17]

Even though its use has been noteworthy in business, the idea of basing planning on a forecast of the market has much in common with nonbusiness enterprises. Certainly a university must be concerned in its planning with its student "market," a government welfare department must gear its plans to meet expected case loads, and church plans must be influenced by the number of communicants expected in an area.

The Nature and Use of the Sales Forecast

The **sales forecast** is a prediction of expected sales, by product and price, for a number of months or years. It is, then, a kind of pro forma sales portion of the traditional income statement for the future.

The sales forecast is the key to internal planning. Business and capital outlays and policies of all kinds are made for the purpose of maximizing profits from expected sales. Although there are some enterprises that need to pay scant attention to sales (for example, the small-city water company or the government defense contractor with a long-term order that has little chance of being canceled or modified), it is a rare business that can overlook the market for long. Even the farmer, who, operating under support prices, may have a guaranteed market for a certain product for a coming year, can hardly ignore market influences as they affect succeeding years or alternative crops.

Smaller companies often make the mistake of believing that sales forecasts are too expensive and of overlooking the variety of sources of data available at little or no cost. The purchasing agent, members of the sales staff, the treasurer, and the production manager are among those who may possess bits and pieces of information, which, gathered together, could make an acceptable forecast. Moreover, the wide range of information available from government and industry sources is neither difficult nor expensive to obtain.

Methods of Sales Forecasting

Methods utilized in sales forecasting may generally be classified as (1) the jury of executive opinion method, (2) the sales force composite method, (3) the users' expectation method, (4) statistical methods, and (5) deductive methods.

1. Jury of executive opinion.   The jury of executive opinion method is perhaps the oldest and simplest method of making sales forecasts since it merely combines and averages the views, many of which may be little more than hunches, of top managers. In most cases, the final estimate is an opinion of the president, based upon a consideration of the opinions of other officers; in other cases, the poll of opinion leads to a rough kind of average estimate. In some cases, the process amounts to little more than group guessing; in other cases, it involves the careful judgment of experienced executives who have studied the underlying factors that influence their company's sales.

This method has the advantage of ease and simplicity, it allows for pooling of experience and judgment, and it need not require the preparation of elaborate economic studies and statistics. An advantage not often cited is that, by forcing top managers to make an estimate, it may put pressure on them to develop pertinent data. On the other hand, such a method has serious drawbacks; for example, forecasts may be based on opinion rather than on facts and analyses.

2. Sales force composite.   One of the commonly used methods of sales forecasting is to obtain from salespeople and sales managers their combined view as to expected sales. The usual technique is to ask salespeople to forecast sales for their districts and have these estimates reviewed by regional sales managers and then by the head-office sales manager. Sometimes salespeople are given guides in the form of company planning premises as to business conditions generally, and often the salespeople's estimates are reviewed by the product specialists, such as the company brand, sales, and advertising managers.

This method is based on the belief that those closest to the sales picture have the best knowledge of the market. Other advantages ascribed to this method are that it places forecasting, initially at least, in the hands of those who must make good on the forecast; it gives a broad sample that makes the total forecast more valid; and it allows an easy breakdown by product, customer, or territory.

On the other hand, the sales force composite method suffers from the fact that salespeople and often even sales executives are apt to be poor forecasters for any period except the immediate future, since they tend to give primary weight to present conditions. Where forecasts are desired for more than the short range, sales personnel normally are at a loss to make sound forecasts because of lack of knowledge of basic social, political, and economic trends. Moreover, under certain conditions—particularly where the forecasts are used for quota purposes—sales personnel incline to pessimism, while in other instances—especially when salespeople want more liberal allowances for expenses, promotion, or advertising—they are inclined to be rather optimistic.

At the same time, most companies have found that forecasts submitted by the sales organization are useful and valuable inputs into the company forecasting effort. It has been found that, when the sales force composite method is properly cross-checked by various other methods, such as review by head-office marketing and sales experts and constant check by salespeople of their estimates of past performance against actual results, it has furnished surprisingly good forecasts.

3. Users' expectation. Many companies, particularly those serving industrial customers in industries composed of a small number of companies or where a few large companies are dominant, find it useful to base their forecasts on expected purchases by these customers. Clearly, if a company can obtain an adequate and reliable information sample of what its customers will buy, even though the actual orders are not in hand, it will have a good basis upon which to develop a sales forecast.

The users' expectation method has clear advantages where other ways of forecasting are inadequate or where the company cannot make a systematic forecast on its own, such as in small companies with limited resources for forecasting, in cases of new products where the users are known, or in instances where a supplier is dependent on plans of major customers. This method is obviously difficult to use in cases where customers are numerous, not easily located, or uncooperative. It is also subject to the difficulty of assessing customer expectations accurately, since the best of these are usually estimates of needs, and not commitments.

4. Statistical methods. The most generally relied upon approach to sales forecasting is the application of various statistical methods. As mathematical techniques have improved and the computer has come into wider use, so have statistics. These statistical methods may be divided into (*a*) trend and cycle, (*b*) correlation analysis, and (*c*) use of mathematical formulas or models.

Trends and cycles. In approaching forecasting through an analysis of trends and cycles, the analyst summarizes a pertinent series of data that reflects dollar or unit sales, units per thousand population, or other basic indicators of sales volume. On the basis of these data the forecast is projected by extrapolation. This analysis is based on the assumption that "what is past is prologue" and that a trend will continue unless something happens to it. It is then up to the analyst to judge whether that "something" will happen. In fact, it is important to the user of a forecast to know whether it represents a mere projection of past trends or a real forecast of what the forecaster expects will happen.

Correlation analysis. One of the widely used statistical methods is correlation analysis, the measurement of the relationship between company sales and one or more other factors. What is usually desired is a close correlation between sales and some broad national index that can be used with a reasonable degree of accuracy, such as gross national product, national income, or consumers' disposable income. Such correlation, either directly or with a lag or lead of a given time period, can give a company a useful and highly reliable basis for sales forecasting.

Virtually every forecaster has found some accurate correlations in using this method. Many companies have found that their sales, aside from industry sales, bear a close relationship to some national index. The problem for the forecaster is, of course, to study the various relationships, with their leads and lags, to find one or more which serve as indicators of the company's sales.

Mathematical formula or model. The third statistical method, one which usually grows out of finding either a trend or correlation analysis relationships, is to develop a mathematical formula to depict the relationship of a number of variables to the company's sales. Often, sales for an individual company are subject to a number of variables. If the relationship of these can be ascertained with reasonable accuracy or if credible assumptions can be made to fill in statistical gaps, a mathematical model very useful to the forecaster can be constructed.

Limitations of statistical methods. Although statistical methods are good for sales forecasting from the standpoint of reliability, they are often subject to certain **drawbacks.** They require research and the use of statistically trained help, which may be costly. It is not always possible to find reliable trends, correlations, or mathematical relationships. Many defense subcontractors have found, for example, that their sales potential is closely related to such vague factors as defense strategy, the course of a conflict, individual program expenditure level, and advances in the art of the industry, none of which bears a reliable correlation with predictable national or industry data. There is also a danger that managers may rely too heavily on statistical relationships and the results implied and thereby miss significant changes which intelligent judgment would have appraised. In any statistical method, it must be realized that the past is used only as a basis for prediction and that the future does not necessarily reflect the past.

5. Deductive methods. No forecast should overlook the opportunity to apply judgment and draw intelligent deductions from facts and relationships. Generally, what is involved is to find out what the present situation is, where the sales are, and why, and then to analyze deductively, by resort to both objective factors and subjective judgment, the factors underlying sales. Although the indications so developed may be put into a mathematical model or merely left as an imprecisely correlated conglomeration of facts and value judgments, they are often a useful check on results arrived at through more scientific methods.

After all, the state of the art of forecasting is such that independent, and often apparently intuitive, appraisal of the sales picture by an intelligent and experienced brain is still an input that no forecaster should overlook. This method has sometimes been referred to as the "lost horse" technique, based upon the old gag about the best way to find a lost horse: Go to where the horse was last seen and ask yourself where you would go if you were a horse.

Combination of Methods

In practice, there is a tendency to combine sales forecasting methods. This is as it should be. The importance of the final forecast for all aspects of company planning makes desirable a forecast system in which every possible input can be utilized. What warms forecasters' hearts and gives them a feeling of reliability is to find that several different forecast indicators, based upon independent approaches and data, all point to the same result. And, even if they do not, the disparity may serve as a warning that a single approach may have overlooked an essential factor.

Sales Forecasting in Practice

To understand sales forecasting techniques, one might examine some typical examples of what companies do.

Starting point: Assumptions about the future.   One large company approaches forecasting by having a staff prepare a forecast of general business conditions, referred to as an "assumption about the future." From this premise of the external business environment is projected a forecast of product sales. The staff takes into account the various factors, both external and internal, that might bear upon sales—such as prices, production capacities, markets, technological changes, competition, and sales promotion plans—and combines them to bring about the forecast.

The basic assumptions for the future are arrived at by the staff and upper managers after consideration of forecasts of gross economic conditions. Then, before the forecast is finished, a series of meetings is held with sales and other company personnel to make sure that all factors have been properly considered. Conferences are also held with staff specialists in production, advertising, research, costs, and pricing. After the forecast weathers these discussions, it goes to the finished products committee of the company, which includes several vice-presidents. When this committee has approved or modified the sales forecast, it then becomes a guide for all managers in planning their budgets and operations.

Starting point: Salespeople.   In another typical case, the initial forecast is made by the salespeople in the field for each of their territories and then modified by the product managers and the sales vice-president to correct for known optimism or pessimism of certain salespeople. A second forecast—based on a combination of historical series and judgment of future conditions as they might affect the company's sales—is prepared by the company's economists after careful study of economic and market statistics. Supplementing these two forecasts, sampling techniques are used to determine actual markets for their products, as disclosed by plans and practices of industrial and other customers. With these three forecasts, prepared independently, top management holds a conference at which the various predictions are appraised and modified. The resulting forecast becomes the basis for company planning and operations.

FIGURE 5-5

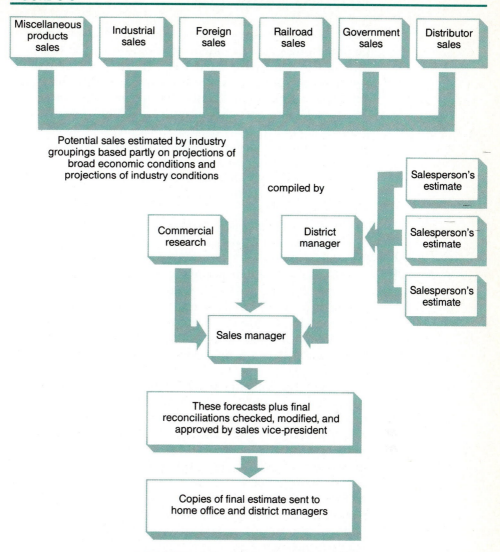

A PROCEDURE FOR SALES FORECASTING.

Starting point: Three sets of sales forecasts.   Another variant found in practice is for the company, as in the previous example, to have three sets of sales forecasts prepared. One set is prepared by industry specialists in home-office sales departments, another set by the commercial research department, and still another by the salespeople in the field. These sets are submitted to the sales manager, who presents all three, plus a forecast that reconciles differences, to the sales vice-president, who, in turn, checks or modifies the reconciled forecast and submits an approved forecast as the planning basis for company operations. An example of such a procedure for sales forecasting is shown in Figure 5-5.

EFFECTIVE PREMISING

Since so many failures occur in planning and planning coordination through poor premising, special attention should be given to this step in planning. It is difficult to identify the factors in a future environment that will affect a manager's plans. But it is also difficult, once these have been identified, to get consistent and meaningful planning premises actually used in practice.

1. Selection of the premises which bear materially on the programs. There are many premises that are of strategic importance to one enterprise but not to another. Thus, top managers of every enterprise, and to a certain extent every manager within it, should select their own premises. This basic question should be asked and answered: What factors in the environment, whether external or internal, will influence most the course of plans for which I am responsible?

2. Development of alternative premises for contingency planning. Since the future cannot be predicted with great certainty, develop plans given different assumptions.

3. Assurance that premises are consistent. One way of making sure is to have the planning staff at headquarters and divisional levels recommend crucial planning premises applicable to an enterprise or a division to the appropriate top executive. Having the top executive approve these premises, usually after consultation with his or her staff, will ensure that the assumptions selected and formulated will be the ones on which the enterprise or division is willing to stake its future.

4. Communication of the premises. One of the first requirements of effective premise communication is to analyze all managers' "need to know," interpret this broadly rather than narrowly, and make sure that premises important for their planning are made available to them. Some companies have found it wise to develop and disseminate to those who need it a manual of planning premises, incorporating assumptions with wide application to planning. These will, of course, be kept current as premises change. They should also be supplemented by the practice of having superiors develop and distribute supplementary planning premises of special concern for managers reporting to them whenever a budget proposal or program recommendation is requested and whenever a major program assignment is made.

In summary, strategies and policies give direction to the enterprise and provide a framework for developing tactics and other action plans. Meaningful premises facilitate consistencies and coordination of plans.

FOR DISCUSSION

1. How can you distinguish between strategies and policies?

2. Are strategies and policies as important in a nonbusiness enterprise (such as a labor union, the State Department, a hospital, or a city fire department) as in a business? Why and how?

3. Why are contingency strategies important?

4. Choose an organization you know and identify its strengths and weaknesses. What are its special opportunities and threats in the external environment?

5. How would you make an organizational appraisal of your college or university? What is the kind of "business" the school is in?

6. How can strategies be implemented effectively?

7. A sales forecast is often regarded both as a plan and as a premise. Comment.

8. Identify major premises which, in your judgment, the Ford Motor Company would need in order to forecast its sales of automobiles for the next 2 years.

9. Can objectives, policies, and procedures be premises in planning?

10. Exactly how would you apply the Delphi technique to premising the major social problems a company will face in the next 10 years?

11. How would you make premising effective?

EXERCISES/ACTION STEPS

1. Take the concepts of strategic planning and relate them to your life. What are your personal strengths and weaknesses? On the basis of this analysis, what would be a suitable (for you) "mission" in this world?

2. Take a major decision problem facing you and outline the more critical planning premises surrounding it. How many of these are matters of knowledge, and how many are matters of forecast? How many are qualitative, and how many are quantitative? How many are within your control?

CASES

CASE 5-1
SEMICONDUCTORS, INC.

Semiconductors, Inc. (SI), is one of the many electronics firms in the West. The firm has been reasonably successful in the past. It now recognizes the threat of Japanese competition. John Henderson, the president, realizes that one of the keys to success in this industry is to be a high-technology innovator. Consequently, he asked a consultant, Martin Rich, to analyze the organization's suitability for becoming a successful high-technology firm.

The consultant's presentation of findings follows: The firm's objectives are mostly for 1 year and pertain primarily to operations. Managers are not rewarded for activities that may be beneficial in the long run. Instead, bonuses are based on the achievement of short-term objectives. Managers, generally speaking, are good "fire fighters," but little effort is expended to prevent problems from occurring. There is little team effort. Each manager focuses on his or her own task. Managers are mostly concerned about the internal operation and care little about the external environment.

The president listened carefully to the report by the consultant. In fact, the findings confirmed his impressions of the organization. But the important point was, What should be done now to overcome these problems?

1. What factors would you consider in assessing the external environment?

2. How would you develop a strategic plan and objectives? Write a mission statement. Give examples of overall company objectives.

3. What would you do to encourage managers to work together toward long-range objectives?

CASE 5-2
McDONALD'S: SERVING FAST FOOD AROUND THE WORLD[18]

Ray Kroc opened the first McDonald's restaurant in 1955. He offered a limited menu of high-quality, moderately priced food served fast in spotless surroundings. McDonald's Q.S.C. & V. (quality, service, cleanliness, and value) was a hit. The chain expanded into every state in the nation. By 1983 it had over 6000 restaurants in the United States.

In 1967 McDonald's opened its first restaurant outside the United States, in Canada. By 1985 international sales represented about one-fifth of McDonald's total revenues. Yet, fast food has barely touched many cultures. While 90 percent of the Japanese in Tokyo have eaten a McDonald's hamburger, few outside the cities know what a hamburger is. In Europe, McDonald's maintains a very small percentage of restaurant sales but commands a large market share of the fast food market.

The taste for fast food, American style, is growing faster abroad than at home. McDonald's international sales have been increasing a large percentage every year. Every day more than 18 million people in over 40 countries eat at McDonald's.

Its traditional menu has been surprisingly successful. People with diverse dining habits have adopted burgers and fries wholeheartedly. Before McDonald's introduced the Japanese to French fries, potatoes were used only to make starch. The Germans thought hamburgers were people from the city of Hamburg.

The fast, family-oriented service, cleanliness, and value accounted for much of McDonald's suc-

cess. McDonald's was one of the first restaurants in Europe to welcome families with children. Not only are children welcomed, in many restaurants they are entertained with crayons and paper, a playland, or maybe Ronald McDonald, who can speak twenty languages.

McDonald's golden arches promise the same basic menu and Q.S.C. & V. in every restaurant. Its products, handling and cooking procedures, and kitchen layout are standardized and strictly controlled.

McDonald's revoked the first French franchises because they failed to meet its standards for fast service and cleanliness, even though they were highly profitable. This may have delayed its expansion in France.

The restaurants are run by local management and crew. Owners and managers must attend the Hamburger University near Chicago to learn how to operate a McDonald's restaurant and maintain Q.S.C. & V. The main campus library and modern electronic classrooms (which include simultaneous translation systems) are the envy of many universities.

McDonald's ensures consistent products by controlling every stage of the distribution. Regional distribution centers purchase products and distribute them to individual restaurants. They will buy from local suppliers, if they can meet detailed specifications. McDonald's has had to make some concessions to available products. For example, it is difficult to introduce the Idaho potato in Europe.

McDonald's uses essentially the same competitive strategy in every country: Be first in a market and establish your brand as rapidly as possible by advertising very heavily. New restaurants are opened with a bang. So many people attended the opening of one Tokyo restaurant that the police closed the street to vehicles. The strategy has helped McDonald's develop a strong market share in the fast food market, even though its U.S. competitors and new local competitors quickly enter the market.

The advertising campaigns are based on local themes and reflect the different environments. In Japan, where burgers are a snack, McDonald's competes against confectioneries and new "fast sushi" restaurants. Many of the charitable causes McDonald's supports abroad have been recommended by the local restaurants.

McDonald's has been willing to relinquish the most control to its Far Eastern operations, where many restaurants are joint ventures with local entrepreneurs who own 50 percent or more of the restaurant.

European and South American restaurants are generally company-operated or franchised (although there are many affiliates—joint ventures—in France). Like U.S. franchises, restaurants abroad are allowed to experiment with the menu. In Japan, hamburgers are smaller because they are considered a snack. The Quarter Pounder didn't make much sense to people on a metric system, so it is called a Double Burger. Some of the German restaurants serve beer, some French restaurants serve wine. Some Far Eastern McDonald's offer oriental noodles. But these new items must not disrupt existing operations.

1. What opportunities and threats did McDonald's face? How did it overcome them? What alternatives could it have chosen?

2. Before McDonald's entered the European market, few people believed that fast food could be successful in Europe. Why do you think McDonald's succeeded? What strategies did it follow? How did these differ from its strategies in Asia?

3. What is McDonald's basic philosophy? How does it enforce this philosophy and adapt to different environments?

REFERENCES

1. P. Petre, "IBM's Misadventures in the Retail Jungle," *Fortune* (July 23, 1984), p. 80.

2. Alfred D. Chandler, Jr. *Strategy and Structure* (Cambridge, Mass.: The M.I.T. Press, 1962). In this excellent historical study, the author analyzes the history of Du Pont, General Motors, Standard Oil Company (New Jersey), and Sears, Roebuck and shows how in each case organization structure followed and reflected strategy.

3. Myron Magnet, "How Top Managers Make a Company's Toughest Decision," *Fortune* (Mar. 18, 1985), pp. 52–57. See also Roger Evered, "The Strategic Decision Process," in Don Hellriegel and John W. Slocum, Jr. (eds.) *Management in the World Today* (Reading, Mass.: Addison-Wesley Publishing Company, 1975).

4. Peter Lorange, Michael F. Scott Morton, and Sumantra Ghoshal, *Strategic Control* (St. Paul: West Publishing Company, 1986).

5. Jaclyn Fierman, "How to Make Money in Mature Markets," *Fortune* (Nov. 25, 1985), pp. 46–53; B. Charles Ames, "Corporate Strategies for a Shrinking Market," *The Wall Street Journal* (Jan. 13, 1986); Kathryn R. Harrigan and Michael E. Porter, "End-Game Strategies for Declining Industries," *Harvard Business Review* (July–August 1983), pp. 111–120.

6. This discussion and the figure have been adapted from Heinz Weihrich, "The TOWS Matrix—A Tool for Situational Analysis," *Long Range Planning,* vol. 15, no. 2 (1982), pp. 54–66.

7. Although we emphasize strategies in this discussion, similar analyses can be made for developing the more detailed tactics and action plans.

8. Bruce D. Henderson, "The Product Portfolio," in *Perspectives* (Boston Consulting Group, 1970); Bruce D. Henderson, "The Experience Curve Revisited" (Boston Consulting Group, undated); Barry Hedly, "Strategy and the 'Business Portfolio,'" *Long Range Planning* (February 1977), pp. 9–15; Bruce D. Henderson, "The Application and Misapplication of the Experience Curve," *Journal of Business Strategy* (Winter 1984).

9. SBUs will be discussed in Chapter 8 of this book.

10. Charles W. Hofer and Dan E. Schendel, *Strategy Formulation: Analytical Concepts* (St. Paul: West Publishing Company, 1978); Walter Kiechel III, "Oh Where, Oh Where Has My Little Dog Gone? or My Cash Cow? or My Star?" *Fortune* (November 1981), pp. 148–154; Richard G. Hamermesh and Roderick E. White, "Manage Beyond Portfolio Analysis," *Harvard Business Review* (January–February 1984), pp. 103–109.

11. Although we use the term "strategies" in this section, some may be policies because there is a great deal of overlap between them, as mentioned earlier in this chapter.

12. Michael E. Porter, *Competitive Strategy* (New York: The Free Press, 1980). See also by the same author *Competitive Advantage* (New York: The Free Press, 1985).

13. Daniel H. Gray, "Uses and Misuses of Strategic Planning," *Harvard Business Review* (January–February 1986), pp. 89–97.

14. Much of this is drawn from Harold Koontz, "Making Strategic Planning Work," *Business Horizons* (April 1976), pp. 37–47.

15. For an excellent discussion of the various approaches to forecasting, see Spyros Makridakis and Steven C. Wheelwright, "Forecasting: Issues and Challenges for Marketing Management," *Journal of Marketing* (October 1977), in Harold Koontz, Cyril O'Donnell, and Heinz Weihrich, *Management: A Book of Readings,* 5th ed. (New York: McGraw-Hill Book Company, 1980), pp. 136–151.

16. See also Frederick J. Parente, Janet K. Anderson, Patrick Myers, and Thomas O'Brien, "An Examination of Factors Contributing to Delphi Accuracy," *Journal of Forecasting,* vol. 3, no. 2 (1984), pp. 173–182.

17. For a thorough study of sales forecasting, see D. L. Hurwood, E. S. Grossman, and E. Bailey, *Sales Forecasting* (New York: The Conference Board, 1978).

18. The case has been based on a variety of sources, including interviews and a visit to Hamburger University, as well as the following:
    Blyskall, Jeff. "The Burger Slows Down," *Forbes* (Oct. 11, 1982), p. 45.
    Katayama, Frederick, H. "Japan's Big Mac," *Fortune* (Sept. 15, 1986), pp. 114–120.
    Kindel, Stephen. "Where's the Growth?" *Forbes* (Apr. 23, 1984), p. 80.
    Kule, Nancy. "Fast Food Expands in Europe," *Restaurant Hospitality* (December 1983).
    Labich, Kenneth. "America's International Winners," *Fortune* (Apr. 14, 1986), pp. 34–46.
    Lang, Joan. "McDonald's Japan," *Restaurant Business* (Nov. 1, 1983), pp. 168–169.
    McDonald's Annual Reports, 1983 and 1984. *Standard & Poor's Industry Survey* (1983).
    "Those Doubts about McDonald's," *Financial World* (June 15, 1983), pp. 38–40.

FOR FURTHER INFORMATION

Ansoff, H. Igor. *Implanting Strategic Management* (Englewood Cliffs, N.J.: Prentice-Hall International, 1984).

Armstrong, J. Scott. *Long-Range Forecasting: From Crystal Ball to Computer,* 2d ed. (New York: Wiley-Interscience, 1985).

Fredrickson, James W. "Strategic Process Research: Questions and Recommendations," *Academy of Management Review* (October 1983), pp. 565–575.

Glueck, William F., and Lawrence R. Jauch. *Business Policy and Strategic Management,* 4th ed. (New York: McGraw-Hill Book Company, 1984).

Leontiades, Milton. *Policy, Strategy, and Implementation—Readings and Cases* (New York: Random House Business Division, 1983).

Lorange, P. *Corporate Planning* (Englewood Cliffs, N.J.: Prentice-Hall, 1980).

Quinn, James B. *Strategies for Change—Logical Incrementalism* (Homewood, Ill.: Richard D. Irwin, 1980).

Robinson, Richard B., Jr., and John. A. Pearce II. "Research Trusts in Small Firm Strategic Planning," *Academy of Management Review* (January 1984), pp. 128–137.

6

Decision Making

CHAPTER OBJECTIVES

After reading this chapter, you should be able to:

1. Analyze decision making as a rational process, with special attention given to evaluating alternatives in the light of the goals sought.

2. Develop alternative courses of action with due consideration of the limiting factor.

3. Select alternatives on the basis of experience and experimentation, as well as research and analysis.

4. Differentiate between programmed and unprogrammed decisions.

5. Understand the differences between decisions under certainty, uncertainty, and risk condition.

6. Select from among alternatives, using risk analysis, decision trees, and preference theory.

7. Recognize the utility of decision support systems.

8. Evaluate the importance of decision making and understand various other factors in decision making.

9. Apply the systems approach to decision making.

*D*ecision making is defined as the selection from among alternatives of a course of action; it is at the core of planning. A plan cannot be said to exist unless a decision—a commitment of resources, direction, or reputation—has been made. Until that point, we have only planning studies and analyses. Managers sometimes see decision making as their central job because they must constantly choose what is to be done, who is to do it, and when, where, and occasionally even how it will be done. Decision making is, however, only a step in planning, even when done quickly and with little thought or when it influences action for only a few minutes. It is also part of everyone's daily living. A course of action can seldom be judged alone because virtually every decision must be geared to other plans. The stereotype of the finger-snapping, button-pushing managerial mogul fades as the requirements of systematic research and analysis preceding a decision come into focus.

THE IMPORTANCE AND LIMITATIONS OF RATIONAL DECISION MAKING

In outlining and discussing the steps in planning in Chapter 3, we were really considering decision making as a major part of planning. As a matter of fact, given an awareness of an opportunity and a goal, the core of planning is really the decision process. Thus, in this context, the process leading to making a decision might be thought of as (1) premising, (2) identifying alternatives, (3) the evaluation of alternatives in terms of the goal sought, and (4) the choosing of an alternative, that is, making a decision.

As you will note, the discussion of decision making in this chapter, although emphasizing the logic and techniques of choosing a course of action, really places decision making as one of the steps in planning.[1]

Rationality in Decision Making

It is frequently said that effective decision making must be rational. But what is rationality? When is a person thinking or deciding rationally?

People acting or deciding rationally are attempting to reach some goal that cannot be attained without action. They must have a clear understanding of alternative courses by which a goal can be reached under existing circumstances and limitations. They also must have the information and the ability to analyze and evaluate alternatives in the light of the goal sought. And, finally, they must have a desire to come to the best solution by selecting the alternative that most effectively satisfies goal achievement.

We seldom achieve complete rationality, particularly in managing.[2] In the first place, since no one can make decisions affecting the past, decisions must operate for the future, and the future almost invariably involves uncertainties. In the second place, it is difficult to recognize all the alternatives that might be followed to reach a goal; this is particularly true when decision making involves opportunities to do something that has not been done before. Moreover, in most

PERSPECTIVE:
COMPAQ VS. IBM

In 1986 Compaq announced a new personal computer model, the Deskpro 386. The new model was based on Intel's 80386 chip, which was considerably faster than the one in the IBM AT model. The decision to market this new computer in 1986 was rather risky and based on incomplete information. It also was a departure from Compaq's previous strategy, which had proved to be very successful. In the past, Compaq followed IBM standards by making a computer that used IBM software.

But with the Deskpro 386, Compaq assumed the lead over the corporate giant IBM, which is expected to market a computer based on the 80386 technology in 1987.

What, then, is Compaq's dilemma? On the one hand, the company may have a head start over its major competitor and gain a considerable market share. On the other hand, the new IBM could include some proprietary features that eventually could make the Deskpro 386 incompatible with IBM's computer. Moreover, the success of a personal computer depends to a large extent on its software (programs). Thus, software writers may not be willing to invest their efforts until it is clear that the Compaq is indeed truly compatible with the IBM computer.[3]

instances, not all alternatives can be analyzed, even with the newest available analytical techniques and computers.

Limited or "Bounded" Rationality

A manager must settle for limited rationality, or "bounded" rationality. In other words, limitations of information, time, and certainty limit rationality even though a manager tries earnestly to be completely rational. Since we cannot be completely rational in practice, managers sometimes allow their dislike of risk—the desire to "play it safe"—to interfere with the desire to reach the best solution under the circumstances. Herbert Simon has called this **satisficing,** that is, picking a course of action that is satisfactory or good enough under the circumstances. Although many managerial decisions are made with a desire to "get by" as safely as possible, most managers do attempt to make the best decisions they can within the limits of rationality and in the light of the size and nature of risks involved.

We will now consider the steps of the decision process in detail.

DEVELOPMENT OF ALTERNATIVES

Assuming that we know what our goals are and agree on clear planning premises, the first step of decision making is to develop alternatives. There are nearly always alternatives to any course of action; indeed, if there seems to be only one way of doing a thing, that way is probably wrong. If we can think of only one course of action, clearly we have not thought hard enough.

The ability to develop alternatives is often as important as selecting correctly from among them. On the other hand, ingenuity, research, and common sense will often unearth so many choices that all of them cannot be adequately evaluated. The manager needs help in this situation, and this help, as well as assistance in choosing the best alternative, is found in the concept of the limiting or strategic factor.

The Principle of the Limiting Factor

A **limiting factor** is something that stands in the way of accomplishing a desired objective. If we recognize the limiting factors in a given situation, we can narrow our search for alternatives to those that will overcome the limiting factors. In the example above, the objective was to turn a loss into a profit. The means for doing so was to acquire some equipment. The limiting factor was the lack of cash and credit. The managers' alternatives were confined to those that would overcome the limiting factor. Their search was accurate, direct, and successful. The **principle of the limiting factor** is as follows: *Only when we recognize and solve for those factors that stand critically in our way to our goal can we select the best alternative course of action.*

Discovering the Limiting Factor

It may not be easy to discover the limiting factor or factors, since they are often obscure. For example, if a company were considering a profit-sharing program, the limiting factors might be tax deductibility and the attitude of employees

---

PERSPECTIVE:
GENERATING ALTERNATIVES IN AN ADVERSE SITUATION

A certain firm once desperately needed some new equipment. Without this equipment, the company could not increase its production or expand its market, and thus it would continue to lose money. The company had lost so much money already, however, that it could not afford to buy new machinery, nor could it borrow the money to do so. It looked as if the only thing to do was to do nothing, but this meant certain bankruptcy.

The officers of the company set out to find alternatives. They located a manufacturer who had the equipment they needed and had not been able to sell it to anyone. He in turn owed money borrowed from a bank to purchase the equipment. The bank agreed to let the manufacturer sell the machines to the firm without taking a down payment on them and arranged for the manufacturer and the firm both to sign a note for the money owed to the bank. The officers also found a competitor who had ordered some new equipment and was willing to sell his old machinery, also without requiring a down payment. Thus, in an apparently hopeless situation, the firm found two reasonable alternatives.

toward the plan. In deciding whether to expand operations, a company m.ght find its limiting factor to be availability of capital, the problems of managing the firm if it got too large, or the attitude of the government antimonopoly agencies.

The search for, and recognition of, limiting factors in planning never ends. For one program at one time, a certain factor may be critical, but, at a later time and for a similar decision, the limiting factor may be something that was relatively unimportant in the earlier planning. Thus, a company might decide to acquire new equipment when the limiting factor was capital availability, only to have the limiting factor become delivery or, later, the training of people to operate the equipment.

EVALUATION OF ALTERNATIVES

Once appropriate alternatives have been found, the next step in planning is to evaluate them and select the one that will best contribute to the goal. This is the point of ultimate decision making, although decisions must also be made in the other steps of planning—in selecting goals, in choosing critical premises, and even in selecting alternatives.

Quantitative and Qualitative Factors

As we compare alternative plans for achieving an objective, we are likely to think exclusively of **quantitative factors.** These are factors that can be measured in numerical terms, such as time or the various types of fixed and operating costs. No one would question the importance of this analysis, but the success of the venture would be endangered if intangible, or qualitative, factors were ignored. **Qualitative or intangible factors** are those that are difficult to measure numerically, such as the quality of labor relations, the risk of technological change, or the international political climate. There are all too many instances where the best of quantitative plans were destroyed by an unforeseen war, a fine marketing plan was made inoperable by a long transportation strike, or a rational borrowing plan was hampered by an economic recession. These illustrations point up the importance of giving attention to both quantitative and qualitative factors when comparing alternatives.

To evaluate and compare the intangible factors in a planning problem and make decisions, we must first recognize these factors and then determine whether a reasonable quantitative measurement can be given them. If not, we should find out as much as possible about them, perhaps rate them in terms of their importance, compare their probable influence on the outcome with that of the quantitative factors, and then come to a decision. This decision may give predominant weight to a single intangible.

Such a procedure allows the manager to decide upon the weight of the total evidence. It does involve fallible personal judgments; however, few managerial decisions can be so accurately quantified that judgment is unnecessary. Decision making is seldom simple. It is not without justification that the successful executive has been cynically described as a person who guesses right.

Marginal Analysis

In evaluating alternatives, we may utilize the techniques of **marginal analysis** to compare additional revenues arising from additional costs. Where the objective is to maximize profits, this goal will be reached, as elementary economics teaches us, when the additional revenues and additional costs are equal. In other words, if additional revenues are greater than additional costs with a larger quantity, more profits can be made by producing more. However, at the point where additional volume costs more than additional revenues, the profit will be larger at a lesser volume.

Marginal analysis can be used in comparing factors other than costs and revenues. For example, to find the best output of a machine, we could vary inputs against outputs until the additional input equals the additional output. This would then be the point of maximum efficiency of the machine. Or, the number of subordinates reporting to a manager might conceivably be increased to the point where additional savings in costs, better communication and morale, and other factors equal additional losses in effectiveness of control, leadership, and similar factors.

Cost Effectiveness Analysis

An improvement on, or variation of, traditional marginal analysis is cost effectiveness, or cost benefit, analysis. **Cost effectiveness analysis** seeks the best ratio of benefits and costs; this means, for example, finding the least costly way of reaching an objective, or, getting the greatest value for given expenditures. Similarly, **cost benefit analysis** also pertains to the ratio of the benefits to costs; it is often not possible, however, to measure benefits of a program accurately. Thus, it is the technique of weighing alternatives that cannot be conveniently reduced to dollars or some other specific measure, as in the case of normal marginal analysis, which is similar to a traditional form of cost benefit analysis.

In its simplest terms, cost effectiveness analysis is a technique for choosing the best plan when the objectives are less specific than sales, costs, or profits. For example, defense objectives may be to deter or repel enemy attack, social objectives may be to reduce air pollution or retrain the unemployed, and business objectives may be to participate in social objectives through a program of training unemployables.

Nonquantifiable objectives can sometimes be given some fairly specific measures of effectiveness. In a program with the general objective of improving employee morale, for example, we can measure effectiveness by such verifiable factors as employee turnover, absenteeism, or volume of grievances and can also supplement these measurements by such subjective inputs as the judgment of qualified experts.

The major features of cost effectiveness analysis are that it makes us focus on the results of a program, helps us weigh the potential benefits of each alternative against its potential cost, and makes us then compare the alternatives in terms of the overall advantages.

Although the decision on cost effectiveness involves the same steps as any planning decision, its major distinguishing features are the following:

1. Objectives are normally oriented to output or end result and usually are not precise.

2. Alternatives ordinarily represent total systems, programs, or strategies for meeting objectives.

3. The measures of effectiveness must be relevant to objectives and set in terms as precise as possible, although some may not be subject to quantification.

4. Cost estimates may include nonmonetary as well as monetary costs.

5. Decision standards, while definite but not usually as specific as cost or profit, may include achieving a given objective at least cost, achieving it with resources available, or providing for a trade-off of cost for effectiveness, particularly in the light of the claims of other programs.

Cost effectiveness analysis can be made most systematic through the use of models and other operations research techniques, which we will describe in Chapter 22. We can develop models to show cost estimated for each alternative, and effectiveness models to show the relationship between each alternative and its effectiveness. Then, models combining these results can be made to show the relationships of costs and effectiveness for each alternative.

SELECTING AN ALTERNATIVE: THREE APPROACHES

When selecting from among alternatives, managers can use three basic approaches: (1) experience, (2) experimentation, and (3) research and analysis. (See Figure 6-1.)

Experience

Reliance on past experience probably plays a larger part than it deserves in decision making. Experienced managers usually believe, often without realizing it, that the things they have successfully accomplished and the mistakes they have made furnish almost infallible guides to the future. This attitude is likely to be more pronounced the more experience a manager has had and the higher in an organization he or she has risen.

To some extent, experience is the best teacher. The very fact that managers have reached their position appears to justify their past decisions. Moreover, the process of thinking problems through, making decisions, and seeing programs succeed or fail does make for a degree of good judgment (at times bordering on intuition). Many people, however, do not profit by their errors, and there are managers who seem never to gain the seasoned judgment required by modern enterprise.

Relying on our past experience as a guide for future action can be dangerous, however. In the first place, most of us do not recognize the underlying reasons for our mistakes or failures. In the second place, the lessons of experi-

FIGURE 6-1

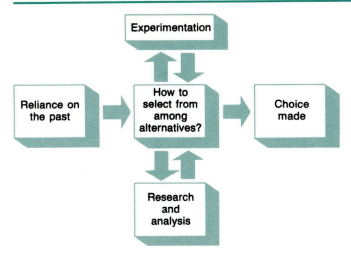

**BASES FOR SELECTING FROM AMONG
ALTERNATIVE COURSES OF ACTION.**

ence may be entirely inapplicable to new problems. Good decisions must be evaluated against future events, while experience belongs to the past.

On the other hand, if we carefully analyze experience rather than blindly follow it, and if we distill from experience the fundamental reasons for success or failure, then experience can be useful as a basis for decision analysis. A successful program, a well-managed company, a profitable product promotion, or any other decision that turns out well may furnish useful data for such distillation. Just as scientists do not hesitate to build upon the research of others and would be foolish indeed merely to duplicate it, managers can learn much from others.

Experimentation

An obvious way to decide among alternatives is to try one of them and see what happens. Experimentation is often used in scientific inquiry. People often argue that it should be employed more often in managing and that the only way a manager can make sure some plans are right—especially in view of the intangible factors—is to try the various alternatives and see which is best.

The experimental technique is likely to be the most expensive of all techniques, especially where a program requires heavy expenditures in capital and personnel and where the firm cannot afford to vigorously attempt several alternatives. Besides, after an experiment has been tried, we may still doubt what it proved, since the future may not duplicate the present. This technique, therefore, should be used only after considering other alternatives.

On the other hand, there are many decisions that cannot be made until the best course of action can be ascertained by experiment. Even reflections on experience or the most careful research may not assure managers of correct decisions. This is nowhere better illustrated than in the planning of a new airplane. The manufacturer may draw from personal experience and that of other plane manufacturers and of new plane users. Engineers and economists may make extensive studies of stresses, vibrations, fuel consumption, speed, space allocation, and other factors. But all these studies do not give every answer to questions about the flight characteristics and economics of a successful plane; therefore, some experimentation is almost always involved in the process of selecting the right course to follow. Ordinarily, a first production, or prototype, airplane is constructed and tested, and, on the basis of these tests, production airplanes are made on a somewhat revised design.

Experimentation is used in other ways. A firm may test a new product in a certain market before expanding its sale nationwide. Organizational techniques are often tried in a branch office or plant before being applied over an entire company. A candidate for a management job may be tested in the job during the incumbent's vacation.

Research and Analysis

One of the most effective techniques for selecting from alternatives when major decisions are involved is research and analysis. This approach means solving a problem by first comprehending it. It thus involves a search for relationships among the more critical of the variables, constraints, and premises that bear upon the goal sought. It is the pencil-and-paper (or, better, the computer-and-printout) approach to decision making.

To solve a planning problem we must break it into its component parts and study the various quantitative and qualitative factors. Study and analysis are likely to be far cheaper than experimentation. Hours of time and reams of paper used for analyses usually cost much less than trying the various alternatives. In building airplanes, if careful research has not preceded the building and testing of the prototype airplane and its parts, we can hardly imagine the resulting costs.

FIGURE 6-2

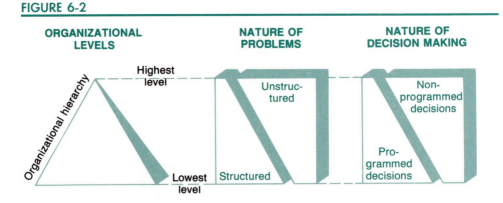

NATURE OF PROBLEMS AND DECISION MAKING IN THE ORGANIZATION.

A major step in the research and analysis approach is to develop a model simulating the problem. Thus, we often make models of a building in the form of extensive blueprints or a three-dimensional rendition. We test models of airplane wings and missiles in a wind tunnel. But the most useful simulation is likely to be a representation of the variables in a problem situation by mathematical terms and relationships. If we can thereby conceptualize a problem we have taken a major step toward its solution. The physical sciences have long relied on mathematical models to do this, and it is encouraging to see this method being applied to managerial decision making.

One of the most comprehensive research-and-analysis approaches to decision making is operations research. Since this is an important tool for production and operations management, we will discuss it more fully in Chapter 22.

PROGRAMMED AND NONPROGRAMMED DECISIONS

We can make a distinction between programmed and nonprogrammed decisions.[4] A **programmed decision,** as shown in Figure 6-2, is applied to structured or routine problems. Lathe operators have specifications and rules that tell them when the part they made can be accepted, when it has to be discarded, and when it can be reworked. Another example of a programmed decision is the reordering of standard items in the inventory. In fact, there is a formula for doing this, as you will see in Chapter 22. This kind of decision is for routine and repetitive work, relying primarily on previously established criteria. You might say that it is decision making by precedent.

Nonprogrammed decisions are used for unstructured, novel, and ill-defined situations of a nonrecurring nature. Examples are the introduction of the Macintosh computer by Apple Computer, Inc., the development of the four-wheel-drive passenger car by Audi, and the marketing of a small video camera by Kodak. In fact, strategic decisions, in general, are nonprogrammed decisions, requiring subjective judgments.

Most decisions are neither completely programmed nor completely nonprogrammed but are a combination of both. As you can see from Figure 6-2, nonprogrammed decisions are mostly made by upper-level managers because upper-level managers have to deal with unstructured problems.[5] Problems on lower levels of the organization are often routine and well structured, requiring less decision discretion by managers and nonmanagers.

DECISION MAKING UNDER CERTAINTY, UNCERTAINTY, AND RISK

Virtually all decisions are made in an environment of at least some uncertainty.[6] However, the degree will vary from relative certainty to great uncertainty. In addition, there are certain risks involved in making decisions.

In a situation involving certainty, we are reasonably sure what will happen when we make a decision. The information is available and is considered to be reliable, and we know the cause and effect relationships.

In a situation of uncertainty, on the other hand, we have only a meager data base, we do not know whether or not the data are reliable, and we are very unsure whether or not the situation may change.[7] Moreover, we cannot evaluate the interactions of the different variables. For example, a corporation that decides to expand its operation in a strange country may know little about its culture, laws, economic environment, or politics. The political situation may be so volatile that even experts cannot predict a possible change in government.

In a risk situation, one may have factual information, but it may be incomplete. To improve decision making one may estimate the objective probabilities of an outcome by using, for example, mathematical models.[8] On the other hand, subjective probability, based on judgment and experience, may be used. Fortunately, there are a number of tools available that help managers to make more effective decisions.

MODERN APPROACHES TO DECISION MAKING UNDER UNCERTAINTY

A number of modern techniques improve the quality of decision making under the normal conditions of uncertainty. Among the most important of these are (1) risk analysis, (2) decision trees, and (3) preference theory.

Risk Analysis

All intelligent decision makers dealing with uncertainty like to know the size and nature of the risk they are taking in choosing a course of action. One of the deficiencies in using the traditional approaches of operations research for problem solving is that many of the data used in a model are merely estimates, and others are based upon probabilities. The ordinary practice is for staff specialists to come up with "best estimates." To give a more precise view of risk, new techniques have been developed.

Virtually every decision is based on the interaction of a number of important variables, many of which have an element of uncertainty but, perhaps, a fairly high degree of probability. Thus, the wisdom of launching a new product might depend upon a number of critical variables: how much it will cost to introduce the product, how much it will cost to produce it, how much of a capital investment will be required, what price can be set for the product, the size of the potential market for it, and the share of total market that it will represent (see Perspective on page 145).

Decision Trees

One of the best ways to analyze a decision is to use so-called decision trees. **Decision trees** sketch in the form of a "tree" the decision points, the chance events, and the probabilities involved in various courses that might be under-

> ## PERSPECTIVE:
> ## INVESTMENT IN A NEW PRODUCT
>
> For a new product investment program, the range of probabilities for a return on investment might be based on different estimates, as follows:
>
> | Rate of return (percent) | Probability of achieving at least rate of return shown |
> | :---: | :---: |
> | 0 | .90 |
> | 10 | .80 |
> | 15 | .70 |
> | 20 | .65 |
> | 25 | .60 |
> | 30 | .50 |
> | 35 | .40 |
> | 40 | .30 |
>
> In other words, there is a 90 percent (.90) chance that the rate of return (or the rate at which the company earns money from its investment) will be at least zero, an 80 percent (.80) chance that it will be at least 10 percent, and so on.
>
> Given such data as these, a manager is better able to assess the probability of accomplishing a best estimate and can see the chances of success that he or she might have if a lesser rate of return would be sufficient.

taken. A common problem occurs in business when a new product is introduced. Managers must decide whether to install expensive permanent equipment so as to ensure production at the lowest possible cost or to undertake cheaper temporary tooling involving a higher manufacturing cost but lower capital investments and lower losses if the product does not sell as well as estimated. In its simplest form, a tree showing the decisions a manager faces in a situation might be similar to that in Figure 6-3.

The decision tree approach makes it possible to see at least the major alternatives and the fact that subsequent decisions may depend upon events in the future. By incorporating probabilities of various events in the tree, we can also comprehend the true probability of a decision leading to the desired results. The "best estimate" may really turn out to be quite risky. One thing is certain: Decision trees and similar decision techniques do replace broad judgments with a focus on the important elements in a decision, bring out into the open premises that are often hidden, and disclose the reasoning process by which decisions are made under uncertainty.

Preference Theory

Preference, or **utility,** theory is based on the notion that individual attitudes toward risk will vary, with some individuals being willing only to take lower risks than indicated by probabilities ("risk averter") and others being willing to take greater risks ("gamblers"). While referred to here as "preference theory," this

FIGURE 6-3

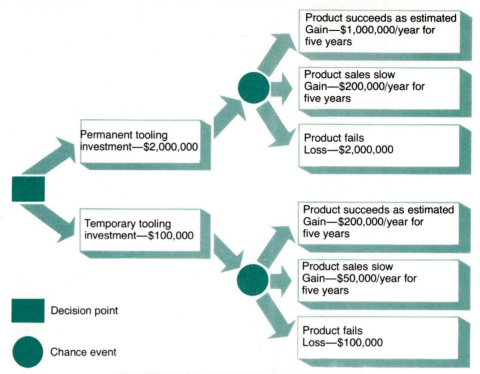

DECISION TREE WITHOUT PROBABILITIES.

technique is more classically called "utility theory." Purely statistical probabilities, as applied to decision making, rest upon the assumption that decision makers will follow them. In other words, it might seem reasonable that if there were a 60 percent chance of a decision's being the right one, we would take it, but this is not necessarily true, since the risk of being wrong is 40 percent and we might not wish to take this risk. Managers avoid risk, particularly if the penalty for being wrong is severe, whether it be in terms of monetary losses, reputation, or job security. If we doubt this, we might ask ourselves whether we would risk, say, $40,000 on the 60 percent chance that we might make $100,000, realizing that there is still a 40 percent chance that we might lose $40,000. We might readily risk $4 on a chance of making $10, and gamblers have been known to risk much more on a lesser chance of success.

Attitudes toward risk. In order to give probabilities practical meaning in decision making, we need better understanding of the individual decision maker's aversion to, or acceptance of, risk. This varies not only with the individual but also with the size of the risk, with the level of the manager in an organization, and according to whether the funds involved are personal or belong to a company.

Higher-level managers are accustomed to taking larger risks than lower-level managers, and their decision areas tend to involve larger elements of risk. A company president may have to take great risks in launching a new product, in selecting an advertising program, or in choosing a vice-president, while a first-level supervisor's risk taking may be limited to hiring or promoting semiskilled workers or approving vacation schedules for subordinates.

Also, the same top managers who may make a decision involving risks of millions of dollars for a company in a given program with a chance of success of, say, 75 percent would not be likely to do that with their own personal fortunes, at least unless they were very large. Moreover, the same manager willing to take a 75 percent risk in one case might not be willing to do so in another. Furthermore, a top executive might "go for" a large advertising program where the chances of success are 70 percent, but might not decide in favor of an investment in plant and equipment unless the probability of success were higher. In other words, attitudes toward risk vary with events, as well as with people and positions.

Personal risk or preference curves.   While we do not know much about attitudes toward risk, we do know that some people are risk averters in some situations and gamblers in others, and that some people have by nature a high aversion to risk and others have a low one. Typical personal risk or preference curves may be drawn as in Figure 6-4. This graph shows both risk averter's and gambler's curves as well as what is referred to as a "personal" curve. The latter, of course, implies that most of us are gamblers when small stakes are involved but that we soon become risk averters when the stakes rise.

Most managers (understandably influenced by the dangers of failure), tend

FIGURE 6-4

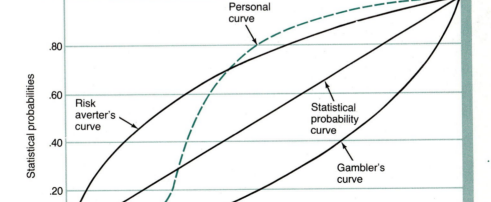

SAMPLE PREFERENCE CURVES.

to be risk averters to some extent and do not in fact play the averages. There-fore, statistical probabilities are not good enough for practical decision making.

Although perhaps too many managers are risk averters and thereby miss opportunities, few are players of pure statistical averages, at least in important decisions. Therefore, individual preference curves could be substituted for statistical probabilities in decision trees. We can do this, at least roughly, by assessing our willingness to take risks in a variety of real or imaginary situations and by developing our own preference curve. Even where we do not do so systematically, those of us who receive recommendations on courses of action from subordinates gain an important advantage if we are aware of the effect of our subordinates' attitude toward risk in making decisions or decision recom-mendations.

EVALUATING THE IMPORTANCE OF A DECISION

Since managers not only must make correct decisions but also must make them as needed and as economically as possible, and since they must do this often, guidelines to the relative importance of decisions are useful. Decisions of lesser importance need not require thorough analysis and research, and they may even be safely delegated without endangering an individual manager's basic responsi-bility. The importance of a decision also depends upon the extent of responsibil-ity, so that what may be of practically no importance to a corporation president may be of great importance to a section head.

If a decision commits the enterprise to heavy expenditure of funds or to an important personnel program, such as a program for management appraisal and training, or if the commitment can be fulfilled only over a long period, such as by the construction of a new chemical plant, it should be subjected to suitable attention at an upper level of management.

Some plans can be easily changed, some have built into them the possibility of a future change of direction, and others involve action difficult to reverse. Clearly, decisions involving inflexible courses of action must be more carefully evaluated than decisions that can be easily changed.

If goals and premises are fairly certain, a decision resting on them tends to be less difficult and to require less judgment and analysis than when they are highly uncertain.

Where the goals, inputs, restrictions, and variables can be accurately mea-sured, like definite inputs in a production machine shop, the importance of the decision, other things remaining the same, tends to be less than where the inputs are difficult to quantify, as in pricing a new consumer product or deciding on its style.

Where the impact of a decision on people is great, its importance is high. A doctor's mistake in a hospital can be fatal to a patient. No one making a decision that affects other people can afford to overlook the needs of those people who accept the decision.

OTHER FACTORS IN DECISION MAKING

There are other factors that influence decision making. They will be discussed in more detail in other chapters.

1. **Personal values and organization culture.** In the strategic planning model shown in the previous chapter, we have seen that an important variable influencing the direction of the enterprise pertained to personal values, primarily of top managers. However, values influence the decision making at all organizational levels, managers and nonmanagers alike. What is true for individuals is also pertinent to the organization as a whole. Thus, the pattern of behavior, shared beliefs, and values of members of an organization do influence decision making and will be discussed in Chapter 11.

2. **Group decision making.** In modern organizations, decisions are often made by groups of individuals, such as by committees or teams.[9] Chapter 10 will discuss these organizational forms of managing.

3. **Creativity and innovation.** Effective decision making requires creativity and innovation.[10] Both aspects will be discussed in Chapter 16.

DECISION SUPPORT SYSTEMS

Decision Support Systems (DSS) use computers to facilitate the decision-making process of semistructured tasks. These systems are designed not to replace managerial judgment but to support it and to make the decision process more effective.[11] The design of an effective DSS requires a thorough knowledge of how managers make decisions.

The availability of mini- and microcomputers as well as communication networks make it possible to access and utilize a great deal of information at low cost. Thus, DSS give managers an important tool for decision making under their own control.

Although there are similarities between Management Information Systems (MIS) and DSS, there are also many differences. Traditionally, the designers of MIS were technical experts, and managers (who had to make the decisions) had only minor inputs. In contrast, DSS focuses on the decision-making process and on managers who, in cooperation with the technical professionals, design the system suitable for a particular position. Managers, having access to data bases in DSS, can manipulate data and explore the effectiveness of alternative courses of action. These and other differences between MIS and DSS are shown in Table 6-1.

Now many software programs are available for microcomputers, such as VisiCalc, Lotus 1-2-3, or Supercalc. The same is true for database software. For example, *INFOWORLD*, the newspaper for the microcomputer industry, evaluated twenty-four such data bases for the IBM PCs and compatible computers

TABLE 6-1 Comparisons between MIS and DSS

MIS	DSS
Focus on structured tasks and routine decisions (e.g., use of procedures, use of decision rules)	Focus on semistructured tasks, requiring managerial judgment
Emphasis on data storage	Emphasis on data manipulation
Often only indirect access to data by managers	Direct data access by managers
Reliance on computer expert	Reliance on manager's own judgment
Access to data possibly requiring a wait for manager's turn	Direct access to computer and data
MIS manager not completely understanding the nature of the decision	Manager knowing decision environment
Emphasis on efficiency	Emphasis on effectiveness

Sources: Peter G. W. Keen and Michael S. Scott Morton, *Decision Support Systems—An Organizational Perspective* (Reading, Mass.: Addison-Wesley Publishing Company, 1978); Ronald R. Wood, "The Personal Computer: How It Can Increase Management Productivity," *Financial Executive* (February 1984); Ernest A. Kallman and Leon Reinharth, *Information Systems for Planning and Decision Making* (New York: Van Nostrand Reinhold, 1984).

(some of these programs may be familiar to you: Cornerstone, Reflex, or Q&A) and ten such programs for the Macintosh computer (e.g., Filemaker, Overvue, and Reflex).[12] Then there are the many integrated programs that may serve as a word processor, spreadsheet, data base, graphics, and communications with names such as Symphony, Framework, or Jazz. Thus, managers can be overwhelmed by the many choices of programs that aid the decision-making process.

PERSPECTIVE:
INVESTMENT DECISIONS IN A HOSPITAL

A decision system can become very complex. The flow diagram of information for proposed investments is shown in Figure 6-5.[13] Now imagine the many other decisions that have to be made in a hospital pertaining to the well-being of patients, providing the basis for fiscal soundness, and balancing the interests of trustees, administrators, and physicians. More recently, some hospitals began thinking strategically by making decisions that related the hospital's strengths and weaknesses with opportunities and threats in the external environment within the framework of its mission. While it might be difficult to diagram all the various decision processes, and one could be overwhelmed by its complexity, the systems nature of decision making must be recognized. The hospital, it must be kept in mind, must not be a closed system but must serve the needs of the community of which it is a part.

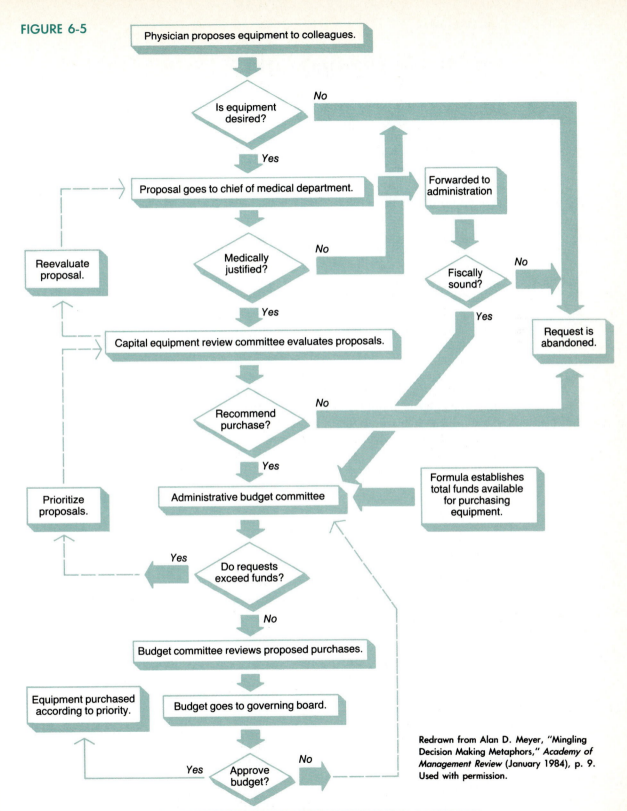

FIGURE 6-5

Physician proposes equipment to colleagues.

Is equipment desired? — No

Yes

Proposal goes to chief of medical department.

Forwarded to administration

Reevaluate proposal.

Medically justified? — No

Fiscally sound? — No

Yes

Yes

Request is abandoned.

Capital equipment review committee evaluates proposals.

Recommend purchase? — No

Yes

Prioritize proposals.

Administrative budget committee

Formula establishes total funds available for purchasing equipment.

Do requests exceed funds? — Yes

No

Budget committee reviews proposed purchases.

Equipment purchased according to priority.

Budget goes to governing board.

Approve budget? — No

Yes

Redrawn from Alan D. Meyer, "Mingling Decision Making Metaphors," *Academy of Management Review* (January 1984), p. 9. Used with permission.

FLOWCHART FOR INVESTMENT DECISIONS IN A HOSPITAL.

THE SYSTEMS APPROACH AND DECISION MAKING

Decisions cannot usually be made, of course, in a closed-system environment. As we have emphasized, many elements of the environment of planning lie outside the enterprise. In addition, every department or section of an enterprise is a subsystem of the entire enterprise; managers of these organizational units must be responsive to the policies and programs of other organization units and of the total enterprise. Moreover, people within the enterprise are a part of the social system, and their thinking and attitudes must be taken into account whenever a manager makes a decision.

Furthermore, even when managers construct a closed-system model, as they may do with operations research decision models, they do so simply to have a workable program to solve. But in so doing, they make certain assumptions as to environmental forces that heavily influence their decision, they enter inputs into their calculations as they are or appear to be at any given time, and they change the construction of their model when forces and developments beyond its boundaries so require (see Perspective on pages 150 and 151).

To say that managers take into account the various elements in the system environment of their problem does not mean, however, that they abdicate their role as decision makers. Someone must select a course of action from among alternatives, taking into account events and forces in the environment of a decision. It is often not feasible, or advisable, to democratize the decision process to the extent that for all decisions a vote is taken from subordinates or the many other persons who may have some immediate or remote interest in the decision. At some point a decision has to be made.

FOR DISCUSSION

1. Why is experience often referred to not only as an expensive basis for decision making but also as a dangerous one? How can a manager make best use of experience?

2. In a decision problem you now know of, how and where would you apply the principle of the limiting factor?

3. Identify five decision problems and recommend programmed or nonprogrammed decisions. If the examples are from an organizational setting, did they occur on upper or lower levels?

4. Draw a decision tree for a decision problem you face.

5. Could you conceptualize an operations research problem in broad terms without the use of mathematics?

6. "Decision making is the primary task of the manager." Comment.

7. How does risk aversion affect your own life? Given a situation, draw your preference curve.

EXERCISES/ACTION STEPS

1. Your boss offers you a promotion to a position in a location that your family does not like. Make the necessary assumptions and then state how and what you would decide.

2. Interview a manager of a local company and obtain information about the decision-making process in the organization. Discuss the concept of bounded rationality and see if it applies to him or her.

CASES

CASE 6-1
OLYMPIC TOY COMPANY

"I expect all the managers in my department to act completely rationally in every decision they make," declared Eleanor Johnson, vice-president of marketing for the Olympic Toy Company. "Every one of us, no matter what his or her position, is hired to be a professional rationalist and I expect all of us not only to know what they are doing and why, but to be right in their decisions. I know that someone has said that a good manager needs only to be right in more than half of his or her decisions. But that is not good enough for me. I would agree that you may be excused for occasionally making a mistake, especially if it is a matter beyond your control, but I can never excuse you for not acting rationally."

"I agree with your idea, Eleanor," said Jill Goldberg, her advertising manager, "and I always try to be rational and logical in my decisions. But would you mind helping me be sure of this by explaining just what 'acting rationally' is?"

1. Explain how the vice-president of marketing might describe what is involved in making rational decisions.

2. If Jill Goldberg then declares that there is no way she can be completely rational, what would you suggest as a reply?

CASE 6-2
KING'S SUPERMARKETS

King's Supermarkets was a chain of twenty-five highly successful supermarkets located in medium-size cities in New England, New York, and New Jersey. It had always been the company's policy to have only one leading store in each of a number of cities of approximately 25,000 to 50,000 population. In each city, the best possible location was sought out and very large stores were developed with attractive buildings, large parking lots, and complete product lines of food and food-related products sold at advertised competitive prices. Although the company had had to close a few poorly located markets over the years, it relied almost entirely for its choice of cities and locations on the instincts of the founder-president, Walter King. The company's record of profits indicated that his judgment had been generally correct over the 25 years since he had opened his first market.

After Walter King's daughter Donna graduated from the university with a degree in business administration and joined the company as assistant to the president, the researching of new city locations was made one of her major assignments. Ms. King felt that the techniques of operations research might be applied to this problem. She pointed out that there must be a "best" city and a "best" location for expansion at any given time and for the future, if only this could be discovered. She insisted that all a company needed to do was to clarify its goals; identify the constraints such as cash available, existing competition, and distance from company warehouses; look at such variables as cost of real estate, money costs, market size and characteristics, local labor markets, and local taxes and regulations; and then put these into a model to come up with a means of identifying the best location.

Her father and the other officers of the company maintained that operations research might be all right for an oil company, a large aerospace company, or even a large bank, but it was too complicated an approach and there were too many intangibles in a matter of a supermarket location. Moreover, for 25 years the company had been successful in relying on the president's judgment, and anyway, neither Mr. King nor any of the other top officers or managers understood advanced mathematics. In addition, they felt that they wanted no part of a company where such major decisions were made by a computer. They pointed out emphatically that they were merchandisers and not computer experts.

Ms. King was not convinced. She was sure that operations research would be a great help in such decisions. But she did not know what to do under the circumstances.

1. Making some reasonable assumptions, show Ms. King and her father how operations research might apply in this case.

2. Draw a rough diagram which shows what factors should be included in an operations research model for this case.

REFERENCES

1. The attempts by a number of management specialists to bring logical order to the decision process are outlined and explained in E. R. Archer, "How To Make a Business Decision: An Analysis of Theory and Practice," *Management Review* (February 1980), pp. 30–37.

2. See James G. March and Herbert A. Simon, *Organizations* (New York: John Wiley & Sons, 1958, 1966).

3. Bro Uttal, "Compaq Bids for PC Leadership," *Fortune* (Sept. 29, 1986), pp. 30–32; Jo E. Davis and Geoff Lewis, "Compaq Is Trying to Steal a March on IBM," *Business Week* (Sept. 22, 1986), p. 30; Edward Warner, "Compaq Introduces 386 PC, Challenges IBM to Match It," *Infoworld* (Sept. 15, 1986), pp. 1, 8.

4. See, for example, Herbert A. Simon, *The New Science of Management Decisions* (Englewood Cliffs, N.J.: Prentice-Hall, 1977).

5. Weston H. Agor, "How Top Executives Use Their Intuition to Make Important Decisions," *Business Horizons* (January–February 1986), pp. 49–53.

6. Strategic decision making often involves a great deal of uncertainty. See Charles R. Schwenk, "Cognitive Simplification Processes in Strategic Decision Making," *Strategic Management Journal* (April–June 1984), pp. 111–128; Weston H. Agor, "How Top Executives Use Their Intuition to Make Important Decisions," _Business Horizons_ (January–February, 1986), pp. 49–53.

7. Charles R. Schwenk, "Cognitive Simplification Processes in Strategic Decision Making," _Strategic Management Journal_, (April–June 1984), pp. 111–128.

8. See also Jitendra V. Singh, "Performance, Slack, and Risk Taking in Organizational Decision Making," _Academy of Management Journal_ (September 1986), pp. 562–585.

9. See also Edwin A. Locke, Gary P. Latham, and David M. Schweiger, "Participation in Decision Making: When Should It Be Used?" _Organizational Dynamics_ (Winter 1986), pp. 65ff.

10. For interesting discussions of the topic, see Andre L. Delbecq and Peter K. Mills, "Managerial Practices That Enhance Innovation," _Organizational Dynamics_ (Summer 1985), pp. 24–34; M. J. Kirton, "Adaptors and Innovators—Why New Initiatives Get Blocked," _Long Range Planning_, vol. 17, no. 2 (1984), pp. 137–143.

11. Peter G. W. Keen and Michael S. Scott Morton, _Decision Support Systems—An Organizational Perspective_ (Reading, Mass.: Addison-Wesley Publishing Company, 1978).

12. Scott Mace, "File Management Software," _Infoworld_ (Sept. 8, 1986), pp. 29–37.

13. Alan D. Meyer, "Mingling Decision Making Metaphors," _Academy of Management Review_ (January 1984), pp. 6–17.

FOR FURTHER INFORMATION

Barnard, Chester I. _The Functions of the Executive_ (Cambridge, Mass.: Harvard University Press, 1964).

Bass, Bernard M. _Organizational Decision Making_ (Homewood, Ill.: Richard D. Irwin, 1983).

Duncan, Jack W. _Decision Making and Social Issues_ (Hinsdale, Ill,: Dryden Press, 1973).

Huber, George P. _Managerial Decision Making_ (Glenview, Ill.: Scott, Foresman and Company, 1980).

Kepner, Charles H., and Benjamin B. Tregoe. _The Rational Manager_ (New York: McGraw-Hill Book Company, 1965).

McCreary, Edward A. "How to Grow a Decision Tree," in Harold Koontz, Cyril O'Donnell, and Heinz Weihrich (eds.), _Management—A Book of Readings_, 5th ed. (New York: McGraw-Hill Book Company, 1980), pp. 182–187.

Meyer, Alan D. "Mingling Decision Making Metaphors," _Academy of Management Review_ (January 1984), pp. 6–17.

Oxenfeldt, Alfred R. "Effective Decision Making for the Business Executive," in Harold Koontz, Cyril O'Donnell, and Heinz Weihrich (eds.), _Management—A Book of Readings_, 5th ed. (New York: McGraw-Hill Book Company, 1980), pp. 170–174.

Simon, Herbert A. _Administrative Behavior_ (New York: The Free Press, 1947).

Staw, Barry M. "The Escalation of Commitment to a Course of Action," _Academy of Management Review_ (October 1981), pp. 577–587.

Ulvila, Jacob W., and Rex V. Brown. "Decision Analysis Comes of Age," _Harvard Business Review_ (September–October 1982), pp. 130–141.

SUMMARY OF MAJOR PRINCIPLES OF PLANNING

Perhaps the best way to summarize Part 2 on planning is to list some of the major principles, or guidelines, that may be used in planning. While others might be added, the most essential guiding principles are the following:

The Purpose and Nature of Planning

The purpose and nature of planning may be summarized by reference to the following principles.

Principle of contribution to objectives. The purpose of every plan and all supporting plans is to promote the accomplishment of enterprise objectives.

Principle of objectives. If objectives are to be meaningful to people, they must be clear, attainable, and verifiable.

Principle of primacy of planning. Planning logically precedes all other managerial functions.

Principle of efficiency of plans. Efficiency of a plan is measured by the amount it contributes to purpose and objectives as offset by the costs required to formulate and operate it and by unsought consequences.

The Structure of Plans

Two major principles dealing with the structure of plans can go far in tying plans together, making supporting plans contribute to major plans, and ensuring that plans in one department harmonize with those in another.

Principle of planning premises. The more thoroughly the individuals who are charged with planning understand and agree to utilize consistent planning premises, the more coordinated enterprise planning will be.

Principle of strategy and policy framework. The more strategies and policies are clearly understood and implemented in practice, the more consistent and effective will be the framework of enterprise plans.

The Process of Planning

Within the process of planning, there are four principles that help in the development of a practical science of planning.

Principle of the limiting factor. In choosing from among alternatives, the more accurately individuals can recognize and solve for those factors which are limiting or critical to the attainment of the desired goal, the more easily and accurately they can select the most favorable alternative.

The commitment principle.   Logical planning should cover a period of time in the future necessary to foresee as well as possible, through a series of actions, the fulfillment of commitments involved in a decision made today.

Principle of flexibility.   Building flexibility into plans will lessen the danger of losses incurred through unexpected events, but the cost of flexibility should be weighed against its advantages.

Principle of navigational change.   The more planning decisions commit us to a future path, the more important it is that we periodically check on events and expectations and redraw plans as necessary to maintain a course toward a desired goal.

The commitment principle and the principles of flexibility and navigational change are aimed at a contingency approach to planning. Although it makes sense to forecast and draw plans far enough into the future to make reasonably sure of meeting commitments, often it is impossible to do so, or the future is so uncertain that it is too risky to fulfill those commitments.

The principle of flexibility deals with that ability to change which is built into plans. The principle of navigational change, on the other hand, implies reviewing plans from time to time and redrawing them if that is required by changed events and expectations. Unless plans have built-in flexibility, navigational change may be difficult or costly.

Organizing

EXTERNAL ENVIRONMENT

Managerial knowledge,
goals of claimants,
and use of inputs
(Part 1. The Basis of
Management Theory
and Science)

Planning
(Part 2)

Organizing
(Part 3)

Staffing
(Part 4)

Leading
(Part 5)

Controlling
(Part 6)

Reenergizing the System

Chapters
7. The Nature and Purpose of Organizing
8. Basic Departmentation
9. Line/Staff Authority and Decentralization
10. Committees and Group Decision Making
11. Effective Organizing and Organizational Culture

Facilitated by communication that also links
the organization with the external environment
(Part 7. Challenges in the Domestic and International Environment)

EXTERNAL ENVIRONMENT

To produce outputs

EXTERNAL ENVIRONMENT

SYSTEMS APPROACH TO MANAGEMENT.

160

The Nature and Purpose of Organizing

CHAPTER OBJECTIVES

After reading this chapter, you should be able to:

1. Realize that the purpose of an organization structure is to establish a formal system of roles that people can perform so that they may best work together to achieve enterprise objectives.

2. Understand the meaning of "organizing" and "organization."

3. Draw a distinction between formal and informal organization.

4. Show how organization structures and their levels are due to the limitations of the span of management.

5. Recognize that the exact number of people a manager can effectively supervise depends on a number of underlying variables and situations.

6. Describe the nature of entrepreneuring and intrapreneuring.

7. Demonstrate the logic of organizing and its relationship to other managerial functions.

8. Make clear that the application of structural organization theory must necessarily take situations into account.

*I*t is often said that good people can make any organization pattern work. Some even assert that vagueness in organization is a good thing in that it forces teamwork, since people know that they must cooperate to get anything done. Surely, however, good people and those who want to cooperate will work together most effectively if they know the parts they are to play in any team operation and how their roles relate to one another. This is as true in business or government as it is in football or in a symphony orchestra. To design and maintain these systems of roles is basically the managerial function of organizing.

For an **organizational role** to exist and to be meaningful to people, it must incorporate (1) verifiable objectives, which, as we indicated in Part 2, are a major part of planning; (2) a clear idea of the major duties or activities involved; and (3) an understood area of discretion or authority, so that the person filling the role knows what he or she can do to accomplish goals.

In addition, to make a role work out effectively, provision should be made for supplying needed information and other tools necessary for performance in that role.

It is in this sense that we think of **organizing** as (1) the identification and classification of required activities, (2) the grouping of activities necessary to attain objectives, (3) the assignment of each grouping to a manager with authority necessary to supervise it (delegation), and (4) the provision for coordination horizontally (on the same or similar organizational level) and vertically (e.g., corporate headquarters, division, and department) in the organization structure.

An organization structure should be designed to clarify who is to do what and who is responsible for what results, to remove obstacles to performance caused by confusion and uncertainty of assignment, and to furnish decision-making and communications networks reflecting and supporting enterprise objectives.

"Organization" is a word many use loosely. Some would say it includes all the behavior of all participants. Others would equate it with the total system of social and cultural relationships. Still others refer to an enterprise, such as the United States Steel Corporation or the Department of Defense, as an "organization." But for most practicing managers, the term **organization** implies a *formalized intentional structure of roles or positions.* The last meaning is generally used in this book, although we sometimes use the term to denote an enterprise.

What do we mean by an "intentional structure of roles"? In the first place, as we implied in defining the nature and content of organizational roles, people working together must fill certain roles. In the second place, the roles people are asked to fill should be intentionally designed to provide that required activities be done and to make sure that activities fit together so that people can work smoothly, effectively, and efficiently in groups. Certainly most managers believe they are organizing when they establish such an intentional structure.

FORMAL AND INFORMAL ORGANIZATION

Many writers on management distinguish between formal and informal organization. Both types are found in organizations, as shown in Figure 7-1. Let us look at them in more detail.

FIGURE 7-1

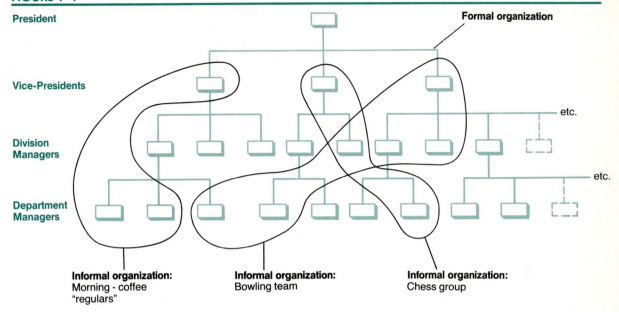

THE FORMAL AND INFORMAL ORGANIZATION.

Formal Organization

In this book, generally, **formal organization** means the intentional structure of roles in a formally organized enterprise. While we speak of an organization as "formal," there is nothing inherently inflexible or unduly confining about it. If the manager is to organize well, the structure must furnish an environment in which individual performance, both present and future, contributes most effectively to group goals.

Formal organization must be flexible. There should be room for discretion for taking advantage of creative talents, and for recognition of individual likes and capacities in the most formal of organizations. Yet, individual effort in a group situation must be channeled toward group and organization goals.

Although the attainment of goals must be the reason for any cooperative activity, we must look further for principles to guide the establishment of effective formal organization. These principles—summarized at the end of Part 3—pertain to the unity of objectives and organizational efficiency.

Informal Organization

Chester Barnard, author of the management classic *The Functions of the Executive,* regarded as informal organization any joint personal activity without conscious joint purpose, even though contributing to joint results.[1] Thus, the informal relationships established in the group of people playing chess during lunchtime may aid in the achievement of organizational goals. It is much easier to ask for help on an organization problem from a person you know, and who may even be in a different department, than from a person you know only as a name on an organization chart. More recently, Keith Davis of Arizona State University, who has written extensively on the topic and whose definition will be used in this book, described the **informal organization** as "a network of personal and social relations not established or required by the formal organization but arising spontaneously as people associate with one another."[2] Thus, informal organizations—relationships not appearing on an organization chart—might include the machine-shop group, the sixth-floor crowd, the Friday evening bowling gang, and the morning coffee "regulars."

An inquiry into why and how these informal organizations exist is a special study in social psychology. These dynamic interpersonal relationships are influenced by the number of people in the group, the actual personnel involved, what the group is concerned with, its changing leadership, and the continuing process of change. Managers must be aware of the informal organization and avoid antagonizing it. They will find it advantageous to use it as they manage subordinates.

ORGANIZATIONAL DIVISION: THE DEPARTMENT

One aspect of organizing is the establishment of departments. The word **department** designates *a distinct area, division, or branch of an organization over which a manager has authority for the performance of specified activities*. A department, as the term is generally used, may be the production division, the sales department, the West Coast branch, the market research section, or the accounts receivable unit. In some enterprises, departmental terminology is loosely applied; in others, especially large ones, a stricter terminology indicates hierarchical relationships. Thus, a vice-president may head a division; a director, a department; a manager, a branch; and a chief, a section.

ORGANIZATION LEVELS AND THE SPAN OF MANAGEMENT[3]

While the reason for organizing is to make human cooperation effective, we find the reason for levels of organization in the limitations of the span of management. In other words, organization levels exist because there is a limit to the number of persons a manager can supervise effectively, even though this limit varies depending on situations. The relationships between the span and the organizational levels are shown in Figure 7-2. A wide span of management is associated with few organizational levels; a narrow span results in many levels.

Choosing the Span

In every organization, it must be decided how many subordinates a superior can manage. Students of management have found that this number is usually four to eight subordinates at the upper levels of organization and eight to fifteen or more at the lower levels. For example, the prominent British consultant Lyndall

FIGURE 7-2

Organization with Narrow Spans

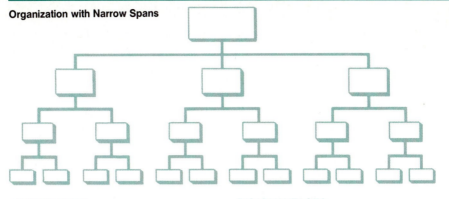

ADVANTAGES
- Close supervision
- Close control
- Fast communication between subordinates and superiors

DISADVANTAGES
- Superiors tend to get too involved in subordinates' work
- Many levels of management
- High costs due to many levels
- Excessive distance between lowest level and top level

Organization with Wide Spans

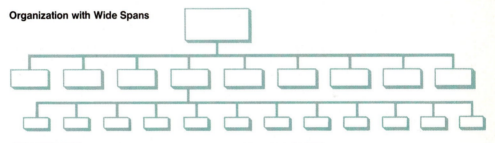

ADVANTAGES
- Superiors are forced to delegate
- Clear policies must be made
- Subordinates must be carefully selected

DISADVANTAGES
- Tendency of overloaded superiors to become decision bottlenecks
- Danger of superior's loss of control
- Requires exceptional quality of managers

ORGANIZATION STRUCTURES WITH NARROW AND WIDE SPANS.

Urwick found "the ideal number of subordinates for all superior authorities . . . to be four," while "at the lowest level of organization, where what is delegated is responsibility for the performance of specific tasks and not for the supervision of others, the number may be eight or twelve."[4] Others find that a manager may be able to manage as many as twenty to thirty subordinates.

In a survey of 100 large companies made by the American Management Association, the number of executives reporting to the presidents varied from one to twenty-four, and only twenty-six presidents had six or fewer subordinates. The median number was nine.[5] In forty-one smaller companies surveyed, twenty-five of the presidents supervised seven or more subordinates, and the

PERSPECTIVE:
MOSES AND THE SPAN OF MANAGEMENT

That the problem of span management is as old as organization itself is apparent from the passages of the Bible dealing with Moses' organizing the exodus of the Israelites. The difficulties that he met and the departmentation he employed to meet them are recounted in Exodus 18:17–26, which records that Moses' father-in-law, noting that Moses was spending so much time supervising so many individuals, advised him as follows:

"The thing thou doest is not good. Thou will surely wear away, both thou and this people that is with thee: for this thing is too heavy for thee; thou art not able to perform it thyself alone. Hearken now unto my voice, I will give thee counsel. . . . Thou shalt provide out of the people able men . . . and place such over them [the people], to be rulers of thousands, and rulers of hundreds, rulers of fifties, and rulers of tens. And let them judge the people at all seasons; and it shall be, that every great matter they shall bring unto thee, but every small matter they shall judge: so shall it be easier for thyself, and they shall bear the burden with thee. If thou shalt do this thing, and God command thee so, then thou shall be able to endure, and all this people shall also go to their place in peace."

Moses thereupon followed his father-in-law's advice. He "chose able men out of all Israel, and made them heads over the people, rulers of thousands, rulers of hundreds, rulers of fifties, and rulers of tens. And they judged the people at all seasons: the hard causes they brought unto Moses, but every small matter they judged themselves."

most common number was eight. Comparable results were found in other studies.

In a very real sense, none of these studies is truly indicative of the actual span of management. For one thing, they measure the span only at or near the top of an enterprise. This is hardly typical of what the span may be throughout the enterprise, particularly since every organizer has experienced the tremendous pressure for a large number of the functions to report to the top executives. It is probable that spans below the top executive are much narrower. Indeed, in a study of more than 100 companies of all sizes, we found a much narrower span in the middle levels of management than at the top.

In addition, the fact that apparently well-managed companies have, among them and certainly within them, widely varying spans indicates that merely counting the numbers in existing spans is not enough to establish what a span ought to be. And this is true even if it could be assumed that, through trial and error, each company has reached the best number. That might prove only that underlying conditions vary, and will be discussed later in this chapter.

Problems with Organization Levels

There is a tendency to regard organization and departmentation as ends in themselves and to gauge the effectiveness of organization structures in terms of clarity and completeness of departments and department levels. Division of activities into departments, and hierarchical organization and the creation of multiple levels, are not completely desirable in themselves.

In the first place, levels are *expensive*. As they increase, more and more effort and money are devoted to managing because of the additional managers, staffs to assist them, and the necessity of coordinating departmental activities, plus the costs of facilities for such personnel. Accountants refer to such costs as "overhead," or "burden," or "general and administrative," in contrast to so-called direct costs. Real production is accomplished by factory, engineering, or sales employees who are, or could logically be accounted for as, "direct labor." Levels above the "firing line" are predominantly staffed with managers whose cost it would be desirable to eliminate, if that were possible.

In the second place, departmental levels *complicate communication*. An enterprise with many levels has greater difficulty communicating objectives, plans, and policies downward through the organization structure than the firm in which the top manager communicates directly with employees. Omissions and misinterpretations occur as information passes down the line. Levels also complicate communication from the "firing line" to the commanding superiors, which is every bit as important as downward communication. It has been well said that levels are "filters" of information.

Finally, numerous departments and levels *complicate planning and control*. A plan that may be definite and complete at the top level loses coordination and clarity as it is subdivided at lower levels. Control becomes more difficult as levels and managers are added, while at the same time the complexities of planning and difficulties of communication make this control more important.

Operational-Management Position: A Situational Approach

The classical school approach to the span of management deals with specifying numbers of subordinates for an effective span. Actual experience does support the classical school opinion that at upper and top levels the span is from three to seven or eight subordinates. However, more recent operational-management theorists have taken the position that there are too many underlying variables in a management situation for us to specify any particular number of subordinates that a manager can effectively supervise. Thus, the **principle of the span of management** states that *there is a limit to the number of subordinates a manager can effectively supervise, but the exact number will depend on the impact of underlying factors.*

In other words, the dominant current guideline is to look for the causes of limited span in individual situations, rather than to assume that there is a widely applicable numerical limit. If we can examine what it is that consumes the time of managers in their handling of their superior-subordinate relationships, and also ascertain what devices can be used to reduce these time pressures, we have an approach that will be helpful in determining the best span in individual cases and also a powerful tool for finding out what can be done to extend the span without destroying effective supervision. There can be no argument that the costs of levels of supervision are such as to make it highly desirable for every individual manager to have as many subordinates as can be effectively supervised.

FACTORS DETERMINING AN EFFECTIVE SPAN

In searching for the answer as to how many subordinates a manager can effectively manage, we discover that—aside from such personal capacities as comprehending quickly, getting along with people, and commanding loyalty and respect—the most important determinant is the manager's ability to reduce the time the superior spends with subordinates. This ability naturally varies with managers and their jobs, but several factors materially influence the number and frequency of such contacts and therefore the span of management (see Table 7-1).

1. Subordinate Training

The better the training of subordinates, the less the impact of necessary superior-subordinate relationships. Well-trained subordinates require not only less of their manager's time but also less contact with them.

Training problems increase in new and more complex industries. Managers in the railroad industry, for example, would—because the technology does not change much—tend to be more completely trained than those in the aerospace

TABLE 7-1 Factors Influencing the Span of Management

Narrow span (a great deal of time spent with subordinates) related to:	Wide spans (very little time spent with subordinates) related to:
Little or no training	Thorough subordinate training
Inadequate or unclear authority delegation	Clear delegation to undertake well-defined tasks
Unclear plans for nonrepetitive operations	Well-defined plans for repetitive operations
Nonverifiable objectives and standards	Verifiable objectives used as standards
Fast changes in external and internal environments	Slow changes in external and internal environments
Use of poor or inappropriate communication techniques, including vague instructions	Use of appropriate techniques such as proper organization structure, written and oral communication
Ineffective interaction of superior and subordinate	Effective interaction between superior and subordinate
Ineffective meetings	Effective meetings
Greater number of specialties at lower and middle levels	Number of specialties at upper levels (top managers concerned with external environment)
Incompetent and untrained manager	Competent and trained manager
Complex task	Simple task
Subordinates' unwillingness to assume responsibility and reasonable risks	Subordinates' willingness to assume responsibility and reasonable risks
Immature subordinates	Mature subordinates

industry. The rapid changes in policy and procedures in the complex electronics and missile industries would increase training problems.

2. Clarity of Delegation of Authority

Although training enables managers to reduce the frequency and extensiveness of time-consuming contacts, the principal cause of the heavy time burdens of superior-subordinate relationships is to be found in poorly conceived and confused organization. The most serious symptom of poor organization affecting the span of management is inadequate or unclear authority delegation. If a manager clearly delegates authority to undertake a well-defined task, a well-trained subordinate can get it done with a minimum of the superior's time and attention. But if the subordinate's task is not one that can be done, if it is not clearly defined, or if the subordinate does not have the authority to undertake it effectively, either the task will not be performed or the manager will have to spend a disproportionate amount of time supervising and guiding the subordinate's efforts.

3. Clarity of Plans

Much of the character of a subordinate's job is defined by the plans to be put into effect. If these plans are well defined, if they are workable, if the authority to undertake them has been delegated, and if the subordinate understands what is expected, little of a supervisor's time will be required. Such is often the case with a production supervisor responsible for largely repetitive operations. Thus, in one large-volume work-clothing manufacturer's plant, production supervisors operated satisfactorily with as many as thirty subordinates.

On the other hand, where plans cannot be drawn accurately and where subordinates must do much of their own planning, they may require considerable guidance. However, if the superior has set up clear policies to guide decisions and has made sure they are consistent with the operations and goals of a department, and if the subordinate understands them, there will certainly be fewer demands on the superior's time than there would be if these policies were indefinite, incomplete, or not understood.

4. Use of Objective Standards

A manager must find out, either by personal observation or through use of objective standards, whether subordinates are following plans. Obviously, good objective standards, revealing with ease any deviations from plans, enable managers to avoid many time-consuming contacts and to direct attention to exceptions at points critical to the successful execution of plans.

5. Rate of Change

Certain enterprises change much more rapidly than others. The rate of change is an important determinant of the degree to which policies can be formulated and the stability of policies maintained. It may explain the organization structure of companies—railroad, banking, and public utility companies, for example—

operating with wide spans of management or, on the other hand, the very narrow span of management used by General Eisenhower during World War II.

The effect of slow change on policy formulation and on subordinate training is dramatically shown in the organization of the Roman Catholic Church. This organization, in terms of durability and stability, can probably be regarded as the most successful in the history of Western civilization. Yet the organization levels are few: in most cases, bishops report directly to the Pope, and parish pastors to bishops, although in some instances bishops report to archbishops. Thus, there are generally only very few levels in this worldwide organization and a consequent wide span of management at each level. Even though it is unquestionably too broad, this extraordinarily wide span is apparently tolerable, partly because of the degree of training possessed by the bishops and, even more, because the rate of change in the Church has been slow. Changes in procedures or policies are developments of decades, and major objectives have remained the same for almost 2000 years.

6. Communication Techniques

The effectiveness with which communication techniques are used also influences the span of management. Objective standards of control are a kind of communications device, but many other techniques reduce the time spent with subordinates.

If every plan, instruction, order, or direction has to be communicated by personal contact and every organization change or staffing problem handled orally, a manager's time will obviously be heavily burdened. Some executives use "assistant-to" positions or administrative staff personnel as a communications device to help them solve their problems with key subordinates. Written recommendations by subordinates, summarizing important considerations, frequently speed decision making. We have seen busy top executives widen their span of management by insisting upon summary presentation of written recommendations, even when these involved enormously important decisions. A carefully reasoned and presented recommendation helps an executive reach a considered decision in minutes, when even the most efficient conference would require an hour.

An ability to communicate plans and instructions clearly and concisely also tends to increase a manager's span. The subordinate who, after leaving a superior's office or receiving instructions, is still in doubt as to what is wanted or what has been said is sure to request further meetings sooner or later. One of the pleasures of being a subordinate is to have superiors who can express themselves well. A manager's casual, easy style may please subordinates, but where this easiness degenerates into confusion and wasted time, the effect is to reduce sharply the effective span of management and often to lower morale as well.

7. Amount of Personal Contact Needed

In many instances, face-to-face meetings are necessary. Many situations cannot be completely handled with written reports, memorandums, policy statements, planning documents, or other communications not calling for personal contact. An executive may find it valuable and stimulating to subordinates to meet and discuss problems in the give-and-take of a conference. There may also be problems of such political delicacy that they can be handled only in face-to-face meetings. This is also true when it comes to appraising people's performance and discussing it with them. And there are other situations where the best way of communicating a problem, instructing a subordinate, or "getting a feel" for how people really think on some matter is to spend time in personal contact.

We wonder, however, whether the high percentage of executive time spent in meetings and committees might be reduced somewhat by better training, better policy making and planning, clearer delegation, more thorough staff work, better control systems and objectives standards, and, in general, better application of sound principles of management. We wonder, also, whether much of the time spent in personal contact might not be much better spent in thought and study.

At the other extreme, many companies seem somewhat unaware of how newer personnel techniques affect first-line supervisors, many of whom appear to have spans of management far beyond their abilities to handle them. Merit rating, insurance programs, grievance procedures, and other personnel matters now requiring supervisors' time in face-to-face relationships have reduced their traditionally wide spans. This is not to say that these innovations are not worth their cost, but span-of-management limitations must be evaluated in the light of these factors. Perhaps we have reached the point where first-level supervisors, with a traditionally large number of people reporting to them, are the most overworked of all managers.

8. Variation by Organization Level

Several research projects have found that the size of the most effective span differs by organization level. In one major study, the researchers developed and tested a model to take into account this variable and found that the degree of specialization by individuals ("person specialization") was the most important variable affecting span, although technology and size also were tested since previous research had concentrated on these.[6] It was found that (1) when a greater number of specialties were supervised, effective spans were less at lower and middle levels of organization but were increased at upper levels, primarily because top-level managers were most concerned with the interface of the enterprise with its external environment, strategic planning, and major policy matters; (2) routineness (lack of variety of work) of an operation appeared to have little effect at any level; and (3) size (in terms of personnel) had little effect at lower levels but a positive effect at middle levels.

Actually, this study is consistent with the impact of variables outlined above. It found what many practitioners have long known: that neither size nor technology has had much to do with an effective span at upper levels of an organization although the variables outlined in this section have.

9. Other Factors

Besides the listed factors, there are others that influence the span of management. For example, a competent and trained manager can effectively supervise more people than one not having these attributes. Furthermore, simple tasks may allow for a wider span than tasks that are complex and include a great variety of activities. There are still other factors that favor a wider span of management, such as the positive attitudes of subordinates toward assumption of responsibility, as well as their willingness to take reasonable risks. Similarly, with more mature subordinates, the superior may delegate more authority, thus widening the span.

The Need for Balance

There can be no doubt that, despite the desirability of a flat organization structure, the span of management is limited by real and important restrictions. Managers may have more subordinates than they can manage effectively, even though they delegate authority, carry on training, formulate plans and policies clearly, and adopt efficient control and communication techniques. It is equally true that as an enterprise grows, the span-of-management limitations force an increase in the number of levels simply because there are more people to supervise.

What is required is more precise balancing, in a given situation, of all pertinent factors. Widening spans and reducing the number of levels may be the answer in some cases; the reverse may be true in others. One must balance all the costs of adopting one course or the other, not only the financial costs but costs in morale, personal development, and the attainment of enterprise objectives. In military organization, perhaps the attainment of objectives quickly and without error would be most important. On the other hand, in a department store operation, the long-run objective of profit may be best served by forcing initiative and personal development at the lower levels of the organization.

ORGANIZATIONAL ENVIRONMENT FOR ENTREPRENEURING AND INTRAPRENEURING

At times, special organizational arrangements need to be made for fostering and utilizing entrepreneurship. Frequently, entrepreneurship is thought to apply to managing small businesses.[7] But other authors expand the concept to apply also to large organizations and to managers carrying out entrepreneurial roles through which they initiate changes to take advantage of opportunities.[8] Although it is common to search for the "entrepreneurial personality," Peter Drucker suggested that this search may not be successful.[9] Instead, one should look for a commitment to systematic innovation, which is a specific activity of entrepreneurs. The essence of entrepreneurship is innovation, that is, goal-oriented change to utilize the enterprise's potential. As entrepreneurs, managers try to improve the situation.

Gifford Pinchot makes a distinction between the intrapreneur and the entrepreneur. Specifically, an **intrapreneur** is a person who focuses on innovation and creativity and who transforms a dream or an idea into a profitable venture by operating *within* the organizational environment. In contrast, the entrepreneur is a person who does the same, but *outside* the organizational setting.[10] But other authors do not make the distinctions, and we will, therefore, also use the term "entrepreneur" for an enterprising person working within and outside the organization.

Since it is the managers' responsibility to create an environment for effective and efficient achievement of group goals, they must promote opportunities for entrepreneurs to utilize their potential for innovation. Entrepreneurs take personal risks in initiating change and they expect to be rewarded for it. Taking of reasonable risk will, at times, result in failure, which must be tolerated. Finally, entrepreneurs need some freedom to pursue their ideas, which, in turn, requires that sufficient authority is delegated.

Innovative persons often have ideas that are contrary to "conventional wisdom." It is quite common that they are not well liked by their colleagues and their contributions are often not sufficiently appreciated. It is, therefore, not surprising, that entrepreneurs leave large companies and start their own businesses. When Steve Wozniak could not get his dream of building a small computer fulfilled at Hewlett-Packard, he left this prestigious firm to form—together with another entrepreneur, Steve Jobs—Apple Computers. Progressive companies, such as IBM or 3M, consciously try to develop an organizational environment that promotes entrepreneurship within the company.

THE STRUCTURE AND PROCESS OF ORGANIZING

In looking at organizing as a process, we can clearly see that several fundamentals must be considered. In the first place, the structure must reflect objectives

**PERSPECTIVE:
POST-IT NOTES[11]**

Even in companies with a policy of promoting entrepreneurship and innovation, the development of new products requires perseverance to transform an idea into reality.

Art Fry, the inventor of Post-it notes, was singing in a church choir. The bookmarks placed in his hymnal fell out after the first church service, making it difficult finding the relevant pages for the second service. The need was clear: An adhesive paper slip that could be easily removed without damaging the paper. However, developing an adhesive with appropriate stickiness was not an easy task. In the past, the 3M Company, where Art Fry worked, was known for providing products with great adhesion. For Art's purpose, however, a material was needed that had sufficient adhesion but also could be removed. The 3M laboratory did not provide much help in the research and development of such a product. Nor did the marketing department think a great deal of his idea. But being an inventor as well as an innovator, Art Fry pursued his goal with great perseverance. The result was the Post-it notes, which turned out to be a very profitable product for 3M.

and plans because activities derive from them. In the second place, it must reflect the authority available to an enterprise's management. Authority in a given organization is a socially determined right to exercise discretion; as such, it is subject to change.

In the third place, organization structure, like any plan, must reflect its environment. Just as the premises of a plan may be economic, technological, political, social, or ethical, so may those of an organization structure. It must be designed to work, to permit contributions by members of a group, and to help people gain objectives efficiently in a changing future. In this sense, a workable organization structure can never be static. There can be no single best organization structure that will work in all kinds of situations. An effective organization structure depends on the situation.

In the fourth place, the organization is staffed with people. The groupings of activities and the authority relationships of an organization structure must take into account people's limitations and customs. This is not to say that the structure must be designed around individuals instead of around goals and accompanying activities. But an important consideration is the kind of people who are to staff it.

The Logic of Organizing

There is a fundamental logic to organizing, as shown in Figure 7-3. Noting that steps 1 and 2 are actually part of planning, we suggest the following six steps:

1. Establishment of enterprise objectives

2. Formulation of supporting objectives, policies, and plans

3. Identification and classification of activities necessary to accomplish these

4. Grouping of these activities in the light of human and material resources available and the best way, under the circumstances, of using them

5. Delegation to the head of each group the authority necessary to perform the activities

6. Tying together of the groups horizontally and vertically, through authority relationships and information flows

Some Misconceptions

Organizing does not imply any extreme occupational specialization, which in many instances makes labor uninteresting, tedious, and unduly restrictive. There is nothing in organization itself that dictates this. To say that tasks should be specific is not to say they must be limited and mechanical. Whether they should be broken down into minute parts—as on a typical assembly line—or be broad enough to encompass the design, production, and sale of a machine is for the organizer to consider in light of the results desired. In any organization, jobs can be defined to allow little or no personal leeway or the widest possible

FIGURE 7-3

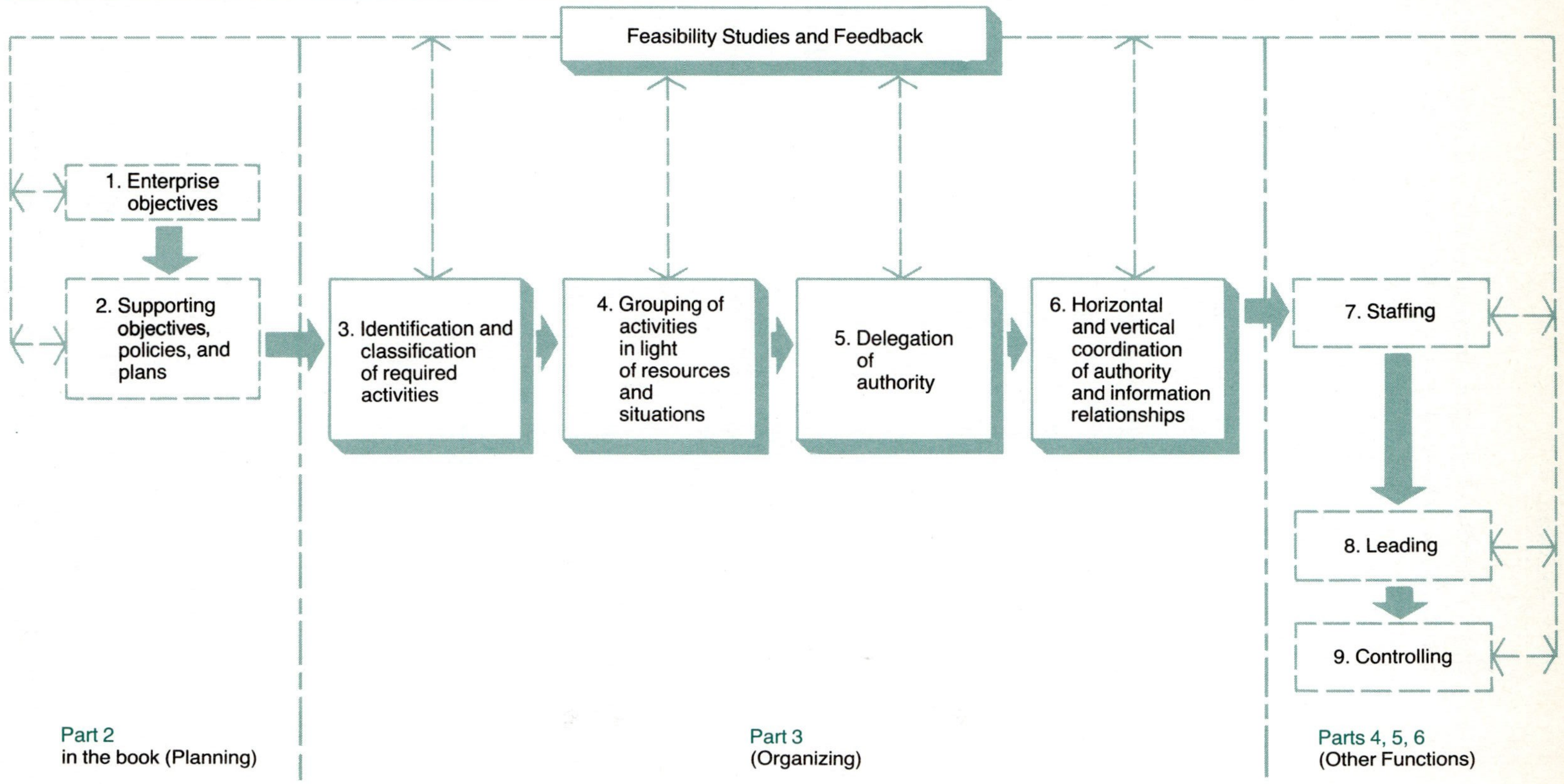

ORGANIZING PROCESS.

discretion. One must not forget that the application of structural organization theory must take into account the situation and that there is no best way to organize.

BASIC QUESTIONS FOR EFFECTIVE ORGANIZING

It is useful to analyze the managerial function of organizing by raising and answering the following questions:

1. What determines the span of management and hence the levels of organization? (Answered in this chapter)

2. What determines the basic framework of departmentation, and what are the strengths and weaknesses of the basic forms? (Answered in Chapter 8)

3. What kinds of authority relationships exist in organizations? (Answered in Chapter 9)

4. How should authority be dispersed throughout the organization structure, and what determines the extent of this dispersion? (Answered in Chapter 9)

5. How can committees be used for effective coordination of activities? (Answered in Chapter 10)

6. How should the manager make organization theory work in practice? (Answered in Chapter 11)

The answers to these questions form a basis for a theory of organizing. When considered along with similar analyses of planning, staffing, leading, and controlling, they constitute an operational approach to management.

FOR DISCUSSION

1. Since people must occupy organization positions and an effective organization depends on people, it is often said that the best organization arises when a manager hires good people and lets them do a job in their own way. Comment.

2. A formal organization is often conceived of as a communications system. Is it? How?

3. Construct a diagram depicting the formal organizations of some enterprises or activity with which you are familiar. How does this organization chart help or hinder the establishment of an environment for performance?

4. Using the same enterprise or activity as in question 3, chart the informal organization. Does it help or hinder the formal organization? Why?

5. Urwick and other writers seem to say that at top levels, the number of persons in the

span of management should not exceed six. Some 750 bishops and some 1200 other persons report directly to the Pope. At one time in the Bank of America organization, over 600 bank managers reported to the chief executive officer. How do you fit these facts with the idea that there is a limit to the number of subordinates a manager can supervise?

6. When you become a manager, what criteria will you favor to determine your span?

EXERCISES/ACTION STEPS

1. Organize a family picnic using the steps suggested in this chapter.

2. Interview a manager in your community and ask him or her how many subordinates he or she has. Are the number of subordinates supervised different at the top, the middle, and the bottom of the organizational hierarchy? What really determines the span of management in this organization? Do you think the span is appropriate for the enterprise?

CASES

CASE 7-1
MEASUREMENT INSTRUMENTS CORPORATION

William B. Richman, president of the Measurement Instruments Corporation, was explaining his organization arrangements to the board of directors. His organization chart is shown on page 178.

When asked by a board member whether he thought he had too many people reporting to him, Mr. Richman replied: "I do not believe in the traditional principle of span of control, or span of management, that managers should have only four or five persons reporting to them. This is what makes waste and bureaucracy. All my subordinates are good people and know what they are doing. All can reach me readily with their problems when they have them. All feel close to the top because they are close to the top. Moreover, I want to know firsthand how every person is doing and to detect any weakness or errors as soon as possible. Furthermore, if a store manager at Sears, Roebuck can have twenty-five to thirty persons reporting to him, I ought to be able to handle nineteen. In addition, too few reporting to a manager doesn't give him enough to do, and I assume that you hired me to give the company my full time."

1. How would you respond to Mr. Richman's arguments?

2. If you were a member of the board of directors, what would you suggest Mr. Richman do?

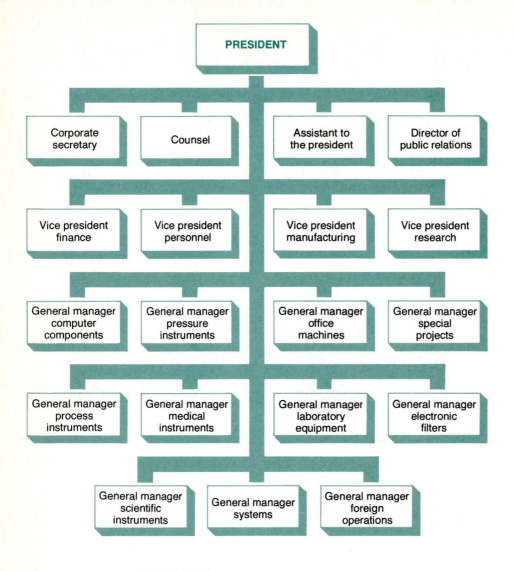

PRESIDENT

Corporate secretary

Counsel

Assistant to the president

Director of public relations

Vice president finance

Vice president personnel

Vice president manufacturing

Vice president research

General manager computer components

General manager pressure instruments

General manager office machines

General manager special projects

General manager process instruments

General manager medical instruments

General manager laboratory equipment

General manager electronic filters

General manager scientific instruments

General manager systems

General manager foreign operations

CASE 7-2
AMERICAN AIRCRAFT COMPANY

The management consultant was lunching with Allen Murray, the president of American Aircraft Corporation. She did this quite often, largely in order to facilitate communication between them.

"This just isn't my day," she told the president. "For instance, I was out in the factory an hour ago, I happened to run into the plant manager, so I asked him, 'Why do you have that conference room filled with people every morn-

ing?' 'Well,' the plant manager replied, 'the people in there, some twenty-two of them, represent assembly, production control, shipping, and accounting. They meet each day for 3 hours. They iron out the problems we have in coordinating effort around here. It is effective as a means of maintaining our shipping schedule.

"Then," she continued, "just as I reached the administration building, I met the sales manager.

He really looked wrung out like a rag. He told me that the weekly Tuesday meeting of department managers had just concluded. It appears that it was my friend's turn to be at the center of the stage explaining the performance reports of his department. Every week his division manager holds a staff meeting given over to reviewing the performance of one of the departments. My friend did say with a spark of malice that next week it will be the turn of engineering."

"I don't see why you are depressed by these events," Mr. Murray remarked.

"Well, it is just this way. I think that these techniques of communication are all wrong. They are expensive, they tend to expose individual managers to criticism before their associates, and they create the wrong circumstances for corrective action. There are other and better means of control. It seems managers agree with theory but never let it influence their practices."

1. Was the consultant right in being depressed about what she had found?

2. What do you believe was wrong with the methods of communication being used?

3. What would you have done to solve the communications problem without having so many long staff meetings?

REFERENCES

1. Chester I. Barnard, *The Functions of the Executive* (Cambridge, Mass.: Harvard University Press, 1938, 1964).

2. Keith Davis and John Newstrom, *Human Behavior at Work* (New York: McGraw-Hill Book Company, 1985) p. 308.

3. In much of the literature of management, this is referred to as the "span of control." Despite the widespread use of this term, we prefer to use "span of management," since the span is one of management and not merely of control, which is only one function of managing.

4. Lyndall Urwick, "Axioms of Organization," *Public Administration Magazine (London)* (October 1955), pp. 348–349. However, in other writings, Urwick modified this position by saying that "no person should supervise more than five, or at the most, six, direct subordinates *whose work interlocks*." See *Notes on the Theory of Organization* (New York: American Management Association, 1952), p. 53.

5. As summarized in *Business Week* (Aug. 18, 1951), pp. 102–103. Healey found similar variations in his study of 409 manufacturing companies in Ohio, although the median was six subordinates. See J. H. Healey, *Executive Co-ordination and Control* (Columbus: Ohio State University Press, 1956), p. 66.

6. Robert D. Dewar and Donald P. Simet, "A Level Specific Prediction of Spans of Control Examining the Effects of Size, Technology, and Specialization," *Journal of the Academy of Management* (March 1981), pp. 5–24.

7. Ricky W. Griffin, *Management* (Boston: Houghton Mifflin Company, 1984), chap. 22.

8. Henry Mintzberg, *The Nature of Managerial Work* (New York: Harper & Row, 1973), chap. 4; James Brian Quinn, "Managing Innovation: Controlled Chaos," *Harvard Business Review* (May–June 1985), pp. 73–84. Entrepreneurship has also been extended to public organizations. See Ravi Ramamurti, "Public Entrepreneurs: Who They Are and How They Operate," *California Management Review* (Spring 1986), pp. 142–158.

9. Peter F. Drucker, "The Discipline of Innovation," *Harvard Business Review* (May–June 1985), pp. 67–72. See also Peter F. Drucker, "A Prescription for Entrepreneurial Management," *Industry Week* (Apr. 29, 1985), pp. 33–40.

10. Gifford Pinchot III, *Intrapreneuring* (New York: Harper & Row, 1985).

11. The story has been reported widely, including the videotape "In Search of Excellence," Pinchot, *Intrapreneuring* (1985), and Lester C. Krogh, "Can the Entrepreneurial Spirit Exist Within a Large Company?" *3M: An Executive Message,* Delivered at the Conference Board, Conference on Research and Development, New York, April 25, 1984.

FOR FURTHER INFORMATION

Barnard, Chester I. *The Functions of the Executive* (Cambridge, Mass.: Harvard University Press 1938, 1964).

Barlett, Christopher A. "MNCs: Get Off the Reorganization Merry-Go-Round," *Harvard Business Review* (March–April 1983), pp. 138–146.

Bowen, Donald D., and Robert D. Hisrich. "The Female Entrepreneur: A Career Development Perspective," *Academy of Management Review* (April 1986), pp. 393–407.

Chandler, Alfred D. *Strategy and Structure* (Cambridge, Mass.: The M.I.T. Press, 1962).

Drucker, Peter F. *Innovation and Entrepreneurship: Practices and Principles* (New York: Harper & Row, 1985). For a review of this book see David E. Gumpert, "Stalking the Entrepreneur," *Harvard Business Review* (May–June 1986), pp. 32–36.

Jackson, John H., and Cyril P. Morgan. *Organization Theory* (Englewood Cliffs, N.J.: Prentice-Hall, 1982).

Katz, Daniel, and Robert L. Kahn. *The Social Psychology of Organizations,* 2d ed. (New York: John Wiley & Sons, 1978).

Koontz, Harold. "Making Theory Operational: The Span of Management," in Harold Koontz, Cyril O'Donnell, and Heinz Weihrich (eds.), *Management: A Book of Readings,* 5th ed. (New York: McGraw-Hill Book Company, 1980), pp. 232–240.

Kuhn, A., and R. D. Beam. *The Logic of Organization* (San Francisco: Jossey-Bass, 1982).

Lawrence, Paul R., and Jay W. Lorsch. *Organization and Environment* (Homewood, Ill.: Richard D. Irwin, 1969).

March, James G., and Herbert A. Simon. *Organizations* (New York: John Wiley & Sons, 1958).

Miner, John B. *Theories of Organizational Structure and Process* (Chicago: Dryden Press, 1982).

Mintzberg, Henry. *Structure in Fives—Designing Effective Organizations* (Englewood Cliffs, N.J.: Prentice-Hall, 1983).

Naisbitt, John, and Patricia Aburdene. *Re-Inventing the Corporation* (New York: Warner Books, 1985). For a review see David E. Gumpert, "Stalking the Entrepreneur," *Harvard Business Review* (May–June 1986), pp. 32–36.

Pearce, John A., II, and Fred R. David. "A Social Network Approach to Organizational Design-Performance," *Academy of Management Review* (July 1983), pp. 436–444.

Scott, William G., Terence R. Mitchell, and Philip H. Birnbaum. *Organization Theory—A Structural and Behavioral Analysis,* 4th ed. (Homewood, Ill.: Richard D. Irwin, 1981).

Van Fleet, David D., and Arthur G. Bedeian. "A History of the Span of Management," *Academy of Management Review* (July 1977), pp. 356–372.

Basic Departmentation

CHAPTER OBJECTIVES

After reading this chapter, you should be able to:

1. Identify the basic patterns of traditional departmentation and analyze their advantages and disadvantages.

2. Analyze matrix organizations, particularly as they have been used in engineering and product management, and outline the steps that can be taken to avoid dangers of disunity of command.

3. Understand the modern departmentation according to strategic business units.

4. Recognize that there is no single pattern of departmentation to use and that responsible managers must select patterns that will assist in accomplishing enterprise objectives in the light of the particular situation.

*T*he limitation on the number of subordinates that can be directly managed would restrict the size of enterprises if it were not for the device of departmentation. Grouping activities and people into departments makes it possible to expand organizations—at least in theory—to an indefinite degree. Departments, however, differ with respect to the basic patterns used to group the activities. We will deal with the nature of these patterns, developed out of logic and practice, and their relative merits in the following sections.

At the outset, let us emphasize that there is no single best way of departmentizing applicable to all organizations or to all situations. The pattern that will be used will depend on given situations and on what managers believe will yield the best results for them in the situation they face.

DEPARTMENTATION BY SIMPLE NUMBERS

Departmentation by simple numbers was once an important method in the organization of tribes, clans, and armies. Although it is rapidly falling into disuse, it still may have certain application in modern society.

The simple-numbers method of departmentizing is achieved by tolling off persons who are to perform the same duties and putting them under a manager. It is, as you recall from the previous chapter, what Moses did in organizing his large group. The essential fact is not what these people do, where they work, or what they work with, but that the success of the undertaking depends only upon the number of people involved in it.

Even though a quick examination may impress an investigator with the number of people departmentized on a human resource basis, the usefulness of this organizational device has declined with each passing century. For one thing, technology has advanced, demanding more specialized and different skills. In the United States, the last stronghold of common labor was agriculture, and even here it is restricted more and more to the harvesting of fewer and fewer crops as farming operations become larger and more specialized.

A second reason for the decline of departmentizing purely by number is that groups composed of specialized personnel are frequently more efficient than those based on mere numbers. The reorganization of the defense forces of the United States on this basis is a case in point. People skilled in the use of different types of weapons have been combined into single units. For example, the addition of artillery and tactical air support to the traditional infantry division makes it a much more formidable fighting unit than if each were organized separately.

A third and long-standing reason for the decline of departmentation by numbers is that it is useful only at the lowest level of the organization structure. As soon as any other factor besides pure human power becomes important, the simple-numbers basis of departmentation fails to produce good results.

DEPARTMENTATION BY TIME

One of the oldest forms of departmentation, generally used at lower levels of the organization, is to group activities on the basis of time. The use of shifts is common in many enterprises where for economic, technological, or other reasons the normal workday will not suffice. Examples of this kind of departmentation can be found in hospitals, where around-the-clock patient care is essential. Similarly, the fire department has to be ready to respond to emergencies at any time. But there are also technological reasons for the use of shifts. A steel furnace, for example, cannot be started and turned off at will. Instead, the process of making steel is continuous and requires workers to work in three shifts.

Advantages

From these few illustrations you can see a number of advantages of departmentation by time. First, services can be rendered that go beyond the typical 8-hour day, often extending to 24 hours a day. Second, it makes possible processes that cannot be interrupted but that require a continuing cycle. Third, expensive capital equipment can be used more than 8 hours a day when workers in several shifts use the same machines. Fourth, some people—students attending classes during the day, for instance—find it convenient to work at night.

Disadvantages

But departmentation by time also has disadvantages. First, supervision may be lacking during the night shift. Second, there is the fatigue factor; it is difficult for most people to switch, for instance, from day to night shift and vice versa. Third, the changing of the shifts may cause problems in coordination and communication. In a hospital, for example, nurses from different shifts attending a patient may not be familiar with the patient's particular problems. In a factory, the night shift may not clean up the machines to be used by the day shift people. Fourth, the payment of overtime rates can increase the cost of the product or service.

DEPARTMENTATION BY ENTERPRISE FUNCTION

The grouping of activities in accordance with the functions of an enterprise—functional departmentation—embodies what enterprises typically do. Since all enterprises undertake the creation of something useful and desired by others, the basic enterprise functions are production (creating utility or adding utility to a good or service), selling (finding customers, patients, clients, students, or members who will agree to accept the good or service at a price or for a cost), and financing (raising and collecting, safeguarding, and expending the funds of the enterprise). It has been logical to group these activities into such departments as engineering, production, sales or marketing, and finance. Figure 8-1 shows a typical functional grouping for a manufacturing company.

Often, these particular terms do not appear in the organization chart. First, there is no generally accepted terminology: Manufacturing enterprises employ the terms "production," "sales," and "finance"; a wholesaler is concerned with such activities as "buying," "selling," and "finance"; and a railroad is involved with "operations," "traffic," and "finance."

A second reason for variance of terms is that basic activities often differ in importance: Hospitals have no selling departments; churches, no production departments. This does not mean that these activities are not undertaken, but merely that they are unspecialized or of such minor importance that they are combined with other activities.

A third reason for the absence of sales, production, or finance departments on many organization charts is that other methods of departmentation may have been deliberately selected. Those responsible for the enterprise may decide to organize on the basis of product, customer, territory, or marketing channel (the way goods or services reach the user).

Functional departmentation is the most widely employed basis for organizing activities and is present in almost every enterprise at some level in the organization structure. The characteristics of the selling, production, and finance functions of enterprises are so widely recognized and thoroughly understood that they are the basis not only of departmental organization but also most often of departmentation at the top level.

Coordination of activities may be achieved through rules and procedures, various aspects of planning (e.g., goals and budgets), the organizational hierarchy, personal contacts, and sometimes liaison departments. Such a department may be used between engineering and manufacturing to handle design or change problems.[1]

Advantages

The most important advantage of functional departmentation is that it is a logical and time-proven method. It is also the best way of making certain that the power and prestige of the basic activities of the enterprise will be defended by the top managers. This is an important consideration among functional managers, for they see on every side the encroachments of staff and service groups, which sometimes threaten the security of the principal line executives. Another advantage is that functional departmentation follows the principle of occupational specialization, thereby making for efficiency in the utilization of people. Still other advantages are that it simplifies training and, because the top managers are responsible for the end results, furnishes a means of tight control at the top.

Disadvantages

In spite of the advantages of functional departmentation, there are times when the claims of other methods seem even stronger. The size of the geographic area

FIGURE 8-1

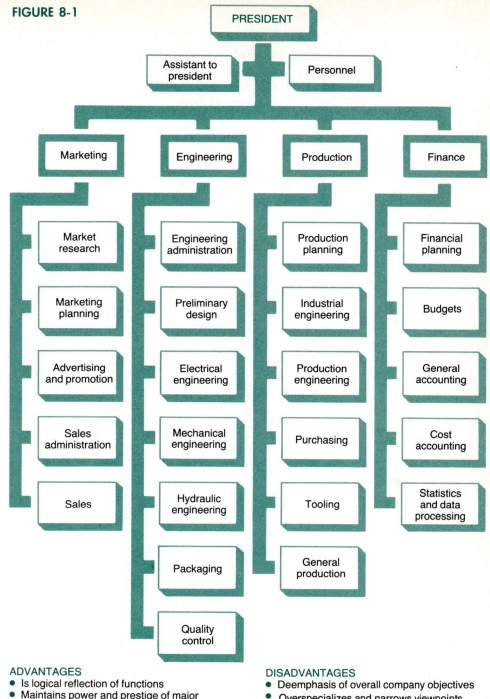

PRESIDENT

Assistant to president

Personnel

Marketing	Engineering	Production	Finance
Market research	Engineering administration	Production planning	Financial planning
Marketing planning	Preliminary design	Industrial engineering	Budgets
Advertising and promotion	Electrical engineering	Production engineering	General accounting
Sales administration	Mechanical engineering	Purchasing	Cost accounting
Sales	Hydraulic engineering	Tooling	Statistics and data processing
	Packaging	General production	
	Quality control		

ADVANTAGES
- Is logical reflection of functions
- Maintains power and prestige of major functions
- Follows principle of occupational specialization
- Simplifies training
- Furnishes means of tight control at top

DISADVANTAGES
- Deemphasis of overall company objectives
- Overspecializes and narrows viewpoints of key personnel
- Reduces coordination between functions
- Responsibility for profits is at the top only
- Slow adaptation to changes in environment
- Limits development of general managers

A FUNCTIONAL ORGANIZATION GROUPING (MANUFACTURING COMPANY).

over which an enterprise operates may call for territorial grouping of activities; the production or purchase of numerous product lines, or of products designed for certain buyer classifications, may call for grouping along product or customer lines. In addition, functional departmentation may tend to de-emphasize overall enterprise objectives. Accountants, production experts, and salespeople, working in specialized departments, often have problems seeing the business as a whole, and coordination among them is frequently difficult to achieve. They develop attitudes and other behavior patterns involving loyalty to a functional department and not to the enterprise as a whole. Such "walls" between functional departments are common and it requires considerable effort to break them down.

Another disadvantage is that only the chief executive officer can be held responsible for profits. In small firms, this is all right, but in large firms the burden becomes too heavy for one person to bear. Also, this kind of departmentation makes it difficult to adapt quickly to environmental changes.[2] What is perhaps most important is that since the lowest general managerial position is that of the president or the executive vice-president, the functionally organized company is not the best training ground for promotable top-management people.

DEPARTMENTATION BY TERRITORY OR GEOGRAPHY

Departmentation based on territory is rather common in enterprises that operate over wide geographic areas. In this case, it may be important that activities in a given area or territory should be grouped and assigned to a manager, for example, as shown in Figure 8-2.

Extent of Use

Territorial departmentation is especially attractive to large-scale firms or other enterprises whose activities are physically or geographically dispersed. However, a plant may be local in its activities and still assign the personnel in its security department on a territorial basis, placing two guards, for example, at each of the south and west gates. Department stores assign floorwalkers on this basis, and it is a common way to assign janitors, window washers, and the like. Business firms resort to this method when similar operations are undertaken in different geographic areas, as in automobile assembly, chain retailing and wholesaling, and oil refining. Many government agencies—the Internal Revenue Service, the Federal Reserve Board, the federal courts, and the Postal Service, among others—adopt this basis of organization in their efforts to provide like services simultaneously across the nation. Territorial departmentation is most often used in sales and in production; it is not used in finance, which is usually concentrated at the headquarters.

Advantages

Departmentation by territory, or geography, offers a number of advantages. It places responsibility at a lower level, encourages local participation in decision

FIGURE 8-2

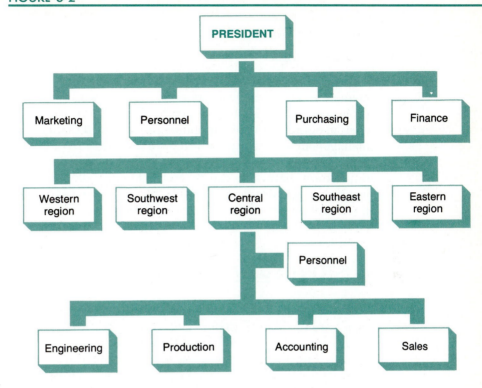

ADVANTAGES

- Places responsibility at a lower level
- Places emphasis on local markets and problems
- Improves coordination in a region
- Takes advantage of economies of local operations
- Better face-to-face communication with local interests
- Furnishes measurable training ground for general managers

DISADVANTAGES

- Requires more persons with general manager abilities
- Tends to make maintenance of economical central services difficult and may require services such as personnel or purchasing at the regional level
- Increases problem of top management control

A TERRITORIAL, OR GEOGRAPHIC, ORGANIZATION GROUPING (MANUFACTURING COMPANY).

making, and improves coordination of activities in a region. Managers can give special attention to the needs and problems of local markets. Thus, they may recruit local salespeople who are familiar with the special situation in the area. Moreover, these salespeople can spend more time selling and less time traveling.

Production may also be organized on a territorial basis by establishing plants in a particular region. This can reduce transportation costs and delivery time. Moreover, labor rates may be lower in certain regions, and producing things locally may create jobs and goodwill in the local community.

Geographic departmentation improves face-to-face communication with local people. Also, since the manager in a territory has to carry out many different functional and managerial activities, this type of organization provides a good training ground for general managers.

Disadvantages

There are also disadvantages in organizing territorially. This kind of departmentation requires more persons with general managerial abilities, and a shortage of them is often a factor limiting the growth of an enterprise. Moreover, geographic departmentation tends to lead to duplication of services. Thus, managers of a territory want to have their own purchasing, personnel, accounting, and other services, services that are also carried out in the home office. This duplication, naturally, can be costly. Finally, geographic departmentation may increase the problem of control by top managers who, at the headquarters, may find it difficult to monitor the activities of the departments located in various territories.

CUSTOMER DEPARTMENTATION

The grouping of activities to reflect a primary interest in customers is common in a variety of enterprises. Customers are the key to the way activities are grouped when each of the different things an enterprise does for them is managed by one department head. The industrial sales department of a wholesaler who also sells to retailers is a case in point. Business owners and managers frequently arrange activities on this basis to cater to the requirements of clearly defined customer groups, and educational institutions offer regular and extension courses to serve different groups of students.

There are difficult decisions to be made in separating some types of customer departments from product departments. For example, in the great central cash markets for agricultural products, the loan officers of commercial banks frequently specialize in fruit, vegetables, or grain even to the point where an individual officer will make loans only on wheat or oranges. This is a case of customer departmentation, since loan service is provided by type of customer. Figure 8-3 illustrates a typical customer departmentation in a large bank.

Advantages

Customer departmentation can address the special and widely varied needs of customers for clearly defined services. The manufacturer who sells to both wholesalers and industrial buyers frequently can meet their special needs by setting up separate departments.

Nonbusiness groups follow similar practices. The extension services of universities, such as night-school divisions, are arranged, with respect to time, subject matter, and sometimes instructors, to appeal to an entirely different group of students from those who attend the university on a full-time day basis. The operations of a United Way drive are arranged on the basis of different "customer" classifications. And departments of the federal government are set

FIGURE 8-3

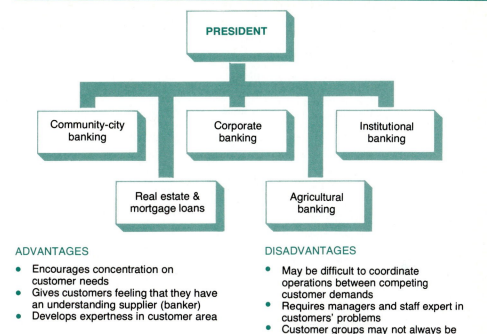

ADVANTAGES

- Encourages concentration on customer needs
- Gives customers feeling that they have an understanding supplier (banker)
- Develops expertness in customer area

DISADVANTAGES

- May be difficult to coordinate operations between competing customer demands
- Requires managers and staff expert in customers' problems
- Customer groups may not always be clearly defined (for example, large corporate firms vs. other corporate businesses)

CUSTOMER DEPARTMENTATION IN A LARGE BANK.

up to care for farmers, business people, industrial workers, the elderly, and other specific groups.

Disadvantages

Customer departmentation is not without certain drawbacks. There is, for instance, the difficulty of coordination between this type of department and those organized on other bases, with constant pressure from the managers of customer departments for special treatment.

Another disadvantage is the possibility of underemployment of facilities and labor-specialized workers in customer groups. In periods of recession, some customer groups may all but disappear, for example, machine-tool buyers; in periods of expansion, the unequal development of customer groups and demands is characteristic.

PROCESS OR EQUIPMENT DEPARTMENTATION

Manufacturing firms often group activities around a process or a type of equipment. Such a basis of departmentation can be found in paint or electroplating

FIGURE 8-4

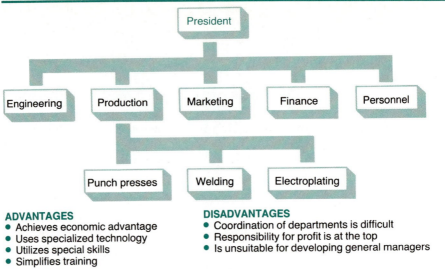

ADVANTAGES
- Achieves economic advantage
- Uses specialized technology
- Utilizes special skills
- Simplifies training

DISADVANTAGES
- Coordination of departments is difficult
- Responsibility for profit is at the top
- Is unsuitable for developing general managers

PROCESS OF EQUIPMENT DEPARTMENTATION.

process grouping or by the arrangement in one plant area of punch presses or automatic screw machines. In this kind of departmentation, people and materials are brought together in order to carry out a particular operation. Figure 8-4 illustrates such an organizational arrangement.

One common example of equipment departmentation is the electronic data-processing department. As installations for data processing have become expensive and complex, with ever-increasing capacities, they have tended to be organized in a separate department. Most large and even medium-size companies have such departments. In some cases, computer stations connected to an enterprise's central computer (or an outside one on a time-sharing or leasing basis), minicomputers, and electronic desk computers have tended to slow the growth of centralized computer departments. However, major data-processing departments will unquestionably continue to exist and to be placed fairly high in the organization structure.

DEPARTMENTATION BY PRODUCT

The grouping of activities on the basis of product or product lines has long been growing in importance in multiline, large-scale enterprises. It can be seen as an evolutionary process. Typically, companies and other enterprises adopting this form were organized by enterprise functions. With the growth of the firm, production managers, sales and service managers, and engineering executives encountered problems of size. The managerial job became complex, and the span of management limited their ability to increase the number of immediate subordinate managers. At this point, reorganization on a product division basis became necessary. This structure permits top management to delegate to a division executive extensive authority over the manufacturing, sales, service, and engineering functions that relate to a given product or product line and to exact a considerable degree of profit responsibility from each of these managers. Figure 8-5 shows an example of a typical product organization grouping for a manufacturing company.[3]

Advantages

Product or product line is an important basis for departmentation because it facilitates the use of specialized capital (e.g., a press for molding car bodies),

FIGURE 8-5

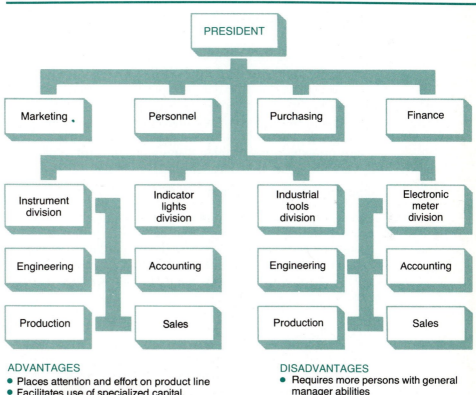

ADVANTAGES

- Places attention and effort on product line
- Facilitates use of specialized capital, facilities, skills, and knowledge
- Permits growth and diversity of products and services
- Improves coordination of functional activities
- Places responsibility for profits at the division level
- Furnishes measurable training ground for general managers

DISADVANTAGES

- Requires more persons with general manager abilities
- Tends to make maintenance of economical central services difficult
- Presents increased problem of top management control

A PRODUCT ORGANIZATION GROUPING (MANUFACTURING COMPANY).

facilitates a certain type of coordination, and permits the maximum use of personal skills and specialized knowledge. For example, the sales effort of a particular person may be most effective when confined to lubricants, or conveyors, or power plants, each of which is best sold by the expert thoroughly familiar with the product. Where the potential volume of business is high enough to fully employ such salespeople, the advantages of product departmentation are significant. If production of an item, or closely related items, is sufficiently large to employ fully specialized facilities, strong pressure may be felt for product departmentation in order to realize economic advantages in manufacturing, assembly, or handling. Note also that this kind of departmentation permits growth and diversity of products and services offered by the firm.

If it is important for activities relating to a particular product to be coordinated, then product departmentation may be preferred. Better timing and customer service can thus sometimes be provided. If sales and engineering efforts are also located in the plant, cooperation with production can be exceptionally good. We will consider later other factors that may reduce this advantage.

Finally, profit responsibility can be exacted from product department managers. Where they supervise the sales, production, engineering, service, and cost functions, they may be held responsible for certain profit goals. They have the responsibility for producing a profit along with other similarly organized groups, and this enables top managers to evaluate more intelligently the contribution of each product line to total profit. Moreover, this kind of departmentation provides a measurable training ground for general managers.

Some Notes of Caution

In considering these advantages, however, it is essential to avoid oversimplification. Product-line managers may be saddled with heavy overhead costs, allocated from the expense of operating the headquarters office, perhaps a central research division, and, frequently, many central service divisions. Product managers understandably resent being charged with costs over which they have no control.

Disadvantages

The disadvantages of product departmentation are similar to those of territorial departmentation. They include the necessity of having more persons with general managerial abilities available, the dangers of increased costs through duplication of central service and staff activities, and the problem of maintaining top-management control. The latter becomes especially important because a product division manager is, to a very great extent, in the same position as the chief executive of a single-product-line company. Enterprises that operate with product divisions must take care, as the General Motors Corporation has done, to place enough decision making and control at the headquarters level that the entire enterprise does not disintegrate.

MATRIX ORGANIZATION

Another kind of departmentation is matrix or grid organization, or project or product management. But, as you will later see, pure project management need not imply a grid or matrix. The essence of matrix organization normally is the combining of functional and product departmentation in the same organization structure. As is shown in Figure 8-6, which depicts matrix organization in an engineering department, there are functional managers in charge of engineering functions with an overlay of project managers responsible for the end product. While this form has been common in engineering and in research and development, it has also been widely used, although seldom drawn as a matrix, in product marketing organization.

We find this kind of organization frequently in construction (such as building a bridge), in aerospace (e.g., designing and launching a weather satellite), in marketing (e.g., advertising campaign for a major new product), in the installation of an electronic data-processing system, or in management consulting firms in which professional experts work together on a project.[4]

Why Matrix Management Is Used

As companies and customers have become increasingly interested in end results, that is, in the final product or completed project, there has been pressure to establish responsibility for ensuring such end results. Of course, this could be accomplished by organizing along traditional product department lines. This is often done, even in engineering, where a project manager is put in charge of all the engineering and support personnel necessary to accomplish an entire project. This kind of organization is depicted in Figure 8-7.

But pure project organization may not be feasible for a number of reasons. For example, the project may not be able to utilize certain specialized engineering personnel or equipment full time, a solid-state physicist may be needed only occasionally, or the project may need only part-time use or an expensive environmental test laboratory or a prototype shop. Also, the project may be of relatively short duration. Although there is no logical reason why an organization structure should not be changed daily or monthly, there is the practical reason that people, particularly highly trained professionals, simply may not tolerate the insecurity of frequent organization change. Another reason why pure project organization may not be feasible is that highly trained professionals (and some that are not so highly trained) generally prefer to be allied organizationally with their professional group. They feel more at home in the functional department; they feel that their professional reputation and advancement will be better served by belonging to such a group than by being allied with a project; and they believe that their superiors, if they are professionals in the same field, will be more likely to appreciate their expertise at times of salary advances, promotions, or layoffs. These feelings ordinarily exist not only among engineers and scientists but also among lawyers, accountants, and university professors.

The reasons for existence of a matrix organization in commercial or indus-

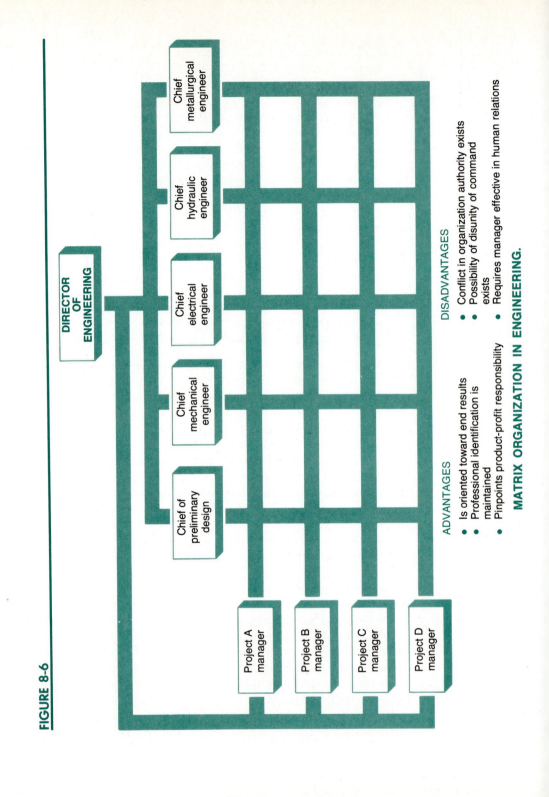

FIGURE 8-6

DIRECTOR OF ENGINEERING

Chief of preliminary design

Chief mechanical engineer

Chief electrical engineer

Chief hydraulic engineer

Chief metallurgical engineer

Project A manager

Project B manager

Project C manager

Project D manager

ADVANTAGES

- Is oriented toward end results
- Professional identification is maintained
- Pinpoints product-profit responsibility

DISADVANTAGES

- Conflict in organization authority exists
- Possibility of disunity of command exists
- Requires manager effective in human relations

MATRIX ORGANIZATION IN ENGINEERING.

194

FIGURE 8-7

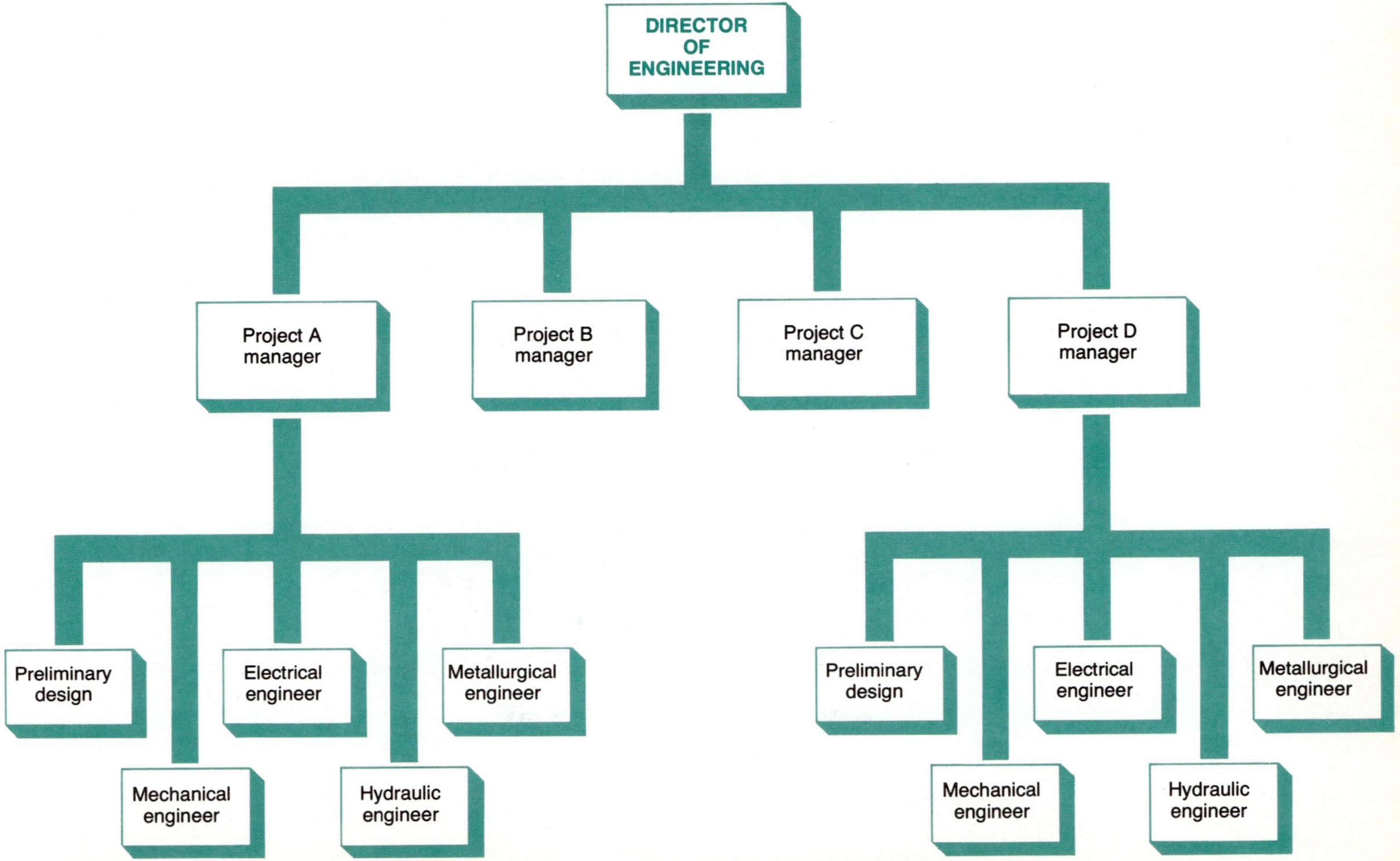

PROJECT ORGANIZATION IN ENGINEERING.

trial product management may be somewhat different. In a soap and detergent company, for example, the top management may want individual responsibility for profit to exist for a given product or brand. If the company had only one product or brand, there would obviously be no problem; the chief executive would have profit responsibility. If the company could organize through the use of an integrated (research, marketing, manufacturing) product division, then the division manager would have profit responsibility. But where, as in a multi-product soap and detergent company, technology and economics dictate that the company can hardly have separate manufacturing facilities or sales forces for each product, the way to get a degree of profit responsibility is to overlay, in some way, a product manager with responsibility for profit for a given brand or product.

Variations in Practice

There are many variations of the project or product manager role. In some cases, the project or product managers have no authority to tell any functional department to do anything. In these cases, they may be only information gatherers, keeping tabs on how their project or product is proceeding and reporting to a top executive when significant deviations from plans occur. Their role might be that of persuader, using knowledge and personal persuasiveness to get results. Obviously, these roles have some very serious drawbacks, particularly if the manager without any organization power whatsoever is actually held responsible for end results. No wonder that turnover among those who hold such positions has been high!

Another variation in practice is simply to draw a grid or matrix, like that in Figure 8-6, showing certain managers in charge of functional departments and others in charge of projects or products. This grid is usually intended to represent a pure case of dual command. The results are predictable. If something goes wrong with a project or product, it is often difficult for a top superior to know whose fault it is and where the difficulties really lie. Also, in such cases, there tend to arise the usual friction, buck passing, and confusion one would expect to result from disunity of command.

Solutions in Engineering and Research and Development

The more sophisticated companies in high-technology industries that have found no alternative to matrix management have solved the problem of confused authority and multiple subordination largely by clarification of the authorities and responsibilities of the functional and project managers. Project managers are normally given authority over the integrity of a total design; they usually have the task of dealing with customers, although in many instances this responsibility will be passed on to the marketing department; they are given authority over budget and in this case become essentially buyers of services from the functional managers; and they are given the authority to work out schedules and priorities for their projects with the functional departments. If they cannot work out priorities because of the claims of other project managers and if they and the other project managers cannot compromise, the matter of priorities goes to a higher authority, usually the manager who has primary responsibility for relationships with all customers.

Under this system, functional managers are given authority over the people in their area and over the integrity of engineering or research work done by them. Thus, between the project manager and the functional manager, much of the problem of disunity of command is eliminated, although there still may be a degree of conflict and uncertainty in such borderline areas as total project design accuracy and integrity.

Solutions in Product Management

Although the Procter & Gamble Company and Libby, McNeil & Libby have successfully used product management in the marketing of their products for many years, and although other prominent companies like Lever Brothers and General Foods have long used it, most of the development of its use has occurred more recently.

As might be expected, the term **product manager** is used in many ways; it may be applied to the general manager of an integrated product division or to someone who is little more than a staff assistant in the marketing head's organization who gathers information and makes recommendations. But a matrix form of organization does not develop until product managers have some degree of authority over functional departments that do not report to them.

Research on the degree of authority granted to product managers shows that in most companies, they may be held to some degree responsible for the success of the brands assigned to them but may be given either little or no authority to accomplish these results; they may merely be assigned the ambiguous role of "charming persuader." It is interesting that this promising organizational device, aiming as it does in a functionally organized company toward giving responsibility for end results to product managers, should repeat the history of vagueness and lack of authority experienced for years in engineering.

However, a number of companies have begun to solve this problem of authority in a way that makes this a real and reasonably workable matrix organization. One of the best solutions is the one that has been used by Procter & Gamble for many years. In this company, a brand manager (located in the advertising department, since the company has long had a policy of preselling through advertising and promotion) derives authority in an interesting way. The brand manager develops the plan for a brand, covering not only advertising but also use of the field sales force, research assistance, packaging, and manufacturing programs, and then negotiates with the various functional departments on the part they will play in the program and the costs involved. After such a comprehensive brand program has been developed, it goes up the line in the company until it and other brand programs are finally approved by the chief executive. Armed with such an approved plan, the brand manager hardly needs any other authority. While the organization chart would not show a grid, the fact is that one exists through authority derived from plans approved at the top.

Problems with Matrix Management

Let us summarize some typical problems found in matrix management.[5]

1. There is the conflict between functional and project managers, both competing for limited resources (e.g., financial and human). Moreover, members on the project team may encounter role ambiguity.

2. Role conflict, role ambiguity, and role overload may result in stress for the functional and project managers as well as for the team members.

3. An imbalance of authority and power as well as horizontal and vertical influence of the project and functional managers can also lead to problems in matrix organizations.[6] If, for example, the functional manager has too much power, work for a project may receive a low priority and delay its completion. An imbalance of authority in favor of the project manager, on the other hand, may result in inefficiencies. The functional manager, for example, may frequently be required to change the machine setup to do work for various projects.

4. Because of the potential conflicts, managers may want to protect themselves against blame by putting everything in writing, resulting in increases in administration costs.

5. Matrix organization requires many time-consuming meetings.[7]

Guidelines for Making Matrix Management Effective[8]

Matrix management can be made more effective by following these guidelines:

1. Define the objectives of the project or task.

2. Clarify the roles, authorities, and responsibilities of managers and team members.

3. Ensure that influence is based on knowledge and information, rather than on rank.

4. Balance the power of functional and project managers.

5. Select an experienced manager for the project who can provide leadership.

6. Undertake organization and team development.

7. Install appropriate cost, time, and quality controls that report deviations from standards in a timely manner.

8. Reward project managers and team members fairly.

STRATEGIC BUSINESS UNITS (SBU)

More recently, companies have been using an organizational device generally referred to as a **strategic business unit (SBU).** These are distinct little businesses set up as units in a larger company to ensure that a certain product or product line is promoted and handled as though it were an independent business. One of the earlier users of this organizational device was the General Electric Company. This special organization unit was introduced to ensure that each product or product line of the hundreds offered by the company got the same attention it would if it were developed, produced, and marketed by an independent company. The device has also been used in some cases by companies for a major product line. Occidental Chemical Company, for example, used it for such products as phosphates, alkalis, and resins.[9]

To be called an SBU, it may have to meet specific criteria.[10] An SBU, for example must (1) have its own mission, distinct from other SBUs, (2) have definable groups of competitors, (3) prepare its own integrative plans, fairly distinct from other SBUs, (4) manage its resources in key areas, and (5) have a proper size—not too large, nor too small. You can see that in practice it might be difficult to define SBUs that meet all of these criteria.

For each SBU a manager (usually a "business manager") is appointed with responsibility for guiding and promoting the product from the research laboratory through product engineering, market research, production, packaging, and marketing, and with bottom-line responsibility for its profitability.[11] Thus, an SBU is given its own missions and goals, and a manager with the assistance of a full-time or part-time staff (people from other departments assigned to the SBU on a part-time basis) to develop and implement strategic and operating plans for the product. The organization of a typical SBU, that for phosphate of the Occidental Chemical Company, is shown in Figure 8-8. You will note that the business manager for phosphates has all the functions reporting to him or her that would be found necessary in a separate company.

Obviously, the major benefit of utilizing an SBU organization is to provide assurance that a product will not get "lost" among other products (usually those with larger sales and profits) in a large company. It preserves the attention and energies of a manager and staff whose job it is to guide and promote a product or product line. It is thus an organizational technique to preserve the entrepreneurial attention and drive so characteristic of the small company. In fact, it is an excellent means of promoting entrepreneurship which is likely to be so lacking in the large company.

CHOOSING THE PATTERN OF DEPARTMENTATION

There is no one best way of departmentizing applicable to all organizations and all situations.[12] Managers must determine what is best by looking at the situation

FIGURE 8-8

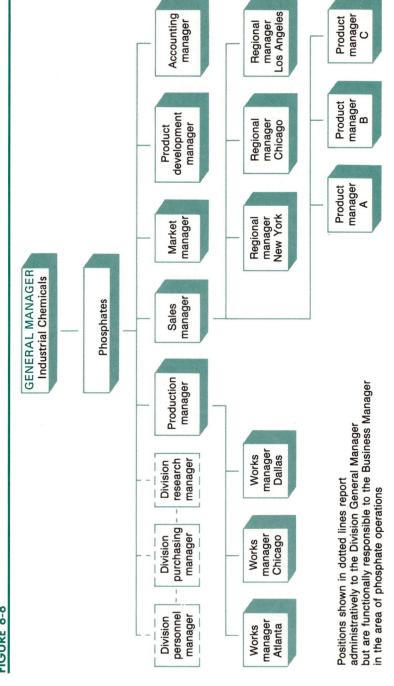

Positions shown in dotted lines report
administratively to the Division General Manager
but are functionally responsible to the Business Manager
in the area of phosphate operations

**TYPICAL STRATEGIC BUSINESS UNIT ORGANIZATION
IN A LARGE INDUSTRIAL CHEMICAL COMPANY.**

they face—the jobs to be done and the way they should be done, the people involved and their personalities, the technology employed in the department, the users being served, and other internal and external environmental factors in the situation. However, if they know the various patterns, their advantages, disadvantages, and dangers, practicing managers should be able to design the organization structure most suitable for their particular operations.[13]

The Aim: Achieving Objectives

Departmentation is not an end in itself but is simply a method of arranging activities to facilitate the accomplishment of objectives. Each method has its advantages and disadvantages. Consequently, the process of selection involves a consideration of the relative advantages of each type at each level in the organization structure. In all cases, the central question concerns the type of organizational environment that the manager wishes to design and the situation being faced. In our discussion of the alternative methods of departmentation, we showed that each method yields certain gains and involves certain costs.

Mixing Types of Departmentation

Another point to be highlighted concerns the mixing of types of departmentation with a functional area. For example, a wholesale drug firm has grouped the buying and selling activities relating to beverages in one product department, but has grouped, on the same level, all other selling activities on a territorial basis. A manufacturer of plastic goods has territorialized both the production and the sale of all its products except dinnerware, which is itself a product department. A functional department manager may, in other words, employ two or more bases for grouping activities on the same organizational levels. Such practices may be justified on logical grounds because the objective of departmentation is not to build a rigid structure, balanced in terms of levels and characterized by consistency and identical bases. The purpose is to group activities in the manner which will best contribute to achieving enterprise objectives. If a variety of bases does this, there is no reason why managers should not take advantage of the alternatives before them.

The logic of this view is frequently ignored by those who design organization structures. For some reason, possibly to make an organization chart look pretty or to maintain control, specialists often insist that all departmentized activities below the primary level of organization be grouped in exactly the same manner. For instance, the organization structure of the Internal Revenue Service at the regional and district levels is essentially the same, despite tremendous variation in district sizes. Firms with multiplants often organize them in the same way; thus, the same departments will be found in virtually all Sears, Roebuck and Company stores.

Creating an identical organization structure in similar enterprise groupings merely to make an organizational chart look nice is really not good practice. The organization planner may think it "looks better," but this is a poor reason for organizing in a particular way. The matter of control, however, is quite different. There may be very important reasons for comparing the operation of similarly organized plants, stores, and agencies. They all may be comparable profit centers; consequently, their managers can be more readily compared within this organization structure. Even though these, and others, are important arguments for similarity of organization structure, we must remember that no one organizes to control; people organize to produce efficiently and effectively. If the latter purpose is sacrificed for the former, the cost of control is too great.

FOR DISCUSSION

1. Some sociologists tell us that organization structuring is a social invention. What do you think they mean? Do they imply that there is a "right" or "wrong" way to organize? What test of whether an organization structure is "right" would you suggest?

2. If you were the president of a company that was organized along functional lines and a consultant suggested that you organize along territorial or product lines, what might concern you in following this recommendation?

3. Why do you think that many large companies have organized along product lines (for example, General Motors or Du Pont), while other large companies have territorial departments (for example, Prudential Life Insurance Company)?

4. Why do most large department store and supermarket chains organize their stores on a territorial basis and then organize the internal store units by products? Give examples from your own experience.

5. Why do most small companies use functionally organized departments?

6. Why are so many federal government agencies organized primarily on a territorial basis?

7. Do you see any reasons why managing by objectives may result in increased use of matrix organizational structures?

8. How does this chapter illustrate a situational approach to management?

EXERCISES/ACTION STEPS

1. Divide the class into groups of four or five students (depending on class size). Assign to each group one (or two if the class is small) kind(s) of departmentation. The groups should discuss (1) the nature of the assigned departmentation, (2) companies that use this departmental arrangement, (3) the advantages of the departmentation, and (4) the disadvantages of the departmentation.

2. Select a company and identify the kind(s) of departmentation(s) used by the enterprise. Draw an organization chart for the firm. Why do you think this company selected the kind of departmentation? Would you recommend a different kind of departmentation? State your reasons for your recommendation.

CASES

CASE 8-1
AGRICULTURAL FERTILIZER DIVISION OF
THE NORTHERN CHEMICAL CORPORATION

At the end of a busy day, a group of middle-level managers of the Agricultural Fertilizer Division of the Northern Chemical Corporation gathered to reflect on their problems. The headquarters of Northern Chemical had recently set up a central data-processing department in Houston, where all the corporation's data processing would be done for its various divisions located over the entire United States. At that time, the data-processing equipment of every division had been taken away from it, each division headquarters office was given a terminal connected to Houston, and each division was required to get any report processing it needed from the Houston facility.

The headquarters of the Agricultural Chemicals Division was located in Sacramento, California. This division had long concentrated on developing and selling fertilizers to the large agricultural growers in the West and on distributing its garden and house plant fertilizers to stores throughout the country. It had been very successful, with sales growing rapidly and profits even faster. But the line managers of the division were quite unhappy about not being able to have their own computer facilities to give them the analyses and reports they needed.

Bill Jacobs, production planning and control supervisor, was particularly disturbed about this move to centralize data processing. "There is no way," said Jacobs, "that I can plan our products, especially with our many products and customers and the demands of our large growers for good service, if Houston runs our programs. They do not always have the data needed in their data bank, and, by the time I get it worked out with them, I have lost much valuable time."

Barry Hill, district sales manager for Northern California, was even unhappier. He pointed out that he often needed to run productivity and profitability studies for large growers and he could not do so unless the division had a computer operation in its own offices in Sacramento. "The growers will never understand why I cannot make these analyses for them quickly and will never understand why they must be made in Houston; they will soon tell me that there are other companies that can serve their needs," moaned Hill.

"You do have a problem," said Mona Fredericks, head of statistical analyses and reports in the division controller's office. "But yours is a small one compared with mine. I have to get many special and regular reports to headquarters, to the division managers, and to all you people in sales, market research, product development, and production. You always want them right now and in the form you can use most easily. How can I do that for you now?"

The frustration reached its peak when Joe Morey, cost control supervisor, startled the group by saying, "Did you know that all the departments in our division are being charged fees each month for Houston's services and that these are higher than the costs when we each had our own little computer system?"

1. Do you agree that these people had a serious problem?

2. If you were one of them, what would you do about it?

3. If you were to look at this purely as an organization problem, what conclusions would you draw?

CASE 8-2
UNIVERSAL FOOD PRODUCTS COMPANY

Alexander Owen, president of the Universal Food Products Company, was tired of being the only one in his company actually responsible for profits. While he had good vice-presidents in charge of finance, sales, advertising, manufacturing, purchasing, and product research, he realized he could not hold any of them responsible for company profits, as much as he would like to. He often found it difficult even to hold them responsible for the contribution of their various areas to company profits. The sales vice-president, for example, had rather reasonably complained that he could not be fully responsible for sales when the advertising was ineffective, when the products customer stores wanted were not readily available from manufacturing, or when he did not have the new products he needed to meet competition. Likewise, the manufacturing vice-president had some justification when he made the point that he could not hold costs down and still be able to produce short runs so as to fill orders on short notice; moreover, financial controls would not allow the company to carry a large inventory of everything.

Mr. Owen had considered breaking his company down into six or seven segments by setting up product divisions with a manager over each with profit responsibility. But he found that this would not be feasible or economical since many of the company's branded food products were produced on the same factory equipment and used the same raw materials, and a salesperson calling on a store or supermarket could far more economically handle a number of related products than one or a few.

Consequently, Mr. Owen came to the conclusion that the best thing for him to do was to set up a system with six product managers reporting to a product marketing manager. Each product manager would be given responsibility for one or a few products and would oversee, for each product, all aspects of product research, manufacturing, advertising, and sales, thereby becoming the person responsible for the performance and profits of the products.

Mr. Owen realized that he could not give these product managers actual line authority over the various operating departments of the company since that would cause each vice-president and his or her department to report to six product managers and the product marketing manager, as well as the president. He was concerned about this problem, but he knew that some of the most successful large companies in the world had used the product manager system. Moreover, one of his friends on a university faculty had told him that he must expect some lack of clearness and some confusion in any organization and that this result might not be bad since it forced people to work together as teams.

Mr. Owen resolved to put in the product manager system as outlined and hope for the best. But he wondered how he could avoid the problem of confusion in reporting relationships.

1. Do you agree with Mr. Owen's program? Would you have done it differently?

2. Exactly what would you do to avoid any confusion in this organization?

REFERENCES

1. Jay R. Galbraith, "Matrix Organization Designs: How to Combine Functional and Project Forms," in Harold Koontz, Cyril O'Donnell, and Heinz Weihrich (eds.), *Management: A Book of Readings*, 5th ed. (New York: McGraw-Hill Book Company, 1980), pp. 292–300.

2. Thomas J. Peters and Robert H. Waterman, Jr., *In Search of Excellence* (New York: Harper & Row, 1982).

3. Product management is also used in nonmanufacturing companies. See, for example, Robert B. Fetter and Jean L. Freeman, "Diagnosis Related Groups: Product Line Management within Hospitals," *Academy of Management Review* (January 1986), pp. 41–54.

4. John M. Stewart, "Making Project Management Work" in Harold Koontz and Cyril O'Donnell (eds.), *Management: A Book of Readings*, 2d ed. (New York: McGraw-Hill Book Company, 1968), pp. 202–213; Kenneth Knight, in Koontz, O'Donnell, and Weihrich, *Management* (1980), pp. 301–312.

5. Based primarily on Knight, in *Management* (1980).

6. Although not directly related to matrix organization, an interesting discussion of power relationships is by Fernando Bartolomé and André Laurent, "The Manager: Master and Servant of Power," *Harvard Business Review*, (November–December 1986), pp. 77–81.

7. For additional information on limitations of matrix management, see Robert A. Pitts and John D. Daniels, "Aftermath of the Matrix Mania," *Columbia Journal of World Business* (Summer 1984), pp. 48–54.

8. Stewart, in *Management* (1968); Knight, in *Management* (1980); Jay Galbraith, *Designing Complex Organizations* (Reading, Mass.: Addison-Wesley Publishing Company, 1973), chap. 5. See also William H. Hoffmann, "Strategy Matrix," *Managerial Planning* (May–June 1985), pp. 4–9, 75.

9. For a discussion of SBUs, see W. K. Hall, "SBUs: Hot, New Topic in the Management of Diversification," *Business Horizons* (February 1978), pp. 13–23.

10. Frederick W. Gluck, "A Fresh Look at Strategic Management," *Journal of Business Strategy* (Fall 1985), pp. 4–19.

11. For a discussion of the effective use of business units see Boris Yavitz and William H. Newman, "What the Corporation Should Provide Its Business Units," *Journal of Business Strategy* (Summer 1982), pp. 14–19.

12. An argument for using relatively simple organizational forms, even for multinational companies, has been made after a study of four Swedish firms by Gunnar Hedlund, "Organization In-Between: The Evolution of the Mother-Daughter Structure of Managing Foreign Subsidiaries in Swedish MNCs," *Journal of International Business Studies* (Fall 1984), pp. 109–122.

13. For an interesting review of books on organizing, see P. H. Ginyer, "Designing Effective Organizations—Book Review Article," *Long Range Planning* (April 1984), pp. 151–156.

FOR FURTHER INFORMATION

Dalton, Dan R., William D. Todor, Michael J. Spendolini, Gordon J. Fielding, and Lyman W. Porter. "Organization Structure and Performance: A Critical Review," *Academy of Management Review* (January 1980), pp. 49–64.

Fredrickson, James W. "The Strategic Decision Process and Organizational Structure," *Academy of Management Review,* (April 1986), pp. 280–297.

Goggin, William C. "How the Multidimensional Structure Works at Dow Corning," *Harvard Business Review* (January–February 1974), pp. 54–65.

Herbert, Theodore T. "Strategy and Multinational Organization Structure: An Interorganizational Relationships Perspective," *Academy of Management Review* (April 1984), pp. 259–271.

Jackson, John H., and Cyril P. Morgan. *Organization Theory—A Macro Perspective for Management,* 2d ed. (Englewood Cliffs, N.J.: Prentice-Hall, 1982).

Mintzberg, Henry. *Structure in Fives—Designing Effective Organizations* (Englewood Cliffs, N.J.: Prentice. Hall, 1983).

Stieglitz, Harold. "On Concepts of Corporate Structure," in Harold Koontz, Cyril O'Donnell, and Heinz Weihrich (eds.), *Management: A Book of Readings,* 5th ed. (New York: McGraw-Hill Book Company, 1980), pp. 266–272.

Line/Staff Authority and Decentralization

CHAPTER OBJECTIVES

After reading this chapter, you should be able to:

1. Understand the nature of authority and power.

2. Distinguish between line and staff, realizing their nature as relationships rather than positions or people.

3. Explain the nature and use of functional authority as a mixture of line and staff.

4. Discuss the nature of centralization, decentralization, and delegation of authority.

5. Explain the factors that generally determine the degree of decentralization.

6. Make recommendations for obtaining the desired degree of decentralization.

7. Recognize the importance of obtaining balance in the centralization and decentralization of authority.

We have discussed the patterns of departmentation. We now consider another essential question: What kind of authority do we find in an organizational structure? The question has to do with the nature of authority relationships—the problem of line and staff. We will also deal with the question: How much authority should be delegated? The answer concerns decentralization of authority.

Without authority—the power to exercise discretion in making decisions— properly placed in managers, various departments cannot become smoothly working units harmonized for the accomplishment of enterprise objectives. Authority relationships, whether vertical or horizontal, are the factors that make organization possible, facilitate departmental activities, and bring coordination to an enterprise.

AUTHORITY AND POWER

Before concentrating on the authority in organization, it will be useful to distinguish between authority and power. **Power** is a much broader concept. It is the ability of individuals or groups to induce or influence the beliefs or actions of other persons or groups.[1] **Authority** in organization is the right in a position (and through it the person occupying the position) to exercise discretion in making decisions affecting others. It is, of course, one type of power, but power in an organization setting.

Although there are many different **bases of power**, the power we are most concerned with in this book is *legitimate* power.[2] It normally arises from position and derives from our cultural system of rights, obligations, and duties whereby a "position" is accepted by people as being "legitimate." In a privately owned business, authority of position arises primarily from the social institution (a "bundle of rights") of private property. In government, this authority arises basically from the institution of representative government. A traffic officer who gives you a traffic ticket gets the power to do so because we have a system of representative government in which we have elected legislators to make and provide for the enforcement of laws.

Power may also come from the *expertness* of a person or a group. This is the power of knowledge. Physicians, lawyers, and university professors may have considerable influence on others because they are respected for their special knowledge. Power may further exist as *referent* power, that is, influence which people or groups may exercise because people believe in them and their ideas. Thus, Martin Luther King had very little legitimate power, but, by the force of his personality, his ideas, and his ability to preach, he strongly influenced the behavior of many people. Likewise, a movie star or a military hero might possess considerable referent power.

In addition, power arises from the ability of some people to grant rewards. Purchasing agents, with little position power, might be able to exercise considerable influence by their ability to expedite or delay a much-needed spare part. Or university professors have considerable *reward* power; they can grant or withhold high grades.

Coercive power is still another type. Although closely related to reward power and normally arising from legitimate power, it is the power to punish, whether by firing a subordinate or withholding a merit increase.

While organization authority is the power to exercise discretion in decision making, it almost invariably arises from the power of position, or legitimate power.[3] When we speak of authority in managerial settings, we usually refer to the power of positions. At the same time, other factors, such as personality and style of dealing with people, are involved in leadership.[4]

LINE AND STAFF CONCEPTS

Much confusion has arisen both in literature and among managers as to what line and staff are; as a result, there is probably no area of management that causes more difficulties, more friction, and more loss of time and effectiveness. Yet line and staff relationships are important as an organizational way of life, and the authority relationships of members of an organization must necessarily affect the operation of the enterprise.

One widely held view of line and staff is that line functions are those that have direct impact on the accomplishment of the objectives of the enterprise. On the other hand, staff functions are to help the line persons to work most effectively in accomplishing the objectives. Those who hold to this view almost invariably classify production and sales (and sometimes finance) as line functions, and purchasing, accounting, personnel, plant maintenance, and quality control as staff functions.

The confusion arising from such a concept is immediately apparent. It is argued that purchasing, for example, merely helps in achieving the main goals of business because, unlike the production departments, such as painting or parts assembly, it is not directly essential. But is purchasing really any less essential to the achievement of company objectives? Could the company not store up painted or assembled parts and get along without these departments for a while as well as it could get along for a while without purchasing? And could not the same question be asked about other so-called staff and service departments, such as accounting, personnel, and plant maintenance? And there is probably nothing that could stop the satisfactory production and sale of most manufactured goods more completely than the failure of quality control.

The Nature of Line and Staff Relationships

A more precise and logically valid concept of line and staff is that they are simply a matter of relationships. Line authority gives a superior a line of authority over a subordinate. It exists in all organizations as an uninterrupted scale or series of steps. Hence, the **scalar principle** in organization: *The clearer the line of authority from the ultimate management position in an enterprise to every subordinate position, the clearer will be the responsibility for decision making and the more effective organization communication will be.* In many large enterprises, the steps are long and complicated, but even in the smallest, the very fact of organization introduces the scalar principle.

PERSPECTIVE:
LINE OR STAFF? WHAT IS YOUR CAREER GOAL?

The goal of many MBA graduates is to work in staff positions, using their analytical skills to advise line managers. In 1985, it has been reported, over a third of Harvard's MBA graduates choose such a career.[5] In earlier years, this percentage was even higher.

In the early and mid-1980s, partly due to the economy, the situation was changing as many large companies reduced their staff. For example, the task of strategy formulation was carried out more frequently by the line managers who also had to implement the strategy, rather than strategic planners in the headquarters. Consequently, people who were used to plan, advise, and analyze business situations, moved into line positions in which they were required to set priorities, make decisions, and motivate people to contribute to the aims of the enterprise.

While some staff personnel made an effective transition into line positions, others failed. One of the problems these "newcomers" encountered was the resentment of the "old-time" managers who saw the positions they aspired to taken by former staff. Clearly, line work is different from staff tasks. Having real authority for executing decisions can be exciting. But not everyone can make this transition. Thus, aspiring managers should carefully analyze their strengths, weaknesses, and motivations before choosing their career paths.

It therefore becomes apparent from the scalar principle that **line** authority is that relationship in which a superior exercises direct supervision over a subordinate—an authority relationship in direct line or steps.

The nature of the **staff** relationship is advisory. The function of people in a pure staff capacity is to investigate, research, and give advice to line managers.

Line and Staff Relationship or Departmentation?[6]

Some managers and writers regard line and staff as types of departments. Although a department may stand in a predominantly line or staff position with respect to other departments, we distinguish line and staff by *authority relationships* and not by what people do.

For example, one may think of the public relations department, to the extent that it is primarily advisory to the top executives, as a staff department. But within the department are line relationships; the director will stand in a line authority position with respect to his or her immediate subordinates. On the other hand, the vice-president in charge of production may head what is clearly and generally known as a line department. His or her job is not primarily advisory to the chief executive officer. If, however, the vice-president counsels the chief executive on overall company production policy, this relationship becomes one of staff.

When one looks at an organization structure as a whole, the general character of line and staff relationships for the total organization emerges. Certain departments are predominantly staff in their relationship to the entire organization. Other departments are primarily line.

Figure 9-1 portrays a simplified organization chart of a manufacturing company. The activities of the director of research and the director of public relations are apt to be mainly advisory to the mainstream of corporate operations and are consequently often considered staff activities. The finance, production,

FIGURE 9-1

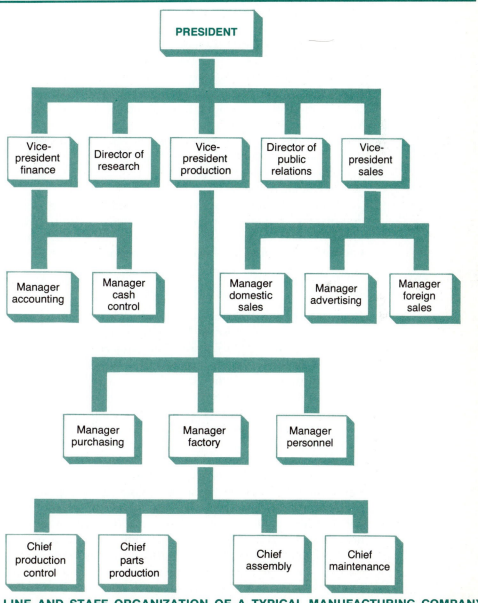

LINE AND STAFF ORGANIZATION OF A TYPICAL MANUFACTURING COMPANY.

and sales departments, with activities generally related to the main corporate functions, are ordinarily considered line departments.

Although it is often convenient and even correct to refer to one department as a line department and to another as a staff department, their activities do not so characterize the departments. Line and staff are characterized by relationships and not by departmental activities.

FUNCTIONAL AUTHORITY

Functional authority *is the right which is delegated to an individual or a department to control specified processes, practices, policies, or other matters relating to activities undertaken by persons in other departments.* If the principle of unity of command were followed without exception, authority over these activities would be exercised only by their line superiors, but numerous reasons—including a lack of special knowledge, lack of ability to supervise processes, and danger of diverse interpretations of policies—explain why they occasionally are not allowed to exercise this authority. In such cases, line managers are deprived of some authority. It is delegated by their common superior to a staff specialist or to a manager in another department.

Functional authority is not restricted to managers of a particular type of department. It may be exercised by line, service, or staff department heads, more often the latter two, because they are usually composed of specialists whose knowledge becomes the basis for functional controls.

Delegation of Functional Authority

We can better understand functional authority if we think of it as *a small slice of the authority of a line superior.* A corporation president, for example, has complete authority to manage a corporation, subject only to limitations placed by such superior authority as the board of directors, the corporate charter and bylaws, and government regulations. In the pure staff situation, the advisers on personnel, accounting, purchasing, or public relations have no part of this line authority, their duty being merely to offer counsel. But when the president delegates to these advisers the right to issue instructions directly to the line organizations, as shown in Figure 9-2, that right is called "functional authority."

The four staff and service executives have functional authority over the line organization with respect to procedures in the fields of accounting, personnel, purchasing, and public relations. What has happened is that the president, feeling it unnecessary that such specialized matters be cleared through him or her, has delegated line authority to staff assistants or managers to issue their own instructions to the operating department. Of course, subordinate managers can use the same device, as when a factory superintendent sets up cost, production control, and quality control supervisors with functional authority to prescribe procedures for the operating supervisors.

FIGURE 9-2

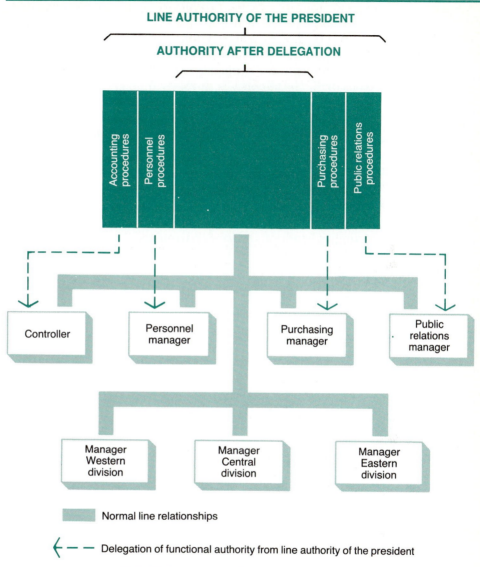

FUNCTIONAL AUTHORITY DELEGATION.

Functional Authority as Exercised by Operating Managers

Operating department heads sometimes have good reason to control some method or process of another operating department. For example, the vice-president in charge of sales may be given functional authority over the manufacturing executives in such sales-related areas as scheduling customer orders, packaging, or making service parts available.

Where a company is organized along product lines, the exercise of functional authority over the product division managers by other executives is rather commonplace. All functions of sales, production, finance, or other operating functions may be placed under a division or product manager. In this case, certain top line officials in charge of a major function of the business might not have a direct line of authority over the product managers. But, to make sure that sales or financial policy is properly followed in the divisions, these officers may be given functional authority, as illustrated in Figure 9-3.

Restricting the Area of Functional Authority

Functional authority should be carefully restricted. A purchasing manager's functional authority, for example, is generally limited to setting the procedures to be used in divisional or departmental purchasing and does not include telling these departments what they can purchase or when. When these managers conduct certain purchasing activities that relate to the whole company, they are acting as heads of service departments. The functional authority of the person-

FIGURE 9-3

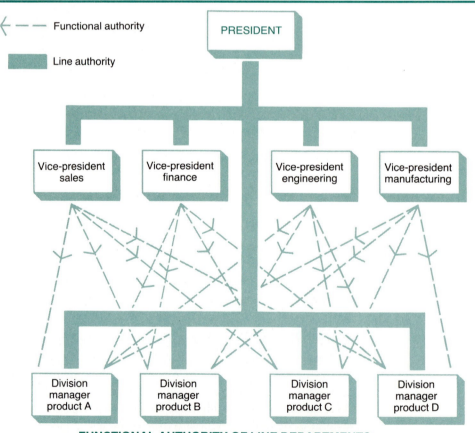

FUNCTIONAL AUTHORITY OF LINE DEPARTMENTS.

nel manager over the general line organization is likewise ordinarily limited to prescribing procedures for handling grievances, for sharing in the administration of wage and salary programs, and for handling vacation procedures and similar matters.

Complications in Exercising Functional Authority

Limiting the area of functional authority is, then, important in preserving the integrity of managerial positions. If a company had, as some do, executives with functional authority over procedures in the fields of personnel, purchasing, accounting, traffic, budgets, engineering, public relations, law, sales policy, and real estate, the complications of authority relationships could be great indeed. A factory manager or a sales manager might have, in addition to an immediate line superior, five, ten, or even fifteen functional bosses. In one case, a factory superintendent was found to be subject to functional authority from eighteen different places. When asked whether, on occasion, some of these instructions were conflicting and confusing, he replied, "Every day!" When asked what he did when this happened, he said that he followed the "decibel system" of management—he paid attention only to those persons who made the most noise. This certainly is an ineffective way of managing.

Although such complexity is often necessary, you can see that it can create serious confusion. Some degree of unity of command is needed, and top-level managers ensure this by delegating functional authority so that it can be exercised at only one level below that of the appointed manager. Thus, in Figure 9-4, the functional authority of the personnel or public relations director should not extend beyond the level of the vice-presidents in charge of finance, sales, and manufacturing. In other words, functional authority should be exercised at the nearest possible point to which it applies in the organization structure, in order to preserve the unity of command of the line executives.

This recommendation may have to be violated. Top managers with functional authority sometimes issue instructions directly to personnel throughout the organization. Where policy or procedure determination is so important that there must be no deviation, both the prestige of the top manager and the necessity for accurate communication may make it necessary and wise to issue such instructions. Issuing them to the responsible line subordinate, as well as to the functional counterpart at the lower level, may not seem to harmfully increase the multiplicity of command. There are needs for centralizing authority that may make this kind of exercise of functional authority unavoidable.

BENEFITS OF STAFF

There are, of course, many important benefits in using staff. The necessity of having the advice of well-qualified specialists in various areas of an organization's operations can scarcely be overestimated, especially as operations become more complex. The United States Army learned this the hard way in 1898: In the Spanish-American War, troops were sent into Cuba in woolen uniforms

FIGURE 9-4

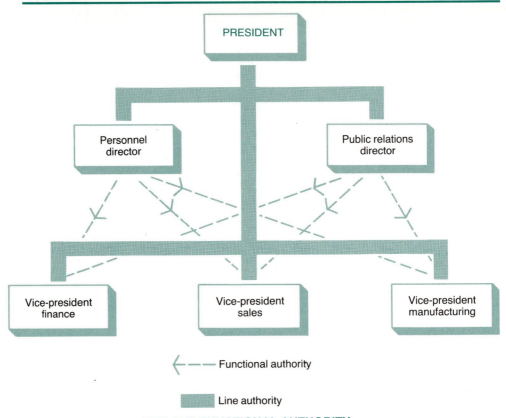

LINE AND FUNCTIONAL AUTHORITY.

despite the tropical heat and were expected to take territory although they lacked accurate road and topographic maps.

Staff advice is far more critical for business, government, and other enterprises today, when operating managers are faced with making decisions requiring expert knowledge in economic, technical, political, legal, and social areas. Moreover, it may be necessary, in many instances where highly specialized knowledge is required, to give specialists some functional authority to make decisions for their bosses.

Another major advantage of staff is that these specialists may be allowed the time to think, to gather data, and to analyze, when their superiors, busy managing operations, cannot do so. It is a rare operating manager, especially at top levels, who has the time, or will take the time, to do those things that a staff assistant can do so well.

Therefore, not only can a staff help line managers to be effective, but, as problems become more complex, staff analysis and advice becomes an urgent necessity. Moreover, despite the dangers of multiple command, even functional authority delegated to staff specialists is often imperative.

LIMITATIONS OF STAFF

Although staff relationships are usually necessary to an enterprise and can do much to make it successful, the nature of staff authority and the difficulty of understanding it lead to certain problems in practice.

The Danger of Undermining Line Authority

Operating managers often view staff personnel with skepticism. Too frequently, a president brings in staff executives, clothes them with authority (frequently very vague), and commands all other managers to cooperate. The proposals of staff specialists are received by the president with enthusiasm, and pressure is brought to bear upon the managers involved to put them into effect. What is actually taking place here is that the authority of department managers is being undermined; yet, grudgingly and resentfully, the proposals will be accepted because all will recognize the high tide of the staff specialists' prestige. A continuation of this situation might harm or even destroy operating departments. Capable managers, not willing to submit to indignity or wait until the tide ebbs, might resign; or they might put the matter bluntly to their boss—fire the staff specialists or get along without the line managers!

Operating departments represent the main line of the enterprise, and their managers gain a degree of indispensability. If staff advisers forget that they are to counsel and not to order, if they overlook the fact that their value lies in the extent to which they strengthen line managers, and if—worse yet—they undermine line authority, they risk becoming expendable. If there is an expendable person in an organization, it is likely to be the staff assistant.

Lack of Staff Responsibility

Advisory departments only propose a plan. Others must make the decision to adopt the plan and put it into operation. This creates an ideal situation for shifting blame for mistakes. The staff will claim that it was a good plan and that it failed because the operating manager was unqualified, uninterested, or intent on sabotage. The manager who must make the plan work will claim that it was a poor plan hatched by inexperienced and impractical theorists.

PERSPECTIVE:
THE ROLE OF THE PERSONNEL MANAGER

In one company, a personnel manager extended his service activities and advisory functions to encompass control over the actual staffing and much of the supervision of subordinates in line departments. For a time, the line managers welcomed this assistance with their personnel problems. But when they realized they no longer controlled their subordinates and when the personnel manager was unwilling to give up control, the resultant outcry forced the president to request his resignation.

Thinking in a Vacuum

The argument that a staff position gives planners time to think is appealing, but it overlooks the possibility that staff may think in a vacuum because staff people do not implement what they recommend. The alleged impracticality of staff recommendations often results in friction, loss of morale, and even sabotage.

Another weakness in the suggestion that planners must be set off from line departments in order to think is the implication that operating managers are without creative ability. They may, indeed, be without specialized knowledge, but this can be furnished by able staff assistants. Good operating managers can analyze plans, see long-range implications, and spot fatal weaknesses far better than most staff assistants.

Managerial Problems

Few would deny the importance of maintaining unity of command. It is not easy for a department head to be responsible to two or more people; at the worker level, it may be disastrous to attempt multiple responsibility. Some disunity in command may be unavoidable, since functional authority relationships are often unavoidable. But managers should remain aware of the difficulties of multiple authority and should either limit it—even with the loss of some uniformity or of the fruits of specialization—or else carefully clarify it.

Furthermore, too much staff activity may complicate a line executive's job of leadership and control. A corporation president may be so busy dealing with the recommendations of a large number of staff assistants and straightening twisted lines of authority that time and attention may not be available for operating departments; or a business may become so intent on making policies and setting procedures that there is little time left to make instruments or provide transportation service.

DECENTRALIZATION OF AUTHORITY

The previous section focused on the kinds of authority relationships such as line, staff, and functional authority. Now we emphasize the dispersion of the authority in the organization.

The Nature of Decentralization

Organization authority is merely the discretion conferred on people to use their judgment to make decisions and issue instructions. **Decentralization** is the tendency to disperse decision-making authority in an organized structure. It is a fundamental aspect of delegation; to the extent the authority is not delegated, it is centralized. How much should authority be concentrated or dispersed through the organization? There could be absolute centralization of authority in one person. But that implies no subordinate managers and therefore no structured organization. Some decentralization exists in all organizations. On the other hand, there cannot be absolute decentralization, for if managers should

FIGURE 9-5

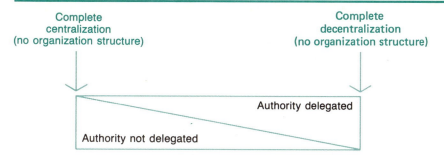

CENTRALIZATION AND DECENTRALIZATION AS TENDENCIES.

delegate all their authority, their status as managers would cease, their position would be eliminated, and there would, again, be no organization. Centralization and decentralization are tendencies; they are qualities like "hot" and "cold," as indicated in Figure 9-5.

Different Kinds of Centralization

The term "centralization" has several meanings:

1. Centralization of performance (further discussed later in this chapter) per-

---

**PERSPECTIVE:
DEGREES OF DECENTRALIZATION**

The **degree of decentralization** is greater:

1. The greater the number of decisions made at lower levels of an organization.

2. The more important the decisions made at lower levels of an organization. For example, the greater the amount of capital expenditure that the plant manager can approve without consulting any superior, the greater the degree of decentralization.

3. The more functions affected by decisions made at lower levels of an organization. Thus, companies that permit only manufacturing decisions to be made at separate branch plants are less decentralized than those that also permit financial and personnel decisions to be made at branch plants.

4. The less checking of a decision with others a manager must do. Decentralization is greater when no check at all must be made, it is less when superiors have to be informed of the decision after it has been made, and it is still less if superiors have to be consulted before the decision is made. The fewer people to be consulted, and the lower they are in the management hierarchy, the greater the degree of decentralization.[7]

tains to the geographic concentration, such as illustrated by a company operating in a single location.

2. **Departmental centralization** refers to the concentration of specialized activities generally in one department. For example, maintenance for a whole plant may be carried out by a single department.

3. **Centralization as an aspect of management** is the tendency to restrict delegation of decision making. A high degree of authority is held at or near the top by managers in the organizational hierarchy.

Decentralization as a Philosophy and Policy

Decentralization implies more than delegation: It reflects a philosophy of organization and management. It requires careful selection of which decisions to push down into the organization structure and which to hold near the top, specific policy making to guide the decision making, proper selection and training of people, and adequate controls. A policy of decentralization affects all areas of management and can be looked upon as an essential element of a managerial system. In fact, without it, managers could not use their discretion to handle the ever-changing situations they face.

DELEGATION OF AUTHORITY

As simple as delegation of authority appears to be, studies have shown that many managers fail because of poor delegation. Delegation is necessary for an organization to exist. Just as no one person in an enterprise can do all the tasks necessary for accomplishing a group purpose, so is it impossible, as an enterprise grows, for one person to exercise all the authority for making decisions. As we saw in Chapter 7, there is a limit to the number of persons managers can effectively supervise and for whom they can make decisions. Once this limit has been passed, authority must be delegated to subordinates, who will make decisions within the area of their assigned duties.

How Authority Is Delegated

Authority is delegated when a superior gives a subordinate discretion to make decisions. Clearly, superiors cannot delegate authority they do not have, whether they are board members, presidents, vice-presidents, or supervisors.

The process of **delegation** involves (1) determination of results expected from a position, (2) assignment of tasks to a position, (3) delegation of authority for accomplishing these tasks, (4) the holding of people in positions responsible for accomplishment of tasks.

In practice, it is impossible to split this process, since expecting a person to accomplish goals without the authority to achieve them is unfair, as is the delegation of authority without knowing for what end results it will be used. Moreover, since his or her responsibility cannot be delegated, a boss has no practical alternative but to hold subordinates responsible for completing their assignments.

Clarity of Delegation

Delegations of authority can be specific or general, written or unwritten. If the delegation is unclear, a manager may not understand the nature of the duties or the results expected. The job assignment of a company controller, for example, may specify such functions as accounting, credit control, cash control, financing, export-license handling, and preparation of financial statistics, and these broad functions may even be broken down into more definite duties. Or a controller may be told merely that he or she is expected to do what controllers generally do.

Specific written delegations of authority are extremely helpful both to the manager who receives them and to the person who delegates. The latter will more easily see conflicts or overlaps with other positions and will also be better able to identify those things for which a subordinate can and should be held responsible.

Sometimes, particularly for new top jobs, delegations cannot be very specific, at least at the outset. If a large company hires for the first time a traffic manager at its various plants, the president may be unclear about the amount of authority called for. But this situation should be remedied as soon as possible. One of the first duties of the new appointee should be to establish a description of the job and to clarify the description with the superior and, ideally, with those other managers on the same level whose cooperation is necessary. Otherwise, organizational frictions, unnecessary meetings and negotiations, jealousies, and numerous other disadvantages are likely to follow. Too many top executives believe they have a happy team of subordinates who do not need specific authority delegations, when, in fact, they have a jealous group of frustrated managers.

If executives fear that specific delegations will result in inflexibility, they can best meet that fear by developing a tradition of flexibility, such as by making necessary changes in organization structure an accepted and expected practice.

Splintered Authority

Splintered authority exists wherever a problem cannot be solved or a decision made without pooling the authority delegations of two or more managers. For example, the superintendent of plant A may see an opportunity to reduce costs through a minor modification in her procedures and those in plant B, but her authority cannot encompass the change. But if the superintendents of the two plants can agree upon the change (and it affects no other managers), all they need to do is to pool their authority and make the decision. Individually, their authority is said to be "splintered." In day-to-day operations of any company, there are many cases of splintered authority. Many managerial conferences are held because of the necessity of pooling authority to make a decision.

Such problems could be handled by merely referring the decision upward until one person can make it. In the case of the two plant superintendents, it might lie within the authority of the vice-president in charge of manufacturing.

PERSPECTIVE:
SPLINTERED AUTHORITY AT THE RAILROAD

One of the authors observed the solution of a problem involving a western railroad with headquarters in Chicago. The problem was relatively minor, but a decision on it in Los Angeles required the consolidated authority of the traffic department, the operating department, and the public relations department. It could have been referred up the line by each of the managers to the president's office, where sufficient authority for making the decision was concentrated. But if such decisions were always handled by upward reference, the president's office would be swamped. In this case, the managers of the three departments in the Los Angeles office met briefly, pooled their delegated authority, and quickly made the decision.

In many cases, the splinters of authority, although far down in the organization, exist in departments that have their common superior only in the office of the president.

Splintered authority cannot be wholly avoided in making decisions. However, recurring decisions on the same matters may be evidence that authority delegations have not been properly made and that some reorganization is required.

Recovery of Delegated Authority

A manager who delegates authority does not permanently dispose of it; delegated authority can always be regained. Reorganization inevitably involves some recovery and redelegation of authority. In a shuffle in an organization, rights are recovered by the responsible head of the firm or a department and then redelegated to managers of new or modified departments; the head of a new department may receive the authority formerly held by other managers. For example, when a reorganization takes quality control responsibility away from a works manager and assigns it to a new manager of quality control reporting to the vice-president in charge of manufacturing, the vice-president has recovered some of the authority formerly delegated to the works manager and has redelegated it, with or without modification, to the new quality control executive.

THE ART OF DELEGATION

Most failures in effective delegation occur not because managers do not understand the nature and principles of delegation but because they are unable or unwilling to apply them. Delegation is, in a way, an elementary act of managing. Yet studies of managerial failures almost invariably find that poor or inept delegation is at or near the top of the list of causes. Much of the reason lies in personal attitudes toward delegation.

Personal Attitudes toward Delegation

Although charting an organization and outlining managerial goals and duties will help in making delegations, and knowledge of the principles of delegation will furnish a basis for it, certain personal attitudes underlie the making of real delegations.

Receptiveness.   An underlying attribute of managers who will delegate authority is a willingness to give other people's ideas a chance. Decision making always involves some discretion, and a subordinate's decision is not likely to be exactly the one a superior would have made. The manager who knows how to delegate must have a minimum of the "NIH (not invented here) factor" and must be able not only to welcome the ideas of others but also to help others and to compliment them on their ingenuity.

Willingness to let go.   A manager who will effectively delegate authority must be willing to release the right to make decisions to subordinates. A great fault of some managers who move up the executive ladder—or of the pioneer who has built a large business from the small beginning of, say, a garage machine shop— is that they want to continue to make decisions for the positions they have left. Corporate presidents and vice-presidents who insist upon confirming every purchase or the appointment of every laborer or secretary do not realize that doing so takes their time and attention from far more important decisions.

Where the size or complexity of the organization forces delegation of authority, managers should realize that there is a kind of law of comparative managerial advantage, somewhat like the law of comparative economic advantage that applies to nations. Well known to economists and logically sound, the law of comparative economic advantage states that a country's wealth will be enhanced if it exports what it produces most efficiently and imports what it produces least efficiently, even though it could produce such imports more cheaply than any other nation. Likewise, managers will enhance their contributions to the firm if they concentrate on tasks that contribute most to the firm's objectives and assign to subordinates other tasks, even though they could accomplish the latter better themselves.

Willingness to let others make mistakes.   Although no responsible manager would sit idly by and let a subordinate make a mistake that might endanger the company or the subordinate's position in the company, continual checking on the subordinate to ensure that no mistakes are ever made will make true delegation impossible. Since everyone makes mistakes, a subordinate must be allowed to make some, and their cost must be considered an investment in personal development.

Serious or repeated mistakes can be largely avoided without nullifying delegation or hindering development of a subordinate. Patient counseling, asking leading or discerning questions, and carefully explaining the objectives and policies are among the tools available to the manager who would delegate well. None of these techniques involves discouraging subordinates with intimidating criticism or harping on their shortcomings.

Willingness to trust subordinates.   Superiors have no alternative to trusting their subordinates, for delegation implies a trustful attitude between them. This trust is sometimes hard to come by. A superior may put off delegation with the thought that subordinates are not well enough seasoned, that they cannot handle people, that they have not yet developed judgment, or that they do not appreciate all the facts bearing on a situation. Sometimes these considerations are true, but then a superior should either train subordinates or else select others who are prepared to assume the responsibility. Too often, however, bosses distrust their subordinates because they do not wish to let go, are threatened by subordinates' successes, do not delegate wisely, or do not know how to set up controls to assure proper use of the authority.

Willingness to establish and use broad controls.   Since superiors cannot delegate responsibility for performance, they should not delegate authority unless they are willing to find means of getting feedback, that is, of assuring themselves that the authority is being used to support enterprise or department goals and plans. Obviously, controls cannot be established and exercised unless goals, policies, and plans are used as basic standards for judging the activities of subordinates. More often than not, reluctance to delegate and to trust subordinates comes from the superior's not having planned carefully enough and having an understandable fear of loss of control.

Guides for Overcoming Weak Delegation

The following are five practical guides to make delegation real:

1. Define assignments and delegate authority in the light of results expected. Or, to put it another way, grant sufficient authority to make possible the accomplishment of goal assignments.

2. Select the person in the light of the job to be done. Although the good organizer will approach delegation primarily from the standpoint of the task to be accomplished, in the final analysis, staffing as a part of the total system of delegation cannot be ignored.

3. Maintain open lines of communication. Since the superior does not delegate all authority or abdicate responsibility and since managerial independence therefore does not exist, decentralization should not lead to insulation. There should be a free flow of information between superior and subordinate, furnishing subordinates information with which to make decisions and to interpret properly authority delegated. Delegations, then, do depend on situations.

4. Establish proper controls. Because no manager can relinquish responsibility, delegations should be accompanied by techniques to make sure the authority is properly used. But if controls are not to interfere with delegation, they must be relatively broad and designed to show deviations from plans rather than interfere with routine actions of subordinates.

5. Reward effective delegation and successful assumption of authority. Managers should be ever-watchful for means of rewarding both effective delegation and effective assumption of authority. Although many of these rewards will be monetary, the granting of greater discretion and prestige—both in a given position and by promotion to a higher position—is often even more of an incentive.

FACTORS DETERMINING THE DEGREE OF DECENTRALIZATION OF AUTHORITY

Managers cannot ordinarily be for or against decentralization of authority. They may *prefer* to delegate authority, or they may like to make all the decisions.

Although the temperament of individual managers influences the extent of authority delegation, other factors also affect it. Most of them are beyond the control of individual managers. Managers may resist their influence, but no successful manager can ignore them.

1. Costliness of the Decision

Perhaps the overriding factor determining the extent of decentralization is, as in other aspects of policy, costliness. As a general rule, the more costly the action to be decided on, the more probable it is that the decision will be made at the upper levels of management. Cost may be reckoned directly in dollars and cents or in such intangibles as the company's reputation, its competitive position, or employee morale. Thus, an airline decision to purchase airplanes will be made at the top levels, while the decision to purchase desks may be made in the second or third echelon of an operating department. Quality control in drug manufacturing, where a mistake might endanger lives, to say nothing of the company's reputation, would normally report to a high level, while the quality inspection in widget manufacturing might report to a much lower one.

The fact that the cost of a mistake affects the decentralization is not necessarily based on the assumption that top managers make fewer mistakes than subordinates. They *may* make fewer mistakes, since they are probably better trained and in possession of more facts, but the controlling reason is the weight of responsibility. Delegating authority is not delegating responsibility; therefore, managers typically prefer not to delegate authority for crucial decisions.

The need for top control depends on the area of decision. In the typical large business, top managers may reasonably feel that they cannot delegate authority over the expenditure of capital funds. The financial aspects of General Motors' operations are centralized under an executive vice-president, who reports to the chairman or vice-chairman of the board of directors rather than to the president. This is an example of the importance of centralization in the area of finance.

2. Desire for Uniformity of Policy

Those who value consistency above all invariably favor centralized authority, since this is the easiest road to such a goal. They may wish to ensure that customers will be treated alike with respect to quality, price, credit, delivery, and service; that the same policies will be followed in dealing with suppliers; or that public relations policies will be standardized.

Uniform policy also has certain internal advantages. For example, standardized accounting, statistics, and financial records make it easier to compare relative efficiencies of departments and keep down costs. The administration of a union contract is facilitated by uniform policy with respect to wages, promotions, vacations, dismissals, and similar matters. Taxes and government regulation entail fewer worries and less change of error with uniform policies.

Yet many enterprises go to considerable length to make sure that some policies will not be completely uniform. Many companies encourage variety in all except major matters, hoping that out of such nonuniformity may come managerial innovation, progress, competition among organizational units, improved morale and efficiency, and supply of promotable managers.

3. Size and Character of the Organization

The larger the organization, the more decisions to be made, and the more places in which they must be made, the more difficult it is to coordinate them. These complexities of organization may require policy questions to be passed up the line and discussed not only with many managers in the chain of command but also with many managers at each level, since horizontal agreement may be as necessary as vertical clearance.

Slow decisions—slow because of the number of specialists and managers who must be consulted—are costly. To minimize this cost, authority should be decentralized wherever feasible. Indeed, the large enterprise that prides itself on the right kind of decentralization may differ widely among companies, depending largely upon the quality of their management.

The costs of large size may be reduced by organizing an enterprise into several units, such as product or territorial divisions. Efficiency may be increased by making the unit small enough for its top executives to be near the point where decisions are made. This makes speedy decisions possible, keeps executives from spending time coordinating their decisions with many others, reduces the amount of paperwork, and improves the quality of decisions by reducing them to manageable proportions.

Also important in determining size is the character of a unit. For decentralization to be thoroughly effective, a unit must possess a certain economic and managerial self-sufficiency. Functional departments, such as sales or manufacturing or engineering, cannot be independent units, while product or territorial departments of the same size can be, encompassing as they do nearly all the functions of an enterprise. It therefore follows that if the uneconomic aspects of size are to be reduced, it is preferable to departmentize along product, territorial, or distribution channel lines.

In the zeal to overcome the disadvantages of size by reducing the size of the decision-making unit, certain shortcomings of decentralization should not be overlooked. When authority is decentralized, a lack of policy uniformity and of coordination may follow. The branch, product division, or other self-sufficient unit may be so preoccupied with its objectives as to lose sight of those of the enterprise as a whole.

4. History and Culture of the Enterprise

Whether authority will be decentralized frequently depends upon the way the business has been built. Those enterprises which, in the main, expand from within—such as Marshall Field and Company and International Harvester Company—show a marked tendency to keep authority centralized, as do those which expand under the direction of their owner-founders. The Ford Motor Company was, under its founder, an extraordinary case of centralized authority; Henry Ford, Sr., prided himself on having no organizational titles in the top management except that of president and general manager, insisting, to the extent he could, that every major decision in that vast company be made by himself.

On the other hand, enterprises that result from mergers and consolidations are likely to show, at least at first, a definite tendency to retain decentralized authority, especially if the unit acquired is already operating profitably. To be sure, this tendency not to rock the boat may be politically inspired rather than based purely on managerial considerations. Certainly, the claim to independence of the once-independent units is especially strong, and many years may have to pass before the chief executive of the consolidated company dares materially to reduce the degree of decentralization.

In some cases, the first influence of a merger or an acquisition may be toward increased centralization. If the controlling group wishes to put in its own management or take immediate advantage of the economies of combined operation, the requirements of policy uniformity and quick action may necessitate centralization.

5. Management Philosophy

The character and philosophy of top executives have an important influence on the extent to which authority is decentralized. Sometimes top managers are despotic, tolerating no interference with the authority they jealously hoard. At other times, top managers keep authority not merely to gratify a desire for status or power but because they simply cannot give up the activities and authorities they enjoyed before they reached the top or before the business expanded from an owner-manager shop.

In many cases, top managers may see decentralization as a way of organizational life that takes advantage of the innate desire of people to create, to be free, and to have status. Many successful top managers find in it a means to promote the desire for freedom to economic efficiency, much as the free enterprise system has been responsible for this country's remarkable industrial progress.

Retaining efficiency and discipline while allowing people to express themselves, to exercise initiative, and to have some voice in the affairs of the organization is the greatest problem large organizations have to solve.

6. Desire for Independence

Individuals and groups often desire a degree of independence from bosses who are far away. It is not at all unusual for West Coast divisions or subsidiaries of companies headquartered in New York to feel somewhat hostile toward directives coming from headquarters managers who are believed not to know West Coast conditions.

Individuals may become frustrated by delay in getting decisions, by long lines of communication, and by the great game of passing the buck. This frustration can lead to dangerous loss of good people, to jockeying by the office politician, and to an attitude of "not rocking the boat" by the less competent seeker of security.

7. Availability of Managers

A real shortage of managers would limit decentralization of authority, since in order to delegate, superiors must have qualified managers to whom to give authority. But too often the scarcity of good managers is used as an excuse for centralizing authority; executives who complain that they have no one to whom they can delegate authority are often trying to magnify their own value to the firm or are confessing a failure to develop subordinates.

There are also managers who believe that a firm should centralize authority because it will then need very few good managers. One difficulty is that the firm that so centralizes authority may not be able to train managers to take over the duties of the top executives, and external sources must be relied upon to furnish necessary replacements.

The key to safe decentralization is adequate training of managers. By the same token, decentralization is perhaps the most important key to training. Many large firms whose size makes decentralization a necessity consciously push decision making down into the organization for the purpose of developing managers; they feel that the best training is actual experience. Since this policy usually carries with it chances for mistakes by a novice, it is good practice to limit, at least initially, the importance of the decisions so delegated.

8. Control Techniques

Another factor affecting the degree of decentralization is the state of development of control techniques. A good manager at any level of the organization cannot delegate authority without having some way of knowing whether it will be used properly. Because some managers do not know how to control, they are unwilling to delegate authority. They may think that it takes more time to correct a mistake than to do the job themselves.

Improvement in statistical devices, accounting controls, the use of computers, and other techniques have helped make possible the current trend toward considerable managerial decentralization. Even the most ardent supporters of decentralization, such as General Motors, Du Pont, and Sears, could hardly take so favorable a view without adequate techniques to show managers, from the top down, whether performance is conforming to plans. To decentralize is not to lose control, and to push decision making down into the organization is not to walk away from responsibility.

9. Decentralized Performance

Decentralized performance refers to *the situation where the managers of an enterprise are dispersed over a geographic area.* The reason for decentralized performance is basically a technical matter depending upon such factors as the economies of division of labor, the opportunities for using machines, the nature of the work to be performed (a railroad has no choice but to spread its performance), and the location of raw materials, labor supply, and customers. This geographic decentralization influences the degree of decentralization of authority.

Authority tends to be decentralized when performance is decentralized, if for no other reason than that the absentee manager is unable to manage, although there are exceptions. For example, some of the large chain store enterprises are characterized by widely decentralized performance, and yet the local manager of a store may have little or no authority over pricing, advertising and merchandising methods, inventory and purchasing, or product line, all of which may be controlled from a central or regional office. The head of a local manufacturing plant of a large organization may have little authority beyond the right to hire and fire, and even then action may be limited by company policy and procedure and by the authority of a centralized personnel department. At the same time, the decentralization of performance limits the ability to centralize authority. The most dictatorial top manager of a national organization based in New York cannot supervise the San Francisco plant as closely as if it were adjacent to the home office.

It does not necessarily follow, however, that when performance is centralized, authority has to be centralized. You may have a company in one location in which authority is greatly decentralized because of the top executive's attitude toward delegation. Nevertheless, in a one-plant situation authority centralization would be easier than if the company had many plants in distant locations.

10. Business Dynamics: The Pace of Change

The pace of change of an enterprise also affects the degree to which authority may be decentralized. If a business is growing fast and facing complex problems of expansion, its managers, particularly those responsible for top policy, may be forced to make a large share of the decisions. But, strangely enough, this very dynamic condition may force these managers to delegate authority and take a calculated risk on the costs of error. Generally this dilemma is resolved in the direction of delegation, and, in order to avoid delegation to untrained subordinates, close attention is given to rapid formation of policies and the acceleration of training in management. An alternative often adopted is to slow the rate of change, including the cause of fast change, expansion. Many top managers have found that the critical factor limiting their ability to meet change and expand a business or other enterprise is the lack of trained personnel to whom authority may be delegated.

In old, well-established, or slow-moving business, there is a natural tendency to centralize or recentralize authority. When few major decisions must be made, the advantages of uniform policy and the economies of having a few well-qualified persons make the decisions cause authority to be centralized. In slow-moving businesses too much centralization may carry danger. New discoveries, vigorous competition from an unexpected source, and political change are only a few of the factors that might introduce conditions requiring change. An over-centralized firm may not be able to meet a situation as well as if authority were decentralized.

11. Environmental Influences

The factors determining the extent of decentralization that we have dealt with so far are largely factors within the enterprise. However, the economics of de-centralization of performance and the character of change include elements well beyond the control of an enterprise's managers. In addition, there are definite external forces affecting the extent of decentralization. Among the most important of these are governmental controls, national unionism, and tax policies.

Government regulation of many facets of business policy makes de-centralization difficult and sometimes impossible. If prices are regulated, sales managers cannot be given much real freedom in determining them. If materials are allocated and restricted, purchasing and factory managers are not free to buy or use any they might wish. If labor may be asked to work only a limited number of hours at a given rate of pay, the local division manager cannot freely set hours and wages.

Top management itself no longer has authority over many aspects of policy and cannot, therefore, delegate authority it does not have. Much authority in areas controlled by government action could still be decentralized. But managers often do not dare trust subordinates to interpret government regulations, especially since the penalties and the public criticism for breaking laws are so serious and since interpretation of most laws is a matter for the specialist.

In the same way, the rise of national unions in the past decades has had a centralizing influence on business. So long as department or division managers can negotiate the terms of a labor contract by dealing either with local unions or with employees directly, authority to negotiate may be delegated by top management to these subordinates. But where, as is increasingly the case, a national union enters into a collective bargaining contract with headquarters management, with the terms of the contract applicable to all workers of a company wherever located, a company cannot chance decentralization of certain decision making any more than it can in the case of government controls.

The tax systems of the national, state, and local governments have had a marked regulatory effect on business. The tax collector, especially the federal tax collector, sits at the elbow of every executive who makes a decision involving funds. The impact of taxation is often a policy-determining factor that over-shadows such traditional business considerations as plant expansion, marketing policies, and economical operations. Uniformity of tax policy becomes of primary importance to company management. This spells centralization because managers without appropriate tax advice cannot be expected to make wise decisions. It may even require a central tax department acting not only in an advisory capacity and as a tax service agency but also with a high degree of functional authority over matters with tax implications.

RECENTRALIZATION OF AUTHORITY

At times an enterprise can be said to recentralize authority—to centralize authority once decentralized. **Recentralization** is normally not a complete reversal of decentralization, for the authority delegations are not wholly withdrawn by the managers who made them. The process is a centralization of authority over a certain type of activity or a certain kind of function, wherever in the organization it may be found.

OBTAINING THE DESIRED DEGREE OF DECENTRALIZATION

In order to obtain the degree of decentralization they want, top managers must understand decentralization; understanding is based upon the knowledge that decentralization cannot mean independence, that it requires establishment of policies to guide decision making along desired courses, that it needs careful delegation of authority by managers who know how and who want to delegate, and that it must be accompanied by controls designed to ensure that delegated authority is used properly. Although the art of authority delegation is basic to proper decentralization, it is apparent that the mere act of delegation is not enough to ensure decentralization.

No manual can indicate how to ensure that authority is properly decentralized or appropriately withheld, but several techniques may be used with some chance of success. One of the most effective of these is to ensure that a system of verifiable objectives is established, that each person is held responsible for achieving certain goals, and that each is given the necessary authority for doing so. Another is merely a technique of organization—providing a statement of each manager's duties and of the responsibility and the degree of authority delegated to that manager. Besides being clear and, preferably, written, the statements should be issued in such a way that any employees may know what they contain, if they need to know.

Another important technique is the example and teaching of a superior, starting at the top of the organization. The character of top leadership in an enterprise affects everyone in an organization. There are in every firm of any size those who will reach out for power, intrude upon activities assigned to others, and bully the timid. Rules and job descriptions are often subject to differences in interpretation, which can be conveniently stretched or limited depending upon the politics in an organization. Their unreliability, despite their obvious usefulness, stands as a warning to executives that the most dependable foundation for achieving a desired degree of decentralization is the education of subordinate managers in the rights of others—teaching them restraint as well as aggressiveness.

One of the means of forcing delegation of authority, particularly in middle and lower levels of organization, is to require managers to have a large number of subordinates and, at the same time, to hold them to a high standard of performance. When the span of management is stretched, there is no alternative but to delegate authority. In order to protect their own performance, managers learn to select good subordinate managers, train them well, establish clear-cut policies, and find efficient means of control. This is said to be the longtime practice of Sears, Roebuck and Company, where store managers are encouraged to have many department managers reporting to them.

Another technique used to force decentralization has been the policy of promoting managers only when they have subordinates able to take their places. To accomplish this end, managers are forced to delegate authority. Moreover, this policy removes a major cause of hoarding authority, the desire of managers to become indispensable by making sure that their duties cannot be handled by any of their subordinates.

Occasionally the problem is how to retain a predetermined degree of authority. Division and branch managers—because they are far away from the home office, often wish to build empires, or want to do a complete job—may assume and oppose central management. The answer to this problem, of course, is primarily one of leadership, clear policy determination, and delegation of authority to and proper training of subordinate managers. But perhaps the principal problem lies in the character of the top executives. If they sit on the fence, do not support the authority delegations they have made, ignore the organization structure, overlook serious deviations from policy, and neglect in other ways to do a thorough managerial job, little can be done to retain any predetermined degree of decentralization.

CLARIFYING DECENTRALIZATION: CHART OF APPROVAL AUTHORIZATION

As in so many areas of managing, conflict, friction, and inefficiencies result from lack of clarification of individual roles. This is nowhere more true in practice than in clarifying the extent and nature of decentralization. This problem can be greatly simplified by means of a chart of executive approval authorizations. The chart is a technique by which the various authority delegations of a company are specified. Since most of these delegations have to do with the right to commit the company for money, most of the chart has to do with expenditure limits.

However, there are other matters, such as certain policies and programs, which can be and often are shown on such a chart.

An excerpt of a chart of approval authorization for a small to medium-sized company is shown in Table 9-1. A list of major decisions (*nature of transaction* in the table) appears on the left-hand side of the chart. This company found it useful to group these decisions under the classifications of personnel, operating expenses, capital expenditures and commitments, prices and sales commitments, and general. Table 9-1 illustrates selected categories. Across the top of the chart are listed the various managers who have authority to make these decisions, along with certain staff or operating personnel who have functional authority or whose consultation is required for advice or information.

The authority and responsibility for developing a chart must rest at the top of a company. Because the chart even distinguishes between decisions that the board of directors reserves for itself and those delegated to operating management, the board must necessarily be called upon to approve at least this area of delegation. An effective board may wish to do more. If its organizational policy is really one of decentralization, with centralized decision making in only certain matters at the top, it may wish to approve the entire chart, or at least enough of it to assure itself that its policy is being followed.

In addition to promoting clarity, the chart has other advantages. It acts as a means of communicating the entire structure of decision making in a company so that people down the line, or in departments whose coordination in a decision is necessary, can see what the decision-making relationships are. Also, in a multidivision company, if there are separate divisional charts as well as a corporate chart, authority may be delegated in varying degrees. Thus, in a large division, more authority may be delegated; or, in a division staffed by less experienced managers, a smaller degree of authority could be delegated. A further advantage is that authority delegations can be changed with greater ease than when they are included in a number of individual position descriptions.

Although the chart of approval authorizations is only a tool, it is an essential one. If it is to work, it should be made a way of life in an enterprise; it must be updated whenever there is any significant change in organization structure or authority delegation and must be communicated to all those in decision-making positions. Along with position descriptions and the formulation of verifiable goals for each position in an enterprise, it helps define the roles which individuals must fill.

BALANCE: THE KEY TO DECENTRALIZATION[8]

To avoid pitfalls, any program for decentralization of authority must take into consideration the advantages and limitations summarized in Table 9-2.

As we have pointed out, strong forces favor the practice of decentralization. At the same time, extensive decentralization is not to be blindly undertaken. Perhaps the principal problem of decentralization is loss of control. No enter-

TABLE 9-1 Chart of Approval Authorization (excerpt)*

Nature of transaction	Department manager	Staff manager	Division director	President (corporate, domestic), board chairperson (international)	Board of directors
		Personnel			
Employment of new personnel:					
Hourly	All	Personnel manager to process and review for consistency with company policy	All exceptions to company policy		
Salaried	All	Personnel manager to process	All over $2000 per month	All over $3000 per month	All over $5000 per month
Wage and salary increases:					
Hourly	All	Personnel manager to process and review for consistency with company policy	All exceptions to company policy		
Salaried	All	Personnel manager to process	All	All resulting in salary over $3000 per month	All resulting in salary over $5000 per month
Moving expenses		To be processed by controller	All	All over $2000 in cost	
Leaves of absence	All	Personnel manager to process	All	All over 30 days	All over 60 days

Operating expenses

Procurement of materials and services (approval of manufacturing and engineering schedule by vice-president of manufacturing and engineering):		
In accordance with approved schedules	Manager of purchasing on all	
Not in accordance with approved schedules	Vice-president of manufacturing and engineering on all. Controller on all exceeding $10,000	All

General

Bank loans for company operations			
Line of credit	Vice-president—finance on all	All	All
Loans within line	Vice-president—finance on all	All	
Loans for buildings and land	Vice-president—finance on all	All	All
Acquisition of financial interest in or loan to any company	Vice-president—finance	All	All

* A person required to approve transactions as outlined in the above chart may authorize another person to sign in case of his or her absence. The person so authorized must affix the proper signature showing his or her initials under such signature.

Source: H. Koontz, *The Board of Directors and Effective Management* (New York: McGraw-Hill Book Company, 1967), pp. 46–49. (Certain limits revised in 1983.)

TABLE 9-2 Advantages and Limitations of Decentralization

Advantages of decentralization

1. Relieves top management of some burden of decision making and forces upper-level managers to let go.
2. Encourages decision making and assumption of authority and responsibility.
3. Gives managers more freedom and independence in decision making.
4. Promotes establishment and use of broad controls which may increase motivation.
5. Makes comparison of performance of different organizational units possible.
6. Facilitates setting up of profit centers.
7. Facilitates product diversification.
8. Promotes development of general managers.
9. Aids in adaptation to fast-changing environment.

Limitations of decentralization

1. Makes it more difficult to have a uniform policy.
2. Increases complexity of coordination of decentralized organizational units.
3. May result in loss of some control by upper-level managers.
4. May be limited by inadequate control techniques.
5. May be constrained by inadequate planning and control systems.
6. Can be limited by the availability of qualified managers.
7. Involves considerable expenses for training managers.
8. May be limited by external forces (national labor unions, governmental controls, tax policies).
9. May not be favored by economies of scale of some operations.

prise can decentralize to the extent that its existence is threatened and the achievement of its goals is frustrated. If organizational disintegration is to be avoided, decentralization must be tempered by selective centralization in certain major policy areas. The company with well-balanced decentralization will probably centralize decisions at the top on such things as financing, overall profit goals and budgeting, major facilities and other capital expenditures, important new product programs, major marketing strategies, basic personnel policies, and the development and compensation of managerial personnel.

The achievement of balance is perhaps one of the greatest accomplishments of Alfred Sloan in his management of General Motors over the years. Although practicing and preaching decentralization, he and his top management team realized that no department or division could be given complete freedom. As a result, this company, as large as it has been, has continued to hold at the very top its major policy and program decisions on matters affecting the soundness and success of the entire company. Yet, once major program and strategy decisions are made at the top, the countless decisions involving their execution have been decentralized to operating divisions.

FOR DISCUSSION

1. Why has there been a conflict between line and staff for so long and in so many companies? Can this conflict be removed?

2. Take as examples a number of positions in any kind of enterprise (business, church, government, or elsewhere). Classify them as line or staff.

3. If the task of a person in a purely staff position is to offer advice, how can an individual receiving this advice make sure that it is independent, well researched, and realistic?

4. How many cases of functional authority in organization have you seen? Analyzing a few, do you agree that they could have been avoided? If avoidance had been possible, would you have eliminated them? If they could not have been avoided or if you had not wanted to eliminate them, how would you remove most of the difficulties which might arise?

5. If you were asked to advise a young college graduate who has accepted a staff position as assistant to a factory manager, what suggestions would you make?

6. Why is poor delegation of authority often found to be the most important single cause of managerial failure?

7. In many foreign countries where companies have grown from within and are often family-owned, very little authority is decentralized. What do you think would explain this? What effect does it have?

8. If you were a manager, would you decentralize authority? State several reasons for your answer. How would you make sure that you did not decentralize too much?

9. Should authority be pushed down into an organization as far as it will go?

EXERCISES/ACTION STEPS

1. Interview a line manager and a staff person of a local company. Ask them what they like and dislike about their jobs. Reflect upon the interviews and ask yourself whether a line or staff position is the major aim of your career plan.

2. Interview two line managers about their views on delegation. Do they think that their superior delegates sufficient authority to them? Also inquire how they feel about delegating authority to their subordinates.

CASES

CASE 9-1
ABC AIRLINES

The president of ABC Airlines, seeing that costs were getting out of control as the company grew, brought in as an assistant a brilliant young man who was a certified public accountant. The assistant was told about the company's problem of rising costs and was asked for his help in solving the problem.

The new assistant gathered a staff of high-quality industrial engineers, financial analysts, and recent top graduates from one of the nation's best-known graduate schools of business administration. After laying out the company's problem, he assigned them to investigate cost problems and management methods in the airline's operations, maintenance, engineering, and sales departments. After a number of studies, the president's assistant found many sources of inefficiency in the various departments and initiated a number of changes in operating practices. In addition, he made many reports to the president outlining in detail the inefficiencies his staff had found and the measures being taken to correct them. These re-

ports also showed, with ample supporting detail, the millions of dollars which his actions were saving the company.

Just as these cost savings programs were being implemented, the vice-presidents in charge of operations, maintenance, engineering, and sales descended on the president and insisted that the assistant be discharged.

1. Why should the assistant who was doing so well be so much resented by the vice-presidents? What went wrong?

2. Assuming that the findings of the assistant and his staff were accurate, what should have been done by the president, the assistant, the vice-presidents, and others to make these findings useful?

CASE 9-2
DECENTRALIZATION AT AMERICAN BUSINESS COMPUTERS AND EQUIPMENT COMPANY

Because of its excellent new products, imaginative marketing, and fine service to company customers, the American Business Computers and Equipment Company grew to be a leader in its field, with sales over $1 billion annually, high profit margins and continually rising stock prices. It became one of the favorites of investors, who enjoyed its fast growth rate and high profits. But the president soon realized that the organization structure, which had served the company so well, no longer fit the company's needs.

For years the company had been organized along functional lines, with vice-presidents in charge of finance, marketing, production, personnel, purchasing, engineering, and research and development. As it grew, the company had expanded its product lines beyond business computers to include electric typewriters, photocopying machines, motion-picture cameras and projectors, computer controls for machine tools, and electric

accounting machines. As time went on, concern had arisen that its organization structure did not provide for profit responsibility below the office of the president, did not appear to fit the far-flung nature of the business now being conducted in many foreign countries, and seemed to accentuate the "walls" impeding effective coordination between the functional departments of marketing, production, and engineering. There seemed to be too many decisions that could not be made at any level lower than the president's office.

As a result, the president decentralized the company into fifteen independent domestic and foreign divisions, each with complete profit responsibility. However, after this reorganization was in effect, he began to feel that the divisions were not adequately controlled. There developed considerable duplication in purchasing and personnel functions, each division manager ran his or her operations without regard to company policies and strategies, and it became apparent to the president that the company was disintegrating into a number of independent parts.

Having seen several large companies get into trouble when a division manager made mistakes and the division suffered large losses, the president concluded that he had gone too far with decentralization. As a result, he withdrew some of the authority delegations to the division managers and required them to get top corporate management approval on such important matters as (1) any capital expenditures over $10,000, (2) the introduction of any new products, (3) marketing and pricing strategies and policies, (4) plant expansion, and (5) changes in personnel policies.

The division general managers were understandably unhappy when they saw some of their independence taken away from them. They openly complained that the company was on a "yo-yo" course, first decentralizing and then centralizing.

The president, worried about his position, calls you in as a consultant to advise him on what to do.

1. In your opinion, what did the president do wrong when he set up the fifteen independent divisions?

2. Do you agree that what the president did to regain control was correct?

3. What would you have done under the circumstances?

4. What specific managerial principles or concepts are illustrated in this case?

REFERENCES

1. The concept of power has been widely discussed in the literature. See, for example, the thorough discussion by Gerald R. Salancik and Jeffrey Pfeffer, "Who Gets Power—and How They Hold on to It: A Strategic-Contingency Model of Power," in David A. Nadler, Michael L. Tushman, and Nina G. Hatvany (eds.), *Managing Organizations—Readings and Cases* (Boston: Little, Brown and Company, 1982), pp. 385–399.

2. John R. P. French, Jr., and Bertram Raven, "The Bases of Social Power," in Walter E. Natemeyer (ed.), *Classics of Organizational Behavior* (Oak Park, Ill.: Moore Publishing Company, 1978), pp. 198–210.

3. But authority patterns may vary with culture. See Trudy Heller, "Changing Authority Patterns: A Cultural Perspective," *Academy of Management Review* (July 1985), pp. 488–495.

4. For a research study on the topic of power see Anthony T. Cobb, "An Episodic Model of Power: Toward an Integration of Theory and Research," *Academy of Management Review* (July 1984), pp. 482–493.

5. Jeff Bailey, "Where the Action Is: Executives in Staff Jobs Seek Line Positions," *The Wall Street Journal* (Aug. 12, 1986); see also David Wessel, "Do as I Do: More Consultants Quit Profession to Start New Businesses," *The Wall Street Journal* (Oct. 15, 1986).

6. Hall L. Logan, "Line and Staff: An Obsolete Concept?" in Harold Koontz, Cyril O'Donnell, and Heinz Weihrich (eds.), *Management: A Book of Readings*, 5th ed. (New York: McGraw-Hill Book Company, 1980), pp. 322–325.

7. Ernest Dale, *Planning and Developing the Company Structure*, Research Report no. 20 (New York: American Management Association, 1952), p. 107.

8. See also John G. Staiger, "What Cannot be Decentralized," in Koontz et al., *Management* (1980), pp. 319–321.

FOR FURTHER INFORMATION

Dale, Ernest. *The Great Organizers* (New York: McGraw-Hill Book Company, 1960).

Dale, Ernest. *Planning and Developing the Company Organization Structure,* Research Report no. 20. (New York: American Management Association, 1952).

Fayol, Henry. *General and Industrial Administration* (New York: Pitman Publishing Corporation, 1949).

Flax, Steven. "The Toughest Bosses in America," *Fortune* (Aug. 6, 1984), pp. 18–23.

Gabarro, John J., and John P. Kotter. "Managing Your Boss," *Harvard Business Review* (January–February 1980), pp. 92–100.

Kiechel, Walter, III. "How to Manage Your Boss," *Fortune* (Sept. 17, 1984), pp. 207–210.

Krein, T.J. "How to Improve Delegation Habits," *Management Review* (May 1982), pp. 58–61.

March, James G., and Herbert A. Simon. *Organizations* (New York: John Wiley & Sons, 1958).

Mintzberg, Henry. "Power and Organization Life Cycles," *Academy of Management Review* (April 1984), pp. 207–224.

Perrow, Charles. "The Bureaucratic Paradox: The Efficient Organization Centralizes in Order to Decentralize," *Organizational Dynamics* (Spring 1977), pp. 3–14.

Scott, William G., Terence R. Mitchell, and Philip H. Birnbaum. *Organization Theory—A Structural and Behavioral Analysis,* 4th ed. (Homewood, Ill: Richard D. Irwin, 1981).

Committees and Group Decision Making[1]

CHAPTER OBJECTIVES

After reading this chapter, you should be able to:

1. Explain the nature of various types of committees.

2. Outline the reasons why committees and groups are used, with special attention to their use in decision making.

3. Present the disadvantages of committees, especially in decision making.

4. Explain the nature of plural executives and the board of directors.

5. Outline the ways committees tend to be misused.

6. Discuss the requirements for using committees effectively.

7. Describe the advantages and disadvantages of small groups other than committees in managing.

*O*ne of the most ubiquitous and controversial devices of organization is the committee. Whether it is referred to as a "board," "commission," "task force," or "team," its essential nature is the same, for the **committee** is *a group of persons to whom, as a group, some matter is committed.* It is this characteristic of group action that sets the committee apart from other organization devices, though, as we will see, not all committees involve group decision making.

Committees are a fact of organizational life. Although committees are widely criticized, properly conducted committee meetings used for the right purpose can result in greater motivation, improved problem solving, and increased output.[2] In a study of subscribers to the *Harvard Business Review,* only 8 percent of the respondents indicated that they would eliminate committees if it were within their power.[3] The problem, then, is not the existence of committees but rather the way they are conducted and where they are used.

THE NATURE OF COMMITTEES

Because of variation in authority assigned to committees, much confusion has resulted as to their nature.

Group Processes in Committees

Some say that groups go through four stages: (1) forming (getting to know each other), (2) storming (determining the objective of the meeting; conflicts arise), (3) norming (the group agrees on norms and some behavior rules), and (4) performance (getting down to the task). While these characteristics may be found in most groups, they may not necessarily follow the sequential steps.[4]

You may also find that people in committees play certain roles. Some seek information, others give information. Some try to encourage others to contribute, others are followers. Finally, some try to coordinate the group's effort or to achieve a compromise in the areas of disagreement, while others take a more aggressive role.

To be effective in a group, one must not only listen to what is said but also observe the nonverbal behavior. Furthermore, noting the seating of members may give some clues of the social bonds among committee participants. Those who know each other often sit next to each other. The seating arrangement may have an impact on the group interaction. You probably have noted that the chairperson sits mostly at the head at a rectangular table. At Daimler Benz, the maker of Mercedes Benz cars, the board of directors sits at a round table to deemphasize the position of the chairperson.

Functions and Formality of Committees

Some committees undertake managerial functions, and others do not. Some make decisions, while others merely deliberate on problems without authority to decide. Some have authority to make recommendations to a manager, who may or may not accept them, while others are formed purely to receive information, without making recommendations or decisions.

A committee may be either line or staff, depending upon its authority. If its authority involves decision making affecting subordinates responsible to it, it is a plural executive—a *line committee;* if its authority relationship to a superior is advisory, then it is a *staff committee.*

Committees may also be formal or informal. If established as part of the organization structure, with specifically delegated duties and authority, they are *formal.* Most committees with any permanence fall into this class. Or they may be *informal,* that is, organized without specific delegation of authority and usually by some person desiring group thinking or group decision on a particular problem. Thus, managers may have a problem on which they need advice from other managers or specialists outside their department and may call a special meeting for the purpose. Indeed, this kind of motivation, plus the occasional need for gathering together in one room all the authority available to deal with an unusual problem, gives rise to many of the numerous conferences in organizational life.

Moreover, committees may be relatively *permanent,* or they may be *temporary.* One would expect formal committees to be more permanent than the informal, although this is not necessarily so. A formal committee might be established by order of a company president, with appropriate provision in the organization structure, for the sole purpose of studying the advisability of building a new factory and be disbanded immediately upon completion of its task. And an informal committee set up by the factory manager to advise upon improvement of product quality or to help coordinate delivery dates with sales commitments might continue indefinitely.

However, the executive who merely calls assistants into the office or confers with department heads is not creating a committee. It is sometimes difficult to draw a sharp distinction between committees and other group meetings. The essential characteristic of the committee is that it is a group charged with dealing with a specific problem or problem areas.

The Use of Committees in Different Organizations

Committees are in wide use in all types of organizations. In government, one finds a large number of standing and special committees of every legislative body; indeed, state and national legislatures are committees, as are the cabinets of the chief executives of the federal and state governments. Committees manage many government agencies such as the Tennessee Valley Authority, the Federal Reserve Board, the Federal Deposit Insurance Corporation, and the Export-Import Bank.

In education, faculties of great universities, jealous of academic freedom and distrustful of administrative power, traditionally circumscribe the authority of presidents and deans with a myriad of committees. In one large university more than 300 standing committees share in administration or advise on policy, ranging from the academic senate and the budget committees to coordinating committees, and committees on alumni records, university welfare, and maintenance of order during examinations.

Religious institutions likewise lean heavily on committees, partly to encourage active participation by members and partly to delimit the authority of leaders. Although their authority may vary widely, depending upon the traditions of the sect, committees—ranging from the church board to the committee in charge of a church supper—are ever present.

Committees are also prevalent in business. A board of directors is a committee, as are its various constituent groups, such as the executive committee, the finance committee, the audit committee, and the bonus committee. Occasionally, one finds a business managed by a management committee instead of a president. And almost invariably under the president there will be a variety of management or policy committees, planning committees, wage and salary review committees, grievance committees, task forces for particular projects, and numerous other standing and special committees. Moreover, at each level of the organization structure, one or more committees are likely to be found. A perhaps extreme example of the use of committees in a large bank is shown in Figure 10-1. Indeed, a survey by Robert H. Hayes & Associates, Inc., of the 500 largest industrial enterprises showed that group management increased from 39 to 70 percent in the early 1970s alone.[5]

The use of formal committees appears to be related to the size of the enterprise. In the study of *Harvard Business Review* subscribers it was found that of the organizations with over 10,000 employees, 94 percent had regular or standing committees. This compares with 64 percent of the enterprises with fewer than 250 employees reporting the use of such committees.[6]

REASONS FOR USING COMMITTEES

One need not look far for reasons for the widespread use of committees. Although the committee is sometimes regarded as having democratic origins and as being characteristic of democratic society, the reasons for its existence go beyond mere desire for group participation. Committees are widely used even in authoritarian organizations, such as Soviet Russia and Communist China.

Group Deliberation and Judgment

Perhaps the most important reason for the use of committees is the advantage of gaining group deliberation and judgment—a variation of the adage that "two heads are better than one." A group of people can bring to bear on a problem a wider range of experience than a single person, a greater variety of opinion, a more thorough probing of the facts, and a more diverse training in specialized aspects. Very few important business problems fall entirely into a single area such as production, engineering, finance, or sales. Most, on the contrary, require more knowledge, experience, and judgment than any individual possesses.

It should not be inferred that group judgment can be obtained only through use of committees. The staff specialist who confers individually with many persons in a given phase of a problem can obtain group judgment without the formation of a committee, as can the executive who asks key subordinates or other specialists for memorandums analyzing a problem and making recommenda-

FIGURE 10-1

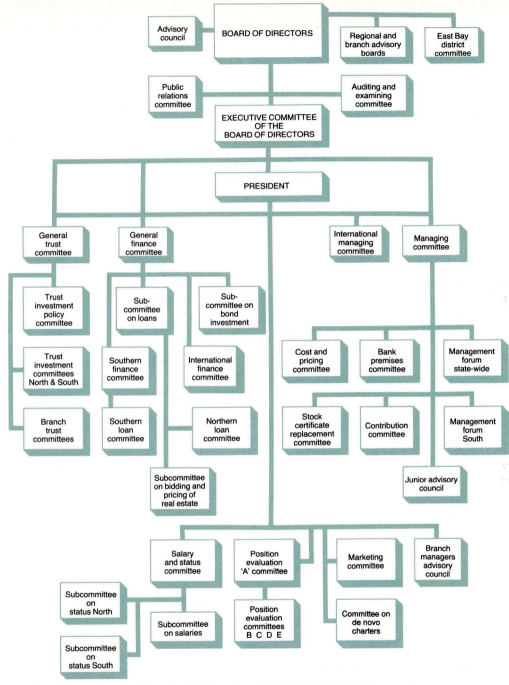

COMMITTEE ORGANIZATION IN A LARGE BANK.

This bank has supplemented its management organization structure with a large number of committees and subcommittees. All these groups exert influence on management policy and decision, and certain committees, such as the position evaluation committee, actually make decisions. Others, such as the advisory council of the board of directors and the regional and branch advisory boards, operate only in an advisory capacity. Likewise, the general trust committees make actual decisions. Most of the committees have as their members senior or other key managers from all the important departments and divisions of the company. The junior advisory council, however, consists of lower-level managers or those about to be placed in a managerial capacity. While it carries on important analyses and projects and advises senior management groups, its primary purpose is training junior managers for future increased responsibilities in the bank.

tions thereon. At times group judgment can thus be obtained more efficiently, in terms of time, without the long deliberations of a committee. The keen manager can usually grasp ideas and the reasoning behind them more quickly from a concise written memorandum than from an oral presentation.

However, one of the advantages of group deliberation and judgment, not to be obtained without an actual meeting, is the stimulation resulting from discussion of ideas and the cross-examination techniques of the committee meeting. Leading, as it does, to clarification of problems and development of new ideas, this interchange has been found to be especially enlightening in policy matters. It is true that sometimes the results obtained by group judgment are superior to those obtained by individual judgment.

Fear of Too Much Authority in a Single Person

Another reason for the widespread use of committees is the fear of delegating too much authority to a single person. This fear, especially pronounced in government, dictated to the framers of the American Constitution not only the establishment of a two-house legislature and a multimember Supreme Court but also the division of the powers of government among the Congress, the Supreme Court, and the President. However, despite this fear of centralized authority, the founders of the American republic placed the *administration* of laws in the hands of a single top executive, recognizing the advantages of this system. Yet, as former President Nixon discovered, the legislature has the power to remove or force the resignation of the chief executive.

Fear of delegating too much authority to an individual has been experienced in educational enterprises and in charitable and religious organizations. Although the willingness of people to be bound by the faith has led to concentration of authority in the head of the Roman Catholic Church, in the various Protestant denominations one finds far less willingness to trust any single executive.

This fear has had less influence in business than in other types of organization. Business enterprises have, for one thing, developed primarily from small beginnings within the institution of private property, with its implications of authority of the owner; workers too, have been free to avoid abuse of power by moving from one company to another; and the overriding importance of efficiency, finally, has favored the single manager. At the same time, the traditional existence of a board of directors as the top managing group of the business corporation may be traced, to a great extent, to the fear of property owners of delegating too much authority to a managing director.

This motive has likewise influenced the formation of many internal business committees. A committee may be established to make recommendations on a problem largely because the president or department head does not wish to take full responsibility for making a decision or to trust the decision to a subordinate. Bonus committees, which may decide on the amount and the distribution of bonuses for outstanding managers, often result from such motivation, and major financial and capital investment policies are developed by committees, partly because of unwillingness to trust a single individual with complete authority to make such important decisions.

Representation of Interested Groups

The desire to have various interested groups represented in policy matters makes itself felt in all branches of government where either law or tradition requires that the two major political parties, various sections of the country, or various pressure groups be represented.

Representation plays a part, too, in the establishment and staffing of committees in business. Boards of directors are often selected on the basis of groups interested in the company and, perhaps more often, on the basis of groups in which the company has an interest. When executives have a particularly difficult internal problem involving managers and specialists in various departments and activities, they may choose committee members in such a way as to give these interested parties representation. They may ostensibly do this in order to get a more balanced group judgment and a more diversified point of view, but they may actually be doing it to ensure that these groups will be represented and will thereby feel a sense of loyalty and commitment to the decision reached.

Coordination of Departments, Plans, and Policies

There is general agreement that committees are very useful for coordinating activities among various organizational units. For example, in one study 90 percent of the respondents agreed with the statement that "committees promote coordination among departments." There was similar agreement on this point among various levels, although lower-middle management agreed slightly less (a little over 80 percent) than upper-middle and top management (about 90 percent agreed with the statement).[7]

Committees are also useful for coordinating planning and the execution of programs. The dynamics of modern enterprise place a heavy burden on its managers to integrate plans and activities. With complications, change, and numerous specialized departments, it is difficult to coordinate every activity, every subordinate plan, and every expenditure.

A committee permits the individuals concerned not only to obtain firsthand a picture of overall plans and of their place in them but also to contribute suggestions on the spot for improvement of plans. Committees also furnish a place where agreement may be reached on the steps in coordination.

Transmission and Sharing of Information

Committees are useful for transmitting and sharing information. All group members affected by a mutual problem or project can learn of it simultaneously, and decisions and instructions can be received uniformly with opportunities for clarification. The time thus saved may be considerable and the spoken word, with its possibilities for overtones and emphasis and the opportunities for clarification, may carry its point better than even carefully written memorandums.

Consolidation of Authority

A manager in a department, branch, or section often has only a portion of the authority necessary to accomplish a program. As noted in Chapter 9, this is known as splintered authority. Good organization practice normally provides managers with the power appropriate to their position. However, this is not possible in every instance, and some matters call for the exercise of authority that the manager at the level concerned does not possess.

One way to handle problems of this sort is to refer them upward in the organizational hierarchy until they reach a point at which the requisite authority exists. But this place is often in the office of the president, and the problem may not be of sufficient importance to be decided at that level.

A customer of a machine-tool manufacturer wished a slight but unusual change in design of a piece of equipment. The customer would approach the sales department, which, if there were no established procedure for handling this change, could not act without the authority of the engineering department, the production department, and the cost estimating department. In this case, the sales manager might establish a special purpose committee to study the problem, to agree on the nature and cost of the change, and to use the combined authority of its members to approve the request.

The informal use of the committee gives much flexibility to organization. However, consolidating splintered authority through a committee should be watched carefully to ascertain whether the organizational structure itself might not be changed to concentrate in one position the appropriate authority to make *recurring* decisions.

Motivation through Participation

Committees permit wide participation in decision making. Persons who take part in planning a program or making a decision usually feel more enthusiastic about accepting and executing it. Even limited participation can be helpful.

The use of committees to motivate subordinates to get behind a program or decision requires skillful handling. It is by no means certain that deliberations of this kind will kindle enthusiastic support, for they can also result in the deepening of existing divisions among participants. On the other hand, there are people who seem to be against every move unless they have been previously consulted. Thus, it requires a skillful chairperson to direct conflicting interests toward common objectives.

Avoidance of Action

It cannot be denied that committees are sometimes appointed by managers when they do not want any action to ensue. One of the surest ways to delay the handling of a problem and even to postpone a decision indefinitely is to appoint a committee, and sometimes many subcommittees, to study the matter, particularly if the membership is carefully selected with delay in mind. In organizations of all kinds, skillful managers resort to this delaying action when they see fit.

DISADVANTAGES OF COMMITTEES

Certain dangers of committees have been so widely publicized that many managers make little use of them.

High Cost in Time and Money

The cost of committee action in time is likely to be considerable. A committee may require members to travel some distance to reach a meeting. During the meeting, all members have the right to be heard, to have their points of view discussed, to challenge and cross-examine the points of view of others, and to analyze the reasons for a considered group conclusion. The spoken word, though valuable for emphasis and clarification, is seldom concise, and the "thinking out loud" that takes place is sometimes a waste of time for those who must listen. If the committee is supposed to reach a unanimous or nearly unanimous decision, the discussion is likely to be lengthy. And if a decision can be reached quickly, the meeting may have been unnecessary in the first place.

The monetary cost of committee discussion can also be very high. One must consider not only the cost of executive time (which for even a $60,000-per-year executive runs to $30 an hour) but even more the cost to the company of loss of the executive time that would otherwise have been devoted to other important duties. However, it is quite possible that the cost of executive time in a group meeting might be less than when a superior meets individually with subordinates.

This cost in time and money becomes all the more disadvantageous when a committee is assigned a problem that could as well, or better, be solved by a single individual or by an individual with the help of a smaller and lesser-paid staff. Thus, the advantages of committee action must be considerable to offset the costs.

Compromise at the Least Common Denominator

Where committees are required to come to some conclusion or to reach some decision, there is danger that their action will be watered down or may even be

---

PERSPECTIVE:
WHAT PEOPLE SAY ABOUT COMMITTEES

Disparaging attitudes are reflected in such definitions of a committee as the following:

"A committee is made up of the unfit selected by the unwilling to do the unnecessary."

"A committee is a place where the loneliness of thought is replaced by the togetherness of nothingness."

"A camel is a horse invented by a committee."

meaningless. If the matter under consideration is so simple that differences of opinion do not exist, the use of committee time is wasteful. If differences of opinion exist, the point at which all or a majority of the committee members can agree will tend to be at the least common denominator. Most often this is not as strong and positive a course of action as that undertaken by an individual, who has only to consider the facts as he or she sees them and then reach a conclusion. Because of the necessity for seeking out common ground, committees often take innocuous action or defer action entirely.

There is the danger of compromising at the level of the least common denominator of agreement. Even committees whose authority delegation requires only majority agreement sometimes develop traditions of unanimity. Small groups of people frequently seek—from feelings of politeness, mutual respect, and humility—to reach conclusions on which all can agree. Since committee members are ordinarily picked from organization equals, reluctance to force a conclusion on a recalcitrant minority is understandable, increasing thereby the probability of weak decisions.

Indecision

Another disadvantage of committees is that the time required for thorough deliberation, the discussion of peripheral or tangential subjects, and the difficulty of reaching agreement often result in adjournment without action.

Committee meetings are often characterized by an official and a hidden agenda. The *hidden agenda* pertains to the disguised individual motives of members. It is not unusual for these motives to prevent the committee from reaching agreement on the official topic of discussion since, if desires and feelings of members are not candidly discussed, members may not really know what the committee, as a group, concludes.

Tendency to Be Self-Destructive

Indecisiveness may give the chairperson or a strong member an opportunity to force the committee into a decision the way he or she wants it to go. Almost invariably, one person in a group emerges as the leader. But when an individual becomes dominant, the nature of the committee as a decision-making group of equals changes, and there actually emerges an executive with a group of followers or advisers. Executives often delude themselves into believing that committees operate on group management principles as a group of equals, when, as a matter of fact, the "team" is composed of subordinate advisers or even yes-sayers following a leader.

Splitting of Responsibility

When authority to study, make recommendations, or arrive at a decision is delegated to a group, the fact is that the authority is dispersed throughout the group. Thus, individual members hardly feel the same degree of responsibility that they would if they personally were charged with the same task. This splitting of responsibility is one of the chief disadvantages of a committee. Since no one can practically or logically feel personally accountable for the actions of a group, no individual feels personally responsible for any action within it.

Tyranny of the Minority

As has been pointed out, committees tend to seek unanimous or near-unanimous conclusions or decisions. Minority members are therefore in a strong position. By their insistence upon acceptance of their position or of a compromise position, they may exercise an unwarranted tyranny over the majority. The minority members of a jury have such power. We recall an important committee of nine members in which a tradition for unanimous agreement developed. One member actually controlled the committee, not through force of leadership but through power to withhold his vote. The matters which he blocked or on which he forced a watered-down conclusion fell in the area of committee authority and responsibility; the committee, though having failed because of his tyranny, provided cover for him. Had he borne individual authority and responsibility for his actions, he could hardly have been the obstructionist he was.

THE PLURAL EXECUTIVE AND THE BOARD OF DIRECTORS[8]

Most committees are nonmanagerial in nature. However, some groups are given the power to make decisions and to undertake one or all of the managerial functions of planning, organizing, staffing, leading, and controlling. It is this latter type of committee that is referred to as the "plural executive."[9]

Origin

The plural executive may be established by law, or it may result from a managerial decision. Examples of the former are the board of directors of a corporation and the plural executive (commission, board) established by various legislatures to operate one of their agencies. In the case of the business corporation, legislatures have traditionally required that the board be elected to act for the stockholders. State and federal legislatures have, especially in recent years, provided for direction of most government agencies by a single manager, but in many instances plural executives are still operating.

Authority

The extent of authority to manage and to make decisions held by a plural executive is not always easy to ascertain. Some, such as the board of directors, clearly have this power, although they may not exercise it. Some companies have been managed from the top, on a day-to-day or weekly basis, by a plural executive, but this is rare.

There are, however, many boards of directors and executive committees of organizations which potentially have the power to manage but actually do not, since decisions are made by a prominent stockholder or a strong leader in the group. Usually, the president is the dominant figure, with the other members often little more than advisers. In other words, the plural executive is not always what it seems, and a single executive often in reality makes the decisions. Then there are other committees established with advisory authority only. Sometimes these actually operate as plural executives if, through tradition, weakness of leadership, or insistence of the chairperson on agreement before a decision is made, they actually make decisions or undertake managerial functions as a group.[10]

Role in Policy Making

The plural executive is often found in the field of strategy or policymaking. Many companies have an executive or management committee to develop major plans and adopt basic strategy. They go by various names: General Motors has its executive and finance committees, United States Rubber Company its operating policy committee, the Sun Chemical Company its management committee, Lockheed Aircraft Corporation its corporate policy committee, and the Koppers Company its policy committee.

The extent of authority of these committees varies considerably, although their influence on decision making is perhaps greater in strategic planning than in any other area. These committees also engage in control, for their concern with strategic plans must be followed up to make sure that events conform to decisions.

Furthermore, these committees are often useful in settling differences of opinion or in the settlement of questions of organizational jurisdiction. The plural executive is an ideal arbitrator of disputes since a determination by a group will usually be accepted by contesting parties as being more impartial than that of a single arbiter. Besides, personality clashes in a given situation are more easily submerged in group action.

Where committees are successful in strategy formulation, they are dependent upon accurate and adequate staff work. A committee can hardly develop a proposal, forecast probable profits and costs from alternative courses of action, or investigate the numerous tangible and intangible factors influencing a basic decision. These are matters for study, and the committee is a notoriously poor study or research device. Therefore, if group deliberation is to be productive, facts and analyses must be developed and presented so that the members have readily available the data upon which to base a decision.

Role in Policy Execution

Many companies and management experts distinguish between strategy/policymaking and execution. It has been said that the former is concerned with the establishment of broad principles by which administration is guided, while the latter is concerned with the daily conduct of the company's affairs—setting standards and procedures to guide and govern execution of policies, establishing controls to ensure adherence to standards, solving interdivisional disputes, improving interdivisional coordination, and meeting various emergencies as they arise.

PERSPECTIVE:
TRENDS IN THE COMPOSITION OF BOARDS

Since the 1960s, more outsiders were selected to the board of directors, and in the 1970s outsiders constituted a majority on many boards of major companies. But in the latter part of the 1980s, many who were called declined the invitation and more insiders are now again favored on many boards.

There are many reasons why people from the outside do not want to serve on the boards of directors.[11] For one, members are increasingly required to study the issues brought before them more carefully, which, in turn, demands a great deal of their time. Moreover, board members are concerned about the possibility of being held liable for their decisions.[12] True, companies may provide liability insurance, but several insurance companies have reduced their coverage, increased the premium, and even withdrawn coverage.[13]

To attract capable directors and to make the board more effective, some ideas for reform have been circulated. Some would like to see that directors have to own stocks in the companies they serve. It is suggested that this would result in more careful deliberation of the issues. Others suggest that board members be nominated by a committee composed of outside members. Still others recommend that members have an independent staff to study the various issues. There is also the idea that the boards should reflect the various claimants. For example, in the early 1980s Douglas A. Frazer of the United Automobile Workers sat on the board of Chrysler. He, in a sense, was required to wear two "hats": He had to represent labor and at the same time he had to consider the overall health of the company and its various claimants. This practice, by the way, is quite common in Germany and other European countries, where, by law, labor must be represented on the board of major companies.

Whatever the changes are going to be, and some seem to be necessary, the role of the board of directors is likely to change in the future.

In companies where this distinction is made, special committees are established in functional areas such as engineering, distribution, manufacturing, public relations, and labor relations. These committees deal with the more specialized and technical aspects of planning. Moreover, such committees may make recommendations to policy committees or may bolster basic policy with detailed plans and programs.

PLURAL VERSUS INDIVIDUAL EXECUTIVE

Committees without managerial authority are far more numerous than those which are true plural executives. While much experience exists in organization with committees and with plural executives, the benefits of group management, as compared to individual management, have not been widely studied.

American Management Association Survey

One attempt to measure the merits of group versus individual managing was made in a study some years ago by the American Management Association.[14] Through interviews with executives and analysis of records of some twenty representative companies, some interesting results were found. Breaking down managing into twelve functions, the survey roughly estimated the proportion of each function that could (1) be exercised effectively by committee action, (2) be exercised effectively by committee action but more effectively by individual action, (3) be exercised by individual action, though helpfully supplemented by committee action, or (4) be effectively exercised only by individual action.

The results of this survey are summarized in Table 10-1. Although the sample is small, the breakdowns rough, and the percentages no more than approximate, the survey (even though some years old) shows what the top executives in some well-managed companies thought of group, as compared to individual, executive action. The survey results indicated a strong preference for the plural executive only in the settling of jurisdictional questions. The emphasis on the superiority of individual action in practically every function of managing is pronounced. Even where committee action was found effective (the first two classifications), though not in all cases as effective as individual action, the score in favor of committees (with one exception) was still not particularly high. While this survey was made some years ago, our experience and study lead us to believe the results are still valid.

TABLE 10-1   Relative Effectiveness of Individual and Committee Action in Functional Activities, Percent

Management function	Can be exercised effectively by committee	Can be exercised by committee but more effectively by individual	Individual initiative essential but may be supplemented by committee	Individual action essential; committee ineffective
Planning	20	20	25	35
Control	25	20	25	30
Formulating objectives	35	35	10	20
Organization	5	25	20	50
Jurisdictional questions	90	10		
Leadership			10	90
Administration	20	25	25	30
Execution	10	15	10	65
Innovation	30	20	20	30
Communication	20	15	35	30
Advice	15	25	35	25
Decision making	10	30	10	50

Evaluation

The foregoing discussion of the plural executive points to certain conclusions. The plural executive succeeds fairly well in helping to coordinate the activities of managers. It has a high potential for aiding in defining objectives, selecting alternative ways of achieving them, and measuring the success attained. In terms of managerial functions, the plural executive is thus especially useful in planning and in certain of the broader aspects of control. However, all the disadvantages of the committee form apply with special force to the true plural executive.

MISUSE OF COMMITTEES

The committee form has often fallen into disrepute through misuse. The five following abuses should be avoided when committees are set up and operated.

As Replacement for a Manager

The weakness of the committee as a managing device has already been noted. Leadership is essentially a quality of individuals. If decision making is to be sharp, clear, prompt, and subject to unquestioned responsibility, it is better exercised by an individual, as is the leading of subordinates.

There are times, it must be admitted, when managerial effectiveness is not an overriding consideration. In certain government agencies the danger of putting too much authority in the hands of an individual may be so great as to supersede questions of pure efficiency. As a matter of fact, before criticizing the waste, duplication, and inefficiency of governmental management, one should face the question of whether these costs are a fair price to pay for curtailing possible abuses of authority. Similarly, in business, a certain area of decision might be so important to the welfare of the company and the dangers of abuse of authority in that area so great that no individual should be entrusted with this power.

One can hardly say that a committee has no place in management, but the advantages of group thinking and participation in policy questions can be gained in most cases through advisory committees. Most business committees function this way, leaving the real decision making and managing to the line executives to whom they report. As Ralph Cordiner, former president of the General Electric Company, has said, "We have no committees to make decisions that individuals should make."

For Research or Study

A group meeting together can hardly engage in research or study, even though it may well weigh and criticize the results of these. When the solution to a problem requires data not available to a committee, no amount of discussion or consideration can turn up the missing information. This is essentially an individual function, even though, of course, individuals may be coordinated into a team with individual research assignments. Most committees, therefore, need a research staff, providing at least analyses of alternative courses of action, historical summaries, or well-considered forecasts.

For Unimportant Decisions

Even where the committee is clothed with advisory authority only, the disadvantages of this device should dictate that its use be limited to important matters. Moreover, no intelligent specialist or manager can help feeling uncomfortable when time is wasted by a group deliberating at length on trivial subjects. This impatience reaches its frustrating climax when a committee member insists on considering at length a question upon which a certain decision is a foregone conclusion.

For Decisions beyond Participants' Authority

Where committees are used for decision making, if committee members with authority attend the meetings or send duly empowered representatives, and if the agenda deals with matters within the competence of the members, no authority problem will be encountered. But too often the executives with the requisite authority cannot or do not attend the meeting. Instead they send subordinates who have not been delegated the superiors' authority or who hesitate to bind the superiors. The result is that the committee cannot function as intended. Delay results while the substitute refers questions to the superior, and much advantage of group decision making and deliberation is lost.

To Consolidate Divided Authority

A disadvantage of departmentalization is that authority is so delegated that, in some cases, no one except the chief executive officer has adequate authority to do what must be done. Even within departments or sections, authority may be so splintered that group meetings are necessary to consolidate authority for making decisions. If divided authority can be eliminated by changing the organization structure and the delegations of authority, recourse to a committee is certainly a misuse of the device.

SUCCESSFUL OPERATION OF COMMITTEES

Managers spend a great deal of time in committees. The use of committees is due not only to the democratic tradition in American social life but also to a growing emphasis on group management and group participation in organizations. In attempting to overcome some of the disadvantages of committees, managers may find the following guidelines useful.

1. Authority

The committee's authority should be spelled out so that members know whether their responsibility is to make decisions, to make recommendations, or merely to deliberate and to give the chairperson some insights into the issue under discussion.

2. Size

The size of the committee is very important. As shown in Figure 10-2, the complexity of interrelationships greatly increases with the size of the group. If the group is too large, there may not be enough opportunities for adequate communication among its members. On the other hand, if the group consists of only three persons, there is the possibility that two may form a coalition against the third member. No precise conclusions can be drawn here about the appropriate size. As a general rule, a committee should be large enough to promote deliberation and include the breadth or expertise required for the job, but not so large as to waste time or foster indecision. The optimum committee size is thought by some to be at least five or six, but not more than fifteen or sixteen. An analysis of small-group research indicates that the ideal committee size may be five when the five members possess adequate skills and knowledge to deal with problems facing the committee.[15] It is obvious that the larger the group, the greater the difficulty in obtaining a "meeting of the minds," and the more time necessary to allow everyone to contribute.

3. Membership[16]

The members of the committee must be selected carefully. If a committee is to be successful, the members must be representative of the interests they are intended to serve. They must also possess the required authority, and be able to perform well in a group. Finally, the members should have the capacity for communicating well and reaching group decisions by integrating group thinking rather than by inappropriate compromise.

4. Subject Matter

The subject must be carefully selected. Committee work should be limited to subject matter that can be handled in group discussion. Certain kinds of subjects lend themselves to committee action, while others do not. Jurisdictional disputes and strategy formulation, for example, may be suitable for group deliberation,

FIGURE 10-2

**INCREASED COMPLEXITY OF RELATIONSHIPS
THROUGH INCREASE IN GROUP SIZE.**

while certain isolated, technical problems may be better solved by an expert in the specialized field. To make committees effective, an agenda and relevant information should be circulated well in advance so that the members can study the subject matter before the meeting.

5. Chairperson

The selection of the chairperson is crucial for an effective committee meeting. Such a person can avoid the wastes and drawbacks of committees by planning the meeting, preparing the agenda, seeing that the results of research are available to the members ahead of time, formulating definite proposals for discussion or action, and conducting the meeting efficiently. The chairperson sets the tone of the meeting, integrates the ideas, and keeps the discussion from wandering.

6. Minutes

Effective communication in committees usually requires circulating minutes and checking conclusions. At times, individuals leave the meeting with varying interpretations as to what was agreed. To avoid this, it is good to take careful minutes of the meeting and circulate them in draft form for correction or modification before the final copy is approved by the committee.

7. Cost Effectiveness

The committee must be worth its cost. It may be difficult to count the benefits, especially such intangible factors as morale, enhanced status of committee members, and the committee's value as a training device to enhance teamwork. But the committee can be justified only if the costs are offset by tangible and intangible benefits.

OTHER GROUPS IN MANAGING

Although committees are of special importance as an organization device, they are really only one of many groups we find in organizations. In addition to committees we find teams, conferences, task forces, and negotiation sessions all involving group activities.

A **group** may be defined as *two or more people acting interdependently in a unified manner toward the achievement of common goals.* A group is more than a collection of individuals; rather, through their interactions, new forces and new properties are created that need to be identified and studied in themselves. The goals may pertain to specific tasks, but it may also mean that the people share some common concerns, values, or ideology. Thus, group members are attracted to each other by some social bonds.

Characteristics of Groups

Groups—and the focus is on groups in the organization—have a number of characteristics. First, group members share one or more common goals, such as the goals of a product group to develop, manufacture, and market a new product. A second characteristic of groups is that they normally require interaction and communication among members. It is impossible to coordinate the efforts of group members without communication. Third, members within a group assume roles. In a product group, for example, individuals are responsible for designing, producing, selling, or distributing a product. Naturally, the roles are in some kind of relationship to each other in order to achieve the group task. Fourth, groups usually are a part of a larger group. The product group may belong to a product division which produces many products of a similar nature. Large groups may also consist of subgroups. Thus, within the product group may be a subgroup specializing exclusively in the selling of the product. Also, groups interface with other groups. Thus, product group A may cooperate with product group B in the distribution of their products. It is evident, then, that the systems point of view, which focuses on the interrelatedness of parts, is essential in understanding the functioning of groups.

There are a number of other sociological characteristics of groups that must be recognized. Groups develop norms, which refer to expected behavior of members belonging to the group. If individuals deviate from the norm, pressure is exerted to make them comply. This can be functional when, for example, a person who frequently shows up late for work is admonished by other group members, but there also are situations in which groups may be dysfunctional. Ambitious, highly motivated employees may be pressed to produce in congruence with generally accepted norms rather than according to their abilities.

PERSPECTIVE:
PRESSURE TOWARD CONFORMITY: HOW WOULD YOU RESPOND?

In a widely publicized experiment, S. E. Asch showed the impact of pressure of the group toward conformity.[17] Members of a small group were asked to match a standard line (8 inches long) with three comparison lines (6¼, 8, and 6¾ inches long—see Figure 10-3). One experimental group member (the naive subject) was not aware that all the other students in the group (confederates of the experimenter) were instructed to give occasionally wrong answers, such as saying that the 6¾-inch line was as long as the 8-inch standard line. The setting was arranged so that the naive subject was one of the last ones to make a judgment. It was found that "innocent" members made wrong choices when the confederates did so unanimously. In later interviews, subjects reported that they wanted to agree with the majority. This illustrates that even in a rather uncomplicated task, people may decide against their better judgment owing to group pressure. These findings explain to some extent the influence of group pressure toward conformity and how it may result in managerial decisions which are less than optimal.

FIGURE 10-3

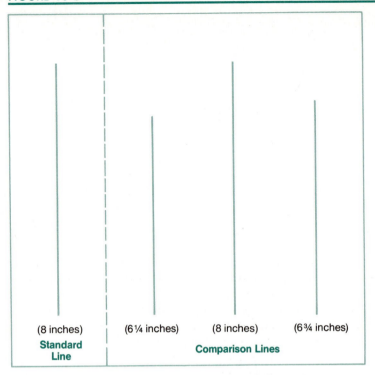

(8 inches)   (6¼ inches)   (8 inches)   (6¾ inches)

Standard Line   **Comparison Lines**

**WHICH COMPARISON LINE IS
THE SAME LENGTH AS THE STANDARD LINE?**

Functions and Advantages of Groups

Groups have many functions. They are powerful in changing behavior, attitudes, and values, and in disciplining members. As noted, deviant members may be pressured to adhere to group norms. In addition, groups are used for decision making, negotiating, and bargaining. Thus, group members with diverse backgrounds may bring different perspectives to the decision-making process. This does not mean, however, that group decisions are always better than individual decisions.

Group concepts are very important for the topics covered in Chapters 17 to 19. Specifically, different group structures influence *communication* patterns. Thus, communication will differ when it is channeled through one key member or when communication flows freely among all the group members. One can hardly consider a number of people a team when each member communicates only with the boss; teamwork requires open communication among all members. Effective group interactions may also affect *motivation*. For example, group members participating in setting objectives may become committed to the achievement of group goals. Finally, *leadership* must be seen in the context of group processes. A grasp of group concepts helps in understanding the interactions between leaders and followers as well as the interactions among all the group members. In short, an understanding of groups is important for carrying out all managerial functions, particularly the function of leading. Groups are a fact of organized and unorganized life. It is important to know how they work and to use them in an effective and efficient manner in situations that favor group actions.

Groups also have advantages for individuals. Groups do provide social satisfaction for their members, a feeling of belonging, and support for the needs of individuals. Another benefit of groups is that they promote communication. It may be the give-and-take in a formal meeting, or it can take the form of the grapevine, which is the informal communication through which group members become aware of "what is really going on in the firm." Groups also provide security. Labor unions are sometimes formed precisely for this reason—to give job security to their members. Finally, groups provide opportunities for promoting self-esteem through recognition from, and acceptance by, peers.

Disadvantages of Groups

Group activities also may present problems. Certainly the disadvantages of committees mentioned above are relevant here. As pointed out in our discussion of committees, when a compromise can be reached only at the lowest common denominator or when decisions must be postponed, the use of groups may be costly in time and money. A chairperson or a strong member may use the group for selfish purposes rather than for the well-being of the enterprise. Responsibility may be divided so that no one feels accountable for a decision. Finally, a few members may tyrannize the group and inhibit its proper functioning. In other words, all the problems and dangers we found in committees are potentially present with groups.

FOR DISCUSSION

1. A prominent novelist-critic of the management scene has said: "I don't think we can go on very much longer with the luxurious practice of hiring ten men to make one man's decision. With all its advantages, professional management tends to encourage bureaucratic corpulence." Comment.

2. Distinguish between a "committee," a "team," and a "group."

3. Where in an organization would you suggest, if anyplace, that committees should be used? Why?

4. What are the reasons for using committees? If there are good reasons, why are committees criticized so much?

5. What is meant by the term "plural executive"?

6. What is the relative effectiveness of individual and committee action in functional activities? Identify the activities that can be undertaken most effectively by a committee.

7. Describe and discuss the nature of misapplications of committees.

8. What would you recommend for making committees effective?

9. What are the major characteristics of groups in organizations?

EXERCISES/ACTION STEPS

1. Discuss one of the cases for this chapter in groups of students. Divide the classes into groups of various sizes (e.g., groups of 3, 6, 9, 12 students). Each group is to analyze the case and make recommendations. Select a spokesperson to present the group's view on the case. On what basis was the spokesperson selected? What are the similarities and differences between a spokesperson and a chairperson? Discuss the advantages and problems encountered in the groups of various sizes. What do you think is the "ideal" group size?

2. Interview two managers and ask about their experiences in committees. Do they have a positive or a negative view of committees? What have they found to be most important to make the committees effective and efficient? What do they think the "ideal" size for a committee is?

CASES

CASE 10-1
THE HUMBOLD RETAIL CHAIN

At a time when most retailers had a decline in earnings, the Humbold Retail Chain showed great increases. The executives at Humbold attribute the profit performance largely to the relatively new managerial style that emphasizes group decision making and personnel policies similar to those used by the Japanese, with an emphasis on job security and nonadversarial relationships with employees as well as with customers.

The current chairman of the board (who, however, is soon to retire) practices consensus management, giving managers ample opportunities to participate in most major decisions. This, in turn, helps managers to understand what is going on at the various levels in the organization. At the same time, the team approach facilitates the development of managers. For example, a committee deals with policy areas such as strategic issues. Through group participation, younger managers become familiar with critical issues facing the firm.

While most managers at Humbold feel that the group management approach is working well, Richard Newstrom, a young manager with a master's degree from a highly respected business school, is not quite as optimistic about this approach. He thinks that managers waste their time in committee meetings and that group decisions are compromises and may not be optimal. In order to emphasize his point he quotes a number of cliches about the weaknesses of committees.

His colleagues, however, point out that the team approach breaks down some of the departmental barriers and facilitates coordination among divisions. They admit that plans developed by a group may be time-consuming, but their implementation is swift. Moreover, they argue that the team approach encourages managers to explore many more alternatives than with individual decision making, and people in different age groups and with different perspectives have an input.

Newstrom does not agree with his colleagues, suggesting that the team approach at Humbold works only because of the managerial style of its chairman, and that as soon as he retires, collaboration among managers will come to an end.

1. What are the advantages and disadvantages of the group decision approach?

2. What accounts for the negative attitudes toward committees?

3. How can committees, or teams, be made more effective?

CASE 10-2
COMMITTEE MANAGEMENT AT
THE UNIVERSITY OF CALIFORNIA

Many universities, notably the larger ones, operate extensively through committee management, especially in the selection and promotion of persons to tenure associate and full professorships. One example of a university where committees are extensively used in this area is embodied by the various campuses of the University of California.

For appointment or promotion to the positions of associate professor or professor (both of which carry tenure), the University of California uses the following steps:

- A candidate is reviewed thoroughly by staffing committee of his or her department or school.

- If a candidate passes there, the action is sent to the chairman or dean for review and then to the executive vice-chancellor of the campus, where it is referred to the campus budget and promotion committee.

- The budget and promotion committee immediately refers the case to a specially appointed ad hoc committee of five faculty members, of whom only one or two may be from the candidate's department or school.

- The ad hoc committee reviews the case and makes a recommendation to the budget and promotion committee.

- The budget and promotion committee reviews the case and makes recommendations to the executive vice-chancellor and chancellor of the campus.

- The executive vice-chancellor and chancellor review the case and, after this review, the case is sent to the academic vice-president of the university with recommendations.

- The university academic vice-president and president review the case and, if their action is favorable, send it with recommended action to the regents of the university for final action.

1. How would you like to be reviewed for selection or promotion by this hierarchy of committees?

2. What strengths or weaknesses do you see in this procedure?

3. Assuming you see certain weaknesses and perhaps dangers in this kind of committee management, what do you suggest be done?

REFERENCES

1. Note that decision making is also discussed in Chapter 6.

2. J. Presley and S. Keen, "Better Meetings Lead to Higher Productivity: A Case Study," _Management Review_ (April 1975), pp. 16–22.

3. R. Tillman, Jr., "Committees on Trial," _Harvard Business Review_ (May–June 1960), pp. 6–12, 162–173. For a discussion of characteristics of committees and their functions, see

John J. Gabarro and Anne Harlan, "Process Observation," in Leonard A. Schlesinger, Robert G. Eccles, and John J. Gabarro, *Managing Behavior in Organizations* (New York: McGraw-Hill Book Company, 1983), pp. 93–100.

4. Walter Kiechel III, "How to Take Part in a Meeting," *Fortune* (May 26, 1986), pp. 177–180.

5. "The Frustrations of the Group Executive," *Business Week* (Sept. 25, 1978), pp. 102–110.

6. Tillman, "Committees" (1960).

7. Tillman, "Committees" (1960).

8. For an excellent and very thorough discussion of the board of directors, see Stanley C. Vance, *Corporate Leadership—Boards, Directors, and Strategy* (New York: McGraw-Hill Book Company, 1983).

9. For an early discussion of the plural executive see William H. Mylander, "Management by the Executive Committee," *Harvard Business Review* (May–June 1955), pp. 51–58.

10. For an early discussion of the functions of the board of directors, see Harold Koontz, *The Board of Directors and Effective Management* (New York: McGraw-Hill Book Company, 1967).

11. Laurie Baum, "The Job Nobody Wants," *Business Week* (Sept. 8, 1986), pp. 56–61; William B. Glaberson and William J. Powell, Jr., "A Landmark Ruling That Puts Board Members in Peril," *Business Week* (Mar. 18, 1985), pp. 56–57; "Inside Look at Life in the Corporate Board Room," *U.S. News & World Report* (Jan. 28, 1985), pp. 71–72.

12. See Rosswell B. Perkins, "Avoiding Director Liability," *Harvard Business Review* (May–June 1986), pp. 8–14.

13. A rather new Delaware law gives some protection to directors from negligence suits. But angry stockholders can still sue them. See Leo Herzel, Richard W. Shepro, and Leo Katz, "Next-to-Last Word on Endangered Directors," *Harvard Business Review* (January–February 1987), pp. 38–43.

14. Ernest Dale, *Planning and Developing the Company Organization Structure*, Research Report no. 20 (New York: American Management Association, 1952), pp. 92–96.

15. See Alan C. Filley, "Committee Management: Guidelines from Social Science Research," *California Management Review* (Fall 1970), pp. 13–21.

16. For an early discussion of membership selection see Cyril O'Donnell, "Ground Rules for Using Committees," *Management Review* (October 1961), pp. 63 ff.

17. See David Krech, Richard S. Crutchfield, and Egerton L. Ballachey, *Individual in Society* (New York: McGraw-Hill Book Company, 1962), pp. 507–508.

FOR FURTHER INFORMATION

Alderfer, Clayton P. "The Invisible Director on Corporate Boards," *Harvard Business Review* (November–December, 1986), pp. 38–52.

Decker, Richard C. and Ross H. Johnson. "How to Make Committees More Effective," in Harold Koontz, Cyril O'Donnell, and Heinz Weihrich (eds.), *Management: A Book of Readings*, 5th ed. (New York: McGraw-Hill Book Company, 1980), pp. 356–359.

Kolb, David A., Irwin M. Rubin, and James M. McIntyre. *Organizational Psychology*, 4th ed. (Englewood Cliffs, N.J.: Prentice-Hall, 1984), Part II.

Vancil, Richard F., and Charles H. Green. "How CEOs Use Top Management Committees," *Harvard Business Review* (January–February 1984), pp. 65–73.

11

Effective Organizing and Organizational Culture

CHAPTER OBJECTIVES

After reading this chapter, you should be able to:

1. Recognize some common mistakes made in organizing.

2. Avoid mistakes in organizing by planning.

3. Show how organizing can be improved by maintaining flexibility and by making staff more effective.

4. Avoid conflict by clarifying the organization structure and ensuring an understanding of organizing.

5. Promote and develop an appropriate organization culture.

6. Recognize that effective organizing depends on the situation.

7. Summarize some major principles or guidelines to be kept in mind in developing organization structure.

*O*rganizing involves developing an intentional structure of roles for effective performance. Organizing requires a network of decision and communication centers for coordinating efforts toward group and enterprise goals. To work, an organization structure must be understood, and principles must be put into practice. As we emphasized at the outset, in organizing, as elsewhere in managing, there is no one best way. What works will always depend on the specific situation.

SOME MISTAKES IN ORGANIZING

Despite their obvious nature and their interference with personal and enterprise goals, the persistence of certain mistakes of organizing is striking evidence of the difficulty of managing, the lack of sophistication of managers, or both.

1. Failure to Plan Properly

It is not unusual to find an enterprise continuing with a traditional organization structure long after its objectives, plans, and external environment have changed. For example, a company may keep its product research department under the control of the manufacturing division long after the business environment has changed from being production-oriented (as in a typical sellers' market) to being marketing-oriented (as in a typical buyers' market). Or a company may continue its functional organization structure when product groupings and the need for integrated, decentralized profit responsibility demand decentralized product divisions.

Also, a company may need managers of a kind not currently available or, just as likely, may find that certain managers have not grown with the company or do not fit current needs. Small, growing businesses often make the mistake of assuming that original employees can grow with the company, only to find that a good engineering designer, made a vice-president of engineering, cannot fill the larger role of the engineering chief, or that a once-adequate production superintendent cannot head a larger manufacturing department.

Another guideline for planning involves properly organizing around people. Organization structure must normally be modified to take people into account, and there is much to be said for trying to take full advantage of employee strengths and weaknesses. But managers organizing primarily around people overlook several facts. In the first place, managers organizing in this way cannot be assured that all bases will be covered and all the necessary tasks will be undertaken. In the second place, there is danger that different people will desire to do the same things, resulting in conflict or multiple command. In the third place, people have a way of coming and going in an enterprise—through retirement, resignation, promotion, or death—which makes organizing around them risky and their positions, when vacated, hard to describe accurately and to fill adequately.

Such mistakes occur when an enterprise fails to plan properly toward a future materially different from the past or present. By looking forward, a manager should determine what kind of organization structure will best serve future needs and what kinds of people will best serve an organization.

2. Failure to Clarify Relationships

The failure to clarify organization relationships, probably more than any other mistake, accounts for friction, politics, and inefficiencies. Since both the authority and the responsibility for action are critical, lack of clarity about them means lack of knowledge of the part members are to play on an enterprise team. This does not imply the need for detailed job descriptions or the possibility that people cannot operate as a team. Although some enterprise leaders have prided themselves on having a team of subordinates without specified tasks and authority lines, any sports coach could tell them that such a team is likely to be a group of jealous, insecure, buck-passing individuals jockeying for position and favor.

3. Failure to Delegate Authority

A common complaint in organization life is that managers are reluctant to push decision making down into the organization. In some businesses where uniformity of policy is necessary and decision making can be handled by one or a few managers, there may be neither the need nor the desire to decentralize authority. But decision-making bottlenecks, excessive referral of small problems to upper echelons, overburdening of top executives with detail, continual "firefighting" and "meeting of crises," and underdevelopment of managers in the lower levels of organization give evidence that failing to delegate authority to the proper extent is decidedly a mistake.

4. Failure to Balance Delegation

Another mistake made in organizing is failure to maintain balanced delegation. In other words, some managers—in their zeal for decentralization—may push decision making too far down in the organization. It may reach down to the very bottom of the structure and a system of independent organizational satellites may develop. Even when it is not taken to this extreme, excessive delegation may cause organization failures.

As we pointed out in the chapter on decentralization, top managers must retain some authority, particularly over decisions of companywide impact and at least enough to review the plans and performance of subordinates. Managers must not forget that there is some authority they should not delegate. Nor should they overlook the fact that they must maintain enough authority to ensure that when they do delegate authority to a subordinate, it will be used in the way and for the purposes intended.

5. Confusion of Lines of Authority with Lines of Information

The problems and costs of levels of organization and departmentation can be reduced by opening wide the channels of information. Unless information is confidential (and businesses and government, as well as other enterprises, overuse this classification), there is no reason why lines of information should follow lines of authority. In other words, relevant information should be widely available to people at all levels of the organization. Information gathering should be separated from decision making, since only the latter requires managerial authority. Enterprises often force lines of information to follow lines of authority when the only reason for following a chain of command is to preserve the integrity of decision-making authority and the clarity of responsibility.

6. Granting Authority without Exacting Responsibility

A significant cause of mismanagement is the assignment of authority without holding a person responsible. Authority delegation is not responsibility delegation; superiors remain responsible for the proper exercise of authority by their subordinates. Any other relationship would lead to organizational chaos. But all those to whom authority is delegated must be willing to be held responsible for their actions.

7. Holding People Responsible Who Do Not Have Authority

A common complaint of subordinates is that superiors hold them responsible for results without giving them the authority to accomplish them. Some of these complaints are unjustified and based on misunderstanding of the fact that subordinates can seldom have unlimited authority in any area because their actions must be coordinated with those of people in other positions and must conform to policy. Subordinates often see their jobs as all-encompassing and forget that their authority must be limited to their own departments and must be within controlling policy guidelines.

Too often, however, complaints are justified; managers, sometimes without realizing they are doing so, hold subordinates responsible for results they have no power to accomplish. This does not happen so frequently where organization lines and duties have been clearly set forth, but where a structure of roles is unclear or confused, it does occur.

8. Careless Application of the Staff Device

There are many valid reasons for using a staff assistant or staff specialist and even building entire advisory departments. However, there is danger that staff people will be used by their superiors to undermine the authority of the very managers they are intended merely to advise.

There is an ever-present danger that top managers may surround themselves with staff specialists and become so preoccupied with the specialists' work as to exclude from their schedule the time and attention needed for their line subordinates; or they may assign problems to their staff that would be more appropriately assigned to line managers.

In other instances, staff personnel exercise line authority that has not been delegated to them. It is easy to understand the impatience of staff specialists who see clearly how a situation should be handled, while the line officer in charge of it seems to be slow and clumsy. The very quality that makes staff specialists valuable—specialized knowledge—also makes them impatient of command. Yet, if they were to exercise authority without clear delegation, they would be not only undermining the authority of the responsible line official but also breaking down the unity of command.

9. Misuse of Functional Authority

Perhaps even more dangerous to good managing are the problems arising from undefined and unrestricted delegation of functional authority. This is especially common because the complexities of modern enterprise often create instances where it is desirable to give a predominantly staff or service department functional authority over activities in other parts of the organization.

In the search for economies of specialization and for advantages of technically expert opinion, managers often unduly exalt staff and service departments at the expense of the operating department. Many line officers—from the vice-president in charge of operations to a first-level supervisor—feel, with justice, that the business is being run by the staff and service departments through their exercise of functional authority. The personnel department, for example, may hire workers for line departments on the basis of psychological test results without consulting with its managers.

10. Multiple Subordination

The principal danger of too much functional authority is the breakdown of unity of command. We have only to look at the various departments of a typical medium-size or large business to see how such a breakdown occurs. The controller prescribes accounting procedures throughout the company. The purchasing director prescribes how and where purchases are to be made. The personnel manager dictates (often according to union contracts or government regulations) how employees shall be classified for pay purposes, how vacations shall be scheduled, and how many hours are to be worked. The traffic manager controls the routing of all freight. The general counsel insists that all contracts bear his or her approval and be made in prescribed form. The public relations director requires that all public utterances of managers and other employees be cleared or meet a prescribed policy line. And the tax director reviews all program decisions for clearance on their tax aspects.

Thus, with all these staff and service specialists having some degree of line authority over other parts of the organization, plus similar groups in divisions and regions, operating managers find themselves subject to the direction of a number of people with functional authority in addition to their principal superiors, who usually have the final decision concerning their pay scales and chances for promotion. It is no wonder that many managers, especially those at lower levels where there are so many functional authorities, feel frustrated.

11. Misunderstanding of the Function of Service Departments

Service departments are often looked upon as rather unconcerned with the accomplishment of major enterprise objectives, when they are, in fact, just as immediately concerned as any operating department. Sometimes people, particularly in so-called line departments, regard a service department as relatively unnecessary, unimportant, and therefore something to be ignored when possible.

On the other hand, many service departments mistakenly look upon their function as an end unto itself rather than a service to other departments. Thus, a purchasing department may not realize that its purpose is to purchase efficiently items ordered by authorized departments; or a statistics department may forget that it exists to furnish data desired by others, rather than to produce reports of its own choosing.

Perhaps the greatest misuse of service departments is summed up in the words "efficient inefficiency." When managers establish service departments, looking more to cost savings than to the efficiency of the entire enterprise, a highly "efficient" service may do an inefficient job of servicing. For example, little is gained in setting up a low-cost central recruiting section if the employees recruited do not meet organization needs.

12. Overorganization and Underorganization

Overorganization usually results from failure to put into practice the idea that the structure of the enterprise is merely a system for making possible efficient performance of people. Managers unduly complicating the structure through creating too many levels ignore the fact that efficiency demands that managers supervise as many subordinates as they can. Narrow spans may reflect misunderstanding of the span-of-management principle, managerial inability to minimize the time requirements of necessary human relationships, or lack of time to manage—a lack often caused by poor assignments and authority delegations. Likewise, the multiplication of staff and service activities or departments may be caused by inadequate delegation to line subordinates and the tendency to regard service specialization and efficiency so narrowly that larger enterprise operations are overlooked.

Managers also overorganize by appointing unnecessary line assistants (for example, assistant or deputy managers). Having a line assistant is justified when managers wish to devote their time to matters outside their department, during their long absences from the office, when they wish to delegate line authority in a given area such as engineering, or during a limited training period for a subordinate to whom full managerial status is soon to be given. Otherwise, the separation of managers from their other subordinates and the confusion as to who is really the superior that result from this practice lead us to conclude that it should be undertaken carefully and sparingly.

Sometimes, excessive procedures are confused with overorganization. Overorganization—particularly if interlaced with functional authority—can lead to excessive procedures. But much of the red tape often blamed on overorganization really results from poor planning. The failure to regard procedures as plans—and to treat them with the respect given other kinds of plans—often results in bewilderingly complex and even unnecessary procedures.

Similarly, too many committees, sapping the time and energies of managers and their staffs, are often blamed on overorganization rather than on poor organization (particularly when committees make decisions better made by individuals). An excess of committees often results from having authority delegated to too many positions or from vague delegation. Such an excess may actually point to underorganization.

AVOIDING MISTAKES BY PLANNING

As with the other functions of managing, establishment of objectives and orderly planning are necessary for good organization. As Urwick said in his classic book, "Lack of design (in organization) is illogical, cruel, wasteful, and inefficient."[1] It is illogical because good design, or planning, must come first, whether one speaks of engineering or social practice. It is cruel because "the main sufferers from a lack of design in organization are those individuals who work in an undertaking." It is wasteful because "unless jobs are clearly put together along lines of functional specialization, it is impossible to train new men (or women) to succeed to positions as the incumbents are promoted, resign or retire." And it is inefficient because, unless based on principles, management will be based on personalities, with the resultant rise of company politics, for "a machine will not run smoothly when fundamental engineering principles have been ignored in construction."

Planning for the Ideal

The search for an ideal organization to reflect enterprise goals under given circumstances is the impetus to planning. The search entails charting the main lines of organization, considering the organizational philosophy of the enterprise managers (for example, whether authority shall be centralized as much as possible or whether the company should divide its operations into semi-independent product or territorial divisions), and sketching out consequent authority relationships. The ultimate form established, like all plans, seldom remains unchanged, and continuous remolding of the ideal plan is normally necessary. Nevertheless, an ideal organization plan constitutes a standard, and, by comparing present structure with it, enterprise leaders know what changes should be made when possible.

An organizer must always be careful not to be blinded by popular notions in organizing, because what may work in one company may not work in another. Principles of organizing have general application, but the background of each company's operations and needs must be considered in applying these principles. Organization structure needs to be tailor-made.

Modification for the Human Factor

If available personnel do not fit into the ideal structure and cannot or should not be pushed aside, the only choice is to modify the structure to fit individual capabilities, attitudes, or limitations. This modification may seem like organizing around people; the difference is that in this case, one is organizing first around the goals to be met and activities to be undertaken, and only then making modifications for the human factor. Thus, planning will reduce compromising the necessity for principle whenever changes occur in personnel.

Advantages of Organization Planning

Planning the organization structure helps determine future personnel needs and required training programs. Without knowing what managerial personnel will be needed and what experience to demand, an enterprise cannot intelligently recruit people and train them.

Furthermore, organization planning can disclose weaknesses. Duplication of effort, unclear lines of authority, overlong lines of communication, excessive red tape, and obsolete practices show up best when desirable and actual organization structures are compared.

AVOIDING ORGANIZATIONAL INFLEXIBILITY

One basic advantage of organization planning is avoidance of organizational inflexibility. Many enterprises, especially those which have been in operation for many years, become too rigid to meet the first test of effective organization structure—ability to adapt to changing environment and meet new contingencies. This resistance to change can cause considerable loss of efficiency in organizations.

Signs of Inflexibility

Some older companies provide ample evidence of inflexibility: an organization pattern no longer suited to the times, a district or regional organization that could be either abolished or enlarged because of improved communications, or a too highly centralized structure for an enlarged enterprise requiring decentralization.

Avoiding Inflexibility through Reorganization

Although reorganization is intended to respond to changes in the enterprise environment, there may be other compelling reasons for reorganization. Those related to the business environment include changes in operations caused by acquisition or sale of major properties, changes in product line or marketing methods, business cycles, competitive influences, new production techniques, labor union policy, government regulatory and fiscal policy, or the current state of knowledge about organizing. New techniques and principles may become applicable, such as that of developing managers by allowing them to manage decentralized semi-independent units of a company. Or new methods may come into use, such as that of gaining adequate financial control with a high degree of decentralization.

Moreover, a new chief executive officer and new vice-presidents and department heads are likely to have some definite organizational ideas of their own. Shifts may be due merely to the desire of new managers to make changes based on ideas formulated through their previous experience or to the fact that their methods of managing and their personalities require a changed organization structure.

Furthermore, reorganization may be caused by demonstrated deficiencies in an existing structure. Some of these arise from organizational weaknesses: excessive spans of management, an excessive number of committees, lack of uniform policy, slow decision making, failure to accomplish objectives, inability to meet schedules, excessive costs, or breakdown of financial control. Other deficiencies may stem from inadequacies of managers. Lack of knowledge or skill on the part of a manager who for some reason cannot be replaced may be avoided by organizing so as to move much of the authority for decision making to another position.

Personality clashes between managers also may be solved by reorganization. Staff-line conflicts may develop to such an extent that they can be resolved only by reorganization.

The Need for Readjustment and Change

In addition to pressing reasons for reorganization, there is a certain need for moderate and continuing readjustment merely to keep the structure from becoming stagnant. "Empire building" (i.e., building up a large organization to make the manager appear to be more important) is not so attractive when all those involved know that their positions are subject to change. As a company president told his subordinates: "Don't bother to build any empires, because I can assure you that you won't be in the same position three years from now." Some managers, realizing that an organization structure must be a living thing, make structural changes merely to accustom subordinates to change.

Much can be said for developing a tradition of change. People who are used to change tend to accept it without the frustration and demoralization that result when need for reorganization is allowed to reach the stage at which change must be revolutionary. On the other hand, a company continually undertaking major reorganization may damage morale, and people may spend much of their time wondering what will happen to them because of organizational changes.

MAKING STAFF WORK EFFECTIVELY

The line-staff problem is not only one of the most difficult that organizations face but also the source of an extraordinarily large amount of inefficiency. Solving this problem requires great managerial skill, careful attention to principles, and patient teaching of personnel.

Understanding Authority Relationships

Managers must understand the nature of authority relationships if they want to solve the problems of line and staff. So long as managers regard line and staff as groups of people or groupings of activities (for example, service departments), confusion will result. Line and staff are authority relationships and many jobs have elements of both. Line means making decisions and acting on them. Staff relationship, on the other hand, implies the right to assist and counsel. In short, the line may "tell," but the staff must "sell" (its recommendations).

Making Line Listen to Staff

If staff counsel and advice are justifiable at all, it is because of the need for assistance either from experts or from those freed from more pressing duties to give such assistance. Obviously, if staff help is not used, it would make sense to abolish it. Line managers should realize that competent staff assistants offer suggestions to aid and not to undermine or criticize. Although line-staff friction may stem from ineptness or overzealousness on the part of staff people, trouble also arises when line executives too carefully guard their authority and resent the very assistance they need.

Line managers should be encouraged or required to consult with staff. Enterprises would do well to adopt the practice of compulsory staff assistance wherein the line must listen to staff. At General Motors, for example, product division managers consult with the headquarters staff divisions before proposing a major program or policy to the top executive or the finance committee. They may not be required to do so, but they are likely to find that this practice results in smoother sailing for their proposals; and if they can present a united front with the staff division concerned, there will unquestionably be a better chance for the adoption to their proposals.

Keeping Staff Informed

Common criticisms of staff are that specialists operate in a vacuum, fail to appreciate the complexity of the line manager's job, or overlook important facts in making recommendations. To some extent, these criticisms are warranted because specialists cannot be expected to know all the fine points of a manager's job. Specialists should take care that their recommendations deal only with matters within their competence, and operating managers should not lean too heavily on a recommendation if it deals only with part of a problem.

Many criticisms arise because staff assistants are not kept informed on matters within their field. Even the best assistant cannot advise properly in such cases. If line managers fail to inform their staff of decisions affecting its work or if they do not pave the way—through announcements and requests for coopera-tion—for staff to obtain the requisite information on specific problems, the staff cannot function as intended. In relieving their superiors of the necessity for gathering and analyzing such information, staff assistants largely justify their existence.

Requiring Completed Staff Work

Many staff persons overlook the fact that in order to be most helpful, their recommendations should be complete enough to make possible a simple positive or negative answer by a line manager. Staff assistants should be problem solvers and not problem creators. They create problems for managers when their advice is indecisive or vague, when their conclusions are wrong, when they have not taken into account all the facts or have not consulted the persons seriously affected by a proposed solution, or when they do not point out to superiors the pitfalls as well as the advantages in a recommended course of action.

Completed staff work implies presentation of a clear recommendation based upon full consideration of a problem, clearance with persons importantly affected, suggestions about avoiding any difficulties involved, and, often, preparation of the paperwork—letters, directives, job descriptions, and specifications—so that a manager can accept or reject the proposal without further study, long conferences, or unnecessary work. Should a recommendation be accepted, thorough staff work provides line managers with the machinery to put it into effect. People in staff positions who learn to do these things can find themselves highly valued and appreciated.

Making Staff Work as a Way of Organizational Life

An understanding of staff authority lays the foundation for an organizational way of life. Wherever staff is used, its responsibility is to develop and maintain a climate of favorable personal relations. Essentially, the task of staff assistants is to make responsible line managers "look good" and to help them do a better job. A staff assistant should not attempt to assume credit for an idea. Not only is this a sure way of alienating line teammates who do not like being shown up by a staff assistant, but operating managers who accept ideas actually bear responsibility for implementation of the proposals.

Even under the best of circumstances, it is difficult to coordinate line and staff authority, for people must be persuaded to cooperate. Staff persons must gain and hold the confidence of their fellow workers. They must keep in close touch with operating departments, know their managers and staffs, and understand their problems. They must, through precept and example, convince their line teammates that their prime interest is the welfare of operating managers, and they must downgrade their own contributions while embellishing those of the persons they assist. People in a staff capacity have succeeded in their role when line executives seek their advice and ask them to study their problems.

AVOIDING CONFLICT BY CLARIFICATION

A major reason for conflict in organizations is that people do not understand their assignments and those of their coworkers. No matter how well conceived an organization structure, people must understand it to make it work. Understanding is aided materially by proper use of organization charts, accurate job descriptions, the spelling out of authority and informational relationships, and the introduction of specific goals for specific positions.

Organization Charts

Every organization structure, even a poor one, can be charted, for a chart merely indicates how departments are tied together along the principal lines of authority. It is therefore somewhat surprising to occasionally find top managers taking pride in not having an organization chart or feeling that the charts should be kept a secret.

Advantages. A prominent manufacturer once said that although he could see some use for an organization chart for his factory, he had refused to chart the organization above the level of factory superintendent. His argument was that charts tended to make people overly conscious of being superiors or inferiors, tended to destroy team feeling, and gave persons occupying a box on the chart too great a feeling of "ownership." Another top executive once said that if an organization is left uncharted, it can be changed more easily, and that the absence of a chart also encourages a competitive drive for higher executive positions on the part of the uncharted middle-management group.

These reasons for not charting organization structures are clearly unsound. Subordinate-superior relationships exist not because of charting but, rather, because of essential reporting relationships. As for a chart's creating a too-comfortable feeling and causing a lack of drive on the part of those who have "arrived," these are matters of top leadership—of reorganizing whenever the enterprise environment demands, of developing a tradition of change, and of making subordinate managers continue to meet adequate and well-understood standards of performance. Managers who believe that team spirit can be produced without clearly spelling out relationships are fooling themselves and preparing the way for politics, intrigue, frustration, buck passing, lack of coordination, duplicated effort, vague policy, uncertain decision making, and other evidences of organizational inefficiency.

Since a chart maps lines of decision-making authority, sometimes merely charting an organization can show inconsistencies and complexities and lead to their correction. A chart also reveals to managers and new personnel how they tie into the entire structure.

Limitations. Organization charts are subject to important limitations. In the first place, a chart shows only formal authority relationships and omits the many significant informal and informational relationships. Figure 11-1 shows many, but not nearly all, of the informal relationships found in a typical organized enterprise. It shows also the major line, or formal, relationships. It does not show how much authority exists at any point in the structure. While it would be interesting to chart an organization with lines of different widths to denote formal authority of varying degrees, authority is not subject to such measurement. And if the multiple lines of informal relationships and of communication were drawn, they would so complicate a chart that it could not be understood.

Many charts show structures as they are supposed to be or used to be, rather than as they really are. Managers hesitate or neglect to redraft charts, forgetting that organization structures are dynamic and that charts should not be allowed to become obsolete.

Another difficulty with organization charts is that individuals may confuse authority relationships with status. The staff officer reporting to the corporation president may be shown at the top of the organization charts, while a regional

FIGURE 11-1

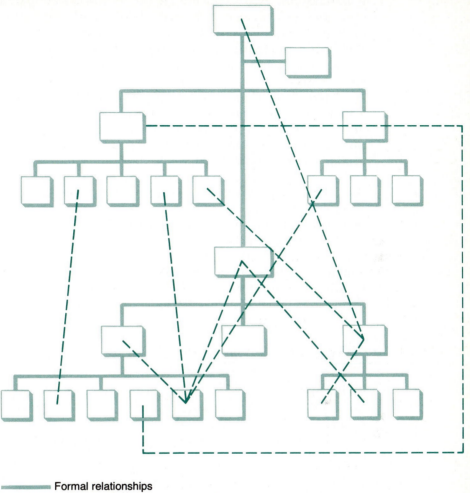

▬▬▬ Formal relationships
– – – – Informal or informational relationships

THE FORMAL AND INFORMAL OR INFORMATIONAL ORGANIZATION.

line officer may be shown one or two levels lower. Although good charting attempts to make levels on the chart conform to levels of enterprise importance, it cannot always do so. This problem can be handled by clearly spelling out authority relationships and by that best indicator of status—salary and bonus levels. No one is likely, for example, to hear that the general manager of Chevrolet in General Motors feels a sense of inferiority because his position on the chart is below that of the company secretary.

Position Descriptions and Charts of Approval Authorizations

Every managerial position should be defined. A good position description informs everyone what the incumbent is supposed to do. A modern position description is not a detailed list of all the activities an individual is expected to undertake, and it certainly does not specify how to undertake them. Rather, it states the basic function of the position, the major end-result areas for which the manager is responsible, and the reporting relationships involved; it makes reference to the current chart of approval authorizations in order to clarify the position's authority and to the current set of verifiable objectives for the end-result areas.

Position descriptions have many benefits. As jobs are analyzed, duties and responsibilities are brought into focus and areas of overlapping or neglected duties come to light. Forcing people to consider what should be done and who should do it is more than worth the effort. Further benefits of job descriptions include the guidance they provide in training new managers, in drawing up candidate requirements, and in setting salary levels. Finally, as a means of control over organization, the position description furnishes a standard against which to judge whether a position is necessary and, if so, what its organization level and exact location in the structure should be.

One of the most powerful tools for defining and clarifying relationships is the chart of executive approval authorizations, discussed in Chapter 9. The authority relationships are clarified by describing organizational positions, showing who has the authority for approving and making commitments, and indicating the functional authority for individual positions.

ENSURING UNDERSTANDING OF ORGANIZING

All the members of an enterprise must understand the structure of their organization in order for that structure to work. This requires teaching. Also, since formal organization is supplemented by informal organization, members of an enterprise must understand the general working of informal as well as formal organization.

Teaching the Nature of Organizing

Many soundly conceived organization plans fail because organization members do not understand them. A well-written organization manual—containing a statement of organization philosophy, programs, charts, and an outline of job descriptions—goes far toward making organizing understandable. If an organization structure is put into written words and charts, it has a better chance of being clear than if it is not. However, because even the best-written words and charts do not always clearly convey the same meaning to every reader, effective managers cannot stop with written clarification. They must teach those in their operation the meaning of the organization structure, their position in it, and the relationships involved.

Managers may do this by individual coaching, through staff or special meetings, or by simply watching how the structure works. If subordinates pass decisions up the line that they should be making themselves, managers can take this opportunity to clarify authority. Likewise, if communication among members of a group seems to be inadequate, managers can look for causes in either a poorly conceived or a poorly understood organization structure. Too many group meetings or too much committee work is a signal for managers to do some investigating. Thus, managers are obligated continually to teach the fundamentals of organizing, for if they do not, their enterprise or department is likely to fail.

Recognizing the Importance of Informal Organization

Another way of making the formal organization work effectively is to recognize and take full advantage of informal organization. The nature of informal organizations and their distinction from formal organizations were discussed in Chapter 7. Many informal organizations arise from the formal organization in which they operate. They include interrelationships that are not usually charted, such as the unwritten rules of organizational conduct, the way to "learn the ropes," who in an enterprise has power not implied by or coming from an organization position, and gossip. One of the best-known examples of an important informal organization, one which seems to exist in every department and organization, is the "grapevine."

The grapevine.   Informal organization tends to exist when members of a formal organization (perhaps a company department) know one another well enough to pass on information—sometimes only gossip—in some way connected with the enterprise. In the typical enterprise—the members of which spend many hours a day deriving material security and status, as well as social satisfaction, from the grapevine—the desire for information concerning the organization and its people is strong enough that such information is rapidly transmitted between persons who know and trust one another.

The grapevine, of course, thrives on information not openly available to the entire group, whether because that information is regarded as confidential, or because formal lines of communication are inadequate to spread it, or because it is of the kind, like much gossip, that would never be formally disclosed. Even managers who conscientiously inform employees through company bulletins or newspapers never so completely or quickly disclose all information of interest as to make the grapevine purposeless.

Since all informal organization serves essential human communication needs, the grapevine is inevitable and valuable. Indeed, an intelligent top manager would probably be wise to feed it accurate information, since it is very effective for quick communication. There is much to be said for a manager's getting a place—personally or through a trusted staff member or secretary—on the company grapevine.

Benefits.   Informal organization brings a kind of cohesiveness to formal organization. It imparts to members of a formal organization a feeling of belonging, of status, of self-respect, and of satisfaction. Many managers, understanding this fact, consciously use informal organizations as channels of communication and molders of employee morale.

PROMOTING AN APPROPRIATE ORGANIZATION CULTURE

The effectiveness of an organization is also influenced by the organization culture, which affects the way the managerial functions of planning, organizing, staffing, leading, and controlling are carried out. (See illustration in Table 11-1.) If given the choice, most people would probably prefer to work in an organization such as environment B, in which one can participate in the decision-making process, one is evaluated on performance criteria rather than on the basis of friendship, one has open communication channels in all directions, and one has the opportunity to exercise a great deal of self-control. In their search for excellent companies, Peters and Waterman, the authors of a best-selling book on management, found that the dominance of a coherent culture characterized these organizations.[2]

But the recognition of the importance of corporate culture is not new at all (although some management gurus want you to believe it).[3] Over 2000 years ago, in 431 B.C., Pericles in ancient Greece eloquently urged the Athenians, who were at war with the Spartans, to adhere to values such as inherent in democracy, informality in communication, the importance of individual dignity, and promotion based on performance. Pericles realized that the underlying values might

TABLE 11-1   Illustrations of Organization Culture and Management Practice

Environment A	Environment B
Planning	
Goals are set in an autocratic manner.	Goals are set with a great deal of participation.
Decision making is centralized.	Decision making is decentralized.
Organizing	
Authority is centralized.	Authority is decentralized.
Authority is narrowly defined.	Authority is broadly defined.
Staffing	
People are selected on the basis of friendship.	People are selected on the basis of performance criteria.
Training is in a narrowly defined specialty.	Training is in many functional areas.
Leading	
Managers exercise directive leadership.	Managers practice participative leadership.
Communication flow is primarily top-down.	Communication flow is top-down, bottom-up, horizontal, and diagonal.
Controlling	
Superiors exercise strict control.	Individuals exercise a great deal of self-control.
Focus is on financial criteria.	Focus is on multiple criteria.

mean victory or defeat. You probably will note that these values are not so different from those espoused by many U.S. companies.

Defining Organization Culture

As it relates to organizations, **culture** is the general pattern of behavior, shared beliefs, and values that members have in common.[4] Culture can be inferred from what people say, do, and think within an organizational setting. It involves the learning and transmitting of knowledge, beliefs, and patterns of behavior over a period of time. This also means that an organization culture is fairly stable and does not change fast.[5] It often sets the tone for the company and establishes implied rules for how people should behave. Many of us have heard slogans that give us a general idea what the company stands for.[6] Here are some examples:

For General Electric, it is "Progress is our most important product."

American Telephone & Telegraph Company is proud of its "universal service."

DuPont makes "better things for better living through chemistry."

Delta Airlines describes its internal climate with the slogan, "the Delta family feeling."

Similarly, IBM wants to be known for its service, Sears for quality and price, Caterpillar for its 24-hour parts service, Polaroid for its innovation, Maytag for its reliability, and so on. Indeed, the orientation of these companies, often expressed in slogans, contributed to the successful conduct of their businesses.

Influence of the Leader on Organization Culture

Managers, and especially top managers, create the climate for the enterprise. Their values influence the direction of the firm. Although the term **value** is used differently, we like to think of a value as a fairly permanent belief about what is appropriate and what is not that guides the actions and behavior of employees in fulfilling the organization's aims. Values can be thought of as forming an ideology that permeates everyday decisions.

In many successful companies, value-driven corporate leaders serve as role models, set the standards for performance, motivate employees, make the company special, and are a symbol to the external environment. It was Edwin Land, the founder of Polaroid, who created a favorable organizational environment for research and innovation. It was Jim Treybig of Tandom in the "Silicon Valley" near San Francisco who made it a point that every person is a human being and deserves to be treated accordingly. It was William Cooper Procter of Procter & Gamble who ran the company with the slogan "Do what is right." It was Theodore Vail of AT&T who addressed the needs of customers by emphasizing service. The organization culture created by corporate leaders can result in managerial functions being carried out in quite different ways.

A clear vision of a common purpose elicits commitment. Moreover, when people participate in the decision-making process and exercise self-direction and

> **PERSPECTIVE:**
> **MERGING CORPORATE CULTURES AT GENERAL MOTORS**
>
> General Motors' chairman Roger B. Smith is attempting to change the company's culture.[7] One of the major tasks is to merge GM's culture with those, very different ones, of the newly acquired firms such as the high-tech aerospace Hughes Aircraft Company and the computer services company Electronic Data System (EDS), headed by the colorful, action-oriented entrepreneur Ross Perot. While GM emphasized bureaucratic processes and procedures, EDS focused on achieving results in a militarylike fashion. While decision making was slow at GM and risk taking usually not rewarded, Hughes, being at the forefront of technology, continuously had to scan the environment for new developments and opportunities, making decisions that, at times, involve a great deal of risk.
>
> To give direction to the divergent cultures, Smith distributes "culture cards" that state the company's mission: "The fundamental purpose of General Motors is to provide products and services of such quality that our customers will receive superior value, our employees and business partners will share our success, and our stockholders will receive a sustained, superior return on their investment."[8]

self-control they feel committed to their own plans. But espoused values need to be reinforced through rewards and incentives, ceremonies, stories, and symbolic actions.[9]

CONTINGENCIES IN ORGANIZING

Throughout this book we have emphasized that to be effective, organizations must adapt to the specific requirement of the situation. Major contributions toward a contingency, or situational, theory of organizing have been made by researchers in the United States and abroad. We will briefly examine some major contributions.

Studies by Burns and Stalker

Tom Burns and G. M. Stalker investigated the relationship between management practices and characteristics of the external environment.[10] Specifically, they interviewed key persons in twenty English and Scottish companies and developed a conceptual scheme with two different systems of management practices. One system was called "mechanistic" and the other "organic."[11]

The **mechanistic** management system appears to be appropriate for relatively stable organization environments. This system is characterized by, among other things, specialized differentiation of tasks, by individuals viewing their tasks as being distinct from the whole, by precisely defined rights and obligations, by a hierarchical structure, by vertical interactions between the superior and the subordinates, and by having instructions and decisions come from the superior.

The **organic** management system, on the other hand, is characterized by individual performance based on knowledge of the task of the whole concern, continued redefinition of tasks through interaction with others, and a great deal of lateral interaction and consultation. This system, it is suggested, is more suitable for coping with unstable and changing conditions and unpredictable problems.

Studies by Woodward

The studies of 100 British firms conducted by Joan Woodward indicate that there is a relationship between organization design and different types of technology.[12] This researcher classified the enterprises into three groups according to increasing degrees of technological complexity: (1) small-batch and unit production making such items as special purpose equipment or custom-made products; (2) large-batch and mass production, as, for example, in the manufacture of items produced in large quantities on the assembly line; and (3) process or continuous flow production, such as that found in chemical firms and oil refineries.

The findings suggest that the more successful firms in the large-batch and mass production category were organized in a manner similar to what Burns and Stalker described as mechanistic.

On the other hand, the small-batch and unit production firms as well as the process or continuous flow production firms were more effective with organic structures. In short, the Woodward research suggests that to be effective, organization design is contingent on production technology.

Studies by Lawrence and Lorsch

Building on the studies by Woodward and Burns and Stalker, the research by Paul R. Lawrence and Jay W. Lorsch focused on the relative stability of environments. Organizations with changing environments demand greater **differentiation,** a term defined as *"the difference in cognitive and emotional orientation among managers in different functional departments."*[13] A company in the plastics industry, for example, working in a dynamic environment, requires considerable differentiation. Such an organization also has a great need for **integration,** a term defined as *"the quality of the state of collaboration that exists among departments that are required to achieve unity of effort by the demands of the environment."*[14] Thus, more unstable environments call for more organic types of organization, using, for example, teams that cut across functions in order to integrate activities.

On the other hand, more stable environments demand less differentiation, and the means for integration may differ from those in dynamic environments. For example, Lawrence and Lorsch found that a company in the container industry with a relatively stable environment was effective in using more mechanistic organizational arrangements such as a managerial hierarchy.

FOR DISCUSSION

1. Many psychologists have pointed to the advantages of "job enlargement"—assignment of tasks that are not so specialized that an individual loses a sense of doing things which are meaningful. Assuming that managers wish to limit specialization of tasks and "enlarge" jobs, can they do so and still apply the basic principles of organizing?

2. Taking an organized enterprise with which you have some familiarity, can you find any of the deficiencies commonly found in organization structures?

3. It is sometimes stated that the typical organization chart is undemocratic in that it emphasizes the superiority and inferiority of people and positions. Comment.

4. What, in your judgment, makes an organization structure "good"? How do "good" organization structures support leadership?

5. What would you need to know to plan an organization structure? How far ahead should you plan it? How would you go about making such a plan?

6. Take an organization you know and discuss its culture. Is the culture helping or hindering the organization in achieving its goals?

EXERCISES/ACTION STEPS

1. Visit a company in your area which is considered a model of effective management. Get any information on this company that gives you some insight into the operation. What makes this organization excellent? Would you like to work for this enterprise? Why or why not?

2. Gather information on a company that is considered poorly managed. If it is a local company, talk to people and read the newspaper. If the firm is not in your area, gather the information from magazines (e.g., *Fortune, Forbes, Business Week*), and newspapers (e.g., *The Wall Street Journal*). What are some of the problems? What would you recommend to make this firm more effective? Present your findings and your recommendations to the class.

CASES

CASE 11-1
THE VGI COMPANY

Egon Schnell was a bright young engineer working for an electronics firm. Although he was very successful as an engineer with the company, and liked his job, which involved developing video games, he decided to leave his job and start his own company. He borrowed money wherever he could get it. Despite his enormous efforts and his good ideas, he failed and almost went bankrupt. Finally, he succeeded after a large retail chain gave him a big order. But success was followed by failure, and failure was succeeded by renewed success.

Employees liked to work at Schnell's company, VGI, where the atmosphere was casual. This climate was conducive to developing new ideas. Yet the competition from large, well-managed companies grew. Still, some brilliant ideas resulted in a great demand for several of the products. In fact, the demand was such that the company could not keep up with production, and there were shortages. But an expansion required capital. Consequently, Mr. Schnell decided to go public and to link up with a large company. This made the owner-entrepreneur several million dollars richer. Mr. Schnell remained as the head of VGI, but his interest in running the company visibly diminished and observers described the firm's state of affairs as "chaotic." Mr. Schnell admitted that he was not a good executive and agreed to a reorganization in which John Newsome assumed the leadership of the company as president. One of the first decisions of the new president was to appoint a new marketing manager to overcome the weakness of the VGI company, which in the past had been dominated by people with technical backgrounds.

Mr. Newsome also exerted strong managerial leadership, developed many new procedures, set specific objectives, and installed strict financial controls. The change from a free-rein to a rather tight managerial approach annoyed many of the old-time engineers. Since there was a great demand for their services, thus providing many job opportunities, many left the company. Some even established their own software company and became direct competitors to their former firm.

1. Why do you think Mr. Schnell was successful at the beginning?

2. Why did employees and especially the engineers, like to work under the free-rein management of Mr. Schnell?

3. Why did Mr. Schnell fail and what would you have done in his place?

4. Do you agree with Mr. Newsome's approach to managing? Why or why not?

CASE 11-2
ORGANIZATION CULTURE AT IBM[15]

Everyone at IBM is expected to follow three fundamental principles: Respect individuals, strive for excellence, and provide the best service. Thomas Watson founded a patriarchy to instill these principles. His successors have maintained them in the face of rapid growth and changing technology by moving toward a more entrepreneurial system.

One way top management shows its respect for individuals is by treating all employees as equals. IBM hires employees for life. No one will lose his job unless he or she consistently fails to meet clear standards or violates the ethics code. There is no distinction between white-, blue-, and pink-collar workers. Many employees will move through line and staff positions over the course of their career. All employees are encouraged to continue their education and prepare themselves

for promotions. Almost all middle- and upper-level positions are filled by existing IBM employees.

New employees undergo up to nine months of training to prepare them for their job and to indoctrinate them in the IBM philosophy. Those who stay rapidly adapt to the corporate culture by dressing conservatively, engaging in competition and team sports, attending various company events, and embracing other aspects of corporate life. Another mark of respect for the individual is the attention top management pays to employee suggestions. The firm has a tradition of open doors at the highest levels. At least once a year, employees discuss matters important to them with their managers. In turn, managers publicly respond to all comments received in suggestion boxes. A suggestion program rewards ideas that reduce costs or improve products or quality control. Between 1975 and 1984, IBM paid workers almost $60 million for suggestions which saved the company $300 million.

Top management monitors employee morale through questionnaires and roundtable discussions at all levels. It holds branch and division managers accountable for any problems and actively helps them improve morale. Most employees are happy being a part of the IBM family and stay with the company for their entire professional life.

IBM is well known for dependable service. Top management emphasizes its commitment to service by focusing on the people who provide that service: the marketing representatives. Most of the top executives, including Thomas Watson, began their career as salesmen.

Representatives are given full responsibility for pleasing customers. If representatives lose an account, the original sales commission for that account is deducted from their salary. Not surprisingly, the representatives spend much of their time helping customers to maintain their system.

Distinction at IBM is based on merit. The system is designed to foster achievers. Managers establish realistic goals and exuberantly reward employees when they reach them. Almost 25 percent of the employees get bonuses, many receive gifts, or a dinner for two, and they receive frequent praise.

The merit system is most obvious in the sales force. Annual sales quotas are set so that approximately 80 percent of the sales representatives will meet them. The representatives' monthly sales are posted on bulletin boards. Managers are expected to help subordinates to meet their goals. Those who achieve their quota join the "100% Club." They attend a lavish three-day annual celebration. The 10 percent of the sales representatives with the highest sales join the "Golden Circle" and celebrate their success at a posh resort. Those who consistently fail to meet quotas are dismissed.

The competition is tempered by a rigorously enforced code of ethics and team spirit. No matter what their levels, managers' successes depend on their teams' efforts. Because the teams are small, managers can give extensive personal attention to their subordinates. In addition, the sales branches hold monthly rallies to review progress and reward top performers.

As IBM grew, the organization became a vast bureaucracy. Growth has spawned many rules and controls. The hierarchy in such a large organization may slow down communication between departments. Thus, despite their immediate superior's attention to their professional needs, some employees feel insignificant and do not know the direction of the company.

IBM's customer orientation helped the firm to respond rapidly to changes in the market despite the bureaucracy. When personal computers became popular, top management realized it had ignored a product its customers wanted. To get a personal computer on the market fast, top management bypassed its bureaucracy by forming an independent business unit (IBU). The vice-president and his team were freed from other duties so that they could devote their full attention to develop, manufacture, and market the IBM personal computer (PC) without interference from the rest of the organization.

The PC team made several revolutionary decisions, including buying components from other companies, using "open architecture" so other companies could provide software and compatible equipment, and distributing the PC through computer stores. Previously, IBM had insisted on providing all computer services and equipment itself, and its technical specifications had been jealously guarded secrets.

IBM is now exploiting opportunities in telecommunications, robotics, electronics, scientific instrumentation, and computer software by buying into existing companies or forming IBUs. The company has also moved toward decentralization, giving individuals more autonomy without relinquishing its founder's basic philosophy.

1. What is IBM's culture? How does it affect employees? What symbols, traditions, and norms typify IBM?

2. How has the culture changed? How did it help

or hinder IBM's adaptation to the external environment?

3. What problems could acquisitions and IBUs create? How should IBM integrate them?

REFERENCES

1. Lyndall Urwick, *The Elements of Administration* (New York: Harper & Row, 1944), p. 38.

2. Thomas J. Peters and Robert H. Waterman, Jr., *In Search of Excellence* (New York: Harper & Row, 1982).

3. John K. Clemens, "A Lesson from 431 B.C.," *Fortune* (Oct. 13, 1986), pp. 161–164.

4. Vijay Sathe, "Some Action Implications of Corporate Culture: A Manager's Guide to Action," *Organizational Dynamics* (Autumn 1983), pp. 4–23; S. R. Luce, "Managing Corporate Culture," *Canadian Business Review* (Spring 1984), pp. 40–43; Stanley M. Davis, "Corporate Culture and Human Resource Management: Two Keys to Implementing Strategy," *Human Resource Planning,* vol. 6, no. 3 (1983), pp. 159–167; Edgar H. Schein, "What You Need to Know about Organizational Culture," *Training and Development Journal* (January 1986), pp. 30–33.

5. B. Littal, "The Corporate Culture Vultures," *Fortune* (Oct. 17, 1983), pp. 66–72.

6. Terrence E. Deal and Allan A. Kennedy, *Corporate Cultures* (Reading, Mass.: Addison-Wesley Publishing Company, 1982), chap. 2.

7. David E. Whiteside, "Roger Smith's Campaign to Change the GM Culture," *Business Week* (Apr. 7, 1986), pp. 84–85; Russell Mitchell, "How General Motors Is Bringing Up Ross Perot's Baby," *Business Week* (Apr. 14, 1986), pp. 96–100; Melinda Grenier Guiles, "GM's Smith Presses for Sweeping Changes, But Questions Arise," *The Wall Street Journal* (Mar. 14, 1985). Partly due to cultural differences, Ross Perot parted with General Motors.

8. Clemens, "A Lesson from 431 B.C.," p. 164.

9. James M. Kouzes, David F. Caldwell, and Barry Z. Posner, "Organizational Culture: How It Is Created, Maintained, and Changed," Presentation by the authors, 1983.

10. Tom Burns and G. M. Stalker, *The Management of Innovation* (London: Tavistock Publications, 1961).

11. For additional discussion see Patrick E. Connor, "Organization Structure and Design," in James E. Rosenzweig and Fremont E. Kast (eds.), *Modules in Management* (Chicago: SRA, Science Research Associates, 1984).

12. Joan Woodward, *Industrial Organization: Theory and Practice* (London: Oxford University Press, 1965), especially chap. 5.

13. Paul R. Lawrence and Jay W. Lorsch, *Organization and Environment* (Homewood, Ill.: Richard D. Irwin, 1969), p. 11.

14. Lawrence and Lorsch, *Organization and Environment* (1969), p. 11.

15. This material has been drawn from a variety of sources including the following: P. H. Dorn, "The Song Remains the Same," *Datamation* (February 1984), pp. 105–110; L. W. Foster, "From Darwin to Now: The Evolution of Organizational Strategies," *Journal of Business Strategy* (Spring 1985), pp. 94–98; B. Jeffery, "With a Little Help From Some Friends," *Datamation* (February 1984), pp. 147–150; D. Kneal, J. Marcom, Jr., and Randall Smith, "IBM: Behind the Monolith—A Special Report," *The Wall Street Journal* (Apr. 7, 1986), pp. 19–22; L. Luciano, "Seeing the Future Work at IBM," *Money* (November 1985); Peter D. Petre, "Meet the Lean, Mean New IBM," *Fortune* (June 13,

1983), p. 69; T. Sweeny, "Corporate Culture," *San Francisco Business* (February 1986), p. 6; Jo Ellen Davis, and Geoff Lewis, "Who's Afraid of IBM?" *Business Week* (June 22, 1987), pp. 68–74.

FOR FURTHER INFORMATION

Cavanagh, Gerald F., Dennis J. Moberg, and Manuel Velasquez. "The Ethics of Organizational Politics," *Academy of Management Review* (July 1981), pp. 363–374.

Davis, Keith, and John Newstrom. *Human Behavior at Work—Organizational Behavior,* 7th ed. (New York: McGraw-Hill Book Company, 1985).

Donaldson, Lex. "Woodward, Technology, Organizational Structure and Performance—A Critique of the Universal Generalization," in Harold Koontz, Cyril O'Donnell, and Heinz Weihrich (eds.), *Management—A Book of Readings,* 5th ed. (New York: McGraw-Hill Book Company, 1980), pp. 369–380.

Frost, Peter J., Larry F. Moore, Meryl Reis Louis, Craig C. Lundberg, and Joanne Martin (eds.). *Organizational Culture* (Beverly Hills, Calif.: Sage Publications, 1985).

Matthews, Glenn H. "Run Your Business or Build an Organization?" *Harvard Business Review,* (March–April 1984), pp. 34–44.

O'Toole, James. *Vanguard Management: Redesigning the Corporate Future* (Garden City, N.Y.: Doubleday & Company, 1985).

SUMMARY OF MAJOR PRINCIPLES, OR GUIDES, FOR ORGANIZING

Although the science of organizing has not yet developed to the point where principles are infallible laws, there is considerable agreement among management scholars and practitioners about a number of them. These principles are truths (or are believed to be truths) of general applicability, although their application is not so precise as to give them the exactness of the laws of pure science. They are more in the nature of essential criteria for effective organizing. The most essential guiding principles of organizing are summarized in this section.

The Purpose of Organizing

The purpose of organizing is to aid in making objectives meaningful and to contribute to organizational efficiency.

Principle of unity of objective. An organization structure is effective if it enables individuals to contribute to enterprise objectives.

Principle of organizational efficiency. An organization is efficient if it is structured to aid the accomplishment of enterprise objectives with a minimum of unsought consequences or costs.

The Cause of Organizing

The basic cause of organization structure is the limitation of the span of management. If there were no such limitation, we might have an unorganized enterprise with only one manager.

Span-of-Management Principle. In each managerial position, there is a limit to the number of persons an individual can effectively manage, but the exact number will depend on the impact of underlying variables.

The Structure of Organization: Authority

Authority is the cement of organization structure, the thread that makes it possible, the means by which groups of activities can be placed under a manager and coordination of organizational units can be promoted. It is the tool by which a manager is able to exercise discretion and to create an environment for individual performance. Some of the most useful principles of organizing are related to authority.

Scalar principle. The clearer the line of authority from the ultimate management position in an enterprise to every subordinate position, the clearer will be the responsibility for decision making and the more effective organization communication will be.

Principle of delegation by results expected.   Authority delegated to all individual managers should be adequate to ensure their ability to accomplish results expected.

Principle of absoluteness of responsibility.   The responsibility of subordinates to their superiors for performance is absolute, and superiors cannot escape responsibility for the organization activities of their subordinates.

Principle of parity of authority and responsibility.   The responsibility for actions cannot be greater than that implied by the authority delegated, nor should it be less.

Principle of unity of command.   The more complete an individual's reporting relationships to a single superior, the smaller the problem of conflicting instructions and the greater the feeling of personal responsibility for results.

Authority-level principle.   Maintenance of intended delegation requires that decisions within the authority of individual managers should be made by them and not be referred upward in the organization structure.

The Structure of Organization: Departmentized Activities

Organization involves the design of a departmental framework. Although there are several principles in this area, one is of major importance: the **principle of functional definition.** The more a position or a department has clear definition of results expected, activities to be undertaken, organization authority delegated, and authority and informational relationships with other positions understood, the more adequately the responsible individual can contribute toward accomplishing enterprise objectives.

The Process of Organizing

The various principles of authority delegation and of departmentation are fundamental truths about the process of organizing. They deal with phases of the two primary aspects of organizing—authority and activity groupings. There are other principles that deal with the process of organizing. It is through their application that we gain a sense of proportion or a measure of the total organizing process.

Principle of balance.   In every structure there is need for balance. The application of principles or techniques must be balanced to ensure the overall effectiveness of the structure in meeting enterprise objectives.

The principle of balance is common to all areas of science and to all functions of the manager. The inefficiencies of broad spans of management must be balanced against the inefficiencies of long lines of communication. The losses from multiple command must be balanced against the gains from expertness and uniformity in delegating functional authority to staff and service departments. The savings of functional specialization in departmentalizing must be balanced against the advantages of establishing profit-responsible, semi-independent product or territorial departments. We see again that the application of management theory depends on the specific situation.

Principle of flexibility.   The more provisions are made for building flexibility in an organizational structure, the more adequately an organization structure can fulfill its purpose.

Devices and techniques for anticipating and reacting to change must be built into every structure. Every enterprise moves toward its goal in a changing environment, both external and internal. The enterprise that develops inflexibilities, whether these are resistance to change, too-complicated procedures, or too-firm departmental lines, is risking inability to meet the challenges of economic, technical, biological, political, and social change.

Principle of leadership facilitation.   The more an organization structure and its delegations of authority enable managers to design and maintain an environment for performance, the more they will help the leadership abilities of those managers.

Since managership depends to a great extent upon the quality of leadership of those in managerial positions, it is important for the organization structure to do its part in creating a situation in which a manager can most effectively lead. In this sense, organizing is a technique of promoting leadership. If the authority allocation and the structural arrangements create a situation in which heads of departments tend to be looked upon as leaders and in which their task of leadership is aided, organization structuring has accomplished an essential task.

Staffing

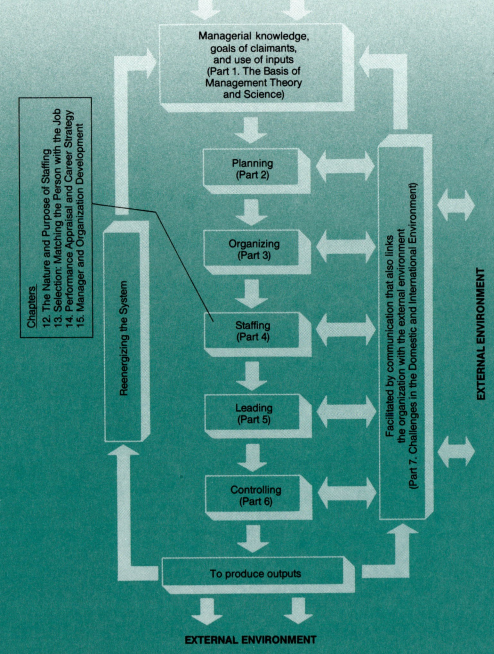

EXTERNAL ENVIRONMENT

Managerial knowledge,
goals of claimants,
and use of inputs
(Part 1. The Basis of
Management Theory
and Science)

Planning
(Part 2)

Organizing
(Part 3)

Staffing
(Part 4)

Leading
(Part 5)

Controlling
(Part 6)

Reenergizing the System

Chapters
12. The Nature and Purpose of Staffing
13. Selection: Matching the Person with the Job
14. Performance Appraisal and Career Strategy
15. Manager and Organization Development

Facilitated by communication that also links
the organization with the external environment
(Part 7. Challenges in the Domestic and International Environment)

EXTERNAL ENVIRONMENT

To produce outputs

EXTERNAL ENVIRONMENT

SYSTEMS APPROACH TO MANAGEMENT.

12

The Nature and Purpose of Staffing

CHAPTER OBJECTIVES

After reading this chapter, you should be able to:

1. Define the managerial function of staffing.

2. Understand what it means to be a manager.

3. Recognize the rewards of managing as well as the stress involved.

4. Describe the systems approach to human resource management.

5. Explain the manager inventory.

6. Understand situational factors in managing including the laws of equal employment opportunity, the role of women in management, and the international environment.

7. Describe factors in the internal environment, including the advantages and problems associated with promotion from within and from outside the organization.

8. Explain the policy of open competition and suggest ways to make staffing more effective.

*F*ew executives would argue with the fact that people are vital for the effective operation of a company. Managers often say that people are their most important asset. Yet the "human assets" are virtually never shown on the balance sheet as a distinct category, although a great deal of money is invested in the recruitment, selection, and training of people. It is for this reason that the late Rensis Likert and his colleagues suggested that we maintain accounts of the valuable human assets. They refer to this process as "human resource accounting."[1] This approach is not without its problems,[2] and there is even conflict among management experts, between the proponents of human resource accounting and the financial people who have to develop the system for measuring the human assets.[3] What is important here is the recognition that staffing is a crucial function of managers and one that may well determine the success or failure of an enterprise.

DEFINITION OF STAFFING

The managerial function of **staffing** is defined as filling, and keeping filled, positions in the organization structure through identifying work-force requirements, inventorying the people available, recruiting, selecting, placing, promoting, appraising, planning the careers, compensating, and training or otherwise developing both candidates and current jobholders to accomplish their tasks effectively and efficiently.[4] It is clear that staffing must be closely linked to organizing, that is, to the setting up of intentional structures of roles and positions.

Many writers on management theory discuss staffing as a phase of organizing. We, however, have identified staffing as a separate managerial function for several reasons. First, the staffing of organizational roles includes knowledge and approaches not usually recognized by practicing managers, who often think of organizing as just setting up a structure of roles, and give little attention to filling these roles. Second, making staffing a separate function allows us to give even greater emphasis to the human element in selection, appraisal, career planning, and manager development. Third, an important body of knowledge and experience has been developed in the area of staffing. The fourth reason for separating staffing is that managers often overlook the fact that staffing is their responsibility—not that of the personnel department. To be sure, this department provides valuable assistance, but it is the job of managers to fill the positions in their organization and keep them filled with qualified people.

DEFINING THE MANAGERIAL JOB

Complete agreement does not exist as to what exactly constitutes the job of a manager. In fact, the nature of managerial tasks has been studied from several different perspectives.[5] One group of writers, known as the *great man school,* studied successful managers and described their behaviors and habits. Although the stories about these people are interesting, the authors usually do not provide an underlying theory to explain the success of their subjects. Other writers—primarily economists—focus on the *entrepreneurial* aspects of managing. Their main concern is profit maximization, innovation, risk taking, and similar activities. Yet another group of writers emphasizes *decision making,* especially the kinds of decisions that cannot be easily programmed. An additional view of the managerial job draws attention to *leadership,* with an emphasis on particular traits and managerial styles. Closely related to this approach is the discussion about *power* and *influence,* that is, the leader's control of the environment and subordinates. Other writers focus their attention on the *behavior of leaders* by examining the content of the manager's job. Finally, the approach favored by Henry Mintzberg is based on observing the *work activities* of managers. It is interesting that the extensive research of the literature by Mintzberg resulted in a grouping of management discussed in Chapter 2 of this book.[6] He found through observations of five executives that their work was characterized by brevity, variety, discontinuity, and action orientation. He also found that executives favor oral communication and that they engage in many activities that link the enterprise with its environment.

We have found it useful, as we have made clear, to organize the key tasks of managers into the five functions of planning, organizing, staffing, leading, and controlling, and these constitute the framework of this book.

REWARDS AND STRESS OF MANAGING

Managers are different; they have different needs, desires, and motives. The topic of motivation will be discussed in its essentials in Chapter 17. The concern here is with some of the general rewards, as well as the stressful aspects, of managing.

Rewards of Managing

Since managerial candidates differ widely in age, economic position, and level of maturity, they want many things, but these usually include opportunity, income, and power.

First, a main concern of managerial candidates is often the opportunity for a progressive career that provides depth and breadth of managerial experience. Related to this is the challenge found in meaningful work. Most people, but perhaps managers especially, want to feel that they make a significant contribution to the aims of an enterprise, and even to society.

Second, managers want to be, and should be, rewarded for their contributions, although the size of the financial rewards has been criticized. The perspective shows the compensation of some of the highest paid executives in 1985.

There is, however, some concern whether the shareholders get their money's worth and whether the compensation is fair. The *Fortune* survey, mentioned above, found that the compensation of the industrial companies increased by 25.3 percent when adjusted for inflation. But the return of the equity of shareholders declined from 13.3 percent in 1976 to 11.5 percent in 1986. At

---

PERSPECTIVE:
FINANCIAL REWARDS OF CEOs

The thirty-sixth annual compensation survey by *Business Week* and Sibson & Co. identified the twenty-five highest-paid executives.[7] The total pay was $12,739,000 for Victor Posner of DWG, $11,426,000 for Lee A. Iacocca of Chrysler, and $8,431,000 for T. Boone Pickens, Jr., the chairman of Mesa Petroleum. Even the 25th-ranked executive, Peter T. Buchanan, president of First Boston, received a total pay of $2,533,000. By far the biggest golden parachute (severance pay) was given to Michel C. Bergerac at Revlon in a total package worth $35 million. A survey of CEOs of the *Fortune 500* largest industrial and the 500 largest service companies showed the median compensation of those surveyed to be $543,400. This figure was considerably higher than in 1976, when it was $209,000.[8]

---

times, then, there is little correlation between executive pay and performance. In another survey, 76 percent of the public thought that top executives are not worth the compensation they receive.[9]

Peter F. Drucker, one of the most perceptive writers on management, suggests that if executive pay is not reformed, Congress will do it.[10] Japan, known for its high productivity, pays its executives about eight times the amount of blue-collar pay. In the United States, the multiplier is much higher. American workers, professionals, and managers are outraged by what they perceive as exorbitant pay for top executives. Unions, for example, were requested to make concessions just to find out later that executives received high bonuses and stock options.[11]

More recently, efforts have been made to link pay to performance and to induce managers to make decisions that are in the long-term interest of the enterprise.[12] At Ford, for example, more emphasis is given to stock grants that reward the achievement of 5-year objectives. These criteria include not only return on equity but also measures such as customer satisfaction, involvement of employees, and product quality. Moreover, performance is compared with that of its competitors. If, for instance, more quality improvements have been made by a competitor, then this will be held against the managers, although quality may have improved at Ford—but not sufficiently.

Stress in Managing

Stress is a very complex phenomenon. It is, therefore, no surprise that there is no commonly accepted definition. A widely used working definition is as follows: *"An adaptive response, mediated by individual differences and/or psychological processes, that is, a consequence of any external (environmental) action, situation, or event that places excessive psychological and/or physical demands on a person."*[13]

Probably the real father of the concept of stress is Hans Selye, who described stress as "the rate of all wear and tear caused by life."[14] Alvin Toffler, the author of *Future Shock,* said, "Dr. Hans Selye knows more about stress than any other scientist alive."[15]

There are many *physical sources* of stress, such as work overload, irregular work hours (e.g., night shift), as well as loss of sleep, loud noises, bright light, or insufficient light. *Psychological sources* of stress may be due to a particular situation, such as having a boring job, being unable to socialize, lack of autonomy, being held responsible for results without sufficient authority, unrealistic objectives, role ambiguity or role conflict, dual-career marriages, and so on. But what might be stressful to one person may be less so to another; people react differently to situations.

Stress can have various *effects* on the individual as well as the organization. There are the physiological effects that may be linked to a variety of illnesses. Then there are psychological effects, such as burnout or boredom. Various kinds of behavior, such as drug and alcohol abuse, inordinate food consumption, accidents, or withdrawal from the stressful situation (absenteeism, excessive labor turnover), may be a reaction to stress. Clearly, not only does the individual suffer but the organization may also be affected by the turnover or impaired decision making of its managers and nonmanagers alike.

Individuals and organizations have attempted to deal with stress in various ways. Individuals, for example, may try to reduce stress through better management of their time, healthful nutrition, exercise, career planning, change in jobs, promotion of psychological health, relaxation,[16] or meditation, and prayer. Organizations may provide counseling or recreation facilities, or improve the job design by matching the person with the job, a topic further discussed in Chapter 13.

Fitting the Needs of the Individual to the Demands of the Job

Managing, then, offers rewards but also involves stress. An individual aspiring to a managerial position should evaluate both the advantages and the disadvantages of managing before pursuing this career. A proper fit between individual needs and the demands of the task will benefit both the individual and the enterprise (further discussed in Chapters 13 through 15). Managers will gain by getting satisfaction and a feeling of competence from their work and enterprises will have a motivated work force.

THE SYSTEMS APPROACH TO HUMAN RESOURCE MANAGEMENT: AN OVERVIEW OF THE STAFFING FUNCTION

Figure 12-1 shows how the managerial function of staffing relates to the total management system.[17] Specifically, enterprise plans (discussed in Part 2 of this book) become the basis for organization plans (Part 3), which are necessary to achieve enterprise objectives. The present and projected organization structure determines the number and kinds of managers required. These demands for managers are compared with available talent through the management in-

FIGURE 12-1

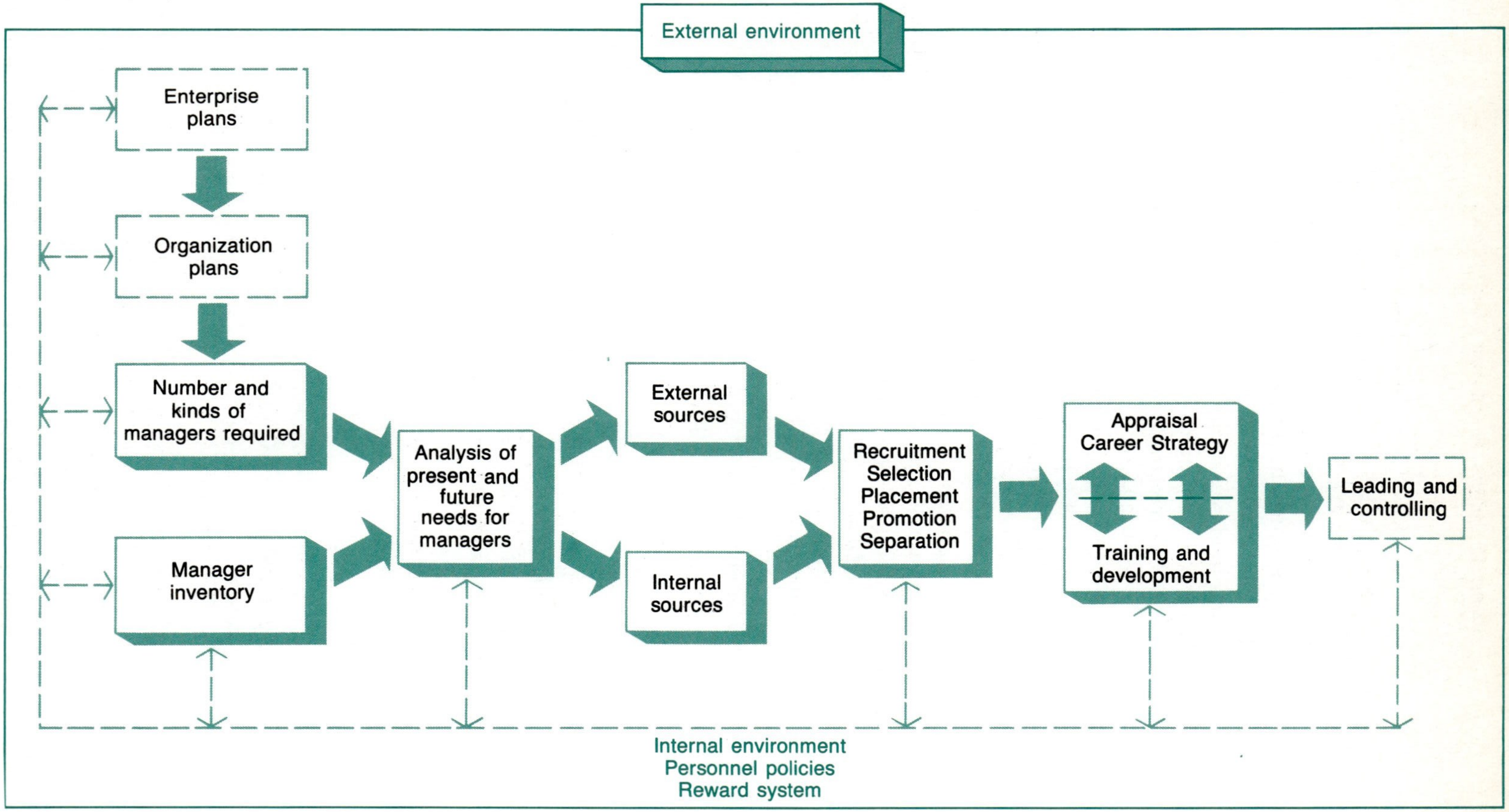

SYSTEMS APPROACH TO STAFFING.

ventory. On the basis of this analysis, external and internal sources are utilized in the processes of recruitment, selection, placement, promotion, and separation. Other essential aspects of staffing are appraisal, career strategy, and training and development of managers.

Staffing, as seen in the model, affects leading and controlling. For instance, well-trained managers create an environment in which people, working together in groups, can achieve enterprise objectives and at the same time accomplish personal goals. In other words, proper staffing facilitates leading (Part 5). Similarly, selecting quality managers affects controlling, for example, by preventing many undesirable deviations from becoming major problems (Part 6).

Staffing requires an open-system approach. It is carried out within the enterprise, which, in turn, is linked to the external environment. Therefore, internal factors of the firm—such as personnel policies, the organizational climate, and the reward system—must be taken into account. Clearly, without adequate rewards it is impossible to attract and keep quality managers. The external environment cannot be ignored either; high technology demands well-trained, well-educated, and highly skilled managers. Inability to meet the demand for such managers may well prevent an enterprise from growing at a desired rate.

Factors Affecting the Number and Kinds of Managers Required

The number of managers needed in an enterprise depends not only upon its size but also upon the complexity of the organization structure, the plans for expansion, and the rate of turnover of managerial personnel. The ratio between the number of managers and the number of employees does not follow any law. It is possible, by enlarging or contracting the delegation of authority, to modify a structure so that the number of managers in a given instance will increase or decrease regardless of the size of an operation.

The annual rate of appointments to managerial positions can be determined by a review of past experience and future expectations. Analysis will also reveal the relative importance of age for retirement, vacancies created by ill health, demotions, and separations, and the steady demand of other enterprises for able young subordinates whom the firm has trained but is unable to hold.

Although the need for determining the number of managers required has been stressed here, it is clear that numbers are only part of the picture. Specifically, the qualifications for individual positions must be identified so that the best-suited managers can be chosen. This kind of detailed analysis of position requirements will be discussed in Chapter 13, on selection of managers.

Determination of Available Managerial Resources: The Management Inventory

It is common for any business, as well as for most nonbusiness enterprises, to keep an inventory of raw materials and goods on hand to enable it to carry on its operations. It is far less common for enterprises to keep an inventory of available human resources, particularly managers, despite the fact that the required number of competent managers is a vital requirement for success. Keeping abreast of the management potential within a firm can be done by the use of an inventory chart,[18] which is simply an organization chart of a unit with managerial positions indicated and keyed as to the promotability of each incumbent.

Figure 12-2 depicts a typical inventory chart. At a glance the controller can see where he or she stands with respect to the staffing function. The controller's successor is probably the manager of general accounting, and this person in turn has a successor ready for promotion. Supporting that person in turn is a subordinate who will be ready for promotion in 1 year, but below that position are one person who does not have potential and two newly hired employees.

The cost accounting manager represents the all-too-frequent case of a person who is acceptable but not promotable. This individual stands in the way of one subordinate who is promotable now. The remaining people in this department represent extremes of nonpromotability and good potential. Overall, the staffing pattern in this department is not satisfactory.

FIGURE 12-2

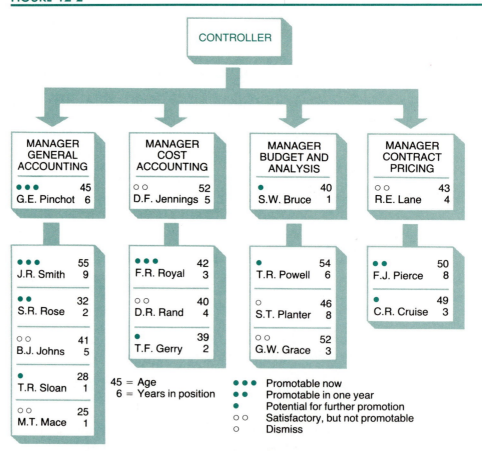

MANAGER INVENTORY CHART.

Note: The age shown on the inventory chart must not be used to discriminate against employees on the basis of their age. (That is illegal.)

The manager of budget and analysis has considerable development to accomplish before being ready for promotion. There is no immediately promotable successor. And to complicate matters, no further potential exists among the remaining two subordinates.

Contract pricing portends some problems. Its manager is not promotable, but there is good potential in the subordinates.

Advantages and Limitations of the Manager Inventory Chart

The manager inventory chart, as seen from the preceding discussion, has certain general advantages:

1. The chart gives an overview of the staffing situation of an organization.

2. Managers who are ready for promotion can now be easily identified. Prompt action in finding a suitable position within the organization may reduce the propensity of managers to seek employment outside the company.

3. The chart also shows the future internal supply of managers by indicating who is promotable in a year or more.

4. Managers who do not perform satisfactorily are identified and the need for training or replacement is indicated.

5. If the organization has insufficient "depth," recruitment and training plans can be initiated immediately to ensure the future supply of managers.

6. Managers who are close to retirement can be identified and preparations can be made for their replacement.

7. The chart facilitates the transfer of managers not only to strengthen weak departments but also to broaden the managers experience.

8. One can identify and prevent the hoarding of promotable people by their immediate superiors, a practice quite common especially in large enterprises. Naturally, superiors dislike depriving themselves of able subordinates by letting them transfer to other organizational units. But the overall interest of the enterprise is more important than the self-interest of an individual manager.

9. Managers can counsel subordinates about their career paths and relate them to employment opportunities within the company.

Despite its many advantages, the manager inventory chart also has limitations:

1. The chart does not show to what position the manager may be promotable. If an opening occurs in another organizational unit, the person who is "promotable now" will not necessarily be able to fit this position since knowledge or skills may be required in specialized areas. A promotable manager in a production department can hardly fill the job of vice-president of sales.

2. The data shown on the chart are not sufficient to make a fair assessment of all the capabilities of individuals. It is still necessary to keep records of the individual's skills, performance, and other biographical information.

3. Although the chart is useful for counseling subordinates, it is often not practical to share the information with all employees. Instead, only the top manager of a division or a department may have this information available.

4. It takes time and effort to keep the chart up to date.

5. Upper-level managers may hesitate to make their charts available to other upper-level managers because they may be afraid they will lose competent subordinates to other organizational units.

Analysis of the Need for Managers: External and Internal Information Sources

As shown in Figure 12-2, the need for managers is determined by enterprise and organizational plans and, more specifically, by an analysis of the number of managers required and the number available as identified through the management inventory. But there are other factors, internal and external, that influence the need for managers. The external forces influencing the demand for and supply of managers include economic, technological, social, political, and legal factors discussed in Chapter 24. For example, economic growth may result in increased demand for the product, which requires an expansion of the work force, thus increasing the demand for managers. At the same time, competing companies may also expand and recruit from a common labor pool, thus reducing the supply of managers. One must also consider the trends in the labor

FIGURE 12-3

PERSONNEL ACTIONS BASED ON MANAGER SUPPLY AND DEMAND WITHIN THE ENTERPRISE.

market, the demographics, and the composition of the community with respect to knowledge and skills of the labor pool and the attitude toward the company. Information about the long-term trends in the labor market may be obtained from several sources. The United States government, for example, publishes the *Monthly Labor Review* and the annual *Manpower Report of the President,* which makes long-term projections. Some trade associations and unions also project the demand for labor.

The data about the need and the availability of personnel give rise to four demand-and-supply situations, each requiring a different emphasis in personnel actions. This is illustrated in the matrix shown in Figure 12-3.

With a high supply of managers and a high demand, the focus will be on selection, placement, and promotion. Consequently, particular efforts are made to match the available managers with enterprise needs most effectively.

A low supply of managers and a high demand requires a different emphasis. If the company favors internal promotions—and most alertly managed firms do—special emphasis would be placed on training and development to enlarge and improve the pool of managers. But this takes time, and planning far in advance of actual needs is essential. Staffing may be based on open competition for available jobs, and managers from outside the firm should also be considered. Thus, recruitment would be another option. In a situation with a high demand for managers within the enterprise, chances are that there is also a general demand for managers in the external environment. It is therefore crucial that compensation be competitive. This is important for retaining managers already employed by the enterprise, and it is also essential for recruiting managers.

A company with a high supply of managers and a low demand has several alternatives available. Either the firm can change plans to take advantage of the managerial assets or it may resort to replacement or "outplacement" (a conscious attempt to help managers find and select other suitable employment), layoffs, demotions, or early retirements.

An enterprise with a low supply of managers and a low demand should be giving special attention to enterprise plans because this situation indicates a degree of stagnation in the firm. Since developing managers is a long process, the company should start developing managers early if there are prospects of growth and changes in demand for managers in the future.

Recruitment, Selection, Placement, and Promotion

After the need for managerial personnel has been determined, a number of candidates may have to be recruited. This involves attracting qualified candidates to fill organizational roles. From these, managers or potential managers are selected; this is the process of choosing from among the candidates the most suitable ones. The aim is to place people in positions where they can utilize their personal strengths and, perhaps, overcome their weaknesses by getting experience or training in those skills in which they need improvement. Finally, placing a manager in a new position within the enterprise often results in a promotion, which normally involves more responsibility. Since recruitment, selection, placement, and promotion are complex processes, they will be discussed in greater detail in Chapter 13.

Managerial Appraisal and Career Planning

Managerial appraisal is closely related to selection, placement, and promotion. One could even argue that appraisal should logically be placed before these other activities. It is true that appraisal serves as a basis for identifying persons within the enterprise who are ready for promotion. On the other hand, the candidates from outside the firm have first to be recruited, selected, and placed before their performance in a given position can be appraised. For this reason, managerial selection precedes appraisal in the model. But there is no doubt that appraisal is closely linked to selection, placement, and promotion, as is indicated by the feedback arrows in Figure 12-1. Career planning is often integrated with the appraisal process and will be discussed in Chapter 14.

Training and Development

In Chapter 15 on manager and organization development, a systematic approach to self-development and the utilization of managers' strengths and potentials, with emphasis on the integration of managerial needs and enterprise demands, will be discussed.

Leading and Controlling

Throughout this book, we have advocated the systems approach to managing. The model in Figure 12-1 shows that the activities in the staffing function must not be viewed in isolation; rather, they are related to leading and controlling. For example, well-selected and well-trained managers provide good leadership and create an environment in which people are motivated and communicate effectively. Likewise, controlling is enhanced by effective staffing. Specifically, what better control is there than preventive control? This means that the higher the quality of selected managers and their subordinates, the lower the need for correcting undesirable deviations from performance standards.

SITUATIONAL FACTORS AFFECTING STAFFING

The actual process of staffing shown in Figure 12-1 is affected by many environmental factors. Specifically, external factors include the level of education, the prevailing attitudes in society (such as the attitude toward work), the many laws and regulations that directly affect staffing, economic conditions, and the supply of and demand for managers outside the enterprise.

But there are also many internal factors that affect staffing. They include, for example, organizational goals, tasks, technology, organization structure, the kinds of people employed by the enterprise, the demand for and the supply of managers within the enterprise, the reward system, and various kinds of policies. Some organizations are highly structured; others are not. For some positions—such as the position of a sales manager—skill in human relations may be of vital importance, while the same skill may be less critical for a research scientist working fairly independently in the laboratory. Effective staffing, then, requires recognition of many external and internal situational factors, but we will focus here on those that have a particular relevance to staffing.

The External Environment

Factors in the external environment do affect staffing to various degrees. These influences can be grouped into educational, sociocultural, legal-political, and economic constraints or opportunities. For example, the high technology used in many industries requires extensive and intensive education. Similarly, managers in the sociocultural environment in the United States generally do not accept orders blindly; they want to become active participants in the decision-making process. Furthermore, now and in the future, managers will have to be more oriented toward the public than they have been in the past, responding to the public's legitimate needs and adhering to high ethical standards.

The economic environment—including the competitive situation—determines the external supply of, and the demand for, managers. Legal and political constraints require firms to follow laws and guidelines issued by various levels of government. Table 12-1 summarizes major federal legislation and orders relat-

TABLE 12-1   Major Federal Laws Governing EEO

Major equal employment opportunity laws	Objectives	Jurisdiction
Equal Pay Act (1963)	Equal pay for equal work regardless of sex	Employers engaged in interstate commerce and most employees of federal, state, and local governments
Title VII of the Civil Rights Act (1964) (As amended in 1972)	Equal Employment Opportunity (EEO) for different races, colors, religions, sexes, and national origins	Employers with fifteen or more employees; unions with fifteen or more members; employment agencies; union hiring halls; institutions of higher education; federal, state, and local governments
Age Discrimination in Employment Act (1967) (As amended from age 65 to 70 in 1978)	EEO for ages 40 to 70	Employers with twenty or more employees; unions with twenty-five or more members; employment agencies; federal, state, and local governments
Vocational Rehabilitation Act (1973)	EEO and reasonable affirmative action for handicapped people	Federal government agencies and government contractors with contracts of $2500 or more
Pregnancy Discrimination Act (1978)	EEO during pregnancy	Same as Civil Rights Act

Source: Keith Davis and John W. Newstrom, *Human Behavior at Work: Organizational Behavior* (New York: McGraw-Hill Book Company, 1985), p. 402. Used with permission.

ing to fair employment that influence the staffing function. We will focus on equal employment opportunity and the role of women in management. In addition, we will discuss the staffing of international businesses.

Equal employment opportunity.   Several laws have been passed that provide for equal employment opportunity (EEO). The laws prohibit employment practices that discriminate on the basis of race, color, religion, national origin, sex, or age (in specified age ranges).[19] EEO is based on federal, state, and local laws, and these laws impact on staffing. Recruitment and selection for promotion must be in compliance with these laws. This means that managers making decisions in these areas must be educated in the laws and how they apply to the staffing function.

Women in management.   In the last decade or so, women have made significant progress in obtaining responsible positions in organizations. Among the reasons for this development are laws governing fair employment practices, changing societal attitudes toward women in the workplace, and the desire of companies to project a favorable image by placing qualified women in managerial positions.

There appears to be some evidence that women also have some difficulty making it to the top. For example, there are no women as major candidates for the chief executive officer's job in the *Fortune 500* corporations. Discrimination has been given as one reason, according to a *Fortune* article.[20] On the other hand, women's representation on boards of directors is increasing.[21] Nevertheless, the total number of women serving on boards is still rather small.

PERSPECTIVE:
CAREER OPPORTUNITIES FOR WOMEN[22]

Opportunities for women occupying managerial positions are increasing. But career advancements may depend on the functional area, on the kind of industry, or on particular companies.

Women are likely to be found at upper levels of management in areas such as personnel or public relations. Certain industries provide faster advancement opportunities than others. Financial services institutions, such as banks, and retailing firms, which traditionally employed large percentages of women, also have more women in managerial positions.

Certain companies have more women managers than other firms. United Airlines, for example, has greatly improved opportunities. While 15 percent of managerial positions were held by women in 1980, the figure was 25 percent in 1985. At Bay Banks in Boston, seven of the nineteen top managers are women. Other companies providing good career opportunities for women are General Electric, Federal Express, and Procter and Gamble.

Some of the gains were due to legal actions. But there are other factors, such as the educational revolution.

Staffing in the international environment.   One must look beyond the immediate external environment and recognize the worldwide changes brought about primarily by advanced communication technology and by the existence of multi-national corporations. It is not unusual for large international firms to have top management teams composed of managers of many different nationalities. However, David A. Heenan and Howard V. Perlmutter stated that only occasionally were foreign nationals included in human resource inventories while parent-country managers of multinational firms were usually included in the human resource pool.[23] In other words, they found mostly Americans in crucial positions of American firms operating abroad. A notable exception was IBM, which has a truly geocentric (world-oriented) management inventory. The geocentric attitude is the basis for viewing the organization as a worldwide entity with global decision making, including staffing decisions. The example of IBM may become the model for many multinational firms in which staffing has a worldwide scope.

The Internal Environment

The internal factors selected for this discussion concern the staffing of managerial positions with personnel from within the firm as well as from the outside, determining the responsibility for staffing, and the need for top management support to overcome resistance to change.

Promotion from within.   Originally, promotion from within implied that workers proceeded into front-line supervisory positions and then upward through the organizational structure. Thus, a firm was pictured as receiving a flow of nonmanagerial employees from which future managers emerged. As used to be said in the railroad industry, "When a president retires or dies, we hire a new office worker."

So long as the matter is considered in general terms, there is little doubt that employees overwhelmingly favor a policy of promotion from within. The banning of outsiders places limits on competition for positions and gives employees of a firm an established monopoly on managerial openings. Employees come to doubt the wisdom of the policy, however, when they are confronted with a specific case of selection of one of their own for promotion. This feeling is present at all levels of the organization, largely because of jealousy or because of rivalry for promotion. The difficulty becomes most evident when selecting a general manager from among the sales, production, finance, or engineering managers. Top managers are often inclined to choose the easy way and avoid problems by selecting an outsider.

Such statements on promotion from within probably represent the general and official attitudes of most corporate executives. There can be little question that many companies place heavy emphasis on the policy for the purpose of encouraging prospective managerial candidates to accept employment, and with the view of fostering long-run commitment and of bolstering employee morale.

PERSPECTIVE:
COMPANIES WITH POLICIES OF PROMOTION FROM WITHIN

Many companies advocate promotion from within. For example, William P. Given, when president of the American Brake Shoe Company, wrote, "It is our policy to give our own people the benefit of advancement as openings occur. We believe that unless we have no one who can possibly qualify it is not fair to our people to hire an outsider." Even more emphatic is the position taken by Sears, Roebuck and Company. In a booklet given to prospective employees is the statement "At Sears the policy of 'promotion from within' is not just a phrase or slogan. It is a fact, insured by specific administrative measures to make sure that it happens." Similarly, Mobil Oil Company states that its policy is to fill all jobs, whenever possible, from within; and Procter & Gamble asserts that it adheres strictly to its policy of promotion from within, and that managers are required to train their successors. It is generally known that a good way to advance is to train subordinates so that they push their boss out of the current job. The policy of promotion from within is a part of the total approach to human resources management at Procter & Gamble that includes an intensive selection process, extensive on-the-job training, and a good compensation system.

It is not always clear whether these same firms give similar assurance to their middle and top functional executives. The saving phrase "whenever possible" is quite sufficient to provide an escape.

Promoting from within the enterprise not only has positive values relating to morale and reputation but also permits taking advantage of the presence of potentially fine managers among the firm's employees. However, even though these positive but unmeasurable values are important, executives should not be blind to the dangers of either overemphasizing this source or relying upon it exclusively.

The assumption underlying the policy of promotion from within is either that new employees are hired with a view to their managerial potential or that, from among the new and old employees, there will emerge a sufficient number of qualified candidates for promotion. The latter assumption is unsafe for modern enterprise. It is increasingly dangerous as our population becomes differentiated in the degree to which its members seek education, since well-educated persons are more likely than the less well educated to be the successful candidates for managerial positions.

The assumption that all employees are hired with a view to their managerial potential is contrary to fact. Indeed, most employees are hired for their skills as machinists, electricians, typists, accountants, engineers, or statisticians. Those who are wanted because of such skills are seldom turned down because they may have low managerial potential.

Another danger presented by an exclusive policy of promoting from within is that it may lead to the selection of persons for promotion who have, perhaps, only imitated their superiors. This is not necessarily a fault, especially if only the best methods, routines, and viewpoints are cultivated, but this is likely to be an unapproachable ideal. The fact is that enterprises often need people from the outside to introduce new ideas and practices. Consequently, there is good reason to avoid a policy of exclusive promotion from within.

Promotion from within in large companies. On the other hand, a policy of promotion from within may be quite suitable for a very large company such as Sears, Du Pont, or General Motors. But even Sears looked outside when the company recruited Philip Purcell as vice-president for corporate planning from the well-known consulting firm of McKinsey & Co. Nevertheless, large business and nonbusiness organizations usually have so many qualified people that promotion from within actually approaches a condition similar to an open-competition policy. Even in these large companies, however, it may be necessary to go outside, as General Motors did when it hired a university professor as vice-president to head its environmental control staff.

The policy of open competition. Managers must decide whether the benefits of a policy of promotion from within outweigh its shortcomings. There are clear-cut reasons for implementing the principle of open competition by opening vacant positions to the best-qualified persons available, whether inside or outside the enterprise. It gives the firm, in the final analysis, the opportunity to secure the services of the best-suited candidates. It counters the shortcomings of an exclusive policy of promotion from within, permits a firm to adopt the best techniques in the recruiting of managers, and motivates the complacent "heir apparent." To exchange these advantages for the morale advantages attributed to internal promotion would appear questionable.

A policy of open competition is a better and more honest means of ensuring managerial competence than obligatory promotion from within. However, it does put the managers who use it under a special obligation. If morale is to be protected in applying an open-competition policy, the enterprise must have fair and objective methods of appraising and selecting its people. It should also do everything possible to help people develop so that they can qualify for promotions.

When these requirements are met, it would be expected that every manager making an appointment to a vacancy or a new position would have available a roster of qualified candidates within the entire enterprise. If people know that their qualifications are being considered, if they have been fairly appraised and have been given opportunities for development, they are far less likely to feel a sense of injustice if an opening goes to an outsider. Other things being equal, present employees should be able to compete with outsiders. If a person has the ability for a position, he or she has the considerable advantage of knowing the enterprise and its personnel, history, problems, policies, and objectives. For the superior candidate, the policy of open competition should be a challenge and not a hindrance to advancement.

Selection of key managers from outside. Key managers are the ones who spark a program and carry it to completion. Although these executives may be found at all organizational levels, key managers will most probably be found at or near the top of the organization structure. They provide the tone, imagination, and judgment which help an enterprise attain its objectives. Since subordinate managers tend to reflect the attitudes of their superiors, their contribution to a program may often be ascribed to the inspiration of outstanding managers.

Often there are reasons for selecting key executives from outside the enterprise. Outside candidates may be considered superior to the internal contenders. For example, when firms reach a position in their development where the outstanding need is for their energies to be directed vigorously toward the solution of marketing problems, they are likely to turn to the outside. Promotion of insiders may not be advisable, since they have brought the enterprise to its stagnant position. Indeed, this is the situation that faced many firms during the 1960s when key marketing executives were brought in to guide firms through a highly competitive period. For similar reasons, production managers were imported during the early decades of the twentieth century, and engineers have more recently been brought into conspicuous positions with firms in the electronics and plastics industries. Here the factors being sought were vision, new ideas, and new applications. And in the same time periods, financial executives seemed to be preferred because of their experience with money and controls and with looking at an organization as a whole.

Responsibility for staffing. While responsibility for staffing should rest with every manager at every level, the ultimate responsibility is with the chief executive officer and the policymaking group of top executives. They have the duty of developing policy, assigning its execution to subordinates, and making certain it is being properly carried out. Policy considerations, for example, include decisions about the development of a staffing program, whether to promote from within or to secure managers from the outside, where to seek candidates, which selection procedure to follow, the kind of appraisal program to use, the nature of manager and organization development, and what promotion and retirement policies to follow.

Line managers should certainly make use of the services of staff members—usually from the personnel department—to assist in recruiting, selecting, placing, promoting, appraising, and training people. In the final analysis, however, it is the manager's responsibility to fill positions with the best qualified persons.

The need for top management support in overcoming resistance to effective staffing. The prestige and power of top management must be brought to bear if staffing is to be effective. Some managers within the organization will resent losing promising subordinates, even though they can make a greater contribution to the enterprise in a different department. Others will resist changes required by managerial and organizational development efforts. There are also those who may be threatened by imaginative and achievement-oriented subordinates. Still others may not see staffing as a pressing matter and neglect it altogether. To overcome these human tendencies, top management involvement in staffing is necessary.

FOR DISCUSSION

1. What differences do you see between staffing for managers and for nonmanagers?

2. What rewards would you expect from becoming a manager? What are some of the negative aspects of being a manager?

3. Why is the function of staffing so seldom approached logically? Briefly describe the systems approach to staffing. How is staffing related to other managerial functions and activities?

4. List and evaluate external factors affecting staffing. Which ones are most critical today? Explain.

5. What are the key characteristics of a manager inventory chart? Discuss the advantages and disadvantages of such a chart.

6. What are the dangers and difficulties in applying a policy of promotion from within?

7. What is meant by a policy of open competition? Do you favor such a policy? Why, or why not?

8. Do you believe that a manager inventory should be kept confidential? Why, or why not?

EXERCISES/ACTION STEPS

1. Take an organization you know and evaluate the effectiveness of the enterprise's recruitment, selection, and appraisal of people. How systematically are these and other staffing activities carried out?

2. Interview two managers and ask them about the most stressful aspects of their job. How do they cope with stress (e.g., exercises, meditation)?

CASES

CASE 12-1
BELDEN ELECTRONICS COMPANY

The Belden Electronics Company (BEC) has an excellent national as well as international reputation, and employees are proud to work for the firm. But the company demands complete loyalty from its employees and even tries to influence their behavior and appearance after work.

Christine Sharp was a bright young woman who had been working for BEC for over 10 years. She was highly respected by her colleagues and did an excellent job as a divisional sales manager, and it was generally agreed that she had excellent

potential for advancement. For 2 months Ms. Sharp had dated Frank Simmons, who worked in the electronics division of a competing company. One day, Ralph Schmidt, Ms. Sharp's boss, approached her about this matter, stating that there might be a possible conflict of interest in the association with an employee of the competitor. He made it clear that BEC has an unwritten policy that demands (and rewards) complete loyalty from all its employees.

Shortly after this emotional confrontation

with her boss, Ms. Sharp was transferred to a nonmanagerial position without any loss in pay. She also noted that even her friends at BEC tried to avoid her. But Ms. Sharp felt very strongly that the company had no business suggesting whom she could and could not see after working hours; as a result, she quit her job.

1. Can a company demand loyalty to the extent indicated in the case? Would your answer be different if Ms. Sharp had access to important company trade secrets?

2. What would you have done in Ms. Sharp's position?

3. What would you have done in the supervisor's position?

CASE 12-2
TEXAS OIL COMPANY

Fred Jenkins and Barbara Eaton, both employees at the Texas Oil Company, sat in the cafeteria and discussed recent happenings in the company. A few months ago, Texas Oil was acquired by one of the largest conglomerate firms, causing a great deal of upheaval among its employees and considerable turnover in personnel. Top management of the conglomerate realized that in order to keep the employees of the newly acquired company happy, it had to provide large salary increases, bonuses, and other benefits. Yet it lost many of Texas Oil's top managers, a fifth of its production people, and many persons involved in oil exploration. While some of the employees left the company for better pay outside the firm, there were also indications that money was not the primary motive for leaving. Becoming a part of a huge conglomerate might seem attractive, but it also involved closer supervision, more bureaucratic rules, and less discretion in decision making. The more formalized approach to managing also created additional paperwork and more formal procedures and controls.

The employees at Texas Oil had been accustomed to a rather laissez-faire managerial approach. This changed, however, when the company became a part of the conglomerate. Despite the conglomerate's attempts to decentralize, the chain of command became much longer, and many managers, especially those with entrepreneurial talent, were frustrated. Fred and Barbara talked about their preferences and whether or not they should leave the company to join a small oil firm known for its informal managerial style. Fred Jenkins favored the small-company atmosphere, but Barbara Eaton liked the status, prestige, and multinational character of the conglomerate.

1. What are the advantages and disadvantages of working for a large, prestigious multinational firm?

2. What are the advantages and disadvantages of working for a small company?

3. What are your preferences? Why?

REFERENCES

1. Rensis Likert, *The Human Organization: Its Management and Value* (New York: McGraw-Hill Book Company, 1967), chap. 9.

2. For a detailed discussion of problems see Phil H. Mirvis and Barry A. Macy, "Human Resource Accounting: A Measurement Perspective," *Academy of Management Review* (April 1976), pp. 74–83.

3. J. D. Powell, H. A. Sciullo, and G. Mattson, "Human Resource Accounting: Why the Delay?" *Journal of Management* (Fall 1976), pp. 25–31.

4. Another term now frequently used for the managerial function of staffing is "human resource management."

5. For a comprehensive review see Henry Mintzberg, *The Nature of Managerial Work* (New York: Harper & Row, 1973), chap. 2.

6. Henry Mintzberg, "The Manager's Job: Folklore and Fact," *Harvard Business Review* (July–August 1975), pp. 49–61.

7. John A. Byrne, "Executive Pay: How the Boss Did in '85," *Business Week* (May 5, 1986), pp. 48–58.

8. Maggie McComas, "Atop the Fortune 500: A Survey of the C.E.O.s," *Fortune* (Apr. 28, 1986), pp. 26–31.

9. "Top Executive Pay Peeves the Public," *Business Week* (June 25, 1984), p. 15; see also "Chrysler Officials' Raises Are Called Lavish by UAW," *The Wall Street Journal* (Apr. 8, 1986); Doron P. Levin, "Chrysler's Iacocca Got a 35% Raise While '85 Net Fell," *The Wall Street Journal* (Apr. 7, 1986).

10. Peter F. Drucker, "Reform Executive Pay or Congress Will," *The Wall Street Journal* (Apr. 24, 1984).

11. The process of determining executive pay has been described by Monci Jo Williams, "Why Chief Executives' Pay Keeps Rising," *Fortune* (Apr. 1, 1985), pp. 66–76.

12. Amanda Bennett, "More Managers Find Salary, Bonus Are Tied Directly to Performance," *The Wall Street Journal* (Feb. 28, 1986); Byrne, "Executive Pay" (1986); "Rewarding Executives for Taking the Long View," *Business Week* (Apr. 2, 1984), pp. 99–100, 108.

13. James L. Gibson, John M. Ivancevich, and James H. Donnelly, Jr., *Organizations*, 5th ed. (Plano, Tex.: Business Publications, 1985), p. 220.

14. Hans Selye, *The Stress of Life*, rev. ed. (New York: McGraw-Hill Book Company, 1976), p. viii.

15. Hans Selye, *Stress without Distress* (New York: The New American Library, 1975), book cover.

16. See for example, Herbert Benson, *The Relaxation Response* (New York: Avon Books, 1975).

17. Figure 12-1 is an overview of the staffing function. The variables not discussed in this chapter, but which also focus on staffing, are enclosed with broken lines.

18. Another term for "inventory chart" is "management replacement chart."

19. See, for example, David G. Scalise and Daniel J. Smith, "Legal Update: When Are Job Requirements Discriminatory?" *Personnel* (March 1986), pp. 41–48.

20. Susan Fraker, "Why Women Aren't Getting to the Top," *Fortune* (Apr. 16, 1984), pp. 40–45.

21. Clare Ansberry, "Board Games," *The Wall Street Journal,* special report (Mar. 24, 1986).

22. Karen Blumenthal, "Room at the Top," *The Wall Street Journal,* special report (Mar. 24, 1986); Irene Pave, "A Woman's Place is at GE, Federal Express, P&G . . . ," *Business Week* (June 23, 1986). See also Karen Pennar and Edward Mervosh, "Women at Work," *Business Week* (Jan. 28, 1985), pp. 80–85; Richard J. Herrnstein, "Are Women Workers Different?" *Fortune* (Apr. 1, 1985), pp. 177–180.

23. David A. Heenan and Howard V. Perlmutter, *Multinational Organization Development* (Reading, Mass: Addison-Wesley Publishing Company, 1979), chap. 3.

FOR FURTHER INFORMATION

Bartolomé, Fernando. "The Work Alibi: When It's Harder to Go Home," *Harvard Business Review* (March–April 1983), pp. 67–74.

Bolt, James F. "Job Security: Its Time Has Come," *Harvard Business Review* (November–December, 1983), pp. 115–123.

Condon, Thomas J., and Richard H. Wolff, "Procedures That Safeguard Your Right to Fire," *Harvard Business Review* (November–December 1985), pp. 16–18.

Cunningham, Mary. *Powerplay: What Really Happened at Bendix* (New York: Linden Press of Simon & Schuster, 1984).

Ivancevich, John M., Michael T. Matteson, and Edward P. Richards III. "Who's Liable for Stress on the Job," *Harvard Business Review* (March–April 1985), pp. 60–72.

Law, Warren A. "A Corporation Is More Than Its Stock," *Harvard Business Review* (May–June 1986), pp. 80–83.

Mills, Quinn D. "Planning With People in Mind," *Harvard Business Review* (July–August 1985), pp. 97–105.

Rowland, Kendrith M., and Gerald R. Ferris, eds. *Current Issues in Personnel Management,* 3d ed. (Boston: Allyn and Bacon, 1986).

Schein, Edgar H. "Increasing Organizational Effectiveness through Better Human Resource Planning and Development," in Harold Koontz, Cyril O'Donnell, and Heinz Weihrich (eds.), *Management: A Book of Readings* (New York: McGraw-Hill Book Company, 1980), pp. 383–395.

Sutton, Charlotte Decker. "Executive Women—20 Years Later," *Harvard Business Review* (September–October 1985), pp. 42–66.

Werther, William B., Jr., and Keith Davis. *Personnel Management and Human Resources* (New York: McGraw-Hill Book Company, 1981).

"You've Come a Long Way, Baby—But Not as Far as You Thought," *Business Week* (Oct. 1, 1984).

Selection: Matching the Person with the Job

CHAPTER OBJECTIVES

After reading this chapter, you should be able to:

1. Summarize important aspects of the systems approach to manager selection.

2. Analyze position requirements and important characteristics of job design.

3. Identify skills and personal characteristics needed by managers.

4. Describe the process of matching manager qualifications with position requirements.

5. Explain the selection process, techniques, and instruments.

6. Discuss the orientation and socialization process of new employees.

*P*lant, equipment, materials, and people do not make a business any more than airplanes, tanks, ships, and people make an effective military force. One other element is indispensable: effective managers. The quality of managers is one of the most important factors determining the continuing success of any organization. It necessarily follows, therefore, that the selection of managers is one of the most critical steps in the entire process of managing. We define **selection** as choosing from among candidates, from within the organization or from the outside, the most suitable person for the current position or for future positions.

SYSTEMS APPROACH TO THE SELECTION OF MANAGERS: AN OVERVIEW

Since qualified managers are critical to the success of an enterprise, a systematic approach is essential to manager selection and to the assessment of present and future needs for managerial personnel.

An overview of the systems approach to selection is illustrated in Figure 13-1. The variables that are closely related to selection, but are not discussed in this chapter, are marked with broken lines in the model. The managerial requirements plan is based on the firm's objectives, forecasts, plans, and strategies. This plan is translated into position and job design requirements which are matched with such individual characteristics as intelligence, knowledge, skills, attitudes, and experience. To meet organizational requirements, managers recruit, select, place, and promote people. This, of course, must be done with due consideration for the internal environment (for example, company policies, supply and demand of managers, and the organizational climate) and the external environment (laws, regulations, availability of managers). After people have been selected and placed in positions, they must be introduced to the new job. This orientation involves learning about the company, its operation, and its social aspects.

The newly placed managers then carry out their managerial and nonmanagerial functions (such as marketing), resulting in managerial performance, which eventually determines enterprise performance. Subsequently, managerial performance is appraised, and managers are rewarded. (See Chapter 14.) On the basis of this evaluation, manager and organization development are initiated (Chapter 15). Finally, appraisal may also become the basis for promotion, demotion, replacement, and retirement decisions.

That is the selection model in brief; now each major variable in the model will receive closer attention.

POSITION REQUIREMENTS AND JOB DESIGN

To select a manager effectively requires a clear understanding of the nature and purpose of the position which is to be filled. An objective analysis of position requirements must be made, and, as far as possible, the job must be designed to

FIGURE 13-1

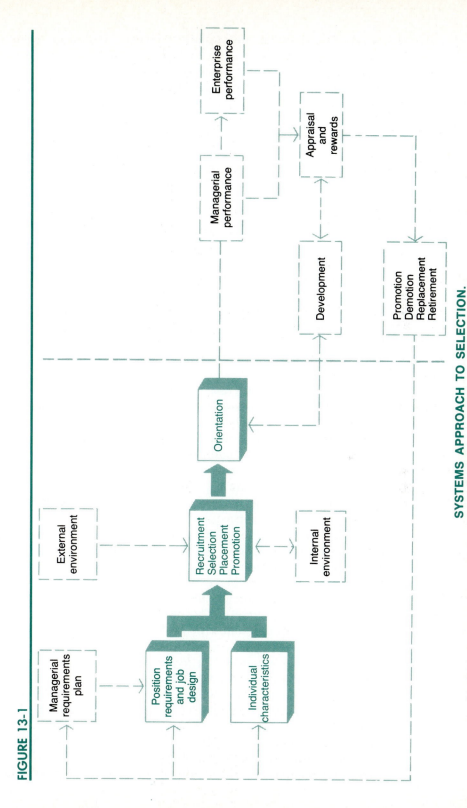

SYSTEMS APPROACH TO SELECTION.

Variables marked with broken lines are staffing and other activities that are discussed in other chapters.

meet organizational and individual needs. In addition, positions must be evaluated and compared so the incumbents can be treated fairly and equitably. Among other factors to consider are the skills required—technical, human, conceptual, and design—since these vary with the level in the organizational hierarchy and the personal characteristics needed by managers.

Identifying Job Requirements

In identifying job requirements, we must answer questions such as these: What has to be done in this job? How is it done? What background knowledge, attitudes, and skills are required? Since positions are not static, we may have to consider additional questions: Can it be done differently? If so, what are the new requirements? To find answers to these and similar questions, we must analyze the job. This can be done through observation, interviews, questionnaires, or even a systems analysis. Thus, a job description, based on job analysis, usually lists important duties, authority-responsibility (although these can also be handled by reference to a chart of approval authorization, discussed in Chapter 9), and the relationship to other positions. More recently, some firms have also included objectives and expected results in job descriptions.

There is, of course, no foolproof rule for designing managerial jobs. Nevertheless, we can avoid mistakes by following some guidelines.

Appropriate scope of the job.   A job too narrowly defined provides no challenge, no opportunity for growth, and no sense of accomplishment. Consequently, good managers will be bored and dissatisfied. On the other hand, a job must not be so broad that it cannot be effectively handled. The result will be stress, frustration, and loss of control.

Full-time challenge of the job.   Sometimes managers are given a job that does not require their full time and effort. They are not challenged by their task and they feel underutilized. Consequently, they often meddle in the work of their subordinates, who then also feel that they do not have sufficient authority and discretion to do their jobs. Some time ago, when a utility company asked for help in solving organizational conflicts, it was found that people did not have full-time jobs; they were quarreling about jobs, duties, and tasks; they were in each other's way. Thus, they channeled their energies against one another instead of toward the aims of the company. The need to design jobs with challenging objectives, duties, and responsibilities should be obvious.

Managerial skills required by the job design.   Generally, the design of the job should start with the tasks to be accomplished. The design is usually broad enough to accommodate people's needs and desires. But some writers on management suggest that we may have to learn to design the job to fit the leadership style of a particular person.[1] It may be especially appropriate to design jobs for exceptional persons, in order to utilize their potential. The problem, of course, is that such a position would probably have to be restructured every time a new manager occupied it. The job description, then, must provide a clear idea of the performance requirements for a person in a particular position, but it must also allow some flexibility so that the employer can take advantage of individual characteristics and abilities.

Any position description is contingent on the particular job and the organization. For example, in a bureaucratic and fairly stable organization environment, the position may be described in relatively specific terms. In contrast, in a dynamic organization with an unstable, fast-changing environment, a job description may have to be more general and most likely will have to be reviewed more frequently. A situational approach to job descriptions and job designs is called for.

Job Design

People spend a great deal of time on the job, and it is therefore important to design jobs so that individuals feel good about their work. This requires an appropriate job structure in terms of content, function, and relationships.

Design of jobs for individuals and work teams.   The focus of job design can be on the individual position or on work groups.[2] First, individual jobs can be enriched by grouping tasks into natural work units. This means putting tasks that are related into one category and assigning an individual to carry out the tasks. A second related approach is to combine several tasks into one job. For example, rather than having the tasks of assembling a water pump carried out by several persons on the assembly line, work stations can be established with individuals doing the whole task of putting the unit together and even testing it. A third way of enriching the job is to establish direct relationships with the client. A systems analyst may present findings and recommendations directly to the managers involved in the systems change rather than reporting to his or her superior who would then make the recommendations to top management. Fourth, prompt and specific feedback should be built into the system whenever appropriate. In one retail store, for example, salespersons received the sales figures for each day and summary figures for each month. Fifth, individual jobs can be enriched through vertical job loading, which is increasing individuals' responsibility for planning, doing, and controlling their job.

Similar arguments can be made for improving the design of jobs for work teams.[3] Jobs should be designed so that groups have a complete task to perform. Moreover, teams may be given authority and freedom to decide how well the jobs shall be performed, giving the groups a great deal of autonomy. Within the team, individuals can often be trained so that they can rotate to different jobs within the group. Finally, rewards may be administered on the basis of group performance, which tends to induce cooperation, rather than competition, among team members.

Factors influencing job design.   In designing jobs, the requirements of the enterprise have to be taken into account. But other factors must be considered in order to realize maximum benefits; they include individual differences, the technology involved, the costs associated with restructuring the jobs, the organization structure, and the internal climate.

People have different needs. Those with unused capabilities and a need for growth and development usually want to have their job enriched and to assume greater responsibility. While some people prefer to work by themselves, others with social needs usually work well in groups. The nature of the task and the technology related to the job must also be considered. While it may be possible for work teams to assemble automobiles, as is done at a Volvo plant in Sweden, it may not be efficient to use the same work design for the high production runs at General Motors in the United States. The costs of changing to new job designs must also be considered. It makes a great deal of difference whether a plant is newly designed or an old plant has to be redesigned and changed to accommodate new job design concepts.

The organization structure must also be taken into account. Individual jobs must fit the overall structure. Autonomous work groups, for example, may work well in a decentralized organization, but they may be inappropriate in a centralized structure. Similarly, the organizational climate influences job design. Groups may function well in an atmosphere that encourages participation, job enrichment, and autonomous work, while they may not fit into an enterprise with an autocratic top-down approach to managerial leadership.

SKILLS AND PERSONAL CHARACTERISTICS NEEDED BY MANAGERS

To be effective, managers need various skills ranging from technical to design. The relative importance of these skills varies according to the level in the organization.

Managerial Skills and the Organizational Hierarchy

Robert L. Katz identified three kinds of skills for administrators.[4] We suggest a fourth—the ability to design solutions.

1. **Technical skill** is knowledge of and proficiency in activities involving methods, processes, and procedures. Thus it involves working with tools and specific techniques. For example, mechanics work with tools, and their supervisors should have the ability to teach these skills to their subordinates. Similarly, accountants apply specific techniques in doing their job.

2. **Human skill** is the ability to work with people; it is cooperative effort; it is teamwork; it is the creation of an environment in which people feel secure and free to express their opinions.

3. **Conceptual skill** refers to the ability to see the "big picture," to recognize significant elements in a situation, to understand the relationships among the elements.

4. **Design skill** connotes the ability to solve problems in ways that will benefit the enterprise. To be effective, particularly at upper organizational levels, managers must be able to do more than see a problem. They must have, in addition, the skill of a good design engineer in working out a practical solution to a problem. If managers merely see the problem and become "problem watchers," they will fail. Managers must also have that valuable skill of being able to design a workable solution to the problem in the light of the realities they face.

The relative importance of these skills may differ at various levels in the organization hierarchy. As shown in Figure 13-2, technical skills are of greatest importance at the supervisory level. Human skills are also helpful in the frequent interactions with subordinates. Conceptual skills, on the other hand, are usually not critical for lower-level supervisors. At the middle-management level,

FIGURE 13-2

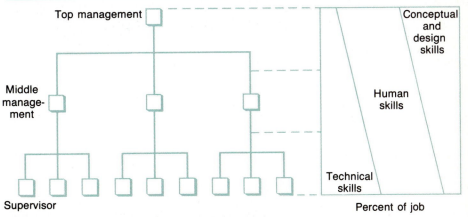

Skills vary in importance at different management levels.

SKILLS AND MANAGEMENT LEVELS.

the need for technical skills decreases; human skills are still essential; the conceptual skills gain in importance. At the top management level, conceptual and design abilities and human skills are especially valuable, but there is relatively little need for technical abilities. It is assumed, especially in large companies, that chief executives can utilize the technical abilities of their subordinates. In smaller firms, however, technical experience may be still quite important.

Analytical and Problem-Solving Abilities

One of the frequently mentioned skills desired of managers is analytical and problem-solving ability. But as Alan Stoneman, former president of the Purex Corporation, used to say: "We have no problems here; all are opportunities; all a problem should be is an opportunity." In other words, managers must be able to identify problems, analyze complex situations, and, by solving the problems encountered, exploit the opportunities presented. They must scan the environment and identify, through a rational process, those factors that stand in the way of opportunities. Thus, analytical skills should be used to find needs of present customers—or potential ones—and then to satisfy these needs with a product or service. It has been amply demonstrated that this opportunity-seeking approach can mean corporate success. For example, Edwin H. Land of Polaroid filled the needs of people who wanted instant photographs. Similarly, Heinz Nordhoff of Volkswagen satisfied those customers in the late 1940s, 1950s, and 1960s who wanted a low-cost, reliable, and fuel-efficient automobile. But problem identification and analysis are not enough. Managers also need the will to implement the solutions; they must recognize the emotions, needs, and motivations of the people involved in initiating the required change as well as those who resist change.

Personal Characteristics Needed by Managers

In addition to the various skills that effective managers need, several personal characteristics are also important. They are (1) a desire to manage, (2) the ability to communicate with empathy, (3) integrity and honesty, and (4) the person's experience—his or her past performance as a manager—which is a very significant characteristic and which should also be considered.

Desire to manage.   The successful manager has a strong desire to manage, to influence others, and to get results through team efforts of subordinates. To be sure, many people want the privileges of the managerial positions, which include high status and salary, but they lack the basic motivation to achieve results by creating an environment in which people work together toward common aims. The desire to manage requires effort, time, energy, and usually long hours of work.

Communication skills and empathy.   Another important characteristic of managers is the ability to communicate through written reports, letters, speeches, and discussions. Communication demands clarity, but even more, it demands *empathy*. This is the ability to understand the feelings of another person and to deal with the emotional aspects of communication. Communication skills are important for effective *intragroup communication,* that is, communication with people in the same organizational unit. As one goes up in the organization, however, *intergroup communication* becomes increasingly important. This kind of communication is not only with other departments but also with groups outside the enterprise: customers, suppliers, governments, the community, and, of course, the stockholders in business enterprises.

Integrity and honesty.   Managers must be morally sound and worthy of trust. Integrity in managers includes honesty in money matters and in dealing with others, effort to keep superiors informed, adherence to the full truth, strength of character, and behavior in accordance with ethical standards.

Many of these qualities, and others, have been cited by top executives of major companies. Henry Ford II, former chairperson of Ford Motor Company, mentioned as appealing qualities honesty, candor, and openness. Similarly, Donald M. Kendall, chairperson of Pepsico, Inc., listed work ethics and integrity as essential characteristics of executives. Noah Dietrich, who ran the Howard Hughes empire for 32 years, identified honesty and candor as the top qualities of his subordinates. His attitude was "I cannot do my job if the executives who report to me do not tell me the truth about their operations."

Past performance as a manager.   Another very important characteristic for selection is past performance as a manager. It is probably the most reliable forecast of a manager's future performance. Of course, an assessment of managerial experience is not possible in selecting first-line supervisors from the ranks, since they have not had such experience. But past accomplishments are important considerations in the selection of middle- and upper-level managers. In a survey of *Fortune 500* companies, most CEOs said that experience within the company was the key to their successful careers.[5]

MATCHING MANAGER QUALIFICATIONS WITH POSITION REQUIREMENTS

After the organizational positions are identified, managers are obtained through recruitment, selection, placement, and promotion. (See variables in Figure 12-1.) There are basically two sources of managerial personnel: People from within the enterprise may be promoted or transferred, and managers may be hired from the outside. For *internal* promotions, a computerized information system may help to identify qualified candidates. It can be used in conjunction with a comprehensive human resource plan. Specifically, it can be utilized to anticipate staff requirements, new openings, attritions, development needs, and career planning.

There are also several *external* sources available, and the enterprise may use different methods in finding qualified managers. Many employment agencies—public and private—locate suitable candidates for positions. Other sources for managers are professional associations, educational institutions, referrals from people within the enterprise, and, of course, unsolicited applications from persons interested in the firm.

Recruitment of Managers

Recruiting involves attracting candidates to fill the positions in the organization structure. Before recruiting begins, the position's requirements—which should relate directly to the task—must be clearly identified. This makes it easier to recruit suitable candidates from the outside. Enterprises with a favorable public image find it easier to attract qualified candidates. A company such as IBM (International Business Machines) has a well-recognized image, while small firms—which frequently offer excellent growth and development opportunities—may have to make great efforts to communicate to the applicant the kinds of products, services, and opportunities the firm offers.

Recruitment in the public sector has many similarities to recruitment in the private sector. However, government regulations or policies may demand that managers adhere to special hiring guidelines. For example, legislation may require that potential employees live within a municipality's boundaries. Another difference is that applicants for public sector positions often have to take competitive tests such as civil service examinations, although an increasing number of privately owned enterprises are using written and oral tests.

Unfortunately, the selection process in government is not always as objective and rational as it should be, and the practice of making decisions on criteria other than competence is probably not unusual. Frederic V. Malek, a former special assistant to the President and now a business executive himself, reports that it is unthinkable for a major corporation to put a person without considerable managerial experience in charge of 5000 people. Yet in government this is not uncommon.[6] Thus, in order to improve the effectiveness and efficiency of government, a better selection process is required.

Information Exchange Contributing to Successful Selection

The exchange of information works two ways in recruitment and selection: An enterprise provides applicants with an objective description of the company and the position, while the applicants provide information about their capabilities. (See Figure 13-3).

Business and other organizations attempt to project a favorable image, stress opportunities for personal growth and development, highlight potential challenges, and indicate promotion possibilities. They also convey information about pay, fringe benefits, and perhaps job security. This can, of course, be overdone, raising unrealistic expectations in the applicant. In the long run, there may be undesirable side effects resulting in low job satisfaction, high turnover, and unfulfilled dreams. Certainly the enterprise should present itself in an attractive light, yet the opportunities should be discussed in a factual and realistic manner, mentioning limitations and even unfavorable aspects of the job.

On the other hand, management should elicit from all the applicants an objective demonstration of their knowledge, skills, abilities, aptitudes, moti-

FIGURE 13-3

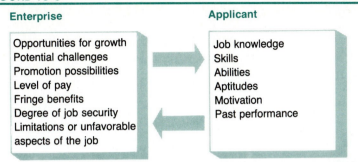

Enterprise

Opportunities for growth
Potential challenges
Promotion possibilities
Level of pay
Fringe benefits
Degree of job security
Limitations or unfavorable
aspects of the job

Applicant

Job knowledge
Skills
Abilities
Aptitudes
Motivation
Past performance

EXCHANGE OF INFORMATION IN SELECTION OF MANAGERS.

vation, and past performance. A number of techniques and instruments can reveal this information; we will discuss them as we continue. To be sure, the collection of data about an applicant can go too far and can become an invasion of privacy. The managerial candidate will tolerate only a reasonable amount of interviewing, testing, and disclosure of personal information. Clearly, managers must exercise restraint and request information that is essential and relevant to the job.

Selection, Placement, and Promotion

Selecting a manager is choosing from among the candidates the one that best meets the position requirements. The selection may be for a specific job opening, or it may be for future managerial requirements. Thus, we can distinguish between the selection and placement approaches to filling organizational positions. In the *selection approach*, applicants are sought to fill a position with rather specific requirements, while in the *placement approach*, the strengths and weaknesses of the individual are evaluated and a suitable position is found or even designed.

Promotion is a change within the organization to a higher position with greater responsibilities and requiring more advanced skills. It usually involves higher status and an increase in pay. The various facets of selection generally apply also to promotion, which may be a reward for outstanding performance or a result of the firm's desire to better utilize the individual's skills and abilities.

Balancing Skills and the Age Factor

There are other important considerations in selection. As we pointed out earlier, managerial positions demand a variety of skills: technical, human, conceptual, and problem-solving. Since one person may not have all the required abilities, others may have to be selected to compensate for any deficiencies. For example, a top manager with excellent conceptual and design skills may need assistance from persons with technical skills. Similarly, a manager with a strong marketing and financial background may have to be complemented by an operations expert.

PERSPECTIVE:
MEET THE YOUNG WORK FORCE[7]

While some observers paint a gloomy picture for the baby-boomers, others look more optimistically into the future. About half of the United States labor force is now under 35, and these men and women will be determining the success of enterprises, and, on a broader scale, the well-being of the country.

Demographics suggest that there may be an oversupply of managers. Yet the salaries of the young managers have not been eroded. Some factors, such as decentralization of organizations, have increased the demand for general managers. On the other hand, the extensive use of computers may have an impact especially on middle managers, as you will see when we discuss management information systems. It seems likely that the competition for managerial jobs is going to increase.

What kind of work force will these managers lead? *Fortune* magazine interviewed about 100 workers across the country and found that they are very much aware of the economic—including the Japanese—challenges. At the same time, they are willing to adapt. In fact, they are eager to learn new skills, are willing to relocate, and are open to changing jobs if necessary. The vitalization of industry will depend to a great extent on the young work force: managers and nonmanagers alike.

Age must also be taken into account when selecting managers. It is not uncommon to find that all vice-presidents and middle managers in a company are in the same age bracket. Problems will thus occur when several managers on a similar organization level retire at the same time. But in selection, managers must not illegally discriminate on the basis of age. Systematic work-force planning can provide for fair distribution of managers in different age groups within the organizational structure.

Dual-Career Couples

Effective selection requires taking into consideration the career of the spouse. Dual-career couples, with both partners working, sometimes have to make some very stressful choices. For example, if both partners have successful careers, the opportunity for a promotion that requires relocation is a particularly painful decision. Merrill Lynch Relocation Management Inc. conducted a survey of 600 major companies and found that 60 percent of relocations involved dual-career couples. It has been estimated that by 1990, it will be 75 percent.[8]

Some companies are accommodating the special needs of dual-career couples by:

■ Having a flexible approach to transfers that involve relocation

■ Considering the needs of both partners in career planning

- Helping to find employment for the spouse either within the company or outside

- Providing maternity leave and day-care services for children.

With the large number of married women in the work force, an increasing number of companies have recognized the stressful situation of dual-career couples through more flexible policies, career planning, personnel selection, placement, and promotion.

The Peter Principle

Errors in selection are possible, perhaps even common. According to Laurence J. Peter and Raymond Hall, authors of *The Peter Principle,* managers tend to be promoted to the level of their incompetence.[9] Specifically, if a manager succeeds in a position, this very success may lead to promotion to a higher position, often one requiring skills that the person does not possess. Such a promotion may involve work that is over the manager's head. While we must not overlook the possibility of individual growth, the Peter Principle can serve as a warning not to take the selection and promotion process lightly.

Responsibility for Selection

The final decision in the selection of a person for a new position should rest with the candidate's prospective superior; only then can the selector be held accountable for the performance of the chosen candidate. It is also advisable to get the opinions of others, especially those with whom the candidate will have working relationships. In addition, the superior of the selector should be involved, approving, rather than actually making, the selection decision. This gives additional assurance that qualifications rather than friendships are the basic reasons for the choice. It also is a way of making more certain that the selecting manager is choosing people with adequate qualifications and potential for growth.

THE SELECTION PROCESS, TECHNIQUES, AND INSTRUMENTS

In this section, we give an overview of the selection process, followed by the discussion of a number of instruments and techniques, including interviews, tests, and the assessment center. For good selection, the information about the applicant should be both *valid* and *reliable*. When we ask if data are **valid,** we raise the question: Are we measuring what we think we are measuring? In selection, validity is the degree to which the data predict the candidate's success as a manager. The information should also have a high degree of **reliability,** a term which refers to the accuracy and consistency of the measurement. For example, a reliable test, if repeated under the same conditions, would give essentially the same results.

The Selection Process

There are some variations of the specific steps in the selection process. For example, the interview of a candidate for a first-level supervisory position may be relatively simple when compared with the rigorous interviews for a top-level executive. Nevertheless, the following broad outline is indicative of the typical process.

First, the selection criteria are established, usually based on the current—and sometimes future—job requirements. These criteria include such items as education, knowledge, skills, and experience. Second, the candidate is requested to complete an application form (this step may be omitted if the candidate for the position is from within the organization). Third, a screening interview is conducted to identify the more promising candidates. Fourth, additional information may be obtained by testing the candidate's qualifications for the position. Fifth, a series of formal interviews are conducted by the manager, his or her superior, and other persons within the organization. Sixth, the information provided by the candidate is checked and verified. Seventh, some organizations require a physical examination. Eight, based on the results of previous steps, a job offer is made or the candidate is informed that he or she has not been selected for the position. Let us examine some parts of the selection process in greater detail.

Interviews

Virtually every manager hired or promoted by a company is interviewed by one or more people. Despite its general use, the interview is considerably distrusted as a reliable and valid means for selecting managers. Various interviewers may weigh or interpret the obtained information differently. Interviewers often do not ask the right questions. They may be influenced by the interviewer's general appearance, which may have little bearing on job performance. They also frequently make up their minds early in the interview, before they have all the information necessary to make a fair judgment.

Several techniques can be used to improve the interviewing process and overcome some of these weaknesses. First, the interviewers should be trained so that they know what to look for. For example, in interviewing people from within the enterprise, they should analyze and discuss past records. They should study the results achieved as well as the way key managerial activities were performed. Chapter 14, on appraisal, shows in greater detail how this can be done. When selecting managers from outside the firm, interviewers find that these data are more difficult to obtain, and they usually get them by checking with the listed references.

Second, the interviewer should be prepared to ask the right questions. There are structured, semistructured, and unstructured interviews. In an *unstructured* interview, an interviewer may say something like, "Tell me about your last job." In the *semistructured* interview, the manager follows an interview guide but may also ask other questions. In a *structured* interview, a set of prepared questions is asked, such as the following:

What were your specific duties and responsibilities in your last job?

What did you achieve in this job and how does this compare with the normal output for this job?

Who could be asked to verify these achievements?

To what extent were these achievements due to your efforts?

What were the contributions of other people?

Who are they?

What did you like and dislike about your job?

What innovations did you make in your job?

Why do you want to change your job?

A third way to improve selection is to conduct multiple interviews utilizing several different interviewers. Thus, several people can compare their evaluations and perceptions. However, not all interviewers should vote in selecting the candidate; rather, this technique provides additional information to the manager who will be responsible for the final decision.

Fourth, the interview is just one aspect of the selection process. It should be supplemented by data from the application form, the results of various tests, and the information obtained from persons listed as references. Reference checks and letters of recommendation may be necessary to verify the information given by the applicant. For a reference to be useful, the person giving the reference must know the applicant well and give a truthful and complete assessment of the applicant. Many people are reluctant to provide complete information, so an applicant's strong points are often overemphasized while his or her shortcomings may be glossed over. The Privacy Act of 1974 and related legislation and judicial rulings have made it even more difficult to obtain objective references. Under this act, the applicant has a legal right to inspect letters of reference unless this right is waived. This is one of the reasons that teachers are sometimes reluctant to make objective and accurate job referrals for their students.

Tests

The primary aim of testing is to obtain data about the applicants that help to predict their probable success as managers. Some of the benefits from testing include finding the best person for the job, obtaining a high degree of job satisfaction for the applicant, and reducing turnover. The most commonly used tests can be classified as follows:

1. **Intelligence tests** are designed to measure mental capacity and to test memory, speed of thought, and ability to see relationships in complex problem situations.

2. **Proficiency and aptitude tests** are constructed to discover interests, existing skills, and potential for acquiring skills.

3. **Vocational tests** are designed to show a candidate's most suitable occupation or where the candidate's interests match the interests of people working in that occupation.

4. **Personality tests** are designed to reveal candidates' personal characteristics and the way candidates may interact with others, thereby giving a measure of leadership potential.

Competent industrial psychologists agree that tests are not accurate enough to be used as the sole way of measuring candidates' characteristics and must be interpreted in the light of each individual's entire history. Second, any test user must know what tests do and what their limitations are; one of the major limitations is uncertainty about whether the tests are really applicable. Even psychologists are not yet highly confident that tests developed thus far are effective in measuring managerial abilities and potentials. Third, before any test is widely used, it should be tried out, if possible on personnel currently employed in an enterprise, to see whether it is valid for employees whose managerial abilities are already known. Fourth, it is also important that tests be administered and interpreted by experts in the field. Finally, tests should not discriminate unfairly and should be consistent with laws and government guidelines.

Assessment Centers

The assessment center is not a location but a technique for selecting and promoting managers. This approach may be used in combination with training. Assessment centers were first used for selecting and promoting lower-level supervisors, but now they are applied to middle-level managers as well. They seem, however, to be inappropriate for top executives. The assessment center technique is not new. It was used by the German and British military in World War II and the American Office of Strategic Services. But its first corporate use in the United States is generally attributed to the American Telephone and Telegraph Company in the 1950s.

Intended to measure how a potential manager will act in typical managerial situations, the usual center approach is to have candidates take part in a series of exercises. During this period they are observed and assessed by psychologists or experienced managers. A typical assessment center will have the candidates do the following:

Take various psychological tests.

Engage in small groups in management games.

Engage in "in-basket" exercises, in which they are asked to handle a variety of matters that they might face in a managerial job.

Participate in a leaderless group discussion of some problem.

Give a brief oral presentation on a particular topic or theme, usually recommending a course of desirable action to a mythical superior.

Engage in various other exercises, such as preparing a written report.

During these exercises, the candidates are observed by their evaluators, who also interview them from time to time. At the end of the assessment center period, the assessors summarize their appraisals of each candidate's performance, compare their evaluations with those of other assessors, come to conclusions with them concerning a candidate's managerial potential, and write a summary report on the candidate. These reports are made available to appointing managers for their guidance. They are also often used as guides for management development. In many cases candidates are given feedback on their evaluation; in other cases feedback is given only when candidates request it. Sometimes the summary evaluation as to promotability remains confidential, even though candidates may be informed by assessors about their performance in the various exercises.

Evidence of the usefulness of the assessment center approach—although not conclusive—is encouraging. Specifically, its reliability seems high enough to suggest that further use is warranted.

Assessment centers do present some problems, however. First, they are costly in terms of time, especially since many effective programs extend over a 5-day period. Second, training assessors is a problem, particularly in those companies which believe, with some justification, that the best assessors are likely to be experienced line managers rather than trained psychologists. Third, although a number of different exercises are used to cover the kinds of things a manager does, questions have been raised as to whether these exercises are the best criteria for evaluation. An even greater problem exists in determining what evaluation measures should be applied to each exercise. Most assessment centers, being highly oriented to individual and interpersonal behavior under various circumstances, may be overlooking the most important element in selecting managers, especially those about to enter the managerial ranks for the first time. That element is motivation—whether or not a person truly wants to be a manager. To be so motivated, candidates must know what managing is, what it involves, and what is required to be a successful manager. Obviously, motivation is a difficult quality to evaluate. However, by making clear to a candidate what managing involves and requires and then asking the candidate to think this over, the interviewer can give the candidate a good basis on which to determine whether he or she really wants to be a manager.

Limitations of the Selection Process

The diversity of selection approaches and tests indicates that there is no one perfect way to select managers. Experience has shown that even carefully chosen selection criteria are still imperfect in predicting performance. Furthermore, there is a distinction between what persons *can do,* that is, their ability to perform, and what people *will do,* which relates to motivation. The latter is a function of the individual and the environment. For example, a person's needs may be different at various times. The organizational environment also changes. The climate of an enterprise may change from one that encourages initiative to a restrictive one because a new top management introduces a different managerial philosophy. Therefore, selection techniques and instruments are not a sure way to predict what people will do, even though they may have the ability to do it.

Testing itself, especially psychological testing, has limitations. Specifically, seeking of certain information may be considered an invasion of privacy. In addition, it has been charged that some tests unfairly discriminate against members of minority groups or women. These complex issues are not easily resolved, yet they cannot be ignored when selecting managers.

Still other concerns in selection and hiring are the time and cost involved in making personnel decisions. It is important to identify such factors as advertising expenses, agency fees, costs of test materials, time spent interviewing candidates, costs for reference checks, medical exams, start-up time required for the new manager to get acquainted with the job, relocation, and orientation of the new employee. When recruiting costs are recognized, it becomes evident that turnover can be very expensive to an enterprise.

ORIENTING AND SOCIALIZING NEW EMPLOYEES

The selection of the best person for the job is only the first step in building an effective management team. Even companies that make great efforts in the recruitment and selection process often ignore the needs of new managers after they have been hired. Yet the first few days and weeks can be crucial for integrating the new person into the organization.

Orientation involves the introduction of new employees to the enterprise, its functions, tasks, and people. Large firms usually have a formal orientation program which explains these features of the company: history, products and services, general policies and practices, organization (divisions, departments, and geographic locations), benefits (insurance, retirement, vacations), requirements for confidentiality and secrecy (especially in defense contracts), safety and other regulations. These may be further described in detail in a company booklet, but the orientation meeting provides new employees with an opportunity to ask questions. Although these formal programs are usually conducted by persons from the personnel department, the primary responsibility for orienting the new manager still rests with the superior.

There is another and perhaps even more important aspect of orientation: the socialization of new managers. **Organizational socialization** is defined in several different ways. A global view includes three aspects: the acquisition of work skills and abilities, the adoption of appropriate role behaviors, and the adjustment to the norms and values of the work group.[10] So, in addition to meeting the specific requirements of the job, new managers will usually encounter new values, new personal relationships, and new modes of behavior. They do not know people they can ask for advice, they do not know how the organization works, and they have a fear of being unsuccessful in the new job. All this uncertainty can cause a great deal of anxiety for the new employee, especially the management trainees. Because the initial experience in an enterprise can be very important for future management behavior, the first contact of trainees should be with the best superiors in the enterprise, people who can serve as models for future behavior.

FOR DISCUSSION

1. What is the systems approach to selection of managers? Why is it called a systems approach? How does it differ from other approaches?

2. What are the important managerial skills? In what ways do you think the need for these skills differs at various levels in the organizational hierarchy?

3. What are some of the factors that are important in designing individual jobs and jobs for work teams? Which ones seem most important to you? Why?

4. What kinds of personal characteristics are important for managerial success?

5. What are the various approaches in the selection of managers? Which approach do you prefer? Why?

6. The Peter Principle has been widely quoted in management circles. What do you think of it? Do you think that it could ever apply to you? Does it mean that all chief executives are incompetent? Explain.

7. What kinds of tests may be used in selecting managers? What are the benefits and limitations of these tests?

8. What is an assessment center? How does it work? Would you like to participate in such a center? Why, or why not?

9. Why are orientation and socialization important?

EXERCISES/ACTION STEPS

1. Take an organization you know and discuss how managers and nonmanagers are recruited and selected. How effective is the recruitment and selection?

2. Go to the library and research the background of successful CEOs. You may begin by looking at the *Fortune* issue of April 28, 1986, or read the biography of Lee Iacocca, the CEO at Chrysler.

CASES

CASE 13-1
CARL WENDOVER

Carl Wendover, an assistant manager of a well-run division, was selected as head of another division. He encountered trouble from the beginning—trouble becoming familiar with the information required by the executive vice-president, trouble with the subordinates he inherited, and trouble in really understanding that he was in trouble. Within a year he was terminated.

The man who selected him was concerned about how he came to make such a mistake. He analyzed the situation carefully and concluded that when Carl Wendover was an assistant manager, he was not trained to operate the division. His then superior simply used him as a staff person and excluded him completely from division operations. The assistant certainly "looked good" to all, but he was merely reflecting the reputation of the well-run division.

1. Exactly why was the mistake in the instance of Carl Wendover made? What defense, if any, could Wendover advance in his behalf?

2. If you were the person who selected Wendover, what would you do to avoid making this mistake again?

3. If you were the executive vice-president, what action, if any, would you take so that such mistakes would be unlikely to occur?

CASE 13-2
THE DENIED PROMOTION

Jerry Nolan worked at the headquarters of the Worldwide Motorbike Company. His task was to process warranty claims and advise service engineers working in the field with distributors throughout the world. Then he heard of an opening for a field engineer.

As a first step, Jerry Nolan approached his immediate superior, Donald Brown, and asked to be considered as field engineer in Jane Smith's department. The idea was rejected with the comment "Let's talk about it later." When Mr. Brown left for a business trip, Jerry approached Jane Smith, the service manager for international operations, who was not only Brown's superior but was also responsible for the field engineers. During the discussion, Ms. Smith, who favored promoting young talent from within the company, recognized that Jerry Nolan was well qualified for the position of field engineer. She promised to talk to Mr. Brown after his return from the trip.

One week later Mr. Brown called Jerry Nolan into his office and opened the conversation as follows: "I heard that you talked to Ms. Smith while I was out of town, about the position of field engineer. I cannot let you take this position. We just switched to a computerized claim-processing system and I need you because you have the broadest experience of any of my seven subordinates." Jerry was shocked. Should he be denied the promotion because he was the best person in the group? Two weeks later, a field engineer was hired from outside the firm. Jerry Nolan wondered what he should do next.

1. If you were Jerry Nolan, what would you do?

2. What do you think about the staffing practices of the company? What policies, if any, would you recommend?

3. What do you think about Mr. Brown's managerial behavior?

REFERENCES

1. See, for example, Fred E. Fiedler, "Engineer the Job to Fit the Manager," *Harvard Business Review* (September–October 1965), pp. 115–122. His theory is discussed in Chapter 18.

2. This discussion of job design is based in part on David A. Nadler, J. Richard Hackman, and Edward E. Lawler III, *Managing Organizational Behavior* (Boston: Little, Brown and Company, 1979), chap. 5.

3. Nadler et al., *Managing Organizational Behavior* (1979). See also the discussion of sociotechnical systems in Chapter 2 of this book.

4. Robert L. Katz, "Skills of an Effective Administrator," *Harvard Business Review* (January–February 1955), pp. 33–42; Robert L. Katz, "Retrospective Commentary," *Harvard Business Review* (September–October 1974), pp. 101–102.

5. Maggie McComas, "Atop the Fortune 500: A Survey of the C.E.O.s," *Fortune* (Apr. 28, 1986), pp. 26–31.

6. Frederic V. Malek, *Washington's Hidden Tragedy* (New York: The Free Press, 1978), p. 68.

7. Myron Magnet, "Baby-Boom Executives Are Making It," *Fortune* (Sept. 2, 1985), pp. 22–28; Michael Brody, "Meet Today's Young American Worker," *Fortune* (Nov. 11, 1985), pp. 90–98.

8. Irene Pave, "Move Me, Move My Spouse: Relocating the Corporate Couple," *Business Week* (Dec. 16, 1985), pp. 57–60.

9. Laurence J. Peter and Raymond Hall, *The Peter Principle* (New York: Bantam Books, 1969). See also Laurence J. Peter, *The Peter Pyramid: Or Will We Ever Get the Point?* reviewed by Peter Shaw, "A Management Guru Peters Out," *The Wall Street Journal* (Jan. 24, 1986).

10. Daniel C. Feldman, "The Multiple Socialization of Organization Members," *Academy of Management Review* (Apr. 1981), pp. 309–318.

FOR FURTHER INFORMATION

Dipboye, Robert L. "Self-Fulfilling Prophecies in the Selection-Recruitment Interview," *Academy of Management Review* (October 1982), pp. 579–586.

Fiedler, Fred E. "Engineer the Job to Fit the Manager," *Harvard Business Review* (September–October 1965), pp. 115–122.

Greer, Charles R. "Countercyclical Hiring as a Staffing Strategy for Managerial and Professional Personnel: Some Considerations and Issues," *Academy of Management Review* (April 1984), pp. 324–330.

Leontiades, Milton. "Choosing the Right Manager to Fit the Strategy," in Arthur A. Thompson, Jr., A. J. Strickland III, and William E. Fulmer (eds.), *Readings in Strategic Management* (Plano, Tex.: Business Publications, 1984), pp. 290–305.

McMurry, Robert M. "Avoiding Mistakes in Selecting Executives," in Harold Koontz, Cyril O'Donnell, and Heinz Weihrich (eds.), *Management: A Book of Readings,* 5th ed. (New York: McGraw-Hill Book Company, 1980), pp. 396–401.

Pascale, Richard T. "Fitting New Employees into the Company Culture," *Fortune* (May 28, 1984), pp. 28–43.

Wanous, J. P. *Organizational Entry: Recruitment, Selection, and Socialization of Newcomers* (Reading, Mass.: Addison-Wesley Publishing Company, 1980).

Performance Appraisal and Career Strategy

CHAPTER OBJECTIVES

After reading this chapter you should be able to:

1. Recognize the importance of effectively appraising managers.

2. Identify the qualities that should be measured in appraising managers.

3. Show what traditional trait appraisals have not been effective.

4. Present a system of managerial appraisal based on evaluating performance against verifiable objectives and performance as a manager.

5. Describe the team approach to evaluation.

6. Identify important aspects of career planning.

Managerial appraisal has sometimes been referred to as the Achilles' heel of managerial staffing. But it is probably a major key to managing itself. It is the basis for determining who is promotable to a higher position. It is also important to management development because if a manager's strengths and weaknesses are not known, it is difficult to determine whether development efforts are aimed in the right direction. Appraisal is, or should be, an integral part of a system of managing. Knowing how well a manager plans, organizes, staffs, leads, and controls is really the only way to ensure that those occupying managerial positions are actually managing effectively. If a business, a government agency, a charitable organization, or even a university is to reach its goals effectively and efficiently, ways of accurately measuring management performance must be found and implemented.

There are other reasons why effective managerial appraisal is important. One of the most compelling arises from the provisions of Title VII of the Civil Rights Act of 1964 (as amended) and the regulations of the Equal Employment Opportunity Commission and the Office of Federal Contract Compliance. These agencies have been highly critical of many appraisal programs, finding them often to result in discrimination, particularly in areas of race, age, and sex. Courts have supported the federal agencies in their insistence that, to be acceptable, an appraisal program must be reliable and valid. That these are rigorous standards is apparent.

Effective performance appraisal should also recognize the legitimate desire of employees for progress in their professions. One way to integrate organizational demands and individual needs is through career management, which can be a part of performance appraisal, as we will see later in this chapter.

THE PURPOSES AND USES OF APPRAISAL

Appraisals serve different organizational and individual needs. We will focus on some important studies.

The Conference Board Study[1]

An extensive study by The Conference Board showed that the *objectives* of appraisal on the basis of the frequency mentioned were the following:

1. Management development
2. Performance appraisal
3. Performance improvement
4. Compensation
5. Potential identification
6. Feedback
7. Work-force planning
8. Communication

However, when respondents were asked how the companies *used* the appraisal, the ranking differed and showed the following results:

1. Performance feedback

2. Compensation administration

3. Promotion decisions

4. Identification of management development needs

5. Work-force planning

6. Validation of selection procedures

The differences between the stated objectives of appraisals and the way they were used may be an important reason for dissatisfaction with the appraisal indicated by some of the personnel managers participating in this study. Note also that the objectives and uses of appraisals have a different orientation. In determining compensation, or often even in evaluating performance, superiors assume the role of judge. In contrast, when the aim is to develop subordinates, managers need to be counselors, helpers, and teachers.

The General Electric Studies

Some of the best-known studies on performance appraisals were done at the General Electric Company.[2] The findings of the initial study showed that (1) criticism had a negative impact on goal accomplishment, (2) praise had little effect, (3) specific goals improved performance, (4) critical appraisal resulted in defensiveness and inferior performance, (5) coaching should be done on a day-to-day basis rather than once a year, (6) joint objective setting, not criticism, improved performance, (7) meetings with the primary purpose of improving performance should not be conducted at the same time that salary or promotion was being considered, and (8) subordinates' participation in setting objectives improved performance.

In light of the findings, General Electric developed a new appraisal program called "Work Planning and Review"—in short, WP&R. This new approach emphasized frequent discussions of performance without summary ratings. Moreover, salary actions were discussed at separate meetings. Finally, problem solving and jointly setting objectives were emphasized. The experience at General Electric suggests that the two purposes of performance appraisal should be separated because if the appraisal is used as the basis for salary action, the superior assumes the role of a judge, while in the attempt to motivate employees, the manager takes the role of a coach. It is through recognizing the split roles in performance appraisal and by setting specific goals mutually agreed upon by the superior and the subordinates that productivity can be improved.

THE PROBLEM OF MANAGEMENT APPRAISAL

Managers have long been reluctant to appraise subordinates. However, in an activity as important as managing, there should be no reluctance to measure performance as accurately as we can. In almost all kinds of group enterprise, whether in work or in play, performance has usually been rated in some way. Moreover, most people, and particularly people of ability, want to know how well they are doing.

It is difficult to believe that the controversy, the misgivings, and even the disillusionment, still so widespread with respect to managerial performance appraisal, have come from the practices of measuring and evaluating. Rather, it appears that they have arisen from the things measured, the standards used, and the way measurement is done.

Managers can understandably take exception, feel unhappy, or resist when they believe that they are evaluating, or being evaluated, inaccurately or against standards that are inapplicable, inadequate, or subjective. However, some light and hope have emerged in the past 30 years and offer promise of making evaluation effective. The interest in evaluating managers by comparing actual performance against preset verifiable objectives or goals is a development of considerable potential.

Even appraisal against verifiable objectives is not enough. It needs to be supplemented by an appraisal of managers as managers. Moreover, neither system is without difficulties and pitfalls, and neither can be operated by simply adopting the technique and doing the paperwork. We must do more. In the first place, it is essential that managing by verifiable objectives, as explained in Chapter 4, be a way of life in an enterprise. In the second place, managers need both a clear understanding of the managerial job and the fundamentals underlying it, and an ability to apply these fundamentals in practice.

CHOOSING THE APPRAISAL CRITERIA

The appraisal should measure both performance in accomplishing goals and plans and performance as a manager. No one wants a person in a managerial role who appears to do everything right as a manager but who cannot turn in a good record of profit making, marketing, controllership, or whatever the area of responsibility may be. Nor should we be satisfied to have a "performer" in a managerial position who cannot operate effectively as a manager. Some star performers may have succeeded through no fault of their own.

Performance in Accomplishing Goals

In assessing performance, systems of appraising against verifiable preselected goals have extraordinary value. Given consistent, integrated, and understood planning designed to reach specific objectives, probably the best criteria of managerial performance relate to the ability to set goals intelligently, to plan programs that will accomplish those goals, and to succeed in achieving them. Those who have operated under some variation of this system often claim that these criteria are adequate and that elements of luck or other factors beyond the manager's control are taken into account when arriving at any appraisal. But, in too many cases, managers who achieve results owing to sheer luck are promoted, and others, who do not achieve expected results because of factors beyond their control, are blamed for failures. Thus, we need a supplement to appraisal against verifiable objectives.

Performance as Managers

The system of measuring performance against preestablished objectives should be supplemented by an appraisal of a manager *as a manager*. Managers at any level also undertake nonmanagerial duties, and these cannot be overlooked. The primary purpose for which managers are hired and against which they should be measured, however, is their performance as managers—that is, they should be appraised on the basis of how well they understand and undertake the managerial functions of planning, organizing, staffing, leading, and controlling. For standards in this area we must turn to the fundamentals of management. But let us first look at some traditional appraisal programs.

TRADITIONAL TRAIT APPRAISALS

For many years, managers have been evaluated against standards of personal traits and work characteristics. Typical trait-rating evaluation systems may list ten to fifteen personal characteristics, such as ability to get along with people, leadership, analytical competence, industry, judgment, and initiative. The list may also include such work-related characteristics as job knowledge, ability to carry through on assignments, production or cost results, or success in seeing that plans and instructions are carried out. However, at least until recent years, personal traits have far outnumbered work-related characteristics. Given these standards, the rater was then asked to appraise subordinates, rating them from unacceptable to outstanding.

Weaknesses of Trait Appraisal

Managers resist doing this type of evaluation or tend to go through the paperwork without knowing exactly how to rate. Even where earnest attempts have been made to "sell" such programs, to indoctrinate managers, and to train them in the meaning of traits so that they can improve their appraisal ability, few managers can or will do them well.

One practical problem of the trait approach to appraisal is that because trait evaluation cannot be objective, serious and fair-minded managers do not wish to utilize their obviously subjective judgment on a matter so important as performance. And employees who receive less than the top rating almost invariably feel that they have been unfairly dealt with.

Another problem is that the basic assumption of trait appraisals is open to question. The connection between performance and possession of specific traits is doubtful. What is evaluated tends to be outside of—separated from—a manager's actual operations. Trait appraisal substitutes someone's opinion of an individual for what that individual really does.

Many managers look upon trait rating as only a paperwork exercise that must be done because someone has ordered it. When people have this attitude, they go through the paperwork and tend to make ratings as painless (for the subordinate and themselves) as possible. Consequently, they tend not to be very discriminating. It is interesting, but hardly surprising, that a study of ratings of navy officers several years ago came up with an arithmetical paradox: that, of all officers of the United States Navy rated over a period of time, some 98.5 percent were outstanding or excellent, and only 1 percent were average!

Trait criteria are at best nebulous. Raters are dealing with a blunt tool, and subordinates are likely to be vague about what qualities they are being rated on. In the hands of most practitioners, it is a crude device, and since raters are painfully aware of this, they are reluctant to use it in a manner that would damage the careers of their subordinates. One of the principal purposes of appraisal is to provide a basis upon which to discuss performance and to plan for improvement. But trait evaluations provide few tangible things to discuss, little on which participants can agree as fact, and therefore little mutual understanding of what is required to obtain improvement.

Attempts to Strengthen Trait Rating

As the deficiencies of trait rating have come to be recognized, a number of changes and additions have been introduced. Some are aimed at making the traits more comprehensible to raters. In a rating form used by a well-known business corporation, a person's "judgment" is defined as his or her capability to recognize the significant from the less significant in arriving at sound conclusions. Likewise, attempts are made to give meanings to various grades under each category.

Often, too, trait and work-quality forms are supplemented by open-ended evaluations in which, without specific guidance, appraisers are asked to supply whatever evidence on performance they feel is pertinent. Sometimes, also, this approach is used for the entire appraisal. Appraisers may be given a broad outline to guide them; for example, they may be asked for comments under such categories as operations, organization, personnel, and financial, and they may be asked specifically to consider such things as quality, quantity, time required to complete work, customer relations, and subordinate employee morale. Although these categories are helpful, experience has shown that they do not greatly improve the quality of ratings.

Attempts have also been made to improve the effectiveness of the rating process. In some systems, subordinates are required to rate themselves, and superiors must compare their ratings with those made by subordinates. In other instances, the superior's superior is asked to rate the former's subordinate or at least to carefully review the evaluation made by the immediate superior. Sometimes, a rater is forced by an appraisal system to rank subordinates from the best to the least able. In still other cases, rating has been done through the use of critical incidents that are assumed to give meaning to the grades given. These incidents are important events or decisions critical for effective performance in a particular job. Such incidents may represent outstanding or unsatisfactory performance.

These and other devices have been used to offset the disadvantages of trait rating. They have helped, but they cannot overcome the fact that traits and work qualities are subjective and are not correlated with what a manager's job really is.

APPRAISING MANAGERS AGAINST VERIFIABLE OBJECTIVES

One widely used approach to managerial appraisal is the system of evaluating managerial performance against the setting and accomplishing of verifiable objectives. As was noted in Chapter 4, a network of meaningful and attainable objectives is basic to effective managing. This is simple logic, since people cannot be expected to accomplish a task with effectiveness or efficiency unless they know what the end points of their efforts should be. Nor can any organized enterprise in business or elsewhere be expected to do so.

The Appraisal Process

Once a program of managing by verifiable objectives is operating, a major phase of appraisal is a fairly easy step. Supervisors determine how well managers set objectives and how well they have performed against them. Where appraisal by results has failed or been disillusioning, this failure has occurred especially because managing by objectives was seen only as an appraisal technique. The system is not likely to work if used only for this purpose. Management by objectives must be a way of managing, a way of planning, as well as the key to organizing, staffing, leading, and controlling. When this is the case, appraisal boils down to whether or not managers have established adequate but reasonably attainable objectives and how they have performed against them in a certain period.

Look at the system of managing and appraising by objectives, as shown in Figure 4-3 (page 90). As you can see, appraising is merely a last step in the entire process.

There are other questions, too. Were the goals adequate? Did they call for "stretched" (high but reasonable) performance?[3] These questions can be answered only by the judgment and experience of a person's superior, although this judgment can become sharper with time and experience, and it may be even more objective if the superior can use the goals of other managers in similar positions for comparison.

In assessing the accomplishment of goals, the evaluator must take into account such considerations as whether the goals were reasonably attainable in the first place, whether factors beyond a person's control unduly helped or hindered in accomplishing goals, and what the reasons for the results were. The reviewer should also note whether an individual continued to operate against obsolete goals when situations changed and revised goals were called for.

Frequency of Performance Reviews

As in any case of control, progress toward goals should be fairly frequently reviewed, since it may be dangerous to limit appraisal to looking at performance once a year. For a top manager, such as a president or a division general manager, progress should probably be reviewed and appraised in fair detail quarterly, and more broadly, in the light of probable accomplishment, for three or four additional quarters in the future. Alert and intelligent managers, hardly wishing to have obsolete objectives, naturally prefer to have both goal setting and evaluation be regular activities, and certainly, in most instances, they will not wish to wait too long to know how they and their subordinates are doing.

For individuals below the top level, quarterly reviews may be enough. And they may not. The real factor is the time span necessary to determine whether a goal is still valid and whether satisfactory progress is being made. For certain positions, such as those of first-level supervisors, reviews probably could be usefully made each month. Note that this task does not necessarily involve much additional work by a superior. It is merely carrying on the function of managing, and actual appraising becomes a relatively easy by-product of the process if we have concentrated on objectives.

Three Kinds of Reviews

The simplified model of performance appraisal shown in Figure 14-1 indicates three kinds of appraisals: (1) a comprehensive review, (2) progress or periodic reviews, and (3) continuous monitoring.

There is general agreement that a *formal comprehensive appraisal* should be conducted at least once a year. But some suggest that such discussions should take place more frequently. Some enterprises do all the reviews within a short period of time each year, while others schedule the appraisal throughout the year, often at the employment anniversary. A case could be made against any rigid schedule of annual performance reviews. Instead, it may be argued, with good reason, that performance should be reviewed, for example, after the completion of a major project. We can conclude that no universally applicable suggestion can be made about the time frame for the formal comprehensive review. It depends on the nature of the task, past company practices, and other situational factors. Once, twice, or even three times may be appropriate for a particular organization or a person who is new in a job.

What is important is that the formal comprehensive reviews are supplemented by frequent *progress* or *periodic reviews*. These reviews can be short and relatively informal, but they help to identify problems or barriers that hinder effective performance. They also keep communication open between the superior and subordinates. Furthermore, priorities can be rearranged and objectives can be renegotiated if warranted by changed situations. It certainly is inappropriate to pursue obsolete or even inappropriate objectives that were agreed upon in an environment of uncertainties.

Finally, there is *continuous monitoring* of performance. This means that when

FIGURE 14-1

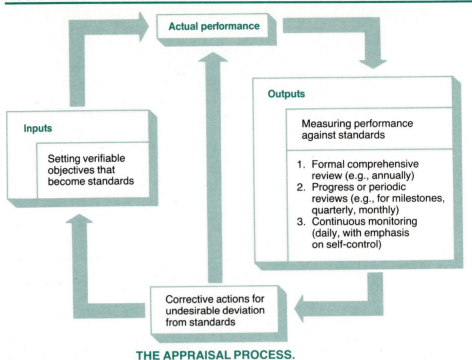

THE APPRAISAL PROCESS.

Redrawn from Heinz Weihrich, *Management Excellence: Productivity through MBO* (New York: McGraw-Hill Book Company, 1985), p. 125.

performance deviates from plans, one does not even wait for the next periodic review. Instead, the superior and the subordinate discuss the situation so that corrective actions can be taken at that time in order to prevent a small deviation from developing into a major problem.

Strengths of Appraisal against Verifiable Objectives

The strengths of appraising against accomplishment of objectives are almost the same as those of managing by objectives. Both are part of the same process, both are basic to effective managing, and both are means of improving the quality of managing.

In the area of appraising, there are special and important strengths. Appraising on the basis of performance against verifiable objectives has the great advantage of being operational. Appraisals are not apart from the job that managers do but are a review of what they actually did as managers.

There are always questions of how well a person did; of whether goals were missed or accomplished, and for what reasons; and of how much in the way of goal attainment should be expected. But information about what a person has done, measured against what that individual agreed was a reasonable target, is available. This information furnishes strong presumptions of objectivity and reduces the element of pure judgment in appraisal. Moreover, the appraisal can be carried on in an atmosphere of superiors working with subordinates and not sitting in judgment on them.

Weaknesses of Appraisal against Verifiable Objectives

As we noted in Chapter 4, there are certain weaknesses in the implementation of managing by objectives. These, of course, apply with equal force to appraisal. One of them is that it is entirely possible for persons to meet or miss goals through no fault of their own. Luck often plays a part in performance. It is possible, for example, that a new product's acceptance will be far beyond expectations and its success will make a marketing manager look exceptionally good, even though the quality of the marketing program and its implementation might actually be poor. Or an unpredictable cancellation of a major military contract might make the record of a division manager look unsatisfactory.

Most evaluators will say that they always take uncontrollable or unexpected factors into account in assessing goal performance, and to a very great extent they do. But it is extremely difficult to do so. In an outstanding sales record, for example, how can anyone be sure how much was due to luck and how much to competence? Outstanding performers are rated highly, at least as long as they perform. Nonperformers can hardly escape having a cloud cast over them.

With its emphasis on accomplishing operating objectives, the system of appraising against these may overlook needs for individual development. Goal attainment tends to be short-run in practice. Even where longer-range goals are put into the system, seldom would they be so long-range as to allow for adequate long-term development of managers. Managers concerned primarily with results might be driven by the system to take too little time to plan, implement, and follow through with programs required for their development and that of their subordinates.

On the other hand, since managing by objectives gives better visibility to managerial needs, development programs can be better pinpointed. If individual development is to be assured, however, goals in this area should be specifically set.

From an appraisal as well as an operating management point of view, perhaps the greatest deficiency of management by objectives is that it appraises operating performance only. Not only is there the question of luck, mentioned previously, but also there are other factors to appraise, notably an individual's *managerial* abilities. This is why an adequate appraisal system must appraise performance as a manager as well as performance in setting and meeting goals.

A SUGGESTED PROGRAM: APPRAISING MANAGERS AS MANAGERS

The most appropriate standards to use for appraising managers as managers are the fundamentals of management. It is not enough to appraise a manager broadly, evaluating only performance of the basic functions of the manager; we should go further.

We believe that the best approach is to utilize the basic techniques and principles of management as standards. If they are basic, as they have been found to be in a wide variety of managerial positions and environments, they should serve as reasonably good standards. As crude as they may be and even though some judgment may be necessary in applying them to practice, they give the evaluator some benchmarks to measure how well subordinates understand and are following the functions of managing. They are definitely more specific and more applicable than evaluations based on such broad standards as work and dress habits, cooperation, intelligence, judgment, or loyalty. They at least focus attention on what may be expected of a manager *as a manager*. And, when used in conjunction with appraisal of the performance of plans and goals, they can help remove much of the weakness in many management appraisal systems.

In brief, the program involves classifying the functions of the manager as done in this book and then dealing with each function by a series of questions. The questions are designed to reflect the most important fundamentals of managing in each area. Although the total list of key questions, the form used, the system of ratings, and the instructions for operating the program are too extensive to be treated in this book,[4] we can look at some sample "checkpoints."

Sample Questions for Appraising Managers as Managers

In the area of *planning*, a manager would be rated by such check questions as the following. Does the manager:

- Set for the departmental unit both short-term and long-term goals in verifiable terms that are related in a positive way to those of superiors and of the company?

- Check plans periodically to see whether they are consistent with current expectations?

- In choosing from among alternatives, recognize and give primary attention to those factors which are limiting or critical to the solution of a problem?

In the area of *organizing,* questions such as the following are asked. Does the manager:

- Delegate authority to subordinates on the basis of results expected of them?

- Refrain from making decisions in that area once authority has been delegated to subordinates?

- Regularly teach subordinates, or otherwise make sure that they understand, the nature of line and staff relationships?

In the three other areas of managing—in staffing, in leading, and in controlling—we ask similar questions. In all, there are seventy-three checkpoints.

Semantics has always been a problem in management. Therefore, we suggest using a standard book on management (such as this one) and referring to the pages that correspond to the check questions.[5] This approach leads to a fair degree of managerial development.

Managers are rated on how well they perform the activities. The scale used is from 0 for "inadequate" to 5 for "superior." To give the numerical ratings more rigor, each rating is defined. For example, "superior" means "a standard of performance which could not be improved under any circumstances or conditions known to the rater."

To further reduce subjectivity and to increase the discrimination among performance levels, we include the requirements that (1) in the comprehensive annual appraisal, incident examples are given to support certain ratings, (2) the ratings are reviewed by the superior's superior, and (3) the raters are informed that their own evaluation will depend in part on how well they discriminate on the ratings of performance levels when evaluating their subordinates. Obviously, objectivity is enhanced by the number (seventy-three) and the specificity of the checkpoint questions.

Advantages of the New Program

Experience with this program in a multinational company showed certain advantages. By focusing on the essentials of management, this method of evaluation gives operational meaning to what management really is. Also, the use of a standard reference text for interpretation of concepts and terms removes many of the semantic and communication difficulties so commonly encountered. Such things as variable budgets, verifiable objectives, staff, functional authority, and delegation take on consistent meaning. Likewise, many management techniques become uniformly understood.

The system, furthermore, has proved to be a tool for management develop-

---

PERSPECTIVE:
PERFORMANCE APPRAISAL: AN ILLUSTRATION

One utility company that had used the management-by-objectives approach successfully in its appraisal program found it desirable to supplement the program with a performance appraisal based on common management responsibilities. The form used for this evaluation, shown in Table 14-1, was based on the ideas discussed above, but it has been greatly simplified. You will note that the program covers all the managerial functions. However, the number of managerial activities graded has been substantially reduced from the seventy-three suggested above. The program provides for frequent performance review so that corrective actions can be taken without delay. Note also that this approach focuses on individual development; if performance of an activity either requires improvement or is unsatisfactory, this must be documented with plans shown for overcoming the weakness.

TABLE 14-1   Performance Appraisal: Common Management Responsibilities

Name	Rated by	Date

To be completed and included as part of the overall appraisal for all unit positions and above who have authority and responsibility for managing human resources.

Needs improvement or Unsatisfactory progress as well as corrective plans must be documented in REMARKS.

Importance weight assigned to Common Management Responsibilities ☐

Performance Rating

	Out-stand-ing	Super-ior	Fully compe-tent	Needs improve-ment	Unsat-isfac-tory
	5	4	3	2	1

1. Planning:

A. Develops and implements effective plans that contain verifiable and realistic goals and objectives.

B. Plans include long-range considerations.

C. Establishes specific quantitative/qualitative work goals or standards to be achieved by subordinates.

REMARKS:

2. Organization / Staffing:*

A. Organizes and staffs consistent with a thorough understanding of job responsibilities.

B. Identifies changes in job responsibilities and effects changes in Position Information Questionnaires.

C. Selects qualified personnel to fill vacancies.

REMARKS:

Performance Progress Review
Month

	J	F	M	A	M	J	J	A	S	O	N	D
A												
B												
C												

3. Delegation / Control:

A. Delegates authority and maintains control consistent with expectations.

B. Control techniques and standards reflect plans and satisfy budget compliance as well as report exceptions in a timely way.

C. Controls provide for optimizing resource utilization.

REMARKS:

4. **Decision Making / Directing:**

   A. Accepts responsibility for making decisions.

   B. Decisions are timely and consistent with plans, programs, and policies.

   C. Qualifies decisions by considering all points of view (subordinates, peer, superior).

   D. Problem solving is effective.

   REMARKS:

5. **Administration:**

   A. Administration of policies and procedures.

   B. Contributes effectively to corporate goals such as Affirmative Action, Safety, EEOC, Minority Contractor, etc.

   C. Sets and administers effective disciplinary standards.

   REMARKS:

6. **Compensation:**

   A. Administration of Performance Planning and Appraisal Program.

   B. Performance appraisal is based on job-related criteria.

   C. Salary administration is fair, equitable, and consistent with corporate wage and salary administration guidelines.

   D. Performance Planning and Appraisal is used as an effective motivating tool and morale builder.

   E. Communicates Performance Planning and Appraisal program and expected results to subordinates effectively.

   REMARKS:

7. **Human Resource Development:**

   A. Provides for subordinate training and development and assists motivated subordinates to prepare for additional responsibility.

   B. Human resource planning and career development procedures are current and realistic.

   C. Subordinates' developmental needs are specifically documented.

   D. Succession plans written for all subordinates.

   E. Actively pursues own personal plan for career development and/or improvement as agreed to with immediate supervisor.

   REMARKS:

Code:

☑ **Fully meeting expectations or better**

Ⓞ **Needs improvement**

Ⓤ **Unsatisfactory**

* The "Performance Progress Review" and "Performance Rating" boxes have been omitted for the managerial responsibilities that follow.

351

ment; in many cases, it has brought to managers' attention certain basics that they may have long disregarded or not understood. In addition, it has been found useful in pinpointing areas where weaknesses exist and to which development should be directed. Finally, as intended, the program acts as a supplement to, and a check on, appraisal of managers' effectiveness in setting and achieving goals. If a manager has an outstanding performance in goal accomplishment but is found to be a less-than-average manager, those in charge would look for the reason. Normally, we would expect a truly effective manager to be effective also in meeting goals.

Weaknesses of the New Program

There are, however, a number of weaknesses or shortcomings in the approach. It applies only to managerial aspects of a given position and not to such technical qualifications as marketing or engineering abilities that might also be important. These, however, can be weighed on the basis of goals selected and achieved. There is also the apparent complexity of the seventy-three checkpoints; to rate on all of them does take time, but the time is well spent.

Perhaps the major shortcoming of the proposed approach to appraising managers as managers is its subjectivity. As we mentioned earlier, some subjectivity in rating each checkpoint was found to be unavoidable. However, the program still has a high degree of objectivity and is far more objective than appraisal of managers only on the broader areas of the managerial functions. At least the checkpoints are specific and go to the essentials of managing.

A TEAM EVALUATION APPROACH[6]

More recently, another approach to performance appraisal has been introduced. The criteria selected for evaluation are, in part, similar to the ones mentioned above and include planning, decision making, organizing, coordinating, staffing, motivating, and controlling. But other factors, such as selling skills, may also be included.

The appraisal involves the person being evaluated in the process, which consists of the following steps:

- Selection of job-related criteria

- Development of examples of observable behavior

- Selection of four to eight raters (peers, associates, other supervisors, and, naturally, the immediate superior)

- Preparation of the rating forms applicable to the job

- Completion of the forms by the raters

- Integration of the various ratings

- Analysis of the results and preparation of the report

This approach has been used not only for appraisal but also for selection of people for promotion, personnel development, and even for dealing with alcoholism.

The advantages suggested by the originators of this approach include a rather high degree of accuracy in appraising people by obtaining several inputs rather than from the superior only. The program can be used to identify raters' biases (e.g., rating others consistently high or low, or giving such ratings to certain groups of people, such as women or those belonging to minority groups). Ratees apparently consider this approach quite fair since they are involved in selecting evaluation criteria as well as the raters. It also allows comparing individuals with each other. Although this approach has been used by a variety of enterprises, additional assessments seem necessary.

FORMULATING THE CAREER STRATEGY[7]

The appraisal of performance should identify the strengths and weaknesses of an individual; this identification can be the starting point for a career plan. The personal strategy should be designed to utilize strengths and overcome weaknesses in order to take advantage of career opportunities. Although there are different approaches to career development, we consider it as a process of developing a personal strategy that is conceptually similar to an organizational strategy. This process is shown in Figure 14-2.

1. Preparation of a Personal Profile

One of the most difficult tasks is to gain insight into oneself; yet this is an essential first step in developing a career strategy. Managers should ask themselves: Am I an introvert or an extrovert? What are my attitudes toward time, achievement, work, material things, and change? The answer to these and similar questions and a clarification of values will help in determining the direction of the professional career.

2. Development of Long-Range Personal and Professional Goals

No airplane would take off without a flight plan including a destination. Yet how clear are managers about the direction of their lives? One often resists career planning because it involves making decisions. By choosing one goal, one gives up opportunities to pursue others; if one studies to become a lawyer, generally one cannot become a doctor. Managers also resist goal setting because uncertainties in the environment cause concern about making commitments. Furthermore, there is the fear of failure to achieve the goals because the nonachievement of objectives is a blow to one's ego.

But by understanding the factors that inhibit goal setting, one can take steps to increase commitment. First, when the setting of performance goals becomes a part of the appraisal process, identifying career goals is easier. Moreover, one does not set career goals all at once. Rather, goal setting is a continuing process that allows flexibility; professional goals can be revised in the light of changing

FIGURE 14-2

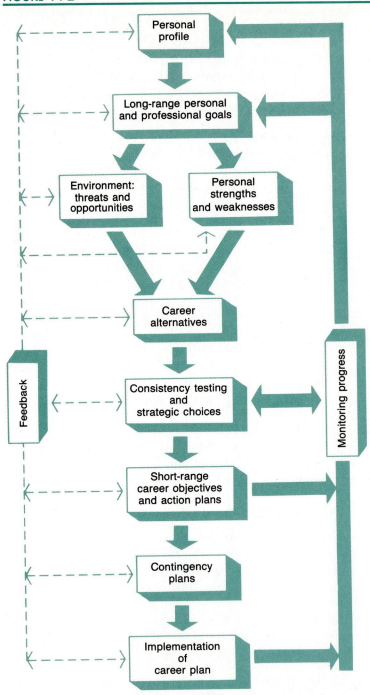

FORMULATION OF CAREER STRATEGY.

circumstances. Another factor that reduces resistance to goal setting is the integration of long-term aims with the more immediate requirement for action. For example, the aim of becoming a doctor makes it easier to study boring subjects that are necessary for the medical degree.

How far in advance should one plan? The answer may be found in the commitment principle discussed in the planning section. It states that planning should cover a period of time necessary for the fulfillment of commitments involved in the decision made today. Therefore, the time frame for career planning will differ with the circumstances. For example, if one wants to become a professor, it is necessary to plan for university studies of 7 to 9 years. On the other hand, if the career goal is to become a taxi driver, the time span is much shorter. At any rate, the long-term aim has to be translated into short-term objectives. Before we discuss these, however, we will make a careful assessment of the external environment with its threats and opportunities.

3. Analysis of the Environment: Threats and Opportunities

In the analysis of the environment within and outside the organization, many diverse factors need to be taken into account. They include economic, social, political, technological, and demographic factors; they also include the labor market, competition, and other factors relevant to a particular situation. For example, joining an expanding company usually provides more career opportunities than working for a mature company that is not expected to grow. Similarly, working for a mobile manager means an increased probability that the position of the superior will become vacant; or one might "ride the coattails" of a competent mobile superior by following him or her through a series of promotions up the organizational hierarchy. At any rate, successful career planning requires a systematic scanning of the environment for opportunities and threats.

One has to be concerned not only about the present but also about the future environment. This requires forecasting. Since there are a great many factors that need to be analyzed, planning one's career necessitates being selective and concentrating on those factors critical to personal success.[8]

4. Analysis of Personal Strengths and Weaknesses

For successful career planning, the environmental opportunities and threats must be matched with the strengths and weaknesses of individuals. Capabilities may be categorized as technical, human, conceptual, or design. As you saw in Figure 13-2, the relative importance of these skills differs for the various positions in the organizational hierarchy, with technical skills being very important on the supervisory level, conceptual skills being crucial for top managers, and human skills being important at all levels.

5. Development of Strategic Career Alternatives

In developing career strategies, several alternatives are usually available. The most successful strategy would be to build on one's strengths to take advantage of opportunities. For example, if one has an excellent knowledge of computers and many companies are looking for computer programmers, one should find many opportunities for a satisfying career. On the other hand, if there is a demand for programmers, and if one is interested in programming but lacks the necessary skills, the proper approach would be a developmental strategy to overcome the weakness and develop these skills in order to take advantage of the opportunities.

It may also be important to recognize the threats in the environment and to develop a strategy to cope with them. A person may have excellent managerial and technical skills but work in a declining company or industry. The appropriate strategy might be to find employment in an expanding firm or in a growing industry.

6. Consistency Testing and Strategic Choices

In developing a personal strategy, one must realize that the rational choice based on strengths and opportunities is not always the most fulfilling one. Although one may have certain skills demanded in the job market, a career in that field may not be congruent with personal values or interests. For example, a person may prefer dealing with people to programming computers. Some may find great satisfaction in specialization, while others prefer to broaden their knowledge and skills.

Strategic choices require trade-offs. Some alternatives involve high risks, others low risks. Some choices demand action now; other choices can wait. Careers that were glamorous in the past may have an uncertain future. Rational and systematic analysis is just one step in the career-planning process, for a choice also involves personal preferences, personal ambitions, and personal values.

7. Development of Short-Range Career Objectives and Action Plans

So far our concern has been with the career direction. But the strategy has to be supported by short-term objectives and action plans which can be a part of the performance appraisal process. Thus, if the aim is to achieve a certain management position that requires a master of business degree, the short-term objective may be to complete a number of courses. Here is an example of a short-term verifiable objective: to complete the course Fundamentals of Management by May 30 with a grade of A. This objective is measurable since it states what will be done, by what time, and the quality of performance (the grade).

Objectives often must be supported by action plans. Continuing with our example, the completion of the management course may require a schedule for attending classes, doing the homework, and obtaining the support of the spouse who may suffer because taking classes takes time that might otherwise be spent with the family. As you can see, the long-term strategic career plan needs to be supported by short-term objectives and action plans.

8. Development of Contingency Plans

Career plans are developed in an environment of uncertainty, and the future cannot be predicted with great accuracy. Therefore, contingency plans based on alternative assumptions should be prepared. While one may enjoy working for a small, fast-growing venture company, it may be wise to prepare an alternative career plan based on the assumption that the venture may not succeed.

9. Implementation of the Career Plan

Career planning may start during the performance appraisal. At that time, the person's growth and development should be discussed. Career goals and personal ambitions can be considered in selecting and promoting, and in designing training and development programs.

10. Monitoring Progress

Monitoring is the evaluation of progress toward career goals and the making of necessary corrections in the aims or plans. While working for a company, an opportune time for assessing career programs would be at the performance appraisal. This is the time not only to review performance against objectives in the operating areas but also to review the achievement of milestones in the career plan. In addition, progress should be monitored at other times, such as at the completion of an important task or project.

FOR DISCUSSION

1. Do you think managers should be appraised regularly? If so, how?

2. What problems may arise from the fact that different managers on the same level appraise differently, some generally rating higher than others?

3. Many firms evaluate managers on such personality factors as aggressiveness, cooperation, leadership, and attitude. Do you think this kind of rating makes sense?

4. An argument has been made in this book for appraising managers on their ability to manage. Should anything more be expected of them?

5. How do you feel about an appraisal system based upon results expected and realized? Would you prefer to be appraised on this basis? If not, why not?

6. What is your assessment of the degree of objectivity or subjectivity of the appraisal approaches suggested in this chapter? Can you suggest any further means of making appraisals more objective?

7. On what basis should your performance in college be appraised?

8. What would you say to a student who tells you that he studies at least 4 hours every day in preparation for the midterm exam and still got only a C?

9. What is your career goal? Have you developed a plan to achieve your goal? If not, why not?

EXERCISES/ACTION STEPS

1. Interview two managers. Ask them what criteria are used for their performance appraisal. Are the criteria verifiable? Do these managers think that the performance evaluation measures their performance in a fair manner?

2. Develop a career plan for yourself. Identify a personal profile for yourself and state your long-range personal and professional goals. What are your strengths and weaknesses? Follow the model shown in this chapter to develop a comprehensive strategic career plan for yourself.

CASES

CASE 14-1
HARDSTONE CORPORATION

William Hardstone, president of the Hardstone Corporation, was interested in putting in a bonus plan for his top managers and their immediate subordinates. The management consultant whom he engaged to help him with the plan strongly recommended that the bonus plan be based on (1) establishing a bonus pool of 8 percent of profits after retaining 12 percent on stockholders' equity plus long-term borrowing, and (2) allocating bonus shares to each person on the basis of position, salary level, and performance on the job.

Mr. Hardstone readily agreed to these principles. The consultant then pointed out that if such a plan were to be instituted, as objective as possible an appraisal of individual performance would be a necessary part of it.

Mr. Hardstone agreed but told the consultant: "I don't want any formal plan of appraisal. I had one once, and all that paperwork was meaningless since everyone was marked 'outstanding' or 'excellent.' I will do my own evaluation and allocate the bonuses to each person. I know how they are all doing and how well they are performing."

1. Do you believe that bonuses should be based, at least in part, on every individual's performance?

2. How would you answer Mr. Hardstone? Is he right, or could he be? What would you suggest?

CASE 14-2
FORESITE INCORPORATED

Carl Fisher was the president of Foresite, Inc., a multidivisional company in the high-technology field. The large company was well known for its technical innovations and the high caliber of its scientists and engineers. But competition was on the increase and the president realized that the success of the firm depended on effective management. It was felt that planning was one of the very weak areas where improvement was needed. Therefore, the president invited John Weigand, a management consultant, to "look at his company" and to explore alternative ways of improving the organization. At the first meeting considerable trust developed between Fisher and Weigand, and in the course of the discussion it was agreed that any major organization intervention should be based on facts (meaning, on data collected from the organization itself). As a first step, Weigand interviewed three major department heads—Ms. Albani, Mr. Johnson, and Mr. Baker—to get an overview of the firm and the quality of its managers. The president agreed, tentatively, to a long-range systematic organizational development effort. However, the immediate problem was to make some selections for key managerial positions.

Managers have to be well versed in all managerial functions, but at this point it was felt that aspects of planning were particularly important. With the guidance of the consultant, Carl Fisher assessed the planning activities of three managers considered for the position of (1) head of the corporate planning group and (2) division manager. He found useful the appraisal approach developed by Harold Koontz and described in the text.

The instructions for rating the candidates for the positions were as follows: In rating each question, give the following marks for each (for each level of rating use only one of two numbers, such as 4.0 or 4.5 for *Excellent;* use no other decimals).

The possible marks were the following:

X = Not applicable to position

N = Do not know accurately enough for rating

5.0 = *Superior:* A standard of performance which could not be improved upon under any circumstances or conditions known to the rater

$\left.\begin{array}{c}4.5\\4.0\end{array}\right\}$ = *Excellent:* A standard of performance which leaves little of any consequence to be desired

$\left.\begin{array}{c}3.5\\3.0\end{array}\right\}$ = *Good:* A standard of performance above the average and meeting all normal requirements of the position

$\left.\begin{array}{c}2.5\\2.0\end{array}\right\}$ = *Average:* A standard of performance regarded as average for the position involved and the people available

$\left.\begin{array}{c}1.5\\1.0\end{array}\right\}$ = *Fair:* A standard of performance which is below the normal requirements of the position, but one that may be regarded as marginally or temporarily acceptable

0.0 = *Inadequate:* A standard of performance regarded as unacceptable for the position involved

The results of the evaluations were as shown in the table on page 360.

To gain greater confidence in his judgment, Carl Fisher also asked two of his vice-presidents to rate the three candidates. Their evaluations were consistent with that of the president.

Assume that all three candidates have similar technical and managerial skills besides those shown in the table and the performance results are similar.

1. Whom would you select as a head of the corporate planning staff? Why?

2. Whom would you choose as manager of the division?

3. What other factors would you consider in making the selection?

4. What training and development would you recommend for each of the managers?

Performance as a Manager

Planning	Florence Albani	Ted Johnson	George Baker
1. Does the manager set for the departmental unit both short-term and long-term goals in verifiable terms (either qualitative or quantitative) that are related in a positive way to those of the superior and the company?	N	3.5	4.5
2. To what extent does the manager make sure that the goals of the department are understood by those who report to him or her?	3.0	3.0	4.0
3. How well does the manager assist those who report to him or her in establishing verifiable and consistent goals for their operations?	3.5	3.0	4.5
4. To what extent does the manager utilize consistent and approved planning premises in planning and see that subordinates do likewise?	4.5	3.5	4.0
5. Does the manager understand the role of company policies in decision making and ensure that subordinates do likewise?	4.5	4.0	4.0
6. Does the manager attempt to solve problems of subordinates by policy guidance, coaching, and encouragement of innovation, rather than by rules and procedures?	4.0	3.0	4.5
7. Does the manager help subordinates get the information they need to assist them in their planning?	4.5	3.5	4.0
8. To what extent does the manager seek out applicable alternatives before making a decision?	4.0	4.0	3.5
9. In choosing from among alternatives, does the manager recognize and give primary attention to those factors which are limiting, or critical, to the solution of a problem?	4.0	N	3.5
10. In making decisions, how well does the manager bear in mind the size and length of commitment involved in each decision?	4.5	4.0	3.5
11. Does the manager check plans periodically to see if they are still consistent with current expectations?	3.0	4.5	4.0
12. To what extent does the manager consider the need for, as well as the cost of, flexibility in arriving at a planning decision?	4.0	4.5	4.5
13. In developing and implementing plans, does the manager regularly consider long-range implications of the decisions along with the short-range results expected?	4.0	4.5	4.0
14. When the manager submits problems to the superior, or when a superior seeks help in solving problems, does he or she submit considered analyses of alternatives (with advantages and disadvantages) and recommended suggestions for solution?	4.0	4.0	3.5
Total number of questions in which ratings are made:	13	13	14
Total score on questions given ratings:	51.5	49.0	56
Average of ratings in Planning:	4.0	3.8	4.0

REFERENCES

1. Robert I. Lazer and Walter S. Wikstrom, *Appraising Managerial Performance: Current Practices and Future Directions* (New York: The Conference Board, 1977).

2. Herbert H. Meyer, Emanuel Kay, and John R. P. French, Jr., "Split Roles in Performance Appraisal," *Harvard Business Review* (January–February 1965), pp. 123–129.

3. For additional questions see the checklist shown in Table 4-2.

4. All the key questions are given in Harold Koontz, *Appraising Managers as Managers* (New York: McGraw-Hill Book Company, 1971), chaps. 5, 6 and apps. 2–5.

5. This has been done, for example, in the text booklet accompanying the cassette recording program "Measuring Managers: A Double-Barreled Approach," by Harold Koontz and Heinz Weihrich (New York: American Management Association, 1981).

6. Mark R. Edwards, Walter C. Borman, and J. Ruth Sproull, "Solving the Double Bind in Performance Appraisal: A Saga of Wolves, Sloths, and Eagles," *Business Horizons* (May–June 1985), pp. 59–68; Mark R. Edwards and J. Ruth Sproull, "Team Talent Assessment: Optimizing Assessee Visibility and Assessment Accuracy, *Human Resource Planning* (Autumn 1985), pp. 157–171; Mark R. Edwards and J. Ruth Sproull, "Confronting Alcoholism Through Team Evaluation," *Business Horizons* (May–June 1986), pp. 78–83.

7. Adapted from Heinz Weihrich, *Management Excellence—Productivity through MBO* (New York: McGraw-Hill Book Company, 1985).

8. For sources that may help you in predicting where the job opportunities will be, see the suggested readings under For Further Information.

FOR FURTHER INFORMATION

Bolles, Richard N. *What Color Is Your Parachute?* (Berkeley, Calif.: Ten Speed Press, 1984).

Business Week's Guide to Careers (New York: McGraw-Hill Book Company. This guide is published several times a year by *Business Week*).

Hall, Douglas T. *Careers in Organizations* (Pacific Palisades, Calif.: Goodyear Publishing Company, 1976).

Latham, Gary P., and Kenneth N. Wexley. *Increasing Productivity through Performance Appraisal* (Reading, Mass.: Addison-Wesley Publishing Company, 1980).

London, Manuel, and Stephen A. Stumpf. *Managing Careers* (Reading, Mass.: Addison-Wesley Publishing Company, 1982).

Mihal, William L., Patricia A. Sorce, and Thomas E. Comte. "A Process Model of Individual Career Decision Making," *Academy of Management Review* (January 1984), pp. 95–103.

Stoner, James A. F., Thomas P. Ference, E. Kirby Warren, and H. Kurt Christensen. *Managerial Career Plateaus—An Exploratory Study* (New York: Center for Research in Career Development, Columbia University, 1980).

Von Glinow, Mary Ann, Michael J. Driver, Kenneth Brousseau, and J. Bruce Prince. "The Design of a Career-Oriented Human Resource System," *Academy of Management Review* (January 1983), pp. 23–32.

Walker, James W., and Thomas G. Gutteridge. *Career Planning Practices: An AMA Survey Report* (New York: AMACOM, 1979).

Weihrich, Heinz. "Strategic Career Management— A Missing Link in Management by Objectives," *Human Resource Management* (Summer/Fall 1982), pp. 58–66.

Wright, John W. *The American Almanac of Jobs and Salaries* (New York: Avon Books, 1982), being crucial for top managers.

15

Manager and Organization Development

CHAPTER OBJECTIVES

After reading this chapter, you should be able to:

1. Distinguish between manager development, managerial training, and organization development.

2. Identify typical failures in manager development, and the necessary premises for an operational-management theory approach to training and development.

3. Discuss the manager development process and training.

4. Describe the various approaches to manager development.

5. Identify changes and sources of conflicts and show how to manage them.

6. Describe the characteristics and processes of organization development.

7. Summarize and briefly explain the major principles, or guides, to staffing and human resource management.

*T*his chapter deals with change. First, the focus is on the change of individuals. Specifically, we deal with manager development and training. But people do not operate in isolation. Consequently, in the second part of this chapter the emphasis shifts to groups of individuals and organizations.

Good executives look to the future and prepare for it. One important way to do this is to develop and train managers so that they are able to cope with new demands, new problems, and new challenges. Indeed, executives have a responsibility to provide training and development opportunities for their employees so that the employees can reach their full potential.

The costs of training represent major investments, and executives are justifiably concerned about the effectiveness of training. It has been estimated that companies spend at least $30 billion per year for education of their work force for formal education classes.[1] Most of the money is spent on in-house training and development. We share the concern for making management education effective and efficient and therefore emphasize in this chapter the need for a systematic approach to manager and organization development. We use the term **manager development** to refer to the progress a person makes in learning how to manage. **Managerial training,** on the other hand, pertains to the programs that facilitate the learning process. There is less agreement on the definition of organization development (OD). We view **organization development** as a systematic, integrated, and planned approach to improving the effectiveness of groups of people and of the whole organization. Organization development uses various techniques for identifying and solving problems.

Especially, then, OD focuses on the total organization (or a major segment of it), while manager development concentrates on the progress individuals make. These approaches support each other and should be integrated to improve the effectiveness of both the managers and the enterprise.

THE NEED FOR EFFECTIVE MANAGER DEVELOPMENT

Many companies have substantial training budgets and large training staffs that design, develop, and "market" programs. Nevertheless, some companies do not get the results they seek.

Management Development Failures

Many of the failures in management development programs can be attributed to an unsystematic approach of training. Much time and money has been spent on management development that does not develop. Before we look at ways to avoid such costly mistakes, some typical problems are highlighted.

Failure of development efforts to support enterprise objectives. The purpose of training is to achieve enterprise objectives and develop professional managers. Unfortunately, there often is little relationship between the training activities and the aims of the firm.

In an effective and efficient training program, managers determine enterprise objectives and integrate them with developmental needs of employees. An enterprise with a need for long-range planning, for example, should match this need with talents and aspirations of managers in the company. Such a situation is shown in Figure 15-1, with the large shaded area indicating a high degree of integration between the enterprise and the managers' development objectives.

Emphasis on programs instead of results.   Some executives take pride in the large number of employees enrolled in management development courses. Unfortunately, benefits derived from attending these meetings are negligible unless they satisfy a clearly defined training need; too often companies emphasize training *activities*, with little concern about training *results*. Many companies have generous training and development budgets, with many employees participating in a great variety of programs, but make no effort to evaluate the effects, if any, on the performance of the employees. Clearly, there is a need for greater concern about the benefits derived from management development.

Limiting manager development to a selected few.   People sometimes think that manager development requires placing a few people with high potential in a training program, while ignoring the rest of the employees. It is, of course, difficult to identify the potential of prospective managers, but to rely on a few trainees is also a gamble. It is even more risky if the trainees are selected on the basis of friendship or kinship with executives, without regard for capabilities. Manager development programs should be available for all qualified employees who aspire to a career in management, and should be based on sound premises.

Operational Management Premises

The operational-management approach to training and development is a situational one that integrates principles, concepts, theory, and behavioral knowledge with management practices to achieve the best results. This approach rests on several assumptions.

FIGURE 15-1

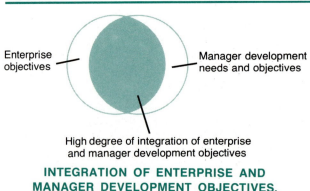

Enterprise objectives

Manager development needs and objectives

High degree of integration of enterprise and manager development objectives

INTEGRATION OF ENTERPRISE AND MANAGER DEVELOPMENT OBJECTIVES.

Active support of the program from top managers.   The support of top executives is essential for any training and development program. But it is particularly important for programs that involve people from different levels of the enterprise, as many organization development efforts do. The support of top managers should go beyond a policy statement regarding training. For best results, it should include their active involvement and participation in development.

Training and development for managers at all levels.   Training is not just for a selected few, nor is it only for those at lower levels. Top management may recognize the training needs of first-line supervisors but not their own. Yet top managers should be trained first, to provide an example of their commitment to the continuing development of all people in the enterprise and also to show that they are up to date on management thinking and techniques before their subordinates know them.

Variety of training and development needs.   Needs vary not only for positions at different levels in the organization hierarchy but also for individuals, since background, requirements, aspirations, and potential are specific to the individual. Consequently, training and development activities should be tailored to these specific and individual needs.

Training and development needs to determine methods.   No program or method fits all needs. Programs and methods should be selected on the basis of how effectively and efficiently they satisfy personal needs and accomplish the developmental objectives of managers and the enterprise.

Theory and practice—hand in hand.   It has been said that nothing is as practical as good theory. There is little doubt that theory provides an excellent framework for learning, but theory and practice must be integrated. Training, which is the teaching of theory and the demonstration of techniques, is one side of the coin;

PERSPECTIVE:
MAKING MANAGEMENT EDUCATION RELEVANT

In order to make business courses more meaningful, many schools invite guest speakers to share their experiences.[2] This creates close ties between business schools and enterprises. Executives become aware of the quality of the school's curriculum and students may find it advantageous to know about the companies when they are looking for a job. Moreover, executives often serve on advisory boards, which makes the schools aware of the needs of the business community. This does not mean, however, that market-driven schools should adopt any management fad.[3] Instead, management education must be broad enough to encompass the teaching of all key managerial activities in planning, organizing, staffing, leading, and controlling.

the other side is the actual practice of managers. The need for management experience is obvious when applying training to practice.

THE MANAGER DEVELOPMENT PROCESS AND TRAINING

Before deciding on specific training and development programs, three kinds of needs must be considered. The needs of the organization include such items as the objectives of the enterprise, the availability of managers, and turnover rates. Needs related to the operations and the job itself can be determined from job descriptions and performance standards. Data about individual training needs can be gathered from performance appraisals, interviews with the jobholder, tests, surveys, and career plans for individuals. Let us look more closely at the steps in the manager development process, focusing first on the present job, then on the next job in the career ladder, and finally on the long-term future needs of the organization. The steps in manager development are depicted in Figure 15-2.

Present Job

Manager development and training must be based on a needs analysis derived from a comparison of actual performance and behavior with required performance and behavior. Such an analysis is shown in Figure 15-3. A district sales manager has decided that the selling of 1000 units is a reasonable expectation, but the actual sales are only 800, 200 units short of the sales target. Analysis of the deviation from the standard might indicate that the manager lacks the knowledge and skills for making a forecast, and that conflicts among subordinate managers hinder effective teamwork. On the basis of this analysis, training needs and methods for overcoming the deficiencies are identified. Consequently, the district sales manager enrolls in courses in forecasting and conflict resolution. Furthermore, organization development efforts are undertaken to facilitate cooperation among organization units.

Next Job

As shown in Figure 15-2, a similar process is applied in the identification of the training needs for the next job. Specifically, present competency is compared with the competency demanded by the next job. For instance, a person who has worked mainly in production may be under consideration for a job as a project manager. This position requires training in functional areas such as engineering, marketing, and even finance. This systematic preparation for a new assignment certainly is a more professional approach than simply thrusting a person into a new work situation without training.

Future Needs

Progressive organizations go one step further in their training and development approach; they prepare for the more distant future. This requires that they

FIGURE 15-2

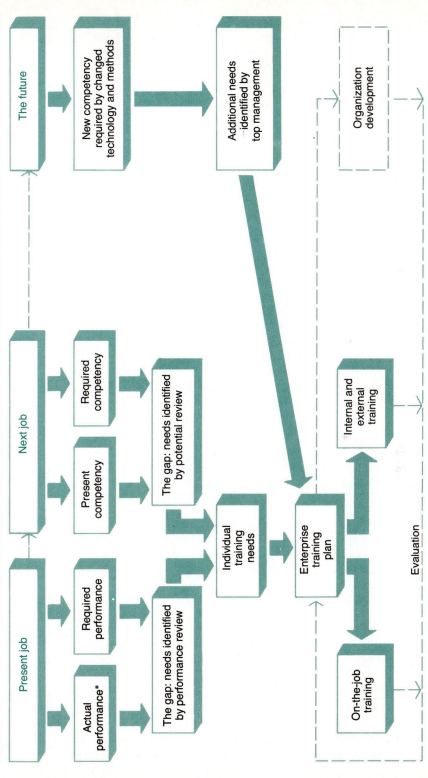

Manager development process and training (including performance measured against verifiable objectives and performance in carrying out managerial functions) can be broken down into detailed steps.

*This includes performance measured against verifiable objectives and performance in carrying out key managerial activities.

Adapted from John W. Humble, *Improving Business Results* [Maidenhead, England: McGraw-Hill Book Company (UK), Ltd., 1968].

FIGURE 15-3

TRAINING NEEDS ANALYSIS.

forecast what new competencies will be demanded by changing technology and methods. For example, energy shortages may again occur, and this requires that managers be trained not only in the technical aspects of energy conservation but also in energy-related long-range planning and creative problem solving. These new demands—created by the external environment—have to be integrated into enterprise training plans which focus on the present and the future. These plans are contingent not only on the training needs but also on the various approaches to manager development that are available.

APPROACHES TO MANAGER DEVELOPMENT: ON-THE-JOB TRAINING

There are many opportunities for development to be found on the job. Trainees can learn and at the same time contribute to the aims of the enterprise. However, because this approach requires competent higher-level managers who can teach and coach trainees, there are limitations to on-the-job training.

Planned Progression

Planned progression is a technique that gives managers a clear idea of their path of development. Managers know where they stand and where they are going. For example, a lower-level manager may have available an outline of the path from superintendent to works manager and eventually to production manager. The manager then knows the requirements for advancement and the means to achieve it. Unfortunately, there may be an overemphasis on the next job instead of on good performance of present tasks. Planned progression may be perceived by trainees as a smooth path to the top, but it really is a step-by-step approach which requires that tasks be done well at each level.

Job Rotation

The purpose of job rotation is to broaden the knowledge of managers or potential managers. The trainees learn about the different enterprise functions by rotating into different positions. They may rotate through (1) nonsupervisory work, (2) observation assignments (observing what managers do, rather than managing themselves), (3) various managerial training positions, and (4) middle-level "assistant" positions, and there is even (5) unspecified rotation to various managerial positions in different departments such as production, sales, and finance.

The theory behind job rotation is good, but there are difficulties. As the term indicates, in some job rotation programs participants do not actually have managerial authority. Instead, they observe or assist line managers, but they do not have the responsibility they would have if they were actually managing. Even in rotations to managerial positions, the participants in the training program may not remain long enough in the position to prove their future effectiveness as managers. Furthermore, when the rotation program is completed, there may be no suitable positions available for the newly trained managers. Despite these drawbacks, if the inherent difficulties are understood by both managers and trainees, job rotation has positive aspects and should benefit trainees.

Creation of "Assistant-to" Positions

"Assistant-to" positions are frequently created to broaden the viewpoints of trainees by allowing them to work closely with experienced managers who can give special attention to the developmental needs of trainees. Managers can, among other things, give selected assignments to test the judgment of trainees. As in job rotation, this approach can be very effective when superiors are also qualified teachers who can guide and develop trainees until they are ready to assume full responsibilities as managers.

Temporary Promotions

Individuals are frequently appointed "acting" managers when, for example, the permanent manager is on vacation, is ill, or is making an extended business trip, or even when a position is vacant. Thus, temporary promotions are a developmental device as well as a convenience to the enterprise.

When the acting manager makes decisions and assumes full responsibility, the experience can be valuable. On the other hand, if such a manager is merely a figurehead, makes no decisions, and really does not manage, the developmental benefit may be minimal.

Committees and Junior Boards

Committees and "junior boards," also known as multiple management, are sometimes used as developmental techniques. These give trainees the opportunity to interact with experienced managers. Furthermore, trainees, usually from the middle, but sometimes from the lower level, become acquainted with a variety of issues that concern the whole organization. They learn about the relationships among different departments and the problems created by the interaction of these organizational units. Trainees may be given the opportunity to submit reports and proposals to the committee or the board and to demonstrate their analytical and conceptual abilities. On the other hand, trainees may be treated in a paternalistic way by senior executives; although trainees are appointed to committees or junior boards, they may not be given opportunities to participate, an omission that might frustrate and discourage them. The program would then be detrimental to their development.

Coaching

On-the-job training is a never-ending process. A good example of on-the-job training is athletic coaching. To be effective, coaching, which is the responsibility of every line manager, must be done in a climate of confidence and trust between superior and trainees. Patience and wisdom are required of superiors, who must be able to delegate authority and give recognition and praise for jobs well done. Effective coaches will develop the strengths and potentials of subordinates and help them to overcome their weakness. To be sure, coaching requires time, but, if done well, it will save time and money and will prevent costly mistakes by subordinates, thus, in the long run, benefiting all—the superior, the subordinates, and the enterprise.

APPROACHES TO MANAGER DEVELOPMENT: INTERNAL AND EXTERNAL TRAINING

Besides on-the-job training, there are many other approaches to developing managers. These programs may be conducted within the company or they may be offered externally by educational institutions and management associations, as indicated in Figure 15-2.

Sensitivity Training, T-Groups, and Encounter Groups

Sensitivity training, also called *T-Group* ("T" stands for training), *encounter group,* or *leadership training,* is a controversial approach to manager development. Although popular in the 1960s and early 1970s, T-groups have lost favor as a managerial training technique in many companies. Still, certain aspects of sensitivity training may be used in team-building efforts. The objectives of sensitivity training generally include (1) better insight into one's own behavior and the way one "appears" to others (2) better understanding of group processes, and (3) development of skills in diagnosing and intervening in group processes.

Although the sensitivity-training process has many variations, one general characteristic is that people interact and then receive feedback on their behavior from the trainer and other group members, who express their opinions freely and openly. The feedback may be candid and direct: "Jim, I do not get a good feeling when you approach the topic the way you just did. Could we talk about it?"

Jim may accept this comment and resolve to change his behavior. But he may also feel hurt and withdraw from the group. The T-group process may lead to personal anxieties and frustrations, but, if properly administered, it can result in collaborative and supportive behavior.

The benefits of sensitivity training must be balanced against the criticisms of it.[4] For example, some people may be psychologically harmed because they simply cannot cope with the concurrent invasions of privacy. Owing to the group pressure and group dynamics, participants may reveal more about themselves than they actually intended to. There also is concern that some trainers may not be qualified to conduct sessions that become highly emotional. Finally, the relevancy of the outcomes of sensitivity training to the work situation has been questioned.

Despite the concerns of researchers and observers, certain enterprises do use T-groups in their development efforts. The following guidelines can help to reduce potential harm and increase effectiveness:

1. Participation in T-groups should be voluntary.

2. Participants should be screened, and those who could be harmed—for example, highly defensive people—should be excluded from this experience.

3. Trainers should be carefully evaluated and their competence clearly established.

PERSPECTIVE:
THE VARIETY OF CONFERENCE PROGRAMS

There is a great variety of conference programs available. The American Management Association offers programs such as these:

- **Time management.** To help managers make better use of their time and the time of their subordinates

- **Managing stress.** To help people in stressful environments such as those with rapidly changing technologies

- **Interpersonal skills.** To be more effective in dealing with people

- **Computer graphics.** To communicate information effectively through the application of graphics

Or consider the sessions offered by the Association for Management Excellence (AME) with topics such as these:

- Increasing productivity through people

- Designing a simple, lean organization

- Developing your entrepreneurial skills

4. Potential participants should be informed about the goals and process before they commit themselves to sensitivity training.

5. Before using sensitivity training, organizations should clearly identify development and training needs and objectives. Given these needs and objectives, other methods should also be considered.

Conference Programs

Conference programs may be used in internal or external training. During conference programs, managers or potential managers are exposed to the ideas of speakers who are experts in their field. Within the company, people may be instructed in the history of the firm and its purposes, policies, and relationships with customers, consumers, and other groups. External conferences may vary greatly, ranging from programs on specific managerial techniques to programs on broad topics, such as the relationship between business and society (see also Perspective on page 371).

These programs can be valuable if they satisfy a training need and are thoughtfully planned. A careful selection of topics and speakers will increase the effectiveness of this training device. Furthermore, conferences can be made more successful by including discussions; two-way communication allows participants to ask for clarification of specific topics particularly relevant to them.

University Management Programs

Besides offering undergraduate and graduate degrees in business administration, many universities now conduct courses, workshops, conferences, institutes, and formal programs for training managers. These offerings may include evening courses, short seminars, live-in programs, a full graduate curriculum, or even programs custom-designed for the needs of individual companies. Some executive development centers even provide career development assistance, with programs designed to fit typical training and development needs of first-line supervisors, middle managers, and top executives.

These programs expose managers to theories, principles, and new developments in management. In addition, there is usually a valuable interchange of experience among managers who, in similar positions, face similar challenges.

Readings

Another approach to development is planned reading of relevant and current management literature. This is essentially self-development. A manager may be aided by the training department, which often develops a reading list of valuable books. This learning experience can be enhanced through discussion of articles and books with other managers and the superior.

Special Training Programs

Management development must take an open-system approach that responds to the needs and demands of the external environment. Recently, government and

PERSPECTIVE:
UNIVERSITY EXECUTIVE PROGRAMS

Many major business schools offer a variety of management development programs. The 1987 Stanford Executive Program, which lasts for 8 weeks, includes topics such as these:

- The functional business areas of accounting, finance, and marketing

- The managerial process and organizational behavior

- Modern methods for quantitative and qualitative decision making

- Assessment of personal values and goals

Besides programs for top executives, the Harvard Business School also offers an intensive 12-week program for functional managers. The MIT Sloan School of Management, located just a short distance from Harvard, offers a 9-week program for senior executives and a 12-month program for middle and upper managers leading to a master's degree in management.

industry have become aware of the need for training programs specifically designed for members of minority groups and individuals who are physically handicapped. Many firms have made special efforts to train these people so that they may utilize their full potential while contributing to the aims of the enterprise.

Evaluation and Transfer

Determining the effectiveness of training programs is difficult. It requires measurements against standards and a systematic identification of training needs and objectives.

In general, developmental objectives include (1) an increase in knowledge, (2) development of attitudes conducive to good managing, (3) acquisition of skills, (4) improvement of management performance, and (5) achievement of enterprise objectives.

If training is to be effective, it is extremely important that the criteria used in the classroom situation resemble as closely as possible the criteria relevant in the working environment. One of the authors observed a T-group which had as its goals openness and frank feedback on each person's conduct in the group. The behavioral change of one of the participants would have had to be rated "excellent" when measured against the T-group criteria. However, when this person attempted to transfer his new values and behavior to the job, he met resistance and outright hostility. Arguments occurred and the result was that this person had to leave the company. Although the person changed, his boss did not; nor did his coworkers or the total work environment. This illustration shows that manager development requires a situational approach in which training objectives, techniques, and methods should be sufficiently congruent with the values, norms, and characteristics of the environment.

MANAGING CHANGE

The forces for change may come from the environment external to the firm, from within the organization, or from the individuals themselves.

Changes That Affect Manager and Organization Development

Several trends, some of them already occurring, will have implications for developing human resources. Here are some illustrations[5]:

1. The increasing use of computers, especially the microcomputers, requires that teachers as well as students become computer-literate.

2. Education extends into the adult life. Lifelong learning becomes a necessity, and educational institutions and enterprises must recognize the special educational needs of adults.

3. The proportion of knowledge workers will increase and the need for skill workers will decrease, which may require more training in knowledge, conceptual, and design skills.

4. The shift from manufacturing to service industries requires retraining in preparation for the new positions.

5. The choice of educational opportunities will increase. For example, many companies already are conducting their own training programs.[6]

6. There may be a greater cooperation and interdependence between the private and the public sector—at least in some countries, such as Canada.

7. Internationalization will continue and managers in different countries must learn to communicate and to adapt to each other. Companies need to train with a global perspective.

There are various ways to respond to these forces. One way is simply to react to a crisis. Unfortunately, this is usually not the most effective response. Another approach is to deliberately plan the change. This may require new objectives or policies, organizational rearrangements, or a change in leadership style and organization culture.

Techniques for Initiating Change

Organizations may be in a state of equilibrium with forces pushing for change on one hand, and forces resisting change with the attempt to maintain the status quo. Kurt Lewin expressed this phenomenon in his **field force theory,** which suggests that an equilibrium is maintained by *driving* forces and *restraining*

FIGURE 15-4

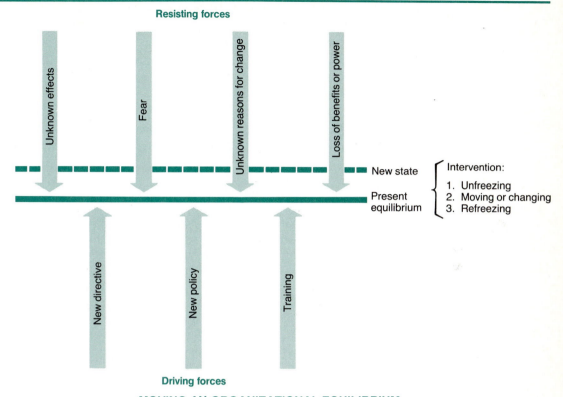

Resisting forces

Unknown effects

Fear

Unknown reasons for change

Loss of benefits or power

New state

Present equilibrium

Intervention:
1. Unfreezing
2. Moving or changing
3. Refreezing

New directive

New policy

Training

Driving forces

MOVING AN ORGANIZATIONAL EQUILIBRIUM.

forces, as shown in Figure 15-4.[7] To initiate change, the tendency is to increase the driving forces; this may indeed produce some movement. However, it usually also increases resistance by strengthening the restraining forces. Another approach, and one that is usually more effective, is to reduce or eliminate the restraining forces and then move to a new level of equilibrium. You may have observed in organizations that resistance to a change in policy was less resisted when those affected by it participated in the change.

The change process may be seen as a three-step process:[8] (1) unfreezing, (2) moving or changing, and (3) refreezing. The first stage, unfreezing, creates motivation for change. If we feel uncomfortable with the present situation, we may see the need for change. It may be an ethical question if and when it is legitimate for the change agent to create discomfort that may initiate change.

The second stage is the change itself. This change may occur through new information, being exposed to new concepts, or looking at the situation from a different perspective.

The third stage is refreezing or stabilizing the change. Change, to be effective, has to be congruent with one's self-concept and one's values. If the change is incongruent with the attitudes and behaviors of others in the organization, chances are that the person will revert back to the old behavior. Thus, reinforcement of the new behavior is essential.

Resistance to Change

There are many reasons why people resist change. Here are some examples:

1. What is not known causes fear and induces resistance. An organizational restructuring can leave a person uncertain about its effect on his or her job. People want to feel secure and have some control over the change.

2. Not knowing the reason for the change also causes resistance. In fact, it is often unclear to those affected why the change is necessary at all.

3. Change may also result in reduction of benefits or a loss of power.

A reduction of resistance can be achieved in many different ways. An involvement of organizational members in planning the change can reduce uncertainty. Communication about the proposed changes also helps to clarify the reasons or effects of the changes. Some approaches focus on the people involved in the change. Others involve changes in the organization structure or the technology. You will recall that the sociotechnical systems approach discussed in Chapter 2 suggests that effective organization requires the consideration of both the social and the technical dimensions in an enterprise. And there are many other approaches to the improvement of organizational effectiveness, such as those discussed later in this chapter.

ORGANIZATIONAL CONFLICT

Conflict is a part of organizational life and may occur within the individual, between individuals, between the individual and the group, and between groups. While conflict is generally perceived as being dysfunctional, it can also be beneficial because it may cause an issue to be presented in different perspectives. One top executive of a major company maintained that when there was no conflict on an issue, it could not have been sufficiently analyzed, and the final decision on the issue was usually postponed until all aspects were critically evaluated.

Sources of Conflict

There are many potential sources of conflict. Today's organizations are characterized by complex relationships and a high degree of interdependence of tasks that can cause frictions. Moreover, the goals of the parties are often incompatible, especially when the parties compete for limited resources. People also have different values and different perceptions of issues. A production manager, for example, may take the position that streamlining the product line and concentrating on a few products can make the organization more productive, while a sales manager may desire a broad product line that will satisfy diverse customer demands. An engineer may want to design the best product regardless of price or whether there is a demand for such a product.

There are other potentials for conflict. There may be conflicts between people in line and staff positions. A superior's autocratic leadership style may cause conflicts. Differing educational backgrounds are potential sources of conflict. Perhaps most often mentioned is lack of communication. Many of these topics are discussed in various chapters of this book.

Managing Conflict

There are different ways of managing conflict, focusing either on interpersonal relationships or on structural changes. *Avoidance* of the situation that causes the conflict is an example of an interpersonal approach.[9] Another way to cope with conflict is through *smoothing*, emphasizing the areas of agreement and common goals and de-emphasizing disagreements. A third way is *forcing*—pushing one's own view on others; this, of course, will cause overt or covert resistance. A traditional way of coping with conflict is to *compromise*, agreeing in part with the other person's view or demand.

Attempts can also be made to *change the behavior* of individuals, a very difficult task indeed. At times, it may also be possible to *reassign* an individual to another organizational unit. In many situations, conflicts are resolved by a *person higher up in the organization* who has sufficient authority to decide an issue. The problem is that the loser may attempt to get even with the winner at a later time, thus perpetuating the conflict. In the *problem-solving* approach to organizational conflicts, differences are openly confronted and the issues are analyzed as objectively as possible.

Another way of coping with conflict is to make structural changes. This means modifying and integrating the *objectives* of groups with different viewpoints. Moreover, the *organization structure* may have to be changed and authority-responsibility relationships clarified. New ways of *coordinating* activities may have to be found. *Tasks* and *work locations* can also be rearranged. In one workroom, for example, machines were placed in a way that prevented conflicting parties from interacting with one another. Often one must not only decide on the necessary changes but also select the appropriate process. For this reason we will turn our attention to organizational development.

ORGANIZATION DEVELOPMENT

Organization development, typically shortened to OD, is a systematic, integrated, and planned approach to improve enterprise effectiveness. It is designed to solve problems that decrease operating efficiency at all levels. Such problems may include lack of cooperation, excessive decentralization, and poor communication.

The techniques of OD may involve laboratory training, managerial-grid training, and survey feedback.[10] Some OD practitioners also use team building, process consultation, job enrichment, organizational behavior modification, job design, stress management, career and life planning, and management by objectives as part of their approach.[11]

The Organization Development Process

Organization development is a situational or contingency approach to improving enterprise effectiveness. Although various techniques are utilized, the process often involves the steps shown in Figure 15-5. An example can illustrate the application of the model.

Consider a firm that experiences certain problems: conflict among organizational units, low morale, customer complaints, and increasing costs (*problem recognition* in the model). The chief executive contacts an OD expert to discuss the situation. The two agree on the necessity of an *organizational diagnosis*. The consultant then collects information from several organizational units, using questionnaires, interviews, and observations. The data are analyzed and prepared for feedback.

The executive confers with other managers and sets up a meeting with them. At the meeting, after some introductory comments, the consultant presents the findings under the headings "relations between departments," "enterprise goals," and "customer relations" (*feedback*). The group then ranks the problems in order of their importance. With the guidance of the consultant, the group discusses the difficulties, identifies the underlying causes, and explores possible solutions.

The role of the consultant is that of a coach facilitating the process. Short lectures and exercises on decision making, team building, and problem solving are integrated into the process. At times, subgroups are established to deal with

FIGURE 15-5

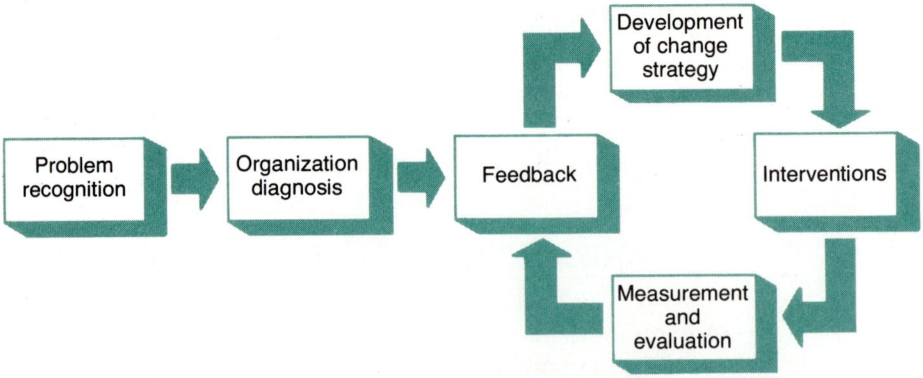

A MODEL OF THE ORGANIZATION DEVELOPMENT PROCESS.

Adapted from H. M. F. Rush, *Organization Development: A Reconnaissance* (New York: National Industrial Conference Board, Inc., 1973), p. 6. Used by permission.

specific issues. The emphasis is on openness and objectivity. The meeting ends with an agreement on a *change strategy.*

The specific *interventions* may include a change in the organization structure, a more effective procedure for handling customer complaints, and the establishment of a team charged with the responsibility of implementing a cost reduction program. Furthermore, the group agrees to meet again in 3 months to *measure and evaluate* the effectiveness of the OD efforts.

Although three phases complete the OD cycle, the effort does not end. Instead, OD becomes a *continuous process*—planned, systematic, and focused on change—that aims at making the enterprise more effective.

Grid Organization Development and Other Methods

One systematic program in organization development is the grid approach.[12] Because the grid itself is discussed in Chapter 18, the emphasis here is on the six phases of grid organization development.

Phase 1 is an introduction to the basic concept of the grid. Robert Blake and Jane Mouton state that the concern for people and the concern for production are not mutually exclusive; they are complementary. The aim of the grid exercise is to develop a high concern for both.

Phase 2 is a continuation of Phase 1, but the focus is on the *team* instead of the individual. In this phase, group members set standards, develop ways to achieve objectives, and identify barriers to achievement of the full potential of the enterprise.

Phase 3 concerns *intergroup development.* It is in this phase that OD really begins. The focus is now on the organization, rather than on individuals. The aim is to reduce conflicts among groups that work together.

Phase 4 involves *organizational goal setting.* In this phase top managers identify the aims of the enterprise and *design an ideal strategic corporate model.* Managers from different enterprise functions, including production, engineering, sales, finance, and personnel, are usually members of this policy-setting team.

Phase 5 is the *implementation of the strategic model.* This phase may extend over several years. Managers from all levels of the organization hierarchy have responsibilities in carrying out the activities necessary to achieve the goals set in the previous phase.

Phase 6 is a *systematic critique.* Managers evaluate achievements as well as mistakes made in the previous phases; they also discuss new challenges.

The managerial grid is but one of several approaches to OD. Another one is the *survey feedback method;* it emphasizes the collection, organization, analysis, and feedback of data to participants. Still another technique of OD is *process consultation,* which is concerned with the role of the consultant in facilitating processes within and between groups. In *team building,* people who work together meet to identify barriers to effective functioning of the group. Then the team members develop change objectives and action plans to make the group more effective in achieving enterprise goals.

As these illustrations demonstrate, the parameters of OD are not clearly defined. Instead, OD is eclectic in the sense that it chooses from a variety of tools, methods, and techniques that facilitate the solving of particular enterprise problems.

OD in Action

General Motors (GM) used OD to improve the effectiveness of its management system. OD as a long-range, situational effort is based on action research and problem-solving techniques.[13] Scientific analysis was used to identify factors that bore on a particular problem. In light of the findings, improvements were made through interventions such as changes in the job content, the organization structure, and the enterprise environment.

At GM's Oldsmobile division, the OD program reduced absenteeism and turnover; the Chevrolet group improved employee job satisfaction; and the Buick division, using a job enrichment program, increased productivity, reduced petty grievances, improved departmental morale, and facilitated better interpersonal relationships.[14]

Organization development is not restricted to business but is widely practiced in the military, which may be a surprise to those who perceive the military as an autocratic, mechanistic organization with values apparently incompatible with OD technologies.[15] The U.S. Army decided in the early 1970s to try a number of new managerial approaches, including OD, which they named "organizational effectiveness" (OE). Among the techniques employed were team building, goal setting, and developmental efforts based on surveys. These decentralized and flexible OE efforts had the strong support of top management, which may have been an important factor in the effectiveness of the program as perceived by respondents in a study.

The OD efforts in the U.S. Navy emphasized survey feedback. The pilot program, called "command development," was not a spectacular success. Nevertheless, the OD efforts were continued under the name "human resource management" (HRM). This program (summarized in Table 15-1) is quite standardized. Although a high percentage of participants felt positive about the program, others did not like the survey or felt that the process was too time-consuming.

The U.S. Air Force does not have a centralized program but relies on a variety of approaches such as laboratory training, team building, survey feedback, and job enrichment. Their results were also mixed. Here, as elsewhere, most claims for the effectiveness of OD are based on testimonials and anecdotes. There is little solid empirical evidence that OD efforts changed the organizations or improved performance.

Although the results of the various kinds of OD efforts in different organizations are mixed, some are encouraging. Still more research needs to be done in a variety of companies under different conditions to make a definitive evaluation of OD. Today, there is still a major gap in research on the cost and effectiveness of OD efforts. No doubt such research is a complex task because it is not easy to

TABLE 15-1 The Navy's Human Resource Management Cycle

Time phasing	Time to conduct	Step activity
Weeks 1–2	1½ days	1. Initial meetings between commanding officer (CO) and consultants
Week 2	½ day	2. Data-gathering planning meetings: Will interview be conducted? What questions? Are additional survey questions desired? Schedule the survey administration
Week 3	1 hour per person	3. Survey administration (mandatory): To all hands
Week 4	As required	4. Conduct interviews (optional)
Week 5	1 day	5. Return survey results to CO: Brief printout format, terms Study and analysis
Weeks 6–7	½ day per working group	6. Survey feedback to work groups (optional): Familiarization with data Source of perceptions? Supervisory self-knowledge Possible solutions/recommendations for action
Weeks 8–9	½ day	7. Action-planning meeting (optional): Develop plans for human resource availability week: OD, equal opportunity, alcohol, drug abuse, and overseas diplomacy
Week 10	1–3 days per group	8. Human resource workshops (optional): Vertical slice of ship or intact work group Modular training packages (standardized series of lectures, films, and exercises on such topics as motivation, communications, MBO, leadership, and race relations)
	2 days	9. Command action-planning workshop (optional): Selected members of crew normally (CO participates part-time) CO approves plan (a command action plan is mandatory)
Week 11	Indefinite	10. Action phase: Implement action plans
Weeks 25–30	½ day	11. Follow-up by consultant: Determine effect of human resource activities through interviews and discussions Meet with CO
Weeks 11–104	As negotiated	12. Follow-on activities (optional): Survey readministered Conduct additional workshops or training activities

Source: D. D. Umstot, "Organization Development Technology and the Military: A Surprising Merger?" *Academy of Management Review,* vol. 5, no. 2 (April 1980), p. 194. Used with permission.

isolate cause and effect relationships. For instance, improved enterprise performance may be attributable to favorable market conditions and not to OD efforts. However, the great interest in measuring productivity—indicated by several writings[16]—may eventually result in development of more sophisticated tools for assessing the effects of OD and other managerial approaches.

FOR DISCUSSION

1. It has been argued that firms have an obligation to train and develop all employees with managerial potential. Do you agree?

2. What are some typical failures in manager development and training? Can you explain these failures? What would you recommend to overcome the shortcomings?

3. Evaluate the advantages and limitations of different approaches to on-the-job training.

4. Evaluate sensitivity training as a technique for training managers. Do you think sensitivity training would make you a better manager? Explain.

5. In the job you now have or the one you expect to have in the future, what kind of coaching and management development would be most beneficial to you?

6. What are the main characteristics of organization development? How does OD differ from manager development? Do you think OD might work in your organization? Explain why or why not.

EXERCISES/ACTION STEPS

1. Take an organization you know and analyze its management development efforts.

2. What kinds of conflicts have you experienced in an organization with which you are familiar? What were the causes of the conflicts? What was done, if anything, about resolving these conflicts?

CASES

CASE 15-1
AEROSPACE, INC.

Jim Smith was the manager of the systems development department of Aerospace, Inc. During his 15 years with the company, he trained many managers and encouraged their development, only to see many of them leave the firm after they got their advanced degrees. The company had a liberal policy of educational reimbursement (75 percent of tuition costs and books), and many engineers (about 50 percent of them have a master's degree in a technical field) took advantage of the educational opportunities.

Joan Harris, an electrical engineer, came to see her boss, Jim Smith, who congratulated her for obtaining her master's degree in business administration, which she received with the assistance of the firm's educational program.

Ms. Harris, to the surprise of Mr. Smith, said that she was leaving the company to go to a competitor because she did not see any opportunities for advancement in the firm.

Mr. Smith was furious because this had happened several times before. He immediately went to see the vice-president of operations and complained about the educational reimbursement policy and the lack of a system approach to staffing.

1. What might be the reason that employees left after receiving their degrees with the help of educational reimbursements?

2. If you were the vice-president, what would you do?

3. How can such labor turnover be prevented?

CASE 15-2
MANAGEMENT DEVELOPMENT AT THE PENDLETON DEPARTMENT STORES CORPORATION

A consultant was discussing the problem of improving the quality of management with a group of executives at the Pendleton Department Stores Corporation headquartered in Chicago. The executive vice-president asked whether there were any broad guidelines in the field of management development. Addressing the consultant, he said, "We know you have had many and varied experiences in the development of managers at all levels in many types of enterprise. Have you reached any conclusions that might approach the quality of general truths or, perhaps, principles?"

"While I would not want to assert that there are principles in this field," the consultant replied, "there are certain convictions that I have about programs for manager development. In the first place, the top manager—whether head of a large division, a region, or the whole enterprise—must know specifically what the proposed program is expected to accomplish, must be convinced that this is the way to go, and must have the patience and willpower to insist that every manager will put the theory into practice.

"In the second place," he continued, "the program must be implemented by operating managers and not by a consultant or the personnel department. Third, every program should be evaluated on the basis of its contribution to company results. And finally, I am certain that when the key top manager loses direct interest in, and contact with, the program, the quality and effectiveness of the program will deteriorate."

"But," said the executive vice-president, "how can we take so direct a part in such programs? We have so many things to do. Anyway, that is the reason we have a training section of the personnel department."

1. Do you agree with the consultant? If so, just how would you accomplish what he suggests be done?

2. What of the executive vice-president's position—how can a top executive do all these things to ensure manager training and still have time to do the rest of his or her job?

REFERENCES

1. Anthony P. Carnevale, "The Learning Enterprise," *Training and Development Journal* (January 1986), p. 18; Lucia Solorzano, "Why Business Spends Billions Educating Workers," *U.S. News & World Report* (Feb. 10, 1986), pp. 50–51.

2. Ed Bean, "By Practicing What It Preaches, Fuqua Wins a Place Among Top Business Schools," *The Wall Street Journal* (May 13, 1986).

3. John A. Byrne, "Business Fads: What's In—And Out," *Business Week* (Jan. 20, 1986), pp. 52–61; Kenneth Dreyfack and John A. Byrne, "When Companies Tell B-Schools What to Teach," *Business Week* (Feb. 10, 1986), pp. 60–61.

4. For an evaluation of sensitivity training see Alan C. Filley, Robert J. House, and Steven Kerr, *Managerial Process and Organizational Behavior*, 2d Ed. (Glenview, Ill.: Scott, Foresman and Company, 1976), pp. 498–503.

5. Based, in part, on Norman B. Wright, "The Revolution Around Us: Human Resource Development in the 80's," *Business Quarterly* (Fall 1984), pp. 6–8.

6. Solorzano, "Why Business Spends Billions" (1986).

7. Kurt Lewin, *Field Theory in Social Science: Selected Theoretical Papers* (New York: Harper & Brothers, 1951).

8. Edgar H. Schein, *Organizational Psychology,* 3d ed. (Englewood Cliffs, N.J.: Prentice-Hall, 1980), Chap. 13; D. D. Warrick, *Managing Organization Change and Development* (Chicago: SRA Science Research Associates, 1984).

9. See Robert R. Blake and Jane S. Mouton, *Building a Dynamic Corporation Through Grid Organization Development* (Reading, Mass.: Addison-Wesley Publishing Company, 1969), chap. 6.

10. A survey feedback approach was used by Xerox and is discussed by Norman Deets and Richard Morano, "Xerox's Strategy for Changing Management Styles," *Management Review* (March 1986), pp. 31–35.

11. For a discussion of the history of OD and the contributions to the field see Wendell L. French, "The Emergence and Early History of Organization Development: With Reference to Influences Upon and Interactions Among Some of the Key Actors," *Group and Organization Studies* (September 1983).

12. Blake and Mouton, *Building a Dynamic Corporation* (1969); Robert R. Blake and Jane S. Mouton, *The Versatile Manager—A Grid Profile* (Homewood, Ill.: Richard D. Irwin, 1981), pp. 157–178.

13. This is the purpose of the concept of double-loop learning as discussed by Chris Argyris, "The Executive Mind and Double-Loop Learning," *Organizational Dynamics* (Autumn 1982), pp. 4–22; Chris Argyris "Double Loop Learning in Organizations," in David A. Kolb, Irwin M. Rubin, and James M. McIntyre (eds.), *Organizational Psychology*, 4th ed. (Englewood Cliffs, N.J.: Prentice-Hall, 1984), pp. 45–58.

14. Stephen P. Robbins, *The Administrative Process* (Englewood Cliffs, N.J.: Prentice-Hall, 1976), pp. 340–345, 347–349.

15. This discussion is drawn from Denis D. Umstot, "Organization Development Technology and the Military: A Surprising Merger?" *Academy of Management Review* (April 1980), pp. 189–201.

16. For more information on improving managerial productivity see, for example, Paul Mali, *Improving Total Productivity* (New York: John Wiley & Sons, 1978); Heinz Weihrich, *Management Excellence—Productivity Through MBO* (New York: McGraw-Hill Book Company, 1985).

FOR FURTHER INFORMATION

Argyris, Chris. *Reasoning, Learning, and Action* (San Francisco: Jossey-Bass, 1982). Book review by Robert P. Vecchio in *Academy of Management Review* (October 1983), pp. 705–706.

Badawy, M. K. *Developing Managerial Skills in Engineers and Scientists* (New York: Van Nostrand Reinhold Company, 1982).

Behrman, Jack N., and Richard I. Levin. "Are Business Schools Doing Their Job?" *Harvard Business Review* (January–February 1984), pp. 140–147.

Fiol, C. Marlene, and Marjorie A. Lyles. "Organizational Learning," *Academy of Management Review* (October 1985), pp. 803–813.

French, Wendell L., Cecil H. Bell, Jr., and Robert A. Zawacki (eds.). *Organization Development—Theory, Practice, and Research* (Plano, Tex.: Business Publications, 1983).

Jaeger, Alfred M. "Organization Development and National Culture: Where's the Fit," *Academy of Management Review* (January 1986), pp. 178–190.

Jenkins, Roger L., Richard C. Reizenstein, and F. G. Rodgers. "Report Cards on the MBA," *Harvard Business Review* (September–October 1984), pp. 20–30.

Kotter, John P., and Leonard A. Schlesinger. "Choosing Strategies for Change," *Harvard Business Review* (March–April 1979), pp. 106–114.

Robey, Daniel, and Steven Altman (eds.). *Organization Development—Progress and Perspectives* (New York: Macmillan Publishing Company, 1982).

Seyna, Eugene J. *Organizational Change in a Complex Organization: A Case Study in MBO* (Ann Arbor: University Microfilms International, 1982).

Smith, David E. "Training Programs for Performance Appraisal: A Review," *Academy of Management Review* (January 1986), pp. 22–40.

Tichy, Noel M. *Managing Strategic Change—Technical, Political, and Cultural Dynamics* (New York: John Wiley & Sons, 1983).

Watson, Charles E. "Getting Management Training to Pay Off," in Harold Koontz, Cyril O'Donnell, and Heinz Weihrich (eds.), *Management: A Book of Readings,* 5th ed. (New York: McGraw-Hill Book Company, 1980), pp. 447–453.

Wexley, Kenneth N., and Gary P. Latham. *Developing and Training Human Resources in Organizations* (Glenview, Ill.: Scott, Foresman and Company, 1981).

White, Louis P., and Kevin C. Wooten. "Ethical Dilemmas in Various Stages of Organizational Development," *Academy of Management Review* (October 1983), pp. 690–697.

SUMMARY OF MAJOR PRINCIPLES, OR GUIDES, OF STAFFING

There are no universally accepted staffing principles. Nevertheless, those listed below are useful as guidelines for understanding the staffing function. These principles are grouped under the purpose and process of staffing.

The Purpose of Staffing

The purpose of staffing is summarized by the following principles.

Principle of the objective of staffing. The objective of managerial staffing is to ensure that organization roles are filled by those qualified personnel who are able and willing to occupy them.

Principle of staffing. The clearer the definition of organization roles and their human requirements, and the better the techniques of manager appraisal and training employed, the higher the managerial quality.

The first principle stresses the importance of desire and ability to undertake the responsibilities of management. There is considerable evidence of failure to achieve results when these qualities are lacking. The second principle rests upon an important body of knowledge concerning management practices. Those organizations that have no established job definitions, no effective appraisals, and no system for training and development will have to rely on coincidence or outside sources to fill positions with able managers. On the other hand, enterprises applying the systems approach to staffing and human resource management will utilize the potentials of individuals in the enterprise more effectively and efficiently.

The Process of Staffing

The following principles indicate the means for effective staffing.

Principle of job definition. The more precisely the results expected of managers are identified, the more the dimensions of their positions can be defined.

This principle is similar to the principle of functional definition discussed in Part 3 on organizing. Since organizational roles are occupied by people with different needs, these roles must have many dimensions—such as pay, status, power, discretion, and possibility of accomplishment—that induce managers to perform.

Principle of managerial appraisal. The more clearly verifiable objectives and required managerial activities are identified, the more precise can be the appraisal of managers against these criteria.

The principle suggests that performance should be measured both against verifiable objectives—as in an appraisal approach based on management by objectives—and against standards of performance as managers. The appraisal of managers as managers considers how well the key managerial activities within the functions of planning, organizing, staffing, leading, and controlling are carried out.

Principle of open competition.   The more an enterprise is committed to the assurance of quality management, the more it will encourage open competition among all candidates for management positions.

Violation of this principle has led many firms to appoint managers with inadequate abilities. Although social pressures strongly favor promotion from within the firm, these forces should be resisted whenever better candidates can be brought in from the outside. At the same time, the application of this principle obligates an organization to appraise its people accurately and to provide them with opportunities for development.

Principle of management training and development.   The more management training and development are integrated with the management process and enterprise objectives, the more effective the development programs and activities will be.

This principle suggests that, in the system approach, training and development efforts are related to the managerial functions, the aims of the enterprise, and the professional needs of managers.

Principle of training objectives.   The more precisely the training objectives are stated, the more likely are the chances of achieving them.

The analysis of training needs is the basis for training objectives that give direction to development and facilitate the measurement of the effectiveness of training efforts. This principle brings into focus the contribution that training makes to the purpose of the enterprise and the development of individuals.

Principle of continuing development.   The more an enterprise is committed to managerial excellence, the more it requires managers to practice continuing self-development.

This principle suggests that in a fast-changing and competitive environment, managers cannot stop learning. Instead, they have to update their managerial knowledge continuously, reevaluate their approaches to managing, and improve their managerial skills and performance to achieve enterprise results.

Leading

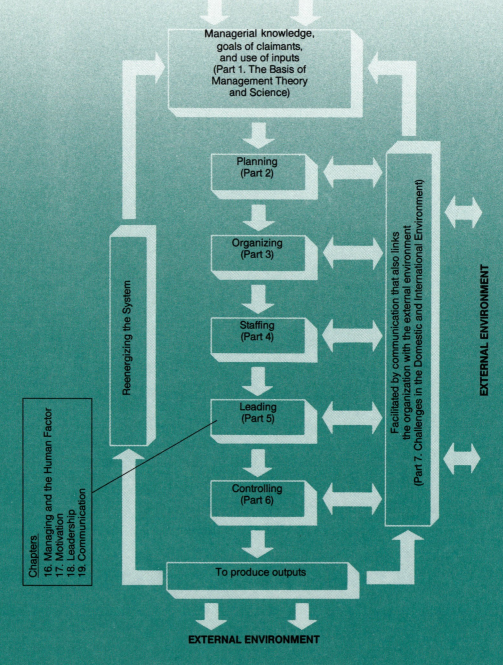

EXTERNAL ENVIRONMENT

Managerial knowledge,
goals of claimants,
and use of inputs
(Part 1. The Basis of
Management Theory
and Science)

Planning
(Part 2)

Organizing
(Part 3)

Staffing
(Part 4)

Leading
(Part 5)

Controlling
(Part 6)

To produce outputs

Reenergizing the System

Facilitated by communication that also links
the organization with the external environment
(Part 7. Challenges in the Domestic and International Environment)

EXTERNAL ENVIRONMENT

Chapters
16. Managing and the Human Factor
17. Motivation
18. Leadership
19. Communication

EXTERNAL ENVIRONMENT

SYSTEMS APPROACH TO MANAGEMENT.

16

Managing and the Human Factor

CHAPTER OBJECTIVES

After reading this chapter, you should be able to:

1. Define the nature of leading and leadership.

2. Describe the basic human factors that affect managing.

3. Explain the various models of the nature of people and their implications for managing.

4. Recognize the need for an eclectic view of behavioral models.

5. Understand the importance of creativity and innovation in managing.

6. Recognize that harmonizing objectives is crucial for effective managing.

*M*anagement and leadership are often thought of as the same thing. Although it is true that the most effective manager will almost certainly be an effective leader and that leading is an essential function of managers, there is more to managing than just leading. As indicated in previous chapters, managing involves doing careful planning, setting up an organization structure that will aid people in achieving plans, and staffing the organization structure with people who are as competent as possible. You will see in Part 6 that the measurement and correction of activities of people through controlling is also an important function of management. However, all these managerial functions accomplish little if managers do not know how to lead people, and to understand the human factor in their operations in such a way as to produce desired results.

The managerial function of **leading** is defined as the process of influencing people so that they will contribute to organization and group goals. In our discussion of this function, we show that the behavioral sciences here make their major contribution to managing. As we analyze the pertinent knowledge in leading, we will focus in Part 5 of this book on the human factor, motivation, leadership, and communication.

In this chapter, we discuss a variety of human factors important for managing. The concept of what people are like influences managerial behavior. Therefore, several models of people will be introduced. Creativity also plays an important role in managing people. Effective managers draw from various theories and experiences in their efforts to harmonize individual and organizational objectives, which is the key to leading.

HUMAN FACTORS IN MANAGING

It is obvious that while enterprise objectives may differ somewhat in various organizations, the individuals involved also have needs and objectives that are especially important to them. It is through the function of leading that managers help people see that they can satisfy their own needs and utilize their potential, while at the same time they contribute to the aims of an enterprise. Managers thus require an understanding of the roles assumed by people, the individuality of people, and their personalities.

Multiplicity of Roles

Individuals are much more than merely a productive factor in management's plans. They are members of social systems of many organizations; they are consumers of goods and services, and thus they vitally influence demand; they are members of families, schools, churches, trade associations, and political parties. In these different roles, they establish laws that govern managers, ethics that guide behavior, and a tradition of human dignity that is a major characteristic of our society. In short, managers and the people they lead are interacting members of a broad social system.

No Average Person

People act in different roles but they are also different themselves. There is no average person. Yet, in organized enterprises, the assumption is often made that there is. Firms develop rules, procedures, work schedules, safety standards, and position descriptions—all with the implicit assumption that people are essentially alike. Of course, this assumption is necessary to a great extent in organized efforts, but it is equally important to acknowledge that individuals are unique—they have different needs, different ambitions, different attitudes, different desires for responsibility, different levels of knowledge and skills, and different potentials.

Unless managers understand the complexity and individuality of people, they may misapply the generalizations about motivation, leadership, and communication. Principles and concepts, although generally true, have to be adjusted to fit the specific situation. In an enterprise, not all the needs of individuals can be completely satisfied, but managers do have considerable latitude in making individual arrangements. Although position requirements are usually derived from enterprise and organization plans, this fact does not necessarily exclude the possibility of arranging the job to fit the person in a specific situation.

The Importance of Personal Dignity

Managing involves achieving enterprise objectives. Achieving results is important, but the means must never violate the dignity of people. The concept of individual dignity means that people must be treated with respect, no matter what their position in the organization. The president, vice-president, manager, first-line supervisor, and worker all contribute to the aims of the enterprise. Each is unique, with different abilities and aspirations, but all are human beings and all deserve to be treated as such.[1]

Considering the Whole Person

We cannot talk about the nature of people unless we consider the whole person, not just separate and distinct characteristics, such as knowledge, attitudes, skills, or personality traits. A person has them all to different degrees. Moreover, these characteristics interact with one another, and their predominance in specific situations changes quickly and unpredictably. The human being is a total person influenced by external factors. People cannot divest themselves of the impact of these forces when they come to work. Managers must recognize these facts and be prepared to deal with them.

BEHAVIORAL MODELS

In order to understand the complexity of people, writers on management have developed several models. Managers, whether they consciously know it or not, have in mind a model of individual and organizational behavior that is based on assumptions about people. These assumptions and their related theories influence managerial behavior.

Over the years, various views about the basic nature of people have been suggested. To deal with all of them would not be practical here. Thus, we focus on selected models by Schein, Porter, and his colleagues, and on McGregor's classic assumptions about people. Furthermore, we examine organization behavior models by Davis and Miles on the macro level.

From the Rational-Economic View to the Complex Person

Edgar H. Schein developed four conceptions about people. First, he noted **rational-economic assumptions** based on the idea that people are primarily motivated by economic incentives.[2] Since these incentives are controlled by the enterprise, people are generally passive and are manipulated, motivated, and controlled by the organization. These assumptions are similar to those listed as Theory X by McGregor, to be discussed shortly.

The second concept, concerning **social assumptions,** is based on Elton Mayo's idea that, basically, people are motivated by social needs. Thus, social forces of the peer group are more important than controls by managers.

The third concept, concerning **self-actualizing assumptions,** suggests that motives fall into five classes in a hierarchy ranging from simple needs for survival to the highest needs of self-actualization with maximum use of a person's potential. According to this conception, people are self-motivated—they want to be, and can be, mature.

The fourth concept, based on **complex assumptions,** presents Schein's own view of people. His underlying assumptions are that people are complex and variable and have many motives which combine into a complex motive pattern. In addition, people are able to learn new motives and to respond to different managerial strategies.

Contrasting Views and Models of People

Because the understanding of the behavior of people is so dependent on their nature, it is no surprise that many attempts have been made to categorize the basic views about the underlying nature of people. Let us explore six models of people identified by Porter and his colleagues[3] and McGregor's Theory X and Theory Y assumptions about the nature of people.

Rational or emotional?   According to the **rational view,** people are seen as behaving rationally: They collect and evaluate information systematically and make decisions based on an objective analysis of the different alternatives available. A manager with this view probably would try to interact with people on a rational basis but would tend to ignore their feelings, their emotions, and the human side of their personalities. The **emotional view** holds that people are ruled primarily by their emotions, some of which are uncontrollable. A manager with this view might, for example, play the role of amateur psychiatrist by trying to unearth the underlying psychological causes of employees' behavior.

Behavioristic or phenomenological?   The **behavioristic view** is that people's behavior is controlled by their environment. Managerial strategies based on this theory would suggest changing the environment to get the desired behavior from subordinates. Directly opposed is the **phenomenological view,** which holds that people are unpredictable, unique, subjective, and relative (rather than being described in absolute terms), but with potential. A manager adopting this model would probably have to understand the complex functioning of the brains of subordinates, because it is there that behavior originates. Since this is not possible, people cannot be understood through scientific and behavioral observation.

Economic or self-actualizing?   According to the **economic view,** people are motivated by economic factors. Thus, it is assumed that people act rationally to get satisfaction from material rewards. Managers with this view probably would see money as the prime (if not the only) way to elicit contributions from subordinates. Furthermore, these managers would create a competitive environment in which people's primary concern is self-interest. In contrast, the **self-actualizing view** holds that people want to increase their competence, they want to develop, and they strive to use their potential. A manager adhering to this model would establish an environment in which people would exercise self-direction and reach their full capabilities thereby.

McGregor's Theory X and Theory Y

Another view about the nature of people has been expressed in two sets of assumptions developed by Douglas McGregor and commonly known as "Theory X" and "Theory Y."[4] Managing, McGregor suggested, must start with the basic question of how managers see themselves in relation to others. This viewpoint requires some thought on the perception of human nature. Theory X and Theory Y are two sets of assumptions about the nature of people. McGregor chose these terms because he wanted neutral terminology without any connotation of being "good" or "bad."

Theory X assumptions.   The "traditional" assumptions about the nature of people, according to McGregor, are included in Theory X as follows:

1. Average human beings have an inherent dislike of work and will avoid it if they can.
2. Because of this human characteristic of dislike of work, most people must be coerced, controlled, directed, and threatened with punishment to get them to put forth adequate effort toward the achievement of organizational objectives.
3. Average human beings prefer to be directed, wish to avoid responsibility, have relatively little ambition, and want security above all.

Theory Y assumptions.   McGregor sees the assumptions under Theory Y as follows:

1. The expenditure of physical effort and mental effort in work is as natural as play or rest.

2. External control and the threat of punishment are not the only means for producing effort toward organizational objectives. People will exercise self-direction and self-control in the service of objectives to which they are committed.

3. The degree of commitment to objectives is in proportion to the size of the rewards associated with their achievement.

4. Average human beings learn, under proper conditions, not only to accept but also to seek responsibility.

5. The capacity to exercise a relatively high degree of imagination, ingenuity, and creativity in the solution of organizational problems is widely, not narrowly, distributed in the population.

6. Under the conditions of modern industrial life, the intellectual potentialities of the average human being are only partially utilized.

These two sets of assumptions obviously are fundamentally different. Theory X is pessimistic, static, and rigid. Control is primarily external, that is, imposed on the subordinate by the superior. In contrast, Theory Y is optimistic, dynamic, and flexible, with an emphasis on self-direction and the integration of individual needs with organizational demands. There is little doubt that each set of assumptions will affect the way managers carry out their managerial functions and activities.

Clarification of the theories.   McGregor was apparently concerned that Theory X and Theory Y might be misinterpreted.[5] The following points will clarify some of the areas of misunderstanding and keep the assumptions in proper perspective. First, Theory X and Theory Y assumptions are just that: They are assumptions only. They are not prescriptions or suggestions for managerial strategies. Rather, these assumptions must be tested against reality. Furthermore, these assumptions are intuitive deductions and are not based on research. Second, Theories X and Y do not imply "hard" or "soft" management. The "hard" approach may produce resistance and antagonism. The "soft" approach may result in laissez-faire management and is not congruent with Theory Y. Instead, the effective manager recognizes the dignity and capabilities, as well as the limitations, of people and adjusts behavior as demanded by the situation. Third, Theories X and Y are not to be viewed as being on a continuous scale, with X and Y on opposite extremes. They are not a matter of degree; rather, they are completely different views of people.

A fourth area of potential misunderstanding is that the discussion of Theory Y is not a case for consensus management, nor is it an argument against the use of authority. Instead, under Theory Y, authority is seen as only one of the many ways a manager exerts leadership. Fifth, different tasks and situations require a variety of approaches to management. At times, authority and structure may be effective for certain tasks, as found in the research by John J. Morse and Jay W. Lorsch.[6] They suggest that different approaches are effective in different situations. Thus, the productive enterprise is one that fits the task requirements to the people and the particular situation.

Behavioral Models in a Historical Perspective

While many models focus on the general nature of people, Keith Davis and John W. Newstrom identify four behavioral models that deal with people within the enterprise context.[7] Specifically, they show how assumptions and related theories influence managerial behavior. Moreover, they suggest that some of these models were emphasized in certain periods in our history.

The autocratic model. The autocratic model prevailed for a long time, especially during the industrial revolution and until the 1920s. The dominant force was power: Managers saw authority as the only means to get things done, and employees were expected to follow orders. The result was high dependency of subordinates on their boss. This dependent relationship was possible because employees at that time lived on the subsistence level. Performance under the autocratic model was, as one might expect, minimal.

The custodial model. The custodial model became popular in the 1890s and 1900s. The managerial orientation was toward the use of money to pay for employee benefits. This model depended on the availability of economic resources of the firm and the ability to pay for those benefits. While employees hoped to obtain security, at the same time they became highly dependent on the enterprise. Rather than producing up to their capacity, however, employees' contributions may be described as passively cooperative.

The supportive model. The supportive model of organizational behavior depends on managerial leadership rather than the use of power or money. The aim of managers is to support employees in their achievement of results. The focus is on participation and involvement of individuals in the managerial process. This model is similar to Theory Y, as discussed by McGregor, and to Rensis Likert's "principle of supportive relationships," which states:

> The leadership and other processes of the organization must be such as to ensure a maximum probability that in all interactions and all relationships with the organization, each member will, in the light of his background, values, and expectations, view the experience as supportive and the one which builds and maintains his sense of personal worth and importance.[8]

The supportive model is found in affluent societies with complex technologies. This model, for example, is widely accepted in theory by managers in the United States, but not necessarily widely practiced.

The collegial model. The collegial model is a further development of the supportive model. This model is based on team concepts and implies partnership among those working on a common task. Employees feel responsible for their own work and their contributions toward shared goals. Control is primarily through self-discipline by the team members. The organizational climate is conducive to self-fulfillment and self-actualization.

The collegial model is particularly suitable for managing professionals with unprogrammed tasks, such as can be found in a research laboratory. But increasingly this model is used in a variety of situations that require behavioral flexibility by responding to changing situations.

A Dual-Model Theory

According to Raymond E. Miles, the managerial task is to integrate organizational variables (goals, technology, and structure) with human variables (capabilities, attitudes, values, needs, and demographic characteristics) into an effective and efficient sociotechnical system.[9] This integration, shown in Table 16-1, is achieved through activities such as directing, selecting, training, appraising, communicating, and controlling. It also includes designing the organization and jobs, developing people, and rewarding individuals for their contributions. The framework, as you will readily recognize, is similar to the managerial activities discussed in this book.

Miles suggests that the manager's own concepts about managing partially determine the way the key managerial activities are carried out. Consequently, he identifies three "theories" of management known as the traditional, the human relations, and the human resources models.[10] In developing these models, Miles draws extensively from McGregor.[11] The traditional model is similar to Theory X while the human resource model is closely related to Theory Y. The human relations model may be seen as Theory X with pseudoparticipation.

The models shown in Table 16-1 begin with assumptions about people; then policies related to these assumptions are described; finally, the expected results are stated. The important point is that managers apparently subscribe not only to one but to two models. One concerns the way they manage subordinates, and the other concerns the way they believe they should be managed by their superiors.

Three managerial models.   In the **traditional model,** emphasis is on control and directing. The underlying assumption is that members of the enterprise will comply if tasks and procedures are specified and members are properly selected, trained, and paid. The **human relations model** is modified and gives attention to social and egoistic needs. Thus, it is recognized that fair treatment and pay are not enough. Nevertheless, the emphasis by managers is still on controlling, although preventive steps are also taken to obtain the desired contributions of enterprise members. The **human resources model** is different. The manager is seen as a developer and facilitator to help subordinates achieve performance aims. There is a great deal of participation in goal setting. Furthermore, if problems occur, several factors—rather than a single cause—are evaluated as potential reasons for the difficulties. Although self-direction and self-control are important to this model, the need for other controls is also recognized.

Separate theories for subordinates and for managers themselves.   On the basis of extensive research evidence, Miles concluded that managers actually believe in

TABLE 16-1   Alternative Theories of Management

Traditional model	Human relations model	Human resources model
Assumptions		
1. Work is inherently distasteful to most people.	1. People want to feel useful and important.	1. Work is not inherently distasteful. People want to contribute to meaningful goals which they have helped establish.
2. What workers do is less important than what they earn for doing it.	2. People desire to belong and to be recognized as individuals.	
3. Few want or can handle work which requires creativity, self-direction, or self-control.	3. These needs are more important than money in motivating people to work.	2. Most people can exercise far more creative, responsible self-direction and self-control than their present jobs demand.
Policies		
1. The manager's basic task is to closely supervise and control his subordinates.	1. The manager's basic task is to make each worker feel useful and important.	1. The manager's basic task is to make use of his "untapped" human resources.
2. He must break tasks down into simple, repetitive, easily learned operations.	2. He should keep his subordinates informed and listen to their objections to his plans.	2. He must create an environment in which all members may contribute to the limits of their ability.
3. He must establish detailed work routines and procedures and enforce these firmly but fairly.	3. The manager should allow his subordinates to exercise some self-direction and self-control on routine matters.	3. He must encourage full participation on important matters, continually broadening subordinate self-direction and control.
Expectations		
1. People can tolerate work if the pay is decent and the boss is fair.	1. Sharing information with subordinates and involving them in routine decisions will satisfy their basic needs to belong and to feel important.	1. Expanding subordinate influence, self-direction, and self-control will lead to direct improvements in operating efficiency.
2. If tasks are simple enough and people are closely controlled, they will produce up to standard.	2. Satisfying these needs will improve morale and reduce resistance to formal authority—subordinates will "willingly cooperate."	2. Work satisfaction may improve as a "by-product" of subordinates' making full use of their resources.

Source: Raymond E. Miles, *Theories of Management: Implications for Organizational Behavior and Development* (New York: McGraw-Hill Book Company, 1975), p. 35. Used with permission.

two models: one for subordinates and the other for themselves. Studies conducted at Stanford University and at the University of California at Berkeley showed a basic agreement about the desirability of the concept concerning participation in decision making by subordinates, sharing of information, and increasing self-control. However, managers did not indicate strong belief in the

PERSPECTIVE:
SOME EXPERIENCES SUPPORTING THE DUAL-MODEL THEORY

The findings by Miles have repeatedly been noted in a variety of our consulting and management development experiences. For example, in seminars on MBO there is little disagreement among participants about the desirability of participation in goal setting; they favor placing responsibility for planning at the level where actions are carried out and providing an environment in which people can use their potential, self-control, self-direction, and accountability for results. Frequently heard from seminar participants are phrases such as "Great idea, but my boss should really attend this session," and "If only top management would practice this participative philosophy." Then, if the same people are observed interacting with their subordinates in the organizational setting, it is not unusual to find that they do not practice what they supposedly believe to be effective. In other words, their position is that the human resources model is effective at their level, but not in their relationships with subordinates.

capabilities of their subordinates and, in fact, exhibited a lack of confidence in them. Nor did these managers think that the capacity for leadership was widely distributed among subordinates. Thus, these managers seemed to reject the human resources model when it came to their own relationships with their subordinates.

The picture was quite different, however, for managers viewing their relationships with their own superiors. There was a tendency for these managers to rate themselves as equal to, or higher than, their superiors on factors such as creativity, ingenuity, flexibility, and willingness to change. In addition, these managers felt that their superiors should use participation, which, in turn, would result in better enterprise performance at their level. In summary, then, these managers appeared to suggest that their superiors should follow practices which would allow them to operate consistently with the human resources model. On the other hand, these same managers, in their relationships with subordinates, seemed to subscribe to the human relations model.

Toward an Eclectic View of Behavioral Models

Which of these many views of individuals is valid? Earlier in this chapter we noted that Schein suggested four conceptions of people, ranging from the rational-economic view to a view that stresses complex motivations. Porter and his colleagues presented six different views about the nature of individuals, and McGregor grouped assumptions into Theory X and Theory Y. Davis's organizational behavior approach identified autocratic, custodial, supportive, and collegial models. And Miles suggested three different models. Which model, then, is valid?

You have seen many similarities among the various models. But it appears that no single model is sufficient to explain the full range of individual and organizational behavior. People behave differently in diverse situations, and, to complicate matters, they even behave differently in similar situations at different times. In some situations people act rationally; in other situations they are guided by emotions. It is the manager's responsibility to create an environment in which people are induced to contribute to the aims of the enterprise. Yet to assume that people can be manipulated ignores their individuality and underestimates their intelligence. Economic rewards certainly are important in an enterprise, but people often want more than money from a job. They usually want to develop their capabilities, their competence, and their potential as well.

The effective manager will take an eclectic approach by drawing from different models that describe the nature of people. At the very least, one must recognize that people are different and do not fit neatly into one conceptual model. They must be treated with respect and dignity, they must be considered as whole persons, and they must be seen in the context of their total environment in which they assume different roles. It is important to realize that different situations require a variety of managerial approaches for utilizing most effectively and efficiently the most valuable resource of the enterprise, namely, people.

CREATIVITY AND INNOVATION

An important factor in managing people is creativity. We can make a distinction between creativity and innovation. The term **creativity** usually refers to the ability and power to develop new ideas. **Innovation,** on the other hand, usually means the use of these ideas. In an organization, this can mean a new product, a new service, or a new way of doing things. Although this discussion centers on the creative process, it is implied that organizations not only generate new ideas but also translate them into practical applications.

The Creative Process

The creative process is seldom simple and linear. Instead it can be thought of as overlapping and interacting phases consisting of (1) unconscious scanning, (2) intuition, (3) insight, and (4) logical formulation.[12]

The first phase, *unconscious scanning,* is difficult to explain because it is beyond consciousness. This scanning usually requires an absorption in the problem which may be vague in the mind. Yet managers working under time constraints often make decisions prematurely rather than dealing thoroughly with ambiguous, ill-defined problems.

The second phase, *intuition,* connects the unconscious with the conscious. This stage may involve the combination of factors that may seem contradictory at first. For example, Donaldson Brown and Alfred Sloan of General Motors conceived in the 1920s the idea of a decentralized division structure with centralized control. These concepts seem to contradict each other. Yet they make sense when one recognizes the underlying principles of (1) giving responsibility for the operations to the general manager of each division, and (2) maintaining centralized control in headquarters over certain functions. It took the intuition of two great corporate leaders to see these two principles interact in the managerial process.

Intuition needs time to work. It requires the finding of new combinations and integration of diverse concepts and ideas. Thus, one must think through the problem. Intuitive thinking is promoted by several techniques, such as brainstorming and synectics, which will be discussed shortly.

Insight is the third phase of the creative process. Insight is mostly the result of hard work. It requires, for example, many ideas to come up with a usable product, a new service, or a new process. Interestingly, insight may come at times when the thoughts are not directly focused on the problem at hand. Moreover, new insights may last for only a few minutes, and effective managers may benefit from having paper and pencil ready to make notes of their creative ideas.

The last phase in the creative process is *logical formulation* or *verification*. Insight needs to be tested through logic or experiment. This may be accomplished by continued work on an idea or by inviting critiques from others. Brown and Sloan's idea of decentralization, for example, needed to be tested against organizational reality.

Techniques to Enhance Creativity

Creativity can be taught.[13] Creative thoughts are often the fruits of extensive efforts, and several techniques are available to nurture those kinds of thoughts, especially in the decision-making process. Some techniques focus on group interactions; others focus on individual actions. As illustrative of the various techniques, two popular ones are brainstorming and synectics.

Brainstorming.   One of the best-known techniques to facilitate creativity has been developed by Alex F. Osborn, who has been called "the father of brainstorming."[14] The purpose of this approach is to improve problem solving by finding new and unusual solutions. In the brainstorming session, a multiplication of ideas is sought. The rules are as follows:

1. No ideas are ever criticized.

2. The more radical the ideas are, the better.

3. The quantity of idea production is stressed.

4. The improvement of ideas by others is encouraged.

Brainstorming, which emphasizes group thinking, was widely accepted after its introduction. However, the enthusiasm was dampened by research which showed that individuals could develop better ideas working by themselves than when working with groups. Additional research, however, showed that in some situations the group approach may work well. This may be the case when the information is distributed among various people or when a poorer group decision is more acceptable than a better individual decision which, for example, may be opposed by those who have to implement it. Also, the acceptance of new ideas is usually greater when the decision is made by the group charged with its implementation.[15]

Synectics.   Originally known as the Gordon technique (named after its creator, William J. Gordon), this system was further modified and became known as synectics.[16] In this approach, the members of the synectics team are carefully selected for their suitability to deal with the problem, a problem which may involve the entire organization.

The leader of the group plays a vital role in this approach. In fact, only the leader knows the specific nature of the problem. This person narrows and carefully leads the discussion without revealing the actual problem itself. The main reason for this approach is to prevent the group from reaching a premature solution to the problem. The system involves a complex set of interactions from which a solution emerges—frequently the invention of a new product.

Limitations of Traditional Group Discussion

Although the techniques of brainstorming and synectics may result in creative ideas, it would be incorrect to assume that creativity flourishes only in groups. Indeed, the usual group discussion can inhibit creativity.[17] For example, group members may pursue an idea to the exclusion of other alternatives. Experts on a topic may not be willing to express their ideas in a group for fear of being ridiculed. Also, lower-level managers may be inhibited in expressing their views in a group with higher-level managers. Pressures to conform can discourage the expression of deviant opinions. The need for getting along with others can be stronger than the need for exploring creative but unpopular alternatives to the solution of a problem. Finally, groups with their needs to arrive at a decision may not make the effort of searching for data relevant to a decision.

The Creative Manager

All too often it is assumed that most people are noncreative and have little ability to develop new ideas. This assumption, unfortunately, can be detrimental to the organization, for in the appropriate environment virtually all people are capable of being creative, even though the degree of creativity varies considerably among individuals.

Generally speaking, creative people are inquisitive and come up with many new and unusual ideas; they are seldom satisfied with the status quo. Although, intelligent, they not only rely on the rational process but also involve the emotional aspects of their personality in problem solving. They appear to be excited about solving a problem, even to the point of tenacity. Creative individuals are aware of themselves and capable of independent judgment. They object to conformity and see themselves as being different.

Unquestionably, creative people can make great contributions to an enterprise. At the same time, however, they may also cause difficulties in organizations. Change—as any manager knows—is not always popular. Moreover, change frequently has undesirable and unexpected side effects. Similarly, unusual ideas, pursued stubbornly, may frustrate others and inhibit the smooth functioning of an organization. Finally, creative individuals may be disruptive by ignoring established policies, rules, and regulations.

We can conclude, then, that the creativity of most individuals is probably underutilized in many cases. Yet unusual innovations can be of great benefit to the firm. Consequently, individual and group techniques can be effectively used to nurture creativity, especially in the area of planning. But creativity is not a substitute for managerial judgment. It is the manager who must determine and weigh the risks involved in pursuing unusual ideas and translating them into innovative practices.

Innovation and Entrepreneurship

Recently, innovation and entrepreneurship has received considerable attention. When hearing these terms, one thinks immediately of success stories of, for example, Steven Jobs of Apple Computers or Ross Perot of Electronic Data Processing (acquired by General Motors). It may be an appealing thought to get rich and get rich quick, often by establishing new companies.[18] While some authors examine the individual entrepreneur, others focus on entrepreneurship in companies.[19]

Peter Drucker suggests that innovation applies not only to high-tech companies but equally to low-tech, established businesses. Worthwhile innovation, rather than being sheer luck, requires systematic and rational work, well organized and managed for results.[20]

What does entrepreneurship imply? It suggests dissatisfaction with how things are and awareness of a need to do things differently. Innovation comes about because of some of the following situations:

1. The unexpected event, failure, or success

2. The incongruous—what is assumed and what really is

3. The process or task that needed improvement

4. Changes in the market or industry structure

5. Changes in demographics

6. Changes in meaning or how things are perceived

7. Innovation based on knowledge

Innovations based solely on bright ideas may be very risky and are, at times, not successful. General Electric's ambitious plans for the "factory of the future" may have been a costly mistake.[21] These plans may have been based on unrealistic forecasts and GE's unrealistic expectation to automate industry. The concept of the new factory expressed the wish of the chairman, who wanted to promote entrepreneurship in an organization that was known to be highly structured.

The most successful innovations are often the mundane ones. Take the

> **PERSPECTIVE:**
> **CREATIVE THINKING AT BELL TELEPHONE LABORATORY**
>
> The Bell Telephone Laboratory has been referred to as "probably the greatest invention factory." The organizational climate in this firm, which allows for great freedom, was probably set many years ago by Theodore Vail, AT&T's president, who himself had an innovative vision in formulating the strategy for the telephone company. In the early 1900s, when the Bell System was almost a monopoly, Vail formalized the purpose of the organization as *providing service*. A simple insight? Perhaps, but it was a significant one because it charted the successful course for the company for many years to come.

Japanese, who make minor innovations (providing, for example, little conveniences that customers like) in their cars or in their electronic equipment.[22] James Brian Quinn found in his research that successful large companies are listening carefully to the needs of their customers. They establish teams that search for creative alternatives to serve their customers—but within a limiting framework and with clear goals in mind.[23]

Innovation is not only relevant to high-tech firms but is also crucial for old-line, traditional companies which may not survive without the infusion of innovation. Managers in those companies must create an environment that fosters entrepreneurial spirit and actions.

HARMONIZING OBJECTIVES: THE KEY TO LEADING

Understanding the human factor in enterprises is important for the managerial function of leading. How a manager views human nature influences the selection of motivational and leadership approaches. A number of models presenting various conceptions of the nature of people have been proposed; however, no single view is sufficient to understand the whole person. Therefore, an eclectic view of the nature of people is suggested.

People do not work in isolation; rather, they work to a great extent in groups toward the achievement of personal and enterprise objectives. Unfortunately, these objectives are not always harmonious. Nor should one take for granted that the goals of subordinates are the same as those of the superior. Therefore, one of the most important single activities of managers is to harmonize the needs of individuals with the demands of the enterprise.

Leading bridges the gap between, on the one hand, logical and well-considered plans, carefully designed organization structures, good programs of staffing, and efficient control techniques, and, on the other hand, the need for people to understand, to be motivated, and to contribute all they are capable of to enterprise and department goals. There is no way that a manager can utilize the desires and goals of individuals to achieve enterprise objectives without knowing what these individuals want. Even then, managers must be able to design an environment that will take advantage of these individual drives. Managers must know how to communicate with and guide their subordinates so that they will see how they serve their own interests by working creatively for an organization.

FOR DISCUSSION

1. What are Theory X and Theory Y assumptions? State your agreements or disagreements with these assumptions. What are some misunderstandings of Theories X and Y?

2. What are some possible implications of Theories X and Y for carrying out the managerial functions of planning, organizing, staffing, leading, and controlling?

3. According to Miles, managers may subscribe to *two* managerial models. What does this actually mean? What has been your experience?

4. According to Davis, different behavioral models within an enterprise have been emphasized at various times in the history of the United States. How can you explain this?

5. Think of a problem that was creatively solved. Did the solution come about through group discussion or was it an individual effort? Reconstruct the steps of the creative process.

6. Do you as a student, as an employee, or as a manager work at your capacity? Why, or why not?

7. Why is harmonizing of personal and enterprise objectives seen as a key to leading?

EXERCISES/ACTION STEPS

1. Interview two managers and ask them what they think about the basic nature of people. For example, do they think that they are basically lazy and need to be controlled? Or do they think that employees want to work and contribute to the company's goals. In preparation for presenting your findings to the class, analyze the managers' responses in light of the theories you learned in this chapter.

2. Read some books and articles on creativity and innovation and try to apply some of the principles, concepts, or theories to your life. You may start by looking at the references for this chapter and suggestions shown in the section For Further Information.

CASES

CASE 16-1
WHAT DO WE KNOW FOR SURE?

The class in management was nearing the conclusion of its study of human behavior. Several members had reported on the research and conclusions of prominent writers in the field. All were quite familiar with the work of Schein, McGregor, Likert, Davis, and Miles.

Hoping to focus attention on the conclusion that might be reached, the professor asked, "Do you feel that the research conducted by these scholars has enabled us to move from hypothesis to truth about the behavior of people?"

One thoughtful student, almost talking to herself, commented: "When I read the work of these investigators, I was convinced that each had a most telling case. I thought that here indeed was truth. Then I recalled that in each instance, these writers were inferring understanding based upon observed behavior. While I was convinced that what people *did* was accurately reported, I could not help but feel that other observers, looking at the same behavior, would have different explanations. Perhaps we will never *know* why people behave as they do. Indeed, I don't understand myself; does the professor understand himself?"

The pragmatist in the class had little use for this line of thought. "What difference does it make," he said, "why people behave in a particular way? Isn't it enough to know that they do so behave? Using this, why can't we establish a motivation system within any enterprise that will work?"

A voice in the back of the room was heard to say, "I'm afraid of generalizations."

1. In your opinion, which of the theories explains best why people behave as they do? Why?

2. Select two theories by authors mentioned in the case and discuss the similarities and differences in their views about the nature of people.

CASE 16-2
CUSTOMER'S ELECTRIC APPLIANCE COMPANY

John Caldwell, the president of the Customer's Electric Appliance Company, had just received the latest report of the state of the firm. He did not like what he read: sales down, costs increased, profits decreased, customer complaints up, and labor turnover extremely high. He immediately asked his secretary to order all the vice-presidents from the functional areas, the controller, and the other key staff personnel to come to his office. At the meeting, Mr. Caldwell stated, "I have just received the report on key indicators and I think the poor performance of the firm is directly attributable to your lack of leadership. This company has become a country club. When I walk through the corridors, I see people standing around as if they were at a cocktail party. Their concern is to do less for more money and more fringe benefits. They have completely forgotten that we are in business to make a profit. You must remember that people want to do as little as possible and to squeeze the last dime out of the company. What is needed is closer supervision and more control. When people are not performing, you warn them once—if they do not shape up, fire them. Recently, several customers complained that they would not get any service if their requests would not result in sales and commissions for the salesperson. I want you to check the salespeople very closely on their dealings with the customers. Do not hesitate to listen in on their telephone conversations. Perhaps you might even make recordings of these conversations and bring them to my attention."

The executives at the meeting nodded approvingly to the president's remarks. Only Carolyn Jung, a 28-year-old staff assistant, raised some questions. She wondered whether the company should go that far in installing controls. In fact, she suggested that people basically want to work, they want to contribute, they want to do a good job, provided opportunities are given. She even suggested that the company perhaps did not really utilize the people's potentials because employees today are better educated than ever before and they want to participate in the decision-making process. She recommended that the president should explain to the employees the company's poor performance and then solicit their help in improving productivity.

The president, stunned by Ms. Jung's comments, said that she must have been misled by some of the new-fangled ideas she might have heard when she recently took courses to complete her M.B.A. degree. Mr. Caldwell then abruptly closed the meeting with the order that all officers come to a meeting scheduled for the following Monday and report on the specific steps each one would undertake to bring the company under control.

1. If you were employed by the firm and attended the meeting (let's say you had been employed for 6 months), what would you have said, if anything?

2. What is the president's view of the nature of people?

3. What are the underlying assumptions about people expressed in Ms. Jung's comments?

4. If you were an outside consultant attending this meeting, what recommendations would you make to the president to improve the human organization?

REFERENCES

1. This is also one of the important messages in the *Second Draft—Pastoral Letter on Catholic Social Teaching and the U.S. Economy,* Oct. 7, 1985. The letter *Economic Justice for All: Catholic Social Teaching and the U.S. Economy* was approved in November 1986.

2. Edgar H. Schein, *Organizational Psychology,* 3d ed. (Englewood Cliffs, N.J.: Prentice-Hall, 1980), pp. 52–101.

3. Lyman W. Porter, Edward E. Lawler III, and J. Richard Hackman, *Behavior in Organizations* (New York: McGraw-Hill Book Company, 1975), chap. 2.

4. Douglas McGregor, *The Human Side of Enterprise* (New York: McGraw-Hill Book Company, 1960).

5. Harold M. F. Rush, *Behavioral Science—Concepts and Management Application* (New York: National Industrial Conference Board, 1969), pp. 13–16; Douglas McGregor, *The Professional Manager* (New York: McGraw-Hill Book Company, 1969), chap. 5.

6. John J. Morse and Jay W. Lorsch, "Beyond Theory Y," *Harvard Business Review* (May–June 1970), pp. 61–68.

7. Keith Davis and John W. Newstrom, *Human Behavior at Work: Organizational Behavior,* 7th ed. (New York: McGraw-Hill Book Company, 1985), pp. 29–34.

8. Rensis Likert and Jane G. Likert, *New Ways of Managing Conflict* (New York: McGraw-Hill Book Company, 1976), p. 108.

9. Raymond E. Miles, *Theories of Management: Implications for Organizational Behavior and Development* (New York: McGraw-Hill Book Company, 1975), especially chap. 2.

10. A theory is defined by Miles in this context as "simply a more or less complete explanation of how and why someone or something behaves, occurs, or responds as he or it does under a given set of circumstances." In Miles, *Theories of Management* (1975), p. 32.

11. See John B. Miner, *Theories of Organizational Behavior* (Hinsdale, Ill.: The Dryden Press, 1980), chap. 10.

12. Much of the discussion of the creative process is based on Michael B. McCaskey, *The Executive Challenge—Managing Change and Ambiguity* (Marshfield, Mass.: Pitman, 1982), chap. 8.

13. Emily T. Smith, "Are You Creative? Research Shows Creativity Can Be Taught—and Companies are Listening," *Business Week* (Sept. 30, 1985), pp. 80–84.

14. Alex F. Osborn, *Applied Imagination,* 3d rev. ed. (New York: Charles Scribner's Sons, 1963).

15. Irvin Summers and David E. White, "Creativity Techniques: Toward Improvement of the Decision Process," *Academy of Management Review* (April 1976), pp. 99–107.

16. William J. Gordon, "Operational Approach to Creativity," *Harvard Business Review* (November–December 1956), pp. 41–51; William J. Gordon, *Synectics* (New York: Harper & Brothers, 1961).

17. George S. Steiner, John B. Miner, and Edmund R. Gray, *Management Policy and Strategy* (New York: Macmillan Publishing Company, 1982), pp. 264–267; Andre L. Delbecq, Andrew H. Van de Ven, and David H. Gustafson, *Group Techniques for Program Planning* (Glenview, Ill.: Scott, Foresman and Company, 1975).

18. For a critical review of some books on entrepreneurship see David E. Gumpert, "Stalking the Entrepreneur," *Harvard Business Review* (May–June 1986), pp. 32–36.

19. Scc also the discussion of "intrapreneurship" mentioned in Chapter 7.

20. Peter F. Drucker, *Innovation and Entrepreneurship—Practices and Principles* (New York: Harper & Row, 1985); Peter F. Drucker, "The Discipline of Innovation," *Harvard Business Review* (May–June 1985), pp. 67–72; John W. Wilson, "The New Economy According to Drucker," *Business Week* (June 10, 1985), pp. 10–12; Everett Groseclose, "A Management Sage's Shibboleths for Success," *The Wall Street Journal* (Oct. 7, 1985).

21. Peter Petre, "How GE Bobbled the Factory of the Future," *Fortune* (Nov. 11, 1985), pp. 52–63.

22. More recently, Japan has been breaking with tradition and now begins funding of basic research. See Stephen K. Yoder, "Going Crazy in Japan," *The Wall Street Journal,* A Special Report on Technology in the Workplace (Nov. 10, 1986).

23. James B. Quinn, "Managing Innovation: Controlled Chaos," *Harvard Business Review* (May–June 1985), pp. 73–84.

FOR FURTHER INFORMATION

Davis, Keith, and John W. Newstrom. *Human Behavior at Work: Organizational Behavior* 7th ed. (New York: McGraw-Hill Book Company, 1985).

Hackman, J. Richard, Edward E. Lawler III, and Lyman W. Porter (eds.). *Perspectives on Behavior in Organization,* 2d ed. (New York: McGraw-Hill Book Company, 1983).

Isenberg, Daniel J. "How Senior Managers Think," *Harvard Business Review* (November–December 1984), pp. 80–90.

McGregor, Douglas. *The Professional Manager* (New York: McGraw-Hill Book Company, 1969).

McFillen, James M. "The Organizing and Managing of Organizational Behavior: A Review of First Edition Organizational Behavior Texts," *Academy of Management Review* (April 1985), pp. 355–365.

Miner, John B. *Theories of Organizational Behavior* (Hinsdale, Ill.: Dryden Press, 1980).

Weihrich, Heinz. "Games Organizational People Play," *Management International Review,* vol. 18, no. 4 (1978), pp. 33–40.

17

Motivation

CHAPTER OBJECTIVES

After reading this chapter, you should be able to:

1. Explain the meanings of motivation, motivators, and satisfaction.

2. Recognize that motives are complex and even conflicting.

3. Explain the various leading theories of motivation and their strengths and weaknesses.

4. Analyze special motivational techniques, with particular emphasis on the quality of working life and job enrichment.

5. Present a system and situational approach to motivation.

Managing requires the creation and maintenance of an environment in which individuals work together in groups toward the accomplishment of common objectives. A manager cannot do this job without knowing what motivates people. The building of motivating factors into organizational roles, the staffing of these roles, and the entire process of leading people must be built on a knowledge of motivation. When we emphasize the importance of knowing and taking advantage of motivating factors, we are not trying to cast managers in the role of amateur psychiatrists. The managers' job is not to manipulate people but, rather, to recognize what motivates people.

The basic element of all human behavior is some kind of activity, whether physical or mental. We can look at human behavior as a series of activities. The question arises as to what activities human beings will undertake at any given time, and why. We know that activities are goal-oriented; that is, people do things that lead them to accomplish something. But individual goals can be baffling. Sometimes people know exactly why they do things; often, however, individual drives lie buried in the subconscious. For example, do you know why you did what you did today and what all your various activities were designed to achieve?

The primary task of managers is to get people to contribute activities that help to achieve the mission and goals of an enterprise or of any department or other organized unit within it. Clearly, to guide people's activities in desired directions requires knowing, to the best of any manager's ability, what leads people to do things, what motivates them.

MOTIVATION AND MOTIVATORS

Human motives are based on needs, whether consciously or subconsciously felt. Some are primary needs, such as the physiological requirements for water, air, food, sleep, and shelter. Other needs may be regarded as secondary, such as self-esteem, status, affiliation with others, affection, giving, accomplishment, and self-assertion. As you can easily imagine, these needs vary in intensity and over time with various individuals.

Motivation

Motivation is a general term applying to the entire class of drives, desires, needs, wishes, and similar forces. To say that managers motivate their subordinates is to say that they do those things which they hope will satisfy these drives and desires and induce the subordinates to act in a desired manner.

The Need-Want-Satisfaction Chain

We can, then, look at motivation as involving a chain reaction—starting out with felt needs, resulting in wants or goals sought, which give rise to tensions (that is, unfulfilled desires), then causing action toward achieving goals, and finally satisfying wants. This chain is shown in Figure 17-1.

PERSPECTIVE: SELF-MOTIVATION

Managers do have a responsibility of providing an environment conducive to performance. But individuals themselves do have a responsibility for self-motivation. One approach is through strategic career management, discussed in Chapter 14. George Odiorne, management professor, scholar, and experienced consultant, made some specific recommendations.[1] Here are some:

1. Set a goal for yourself and do not lose sight of it. Lee Iacocca (currently president at Chrysler) set the goal of becoming vice-president at the Ford Motor Company by age 35, and for 15 years this aim motivated him and guided his behavior.

2. Supplement your long-term objectives with short-term goals and specific actions. It has been said that to get something done is to begin.

3. Learn a challenging new task each year. Learning to become a manager does not stop with a bachelor's or master's degree in business. A degree is the real beginning, not the end, of learning. Learning and applying the new microcomputer technology might be such a challenging task.

4. Make your job a different one. Set improvement objectives for your position. With some imagination, you probably can considerably increase your productivity.

5. Develop an area of expertise. Build on your strengths or develop one of your weaknesses into a strength. You might want to be known as the best accountant or the best engineer in your specific area of competence.

6. Give yourself feedback and reward yourself. Setting verifiable goals provides you with a standard against which you can measure your performance. Why not have a special dinner to celebrate your accomplishments?

The chain explanation is complex. In the first place, except for physiological needs, such as hunger, needs are not independent of a person's environment. We can easily see also that many physiological needs are stimulated by environmental factors: The smell of food may make us feel hungry, a high thermometer reading may make us suddenly feel hot, or the sight of a cold drink may cause an overwhelming thirst.

Environment has a major influence on our perception of secondary needs. The promotion of a colleague may kindle our desire for a higher position. A challenging problem may whet our desire to accomplish something by solving it. A congenial social group may increase our need for affiliation, and, of course, being alone more than we want to be can give us strong motivation for wanting to be with people.

In the second place, the need-want-satisfaction chain does not always operate as simply as portrayed. Needs do cause behavior. But needs also may result

FIGURE 17-1

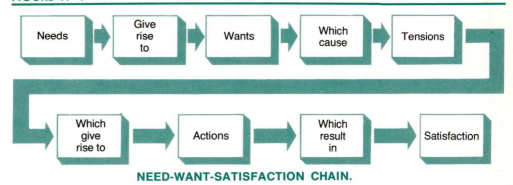

NEED-WANT-SATISFACTION CHAIN.

from behavior. Satisfying one need may lead to a desire to satisfy more needs. For example, a person's need for accomplishment may be made keener by the satisfaction gained from achieving a desired goal, or it may be dulled by failure. The one-way nature of the chain has also been challenged by the work of some biological scientists who have found that needs are not always the cause of human behavior but may be a result of it. In other words, behavior is often what we do and not why we do it.

The Complexity of Motivation

It takes only a moment's thought to realize that at any given time, an individual's motives may be quite complex and often conflicting. A person may be motivated by a desire for economic goods and services (groceries, a better house, a new car, or a trip), and even these desires may be complex and conflicting (should one buy a new house or a new car?). At the same time an individual may want self-esteem, status, a feeling of accomplishment, or relaxation (who has not felt a conflict-between the time demands of a job and the desire to play golf or to go to a movie?).

Motivators.   **Motivators** are things which induce an individual to perform. While motivations reflect wants, motivators are the identified rewards, or incentives, that sharpen the drive to satisfy these wants. They are also the means by which conflicting needs may be reconciled or one need heightened so that it will be given priority over another.

A manager can do much to sharpen motives by establishing an environment favorable to certain drives. For example, people in a business which has developed a reputation for excellence and high quality tend to be motivated to contribute to this reputation. Similarly, the environment of a business in which managerial performance is effective and efficient tends to breed a desire for high-quality management among most, or all, managers and personnel.

A motivator, then, is something that influences an individual's behavior. It makes a difference in what a person will do. Obviously, in any organized enterprise, managers must be concerned about motivators and also inventive in

FIGURE 17-2

DIFFERENCES BETWEEN MOTIVATION AND SATISFACTION.
Motivation is the drive to satisfy a want (achieve an outcome); satisfaction is experienced when the outcome has been achieved.

their use. People can often satisfy their wants in a variety of ways. A person can, for example, satisfy a desire for affiliation by being active in a social club rather than in a business, meet economic needs by performing a job just well enough to get by, or satisfy status needs by spending time working for a political party. What a manager must do, of course, is to use those motivators which will lead people to perform effectively for the enterprise that employs them. No manager can expect to hire the whole person since people always have desires and drives outside the enterprise. But if a company or any other kind of enterprise is to be efficient and successful, enough of every person's drives must be stimulated and satisfied to ensure effective performance.

The difference between motivation and satisfaction.   **Motivation** refers to the drive and effort to satisfy a want or goal. **Satisfaction** refers to the contentment experienced·when a want is satisfied. In other words, motivation implies a drive toward an outcome, and satisfaction is the outcome already experienced, as you can see in Figure 17-2.

From a management point of view, then, a person might have high job satisfaction but have a low level of motivation for the job, or the reverse might be true. There is understandably the probability that highly motivated persons with low job satisfaction will look for other positions. Likewise, those people who find their positions rewarding but are being paid considerably less than they desire or think they deserve will probably search for other jobs.

MOTIVATION: THE CARROT AND THE STICK

In examining the various leading theories of motivation and motivators, we seldom now hear reference to the carrot and the stick. This metaphor relates, of course, to the use of rewards and penalties in order to induce desired behavior.

It comes from the old story that to make a donkey move one must put a carrot in front of him or jab him with a stick from behind.

Despite all the researches and theories of motivation that have come to the fore in recent years, reward and punishment are still considered strong motivators. For centuries, however, they were too often thought of as the only forces that could motivate people. As we shall see in the succeeding sections, there are many other motivators.

At the same time, in all theories of motivation, the inducements of some kind of "carrot" are recognized. Often this is money in the form of pay or bonuses. Even though money is not the only motivating force, it has been and will continue to be an important one. The trouble with the money "carrot" approach is that too often everyone gets a carrot, regardless of performance, through such practices as salary increases and promotion by seniority, automatic "merit" increases, and executive bonuses not based on individual manager performance. It is as simple as this: If a person put a donkey in a pen full of carrots and then stood outside with a carrot, would the donkey be encouraged to come out of the pen?

The "stick" in the form of fear—fear of loss of job, loss of income, reduction of bonus, demotion, or some other penalty—has been and continues to be a strong motivator. Yet it is admittedly not the best kind. It often gives rise to defensive or retaliatory behavior, such as union organization, poor-quality work, executive indifference, failure of a manager to take any risks in decision making, or even dishonesty. But fear of penalty cannot be overlooked. And most managers never fully appreciate the power of their position. Whether they are first-level supervisors or chief executives, the power of their position to give or withhold rewards or impose penalties of various kinds gives them an ability to control, to a very great extent, the economic and social well-being of their subordinates. It is hardly a wonder that many subordinates are "yes-sayers" who simply agree with their superiors rather than using their considered judgment.

THE HIERARCHY OF NEEDS THEORY

One of the most widely mentioned theories of motivation is the hierarchy of needs theory put forth by psychologist Abraham Maslow.[2] Maslow saw human needs in the form of a hierarchy, ascending from the lowest to the highest, and he concluded that when one set of needs was satisfied, this kind of need ceased to be a motivator.

The Need Hierarchy[3]

The basic human needs placed by Maslow in an ascending order of importance and shown in Figure 17-3 are these:

1. **Physiological needs.** These are the basic needs for sustaining human life itself, such as food, water, warmth, shelter, and sleep. Maslow took the

FIGURE 17-3

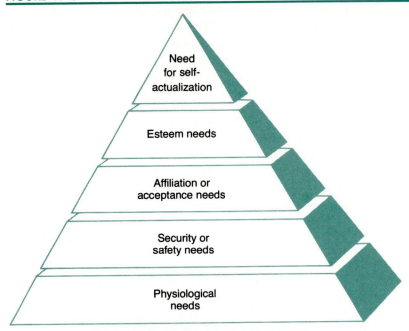

MASLOW'S HIERARCHY OF NEEDS.

position that until these needs are satisfied to the degree necessary to maintain life, other needs will not motivate people.

2. **Security, or safety, needs.** These are the needs to be free of physical danger and the fear of loss of a job, property, food, or shelter.

3. **Affiliation, or acceptance, needs.** Since people are social beings, they need to belong, to be accepted by others.

4. **Esteem needs.** According to Maslow, once people begin to satisfy their need to belong, they tend to want to be held in esteem both by themselves and by others. This kind of need produces such satisfactions as power, prestige, status, and self-confidence.

5. **Need for self-actualization.** Maslow regards this as the highest need in his hierarchy. It is the desire to become what one is capable of becoming—to maximize one's potential and to accomplish something.

Questioning the Need Hierarchy

Maslow's concept of a hierarchy of needs has been subjected to considerable research. E. Lawler and J. Suttle collected data on 187 managers in two different organizations over a period of 6 months to 1 year.[4] They found little evidence to support Maslow's theory that human needs form a hierarchy. They did note, however, that there were two levels of needs—biological and other needs—and that the other needs would emerge only when biological needs were reasonably satisfied. They found, further, that at the higher level, the strength of needs varied with the individual; in some individuals, social needs predominated, and in others, self-actualization needs were strongest.

In another study of Maslow's needs hierarchy involving a group of managers over a period of 5 years, Douglas T. Hall and Khalil Nougaim did not find strong evidence of a hierarchy.[5] They found that as managers advance in an organization, their physiological and safety needs tend to decrease in importance, and their needs for affiliation, esteem, and self-actualization tend to increase. They insisted, however, that the upward movement of need prominence resulted from upward career changes and not from the satisfaction of lower-order needs.

THE MOTIVATION-HYGIENE APPROACH TO MOTIVATION

Maslow's need approach has been considerably modified by Frederick Herzberg and his associates.[6] Their research purports to find a **two-factor theory** of motivation. In one group of needs are such things as company policy and administration, supervision, working conditions, interpersonal relations, salary, status, job security, and personal life. These were found by Herzberg and his associates to be only dissatisfiers and not motivators. In other words, if they exist in a work environment in high quantity and quality, they yield no dissatisfaction. Their existence does not motivate in the sense of yielding satisfaction; their lack of existence would, however, result in dissatisfaction. They were consequently referred to as "hygiene" factors.

In the second group, Herzberg listed certain **satisfiers**—and therefore **motivators**—all related to **job content.** They included achievement, recognition, challenging work, advancement, and growth in the job. Their existence will yield feelings of satisfaction or no satisfaction (not dissatisfaction). As we can see from Figure 17-4, the factors identified by Herzberg are similar to those suggested by Maslow.

The first group of factors (the *dissatisfiers*) Herzberg called **maintenance, hygiene,** or **job context** factors. Their presence will not motivate people in an organization; yet they must be present, or dissatisfaction will arise. The second group or the job-content factors, he found to be the real motivators because they have the potential of yielding a sense of satisfaction. Clearly, if this theory of motivation is sound, managers must give considerable attention to upgrading job content.

The Herzberg research has not gone unchallenged.[7] Some researchers question Herzberg's methods, saying that his investigation methods tended to prejudice his results. For example, the well-known tendency of people to attribute good results to their own efforts and to blame others for poor results is thought to have prejudiced Herzberg's findings. Other researchers, not following his methods, have arrived at conclusions not supporting Herzberg's theory.

FIGURE 17-4

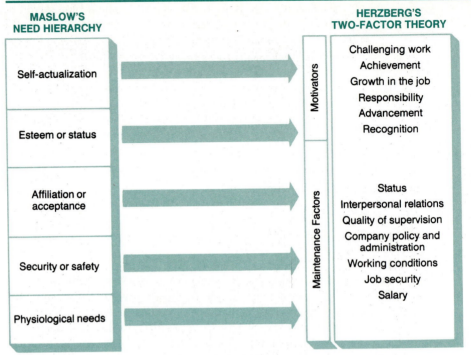

COMPARISON OF MASLOW'S AND HERZBERG'S THEORIES
OF MOTIVATION.

THE EXPECTANCY THEORY OF MOTIVATION

Another approach, one that many believe goes far in explaining how people are motivated, is the expectancy theory. One of the leaders in advancing and explaining this theory is the psychologist Victor H. Vroom. He holds that people will be motivated to do things to reach a goal if they believe in the worth of that goal and if they can see that what they do will help them in achieving it.[8] In a sense, this is a modern expression of what Martin Luther observed centuries ago when he said that "everything that is done in the world is done in hope."

In greater detail, Vroom's theory is that people's motivation toward doing anything will be determined by the value they place on the outcome of their effort (whether positive or negative), multiplied by the confidence they have that their efforts will materially aid in achieving a goal. In other words, Vroom makes the point that motivation is a product of the anticipated worth that an individual places on a goal and the chances he or she sees of achieving that goal. Using his own terms, Vroom's theory may be stated as:

$$\text{Force} = \text{valence} \times \text{expectancy}$$

where **force** is the strength of a person's motivation, **valence** is the strength of an individual's preference for an outcome, and **expectancy** is the probability that a particular action will lead to a desired outcome. When a person is indifferent about achieving a certain goal, a valence of zero occurs, and there is a negative valence when the person would rather not achieve the goal. The result of either would be, of course, no motivation. Likewise, a person would have no motivation to achieve a goal if the expectancy were zero or negative. The force exerted to do something will depend on *both* valence and expectancy. Moreover, a motive to accomplish some action might be determined by a desire to accomplish something else. For example, a person might be willing to work hard to get out a product for a valence in the form of pay. Or a manager might be willing to work hard to achieve company goals in marketing or production for a promotion or pay valence.

The Vroom Theory and Practice

One of the great attractions of the Vroom theory is that it recognizes the importance of various individual needs and motivations. It thus avoids some of the simplistic features of the Maslow and Herzberg approaches. It does seem more realistic. It fits the concept of harmony of objectives, explained in Chapter 16: that individuals have personal goals different from organization goals, but that these can be harmonized. Furthermore, Vroom's theory is completely consistent with the system of managing by objectives.

The strength of Vroom's theory is also its weakness. His assumption that senses of value vary among individuals at different times and in various places appears to fit real life more accurately. It is consistent also with the idea that a manager's job is to *design* an environment for performance, necessarily taking into account the differences in various situations. On the other hand, Vroom's theory is difficult to apply in practice. Despite its difficulty in application, the logical accuracy of Vroom's theory indicates that motivation is much more complex than the approaches of Maslow and Herzberg seem to imply.

The Porter and Lawler Model

Lyman W. Porter and Edward E. Lawler III derived a substantially more complete model of motivation, built in large part on expectancy theory. In their study, they have applied this model primarily to managers.[9] It is summarized in Figure 17-5.

As this model indicates, the amount of effort (the strength of motivation and energy exerted) depends on the value of a reward plus the amount of energy a person believes is required and the probability of receiving the reward. The perceived effort and probability of actually getting a reward are, in turn, also influenced by the record of actual performance. Clearly, if people know they can do a job or if they have done it, they have a better appreciation of the effort required and know better the probability of rewards.

Actual performance in a job (the doing of tasks or the meeting of goals) is determined principally by effort expended. But it is also greatly influenced by an

FIGURE 17-5

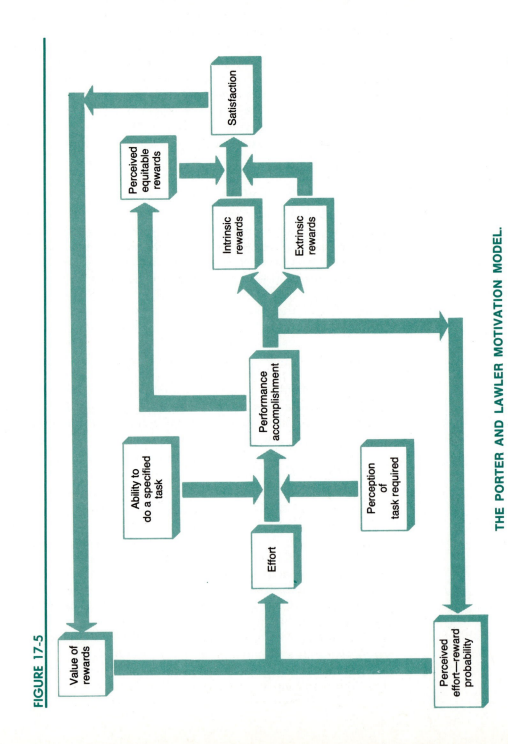

THE PORTER AND LAWLER MOTIVATION MODEL.

Adapted from L. W. Porter and E. E. Lawler, *Managerial Attitudes and Performance* (Homewood, Ill.: Richard D. Irwin, Inc., 1968), p. 165.

individual's ability (knowledge and skills) to do the job and by his or her perception of what the required task is (the extent to which the person understands the goals, required activities, and other elements of a task). Performance, in turn, is seen as leading to intrinsic rewards (such as a sense of accomplishment or self-actualization) and extrinsic rewards (such as working conditions and status). These rewards, tempered by what the individual sees as equitable, lead to satisfaction. But performance also influences sensed equitable rewards. As you can understand, what the individual sees as a fair reward for effort will necessarily affect the satisfaction derived. Likewise, the actual value of rewards will be influenced by satisfaction.

Implications for Practice

The Porter and Lawler model of motivation, while more complex than other theories of motivation, is almost certainly a more adequate portrayal of the system of motivation. To the practicing manager, this model means that motivation is not a simple cause and effect matter. It means, too, that managers should carefully assess their reward structures and that through careful planning, managing by objectives, and clear definition of duties and responsibilities by good organization structuring, the effort-performance-reward-satisfaction system can be integrated into an entire system of managing.

EQUITY THEORY

An important factor in motivation is whether individuals perceive the reward structure as being fair. One way of addressing this issue is through **equity theory,** which refers to the individuals' subjective judgments about the equity or fairness of the reward they got in relationship to the inputs (which include many factors such as effort, experience, education and so on) in comparison with others. J. Stacy Adams has received a great deal of credit for the formulation of the equity (or inequity) theory.[10] The essential aspects of the equity theory may be shown as follows:

$$\frac{\text{Outcomes by a person}}{\text{Inputs by a person}} = \frac{\text{outcomes by another person}}{\text{inputs by another person}}$$

There should be a balance of the outcomes/inputs relationship for one person in comparison with another person.

If people feel they are inadequately rewarded, they may be dissatisfied, reduce the quantity or quality of output, or leave the organization.

If people perceive the rewards as equitable, they probably will continue at the same level of output.

If people think that the rewards are greater than what is considered equitable, they may work harder. It is also possible that some may discount the reward.

One of the problems is that people may overestimate their own contributions and the rewards others receive.

Certain inequities may be tolerated for some time by employees.[11] But the prolonged feelings of inequity may result in strong reactions to an apparently minor occurrence. For example, an employee being reprimanded for being a few minutes late may get angry and decide to quit the job, not so much because of the reprimand but because of long-standing feelings that the rewards for this person's contributions are inequitable in comparison with others. In another illustration, a person may be very satisfied with a weekly salary of $500 until he or she finds out that another person doing similar work gets $10 more.

REINFORCEMENT THEORY

Psychologist B. F. Skinner of Harvard developed an interesting—but controversial—technique for motivation. This approach, called **positive reinforcement** or **behavior modification**[12] holds that individuals can be motivated by proper design of their work environment and praise for their performance, and that punishment for poor performance produces negative results.

Skinner and his followers do far more than praise good performance. They analyze the work situation to determine what causes workers to act the way they do, and then they initiate changes to eliminate troublesome areas and obstructions to performance. Specific goals are then set with workers' participation and assistance, prompt and regular feedback of results is made available, and performance improvements are rewarded with recognition and praise. Even when performance does not equal goals, ways are found to help people and praise them for the good things they do. It has also been found highly useful and motivating to give people full information on a company's problems, especially those in which they are involved.

This technique sounds almost too simple to work, and many behavioral scientists and managers are skeptical about its effectiveness. However, a number of prominent companies have found that approach beneficial. Emery Air Freight Corporation, for example, observed that this approach saved the company a substantial amount of money by merely inducing employees to take great pains to be sure that containers were properly filled with small packages before shipment.[13]

Perhaps the strength of the Skinner approach is that it is so closely akin to the requirements of good managing. It emphasizes removal of obstructions to performance, careful planning and organizing, control through feedback, and the expansion of communication.

McCLELLAND'S NEEDS THEORY OF MOTIVATION

David C. McClelland has contributed to the understanding of motivation by identifying three types of basic motivating needs.[14] He classified them as need for power (n/PWR), need for affiliation (n/AFF), and need for achievement (n/ACH). Considerable research has been done on methods of testing people with respect to these three types of needs, and McClelland and his associates have done substantial research, especially on the need for achievement.[15]

All three drives—power, affiliation, and achievement—are of particular relevance to management since all must be recognized to make an organized enterprise work well. Because any organized enterprise and every department of it represent groups of individuals working together to achieve goals, the need for achievement is of paramount importance.

The Need for Power

McClelland and other researchers have found that people with a high need for power have a great concern for exercising influence and control.[16] Such individuals generally are seeking positions of leadership; they are frequently good conversationalists, though often argumentative; they are forceful, outspoken, hardheaded, and demanding; and they enjoy teaching and public speaking.

The Need for Affiliation

People with a high need for affiliation usually derive pleasure from being loved and tend to avoid the pain of being rejected by a social group. As individuals, they are likely to be concerned with maintaining pleasant social relationships, to enjoy a sense of intimacy and understanding, to be ready to console and help others in trouble, and to enjoy friendly interaction with others.

The Need for Achievement[17]

People with a high need for achievement have an intense desire for success and an equally intense fear of failure. They want to be challenged, set moderately difficult (but not impossible) goals for themselves, and take a realistic approach to risk; they are not likely to be gamblers but, rather, prefer to analyze and assess problems, assume personal responsibility for getting a job done, like specific and prompt feedback on how they are doing, tend to be restless, like to work long hours, do not worry unduly about failure if it does occur, and tend to like to run their own shows.

How McClelland's Approach Applies to Managers

In researches made by McClelland and others, entrepreneurs—people who start and develop a business or other enterprise—showed very high need-for-achievement and fairly high need-for-power drives but were quite low in their need for affiliation. Managers generally showed high on achievement and power and low on affiliation, but not so high or low as entrepreneurs.

McClelland found the patterns of achievement motivation clearest in people in small companies, with the president normally having very high achievement motivation. In large companies, interestingly enough, he found chief executives to be only average in achievement motivation and often stronger in drives for power and affiliation. Managers in the upper-middle level of management in such companies rated higher than their presidents in achievement motivation.

Perhaps, as McClelland indicated, these scores are understandable. The chief executive had "arrived," and those below are striving to advance.

The question is often raised as to whether all managers should rate high on achievement motivation. People who do rate high tend to advance faster than those who do not. But because so much of managing requires other characteristics besides achievement drive, every company should probably have many managers who, while possessing fairly strong achievement motivation, also have a high need for affiliation. This latter need is important for working with people and for coordinating the efforts of individuals working in groups.

SPECIAL MOTIVATIONAL TECHNIQUES

After looking at the theories of motivation, we may well ask what they mean to managers. What are some of the major motivational techniques managers can use? While motivation is so complex and individualized that there can be no single best answer, we can identify some of the major motivational techniques.

Money

As we mentioned earlier in the discussion of the carrot and the stick, money can never be overlooked as a motivator. Whether in the form of wages, piecework (getting paid for units produced at a certain quality level) or any other incentive pay, bonuses, stock options, company-paid insurance, or any of the other things that may be given to people for performance, money is important. And, as some writers have pointed out, money is often more than monetary value. It can also mean status or power.

Economists and most managers have tended to place money high on the scale of motivators,[18] while behavioral scientists tend to place it low. Probably neither view is right.[19] But if money is to be the kind of motivator that it can and should be, managers must remember several things.

First, money, as money, is likely to be more important to people who are raising a family, for example, than to people who have "arrived" in the sense that their money needs are not so urgent. Money is an urgent means of achieving a minimum standard of living, although this minimum has a way of getting higher as people become more affluent. For example, an individual who was once satisfied with a small house and a low-priced car may now be able to derive the same satisfaction only from a large and comfortable house and a fairly luxurious automobile. And yet we cannot generalize in even these terms. For some people, money will always be of the utmost importance, while for others, it may never be.

Second, it is probably quite true that in most kinds of businesses and other enterprises, money is used as a means of keeping an organization adequately staffed, and not primarily as a motivator. Various enterprises make wages and salaries competitive within their industry and their geographic area so as to attract and hold people.

Third, money as a motivator tends to be dulled somewhat by the practice of making sure that salaries of various managers in a company are reasonably

**PERSPECTIVE:
THE OTHER SIDE OF THE COIN**

The lure of money and power can lead to inappropriate and illegal actions. Ivan F. Boesky has been accused of insider trading that resulted in huge personal profits—and a $100 million fine. The scandal, one of the worst on Wall Street since the 1920s, has shaken the public confidence with fear that stock trading may be rigged.[20] While money is often used for motivating, it also addresses itself to human greed that dulls the conscience and may result in unethical and illegal behavior.

similar. In other words, we often take great care to be sure that people on comparable levels are given the same, or nearly the same, compensation. This is understandable, since people usually evaluate their compensation in the light of what their equals are receiving.

Fourth, if money is to be an effective motivator, people in various positions, even though at a similar level, must be given salaries and bonuses that reflect their individual performance. Perhaps we are committed to the practice of comparable wages and salaries. But a well-managed company need never be bound to the same practice with respect to bonuses. In fact, it appears that, unless bonuses to managers are based to a major extent on individual performance, an enterprise is not buying much motivation with them. The way to ensure that money has meaning as a reward for accomplishment and as a way of giving people pleasure from accomplishment is to base compensation as much as possible on performance.

It is almost certainly true that money can motivate only when the prospective payment is large relative to a person's income. The trouble with many wage and salary increases, and even bonus payments, is that they are not large enough to motivate the receiver. They may keep the individual from being dissatisfied and from looking for another job, but unless they are large enough to be felt, they are not likely to be a strong motivator.[21]

Participation

One technique that has been given strong support as the result of motivation theory and research is the increased awareness and use of participation. There can be no doubt that only rarely are people not motivated by being consulted on action affecting them—by being "in on the act." There is also doubt that most people in the center of an operation have knowledge both of problems and of solutions to them. As a consequence, the right kind of participation yields both motivation and knowledge valuable for enterprise success.

Participation is also a means of recognition. It appeals to the need for affiliation and acceptance. And, above all, it gives people a sense of accomplishment. But encouraging participation should not mean that managers weaken their positions. Although they encourage participation of subordinates on matters where the latter can help, and although they listen carefully, on matters requiring their decision they must decide themselves. The best subordinates would not have it any other way, and few subordinates can ever have respect for a wishy-washy superior.

Quality of Working Life (QWL)

One of the most interesting approaches to motivation is the *quality of working life* (QWL) program, which is a systems approach to job design and a promising development in the broad area of job enrichment, combined with a grounding in the sociotechnical systems approach to management (see Chapter 2). QWL is not only a very broad approach to job enrichment but also an interdisciplinary field of inquiry and action combining industrial and organization psychology and sociology, industrial engineering, organization theory and development, motivation and leadership theory, and industrial relations. Although QWL rose to prominence only in the 1970s, there are now hundreds of case studies and practical programs, and a number of QWL centers, primarily in the United States, Great Britain, and Scandinavia.[22]

QWL has received enthusiastic support from a number of sources. Managers have regarded it as a promising means of dealing with stagnating productivity, especially in the United States and Europe. Workers and union representatives have also seen it as a means of improving working conditions and productivity and as a means of justifying higher pay. Government agencies have been

PERSPECTIVE:
QWL IN ACTION

In developing a QWL program, certain steps are normally undertaken. Usually, a labor-management steering committee is set up, ordinarily with a QWL specialist or staff, with the charge of coming up with ways of enhancing the dignity, attractiveness, and productivity of jobs through job enrichment and redesign. The participation of workers and their unions (if an operation is unionized) in the effort is thought to be very important, not only because of the exercise of industrial democracy but also because of the great practical advantage that people on a job are best able to identify what would enrich the job for them and make it possible for them to be more productive. This typical QWL technique tends to solve the problem encountered in many job enrichment cases where workers have mistakenly not been asked what would make the job more interesting for them.

Out of the deliberations of this committee, a number of changes may be suggested in the design of jobs and in the entire working environment. The recommendations of the committees may extend to such matters as reorganization of the organization structure, means of improving communication, problems that may never have surfaced before and their solutions, changing work arrangements through technical modifications such as the redesign of an assembly line, better quality control, and other things that might improve organization health and productivity.

attracted to QWL as a means of increasing productivity and reducing inflation and as a way of obtaining industrial democracy and minimizing labor disputes.

It is no wonder that QWL, with such possible important yields, has been spreading fast, especially in our larger companies. Nor is it a surprise that leaders in adopting QWL programs should be such well-managed companies as General Motors, Procter & Gamble, American Aluminum (ALCOA), and AT&T.

JOB ENRICHMENT

Research and analysis of motivation point to the importance of making jobs challenging and meaningful. This applies to the jobs of managers as well as to those of nonmanagers. Job enrichment is related to Herzberg's theory of motivation, where factors such as challenge, achievement recognition, and responsibility are seen as the real motivators. Even though his theory has not gone unchallenged, it has led to a widespread interest in both the United States and overseas in developing ways to enrich job content, particularly for nonmanagerial employees.

Job enrichment should be distinguished from job enlargement (but some authors do not make this distinction). **Job enlargement** attempts to make a job more varied by removing the dullness associated with performing repetitive operations. It means enlarging the scope of the job by adding similar tasks without enhancing responsibility. For example, a production line worker may install not only the bumper on a car but also the front hood. Critics would say that this is simply adding one dull job to another, but it does not increase the worker's responsibility. In **job enrichment,** the attempt is to build into jobs a higher sense of challenge and achievement. A job may be enriched by variety. But it also may be enriched by (1) giving workers more freedom in deciding about such things as work methods, sequence, and pace, or the acceptance or rejection of materials; (2) encouraging participation of subordinates and interaction between workers; (3) giving workers a feeling of personal responsibility for their tasks; (4) taking steps to make sure that workers can see how their tasks contribute to a finished product and the welfare of an enterprise; (5) giving people feedback on their job performance, preferably before their supervisors get it; and (6) involving workers in analysis and change of physical aspects of the work environment, such as layout of office or plant, temperature, lighting, and cleanliness.

The Claims of Job Enrichment

A number of companies have introduced programs of job enrichment. The first company to do so on a fairly large scale was Texas Instruments, and other companies, such as AT&T, Procter & Gamble, and General Foods, have had considerable experience with it. In all these companies, claims have been made that productivity was increased, that absenteeism and turnover were reduced, and that morale improved.

Perhaps the most glowing claims for job enrichment are contained in the report of a study made by the U.S. Department of Health, Education, and Welfare, published in 1973.[23] As the result of an analysis of worker attitudes and the quality of working life, this study concluded that (1) the primary cause of dissatisfaction of workers is the nature of their work—the quality of their working life—and (2) blue-collar workers will work harder if their jobs are enriched and expanded so as to give them greater control over their work and more freedom from their supervisor.

Limitations of Job Enrichment

Even the strongest supporters of job enrichment readily admit that there are limitations in its application.[24] One of these is technology. With specialized machinery and assembly line techniques, it may not be possible to make all jobs very meaningful. Another limitation is cost. General Motors tried six-person and three-person teams in the assembly of motor homes but found that this approach was too difficult, slow, and costly. On the other hand, two Swedish auto manufacturers, Saab and Volvo, have used the team approach and have found costs to be only slightly higher, but they believe that this increase was more than offset by reductions in absenteeism and turnover. Another problem has been the difficulty of enriching any job that requires low levels of skill.

There is also some question as to whether workers really want job enrichment, especially of the kind that changes the basic content of their jobs. Various surveys of worker attitudes, even the attitudes of assembly line workers, have shown that a high percentage of workers are not dissatisfied with their jobs and that few want "more interesting" jobs. What these workers seem to want above all is job security and pay. Moreover, workers are concerned that changing the nature of the task to increase productivity may mean a loss of jobs.

The limitations of job enrichment apply mainly to jobs requiring low skill levels. The jobs of highly skilled workers, professionals, and managers already contain varying degrees of challenge and accomplishment. Perhaps these could be enriched considerably more than they are. But this can probably be done best by modern management techniques such as managing by objectives, utilizing more policy guidance with delegation of authority, introducing more status symbols in the form of titles and office facilities, and tying bonus and other rewards more closely to performance.

Problems with Job Enrichment

On the surface, job enrichment as a response to motivating factors is an attractive idea. But it apparently has not worked as well as anticipated. There do seem to be a number of problems in the way it has been approached.

One of the major problems appears to be the tendency for top managers and personnel specialists to apply their own scale of values of challenge and accomplishment to other people's personalities. Some people are challenged by jobs that would appear dull to many of us. In one company, an employee who had spent his life doing no more than keeping daily records of orders received honestly felt he had one of the most important jobs in the company. In another business, a woman who had had a job-enriched position with a variety of tasks told her supervisor that she was greatly relieved to be freed of such responsibility when she was given a repetitive assembly line job. Similarly, a woman who was found to have considerable leadership ability in her outside activities with the Girl Scouts and Parent-Teacher Association turned down a supervisory position because her present job allowed her to think about the problems and programs she was interested in outside the company.

Another difficulty is that job enrichment is usually imposed on people; they are told about it, rather than being asked whether they would like it and how their jobs could be made more interesting. This appeared to be, at least in part, the problem General Motors encountered in enlarging the jobs of assembly line workers at the Vega plant in Lordstown, where workers interpreted the attempts to make jobs more varied and meaningful as only a scheme of the company to get them to work harder. We can never overlook the importance of consultation, of getting people involved.

Also, there has been little or no support of job enrichment by union leaders. If job enrichment were so important to workers, one would think that it would be translated into union demands, a move that apparently has seldom occurred.

Making Job Enrichment Effective

Several approaches can be used to make job enrichment appeal to higher-level motivations. First, we need a better understanding of what people want. As certain motivation researchers have pointed out, wants vary with people and situations. Research has shown that workers with few skills want such factors as job security, pay, benefits, less restrictive plant rules, and more sympathetic and understanding supervisors. As we move up the ladder in an enterprise, we find that other factors become increasingly important. But little job enrichment research has been done on high-level professionals and managers.

Second, if productivity increases are the main goal of enrichment, the program must show how workers will benefit. For example, in one company with fleets of unsupervised two-person service trucks, a program of giving these employees 25 percent of the cost savings from increased productivity, while still making it clear that the company would profit from their efforts, resulted in a startling rise in output and a much greater interest in these jobs.

Third, people like to be involved, to be consulted, and to be given an opportunity to offer suggestions. They like to be considered as people. In one aerospace missile plant, increased morale and productivity, as well as greatly reduced turnover and absenteeism, resulted from the simple technique of having all employees' names on placards at their work stations and of having each program group—from parts production and assembly to inspection—work in an area in which machines and equipment were painted a different color.

Fourth, people like to feel that their managers are truly concerned with their welfare. Workers like to know what they are doing and why. They like feedback on their performance. They like to be appreciated and recognized for their work.

A SYSTEMS AND CONTINGENCY APPROACH TO MOTIVATION

The foregoing analysis of theory, research, and application demonstrates that we must consider motivation from a systems and contingency point of view. Given the complexity of motivating people with varying personalities and in different situations, risks of failure exist when any single motivator, or group of motivators, is applied without taking into account these variables. Human behavior is not a simple matter but must be looked upon as a system of variables and interactions of which certain motivating factors are an important element.

Dependence of Motivation on Organizational Climate

Motivating factors definitely do not exist in a vacuum. Even individual desires and drives are conditioned by physiological needs or by needs arising from a person's background. But what people are willing to strive for is also affected by the organizational climate in which they operate. At times a climate may curb motivations; at other times it may arouse them.

Motivation, Leadership, and Managership

The interaction of motivation and organizational climate not only underscores the systems aspects of motivation but also emphasizes how motivation both depends on and influences leadership styles and management practice. Both leaders and managers (who, if effective, will almost certainly be leaders) must respond to the motivations of individuals if they are to design an environment in which people will perform willingly.[25] Likewise, they can design a climate that will arouse or reduce motivation. We will discuss styles of leadership in Chapter 18.

As for the ways and means by which managers design an environment for performance, they are really the subject of this entire book. In short, managers do this when they see that verifiable goals are set, strategies are developed and communicated, and plans to achieve objectives are made. They do it also in designing a system of organizational roles in which people can be effective (it should be pointed out in this connection that "organization structure" is not used here in the restrictive bureaucratic sense). Managers do it also when they make sure that the structure is well staffed. Their styles of leadership and their ability to solve communication problems are also central to managing. And managers do much to create an effective environment when they make sure that control tools, information, and approaches furnish people with the feedback knowledge they must have for effective motivation.

FOR DISCUSSION

1. What is motivation? How does effective managing take advantage of, and contribute to, motivation?

2. Why is the need-want-satisfaction chain too simplified an explanation of motivation?

3. Why has the Maslow theory of needs been criticized? To what extent, if any, is it valid?

4. Compare and contrast the Maslow and Herzberg theories of motivation. On what grounds has the Herzberg theory been criticized? Why would you suspect that Herzberg's approach has been so popular with practicing managers?

5. Explain Vroom's expectancy theory of motivation. How is it different from the Porter and Lawler approach? Which appeals to you as being more accurate? Which is more useful in practice?

6. Explain McClelland's theory of motivation. How does it fit into a systems approach? What does the impact of organizational climate show?

7. "You cannot motivate managers. They are self-propelled. You just get out of their way if you really want performance." Comment.

8. To what extent, and how, is money an effective motivator?

9. What motivates you in striving toward excellence in your work at school? Are these motivating forces shown in any of the models discussed in this chapter?

EXERCISES/ACTION STEPS

1. The instructor may take a survey in the class and ask the students to respond to two questions: (1) "Can you describe in detail when you felt exceptionally good about your job?" and (2) "Can you describe in detail when you felt exceptionally bad about your job?" Students should write the answers on a sheet of paper. Then each individual should be encouraged to share his or her good and bad work experiences with the class. The instructor can classify these responses according to Herzberg's two-factor theory and point out the weakness in this research design.

2. Collect information on an organization you know and identify the reasons why people contribute to the goals of the enterprise.

CASES

CASE 17-1
MOTIVATION AT THE BRADLEY CLOTHING COMPANY

Alice Johnson, personnel manager of the Bradley Clothing Company (manufacturer of women's clothing and accessories), had just returned from a management development seminar where considerable attention had been given to motivation and especially the theories of Maslow and Herzberg. Impressed by Maslow's clear hierarchy of needs and Herzberg's motivator-hygiene theory, she felt that the company could immediately make practical use of them. She liked the simplicity of these two approaches to motivation, and, feeling that the company's wage and salary levels were among the best in the industry, she was convinced that the company should concentrate on Herzberg's motivators.

As a result, she was able to persuade the executive committee of the company to embark on various programs emphasizing recognition, advancement, greater personal responsibility, achievement, and making work more challenging.

After the programs had been in operation for a number of months, she was puzzled to find that the results were not what she had expected.

Clothing designers did not seem to react enthusiastically to the programs. Some felt they already had a challenging job, that their sense of achievement was fulfilled by exceeding their sales quotas, that their recognition was in their commission checks, and that all these new programs were a waste of time for them. Cutters, seamsters, pressers, and packagers had mixed feelings. Some responded favorably to the recognition they got as a result of the new programs, but others regarded them as a managerial scheme to get them to work harder without any increase in pay. Their union business agent, agreeing with the latter group, openly criticized the programs.

With reactions so variable, Ms. Johnson came under considerable criticism by the company's top officers, who believed they had been taken in by an overzealous personnel manager. On discussing the problem with the company's management consultant, Ms. Johnson was advised that she had taken too simplistic a view of human motivations.

1. Why do you believe this program caused so much difficulty?

2. Why did the management consultant say that Ms. Johnson had taken too simplistic a view of human motivation?

3. If you were Ms. Johnson, what would you have done?

CASE 17-2
CONSOLIDATED MOTORS CORPORATION

One of the problems that had long concerned the top managers of the Consolidated Motors Corporation was the lack of workers' interest in doing their jobs on both the components and the final car assembly lines, with the result that quality had to be ensured by the inspection department. For those cars that could not meet final inspection, the company found its only answer to be the setting up of groups of highly skilled mechanics in a special shop where quality problems were fixed at the end of the line. Not only was this costly but it also caused considerable concern since most of the problems were the result of lack of care in assembling components and of the design of the automobile itself.

At the urging of the company president, the division general manager called a meeting of his key department heads to see what could be done about the problem.

Bill Burroughs, production manager, claimed that some of the problems were a matter of engineering. He held that if only engineering would design components and the automobile carefully enough, many quality problems would disappear.

He also blamed the personnel department for not selecting workers more carefully and for not getting the union business agent involved in the problem. He pointed out especially that there was a high turnover, more than 5 percent per month among assembly workers, and that absenteeism on Mondays often reached 20 percent. His position was that no production department could operate effectively with this kind of labor force.

Charles Wilson, chief engineer, held that the components and cars were engineered well enough and that if engineering tolerances were any more strict, the fitting of parts would be so difficult and time-consuming that the company's automobiles would be too costly to make.

Alice Turner, the personnel manager, accounted for the personnel problems in several ways. First, she pointed out that her department had little or no control over whom the company hired or kept, in view of the strong labor union the company had. Second, she observed that assembly work was dull, deadening drudgery and that the company should not expect people to have much interest in this work beyond their paychecks.

But Ms. Turner did say she was convinced that the company could develop more worker interest and consequently higher-quality work and less absenteeism and turnover if assembly jobs could be enlarged. When asked what she would suggest, Ms. Turner recommended that the company do two things. One was to have workers handle several operations on the assembly line and work as a team, instead of doing only one simple task. A second was to rotate workers each week from one location on the line to a completely different one in order to give them new and more challenging work.

These suggestions were adopted and put into effect. To everyone's surprise, workers expressed great dissatisfaction with the new program. After a week, the assembly lines were closed down by a strike, the workers claiming that the new program was only a management scheme to get them to do more work than they had done before and to train them to replace other workers without any increase in pay.

The division manager and the personnel manager were surprised. When asked by the division manager what had happened, Ms. Turner could only say: "This is a mystery to me. We make their jobs more interesting, and they strike!"

1. What do you believe went wrong with the program?

2. What would you have done if you had been the personnel manager? Would you have used this program, a different one, or none at all? Why?

REFERENCES

1. Most of the recommendations are based on *The George Odiorne Letter* (Nov. 8, 1985).

2. Abraham Maslow, *Motivation and Personality* (New York: Harper & Row, 1954).

3. A variation of Maslow's hierarchy of needs theory of motivation has been suggested by Clayton P. Alderfer, which he refers to as ERG (existence, relatedness, and growth) theory of needs. See his *Existence, Relatedness, and Growth: Human Needs in Organizational Settings* (New York: The Free Press, 1972).

4. Edward Lawler III and J. Lloyd Suttle, "A Causal Correlation Test of the Need-Hierarchy Concept," *Organizational Behavior and Human Performance* (April 1972), pp. 265–287.

5. Douglas T. Hall and Khalil Nougaim, "An Examination of Maslow's Hierarchy in an Organization Setting," *Organizational Behavior and Human Performance* (February 1968), pp. 12–35. For an additional evaluation of the need-hierarchy theory see John B. Miner, *Theories of Organizational Behavior* (Hinsdale, Ill.: The Dryden Press, 1980), chap. 2.

6. Frederick Herzberg, Bernard Mausner, Robert A. Peterson, and D. Capwell, *Job Attitudes: Review of Research and Opinion* (Pittsburgh: Psychological Services of Pittsburgh, 1957); Frederick Herzberg, Bernard Mausner, and Barbara B. Snyderman, *The Motivation to Work* (New York: John Wiley & Sons, 1959).

7. See, for example, H. Randolph Bobbitt and O. Behling, "Defense Mechanism as an Alternate Explanation of Herzberg's Motivator-Hygiene Results," *Journal of Applied Psychology* (January 1972), pp. 24–27; D. A. Ondrack, "Defense Mechanism and the Herzberg Theory: An Alternate Test, *Academy of Management Journal* (March 1974), pp. 79–89; Edwin A. Locke and Roman J. Whiting, "Sources of Satisfaction and Dissatisfaction among Solid Waste Management Employees," *Journal of Applied Psychology* (April 1974), pp. 145–156.

8. Victor H. Vroom, *Work and Motivation* (New York: John Wiley & Sons, 1964). See also David A. Nadler and Edward E. Lawler III, "Motivation: A Diagnostic Approach," in J. Richard Hackman, Edward E. Lawler III, and Lyman W. Porter (eds.), *Perspectives on*

Behavior in Organizations, 2d ed. (New York: McGraw-Hill Book Company, 1983), pp. 67–87.

9. Lyman W. Porter and Edward E. Lawler III, *Managerial Attitudes and Performance* (Homewood, Ill,: Richard D. Irwin, 1968); Cynthia M. Pavett, "Evaluation of the Impact of Feedback on Performance and Motivation," *Human Relations* (July 1983), pp. 641–654.

10. J. Stacy Adams, "Toward an Understanding of Inequity," *Journal of Abnormal and Social Psychology,* vol. 67 (1963), p. 422–436; J. Stacy Adams, "Inequity in Social Exchange," in L. Berkowitz (ed.), *Advances in Experimental Social Psychology* (New York: Academic Press, 1965), pp. 267–299.

11. Richard A. Cosier and Dan R. Dalton, "Equity Theory and Time: A Reformulation," *Academy of Management Review* (April 1983), pp. 311–319. See also Richard C. Huseman, John Hatfield, and Edward W. Miles, "A New Perspective on Equity Theory: The Equity Sensitivity Construct," *Academy of Management Review* (April 1987), pp. 222–234.

12. Fred Luthans and Robert Kreitner, *Organizational Behavior Modification and Beyond: An Operant and Social Learning Approach* (Glenview, Ill.: Scott, Foresman and Company, 1984).

13. For an extensive discussion of the benefits of behavior modification see W. Clay Hamner and Ellen P. Hamner, "Behavior Modification on the Bottom Line," in J. Richard Hackman et al., *Perspectives on Behavior* (1983), pp. 310–324.

14. David C. McClelland, *The Achievement Motive* (New York: Appleton-Century-Crofts, 1953), *Studies in Motivation* (New York: Appleton-Century-Crofts, 1955), and *The Achieving Society* (Princeton, N.J.: D. Van Nostrand Company, 1961). See also his "Achievement Motivation Can Be Developed," *Harvard Business Review* (January–February 1965), pp. 6–24, 178, and (with David G. Winter) *Motivating Economic Achievement* (New York: The Free Press, 1969).

15. For a thorough evaluation of the theory see John B. Miner, *Theories of Organizational Behavior* (1980), chap. 3.

16. See, for example, David C. McClelland and David H. Burnham, "Power Is the Great Motivator," *Harvard Business Review* (March–April 1976), pp. 100–110.

17. David C. McClelland, "That Urge to Achieve," in Max D. Richards (ed.), *Readings in Management,* 7th ed. (Cincinnati: South-Western Publishing Co., 1986), pp. 367–375.

18. See, for example, the discussion of pay in Chapter 16. See also Aaron Bernstein and Michael A. Pollock, "Executive Pay: Who Made the Most," *Business Week* (May 5, 1985), pp. 78–103.

19. George S. Odiorne, "When Money Has Lost Its Motivational Power, What Else Can You Use to Motivate Your People?" *The George Odiorne Letter* (Mar. 21, 1986), pp. 1–3.

20. William B. Glaberson, Jeffrey M. Laderman, Christopher Power, and Vicky Cahan, "Who'll Be the Next to Fall?" *Business Week* (Dec. 1, 1986), pp. 28–30; Chris Welles and Gary Weiss "A Man Who Made a Career of Tempting Fate," *Business Week* (Dec. 1, 1986), pp. 34–35.

21. For the discussion of a compensation plan see Jay R. Schuster, "Compensation Plan Design," *Management Review* (May 1985), pp. 21–25. Also, more recently, employee ownership has become more common. See J. C. Louis, "Employee Ownership: The Rising Tide," *Management Review* (March 1985), pp. 40–43.

22. For a pioneering work in this field see Louis E. Davis and Albert B. Cherns, *Quality of Working Life* (New York: The Free Press, 1975). Among the more prominent Quality of Working Life Centers are the Tavistock Institute in Great Britain, under Eric L. Trist; the Center at the University of California, Los Angeles, under Louis E. Davis; and The Institute for Social Research in Industry in Trondheim, Norway, under M. Elder.

23. DHEW, *Work in America* (Washington: Government Printing Office, 1973). See also

Antone Alber, "Job Enrichment for Profit," *Human Resource Management* (Spring 1979), pp. 15–25.

24. The appropriateness of job enrichment depends on the situation. The need for balancing internal and external factors has been pointed out by Randall B. Dunham, Jon L. Pierce, and John W. Newstrom, "Job Context and Job Content: A Conceptual Perspective," *Journal of Management* (Fall–Winter 1983), pp. 187–202.

25. Zaleznik makes a distinction between managers and leaders. But the difference is primarily in the way he describes managers (in a rather negative way), which certainly is not our view of an effective manager. See Abraham Zaleznik, "Managers and Leaders: Are They Different?" *Harvard Business Review* (May–June 1986), p. 48.

FOR FURTHER INFORMATION

Bylinsky, G. "America's Best-Managed Factories," *Fortune* (Mar. 28, 1984), pp. 16–24.

Guest, Robert H. "Quality of Work Life—Learning from Tarrytown," *Harvard Business Review* (July–August 1979), pp. 76–87.

Haynes, Robert S., Randall C. Pine, and H. Gordon Fitch. "Reducing Accident Rates With Organizational Behavior Modification," *Academy of Management Journal* (June 1982), pp. 407–416.

Hofstede, Geert. "The Cultural Relativity of the Quality of Life Concept," *Academy of Management Review* (July 1984) pp. 389–398.

Klein, Janice A. "Why Supervisors Resist Employee Involvement," *Harvard Business Review* (September–October 1984), pp. 87–95.

Lawler, Edward E. "Merit Pay: Fact or Fiction?" *Management Review* (April 1981), pp. 50–53.

Miner, John B. *Theories of Organizational Behavior* (Hinsdale, Ill.: The Dryden Press, 1980).

Mitchell, Terence R. "Motivation: New Directions for Theory, Research, and Practice," *Academy of Management Review* (January 1982), pp. 80–88.

Richards, Max D. *Readings in Management,* 7th ed. (Cincinnati: South-Western Publishing Co., 1986), chap. 10.

Rice, Robert W., Dean B. McFarlin, Raymond G. Hunt, and Janet P. Near. "Organizational Work and the Perceived Quality of Life: Toward a Conceptual Model," *Academy of Management Review* (April 1985), pp. 296–310.

Spicer, Michael W. "A Public Choice Approach to Motivating People in Bureaucratic Organizations," *Academy of Management Review* (July 1985), pp. 518–526.

Stanton, Erwin S. "A Critical Reevaluation of Motivation, Management and Productivity," in James H. Donnelly, Jr., James L. Gibson, and John M. Ivancevich (eds.), *Perspectives on Management,* 5th ed. (Plano, Tex.: Business Publications, 1984), pp. 188–196.

Leadership

CHAPTER OBJECTIVES

After reading this chapter, you should be able to:

1. Define leadership and identify its ingredients.

2. Describe the trait approaches to leadership and recognize their limitations.

3. Discuss various leadership styles based on the use of authority.

4. Explain Likert's four systems of management.

5. Identify the two dimensions of Blake and Mouton's managerial grid and the resulting extreme leadership styles.

6. Recognize that leadership could be seen as a continuum.

7. Explain the contingency approach to leadership.

8. Describe the path-goal approach to leadership effectiveness.

Although some people treat the terms "managership" and "leadership" as synonyms, we believe they should be distinguished. As a matter of fact, there can be leaders of completely unorganized groups, but there can be managers, as conceived here, only where organized structures create roles. There are also important analytical advantages in separating leadership from managership. It permits leadership to be singled out for study without the encumbrance of qualifications relating to the more general issue of managership.

Leadership is an important aspect of managing. As we will show in this chapter, the ability to lead effectively is one of the keys to being an effective manager; also, undertaking the other essentials of managing—doing the entire managerial job—has an important bearing on ensuring that a manager will be an effective leader. Managers must exercise all the functions of their role in order to combine human and material resources to achieve objectives. The key to doing this is the existence of a clear role and a degree of discretion or authority to support managers' actions.

The essence of leadership is followership.[1] In other words, it is the willingness of people to follow that makes a person a leader. Moreover, people tend to follow those whom they see as providing a means of achieving their own desires, wants, and needs.

Leadership and motivation are closely interconnected. By understanding motivation, we can appreciate better what people want and why they act as they do. Also, as noted in the previous chapter, leaders may not only respond to subordinates' motivations but also arouse or dampen them by means of the organizational climate they develop. Both these factors are as important to leadership as they are to managership.

DEFINING LEADERSHIP

Leadership has different meanings to various authors.[2] We define **leadership** as influence, the art or process of influencing people so that they will strive willingly and enthusiastically toward the achievement of group goals. Ideally, people should be encouraged to develop not only willingness to work but also

PERSPECTIVE:
LEADER- FOLLOWERSHIP AT MCDONALD'S

An example of leadership-followership can be found in the story of McDonald's hamburger franchise.[3] Although Ray Kroc, the founder, has passed away, his philosophy has become a legend that continues. Chairman Fred Turner stays with hamburgers and fries even though other opportunities for company growth are available. He also continues to use Kroc's motto, expressed in the acronym QSCV (quality, service, cleanliness, and value). Leadership requires followership, and Turner has followed Kroc's footsteps since he joined the company at age 23.

> ### PERSPECTIVE:
> ### LEADERSHIP AT SOUTHWEST AIRLINES
>
> Let us consider the leadership style of Herbert Kelleher, the chairman of Southwest Airlines.[4] He attempts to create a family feeling among his employees by remembering their names and personally sending out birthday cards. In an attempt to stay competitive in the deregulated airline industry, he asked for, and received, considerable concessions from employees and their union. His hands-on leadership style won him the respect and followership of his employees. The austerity measures apply equally to management and employees. His office, for example, is in a barrack-style building. Leading by example those who follow him, he seems concerned about both the tasks to be done and people who work for him.

willingness to work with zeal and confidence. Zeal is ardor, earnestness, and intensity in the execution of work; confidence reflects experience and technical ability. Leaders act to help a group attain objectives through the maximum application of its capabilities. They do not stand behind a group to push and prod; they place themselves before the group as they facilitate progress and inspire the group to accomplish organizational goals. A good example is an orchestra leader, whose function is to produce coordinated sound and correct tempo through the integrated effort of the musicians. Depending upon the quality of the director's leadership, the orchestra will respond.

INGREDIENTS OF LEADERSHIP

Every group of people that performs near its total capacity has some person as its head who is skilled in the art of leadership. This skill seems to be a compound of at least four major ingredients: (1) the ability to use power effectively and in a responsible manner, (2) the ability to comprehend that human beings have differing motivation forces at different times and in different situations, (3) the ability to inspire, and (4) the ability to act in a manner that will develop a climate conducive to responding to and arousing motivations.

The first ingredient of leadership is power. The nature of power and the differences between power and authority were discussed in Chapter 9.

The second ingredient of leadership is a fundamental understanding of people. As in all practices, it is one thing to know motivation theory, kinds of motivating forces, and the nature of a system of motivation, and another thing to be able to apply this knowledge to people and situations. A manager or any other leader who at least knows the present state of motivation theory and who understands the elements of motivation is more aware of the nature and strength of human needs and is more able to define and design ways of satisfying them and to administer so as to get the desired responses.

The third ingredient of leadership seems to be a rare ability to inspire followers to apply their full capabilities to a project. While the use of motivators seems to center on subordinates and their needs, inspiration also comes from group heads. They may have qualities of charm and appeal that give rise to loyalty, devotion, and a strong desire on the part of followers to promote what leaders want. This is not a matter of need-satisfaction; it is, rather, a matter of people giving unselfish support to a chosen champion. The best examples of inspirational leadership come from hopeless and frightening situations: an unprepared nation on the eve of battle, a prison camp with exceptional morale, or a defeated leader undeserted by faithful followers. Some may argue that such devotion is not entirely unselfish, that it is in the interests of those who face catastrophe to follow a person they trust. But few would deny the value of personal appeal in either case.

A fourth ingredient of leadership has to do with the style of the leader and the climate he or she develops. We have seen in Chapter 17 how much the strength of motivation depends on expectancies, perceived rewards, the amount of effort believed to be required, the task to be done, and other factors which are part of an environment. We have seen also how an organizational climate influences motivation. Awareness of these factors has led to considerable research on, and the development of various theories of, leadership behavior. The views of those who have long approached leadership as a psychological study of interpersonal relationships have tended to converge with ours. As will be recalled, we see the primary tasks of managers as the design and maintenance of an environment for performance.

Almost every role in organized enterprise is made more satisfying to participants and more productive for the enterprise by those who can help others fulfill their desire for such things as money, status, power, or pride of accomplishment. The fundamental principle of leadership is this: _Since people tend to follow those who, in their view, offer them a means of satisfying their own personal goals, the more managers understand what motivates their subordinates and how these motivations operate, and the more they reflect this understanding in carrying out their managerial actions, the more effective they are likely to be as leaders._

Because of the importance of leadership to all kinds of group action, there is a considerable volume of theory and research concerning it.[5] It is difficult to summarize such a large body of research in a form relevant to day-to-day management. However, in the succeeding pages we shall identify several major types of leadership theory and research and outline some basic kinds of leadership styles.

TRAIT APPROACHES TO LEADERSHIP

Prior to 1949, studies of leadership were based largely on an attempt to identify the traits that leaders possess.[6] Starting with the "great man" theory that leaders are born and not made, a belief dating back to the ancient Greeks and Romans, researchers have tried to identify the physical, mental, and personality traits of various leaders. The "great man" theory lost much of its acceptability with the rise of the behaviorist school of psychology, which emphasizes that people are not born with traits other than inherited physical characteristics and perhaps tendencies toward good health.

Various studies of traits have been made.[7] Ralph M. Stogdill found that various researchers identified five physical traits related to leadership ability (such as energy, appearance, and height), four intelligence and ability traits, sixteen personality traits (such as adaptability, aggressiveness, enthusiasm, and self-confidence), six task-related characteristics (such as achievement drive, persistence, and initiative), and nine social characteristics (such as cooperativeness, interpersonal skills, and administrative ability).[8]

Edwin Ghiselli noted significant correlations between leadership effectiveness and traits of intelligence, supervisory ability, initiative, self-assurance, and individuality in ways of doing work.[9] At the same time, extremely high or low intelligence reduces the leader's effectiveness.[10] In other words, the intelligence level of the leader should not be too different from that of the subordinates. In general, however, the study of leaders' traits has not been a very fruitful approach to explaining leadership. Not all leaders possess all the traits, and many nonleaders may possess most or all of them. Also, the trait approach gives no guidance as to *how much* of any trait a person should have. Furthermore, the dozens of studies that have been made do not agree as to what traits are leadership traits or what their relationships are to actual instances of leadership. Most of these so-called traits are really patterns of behavior.

LEADERSHIP BEHAVIOR AND STYLES

There are several theories on leadership behavior and style. In this section we will focus on (1) leadership based on the use of authority, (2) Likert's four systems of managing, (3) the managerial grid, and (4) leadership involving a variety of styles, ranging from a maximum to a minimum use of power and influence.

Styles Based on Use of Authority

Some earlier explanations of leadership styles classified them on the basis of how leaders use their authority. Leaders were seen as applying three basic styles. The **autocratic** leader was defined as one who commands and expects compliance, who is dogmatic and positive, and who leads by the ability to withhold or give rewards and punishment. The **democratic,** or **participative,** leader consults with subordinates on proposed actions and decisions and encourages participation from them. This type of leader was seen as ranging from the person who does not take action without subordinates' concurrence to the one who makes decisions but consults with subordinates before doing so.

The third type of leader uses his or her power very little, if at all, giving subordinates a high degree of independence, or **free rein,** in their operations. Such leaders depend largely on subordinates to set their own goals and the means of achieving them, and they see their role as one of aiding the operations of followers by furnishing them information and acting primarily as a contact

FIGURE 18-1

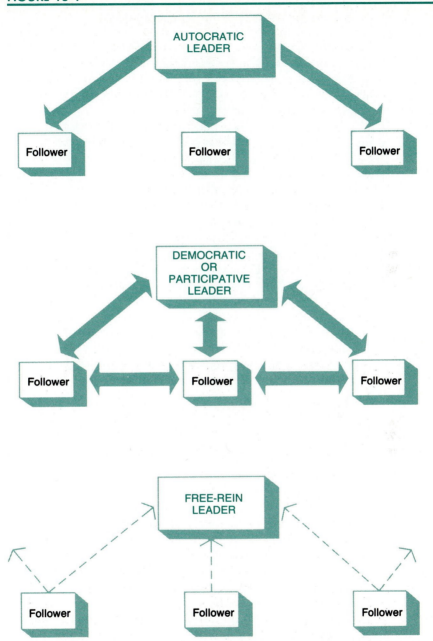

THE FLOW OF INFLUENCE WITH THREE LEADERSHIP STYLES.

with the group's external environment. Figure 18-1 illustrates the flow of influence in the three leadership situations.

There are variations within this simple classification of leadership styles.

PERSPECTIVE:
MANAGEMENT BY WALKING AROUND (MBWA)

Leadership demands information about what is really going on in the organization. Managers who never leave the office, and who rely on formal communication channels, may receive only the information that places subordinates in a favorable light. To overcome the isolation, managers need to supplement the formal with the informal communication.

In their search for excellent companies, Peters and Waterman noted that managers at United Airlines practiced what has been labeled as "Management by Walking Around."[11] A similar practice is called "Management by Wandering Around" at Hewlett Packard. The aim is to improve informal communication channels by walking through the plant.

However, a survey of CEOs of *Fortune 500* enterprises showed that lower-level employees get only little time from CEOs.[12] Prof. Henry Mintzberg, who previously studied the activities of executives, interpreted the findings as showing that management by walking around is not very prevalent in these large companies. Managers spend a lot of time with those who are at similar organizational levels.

Some autocratic leaders are seen as "benevolent autocrats." Although they listen considerately to their followers' opinions before making a decision, the decision is their own. They may be willing to hear and consider subordinates' ideas and concerns, but when a decision is to be made, they may be more autocratic than benevolent.

A variation of the participative leader is the person who is supportive. Leaders in this category may look upon their task as not only consulting with followers and carefully considering their opinions but also doing all they can to support subordinates in accomplishing their duties.

The use of any style will depend on the situation. A manager may be highly autocratic in an emergency; one can hardly imagine a fire chief holding a long meeting with the crew to consider the best way of fighting a fire. Managers may also be autocratic when they alone have the answers to certain questions.

A leader may gain considerable knowledge and a better commitment on the part of persons involved by consulting with subordinates. We saw that this was true in developing verifiable objectives under systems of managing by objectives. Furthermore, a manager dealing with a group of research scientists may give them free rein in developing their inquiries and experiments. But the same manager might be quite autocratic in enforcing a rule concerning protective covering to be worn when handling certain potentially dangerous chemicals.

Likert's Four Systems of Management

Prof. Rensis Likert and his associates at the University of Michigan have studied the patterns and styles of leaders and managers for three decades.[13] In the course of these researches, Likert has developed certain ideas and approaches

rated.[15] Likert and his associates realize the need for clarity in role definitions, but at the same time they suggest, for example, matrix departmentation, which usually increases role conflict and uncertainty. Since System 4 approaches are often introduced when companies are profitable, the results attributed to the survey feedback method may actually be due to general prosperity of the firm. It appears, then, that those evaluating System 4 theories should take careful account of the surrounding circumstances. For the practicing manager this means that the benefits attributed to System 4 theory must be viewed with some caution.

The Managerial Grid

One of the widely known approaches to defining leadership styles is the *managerial grid,* developed some years ago by Robert Blake and Jane Mouton.[16] Building on previous research that showed the importance of a manager's having concern both for production and for people, Blake and Mouton devised a clever device to dramatize this concern. This grid, shown in Figure 18-3, has been used throughout the world as a means of managerial training and of identifying various combinations of leadership styles.

The grid dimensions. The grid has two dimensions: concern for people and concern for production. As Blake and Mouton have emphasized, their use of the phrase "concern for" is meant to convey "how" managers are concerned about production or "how" they are concerned about people, and not such things as "how much" production they are concerned about getting out of a group.

"Concern for production" includes the attitudes of a supervisor toward a wide variety of things, such as the quality of policy decisions, procedures and processes, creativeness of research, quality of staff services, work efficiency, and volume of output. "Concern for people" is likewise interpreted in a broad way. It includes such elements as degree of personal commitment toward goal achievement, maintenance of the self-esteem of workers, placement of responsibility on the basis of trust rather than obedience, provision of good working conditions, and maintenance of satisfying interpersonal relations.

The four extreme styles. Blake and Mouton recognize four extremes of style. Under the **1.1** style (referred to as "impoverished management"), managers concern themselves very little with either people or production and have minimum involvement in their jobs; to all intents and purposes, they have abandoned their jobs and only mark time or act as messengers communicating information from superiors to subordinates. At the other extreme are the **9.9** managers, who display in their actions the highest possible dedication both to people and to production. They are the real "team managers" who are able to mesh the production needs of the enterprise with the needs of individuals.

Another style is **1.9** management (called "country club management" by some), in which managers have little or no concern for production but are concerned only for people. They promote an environment where everyone is relaxed, friendly, and happy and no one is concerned about putting forth

FIGURE 18-3

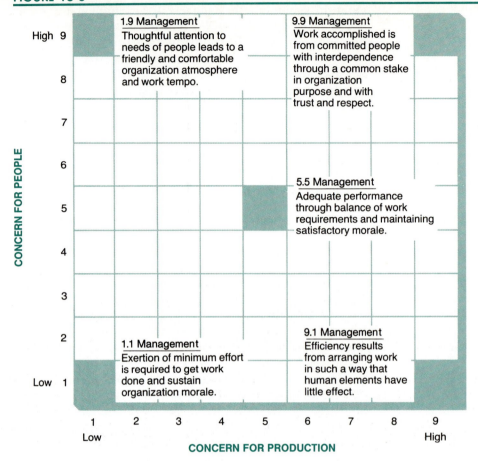

THE MANAGERIAL GRID.

Adapted from R. R. Blake and J. S. Mouton, *The Managerial Grid* (Houston, Texas: Gulf Publishing Company, 1964), p. 10.

coordinated effort to accomplish enterprise goals. At another extreme are the **9.1** managers (sometimes referred to as "autocratic task managers"), who are concerned only with developing an efficient operation, who have little or no concern for people, and who are quite autocratic in their style of leadership.

Using these four extremes as points of reference, every managerial technique, approach, or style can be placed somewhere on the grid. Clearly, **5.5** managers have medium concern for production and for people. They obtain adequate, but not outstanding, morale and production. They do not set goals too high, and they are likely to have a rather benevolently autocratic attitude toward people.

The managerial grid is a useful device for identifying and classifying managerial styles. But it does not tell us *why* a manager falls in one part or another of the grid. To find this out, we have to look at underlying causes, such as the personality of the leader or those of the followers, the ability and training of managers, the enterprise environment, and other situational factors that influence how both leaders and followers act.

Leadership as a Continuum

The adaptation of leadership styles to different contingencies have been well characterized by Robert Tannenbaum and Warren H. Schmidt, developers of the concept of a leadership continuum.[17] As is shown in Figure 18-4, they see leadership as involving a variety of styles, ranging from one that is highly boss-centered to one that is highly subordinated-centered. These vary with the degree of freedom a leader or manager grants to subordinates. Thus, instead of suggesting a choice between the two styles of leadership—authoritarian or democratic—this approach offers a range of style, with no suggestion that one is always right and another is always wrong.

PERSPECTIVE:
LEADERSHIP AT ITALTEL

When Marisa Bellisario became director and CEO of ITALTEL in 1981, a state-owned telecommunication equipment manufacturer in Italy, the company was in trouble: high losses, large debts, insufficient research and development, and an overstaffed, unionized organization.[19] Ms. Bellisario took some major steps to turn the company around and to improve productivity. Here are some examples of the new direction:

- Restructuring the organization into business units

- Reducing employees by more than one-third between 1980 and 1985, which was accomplished through open communication and cooperation with the union

- Leading the company into electronics, which required retraining of employees

- Developing a program to upgrade low-skilled women in the work force

- Pushing for intra-European cooperation with other companies in France, England, and West Germany

- Improving efficiency through innovation in products and manufacturing processes

   Leadership such as this has to be analyzed in terms of the characteristics of the leader (technical, human, conceptual, and design skills), the good relations with the followers, especially the unionized work force, and the situation which in the early 1980s demanded a strong leader to deal with the crisis.

FIGURE 18-4

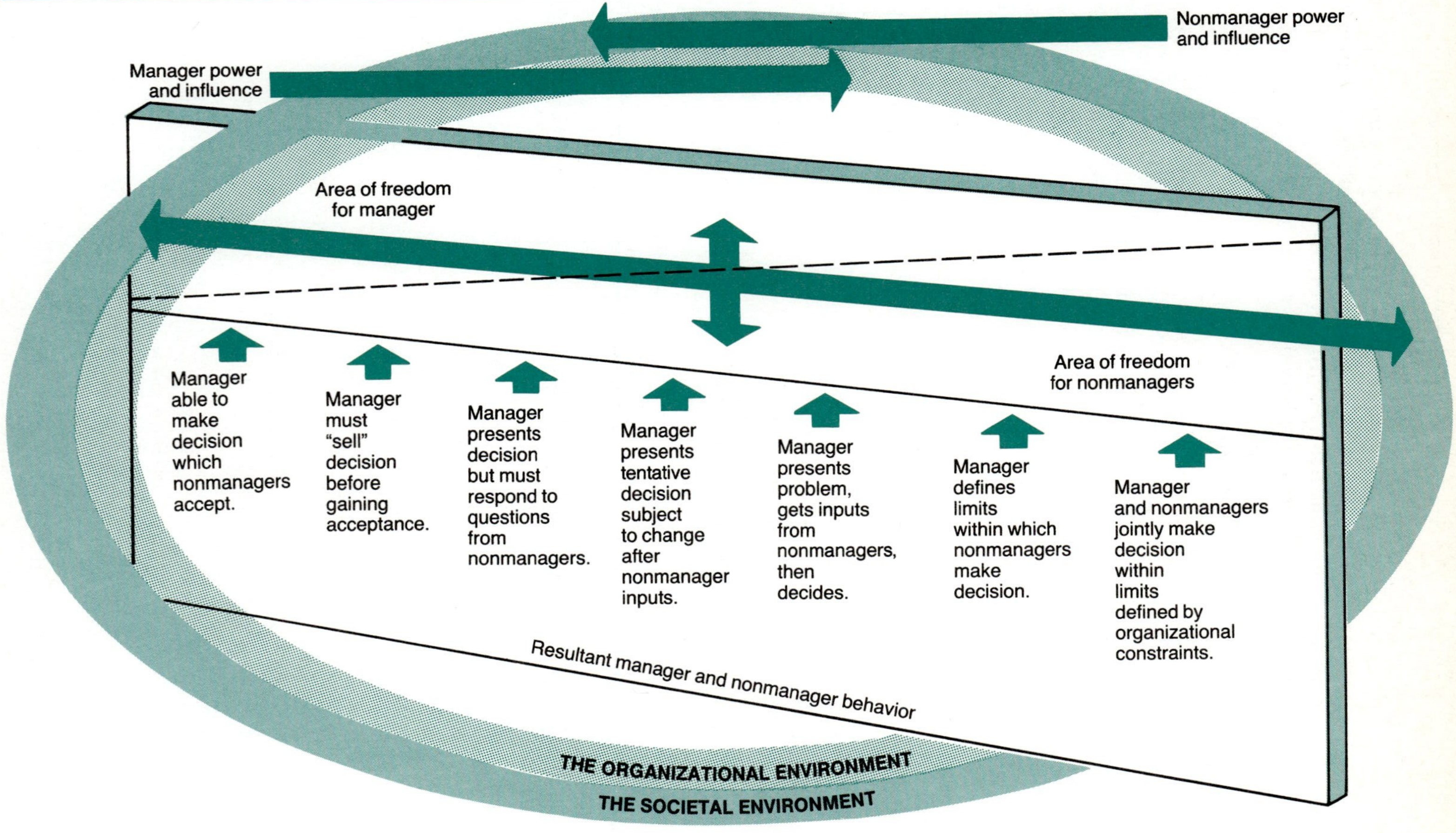

CONTINUUM OF MANAGER-NONMANAGER BEHAVIOR.

Used with permission from R. Tannenbaum and W. H. Schmidt, "Retrospective Commentary" on "How to Choose a Leadership Pattern," *Harvard Business Review,* vol. 51, no. 3 (May–June 1973), p. 167.

The continuum theory recognizes that what style of leadership is appropriate depends on the leader, the followers, and the situation. Tannenbaum and Schmidt saw the most important elements that may influence a manager's style along a continuum as (1) the forces operating in the manager's personality, including his or her value system, confidence in subordinates, inclination toward leadership styles, and feelings of security in uncertain situations; (2) the forces in subordinates (such as their willingness to assume responsibility, their knowledge and experience, their tolerance for ambiguity, and so on) that will affect the manager's behavior; and (3) the forces in the situation, such as organization values and traditions, how effectively subordinates work as a unit, the nature of a problem and whether authority to handle it can be safely delegated, and the pressure of time.

In reviewing in 1973 their continuum model, which was first formulated in 1958, Tannenbaum and Schmidt placed circles around their model, as shown in Figure 18-4, to represent the influences on style imposed both by the organizational environment and the societal environment.[18] This was done to emphasize the open-system nature of leadership styles and the various impacts both of the organizational environment and of the social environment outside an enterprise. In their 1973 commentary, the authors put increased stress on the interdependency of leadership style and environmental forces—such as labor unions, greater pressures for social responsibility, the civil rights movement, and the ecology and consumer movements—that challenge the rights of managers to make decisions or handle their subordinates without considering interests outside the organization.

SITUATIONAL, OR CONTINGENCY, APPROACHES TO LEADERSHIP

As disillusionment with the "great man" and trait approaches to understanding leadership increased, attention turned to the study of situations and the belief that leaders are the product of given situations. A large number of studies have been made on the premise that leadership is strongly affected by the situation from which the leader emerges and in which he or she operates. That this is a persuasive approach is indicated by the rise of Hitler in Germany in the 1930s, the earlier rise of Mussolini in Italy, the emergence of Franklin Delano Roosevelt in the Great Depression of the 1930s in the United States, and the rise of Mao Tse-tung in China in the period after World War II. This approach to leadership recognizes that there exists an interaction between the group and the leader. It supports the follower theory that people tend to follow those whom they perceive (accurately or inaccurately) as offering them a means of accomplishing their own personal desires. The leader, then, is the person who recognizes these desires and does those things, or undertakes those programs, designed to meet them.

Situational, or contingency, approaches obviously have much meaning for managerial theory and practice. They also tie into the system of motivation discussed in Chapter 17, and have meaning for practicing managers who must take into account the situation when they design an environment for perform-ance.

Fiedler's Contingency Approach to Leadership

Although their approach to leadership theory is primarily one of analyzing leadership style, Fred E. Fiedler and his associates at the University of Illinois have suggested a contingency theory of leadership.[20] This means that people become leaders not only because of the attributes of their personalities but also because of various situational factors and the interactions between the leaders and group members.

Critical dimensions of the leadership situation. On the basis of his studies, Fiedler described *three critical dimensions* of the leadership situation that help determine what style of leadership will be most effective:

1. **Position power.** This is the degree to which the power of a position, as distinguished from other sources of power, such as personality or expertise, enables a leader to get group members to comply with directions; in the case of managers, this is the power arising from organizational authority. As Fiedler points out, a leader with clear and considerable position power can obtain good followership more easily than one without such power.

2. **Task structure.** With this dimension, Fiedler had in mind the extent to which tasks can be clearly spelled out and people held responsible for them. Where tasks are clear (in contrast to situations where tasks are vague and unstruc-tured), the quality of performance can be more easily controlled, and group members can be held more definitely responsible for performance.

3. **Leader-member relations.** This dimension, which Fiedler regarded as most important from a leader's point of view since position power and task struc-ture may be largely under the control of an enterprise, has to do with the extent to which group members like and trust a leader and are willing to follow that leader.

Leadership styles. To approach his study, Fiedler set forth two major styles of leadership. One of these is primarily task-oriented, and a leader gains satisfac-tion from seeing tasks performed. The other is oriented primarily toward achieving good interpersonal relations and toward attaining a position of per-sonal prominence.

Favorableness of situation was defined by Fiedler as the degree to which a given situation enables a leader to exert influence over a group. To measure leadership styles and determine whether a leader is chiefly task-oriented, Fiedler used an unusual testing technique. He based his findings on two types of sources: (1) scores on the *least preferred coworker* (LPC)—these were ratings made by people in a group as to those with whom they would least like to work; and (2) scores on *assumed similarity between opposites* (ASO)—ratings based on the degree to which leaders see group members to be like themselves, on the assumption that people will like best, and work best with, those who are seen as most like themselves. Now the LPC scale is most commonly used in research. In developing this scale, respondents were asked the traits of a person with whom they could work least well.[21] The person was to be described on sixteen items that were scaled, such as the following:

Pleasant : _____ : _____ : _____ : _____ : _____ : _____ : _____ : _____ : Unpleasant

Rejecting : _____ : _____ : _____ : _____ : _____ : _____ : _____ : _____ : Accepting

In his studies using this method, supported also by studies of others, Fiedler found that people who rated their coworkers high (that is, in favorable terms) were those who derived major satisfaction from successful interpersonal relationships. People who rated their "least preferred coworker" low (that is, in unfavorable terms) were seen as deriving their major satisfaction from task performance.

From his research, Fiedler came to some interesting conclusions. Recognizing that personal perceptions may be unclear and even quite inaccurate, Fiedler nonetheless found the following to be true:

> Leadership performance depends as much on the organization as it depends on the leader's own attributes. Except perhaps for the unusual case, it is simply not meaningful to speak of an effective leader or an ineffective leader; we can only speak of a leader who tends to be effective in one situation and ineffective in another. If we wish to increase organizational and group effectiveness we must learn not only how to train leaders more effectively but also how to build an organizational environment in which the leader can perform well.[22]

Fiedler's contingency model of leadership can be summarized by reference to Figure 18-5. This figure is really a summary of Fiedler's research, in which he found that in "unfavorable" or "favorable" situations the task-oriented leader would be the most effective. In other words, when leader position power is weak, the task structure is unclear, and leader-member relations are moderately poor, the situation is unfavorable for the leader and the most effective leader will be one who is task-oriented. (Note the dots in the lower right-hand corner in Figure 18-5. Each dot represents findings from a research study.) Likewise, at the other extreme, where position power is strong, the task structure is clear, and leader-member relations are good—a favorable situation for the leader—Fiedler found that the task-oriented leader was also most effective. However, where the situation was only moderately unfavorable or favorable (the middle of the scale in the figure), the human-relations-oriented leader was found to be most effective.

In a highly structured situation, such as in the military during a war, where the leader has a strong position power and good relations with members, there is a favorable situation in which task orientation is most appropriate. The other extreme, an unfavorable situation with moderately poor relations, an unstructured task, and weak position power, also suggests task orientation by the leader, who may reduce anxiety or ambiguity that could be created by the loosely structured situation. Between the two extremes (the middle of the scale in Figure 18-5), the suggested approach emphasizes cooperation and good relations with people.

Fiedler's research and management.   In reviewing Fiedler's research, one finds that there is nothing automatic or "good" in either the task-oriented or the people-satisfaction-oriented style. Leadership effectiveness depends upon the various elements in the group environment. This might be expected. Cast in the desired role of leaders, managers who apply knowledge to the realities of the group reporting to them will do well to recognize that they are practicing an art. But in doing so, they will necessarily take into account the motivations to which people will respond and their ability to satisfy them in the interest of attaining enterprise goals.

Several scholars have put Fiedler's theory to the test in various situations. Some have questioned the meaning of the LPC score, and others suggest that the model does not explain the causal effect of the LPC score on performance. Some of the findings are not statistically significant and situational measures may not be completely independent of the LPC score.

Despite criticism, it is important to recognize that effective leadership style depends on the situation. Although this idea may not be new, Fiedler and his colleagues drew attention to this fact and stimulated a great deal of research.

The Path-Goal Approach to Leadership Effectiveness

The path-goal theory suggests that the main function of the leader is to clarify and to set goals with subordinates, to help them to find the best path for achieving them, and to remove obstacles. Proponents of this approach have studied leadership in a variety of situations.[23] As stated by Robert House, the theory builds on various motivational and leadership theories of others.[24]

In addition to the expectancy theory variables, other factors contributing to effective leadership should be considered. These situational factors include (1) characteristics of subordinates, such as their needs, self-confidence, and abilities; and (2) the work environment, including such components as the task, the reward system, and the relationship with coworkers (see Figure 18-6).

Leader behavior is categorized into four groups:

1. Supportive leadership behavior gives consideration to the needs of subordinates, shows a concern for their well-being, and creates a pleasant organizational climate. It has the greatest impact on subordinates' performance when they are frustrated and dissatisfied.

2. Participative leadership allows subordinates to influence the decisions of their superiors and can result in increased motivation.

3. Instrumental leadership gives subordinates rather specific guidance and makes it clear what is expected of them; this includes aspects of planning, organizing, coordinating, and controlling by the leader.

4. Achievement-oriented leadership involves setting challenging goals, seeking

FIGURE 18-5

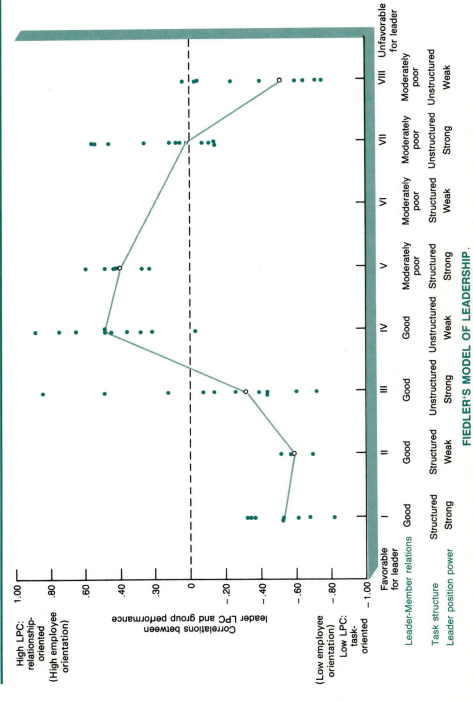

FIEDLER'S MODEL OF LEADERSHIP.

Adapted from F. E. Fiedler, *A Theory of Leadership Effectiveness* (New York: McGraw-Hill Book Company, 1967), p. 146. Used with permission.

FIGURE 18-6

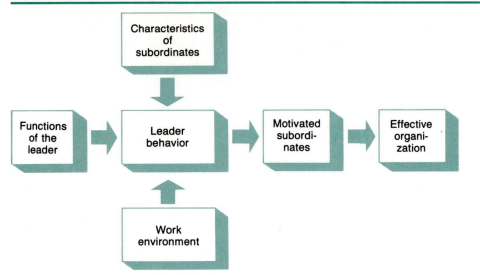

PATH–GOAL APPROACH TO LEADERSHIP EFFECTIVENESS.

improvement of performance, and having confidence that subordinates will achieve high goals.

Rather than suggesting that there is one best way to lead, this theory suggests that the appropriate style depends on the situation. Ambiguous and uncertain situations can be frustrating for subordinates and a more task-oriented style may be called for. In other words, when subordinates are confused, then the leader may tell them what to do and show them a clear path to goals. On the other hand, in a routine task, such as can be found on the assembly line, additional structure (usually provided by a task-oriented leader) may be considered redundant and subordinates may see this as overcontrolling. This, in turn, may be dissatisfying. To put it differently, employees want the leader to stay out of their way because the path is already clear enough.

The theory proposes that the behavior of the leader is acceptable and satisfies subordinates to the extent that they see it as a source for their satisfaction. Another proposition of the theory is that the behavior of the leader increases the effort of subordinates, that is, is motivating, insofar as (1) this behavior makes the satisfaction of the needs of subordinates dependent on effective performance, and (2) the behavior enhances subordinates' environment through coaching, directing, supporting, and rewarding.

The key to the theory is that the leader influences the paths between behavior and goals. The leader can do this by defining positions and task roles, by removing obstacles to performance, by enlisting the assistance of group members in setting goals, by promoting group cohesiveness and team effort, by increasing opportunities for personal satisfaction in work performance, by reducing stresses and external controls, by making expectations clear, and by doing other things that meet people's expectations.

The path-goal theory makes a great deal of sense to the practicing manager. At the same time, one must realize that the model needs further testing before the approach can be used as a definite guide for managerial action.

FOR DISCUSSION

1. What do you see as the essence of leadership?

2. How are leadership theory and styles related to motivation?

3. Why has the trait approach as a means of explaining leadership been so open to question?

4. Can you see why the managerial grid has been so popular as a training device?

5. For a business or political leader you admire, identify his or her style of leading by applying the managerial grid or the continuum-of-behavior model of Tannenbaum and Schmidt.

6. What is Fiedler's theory of leadership? Applying it to cases of leaders you have known, do you perceive it as being accurate?

7. What are the advantages and limitations of the path-goal approach to leadership?

8. If you were selected the group leader for a class project (for example, to make a case study of a particular company), which leadership style or what behavior would you use? Why?

EXERCISES/ACTION STEPS

1. Analyze a situation in which you were the leader. Which leadership approach discussed in this chapter helps you to explain why you were a leader?

2. Analyze a case in this book by using the group approach. Specifically, the class should be divided into groups of about five students. Each group should select a "spokesperson" who should present the analysis of the case to the class. For each group, one observer (this person should not be a participant in the case discussion) should describe the interactions in the group. Was there a leader in the group? If the answer is "yes," why was he or she considered a leader? Was it due to the leader's personality, the other group members (followers), or the nature of the task (situation)? Explain the group processes in light of any leadership theory or concepts discussed in this chapter.

CASES

CASE 18-1
LEADERS IN GOVERNMENT DEPARTMENTS AND AGENCIES

"The trouble with government departments and agencies today," said Sen. Paul Murphy, chairman of the Special Committee to Improve Government Management, "is that we have many managers, or administrators, who get high salaries, but too few leaders. I tell you that leaders are born and not made by any management development program you people have. We put people in positions of responsibility and expect them to be leaders. What we should do is to select people for government administrative positions who have demonstrated such personality traits as intelligence, energy, drive, initiative, enthusiasm, honesty, self-assurance, ability to get along with people, and ability to inspire confidence in their subordinates."

"But," responded Helen Baxter, Civil Service Commission management recruitment administrator, "you do not understand, Senator. We need people who are managers to head up our departments, divisions, and sections. Personal traits and qualities may be essential to political leaders. However, in government management we need persons who are concerned with getting

tasks done as well as concerned with people. Well-known and respected psychologists, such as Dr. Fred Fiedler, Dr. Rensis Likert, Dr. Robert Blake, Dr. Jane Mouton, Dr. Robert Tannenbaum, and Dr. Warren Schmidt, have made all this clear in their theories and researches."

At that point, Senator Murphy declared: "I don't care what these psychologists say. What do they know about leaders? Our government departments and agencies have long suffered from lack of leadership at all levels and I want the Civil Service Commission to do something to ensure that we have leaders in administrative positions."

1. To what extent do you agree with Senator Murphy?

2. If you were Helen Baxter, how would you respond to the senator?

3. Combine the research and theories of Fiedler, Likert, Blake and Mouton, Tannenbaum and Schmidt, and others, and come up with an answer on how the government can be assured that government administrators will become effective leaders.

CASE 18-2
PALMER MACHINERY COMPANY

Palmer Machinery Company has encountered hard times, not only owing to an economic recession but also because of the competition from products imported from Japan. In the past, labor relations have been rather poor. The unions usually asked for big pay increases for the workers and got them. But things have changed during the last few months, and labor and management have

realized that they are in for some bad times ahead.

The company maintains it is in a precarious condition and asks labor for concessions and givebacks. The union calls a membership meeting and discusses the situation of the company. While Ann Stewart, an assembler, thinks that she is overpaid and argues for a wage reduction, the majority of those present disagree and do not want to make any concession. In fact, there is a great mistrust of management's intentions, and the workers feel that giving concessions will encourage the company to ask for additional ones. After a long discussion some workers are more agreeable to concessions if management makes similar sacrifices. But management does not make any commitments. During the next few weeks the situation gets worse, and faced with a layoff, the union agrees to some cutbacks with an understanding that employees will share in some way in the profits of the company when things get better.

One month later, a survey of salaries of executives of major companies published in a national magazine shows that executives of their company received a substantial increase in compensation. One worker remarks: "You just cannot trust top management. I wish we had a situation as in Japan where in hard times the dividends are cut first, then the salary of top management is reduced, and later middle-level managers get a pay cut; the workers' pay is affected last."

1. Do you think the workers should have made concessions and agreed to givebacks?

2. If you were the president of the company, how would you have handled the situation?

3. What do you think of the Japanese approach to dealing with economic problems?

REFERENCES

1. For a review of research on followership see Trudy Heller and Jon Van Til, "Leadership and Followership: Some Summary Propositions," *Journal of Applied Behavioral Science*, Vol. 18, No. 3 (1982), pp. 405–414. For other discussions see William Litzinger and Thomas Schaefer, "Leadership through Followership," *Business Horizons* (September–October 1982), pp. 78–81.

2. See Bernard M. Bass, *Stogdill's Handbook of Leadership: A Survey of Theory and Research,* rev. ed. (New York: The Free Press, 1981).

3. M. J. Williams, "McDonald's Refuses to Plateau," *Fortune* (Nov. 12, 1984), pp. 34–40.

4. "Why Herb Kelleher Gets So Much Respect from Labor," *Business Week* (Sept. 24, 1984), pp. 112–114.

5. For an evaluation of the extensive research see John B. Miner, "The Validity and Usefulness of Theories in an Emerging Organizational Science," *Academy of Management Review* (April 1984), pp. 296–306.

6. For a discussion of leadership traits see Gary A. Yukl, *Leadership in Organizations* (Englewood, N.J.: Prentice-Hall, 1981), chap. 4.

7. David A. Kenny and Stephen J. Zaccaro, "An Estimate of Variance Due to Traits in Leadership," *Journal of Applied Psychology* (November 1983), pp. 678–685.

8. Ralph M. Stogdill, *Handbook of Leadership: A Survey of Theory and Research* (New York: The Free Press, 1974). See also his earlier study, "Personal Factors Associated with Leadership: A Survey of the Literature," *Journal of Psychology*, vol. 25 (1948), pp. 35–71.

9. Edwin E. Ghiselli, "Managerial Talent," *American Psychologist* (October 1963), pp. 632–641.

10. Edwin E. Ghiselli, *Explorations in Managerial Talent* (Pacific Palisades, Calif.: Goodyear Publishing Company, 1971).

11. Thomas J. Peters and Robert H. Waterman, Jr. *In Search of Excellence* (New York: Harper & Row, 1982), chap. 5.

12. Maggie McComas, "Atop of the Fortune 500: A Survey of the C.E.O.s," *Fortune* (Apr. 28, 1986), pp. 26–31.

13. See especially his *New Patterns of Management* (New York: McGraw-Hill Book Company, 1961) and *The Human Organization* (New York: McGraw-Hill Book Company, 1967), from which material in this section has been drawn. Also see Rensis Likert and Jane G. Likert, *New Ways of Managing Conflict* (New York: McGraw-Hill Book Company, 1976).

14. John B. Miner, *Theories of Organizational Structure and Process* (Hinsdale, Ill.: Dryden Press, 1982), chap. 2.

15. David G. Bowers, "Hierarchy, Function and the Generalizability of Leadership Practices," in James G. Hunt and Lars L. Larson (eds.), *Leadership Frontiers* (Kent, O.: Kent State University Press, 1975), pp. 167–180.

16. Robert R. Blake and Jane Mouton, *The Managerial Grid* (Houston, Tex.: Gulf Publishing Company, 1954) and *Building a Dynamic Corporation through Grid Organization Development* (Reading, Mass.: Addison-Wesley Publishing Company, 1969). The grid concept has been further refined in Robert R. Blake and Jane S. Mouton, *The Versatile Manager: A Grid Profile* (Homewood, Ill.: Richard D. Irwin, 1981) and by the same authors, *The Managerial Grid III* (Houston, Tex.: Gulf Publishing, 1985).

17. Robert Tannenbaum and Warren H. Schmidt, "How to Choose a Leadership Pattern," *Harvard Business Review* (March–April 1958), pp. 95–101. See also Heinz Weihrich, "How to Change a Leadership Pattern," *Management Review* (April 1979), pp. 26–28, 37–40.

18. Tannenbaum and Schmidt, "How to Choose a Leadership Pattern," reprinted with a commentary by the authors in *Harvard Business Review* (May–June 1973), pp. 162–180.

19. A variety of sources have been consulted, including Lawrence Ingrassia, "A Revitalized ITALTEL Wants to Test Wings in the Global Market," *The Wall Street Journal* (June 17, 1985); Parker Hodges, "The Continental Challenge," *Datamation* (Nov. 1, 1985); "ITALTEL's New Chief Gets What She Wants," *Business Week* (Apr. 30, 1984); "European Companies Link Up for Strategic Growth," *International Management* (June 1985); and personal correspondence.

20. Fred E. Fiedler, *A Theory of Leadership Effectiveness* (New York: McGraw-Hill Book Company, 1967). See also Fred E. Fiedler and Martin M. Chemers, *Leadership and Effective Management* (Glenview, Ill.: Scott, Foresman and Company, 1974); Fred E. Fiedler and Martin M. Chemers, with Linda Mahar, *Improving Leadership Effectiveness* (New York: John Wiley & Sons, 1977).

21. Fiedler, *A Theory of Leadership Effectiveness* (1967), p. 41.

22. Fiedler, p. 261.

23. For a meta-analysis of the research on the path-goal theory see Julie Indvik, "Path-Goal Theory of Leadership: A Meta-Analysis," in John A. Pearce II and Richard B. Robinson, Jr. (eds.), *Best Papers Proceedings, Academy of Management* (Chicago: Forty-Sixth Annual Meeting of the Academy of Management, 1986), pp. 189–192.

24. Robert J. House, "A Path-Goal Theory of Leadership Effectiveness," *Administrative Science Quarterly* (September 1971), pp. 321–338; Robert J. House and Terence R. Mitchell, "Path-Goal Theory of Leadership," in Harold Koontz, Cyril O'Donnell, and Heinz Weihrich (eds.), *Management: A Book of Readings*, 5th ed. (New York: McGraw-Hill Book Company, 1980), pp. 533–540; Alan C. Filley, Robert J. House, and Steven Kerr, *Managerial Process and Organizational Behavior* (Glenview, Ill., Scott, Foresman and Company, 1976), chap. 12.

FOR FURTHER INFORMATION

Bass, Bernard M. *Stogdill's Handbook of Leadership: A Survey of Theory and Research,* rev. ed. (New York: The Free Press, 1981).

Boyatzis, Richard E. *The Competent Manager: A Model for Effective Performance* (New York: John Wiley & Sons, 1982).

Graeff, Claude L. "The Situational Leadership Theory: A Critical View," *Academy of Management Review* (April 1983), pp. 285–291.

Hersey, Paul, and Kenneth H. Blanchard. *Management of Organizational Behavior: Utilizing Human Resources,* 3d ed. (Englewood Cliffs, N.J.: Prentice-Hall, 1977).

Hurst, David K. "Of Boxes, Bubbles, and Effective Management," *Harvard Business Review* (May–June 1984), pp. 78–88.

McConkey, Dale D. "Participative Management: What It Really Means in Practice," *Business Horizons* (October 1980), pp. 66–73.

"What It Takes to Be a Leader," *Harvard Business Review* (1981). This is a special issue on leadership with several articles by various authors.

19

Communication

CHAPTER OBJECTIVES

After reading this chapter, you should be able to:

1. Describe the communication function in an organization.

2. Diagram a model of the basic communication process.

3. Explain the flow of communication in an organization.

4. Describe the characteristics of written, oral, and nonverbal communication.

5. Identify barriers and breakdowns in communication and suggest approaches to improve it.

6. Describe the role of the electronic media in communication.

7. Identify the major principles, or guides, for leading.

Although communication applies to all phases of managing, it is particularly important in the function of leading. We define **communication** as the transfer of information from the sender to the receiver, with the information being understood by the receiver. This definition, then, becomes the basis for the communication process model—discussed in greater detail later—which focuses on the sender of the communication, the transmission of the message, and the receiver of the message. The model also draws attention to noise, which interferes with good communication, and feedback, which facilitates communication. Finally, we will describe the impact of the electronic media on communication.

THE COMMUNICATION FUNCTION IN ORGANIZATIONS

It is no exaggeration to say that the communication function is the means by which organized activity is unified. It may be looked upon as the means by which social inputs are fed into social systems. It is also the means by which behavior is modified, change is effected, information is made productive, and goals are achieved. Whether we are considered a church, a family, a scout troop, or a business enterprise, the transfer of information from one individual to another is absolutely essential.

The Importance of Communication

Over the years, the importance of communication in organized effort has been recognized by many authors. Chester I. Barnard, for example, viewed communication as the means by which people are linked together in an organization to achieve a common purpose.[1] This is still the fundamental function of communication. Indeed, group activity is impossible without communication because coordination and change cannot be effected.

Psychologists have also been interested in communication. They emphasize human problems that occur in the communication process of initiating, transmitting, and receiving information. They have focused on the identification of barriers to good communication, especially those that involve interpersonal relationships. Sociologists and information theorists, as well as psychologists, have concentrated on the study of communication networks.

The Purpose of Communication

In its broadest sense, the purpose of communication in an enterprise is to effect change—to influence action toward the welfare of the enterprise. Communication is essential for the *internal* functioning of enterprises because it integrates the managerial functions. Especially, communication is needed to (1) establish and disseminate goals of an enterprise, (2) develop plans for their achievement, (3) organize human and other resources in the most effective and efficient way, (4) select, develop, and appraise members of the organization, (5) lead, direct, motivate, and create a climate in which people want to contribute, and (6) control performance.

FIGURE 19-1

THE MANAGEMENT PROCESS

Planning Organizing Staffing Leading Controlling

Communication

External Environment
- Customers
- Suppliers
- Stockholders
- Governments
- Community
- Others

THE PURPOSE AND FUNCTION OF COMMUNICATION.

Figure 19-1 graphically shows not only that communication facilitates the managerial functions but that communication also relates an enterprise to its *external* environment. It is through information exchange that managers become aware of the needs of customers, the availability of suppliers, the claims of stockholders, the regulations of governments, and the concerns of a community. It is through communication that any organization becomes an open system interacting with its environment, a fact whose importance is emphasized throughout this book.

THE COMMUNICATION PROCESS

Simply stated, the communication process, diagrammed in Figure 19-2, involves the sender who transmits a message through a selected channel to the receiver. Let us examine closely the specific steps in the process.

The Sender of the Message

Communication begins with the sender, who has a *thought* or an idea, which is then encoded in a way that can be understood by both the sender and the receiver. We usually think of *encoding* a message into the English language, but

FIGURE 19-2

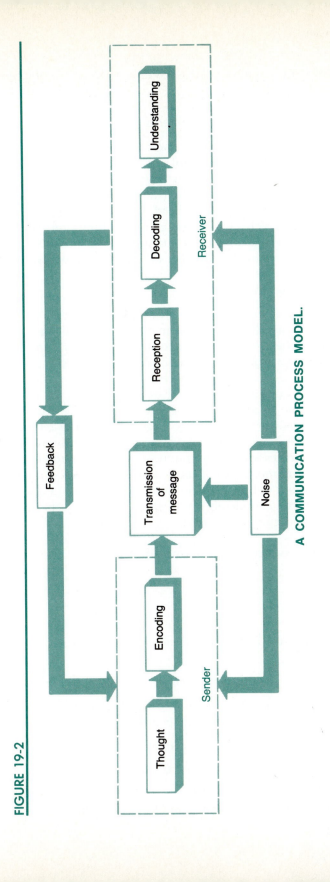

A COMMUNICATION PROCESS MODEL.

there are many other ways of encoding, such as translating the thought into computer language.

Use of a Channel to Transmit the Message

The information is transmitted over a *channel* that links the sender with the receiver. The message may be oral or written, and it may be transmitted through a memorandum, a computer, the telephone, a telegram, or television. Television, of course, also facilitates the transmission of gestures and visual clues. At times, two or more channels are used. In a telephone conversation, for instance, two people may reach a basic agreement that they later confirm by a letter. Since many choices are available, each with advantages and disadvantages, the proper selection of the channel is vital for effective communication.

The Receiver of the Message

The receiver has to be *ready* for the message so that it can be decoded into thought. A person thinking about an exciting football game may pay insufficient attention to what is being said about an inventory report, for example, thus increasing the probability of a communication breakdown. The next step in the process is *decoding,* in which the receiver converts the message into thoughts. Accurate communication can occur only when both the sender and the receiver attach the same or at least similar meanings to the symbols that compose the message. A message encoded into French requires a receiver who understands French. This is obvious; less obvious, and frequently overlooked, is the use of technical or professional jargon that may be understood by the recipient of the message. So communication is not complete unless it is understood. *Understanding* is in the mind of both the sender and the receiver. Persons with closed minds will normally not completely understand messages, especially if the information is contrary to their value system.

Noise and Feedback in Communication

Unfortunately, communication is affected by *noise*, which is anything—whether in the sender, the transmission, or the receiver—that hinders communication. For example:

- A noise or a confined environment may hinder the development of a clear thought.
- Encoding may be faulty because of the use of ambiguous symbols.
- Transmission may be interrupted by static in the channel, such as may be experienced in a poor telephone connection.
- Inaccurate reception may be caused by inattention.
- Decoding may be faulty because the wrong meaning may be attached to words and other symbols.
- Understanding can be obstructed by prejudices.

■ Desired change may not occur because of the fear of possible consequences of the change.

To check the effectiveness of communication, *feedback* is essential. We can never be sure whether or not a message has been effectively encoded, transmitted, decoded, and understood until it is confirmed by feedback. Similarly, feedback indicates whether individual or organizational change has taken place as a result of communication.

Situational and Organizational Factors in Communication

Many situational and organizational factors affect the communication process. Such factors in the external environment may be educational, sociological, legal-political, and economic. For example, a repressive political environment will inhibit the free flow of communication. Another situational factor is geographic distance. A direct face-to-face communication is different from a telephone conversation with another person on the other side of the globe and different from an exchange of cables or letters. Time must also be considered in communication. The busy executive may not have sufficient time to receive and send information accurately. Other situational factors that affect communication within the enterprise include the organization structure, managerial and non-managerial processes, and technology. An example of the latter is the pervasive impact of computer technology on handling very large amounts of data.

In summary, the communication model provides an overview of the communication process, identifies the critical variables, and shows their relationships. This, in turn, helps managers to pinpoint communication problems and to take steps to solve them, or even better, to prevent the difficulties from occurring in the first place.

COMMUNICATION IN THE ENTERPRISE

In today's enterprises, information must flow faster than ever before. Even a short stoppage on a fast-moving production line can be very costly in lost output. It is, therefore, essential that production problems be communicated quickly for corrective action. Another important element is the amount of information, which has greatly increased over the years, frequently causing an information overload. What is often needed is not more information, but relevant information. It is necessary to determine what kind of information the manager needs to have for effective decision making. To obtain this information frequently requires getting information from managers' superiors and subordinates and also from departments and people elsewhere in an organization.

The Manager's Need to Know

To be effective, a manager needs information necessary to carry out managerial functions and activities. Yet even a casual glance at communication systems shows that managers often lack vital information for decision making, or they may get too much information, resulting in overload. It is evident that managers must be discriminating in selecting information. A simple way for a manager to start is to ask, "What do I really need to know for my job?" Or, "What would happen if I did not get this information on a regular basis?" It is not maximum information a manager needs but pertinent information. Clearly, there is no universally applicable communication system; rather, it must be tailored to the manager's needs.

The Communication Flow in the Organization

In an effective organization, communication flows in various directions: downward, upward, and crosswise. Traditionally, *downward* communication was emphasized, but there is ample evidence that if communication flows only downward, problems will develop. In fact, one could argue that effective communication has to start with the subordinate, and this means primarily *upward* communication. Communication also flows *horizontally,* that is, between people on the same or similar organizational levels, and *diagonally,* involving persons from different levels who are not in direct reporting relationships with one another. You can see the different kinds of information flows in Figure 19-3.

Downward communication.   Downward communication flows from people at higher levels to those at lower levels in the organizational hierarchy. This kind of communication exists especially in organizations with an authoritarian atmosphere. The kinds of media used for downward *oral* communication include instructions, speeches, meetings, the telephone, loudspeakers, and even the grapevine. Examples of *written* downward communication are memoranda, letters, handbooks, pamphlets, policy statements, procedures, and electronic news display.[2]

Unfortunately, information is often lost or distorted as it comes down the

FIGURE 19-3

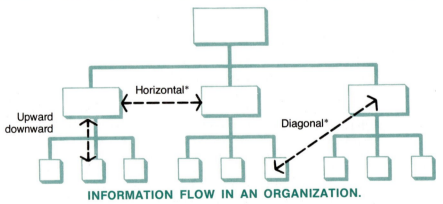

INFORMATION FLOW IN AN ORGANIZATION.

* Since horizontal and diagonal communication flows have some common characteristics, we call them crosswise communication and discuss them together later in this chapter.

chain of command. Top management's issuance of policies and procedures does not ensure communication. In fact, many directives are not understood or even read. Consequently, a feedback system is essential for finding out whether information was perceived as intended by the sender.

Downward flow of information through the different levels of the organization is time-consuming. Indeed, delays may be so frustrating that some top managers insist that information be sent directly to the person or group requiring it.

Upward communication.   Upward communication travels from subordinates to superiors and continues up the organizational hierarchy. Unfortunately, this flow is often hindered by managers in the communications chain who filter the messages and do not transmit all the information—especially unfavorable news—to their bosses. Yet objective transmission of information is essential for control purposes. Upper management needs to know specifically about production performance, marketing information, financial data, what lower-level employees are thinking, and so on.

Upward communication is primarily nondirective and is usually found in participative and democratic organizational environments. Typical means for upward communication—besides the chain of command—are suggestion systems, appeal and grievance procedures, complaint systems, counseling sessions, joint setting of objectives, the grapevine, group meetings, the practice of open-door policy, morale questionnaires, the exit interview, and the ombudsperson.

The concept of the **ombudsperson** was used relatively little in the United States until recently. It originated in Sweden, where a civil servant could be approached by a citizen to investigate complaints about the governmental bureaucracy. Now some U.S. companies have established a position for a person who investigates employees' concerns. Anheuser-Busch, Control Data, General Electric, McDonnell Douglas, and AT&T are just a few of the companies using the ombudsperson for promoting upward communication. There is now even a Corporate Ombudsman Association. At General Dynamics, over 3000 calls to the ombudsperson in 1986 suggest that workers trust the person in such a position.[3] Companies have found that the position of the ombudsperson can provide a valuable upward communication link and avert front-page scandals and legal costs by bringing improprieties to the attention of the appropriate person before they become major problems.

Effective upward communication requires an environment in which subordinates feel free to communicate. Since the organizational climate is greatly influenced by upper management, the responsibility for creating a free flow of upward communication rests to a great extent—although not exclusively—with superiors (see also Perspective on page 468).

Crosswise communication.   Crosswise communication includes the *horizontal* flow of information, with people on the same or similar organizational levels, and *diagonal* flow, with persons at different levels who have no direct reporting relationships. This kind of communication is used to speed information flow, to improve understanding, and to coordinate efforts for the achievement of orga-

PERSPECTIVE:
LACK OF UPWARD COMMUNICATION

The lack of upward communication can be disastrous. In the 1986 space shuttle disaster vital information apparently did not reach the top management at NASA.[4] Other examples of a breakdown of upward communication are these: Bank of America's top officials were surprised about the poor quality of their mortgage portfolio, which resulted in losses for the bank. E. F. Hutton's executives were apparently unaware of the incorrect check-writing scheme by their lower-level managers.

In some organizations, upward communication is hindered by the organization culture and climate that "punishes" managers who communicate bad news or information with which top management does not agree. Indeed, the tendency to report only good news upward is quite common. Yet correct information is absolutely necessary for managing an enterprise.

So what can managers do to facilitate the free flow of information? First, managers must create an informal climate that encourages upward communication. An open-door policy is only useful when it is practiced. Second, the formal structure of information flow must be clear. Third, managers can learn a great deal by just wandering through the corridors. Hewlett Packard is often mentioned as an example of open communication by the practice of "management by wandering around."

nizational objectives. A great deal of communication does not follow the organizational hierarchy but cuts across the chain of command.

The enterprise environment provides many occasions for *oral* communication. They range from the informal meeting of the company bowling team and lunch hours spent together to the more formal conferences and committee and board meetings. This kind of communication also occurs when individual members of different departments are grouped into task teams or project organizations. Finally, communication cuts across organizational boundaries when, for example, staff with functional or advisory authority interacts with line managers in different departments.

In addition, *written* forms of communication keep people informed about the enterprise. These written forms include the company newspaper or magazine and bulletin boards. Modern enterprises use many kinds of oral and written crosswise communication patterns to supplement the vertical flow of information.

Because information may not follow the chain of command, proper safeguards need to be taken to prevent potential problems. Specifically, *crosswise* communication should rest on the understanding that (1) crosswise relationships will be encouraged wherever they are appropriate, (2) subordinates will refrain from making commitments beyond their authority, and (3) subordinates will keep superiors informed of important interdepartmental activities. In short, crosswise communication may create difficulties, but it is a necessity in many enterprises in order to respond to the needs of the complex and dynamic organizational environment.

Written, Oral, and Nonverbal Communication

Written and oral communication media have favorable and unfavorable characteristics; consequently, they are often used together so that the favorable qualities of each can complement the other. In addition, visual aids may be used to supplement both oral and written communications. For example, the lecture in the management training session may be made more effective when written handouts, transparencies, videotapes, and films are used. Evidence has shown that when a message is repeated through several media, the people receiving it will more accurately comprehend and recall it.

In selecting the media, one must consider the communicator, the audience, and the situation. An executive who feels uncomfortable in front of a large audience may choose written communication rather than a speech. On the other hand, certain audiences who may not read a memo may be reached and become motivated by direct oral communication. Situations may also demand a specific medium. For example, President Reagan, an effective communicator, used press conferences in trying to clarify the arms shipments to Iran. Face-to-face interaction was demanded by the news media to deal with the many aspects of the transactions.

Written communication.   Written communication has the *advantage* of providing records, references, and legal defenses. We can carefully prepare the message and direct it to a large audience through mass mailings. Written communication can also promote uniformity in policy and procedure and can reduce costs, in some cases.

The *disadvantages* are that written messages may create mountains of paper, may be poorly expressed by ineffective writers, and may provide no immediate feedback. Consequently, it may take a long time to know whether a message has been received and properly understood.

Oral communication.   A great deal of information is communicated orally. Oral communication can be a face-to-face meeting of two people, or a manager addressing a large audience; it can be formal or informal, and it can be planned or accidental.

The *advantages* of oral communication are that it can provide for speedy interchange with immediate feedback. People can ask questions and clarify points. In a face-to-face interaction, the effect can be noted. Furthermore, a meeting with the superior may give the subordinate a feeling of importance. Clearly, informal or planned meetings can greatly contribute to the understanding of the issues.

However, oral communication also has *disadvantages*. It does not always save time, as any manager knows who has attended meetings in which no results or agreements were achieved. These meetings can be costly in terms of time and money.

Nonverbal communication.   We communicate in may different ways. What we say can be reinforced (or contradicted) by nonverbal communication, such as facial expressions and body gestures. Nonverbal communication is expected to support the verbal. But it does not always do so. For example, an autocratic manager who pounds a fist on the table while announcing that from now on participative management will be practiced certainly creates a credibility gap. Similarly, managers who state that they have an open-door policy, but then have a secretary carefully screen people who want to see the boss, create an incongruency between what they say and the way they behave. Clearly, nonverbal communication may support or contradict verbal communication, giving rise to the saying that actions often speak louder than words.

BARRIERS AND BREAKDOWNS IN COMMUNICATION

It is probably no surprise that managers frequently cite communication breakdowns as one of their most important problems. However, communication problems are often symptoms of more deeply rooted problems. For example, poor planning may be the cause for uncertainty about the direction of the firm. Similarly, a poorly designed organization structure may not clearly communicate organizational relationships. Vague performance standards may leave managers uncertain about what is expected of them. Thus, the perceptive manager will first look for the causes of communication problems instead of just dealing with the symptoms. Barriers can exist in the sender, in the transmission of the message, in the receiver, or in the feedback.

Lack of Planning

Good communication seldom happens by chance. Too often people start talking and writing without first thinking, planning, and stating the purpose of the message. Yet giving the reasons for a directive, selecting the most appropriate channel, and choosing proper timing can greatly improve understanding and reduce resistance to change.

Unclarified Assumptions

Often overlooked, yet very important, are the uncommunicated assumptions that underlie messages. A customer may send a note that she will visit a vendor's plant. Then she may assume that the vendor will meet her at the airport, reserve a hotel room, arrange for transportation, and set up a full-scale review of the program at the plant. But the vendor may assume that the customer is coming to town mainly to attend a wedding and will make a routine call at the plant. These unclarified assumptions in both instances may result in confusion and the loss of goodwill.

Semantic Distortion

Another barrier to effective communication can be attributed to semantic distortion, which can be deliberate or accidental. An advertisement saying,

"We sell for less," is deliberately ambiguous; it raises the question: Less than what? Words may evoke different responses. To some people, the word "government" may mean interference or deficit spending; to others, the same word may mean help, equality and justice.

Poorly Expressed Messages

No matter how clear the idea in the mind of the sender of communication, it may still be marked by poorly chosen words, omissions, lack of coherence, poor organization of ideas, awkward sentence structure, platitudes, unnecessary jargon, and a failure to clarify the implications of the message. This lack of clarity and precision, which can be costly, can be avoided through greater care in encoding the message.

Communication in the International Environment

Communication in the international environment becomes even more difficult because of different languages, cultures, and etiquette.[5] Translating advertising slogans is very risky. The slogan "Put a Tiger in Your Tank" by Exxon was very effective in the United States, yet it is an insult to the people in Thailand. Colors have different meanings in various cultures. Black is often associated with death in many Western countries, while in the Far East, white is the color of mourning. In business dealings it is quite common in the United States to communicate on a first-name basis. In most cultures, especially in those with a pronounced hierarchical structure, persons generally address one another by their last names.[6]

To overcome communication barriers in the international environment, large corporations have taken a variety of steps. Volkswagen, for example, provides extensive language training. Furthermore, the company maintains a large staff of translators. Frequently, local nationals who know both the language and the culture are hired for top positions. Foreign firms find it advantageous to hire students from their country attending universities in the United States.

Loss by Transmission and Poor Retention

In a series of transmissions from one person to the next, the message becomes less and less accurate. Poor retention of information is another serious problem. This makes the necessity for repetition of the message and the use of several channels rather obvious. Consequently, companies often use more than one channel to communicate the same message.

Poor Listening and Premature Evaluation

There are many talkers but few listeners. Everyone probably has observed people entering a discussion with comments that have no relation to the topic. One reason may be that these persons are pondering their own problems—such as preserving their own egos or making a good impression on other group members—instead of listening to the conversation. Listening demands full attention and self-discipline. It also means avoiding premature evaluation of what the other person has to say. A common tendency is to judge, to approve or disapprove what is being said, rather than trying to understand the speaker's frame of reference. Yet listening without making hasty judgments can make the whole enterprise more effective and more efficient. For example, sympathetic listening can result in better labor-management relations and greater understanding among managers; specifically, sales personnel may better understand the problems of production people, and the credit manager may realize that an overrestrictive credit policy may lead to a disproportionate loss in sales. In short, listening with empathy can reduce some of the daily frustrations in organized life and result in better communication.

Impersonal Communication

Effective communication is more than simply transmitting information to employees. It requires face-to-face communication in an environment of openness and trust. The following story illustrates how this simple but effective communication technique may be overlooked.

This occurrence illustrates that real improvement of communication often requires not expensive and sophisticated (and impersonal) communication media but the willingness of superiors to engage in face-to-face communication. This informal gathering without status trappings or a formal authority base may be threatening to a top executive, but it may be worth taking the risk to benefit from better communication.

Distrust, Threat, and Fear

Distrust, threat, and fear undermine communication. In a climate containing these forces, any message will be viewed with skepticism. Distrust can be the result of inconsistent behavior by the superior, or it can be due to past experiences in which the subordinate was punished for honestly reporting unfavorable, but true, information to the boss. Similarly, in the light of threats—whether

---

PERSPECTIVE:
THE CLOSED-CIRCUIT TELEVISION FAILURE[7]

A company was about to install a sophisticated $300,000 closed-circuit television system to improve the transmission of information to employees. When a management consultant recommended instead that the president should join his people during the coffee break, rather than sipping his coffee in a closed group of top executives, he was skeptical. This suggestion seemed radical, but he agreed to try it. The experiment was a failure because the president found that his employees would not talk to him. After some soul-searching, the president tried once more meeting with his employees face to face during the coffee break, but this time he talked about *their* concern (the opening of a European plant that could result in the elimination of jobs). To the president's surprise, employees talked openly about what was on their minds. In fact, the communication went so well that the president requested that his executive group mingle with their people for "kaffeeklatsches."

real or imagined—people tend to tighten up, become defensive, and distort information. What is needed is a climate of trust, which facilitates open and honest communication.

Insufficient Period for Adjustment to Change

The purpose of communication is to effect change that may seriously concern employees: shifts in the time, place, type, and order of work, or shifts in group arrangements or skills to be used. Some communications point to the need for further training, career adjustment, or status arrangements. Changes affect people in different ways, and it may take time to think through the full meaning of a message. Consequently, it is important to efficiency not to force change before people can adjust to its implications.

Information Overload

One might think that more and unrestricted information flow would help to overcome communication problems. But unrestricted flow may result in too much information. People respond to information overload in various ways.[8] First, they may *disregard* certain information. A person getting too much mail may simply ignore letters that should be answered. Second, if they are overwhelmed with too much information, people *make errors* in processing it. For example, they may leave out the word "not" in a message, which reverses the intended meaning. Third, people may *delay* processing information either permanently or with the intention of catching up in the future. Fourth, a person may *filter* information. Filtering may be helpful when the most pressing and most important information is processed first and the less important messages receive lower priority. However, chances are that attention will be given first to matters that are easy to handle, while more difficult but perhaps critical messages are ignored. Finally, people respond to information overload by simply *escaping* from the task of communication. In other words, they ignore information or they do not communicate information because of an overload.

Some responses to information overload may be adaptive tactics that can, at times, be functional. For example, delaying the processing of information until the amount is reduced can be effective. On the other hand, withdrawing from the task of communicating is usually not a helpful response. Another way to approach the overload problem is to reduce the demands for information. Within an enterprise, this may be accomplished by insisting that only essential data be processed, such as information showing critical deviations from plans. Reducing the external demand for information is usually more difficult because these demands are less controllable by managers. An example may be the government's demand for detailed documentation on governmental contracts. Companies that do business with the government simply have to comply with these requests.

Other Communication Barriers

Besides the mentioned barriers to effective communication, there are many others. In *selective perception* people tend to perceive what they expect to perceive.

In communication this means that we hear what we want to hear and ignore other relevant information.

Closely related to perception is the influence of *attitude*, which is the predisposition to act or not to act in a certain way; it is a mental position regarding a fact or state. Clearly, if we have made up our minds, we cannot objectively listen to what is said.

Still other barriers to communication are differences in *status* and *power* between the sender and the receiver of communication. Also, when information has to pass through several *levels* in the organization hierarchy, it tends to be distorted.

TOWARD EFFECTIVE COMMUNICATION

The communication process model introduced at the beginning of this chapter (Figure 19-2) helps to identify the critical elements in the communication process. At each state, breakdowns can occur—in the encoding of the message by the sender, in the transmission of the message, and in the decoding and understanding of the message by the receiver. Certainly noise can interfere with effective communication at each stage of the process.

There are several approaches that can be used to improve communication. The first one is to make a communication audit. The findings then become the basis for organization and system changes. The second approach is to apply communication techniques, with the focus on interpersonal relations and listening.

The Communication Audit

One way to improve communication in the organization is the communication audit.[9] It is a tool for auditing communication policies, networks, and activities. Organizational communication is viewed as a group of communication factors related to organizational goals, as shown in Figure 19-4.

What is interesting in this model is that communication is considered not for its own sake but rather as a means to achieve organizational goals, a fact sometimes forgotten by those concerned only with interpersonal relations. This model is consistent with our systems model of the operational approach to managing (see Figure 1-3 in Chapter 1). In our model, as you will recall, the communication system integrates the managerial functions of planning, organizing, staffing, leading, and controlling. In addition, it is important to remember that the communication system has another function, namely, to link the enterprise with its environment.

The four major communication networks that need to be audited are as follows:

1. The regulative or task-related network pertaining to policies, procedures, rules, and superior-subordinate relationships

FIGURE 19-4

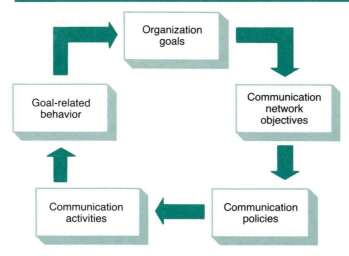

**RELATIONSHIP OF COMMUNICATION FACTORS
TO ORGANIZATION GOALS.**

From H. H. Greenbaum, "The Audit of Organizational Communication," *Academy of Management Journal,* vol. 17, no. 4 (December 1974), p. 743. Used by permission.

2. The innovative network, which includes problem solving, meetings, and suggestion for change

3. The integrative network, which consists of praise, rewards, promotions, and those items that link enterprise goals with personal needs

4. The informative-instructive network, which includes company publications, bulletin boards, and the grapevine[10]

The communication audit, then, is a tool for analyzing communication related to many key managerial activities. It is used not only when problems occur but to prevent them in the first place. The format of the audit can take many shapes and may include observations, questionnaires, interviews, and analyses of written documents. Although the initial audit of the communication system is highly desirable, it needs to be followed by periodic reports.

Guidelines for Improving Communication

Effective communication is the responsibility of all persons in the organization, managers as well as nonmanagers, who work toward a common aim. Whether communication is effective can be evaluated by the intended results. The following guidelines can help to overcome the barriers to communication.

1. Senders of messages must clarify in their minds what they want to communicate. This means that one of the first steps in communicating is to clarify the purpose of the message and make a plan to achieve the intended end.

2. The planning of the communication should not be done in a vacuum. Instead, others should be consulted and encouraged to participate: to collect the facts, analyze the message, and select the appropriate media. For example, you may ask a colleague to read an important memo before you distribute it throughout the organization. The content of the message should fit the level of knowledge of the recipients of the message and the organizational climate.

3. Consider the needs of the receivers of the information. Whenever appropriate, communicate something that is of value to them, in the short run as well as in the more distant future. At times, unpopular actions that affect employees in the short run may be more easily accepted if they are beneficial to them in the long run. For instance, shortening the workweek may be more acceptable if it is made clear that this action will strengthen the competitive position of the company in the long run and avoid layoffs.

4. There is a saying that the tone makes the music. Similarly, in communication the tone of voice, the choice of language, and the congruency between what is said and how it is said influence the reactions of the receiver of the message. An autocratic manager ordering subordinate supervisors to practice participative management will create a credibility gap that will be difficult to overcome.

5. Too often information is transmitted without communicating, since communication is complete only when the message is understood by the receiver. And one never knows whether communication is understood unless the sender gets feedback. This is accomplished by asking questions, requesting a reply to a letter, and encouraging receivers to give their reactions to the message.

6. The function of communication is more than transmitting information. It also deals with emotions that are very important in interpersonal relationships between superiors, subordinates, and colleagues in an organization. Furthermore, communication is vital for creating an environment in which people are motivated to work toward the goals of the enterprise while, at the same time, they achieve their personal aims. Another function of communication is control. As we have seen in the discussion of management by objectives (MBO), control does not necessarily mean top-down control. Instead, the MBO philosophy emphasizes self-control, which demands clear communication with an understanding of the criteria against which performance is measured.

7. Effective communicating is the responsibility not only of the sender but also of the receiver of the information. Thus, listening is an aspect that needs additional comment.

Listening: The Key to Understanding

The rushed, never-listening manager will seldom get an objective view of the functioning of the organization. Time, empathy, and concentration on the communicator's messages are prerequisites to understanding. People want to be heard, want to be taken seriously, want to be understood. Thus, the manager must avoid interrupting subordinates and putting them on the defensive. It is also wise both to give and to ask for feedback, for without it one can never be sure whether the message is understood. To elicit honest feedback, an atmosphere of trust and confidence and a supportive leadership style are desirable, with a de-emphasis on status (such as barricading one's self behind an extrawide executive desk).

Listening is a skill that can be developed. Keith Davis and John W. Newstrom proposed ten guides to improve listening: (1) Stop talking, (2) put the talker at ease, (3) show the talker that you want to listen, (4) remove distractions, (5) empathize with the talker, (6) be patient, (7) hold your temper, (8) go easy on arguments and criticism, (9) ask questions, and (10) stop talking! The first and the last guides are the most important; we have to stop talking before we can listen.[11]

Carl R. Rogers and F. J. Roethlisberger suggest a simple experiment.[12] It goes like this. The next time you have an argument try to use the following simple rule: A person may speak only after the ideas and feelings of the previous speaker are repeated accurately to the speaker's satisfaction. This rule sounds simple yet is difficult to practice. It requires listening, understanding, and empathy. But managers who have used this technique have reported a considerable number of cases in which they were not communicating accurately.

Some Tips for Improving Written Communication

Effective writing may be the exception rather than the rule; nor do education and intelligence guarantee good writing. Many people fall into the habit of using technical jargon that can be understood only by experts in the same field. Common problems in written communications are that writers omit the conclusion or bury it in the report, are too wordy, and use poor grammar, ineffective sentence structure, and incorrect spelling. Yet a few guidelines may do much to improve written communication.[13]

Use simple words and phrases.

Use short and familiar words.

Use personal pronouns (such as "you") whenever appropriate.

Give illustrations and examples; use charts.

Use short sentences and paragraphs.

Use active verbs, such as "The manager _plans_ . . ."

Avoid unnecessary words.

John Fielden suggests that the writing style should fit the situation and the effect you want to achieve.[14] Specifically, he recommends a _forceful_ style when the writer has power; the tone should be polite but firm. The _passive_ style is appropriate when the writer is in a position lower than that of the recipient of the message. The _personal_ style is recommended for communicating good news and making persuasive requests for action. The _impersonal_ style is generally right for conveying negative information. The _lively_ or _colorful_ style is suitable for good-news items, advertisements, and sales letters. On the other hand, a _less_ *colorful* style, combining the impersonal with the passive, may be appropriate for common business writing.

DOUBLE-LOOP LEARNING

One of the problems encountered in organizations is that unpleasant informa- tion is incorrectly, if at all, reported upward in the organizational hierarchy. The inability of top management to obtain correct information about the true state of the organization arises, according to Chris Argyris of Harvard University, from the way people learn in the organization.[15]

The traditional norm for learning is single-loop learning. This is, essentially, comparing performance against standards and then correcting undesirable de- viations. An example may be the thermostat that corrects the room temperature by either heat or cool air when it falls below or exceeds certain levels. We will learn more about this kind of control system in Part 6 in this book.

But there is another kind of organizational learning: double-loop learning, which questions the assumptions underlying organizational objectives and pol- icies. Thus, it is not enough to note that there are deviations from standards, but one has to question whether or not the objectives were appropriate in the first place.

Double-loop learning does occur in organizations. Unfortunately, it is often in response to a crisis in the external or the internal environment, or even crises created by managers to shake up the organization. That this is costly in terms of time, energy, and money is evident. For one thing, actions may be too late to be effective, while problems could have been prevented through open communica- tion. Also, people may become inactive as they wait until someone else addresses the problem.

What, then, can be done to encourage double-loop learning? One solution would be to educate the organization's members through seminars and work- shops. But this approach may not have long-lasting effects and people are likely to revert to their old behavior. A better way may be to develop assumptions underlying double-loop learning. This means making decisions that are based on valid information that can be tested. Thus, employees learn to test objectives, policies, and assumptions. The norms in the environment have to say that it is all right to take risks, to be open, and to trust others. People also have to develop an understanding of their own assumptions about objectives and policies. Clearly, in such an environment, upward communication is enhanced, which, in turn, should result in better decisions and greater organizational effectiveness. Dou- ble-loop learning, according to Argyris, is still in its infancy and awaits further testing.

ELECTRONIC MEDIA IN COMMUNICATION

Managers have studied and are gradually adopting various electronic devices that improve communication. Electronic equipment includes mainframe com- puters, minicomputers, personal computers, electronic mail systems, and electronic typewriters, the cellular telephone that lets you make telephone calls from your car, and the beeper that keeps you in contact with the office. The impact of computers on all phases of the management process will be discussed later in connection with the management information systems and will therefore be mentioned only briefly here. Let us first look at telecommunication in general and at the increasing use of teleconferencing in particular.

Telecommunication

Although telecommunication is just emerging, a number of companies have already effectively utilized the new technology in a variety of ways, as shown by the examples that follow.[16]

- A large bank supplies the hardware and software to its customers so that they can easily transfer funds to their suppliers.

- Several banks now make bank-by-phone services available even to individuals.

- Facsimile mail service assures delivery of a document across the country within hours.

- Car companies can stay in close contact with their suppliers, informing them about their needs and thus reducing inventory costs.

- Telecommunication can also provide an important link for just-in-time inventory systems.

- Airlines and trucking firms can keep track of the locations of their equipment, and the airline reservation system facilitates making travel arrangements.

- One large medical supply company gained a competitive edge by providing hospital purchasing agents with the opportunity to enter supply orders directly at the computer terminal.

- Many firms now have detailed personnel information—including performance appraisals and career development plans—in a data bank.

As you can see, there are many applications of telecommunication. But to make telecommunication systems effective, the technical experts must make every effort to identify the real needs of managers and customers and to design systems that are useful.[17] Let us now turn to a specific application of the new technology: teleconferencing.

Teleconferencing

For some time now companies such as IBM, Bank of America, and Hughes have used teleconferencing.[18] However, the systems vary widely, including audio systems, audio systems with snapshots displayed on the video monitor, and live video systems. You can see, therefore, that the term "teleconferencing" is difficult to define. In general, most people think of a **teleconference** as a group of people interacting with each other using audio and video media with moving or still pictures.

Full-motion video is frequently used to hold meetings among managers. Not only do they hear each other but they can also see each other's expressions or discuss some visual display. This kind of communication is, of course, rather expensive, and audio in combination with still video may be used instead. This method of communicating may be useful for showing charts or illustrations when conducting a technical discussion.

Advantages.   Some of the potential advantages of teleconferencing include savings in travel expenses and travel time. Also, conferences may be held when the need arises without making travel plans long in advance. Teleconferencing allows meetings to be held more frequently, improving communication between, for example, headquarters and the geographically scattered divisions.

Disadvantages.   But there are also drawbacks to teleconferencing. Because of the ease in arranging meetings in this manner, they may be held more often than necessary. Moreover, since this approach uses rather new technology, the equipment is subject to breakdowns. Most important, perhaps, teleconferencing is still a poor substitute for meeting with other persons face to face. Despite these limitations, we can expect increased use of teleconferencing in the future.

The Use of Computers for Information Handling

Electronic data processing now makes it possible to handle large amounts of data and to make information available to a large number of people. Thus, one can obtain, analyze, and organize timely data quite inexpensively. But it must never be forgotten that data are not necessarily information; information must inform someone. The new computer graphics can inform visually, displaying important company information. At PepsiCo Inc., managers, instead of digging through reams of computer printouts, now can quickly display a colored map showing their competitive picture.[19] There will be more about the impact of the computer on the process of managing in Chapter 21.

FOR DISCUSSION

1. Briefly describe the communication process model. Select a communication problem and determine the cause(s) by applying the model in your analysis.

2. List different channels for transmitting a message. Discuss the advantages and disadvantages of the various channels.

3. What are some kinds of downward communication? Discuss those used most frequently in an enterprise you are familiar with. How effective are the various types?

4. What are some problems in upward communication? What would you suggest to overcome the difficulties?

5. What are the advantages and disadvantages of written and oral communication? Which do you prefer? Under what circumstances?

6. What is information overload? Do you ever experience it? How do you deal with it?

7. How well do you listen? How could you improve your listening skills?

EXERCISES/ACTION STEPS

1. Take a situation you experienced at home or at work and identify communication problems you observed or experienced. Discuss how the communication model in this chapter can help you to locate the problems.

2. Go to the library and do research on a public person who communicates well (such as President Reagan). Discuss this person's characteristics as they relate to communication.

CASES

CASE 19-1
HAYNES FASHION STORES, INCORPORATED

Joyce Haynes, just graduated from college, joined her father, Dudley Haynes, president of Haynes Fashion Stores, Incorporated, a chain of thirty women's apparel stores in the New England area. The company had been founded by Ms. Haynes's grandfather over 50 years ago. With her grandfather's and, for the past 20 years, her father's drive and knowledge of women's fashions and of how to buy and sell them, the company had developed from a single store in Hartford, Connecticut, to a fairly large and highly profitable chain of stores. Dudley Haynes was much like his father before him. He knew what he was doing and how to do it, and he prided himself on being able to keep his hands on details in buying, advertising, and store management. Every one of his store managers, as well as his top vice-presidents and headquarters staff people, met with the president every 2 weeks in Hartford. Between these meetings, Mr. Haynes spent 2 or 3 days each week visiting the stores and working with store managers.

But his major worries were communication and motivation. He felt that, at the conferences he held, all his managers and staff people listened carefully. But judging from what they did, he began to wonder whether they heard him or whether they indeed had listened carefully. He observed that many of his policies were not being strictly followed in the stores; he often had to

rewrite advertising copy; in some of the stores the employees had joined the clerks union; and he increasingly heard of things he did not like. Among them were reports that many of his employees and even some of his managers felt that they did not know what the Haynes company was trying to do and believed they could do better if they had a chance to communicate with Mr. Haynes and his vice-presidents at the headquarters. He also had a strong feeling that many of his managers in headquarters and in the stores, as well as most of the store clerks, were merely doing their jobs without showing any real imagination or drive. He was also concerned that some of his best people had quit and taken positions with a competitor.

When his daughter walked into his office to take a position as his special assistant, he said, "Joyce, I am worried about how things are going. Apparently, my two problems are communication and motivation. Now, I know that you took some courses in management in school. I have heard you talk of the problems, barriers, and techniques of communication. I have heard from you about some fellows—Maslow, Herzberg, Vroom, McClelland, and others—who you thought knew a great deal about motivation. While I doubt that these psychology types knew much about business and I feel that I know what motivates people—primarily money, good bosses, and a good place to work—I wonder if you have learned anything that will help me to communicate better. I hope so, for that college education of yours has cost me a lot of money. What do you suggest?"

1. If you were Ms. Haynes, what would you say to your father?

2. How would you go about analyzing the communication problem, and what problems do you see already from the case?

3. How would you suggest that the motivation and communication theories you have studied might be applied to the Haynes Fashion Stores? Is there anything else you would want to know?

4. How would you apply the Rogers and Roethlisberger experiment discussed in this chapter to the case?

CASE 19-2
HOME RADIO AND TELEVISION COMPANY

Robert Gates founded a small radio manufacturing plant in Detroit in the 1930s. From this small start came one of the nation's largest radio, television, and allied products companies. By 1965 its sales approached $300 million annually, with 15,000 employees and ten manufacturing locations. Throughout its growth the founder remained the active, imaginative, and driving force of the company. In earlier days every manager and worker knew him, and he was able to call most of them by their first names, so even after the company grew fairly large, people felt that they knew the founder and chief executive, and this strong feeling of personal loyalty had much to do with the fact that the company was never unionized.

However, as the company prospered and grew, Mr. Gates worried that it was losing its "small-company" spirit. He also worried that communications were suffering, that his objectives and philosophy were not being understood in the company, that much wasteful duplication was occurring through poor knowledge of what others in the company were doing, and that new product development and marketing were suffering as a result. Likewise, he was concerned that he had lost touch with the people.

To solve the communication problem, he hired and had report to him a director of communication. Between the two, they put into effect every communication device they found other companies using: bulletin boards in every office and plant throughout the country; a revitalized company newspaper carrying much company and personal news affecting all locations; "Company Facts" books for every employee, giving significant information about the company; regular profit-sharing letters; company-sponsored courses to teach communication; monthly 1-day meetings at headquarters for the top 100 executives; annual 3-day meetings of 1200 managers of all levels at a resort area; and a large number of special committees to discuss company matters.

After much time, effort, and expense, Mr. Gates was disappointed to find that his problems of communication and of the small-company feeling still existed and that the results of his programs did not seem to be significant.

1. Why do you think that Mr. Gates was disappointed? Should he have been?

2. What do you see as the company's real communication problem?

3. What would you suggest to improve communication in the company?

4. Was Mr. Gates right in believing that communication would solve his problem in maintaining the "small-company" spirit?

REFERENCES

1. Chester I. Barnard, The Functions of the Executive (Cambridge, Mass.: Harvard University Press, 1938).

2. Walter Kiechel III, "No Word from on High," *Fortune* (Jan. 6, 1986), pp. 125–126.

3. Michael Brody, "Listen to Your Whistleblower," *Fortune* (Nov. 24, 1986), pp. 77–78.

4. Michael Brody, "NASA's Challenge: Ending Isolation at the Top," *Fortune* (Mar. 12, 1986), pp. 26–32.

5. See John D. Daniels, Ernest W. Ogram, Jr., and Lee H. Radebaugh, *International Business,* 3d ed. (Reading, Mass.: Addison-Wesley Publishing Company, 1982), chaps. 4 and 19; Simcha Ronen, *Comparative and Multinational Management* (New York: John Wiley & Sons, 1986), chap. 4.

6. V.H. Kirpalani, *International Marketing* (New York: Random House, 1985), chap. 4.

7. Roger D'Aprix, "The Oldest (and Best) Way to Communicate With Employees," *Harvard Business Review* (September–October 1982), pp. 30–32.

8. For a detailed discussion of this topic, see Miller's analysis of information overload in Daniel Katz and Robert L. Kahn, *The Social Psychology of Organizations* (New York: John Wiley & Sons, 1978), pp. 451–455.

9. Howard H. Greenbaum, "The Audit of Organizational Communication," *Academy of Management Journal* (December 1974), pp. 739–754.

10. Howard H. Greenbaum and N. D. White, "Biofeedback at the Organizational Level: The Communication Audit," *Journal of Business Communication* (Summer 1976), pp. 3–15.

11. Keith Davis and John W. Newstrom, *Human Behavior at Work: Organizational Behavior,* 7th ed. (New York: McGraw-Hill Book Company, 1985), p. 436.

12. Carl R. Rogers and F. J. Roethlisberger, "Barriers and Gateways to Communication," *Business Classics: Fifteen Key Concepts for Managerial Success* (Boston: Resident and Fellows of Harvard College, 1975), pp. 44–50.

13. Davis and Newstrom, *Human Behavior at Work* (1985), p. 438.

14. John S. Fielden, "What Do You Mean You Don't Like My Style?" *Harvard Business Review* (May–June 1982), pp. 128–138.

15. Chris Argyris, "Double Loop Learning in Organizations," *Harvard Business Review* (September–October 1977), pp. 105–115. See also Chris Argyris, "The Executive Mind and Double-Loop Learning," *Organizational Dynamics* (Autumn 1982), pp. 5–22.

16. Eric K. Clemons and F. Warren McFarlan, "Telecom: Hook Up or Lose Out," *Harvard Business Review* (July–August 1986), pp. 91–97; Anne R. Field and Catherine L. Harris, "The Information Business," *Business Week* (Aug. 25, 1986), pp. 82–90.

17. For a series of articles on telecommunications see *The Wall Street Journal—A Special Report—Telecommunications* (Feb. 24, 1986).

18. Robert Johansen and Christine Bullen, "What to Expect from Teleconferencing," *Harvard Business Review* (March–April 1984), pp. 164–174.

19. "Management Warms Up to Computer Graphics," *Business Week* (Aug. 13, 1984), pp. 96–101.

FOR FURTHER INFORMATION

American Management Association. "Ten Commandments of Good Communication," in Harold Koontz, Cyril O'Donnell, and Heinz Weihrich (eds.). *Management: A Book of Readings,* 5th ed. (New York: McGraw-Hill Book Company, 1980) pp. 565–566.

Argyris, Chris. "Skilled Incompetence," *Harvard Business Review* (September–October 1986), pp. 74–79.

Axley, Stephen R. "Managerial and Organizational Communication in Terms of the Conduit Metaphor," *Academy of Management Review* (July 1984), pp. 428–437.

Fielden, John. "What Do You Mean I Can't Write?" in *Business Classics: Fifteen Key Concepts for Managerial Success* (Boston: President and Fellows of Harvard College, 1975), pp. 125–133.

Flesch, Rudolf. *The Art of Plain Talk* (New York: P. F. Collier & Son, 1967).

"It's Rush Hour for 'Telecommuting,'" *Business Week* (Jan. 23, 1984), pp. 99–102.

Nichols, Ralph G., and Leonard A. Stevens. *Are You Listening?* (New York: McGraw-Hill Book Company, 1957).

Rowe, Mary P., and Michael Baker. "Are You Hearing Enough Employee Concerns?" *Harvard Business Review* (May–June 1984), pp. 127–135.

Schein, Edgar H. "Improving Face-to-Face Relationships," *Sloan Management Review* (Winter 1981), pp. 43–52.

Strunk, William Jr., and E. B. White. *The Elements of Style,* 3d ed. (New York: Macmillan Publishing Company, 1979).

Vallee, Jacques. *Computer Message Systems* (New York: McGraw-Hill Book Company, 1984.)

SUMMARY OF MAJOR PRINCIPLES, OR GUIDES, OF LEADING

For the managerial function of leading, several principles, or guidelines, can be summarized. They are the following:

Principle of harmony of objectives.   The more managers can harmonize the personal goals of individuals with the goals of the enterprise, the more effective and efficient the enterprise will be.

Principle of motivation.   Since motivation is not a simple cause-and-effect matter, the more managers carefully assess a reward structure, look upon it from a situation and contingency point of view, and integrate it into the entire system of managing, the more effective a motivational program will be.

Principles of leadership.   Since people tend to follow those who, in their view, offer them a means of satisfying their personal goals, the more managers understand what motivates their subordinates and how these motivators operate, and the more they reflect this understanding in carrying out their managerial actions, the more effective they are likely to be as leaders.

Principle of communication clarity.   Communication tends to be clear when it is expressed in a language and transmitted in a way that can be understood by the receiver.

The responsibility of the sender is to formulate the message so that it is understandable to the receiver. This responsibility pertains primarily to written and oral communication and points to the necessity for planning the message, stating the underlying assumptions, and applying the generally accepted rules for effective writing and speaking.

Principle of communication integrity.   The greater the integrity and consistency of written, oral, and nonverbal messages, as well as of the moral behavior of the sender, the greater the acceptance of the message by the receiver.

Principle of supplemental use of informal organization.   Communication tends to be more effective when managers utilize the informal organization to supplement the communication channels of the formal organization.

Informal organization is a phenomenon managers must accept. Information, true or not, flows quickly through the informal organization. Consequently, managers should take advantage of this device to correct misinformation and to provide information that cannot be effectively sent or appropriately received through the formal communication system.

Controlling

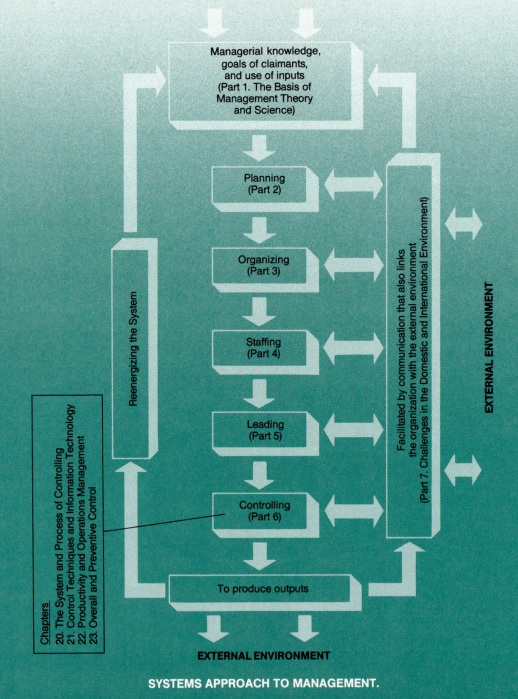

EXTERNAL ENVIRONMENT

Managerial knowledge,
goals of claimants,
and use of inputs
(Part 1. The Basis of
Management Theory
and Science)

Planning
(Part 2)

Organizing
(Part 3)

Staffing
(Part 4)

Leading
(Part 5)

Controlling
(Part 6)

Reenergizing the System

To produce outputs

Facilitated by communication that also links
the organization with the external environment
(Part 7. Challenges in the Domestic and International Environment)

EXTERNAL ENVIRONMENT

EXTERNAL ENVIRONMENT

Chapters
20. The System and Process of Controlling
21. Control Techniques and Information Technology
22. Productivity and Operations Management
23. Overall and Preventive Control

SYSTEMS APPROACH TO MANAGEMENT.

20

The System and Process of Controlling

CHAPTER OBJECTIVES

After reading this chapter, you should be able to:

1. Describe the basic control process.

2. Enumerate and explain the critical control points and standards.

3. Illustrate applications of the feedback system.

4. Demonstrate that because of the time lags in feedback control, real-time information will not solve all the problems of management control.

5. Show that feedforward control systems can make management control more effective.

6. List and explain the requirements for effective controls.

*T*he managerial function of **controlling** is the measurement and correction of performance in order to make sure that enterprise objectives and the plans devised to attain them are accomplished. Planning and controlling are closely related. In fact, some writers on management think that these functions cannot be separated. We consider it wise to separate them conceptually, however, and therefore discuss them in Parts 2 and 6 of this book. Still, planning and controlling may be viewed as the blades of a pair of scissors; the scissors cannot work unless there are two blades. Without objectives and plans, control is not possible, because performance has to be compared against some established criteria.

Controlling is the function of every manager from president to supervisor. Some managers, particularly at lower levels, forget that the primary responsibility for the exercise of control rests in every manager charged with the execution of plans. Occasionally, because of the authority of upper-level managers and their resultant responsibility, top- and upper-level control is so emphasized that people assume that little controlling is needed at lower levels. Although the scope of control varies among managers, those at all levels have responsibility for the execution of plans, and control is therefore an essential managerial function at every level.

Although control is often treated superficially in management literature, Giovanni B. Giglioni and Arthur G. Bedeian found a valuable body of knowledge in the following areas: control concepts, the process of control, characteristics of control systems, the problems encountered in control and the lessons learned from them, the variety of control models and techniques, and some principles for effective and efficient control.[1] We will discuss all these topics in Part 6, as well as others such as management information systems, and tools for production and operation management.

THE BASIC CONTROL PROCESS

Control techniques and systems are essentially the same for cash, office procedures, morale, product quality, or anything else. The **basic control process,** wherever it is found and whatever is being controlled, involves three steps: *(1) establishing standards, (2) measuring performance against these standards, and (3) correcting variations from standards and plans.*

1. Establishment of Standards

Because plans are the yardsticks against which managers devise controls, the first step in the control process logically would be to establish plans. However, since plans vary in detail and complexity and since managers cannot usually watch everything, special standards are established. Standards are by definition simply criteria of performance. They are the selected points in an entire planning program at which measures of performance are made so as to give managers signals as to how things are going without their having to watch every step in the execution of plans.

There are many kinds of standards. Among the best are verifiable goals or objectives, as suggested in the discussion of managing by objectives. (See Chapter 4.) You will learn more about standards, especially about those that point out deviations at critical points, in the next section.

2. Measurement of Performance

Although such measurement is not always practicable, the measurement of performance against standards should ideally be on a forward-looking basis so that deviations may be detected in advance of their occurrence and avoided by appropriate actions. The alert, forward-looking manager can sometimes predict probable departures from standards. In the absence of such ability, however, deviations should be disclosed as early as possible.[2]

If standards are appropriately drawn and if means are available for determining exactly what subordinates are doing, appraisal of actual or expected performance is fairly easy. But there are many activities for which it is difficult to develop accurate standards, and there are many activities that are hard to measure. It may be quite simple to establish labor-hour standards for the production of a mass-produced item, and it may be equally simple to measure performance against these standards, but if the item is custom-made, the appraisal of performance may be a formidable task because standards are difficult to set.

Moreover, in the less technical kinds of work, not only may standards be hard to develop but also appraisal will be difficult. For example, to control the work of the finance vice-president or the industrial relations director is not easy because definite standards are not easily developed. The superior of these managers often relies on vague standards, such as the financial health of the business, the attitude of labor unions, the absence of strikes, the enthusiasm and loyalty of subordinates, the expressed admiration of business associates, and the overall success of the department (often measured in a negative way by lack of evidence of failure). The superior's measurements are often equally vague. At the same time, if the department seems to be making the contribution expected of it at a reasonable cost and without too many serious errors, and if the measurable accomplishments give evidence of sound management, a general appraisal may be adequate. The point is that, as jobs move away from the assembly line, the shop, or the accounting machine, controlling them becomes more complex and often even more important.

3. Correction of Deviations

Standards should reflect the various positions in an organization structure. If performance is measured accordingly, it is easier to correct deviations. Managers know exactly where, in the assignment of individual or group duties, the corrective measures must be applied.

Correction of deviations is the point at which control can be seen as a part of the whole system of management and can be related to the other managerial functions. Managers may correct deviations by redrawing their plans or by modifying their goals. (This is an exercise of the principle of navigational change.) Or they may correct deviations by exercising their organizing function through reassignment or clarification of duties. They may correct, also, by additional staffing, by better selection and training of subordinates, or by that ultimate restaffing measure—firing. Or, again, they may correct through better leading—fuller explanation of the job or more effective leadership techniques.

CRITICAL CONTROL POINTS AND STANDARDS

Standards are yardsticks against which actual or expected performance is measured. In a simple operation, a manager might control through careful personal observation of the work being done. However, in most operations this is not possible because of the complexity of the operations and the fact that a manager has far more to do than personally observe performance for a whole day. A manager must choose points for special attention and then watch them to be sure that the whole operation is proceeding as planned.

The points selected for control should be *critical,* in the sense either of being limiting factors in the operation or of showing better than other factors whether plans are working out. With such standards, managers can handle a larger group of subordinates and thereby increase their span of management, with resulting cost savings and improvement of communication. The **principle of critical-point control,** one of the more important control principles, states: *Effective control requires attention to those factors critical to evaluating performance against plans.*

There are, however, no specific catalogs of controls available to all managers because of the peculiarities of various enterprises and departments, the variety of products and services to be measured, and the innumerable planning programs to be followed.[3] At the same time, a number of types of critical-point standards have been used. Nonetheless, all managers must tailor their own controls and control standards to fit their individual needs.

Questions for Selecting Critical Points of Control

The ability to select critical points of control is one of the arts of management, since sound control depends on them. In this connection, managers must ask themselves such questions as these: What will best reflect the goals of my department? What will best show me when these goals are not being met? What will best measure critical deviations? What will inform me as to who is responsible for any failure? What standards will cost the least? For what standards is information economically available?

Types of Critical-Point Standards

Every objective, every goal of the many planning programs, every activity of these programs, every policy, every procedure, and every budget become standards against which actual or expected performance might be measured. In practice, however, standards tend to be of the following types: (1) physical standards, (2) cost standards, (3) capital standards, (4) revenue standards, (5) program standards, (6) intangible standards, (7) goal standards, and (8) strategic plans as control points for strategic control.

1. Physical standards.   Physical standards are nonmonetary measurements and are common at the operating level where materials are used, labor is employed, services are rendered, and goods are produced. They may reflect quantities such as labor-hours per unit of output, pounds of fuel per horsepower produced, ton-miles of freight traffic carried, units of production per machine-hour, or feet of wire per ton of copper. Physical standards may also reflect quality, such as hardness of bearings, closeness of tolerances, rate of climb of an airplane, durability of a fabric, or fastness of a color.

2. Cost standards.   Cost standards are monetary measurements and, like physical standards, are common at the operating level. They attach monetary values to the costs of operations. Illustrative of cost standards are such widely used measures as direct and indirect cost per unit produced, labor cost per unit or per hour, material cost per unit, machine-hour costs, costs per plane reservation, selling costs per dollar or unit of sales, and costs per foot of oil well drilled.

3. Capital standards.   There are a variety of capital standards, all arising from the application of monetary measurements to physical items. They have to do with the capital invested in the firm rather than with operating costs and are therefore related primarily to the balance sheet rather than the income statement. Perhaps the most widely used standard for new investment, and for overall control, is return on investment. The typical balance sheet will disclose other capital standards, such as ratios of current assets to current liabilities, debt to net worth, fixed investment to total investment, cash and receivables to payables, and notes or bonds to stock, and the size and turnover of inventories.

4. Revenue standards.   Revenue standards arise from attaching monetary values to sales. They may include such standards as revenue per bus passenger-mile, average sale per customer, or sales per capita in a given market area.

5. Program standards.   A manager may be assigned to install a variable budget program, a program for formally following the development of new products, or a program for improving the quality of a sales force. Although some subjective judgment may have to be applied in appraising program performance, timing and other factors can be used as objective standards.

6. Intangible standards.   More difficult to set are standards not expressed in either physical or monetary measurements. What standard can a manager use for determining the competence of the divisional purchasing agent or personnel director? What can one use for determining whether the advertising program meets both short- and long-term objectives? Or whether the public relations program is successful? Are supervisors loyal to the company's objectives? Is the office staff alert? Such questions show the difficulty of establishing standards or goals for clear quantitative or qualitative measurement.

Many intangible standards exist in business, partially because adequate research into what constitutes desired performance has not been done above the level of the shop, the district sales office, the shipping room, or the accounting department. Perhaps a more important reason is that where human relationships count in performance, as they do above the basic operating levels, it is very hard to measure what is "good," "effective," or "efficient." Tests, surveys, and sampling techniques developed by psychologists and sociometrists have made it possible to probe human attitudes and drives, but many managerial controls over interpersonal relationships must continue to be based upon intangible standards, considered judgment, trial and error, and even, on occasion, sheer hunch.

7. Goals as standards.   With the present tendency for better-managed enterprises to establish an entire network of verifiable qualitative or quantitative goals at every level of management, the use of intangible standards, while still important, is diminishing. In complex program operations as well as in the performance of managers themselves, modern managers are finding that through research and thinking it is possible to define goals that can be used as performance standards. While the quantitative goals are likely to take the form of the standards outlined above, definition of qualitative goals represents an important development in the area of standards. For example, if the program of a district sales office is spelled out to include such elements as training salespeople in accordance with a plan with specific characteristics, the plan and its characteristics themselves furnish standards which tend to become objective and, therefore, "tangible."

8. Strategic plans as control points for strategic control.   A great deal has been written about strategic planning. But relatively little is known about strategic control. A recent book on the topic considers **strategic control** as the systematic monitoring at strategic control points as well as modifying the organization's strategy on the basis of this evaluation.[4] The authors agree with our position that planning and controlling are closely related. Therefore, strategic plans require strategic control. Moreover, since controls facilitate comparisons of the intended with actual performance, it also provides opportunities for learning, which, in turn, is the basis for organization change. Finally, through the use of strategic control one gains insights not only about organizational performance but also about the ever-changing environment by monitoring it.

CONTROL AS A FEEDBACK SYSTEM

Managerial control is essentially the same basic process as is found in physical, biological, and social systems. Many systems control themselves through information feedback which shows deviations from standards and initiates changes. In other words, systems use some of their energy to feed back information that compares performance with a standard and initiates corrective action. A simple feedback system was shown earlier in Chapter 3 (see Figure 3-2).

Management control is usually perceived as a feedback system similar to that which operates in the usual household thermostat.[5] This can be seen clearly by

PERSPECTIVE:
EXAMPLES OF FEEDBACK SYSTEMS

The steam engine governor is a simple mechanical feedback system; in other words, it is a system of feedback of information for control. In order to control an engine's speed under different load conditions, weights (balls) are whirled. As the speed increases, centrifugal force makes these weights exercise an outward thrust, which force in turn transmits a message to cut down the input of steam and thereby reduce the speed. As speed is reduced, the reverse occurs. Likewise, in the human body, a number of feedback systems control temperature, blood pressure, motor reactions, and other conditions. Another example of feedback is the grade a student receives on a midterm test. This is intended, of course, to give students information as to how they are doing, and, if performance is less than desirable, to send a signal suggesting improvement. And in social systems, even excluding the managed formal organizations, one also finds feedback. For example, in the social system of baseball, there are such standards as three strikes and out, and even the seventh-inning stretch, which are accomplished, essentially, by the feedback of information which corrects those who would deviate.

looking at the feedback process in management control shown in Figure 20-1. This system places control in a more complex and realistic light than would regarding it merely as a matter of establishing standards, measuring performance, and correcting for deviations. Managers do measure actual performance, compare this measurement against standards, and identify and analyze deviations. But then, to make the necessary corrections, they must develop a program for corrective action and implement this program in order to arrive at the performance desired.

FIGURE 20-1

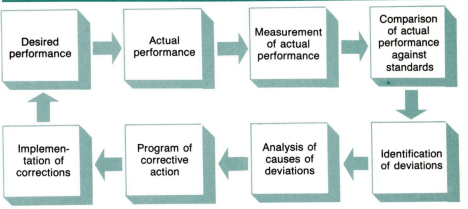

FEEDBACK LOOP OF MANAGEMENT CONTROL.

REAL-TIME INFORMATION AND CONTROL

One of the interesting advances arising from the use of the computer and electronic gathering, transmission, and storage of data is the development of systems of real-time information. This is information about what is happening while it is happening. It is technically possible through various means to obtain real-time data on many operations. For years, airlines have obtained information about vacant seats simply by pushing a flight number, trip segment (for example, Los Angeles to New York), and date into a memory system that immediately responds with information as to whether seats are available. Supermarkets and department stores have electronic cash registers in operation that transmit data on every sale immediately to a central data storage facility, where inventory, sales, gross, profit, and other data can be obtained as they occur. A factory manager can have a system that reports at any time the status of production programs in terms of such things as the production point reached, labor-hours accumulated, and whether a project is late or on time in the manufacturing process.

Some people see real-time information as a means of getting real-time control in areas of importance to managers—in other words, control effected at the very time information shows a deviation from plans. But reference to the management control feedback loop in Figure 20-1 shows that real-time information does not, except possibly in the simplest and most unusual cases, make possible real-time control. It is possible in many areas to collect real-time data measuring performance. It may also be possible in many of these cases to compare these data with standards and even to identify deviations. But the analysis of causes of deviations, the development of programs of correction, and the implementation of these programs are likely to be time-consuming tasks.

In the case of quality control, for example, it may take considerable time to discover what is causing factory rejects and more time to put corrective measures into effect. In the more complex case of inventory control, particularly in a manufacturing company where there are many items—raw materials, component parts, goods in process, and finished goods—the correction time may be very long. Once it is learned that an inventory is too high, the steps to get it back to the desired level may take a number of months. And so it goes with most instances of management control problems: Time lags are unavoidable.

This does not mean that prompt measurement of performance is unimportant. The sooner managers know that activities for which they are responsible are not proceeding in accordance with plans, the faster they can take action to make corrections. But there is always the question of whether the cost of gathering real-time data is worth the few days saved. Often it is, as in the case of the airline business, where ready information on availability of seats is likely to be crucial to serving customers and filling airplanes. But in a major defense company producing one of the highest-priority defense equipment items, there was little real-time information in an otherwise highly sophisticated control information system. Even for this program, the benefit of gathering real-time data was thought not to be worth the expense because the correction process took so long.

FEEDFORWARD CONTROL[6]

The time lag in the management control process shows that control must be directed toward the future if it is to be effective. It illustrates the problem of only using feedback from the output of a system and measuring this output as a means of control. It shows the deficiency of historical data such as those received from accounting reports. One of the difficulties with such historical data is that they tell business managers in November that they lost money in October (or even September) because of something that was done in July. At this late time, such information is only a distressingly interesting historical fact.

What managers need for effective control is a system that will tell them, in time to take corrective action, that problems will occur if they do not do something about them now. Feedback of output of a system is not good enough for control. This kind of feedback is not much more than a postmortem, and no one has found a way to change the past.

Future-directed control is largely disregarded in practice, mainly because managers have been so dependent for purposes of control on accounting and statistical data.[7] To be sure, in the absence of any means of looking forward, reference to history, on the questionable assumption that what is past is prologue, is admittedly better than no reference at all.

Techniques of Future-Directed Control

Neglect of future-directed control does not mean that nothing has been done. One common way many managers have practiced it is through careful and repeated forecasts using the latest available information, comparing what is desired with the forecasts, and introducing program changes so that forecasts can be made more promising. For example, a company may make a sales forecast that indicates that sales will be at a lower level than desirable. At this time, managers may develop new plans for advertising, sales promotion, or introduction of new products so as to improve the sales forecast.

Likewise, most businesses and other enterprises engage in future-directed control when managers carefully plan the availability of cash to meet requirements. Businesses, for example, would hardly find it wise to wait for a report at the middle or end of May to find out whether they had enough cash in the banks to cover checks issued in April.

One of the better techniques of future-directed control in use today is the technique of network planning, exemplified by PERT (Program Evaluation and Review Technique) networks, to be discussed in Chapter 21. This technique of planning and control enables managers to see that they will have problems in such areas as costs or on-time delivery unless they take action now.

Feedforward in Engineering

In recent years, particularly in chemical and electrical process systems, engineers have designed systems of feedforward control. For example, it was found that, because of surges in water usage, thermostatic control of water temperature with measurements of the outlet was not good enough for holding constant temperatures required for water being mixed into certain chemical compounds. As a result, process engineers designed systems whereby the needs for various quantities of water could be anticipated so that temperature could be controlled in advance of the outlet.

Feedforward in Human Systems

Interestingly enough, we find many examples of feedforward in human systems. A motorist, for example, who wishes to maintain a constant speed in going up a hill would not usually wait for the speedometer to signal a drop in speed before depressing the accelerator. Instead, knowing that the hill represents a disturbing variable in the system, the driver would likely correct for this by pressing the accelerator before speed falls. Likewise, a hunter will always aim ahead of a duck's flight to correct for the time lag between a shot and a hoped-for hit.

Feedforward versus Feedback Systems

Simple feedback systems measure outputs of a process and feed into the system or the inputs of a system corrective actions to obtain desired outputs. For most management problems, because of time lags in the correction process, this is not good enough. Feedforward systems monitor *inputs* into a process to ascertain whether the inputs are as planned; if they are not, the inputs, or perhaps the process, are changed in order to obtain desired results.

The nature of a feedforward as compared with a feedback system is depicted in Figure 20-2.

In a sense, we could say that a feedforward control system is really a kind of feedback system. This is true, but the information feedback is at the input side of the system so that corrections can be made before the system output is affected.

FIGURE 20-2

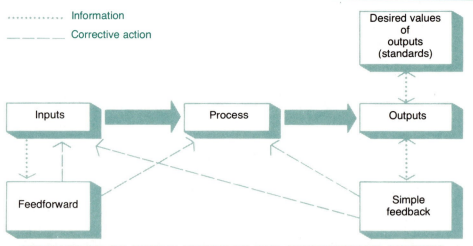

COMPARISON OF SIMPLE FEEDBACK AND FEEDFORWARD SYSTEMS.

Also, no one would deny that, even with a feedforward system, a manager would still want to measure final system output since nothing can be expected to work perfectly enough to ensure that the final output will always be exactly what is desired.

Feedforward in Management

To give you an idea of what feedforward means in management control, let us look at examples of cash and inventory planning systems. Figures 20-3 and 20-4 illustrate what is involved.

The somewhat simplified schematic figures of input variables shown in the charts for cash and for inventory planning and control indicate that if managers are to exercise effective control over either cash or inventories, they must identify each as an interacting system. As can be seen in each instance, some of the variables interact, and some have either a negative or a positive effect on either cash or inventory.

Also, if the system of variables and their impact on a process are accurately portrayed—and each enterprise should design its own system appropriate to the realities of its situation—a deviation from any planned input can result in an unplanned output unless something is done about it in time. For example, in the case of the inventory model, if purchase deliveries are greater than planned or if factory usage turns out to be less than planned, the result will be a higher-than-planned inventory unless corrective action is taken. Of course, to make feedforward work in practice, inputs must be carefully monitored.

In the best kind of feedforward control program, the model of input variables should include inputs in the system model that materially influence the key inputs. For example, purchase deliveries tend to increase inventories. But these deliveries are, of course, dependent on orders placed, and the placing of orders is in turn dependent on other factors.

The system of feedforward may appear to be rather complex. But for major problem areas, at least, it should not be difficult to identify system input variables, to see them as an interacting system, and to computerize the model. From that point it should be an easy matter to gather information on the inputs and to determine on a regular basis their effect on the desired end result. Certainly, in view of its importance to meaningful management control, this would not appear to be too much trouble to take.

One of the problems in all feedforward control systems is the necessity to watch for what engineers call "disturbances." These are factors which have not been taken into account in the input model but which may have an impact on the system and desired end results. Obviously, it would be impracticable to take into account in a model all inputs that might possibly affect the operation of a program. For example, for a company with a long history of adequate flow of bank loans for financing needs, the possibility that the company's bank may suddenly have to restrict credit might not have been a variable put into the input system. Or the bankruptcy of a large customer or supplier might be an unanticipated, and unprogrammed, input variable. Since unprogrammed events do sometimes occur and may upset a desired output, monitoring of regular inputs

FIGURE 20-3

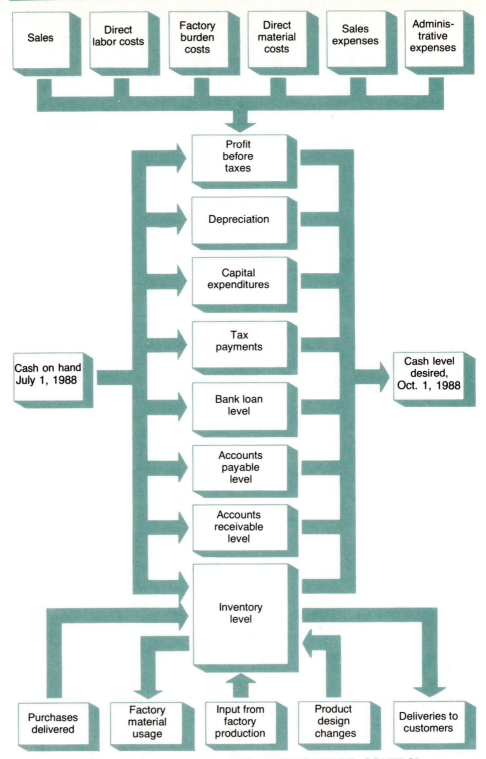

SYSTEM OF INPUTS FOR CASH FEEDFORWARD CONTROL.

FIGURE 20-4

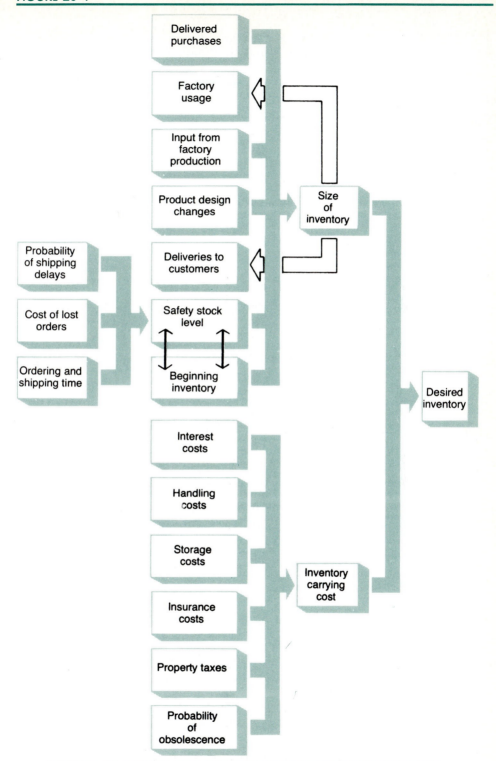

SYSTEM OF INPUTS FOR FEEDFORWARD INVENTORY CONTROL.

must be supplemented by watching for, and taking into account, unusual and unexpected "disturbances."

Requirements for Feedforward Control

The requirements for a workable feedforward control system may be summarized as follows:

1. Make a thorough and careful analysis of the planning and control system and identify the more important input variables.

2. Develop a model of the system.

3. Take care to keep the model up to date; in other words, the model should be reviewed regularly to see whether the input variables identified and their interrelationships continue to represent realities.

4. Collect data on input variables regularly and put them into the system.

5. Regularly assess the variations of actual input data from planned-for inputs and evaluate the impact on expected end results.

6. Take action. Like any other technique of planning and control, all that the system can do is to show people problems; they must obviously take action to solve them.

REQUIREMENTS FOR EFFECTIVE CONTROLS

All alert managers want to have an adequate and effective system of controls to assist them in making sure that events conform to plans.[8] It is sometimes not realized that the controls used by managers must be designed for the specific task and person they are intended to serve. While the basic process and the fundamentals of control are universal, the actual system requires special design.

Indeed, we can say that if controls are to work, they must be specially tailored. In short, they must be tailored to plans and positions, to the individual managers and their personalities, and to the needs for efficiency and effectiveness.

Tailoring Controls to Plans and Positions

All control techniques and systems should reflect the plans they are designed to follow. Every plan and every kind and phase of an operation has unique characteristics. What managers need is the information that will tell them how the plans for which they are responsible are progressing. Certainly the information needed for following the progress of a marketing program will be quite different from that needed to check on a production plan.

In the same way, controls should be tailored to positions. What will do for a vice-president in charge of manufacturing will certainly not be appropriate for a shop supervisor. Controls for the sales department will differ from those for the finance department, and these from controls for the purchasing department. And a small business will need some controls different from those for a large business. The very nature of control emphasizes the fact that the more controls are designed to deal with and reflect the specific nature and structure of plans, the more effectively they will serve managerial needs.

Certain techniques, such as budgets, standard hours and costs, and various financial ratios, have general application in various situations. However, none of these widely used techniques is completely applicable in any given situation. Managers must always be aware of the critical factors in their plans and operations requiring control, and they must use techniques and information suited to them.

Controls should also reflect the organization structure. As the principal means of clarifying the roles of people in an enterprise, organization structure shows who is responsible for the execution of plans and for any deviation from them. Controls must therefore reflect the organization structure, and the more carefully controls are designed to reflect the place in the organization where responsibility for action lies, the more they will enable managers to correct deviations from plans. For example, unless product costs are accumulated so as to fit the organization structure of the manufacturing department, and unless each factory superintendent and supervisor knows the costs incurred by his or her department in the production of an item, actual costs may be out of line without any of these managers knowing whether he or she is responsible. Fortunately, cost accountants have recognized the importance of relating cost data to organization structure, and the places where costs are incurred, now typically used in industry, provide data appropriate for each manager and his or her responsibility.

Tailoring Controls to Individual Managers

Controls must also be tailored to individual managers. Control systems and information are of course intended to help individual managers carry out their function of control. If they are not of a type that a manager can or will understand, they will not be useful. It really does not matter whether people cannot understand a control technique or control information or whether they are just unwilling to understand it. In either case, it is not understood. What individuals cannot understand they will not trust. And what they do not trust they will not use.

Some people—for instance, certain statisticians and accountants—like their information in the form of complex tables of data or voluminous computer printouts. In such cases, let them have it that way. Other people like their information in chart form; if so, it should be furnished this way. And a few people—for instance, scientists and mathematicians—may even like their information in mathematical model form; in this event, it should be given to them that way. It is sometimes said that if people will not understand the information they need in any other way, we might consider giving it to them in comic-book form. The important thing is that people get the information they need in a form they will understand and use.

What is said about tailoring information for understanding is true also of control techniques. Even quite intelligent people may be "turned off" by some of the sophisticated techniques of the expert. Sophisticated techniques of planning and control, like variable budgeting or network planning, can fail in practice solely because the systems either were not comprehensible to the people who had to use them or appeared to be too complex for them. Experts in these matters must not try to show others how expert they are but should, rather, design a system at the level of ready comprehension so that people will use it. If we can get 80 percent of the benefit with a fairly crude system, this is far better than obtaining no benefit from a more perfect, but unworkable, system.

Controls Pointing Up Exceptions at Critical Points

One of the most important ways of tailoring controls to needs for efficiency and effectiveness is to make sure that they are designed to point up exceptions. In other words, by concentrating on exceptions from planned performance, managers can use controls based on the time-honored exception principle to detect those places where their attention is required.

But it is not enough merely to look at exceptions. Some deviations from standards have little meaning, and others have a great deal. Small deviations in certain areas may have greater significance than larger exceptions in other areas. A manager, for example, might be concerned if the cost of office labor deviated from budget by 5 percent but might be unworried if the cost of postage stamps deviated from budget by 20 percent.

Consequently, the exception principle must be accompanied in practice by the *principle of critical-point control.* It is not enough just to look for exceptions; we must also look for them at critical points. It is true that the more that managers concentrate their control efforts on exceptions, the more efficient their control will be. But this principle had best be considered in the light of the fact that effective control requires managers to pay primary attention to those things which are most important.

Objectivity of Controls

Management necessarily has many subjective elements, but whether a subordinate is doing a good job should ideally not be a matter for subjective determination. Where controls are subjective, a manager's or a subordinate's personality may influence judgments of performance and make them less accurate; but people have difficulty in explaining away control of their performance, particularly if the standards and measurements are kept up to date through periodic review. This requirement may be summarized by saying that effective control requires objective, accurate, and suitable standards.

Flexibility of Controls

Controls should remain workable in the face of changed plans, unforeseen circumstances, or outright failures. If controls are to remain effective despite failure or unexpected changes of plans, they must be flexible

The need for flexible control can readily be illustrated. A budget system may project a certain level of expenses and grant authority to managers to hire labor and purchase materials and services at this level. If, as is usually the case, this budget is based on a forecast of a certain level of sales, it may become meaningless as a system of control if the actual sales volume is considerably above or below the forecast. Budget systems have been brought into ill repute among some companies because of inflexibility in such circumstances. What is needed, of course, is a system that will reflect sales variations as well as other deviations from plans. This requirement is provided by the flexible, or variable, budget, as we will see in Chapter 21.

Fitting the Control System to the Organizational Climate

To be most effective, any control system or technique must fit the organizational climate. For example, a tight control system applied in an organization where people have been given considerable freedom and participation may go so strongly against the grain that it will be doomed to failure. On the other hand, if subordinates have been managed by a superior who allows little participation in decision making, a generalized and permissive control system would hardly succeed. People with a low desire to participate, or who have not been accustomed to participating, are likely to want to have clear standards and measurements and to want to be told what to do.

Economy of Controls

Controls must be worth their cost. Although this requirement is simple, it is often difficult to accomplish in practice. A manager may have difficulty in ascertaining what a particular control system is worth or what it costs. Economy is relative, since the benefits vary with the importance of the activity, the size of the operation, the expense that might be incurred in the absence of control, and the contribution the system can make.

A limiting factor of control systems is their cost; this, in turn, will depend a great deal on managers' selecting for control only critical factors in areas important to them. If tailored to the job and to the size of the enterprise, control will probably be economical. One of the economies of large-scale enterprise is being able to afford expensive and elaborate control systems. Often, however, the magnitude of the problems, the wider area of planning, the difficulty of coordinating plans, and poor management communication in a large organization require such expensive controls that their overall efficiency suffers in comparison with lesser controls in a small business. Control techniques and approaches are efficient when they bring to light the causes of actual or potential deviations from plans with the minimum of costs.

Controls Leading to Corrective Action

An adequate system will disclose where failures are occurring and who is responsible for them, and it will ensure that some corrective action is taken. Control is justified only if deviations from plans are corrected through appropriate planning, organizing, staffing, and leading.

FOR DISCUSSION

1. Planning and control are often thought of as a system; control is also often referred to as a system. What is meant by these observations? Can both statements be true?

2. Why is real-time information not good enough for effective control?

3. What is feedforward control? Why is it important to managers? Besides the examples of cash and inventory control mentioned in this chapter, can you think of any other areas where feedforward would be used? Selecting one of these, how would you proceed?

4. If you were asked to institute a system of "tailored" controls in a company, how would you go about it? What would you need to know?

5. Develop a set of standards for any area of interest to you where you might wish to exercise effective control.

EXERCISES/ACTION STEPS

1. Design a control system for measuring the progress you make in your course work. Apply the feedback and feedforward concepts discussed in this chapter.

2. Interview two managers about the controls used in their companies. Can you identify standards against which performance can be accurately measured? How is performance measured against the standard and how timely are deviations reported? If deviations are detected, how long does it take before corrections are made in specific situations?

CASES

CASE 20-1
THE KAPPA CORPORATION

As George House, vice-president of finance, and Helen Robbins, controller, walked into the office of Adrian Barnes, chairperson and chief executive officer of Kappa Corporation, they were met with the following outburst from the company's top officer:

"Why doesn't someone tell me things? Why can't I know what is going on around here? Why am I kept in the dark? No one informs me on how the company is going, and I never seem to hear of our problems until they become crises. Now, I want you both to work out a system where I can be kept informed, and I want to know by next Monday how you will do it. I am tired of being isolated from the things I must know if I am to take responsibility for this company."

After George House had left Mr. Barnes's office, he turned to his controller and muttered, "That silly jerk! Everything he wants to know or could possibly want to know is in that stack of reports on the table in back of his desk."

1. Who was right—Adrian Barnes or George House? Was Barnes getting information?

2. What would you do to make sure that the chairperson did get the information he needed for control purposes?

CASE 20-2
HANOVER SPACE AND ELECTRONICS CORPORATION

Warren Hanover, president of Hanover Space and Electronics Corporation, and the presidents of other large defense contractors had just met with the secretary of defense in Washington. The secretary had impressed on the group of presidents the fact that the government must insist on better management and tighter control by defense contractors in order to get more product from increasingly scarce defense dollars, especially in view of the sharp inflation of recent years. The secretary had strongly emphasized that, from now on, the Defense Department would carefully examine management practices of contractors and, at the very least, would not give any major contract to a company that did not have a strong, effective control system.

Warren Hanover, as well as the other presidents, got the message. On his return to his headquarters in Kansas City, he immediately called in his administrative vice-president, told him of the secretary's position, and ordered him to install an effective control system. The administrative vice-president, in turn, called in the corporation controller and passed the order on to him. The controller then assigned the task to his staff assistant, asking her to scour the literature on control to find a system the company could adopt and to present a proposal to him within a week.

At the end of the week, the staff assistant had to report to the controller that she had not found a control system suitable for the company, despite the fact that she had reviewed dozens of books and journal articles.

1. Could the staff assistant have found a suitable control system if she had looked far enough?

2. If you were the staff assistant, what would you suggest be done to develop an effective control system?

REFERENCES

1. For an excellent summary of pioneering writers on control, see Giovanni B. Giglioni and Arthur G. Bedeian, "A Conspectus of Management Control Theory: 1900–1972," *Academy of Management Journal* (June 1974), pp. 292–305.

2. Richard L. Daft and Norman B. Macintosh, "The Nature and Use of Formal Control Systems for Management Control and Strategy Implementation," *Journal of Management* (Fall 1984), pp. 43–66.

3. For different kinds of control, such as control-problem avoidance, control of specific actions, control of results, and control of personnel, see Kenneth A. Merchant, "The Control Function of Management," in Max D. Richards (ed.), *Readings in Management,* 7th ed. (Cincinnati: South-Western Publishing Company, 1986), pp. 285–301.

4. Peter Lorange, Michael F. Scott Morton, and Sumantra Ghoshal, *Strategic Control* (St.

Paul: West Publishing Company, 1986), p. xvii. See also Richard L. Daft and Norman B. Macintosh, "The Nature and Use of Formal Control Systems for Management Control and Strategy Implementation," *Journal of Management* (Spring 1984), pp. 43–66.

5. There are also limitations and problems in relying on feedback. See Geert Hofstede, "The Poverty of Management Control Philosophy," in Richards, *Readings* (1986), pp. 302–315. We will discuss some of the limitations of traditional controls in a later chapter under the topic "preventive controls."

6. For a discussion of feedforward control techniques, see Harold Koontz and Robert W. Bradspies, "Managing through Feedforward Control," in Harold Koontz, Cyril O'Donnell, and Heinz Weihrich (eds.), *Management: A Book of Readings*, 5th ed. (New York: McGraw-Hill Book Company, 1980), pp. 576–585. Much of the material in this section is drawn from that paper.

7. The idea of future-directed control was emphasized by one of the authors many years ago. See Harold Koontz, "A Preliminary Statement of Principles of Planning and Control," *Academy of Management Journal* (April 1958), pp. 45–61. Now many authors discuss this concept using different names. For example, the term "Steering Controls" has been used by James A. F. Stoner and Charles Wankel, *Management*, 3d ed. (Englewood Cliffs, N.J.: Prentice-Hall, 1986), p. 579; and John R. Schermerhorn, Jr., *Management for Productivity*, 2d ed. (New York: John Wiley & Sons, 1986), p. 402.

8. See also Robert N. Anthony, John Dearden, and Norton M. Bedford, *Management Control Systems*, 5th ed. (Homewood, Ill.: Irwin, 1984).

FOR FURTHER INFORMATION

Banks, Robert L., and Steven C. Wheelwright. "Operations vs. Strategy: Trading Tomorrow for Today," *Harvard Business Review* (May–June 1979), pp. 112–120.

Flamholtz, Eric. "Organizational Control Systems as a Managerial Tool," *California Management Review* (Winter 1979), pp. 50–59.

McFarlan, F. Warren, James L. McKenney, and Philip Pyburn. "The Information Archipelago—Plotting a Course," *Harvard Business Review* (January–February 1983), pp. 145–156.

McFarlan, F. Warren, and James L. McKenney. "The Information Archipelago—Governing the New World," *Harvard Business Review* (July–August 1983), pp. 91–99.

Michael, Steven R. "Feedforward versus Feedback Control," *Managerial Planning* (November–December 1980), pp. 34–38.

Mills, Peter K. "Self-Management: Its Control and Relationship to Other Organizational Properties," *Academy of Management Review* (July 1983), pp. 445–453.

Smith, Howard L., Myron D. Fottler, and Borje O. Saxberg. "Cost Containment in Health Care: A Model for Management Research," *Academy of Management Review* (July 1981), pp. 397–407.

Control Techniques and Information Technology

CHAPTER OBJECTIVES

After reading this chapter, you should be able to:

1. Explain the nature of budgeting and types of budgets.

2. Present modern techniques of budgeting, including variable and zero-base budgets.

3. Describe nonbudgetary control devices.

4. Analyze time-event networks as a major technique of control.

5. Explain the nature and problems of program budgeting.

6. Discuss the special need for effective procedures planning and control.

7. Describe the nature and applications of information technology.

8. Recognize the importance of computers in handling information.

9. Explain the challenges created by the new information technology.

Although the basic nature and purpose of management control do not change, a variety of tools and techniques have been used over the years to help managers control. As you will see, all these techniques are in the first instance tools for planning. They illustrate the fundamental truth that the task of controls is to make plans succeed; naturally, in doing so, controls must reflect plans; and planning must precede control.

Some of these tools may be classed as traditional in the sense that they have long been used by managers, although variable budgeting and zero-base budgeting, for example, are refinements of traditional budgeting. Others, like Program Evaluation and Review Technique (PERT) and program budgeting, represent a newer generation of planning and control tools. While there are many more of these than discussed here, the newer tools generally reflect the systems techniques long used in the physical sciences. Operations research, discussed in Chapter 22, is such a technique. Since information is vital for managing effectively, we discuss in this chapter the newer information technology and its challenges, as well as the use of computers.

In spite of all the newer techniques of planning and control, the traditional tools are still extremely important.

CONTROL TECHNIQUES: THE BUDGET[1]

A widely used device for managerial control is the budget. Indeed, it has sometimes been assumed that budgeting is *the* device for accomplishing control. However, many nonbudgetary devices are also essential.

The Concept of Budgeting

Budgeting is the formulation of plans for a given future period in numerical terms. As such, budgets are statements of anticipated results, in financial terms—as in revenue and expense and capital budgets—or in nonfinancial terms—as in budgets of direct-labor-hours, materials, physical sales volume, or units of production. It has sometimes been said, for example, that financial budgets represent the "dollarizing" of plans.

The Purpose of Budgeting

By stating plans in terms of numbers and breaking them into parts that parallel the parts of an organization, budgets correlate planning and allow authority to be delegated without loss of control. In other words, reducing plans to numbers forces a kind of orderliness that permits the manager to see clearly what capital will be spent by whom and where, and what expense, revenue, or units of physical input or output the plans will involve. Having ascertained this, the manager can more freely delegate authority to effect the plan within the limits of the budget. Moreover, a budget, to be useful to a manager at any level, must reflect the organizational pattern. Only when plans are complete, coordinated, and developed enough to be fitted into departmental operations can a useful departmental budget be prepared as an instrument of control.

Types of Budgets

There are many types of budgets. They may be classified into several basic types, with a budget summary (discussed in Chapter 23) portraying the total planning picture of all the budgets: (1) revenue and expense budgets, (2) time, space, material, and product budgets, (3) capital expenditure budgets, and (4) cash budgets.

1. Revenue and expense budgets.   By far the most common budgets spell out plans for revenues and operating expenses in dollar terms. The most basic of these is the sales budget (for a simple example see Table 21-1), the formal and detailed expression of the sales forecast. Just as the sales forecast is the cornerstone of planning, so is the sales budget the foundation of budgetary control. Although a company may budget other revenues, such as expected income from rentals, royalties, or miscellaneous sources, the revenue from sales of products or services furnishes the principal income to pay operating expenses and yield profits.

Operating expense budgets of the typical enterprise can be as numerous as the expense classifications in its chart of accounts and the units of organization in its structure. These budgets may deal with individual items of expense, such as travel, data processing, entertainment, advertising, telephone, insurance, and many others. Sometimes a department head will budget only major items and lump together other items in one control summary. For example, if the manager of a small department is expected to take one business trip a year at a cost of $720, budgeting this cost each month at $60 would mean little for monthly planning or control.

2. Time, space, material, and product budgets.   Many budgets are better expressed in quantities other than in monetary terms. Although such budgets are

TABLE 21-1   A Typical Sales Budget
(For the Year Ending December 31, 1990)

Product and area	Unit sales volume	Unit selling price	Total sales
Product A:			
Area 1	26,000	$10	$260,000
Area 2	15,000	10	150,000
Area 3	20,000	10	200,000
Total			$610,000
Product B:			
Area 1	30,000	$15	$450,000
Area 2	20,000	15	300,000
Area 3	22,000	15	330,000
Total			$1,080,000
Total revenue from sales			$1,690,000

usually translated into monetary terms, they are much more significant at a certain stage in planning and control if they are expressed in terms of quantities. Among the more common of these are the budgets for direct-labor-hours, machine-hours, units of materials, square feet allocated, and units produced. Most firms budget product output, and most production departments budget their share of the output of components of the final product. In addition, it is common to budget labor, either in labor-hours, labor-days, or by types of labor required. Obviously, such budgets cannot be well expressed in monetary terms since the dollar cost would not accurately measure the resources used or the results intended.

3. Capital expenditure budgets.   Capital expenditure budgets outline specifically capital expenditures for plant, machinery, equipment, inventories, and other items. Whether for a short or a long term, these budgets require care since they give definite form to plans for spending the funds of an enterprise. Since capital is generally one of the most limiting factors of any enterprise and since a business takes a long time to recover its investment in plant and equipment through charges as costs, thereby leading to a high degree of inflexibility, capital expenditure budgets should usually be tied in with fairly long-range planning.

4. Cash budgets.   The cash budget is simply a forecast of cash receipts and disbursements against which actual cash "experience" is measured. Whether called a budget or not, this is perhaps the most important single control of an enterprise. The availability of cash to meet obligations as they fall due is the first requirement of existence, and handsome business profits do little good when tied up in inventory, machinery, or other noncash assets. Cash budgeting also shows availability of excess cash, thereby making possible planning for profit-making investment of surpluses.

Dangers in Budgeting

Budgets are used for planning and control. Unfortunately, some budgetary control programs are so complete and detailed that they become cumbersome, meaningless, and unduly expensive.

Overbudgeting.   There is danger in overbudgeting through spelling out minor expenses in detail and depriving managers of needed freedom in managing their departments. For example, a department head in a poorly budgeted company was hindered in an important sales promotion because expenditures for office supplies exceeded budgeted estimates; new expenditures had to be limited, even though his total departmental expenses were well within the budget and he had funds to pay personnel for writing sales promotion letters. In another department, expenses were budgeted in such useless detail that the cost of budgeting of many items exceeded the expenses controlled.

Overriding enterprise goals.   Another danger lies in allowing budgetary goals to become more important than enterprise goals. In their zest to keep within budget limits, managers may forget that they owe primary loyalty to enterprise objectives. In one company with a budgetary control program, the sales department could not obtain needed information from the engineering department on the grounds that the latter's budget would not stand such expense! This conflict between partial and overall control objectives, the excessive departmental independence generated, and the lack of coordination are symptoms of inadequate management since plans should constitute a supporting and interlocking network and every plan should be reflected in a budget in a way that will aid in achieving enterprise goals.

Hiding inefficiencies.   Another danger in budgeting is that it may be used to hide inefficiencies. Budgets have a way of growing from precedent, and that a certain expenditure was made in the past can become evidence of its reasonableness in the present; if a department once spent a given amount for supplies, this cost becomes a minimum for future budgets. Also, managers sometimes learn that budget requests are likely to be pared down in the course of final approval, and therefore they ask for much more than they need. Unless budget making is accomplished by constant reexamination of standards and conversion factors by which planned action is translated into numerical terms, the budget may become an umbrella under which slovenly and inefficient management can hide.

Inflexibility.   Perhaps inflexibility is the greatest danger in budgets. Even if budgeting is not used to replace managing, the reduction of plans to numerical terms gives them a kind of misleading definiteness. It is entirely possible that events will prove that a larger amount should be spent for this kind of labor or that kind of material and a smaller amount for another, or that sales will exceed or fall below that amount forecast. Such differences may make a budget obsolete almost as soon as it is made, and, if managers must stay within the straitjacket of their budgets in the face of such events, the usefulness of budgets is reduced or nullified. This is especially true where budgets are made for long periods in advance.

Variable Budgets

Because of the dangers arising from inflexibility in budgets and because maximum flexibility consistent with efficiency underlies good planning, attention has been increasingly given to variable or flexible budgets. These are designed to vary usually as the volume of sales or some other measure of output varies and so are limited largely to expense budgets. The variable budget is based upon an analysis of expense items to determine how individual costs *should* vary with volume of output. Some costs do not vary with volume, particularly in so short a period as a month, 6 months, or a year. Among these are depreciation, property taxes and insurance, maintenance of plant and equipment, and costs of keeping a minimum staff of supervisory and other key personnel. Some of these standby, or period, costs—such as those of maintaining a minimum number of key or trained personnel for advertising or sales promotion and for research—depend upon managerial policy.

Costs that vary with volume of output range from those that are completely variable to those that are only slightly variable. The task of variable budgeting is to select some unit of measure that reflects volume, to inspect the various categories of costs (usually by reference to the chart of accounts), and, by statistical studies, methods of engineering analyses, and other means, to determine how these costs should vary with volume of output. At this stage, each category of cost is related to volume, sometimes with recognition of "steps" as volume increases. Each department is given these variable cost items, along with definite dollar amounts for its fixed, or standby, costs. Periodically—usually each month—department heads are then given the volume forecast for the immediate future, from which is calculated the dollar amounts of variable costs that make up the budget. In this way, a basic budget can be established for 6 months or a year in advance, but be made variable with shorter-term changes in sales and output.

As you can see, Figure 21-1 is based on the assumption that period costs will remain the same for a volume output of 0 to 6000 units. In most cases, a variable budget will represent a range of output where plant, managerial, organizational,

FIGURE 21-1

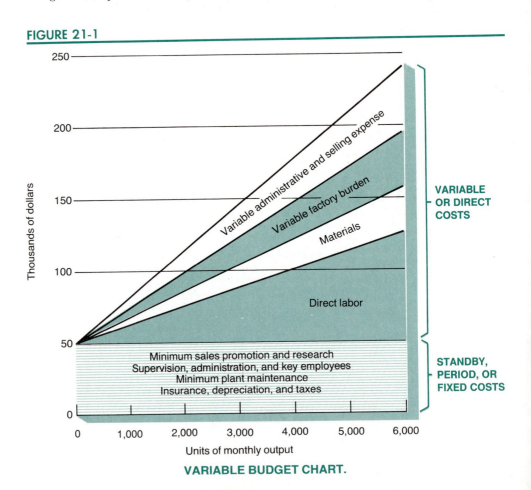

VARIABLE BUDGET CHART.

PERSPECTIVE:
EXAMPLE OF A VARIABLE BUDGET

A typical variable budget resulting from such an analysis is shown in Table 21-2. The table shows an expense budget for an entire company based on a range of expected monthly sales volume of $575,000 to $875,000. The assumption is that if sales were thought to be below $575,000, the company would probably have to reorganize its operations to profitably sustain this smaller volume. On the other hand, if monthly sales rose above $875,000, an expansion of company plant and organization would require a completely new variable budget.

and other elements of period cost will be the same. But, in practice, this may be over a range of 3000 to 10,000 units. If it were less than 3000 units, a different variable budget would be required with the level of period costs more suitable for the smaller volume; if it were more than 10,000 units, another variable budget would be necessary to reflect the level of period costs necessitated by a larger operation.

When using the various kinds of variable budgets, department managers must still make future plans. It may be easy to tell a certain supervisor that during the month of May he can have twelve trained electronic assemblers, then, several weeks later, that he may have fifteen in June, and a month later, that his budget for July will permit his having only ten. But the problems of hiring and training competent personnel make accomplishing these variations more costly than they are worth. In other words, efficiency may demand that department managers not vary certain of their expenses with short-term variations in vol-

TABLE 21-2   A Typical Variable Budget for an Entire Company
(In Thousands of Dollars)

	Monthly sales volume						
Item of expense	$575	$625	$675	$725	$775	$825	$875
Material	$184	$200	$216	$232	$248	$264	$280
Direct labor	70	76	82	88	94	100	106
Overhead costs	150	155	161	168	170	171	174
Cost of production	$404	$431	$459	$488	$512	$535	$560
Engineering	$ 35	$ 36	$ 38	$ 38	$ 38	$ 38	$ 40
Research and development	10	10	10	10	12	12	12
Sales and advertising	64	66	69	72	73	74	75
Administrative costs	60	62	63	63	64	65	66
Total costs	$573	$605	$639	$671	$699	$724	$753
Profit from operations	$2	$20	$36	$54	$76	$101	$122
Percentage of profit to sales	0.3%	3.2%	5.4%	7.5%	9.8%	12.3%	14%

ume. In the search for flexibility in budgets, as with other tools of management, an intelligent manager will not lose sight of basic objectives and efficiencies by blindly following any system.

Variable budgets work best when sales or other measures of volume can be reasonably well forecast and when longer-range plans are made, so that the level of expense will not have to be changed so often and on such short notice as to make the job of supervisors intolerable. Under these circumstances, one might well ask: What are the advantages of variable budgeting? Although a fixed budget will work as well with good plans and sales forecasts, a variable budget *forces* study of, and preoccupation with, factors which translate work load into labor or expense needs. Carefully worked-out conversion factors—worked out and applied in advance—are necessary for any good budgeting. This, rather than flexibility itself, appears to be the principal advantage of variable budgeting.

Alternative and Supplementary Budgets

Another method of obtaining variable budgeting is to establish **alternative budgets**. Sometimes a company will establish budgets for a high level of operation, a medium level, and a low level, and the three budgets will be approved for the company as a whole and for each organizational segment for 6 months or a year in advance. Then, at stated times, managers will be informed as to which budget to use in their planning and control. Alternative budgets are a modification of variable budgets, the latter being virtually infinitely variable instead of being limited to a few alternatives.

Budget flexibility is also obtained with a plan referred to as the **supplemental monthly budget**. Under this plan, a 6-month or 1-year budget is prepared for the primary purpose of outlining the framework of the company's plans, coordinating them among departments, and establishing department objectives. This is a basic or minimum budget. Then a supplementary budget is prepared each month on the basis of the volume of business forecast for that month. This budget gives each manager authority for scheduling output and spending funds above the basic budget if, and to the extent that, the shorter-term plans so justify. It avoids some of the detailed calculations necessary under the typical variable budget. But these budget approaches do not usually have the advantage of forcing complete analysis of all costs and relating them to volume.

Zero-Base Budgeting

Another type of budgeting, the purpose of which has much in common with the purpose of a well operated system of variable budgeting, is **zero-base budgeting**. The idea behind this technique is to divide enterprise programs into "packages" composed of goals, activities, and needed resources and then to calculate costs for each package from the ground up. By starting the budget of each package from base zero, costs are calculated afresh for each budget period, thus avoiding the common tendency in budgeting to look only at changes from a previous period.

This technique has generally been applied to so-called support areas, rather than to actual production areas, on the assumption that there is some room for discretion in expenditures for most programs in such areas as marketing, research and development, personnel, planning, and finance. The various programs thought to be desirable are costed and reviewed in terms of their benefits to the enterprise and are then ranked in accordance with those benefits and selected on the basis of which package will yield the benefit desired.

The principal advantage of this technique is, of course, the fact that it forces managers to plan each program package afresh. As managers do so, they review established programs and their costs in their entirety, along with newer programs and their costs.

Effective Budgetary Control

If budgetary controls are to work well, managers must remember that budgets are designed only as tools and not to replace managing, that they have limitations, and that they must be tailored to each job. Moreover, they are the tools of all managers and not only of the budget administrator or the controller. The only persons who can administer budgets, since they are plans, are the managers responsible for budgeted programs. No successful budget program can be truly "directed" or "administered" by a budget director. This staff officer can assist in the preparation and use of budgets by the responsible managers, but, unless the entire company management is to be turned over to the budget officer, this person should not be given the job of making budget-commitment or expenditure decisions.

Top management support.   To be most effective, budget making and administration must receive the wholehearted support of top management. To establish an office of budget administrator by decree and then forget about it leads to haphazard budget making and to saddling subordinate managers with another procedure or set of papers to prepare. On the other hand, if top management actively supports budget making and grounds a budget firmly on plans, requires divisions and departments to make and defend their budgets, and participates in this review, then budgets encourage alert management throughout the organization.

Participation.   Related to the participation of top management, another means of making budgets work is to make sure that all managers expected to operate and live under budgets have a part in their preparation. Real participation in budget making is necessary to ensure success. Most budget administrators and controllers recognize this fact, but too often in practice participation amounts to managers' being simply pressured to "accept" budgets.

Although budgets do furnish a means of delegating authority without loss of control, there is danger, as noted earlier, that they will be so detailed and inflexible that little real authority is, in fact, delegated. Some executives even believe that the best budget to give managers is one that lumps all their allowable expenditures for a period of time into a single amount and then gives them complete freedom as to how these funds are to be spent in pursuance of the company's goals. This kind of decentralization has much to recommend it, although better planning and control might be achieved by allowing the department manager real participation in budget making. It may be well, however, to allow department managers a reasonable degree of latitude in changing their budgets and in shifting funds, as long as they meet their *total* budgets.

Standards. One of the keys to making budgeting work is to develop and make available standards by which programs and work can be translated into needs for labor, operating expenses, capital expenditures, space, and other resources. Many budgets fail for lack of such standards, and some upper-level managers hesitate to allow subordinates to submit budget plans for fear that they may have no logical basis for reviewing budget requests. With conversion factors available, superior managers can review such requests and justify their approval or disapproval of them. Moreover, by concentrating on the resources required to do a planned job, managers can base their request on what they need to have for meeting output goals and improving performance. They no longer must cope with arbitrary across-the-board budget cuts—a very frustrating technique. In fact, across-the-board cuts are the surest evidence of poor planning and loss of control.

Information. Finally, if budgetary control is to work, managers need ready information as to actual and forecast performance under budgets by their departments. This information must be designed to show them how well they are doing. Unfortunately, however, such information is usually not available until it is too late for the manager to avoid budget deviations.

TRADITIONAL NONBUDGETARY CONTROL DEVICES

There are, of course, many traditional control devices not connected with budgets, although some may be related to, and used with, budgetary controls. Among the more important of them are (1) statistical data, (2) special reports and analyses, (3) the operational audit, and (4) personal observation.

1. Statistical Data

Statistical analyses of the innumerable aspects of an operation and the clear presentation of statistical data, whether of a historical or a forecast nature, are important to control. It is probably safe to say that most managers understand statistical data best when they are presented in chart or graphic form, since trends and relationships are then easier to see. Moreover, if data are to be meaningful, even when presented on charts, they should be formulated in such a way that comparisons to some standard can be made. What is the significance of a 3 or a 10 percent rise or fall in sales or costs? Who is responsible? Clear presentation of statistical data in graphic, tabular, or chart form is an art that requires imagination.

Moreover, since no manager can do anything about history, it is essential that statistical reports show trends so that the viewer can extrapolate where things are going. This means that most data, when presented on charts, should be made available as averages to rule out variations due to accounting periods, seasonal factors, accounting adjustments, and other periodic variations. In the 12-month moving average, for example, the total for 12 consecutive months, divided by 12, is used. You can see the difference in clarity from the comparative data presented graphically in Figure 21-2.

2. Special Reports and Analyses

For control purposes, special reports and analyses help in particular problem areas. Although routine accounting and statistical reports furnish a good share

FIGURE 21-2

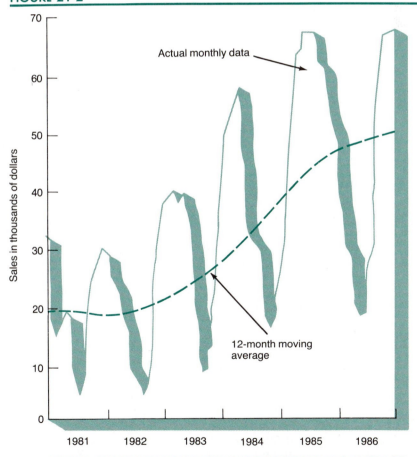

ACTUAL MONTHLY DATA VERSUS 12-MONTH MOVING AVERAGE.
Sales of company X, 1981–1986.

of necessary information, there are often areas in which they are inadequate. One successful manager of a complicated operation hired a small staff of trained analysts and gave them no assignment other than that of investigating and analyzing operations under his control. This group developed a surprising sense for situations where things did not seem just right. Almost invariably, their investigation disclosed opportunities for cost improvement or better utilization of capital that no statistical chart would have revealed.

It may be that some of the funds being spent for elaborate information programs could be more profitably spent for special analyses. Their nonroutine nature can highlight the unusual and, in so doing, reveal places for significant improvement in efficiency. In the routine search for pennies and accounting for them, opportunities for saving dollars may be overlooked.

3. The Operational Audit

Another effective tool of managerial control is the internal audit, or, as it is now coming to be called, the operational audit. **Operational auditing**, in its broadest sense, is the regular and independent appraisal, by a staff of internal auditors, of the accounting, financial, and other operations of a business. Although often limited to the auditing of accounts, in its most useful form operational auditing includes appraisal of operations generally, weighing actual results against planned results. Thus, operational auditors, in addition to assuring themselves that accounts properly reflect the facts, also appraise policies, procedures, use of authority, quality of management, effectiveness of methods, special problems, and other phases of operations.

4. Personal Observation

One should never overlook the importance of control through personal observation. Budgets, charts, reports, ratios, auditors' recommendations, and other devices are essential to control. But the manager who relies wholly on these devices and sits, so to speak, in a soundproof control room reading dials and manipulating levers can hardly expect to do a thorough job of control. Managers, after all, have the task of seeing that enterprise objectives are accomplished by *people,* and although many scientific devices aid in ensuring that people are doing that which has been planned, the problem of control is still one of measuring activities of human beings. It is amazing how much information an experienced manager can get from personal observation even from an occasional walk through a plant or an office. In some companies this is called "management by walking around."

TIME-EVENT NETWORK ANALYSES

Another planning and control technique is a time-event network analysis called Program Evaluation and Review Technique (PERT). Before the development of PERT, there were other techniques designed to watch how the parts of a program fit together during the passage of time and events.

Gantt Charts

The first of these techniques were the chart systems (see Figure 21-3) developed by Henry L. Gantt early in the twentieth century and culminating in the bar chart bearing his name. Although simple in concept, this chart, showing time relationships between "events" of a production program, has been regarded as revolutionary in management. What Gantt recognized was that total program goals should be regarded as a series of interrelated supporting plans (or events) that people can comprehend and follow. The most important developments of such control reflect this simple principle and also such basic principles of control as picking out the more critical elements of a plan to watch carefully.

Milestone Budgeting

As the result of the development of further techniques from the principles of the Gantt chart, and with better appreciation of the network nature of programs, "milepost" or "milestone" budgeting and PERT have been devised, contributing much to better control of many projects and operations. Used by an increasing number of companies in recent years in controlling engineering and development, milepost or milestone budgeting breaks a project down into controllable pieces and then carefully follows them. As we pointed out in the discussion of planning, even relatively simple projects contain a network of supporting plans or projects. In this approach to control, milestones are defined as identifiable segments. When accomplishment of a given segment occurs, cost or other results can be determined.

Program Evaluation and Review Technique (PERT)

Developed by the Special Projects Office of the United States Navy,[2] PERT was first formally applied to the planning and control of the Polaris Weapon System in 1958 and worked well in expediting the successful completion of that program. For a number of years, it was so enthusiastically received by the armed services that it became virtually a required tool for major contractors and

PERSPECTIVE:
PLANNING AND CONTROL IN ENGINEERING

The best way to plan and control an engineering project is to break it down into a number of events—for example, completion of preliminary drawings, an experimental model, a package design, a packaged prototype, and a production design. Or a project might be broken down vertically into subprojects—for example, the design of a circuit, a motor, a driving mechanism, a sensing device, a signal feedback device, and similar components—that can be designed individually, in a time sequence, to be ready when needed. Milestone budgeting allows a manager to see a complex program as a series of simpler parts and thus to maintain some control through knowing whether a program is succeeding or failing.

FIGURE 21-3

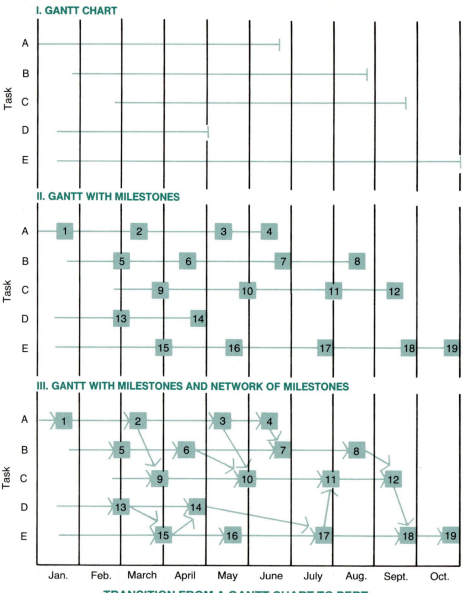

TRANSITION FROM A GANTT CHART TO PERT

The Gantt chart in I above shows the scheduled time of accomplishing a task, such as procurement (Task A), and the related schedules of doing other tasks, such as manufacture of parts (Task B). When each of these tasks is broken down into milestones, such as the preparation of purchase specifications (Task A-1), and when network relationships among the milestones of each task to those of other tasks are worked out, the result provides the basic elements of a PERT chart.

subcontractors in the armament and space industry. Although PERT is no longer much heard of in defense and space contracts for reasons that will be noted presently, its fundamentals are still essential tools of planning and control. Moreover, in a host of nongovernmental applications, including construction, engineering and tooling projects, and even such simple things as the scheduling of activities to get out monthly financial reports, PERT or its companion network technique, CPM (Critical Path Method), may be profitably used.

Major features.   In a sense, PERT is a variation of milestone budgeting. It uses a time-event network analysis, as shown in Figure 21-4. This very simple example illustrates the basic nature of PERT. Each *circle* represents an event—a supporting plan whose completion can be measured at a given time. The circles are

FIGURE 21-4

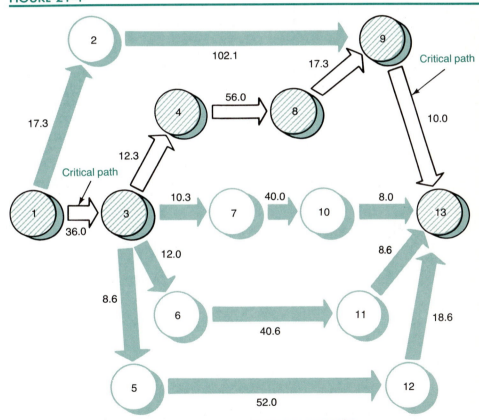

PERT FLOW CHART: TIME IN WEEKS.

Major assembly of an airplane. Events (major milestone of progress) are: (1) order program go-ahead; (2) initiate engine procurement; (3) complete plans and specifications; (4) complete fuselage drawings; (5) submit GFAE* requirements; (6) award tail assembly subcontract; (7) award wings subcontract; (8) complete manufacture of fuselage; (9) complete assembly of fuselage engine; (10) receive wings from subcontractors; (11) receive tail assembly from subcontractors; (12) receive GFAE; (13) complete aircraft.
*Note: GFAE stands for government-furnished airplane equipment.

numbered in the order in which the events occur. Each *arrow* represents an activity—the time-consuming element of a program, the effort that must be made between events; *activity time* is the elapsed time required to accomplish an event represented by the numbers beside the arrows.

In this example, only a single time is shown, but in the original PERT program there were *three time estimates:* "optimistic" time, an estimate of time required if everything goes exceptionally well; "most likely" time, an estimate of what the project engineer really believes necessary to do the job; and "pessi-mistic" time, an estimate based on the assumption that some logically conceivable bad luck—other than a major disaster—will be encountered. These estimates are often included in PERT because it is very difficult, in many engineering and development projects, to estimate time accurately, and partly, it is believed, because engineers will be willing to make a variety of estimates and will do their best to beat the pessimistic estimate. When several estimates are made, they are usually averaged, with special weight given to the most likely estimate; a single estimate is then used for calculations.

The next step is to compute the *critical path,* that is, the sequence of events which takes the longest time and which has zero (or the least) slack time. In Figure 21-4, the critical path is indicated as that following events 1-3-4-8-9-13. Over this path, the activity time for this sequence of events is 131.6 weeks; if promised delivery is in 135 weeks, even this critical path would have been completed 3.4 weeks ahead of time. Some of the other paths are almost as long as the critical path. For example, the path 1-2-9-13 is 129.4 weeks. This is not unusual in PERT charts, and it is customary to identify several crucial paths in order of importance. Although the critical path has a way of changing as key events are delayed in other parts of the program, identifying it at the start makes possible close watching of this particular sequence of events to ensure the total program's being on schedule.

Typical PERT analyses run into hundreds or thousands of events. Even though smaller PERT analyses—including the input of event accomplishment and the frequent calculation of critical path—can be done manually, it is esti-mated that when upward of approximately 200 to 300 events are involved, it is virtually impossible to handle the calculations without an electronic computer.

It is customary to summarize very large and complex time-event networks by subnetworks and to prepare the summarized network for top-management consideration. Thus, the top-management network might include some forty or fifty major events, each a summary of a number of subsidiary events. In fact, it is possible to group, or to break down, events so as to have a PERT network appropriate to every level of management.

Strengths and weaknesses. There are five important *advantages* of PERT. First, it forces managers to plan, because it is impossible to make a time-event analysis without planning and seeing how the pieces fit together. Second, it forces planning all down the line, because each subordinate manager must plan the event for which he or she is responsible. Third, it concentrates attention on critical elements that may need correction. Fourth, it makes possible a kind of forward-looking control; a delay will affect succeeding events, and possibly the whole project, unless the manager can somehow make up the time by shortening that of some action in the future. Fifth, the network system with its subsystems permits managers to aim reports and pressure for action at the right spot and level in the organization structure at the right time.

PERT also has certain *limitations.* Because of the importance of activity time to its operation, it cannot be useful when a program is nebulous and no reasonable "guesstimates" of schedule can be made; even here, however, insurance can be "bought" by such practices as putting two or more groups of people to work on an event when costs permit. PERT is also not practicable for routine planning of recurring events, such as mass production; although it could be used here, once a repetitive sequence of events is clearly worked out, so elaborate a continuing control is not required. A major disadvantage of PERT has been its emphasis on time only, not on costs. While this focus is suitable for programs where time is of the essence or where, as so often is the case, time and costs have a close direct relationship, the tool is more useful when considerations other than time are introduced into it. (There is, however, another program called PERT/COST which does consider costs.)

PERT is not a cure-all. It will not *do* the planning, although it *forces* planning. It will not make control automatic, although it establishes an environment where sound control principles can be appreciated and used. And it apparently involves rather less expense than might be thought. Setting up the network, its analysis, and its interpretation, and reporting from it probably require little, if any, more expense than most other planning and control techniques, unless, of course, these are made unduly complicated.

PROGRAM BUDGETING

One of the widely publicized tools of planning and control, used primarily in government operation but applicable to any kind of enterprise, is **program planning and budgeting (PPB)**, or, more simply, **program budgeting**. Although really not more, at least in its fundamentals, than what budgeting should always be, its emphasis and approach deserve analysis.

What Program Budgeting Is

Program budgeting is basically a means for providing a systematic method for allocating the resources of an enterprise in ways most effective to meet its goals. By emphasizing goals and programs to meet them, it overcomes the ordinary weakness of all kinds of budgets, even in business, of being too closely tied to the time frames of accounting periods of months, quarters, or years. By concentrating on goals and programs in the light of available resources, it stresses the desirability of assessing costs against benefits when selecting the best course toward accomplishing a program goal.

Problems in Applying Program Budgeting in Government

For most government agencies, program budgeting has not been the great tool in practice that its logic would imply. There are a number of reasons why it has not.

In the first place, many federal, state, and local government executives, particularly at the middle and lower levels of management, do not understand the philosophy and theory of the technique; they have been given directives and forms but have not really known what the system entails. A second major hurdle has been the lack of clearly defined goals; obviously, no one can plan and budget for an unknown or fuzzy goal. Another difficulty is the lack of attention to planning premises; even with clear program goals, the program budgeter is in the dark without knowledge of critical planning premises. Another problem arises from the long tradition in government of line budgeting, and most legislators, accustomed to line budgets, often will not tolerate other budgets unless they are recast in a line-item form. Also, many government budgetary divisions or staffs have been reluctant to make the change from their practice and procedures of annual budgets to longer-range program budgets. Other roadblocks include the fact that accounting data are seldom consistent with program budgeting, the lack of information in many areas to make meaningful cost effectiveness analyses, and the political problems of reorganizing government departments to improve concentration of program responsibility.

PROCEDURES PLANNING AND CONTROL

Procedures present a rewarding area of planning and control to which a systems approach can be applied. They are desirable tools for efficiently getting things done in a given way or for control. But procedures can also make for departmental rigidity that thwarts innovation and response to change. Although they *should* be designed to implement plans and to respond to change, they too often are not.

Effective planning and control of procedures depend on recognizing that they are inherently systems. Procedures normally extend into various departments, and it is a rare procedure which does not concern itself with more than two. This increases the importance of their control. Accounting departments, for example, tend to regard their procedures as concerned purely with their function, and yet a simple payroll or expense account procedure reaches into every nook and cranny of the company and affects many nonaccounting activities. Personnel, purchasing, and other functional departmental procedures do likewise.

How Procedures Get Out of Control

Procedures often get out of control because of the specialized approach of each organization function in setting them up for its particular operation. Accounting procedures may conflict with, or overlap, purchasing procedures, differ slightly from personnel procedures, and somewhat duplicate sales department procedures. Duplication, overlapping, and conflict are usually elusive and partial; there is rarely either complete duplication or clear disagreement. Commonly, different forms and records are called for, though they use the same subject matter. This, of course, can be expensive.

Procedures also get out of control when managers try to use them to solve problems instead of solving the problems through better policies, clearer delegations, or improved direction. Then again, many procedures are instituted to correct a mistake which might never be made again. In one case, a division head ordered development of a complete system of procedures to prevent duplicating one serious customer complaint. This had happened only once. A clear policy statement, simple routing of complaints, and assigning the handling of complaints to the service manager would have taken care of the situation and avoided any recurrence.

Procedures also evade control by becoming obsolete, either because they are not kept up to date or because failure to police them permits deviations in practice. Moreover, procedures have a way of becoming customs, ingrained in departments and in individuals who have a stubborn resistance to change. And managers find it expedient to impose new procedures on the old, a haphazard practice.

Finally, a major reason why procedures get out of control is that managers are often not clear as to what procedures should do, how much they cost, when they are duplicated, how to overhaul them, and how to control them. And to top all this, managers often fail to obtain the interest and support of top managers in the tedious and unromantic planning and control procedures. There are, however guidelines that make the planning and control of procedures more effective as shown in the following.

Guidelines for Effective Procedures

1. Minimize procedures.   Limit procedures to those situations in which they are clearly called for. The costs of procedures in paper handling, stifled thinking, delay, and lack of responsiveness to change are such as to make a concerned manager think twice before initiating them. Managers must weigh the potential gain in money or necessary control against the disadvantages and costs.

2. Make sure procedures are plans.   Since procedures are plans, they must be designed to reflect and help accomplish enterprise (not just departmental) objectives and policies. Have they been planned? If they are necessary, are they designed effectively and efficiently to accomplish plans? For example, a procedure to handle orders for spare parts or repair defective parts should expedite a job so as to meet customer service standards without undue delay.

3. Analyze procedures.   Procedures should be carefully analyzed to ensure a minimum of duplication, overlapping, and conflict. To do this, the procedures must be visualized. This, in turn, necessitates mapping them with their various steps identified and interrelated. That this is not always easy is exemplified by a defense material procedure which, when charted, took a piece of paper 27 feet long and involved over 250 related required actions!

4. Recognize procedures as systems.   Any given procedure, whether it specifies the handling of payroll, procurement, inventory planning and control, or other of the many uses, is in itself a system of interrelated activities normally in a network rather than a pure linear form. Therefore, groups of procedures are usually interrelated systems.

5. Estimate the cost of procedures.   The analysis of procedures should include an estimate of what its operation will cost. While some costs cannot be ascertained, such as the cost of possible frustration to those involved, an estimate may bring into sharper focus the answer to the question: Is this procedure worthwhile?

6. Police the operation of procedures.   To be sure that procedures are needed and are doing the job intended, they must be policed. This requires three steps: (1) Knowledge of procedures must be made available in manual or other form to those who must follow them. (2) Employees must be taught how to operate under them, and, ideally, why the procedures are necessary and what purpose they are designed to serve. (3) There must be machinery to ensure that people do understand and are employing up-to-date procedures and that they are doing the job intended. This requires constructive auditing.

Procedures Analysis and Electronic Data Processing

An encouraging consequence of present systems and procedures planning and the analysis of procedures as systems is that they are often programmed on electronic data processing (EDP) equipment. However, there remains the danger that the systems and procedure expert will become so enamored of programming as to forget that electronic automation of procedures can reflect the system of procedures only as it exists.

Despite this danger, EDP has stimulated broad analysis and improvement of procedures. A strong effort needs to be made to ensure that the procedure is workable and clear before it is automated. Nevertheless, the systems approach of the programmer forces an orderly approach to procedure analysis. Since, at the very least, a procedure cannot be put on a machine without having been mapped, the very process of mapping often shows up the existence of overlapping and the need for simplification, as well as the means of achieving it.

The need is great for experts who understand the nature of procedures as a management tool and their importance in accomplishing enterprise objectives. Systems and procedure analysis—like improved information technology, discussed next—is high-level, difficult, and challenging work.

INFORMATION TECHNOLOGY

The systems model of management shows that communication is needed for carrying out the managerial functions and to link the organization with its external environment. The Management Information System (MIS) provides the communication link that makes managing possible.

PERSPECTIVE:
PLANNING AND CONTROL AT VOLKSWAGEN

Siegfried Hoehn, director of strategy and investment at Volkswagen A.G. (VW), writing from the perspective of a practitioner, points out that the information system affects the whole system of managing, but especially planning and controlling.[3] Figure 21-5 provides an overview of the planning and control model used by the VW Group.

Although the planning and control system at VW is quite comprehensive, Hoehn suggests that new developments in information technology will change planning and control in the future. Some of the trends include the use of integrative systems, multifunction terminals, telecommunication networks, and computer systems. Moreover, greater decentralization allows tailoring the system to the specific functions of the users. The application of the computers facilitates the automation of the workplaces with computers doing more of the routine work.[4]

The term **management information system** has been used differently by various authors. We define it as: *A formal system to gather, integrate, compare, analyze, and disperse information internal and external to the enterprise in a timely, effective, and efficient manner.*

The management information system has to be tailored to specific needs and may include *routine* information, such as monthly reports, information that points out *exceptions*, especially at critical points, and information necessary to *predict* the future. The guidelines for designing a management information system are similar to designing systems and procedures and other control systems. Since they have been discussed elsewhere, they need not be elaborated here.

Electronic equipment permits fast and economical processing of huge amounts of data. The computer can, with proper programming, process data toward logical conclusions, classify them, and make them readily available for a manager's use. In fact, data do not become information until they are processed into a usable form that informs.

Expanding Basic Data

The focus of attention on management information, coupled with its improved processing, has led to the reduction of long-known limitations. Managers for years have recognized that traditional accounting information, aimed at the calculation of profits, has been of limited value for control. Yet in many companies this has been virtually the only regularly collected and analyzed type of data. Managers need all kinds of nonaccounting information about the external environment such as social, economic, political, and technical developments. In addition, managers need nonaccounting information on internal operations. The information should be qualitative as well as quantitative.

While not nearly enough progress has been made in meeting these require-

FIGURE 21-5

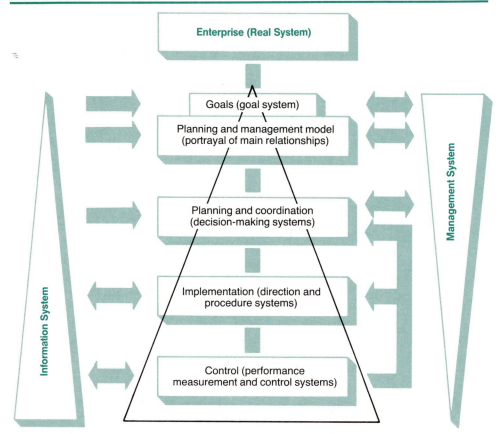

**INFORMATION, PLANNING, AND CONTROL
IN THE MANAGEMENT SYSTEM OF THE VOLKSWAGEN GROUP.**

From Siegfried Hoehn, "How Information Technology Is Transforming Corporate Planning," *Long Range Planning* (August 1986), p. 19. Used with permission.

ments, the computer, plus operations research, has led to enormous expansion of available managerial information. One sees this especially in relation to data on marketing, competition, production and distribution, product cost, technological change and development, labor productivity, and goal accomplishment.

Information Indigestion

Managers who have experienced the impact of better and faster data processing are justly concerned with the danger of information indigestion. Their appetite for figures whetted, the data originators and processors are turning out material at an almost frightening rate. Managers are complaining of being buried under printouts, reports, projections, and forecasts which they do not have time to read or cannot understand or which do not fill their particular needs.

Intelligence Services

One attempt at solving the information overload is the establishment of an intelligence service and the development of a new profession of intelligence experts. The service would be provided by specialists who know (or find out) what information managers need and who would know how to digest and interpret such information for managerial use. Some companies have established organizational units under such names as "administrative services" or "management analyses and services" for making information understandable and useful.[5]

THE USE OF COMPUTERS IN HANDLING INFORMATION

The computer can store, retrieve, and process information. Often a distinction is made between kinds of computers. The *mainframe* is a full-scale computer. Such a computer is capable of handling huge amounts of data, often costing millions of dollars. Some of these "supercomputers" are used for engineering, simulation, and the manipulation of large data bases. The *minicomputer* has less memory and is smaller than the mainframe. This kind of computer is often connected with peripheral equipment. The *microcomputer* is still smaller and may be a desk computer, home computer, personal computer, portable computer, or a computer for a small business system. Increasingly, however, minicomputers are used by large organizations either as a stand-alone computer or as a part of a network.

But the distinction between the various classes of computers is disappearing. With the introduction of the new microcomputers based on the 80386 microprocessor, these computers have become very powerful. However, the full utilization of the hardware (the computers) depends to a considerable degree on the lagging development of the software programs.

Among the many business applications of the computer are material requirements planning, manufacturing resource planning, computer-aided control of manufacturing machinery, project costing, inventory control, and purchasing. The computer also aids design and engineering, an application which made the U.S. space program possible. Then there are the many uses in processing financial information such as accounts receivable and accounts payable, payroll, capital budgeting, and financial planning.

The Impact of Computers on Managers at Different Organizational Levels

Information needs differ at various organizational levels. Therefore, the impact of computers will also be different.

At the *supervisory level* activities are usually highly programmable and repetitive. Consequently, the use of computers is widespread at this level. Scheduling, daily planning, and controlling of the operation are just a few examples.

Middle-level managers, such as department heads or plant managers, usually have responsibility for administration and coordination. But much of the information important to them is now also available to top management if the company has a comprehensive information system. For this reason, some people think that the need for middle-level managers will be reduced by the computer. Others predict that their roles may be expanded and changed.

Top-level managers are responsible for the strategy and overall policy of the organization.[6] They are not only determining the general direction of the company but also are responsible for the appropriate interaction between the enterprise and its environment. Clearly, the tasks of CEOs are not easily programmable. Yet top managers can use the computer to retrieve information from a data base that aids the application of decision models.[7] This enables the company to make timely responses to changes in the external environment. Still, the use of the computer will probably less severely affect the jobs of top managers than those at the lower levels.

The Application and Impacts of Microcomputers

The personal computer (PC) is becoming increasingly appealing to managers because it is flexible and relatively inexpensive, and can be used more quickly than the mainframe computer. Its applications include the following:

Budget preparation	Simulation models
Graphic presentations	Forecasting
Electronic spread sheets	Electronic mail
Financial analyses	Tapping into data bases
Word processing	Time sharing

The implications of the increasing use of the microcomputer are manifold. There is a need for specialized staff support, education for managers and nonmanagers, and a redefinition of jobs. For example, the distinction between line and staff is becoming less clear. The information that was formerly gathered by staff can now be obtained with ease by other managers by accessing a common data base. On the other hand, information that was the prerogative of upper-level managers can also be made available to personnel at lower levels, possibly resulting in the shift of power to lower levels in the organization. But not all information should be accessible to all people in the company. Thus, one of the problems currently faced by many firms is maintaining the security of information.

CHALLENGES CREATED BY INFORMATION TECHNOLOGY

Securing the unauthorized use of information is just one of many challenges. Others are the reduction in resistance to the use of computers, speech recognition devices, and computer networks.

Resistance to Computer Application

While high school students may feel comfortable using the computer, some managers fear it. One study revealed that the typical executive affected by this phobia is a male about 50 years old who has worked most of the time for the same company. This fear might explain why certain managers are reluctant to use the computer. Naturally, they do not want to look unskilled when they are not able to understand the new technology and do not have the typing skills often necessary for submitting data to the computer. In the past, typing was considered the task of the secretary, not the manager.

Another survey of CEOs of *Fortune 500* companies showed that over 50 percent of the respondents never used the computer and over 70 percent of them did not have a computer in their offices.[8] On the other hand, a majority of the top executives thought that computers assist managers in doing their jobs, suggesting that computers are considered useful below the level of CEO. Those not favorably inclined to the use of computers made various comments, such as saying that their time is too valuable to learn computer skills.

The application of graphics can help to overcome the resistance to computers. Instead of being buried in reams of computer outputs, information is displayed as easy-to-understand graphics. PepsiCo, for example, invested $250,000 in decision-support graphics over 3 years, generating 80,000 charts and slides.[9] At any rate, as more sophisticated technology makes the use of the computer easier, its acceptance is likely to increase.

Speech Recognition Devices

Another way to encourage the use of computers is through speech recognition devices.[10] The aim is to input data into the computer by speaking in a normal manner, rather than through the use of the keyboard. Several companies are working on such devices, but it may still take several years before they can be widely applied, although simple speech recognition has been in limited use for some time. Just expanding the vocabulary through larger memory is not enough. Imagine the program sophistication needed to distinguish between similar sounds such as "then" and "than," "to" and "too" and "two." Despite the complex problems, some think that the efforts made in this area will result in some products that may revolutionize office operation.

Telecommuting

The widespread use of computers and the east of linking them through telephone lines to the mainframe company computer has led to **telecommuting**. This means that a person can work at home at the computer terminal instead of commuting to work. Some of the advantages claimed include a greater flexibility in scheduling work, the avoidance of traffic congestion, and a reduced need for office space.

The futurist Alvin Toffler envisioned an "electronic cottage" with computer terminals installed at home. But John Naisbitt in his book *Megatrends* is skeptical of the idea and suggested that after some time of telecommuting, workers will miss the office gossip and the human interactions with fellow workers.[11] Some companies who have contracted work to telecommuters have been criticized for not providing the benefits usually given to office workers. At Pacific Bell, however, participants in the voluntary program are considered full-time employees.[12] Moreover, some employees go to the office at least once a week to check their mail and to mingle with coworkers.

With the increasing traffic congestion, especially in metropolitan areas, one may see a somewhat greater use of telecommuting. But it is doubtful that it will replace the office as we know it today.[13]

FIGURE 21-6

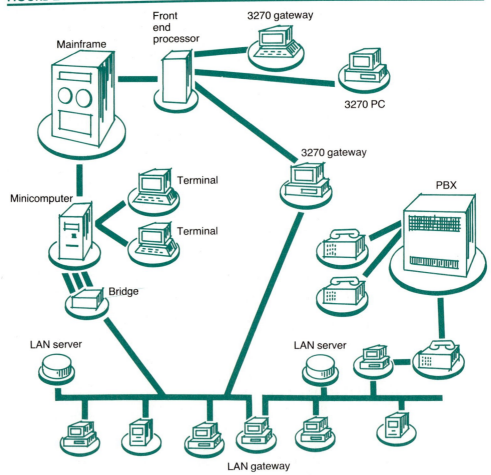

THE OFFICE OF TOMORROW.

In the office of the future, all electronic components will be connected, providing even greater productivity through new applications.

Courtesy of Businessland, Inc., from "The Businessland Technology Forum on Networking," 1986.

Computer Networks

The widespread use of stand-alone computers often results in duplication of efforts. The data base in the mainframe or the minicomputer, for example, may not be accessible from the desktop computer. Therefore, computer networks have been developed that link workstations with each other, with larger computers, and with peripheral equipment, as illustrated in Figure 21-6.

Persons at several workstations can communicate with each other as well as access other computers.[14] Moreover, workstations can be connected to costly hardware that may be underutilized by a single user. For example, several users can share laser printers or tape backup units that ensure saving of the data files. There are many other applications of computer networks such as electronic mail, the gathering and dissemination of industry data, and future trends. Although computer networking is still in its infancy, new technological developments rapidly change the system of information handling.

FOR DISCUSSION

1. The techniques of control appear to be as much techniques of planning as they are of control. In what ways is this true? Why would you expect it to be so?

2. "Variable budgets are flexible budgets." Discuss.

3. It is often claimed that an operating expense budget must be set at a level lower than expected in order to ensure the attainment of cost and profit goals. Do you agree?

4. To what extent, and how, can budgeting be approached on a grass roots basis, that is, from the bottom of the organization upward?

5. If you were going to institute a program of special control reports and analyses for a top manager, how would you go about it?

6. PERT is a management invention that takes basic principles and knowledge and, through design to get a desired result, comes up with a useful technique of planning and control. Analyze PERT with this in mind.

7. Why has program budgeting been regarded as so important in government? If you were to introduce it in a government department, how would you proceed? What would you need to do so?

EXERCISES/ACTION STEPS

1. Take PERT and use it to plan your college study program. What are the advantages in using this technique? What are some problems?

2. Take an organization you know and show how it uses computers.

CASES

CASE 21-1
THE ELECTRICAL CONSTRUCTION COMPANY

Independent auditors had just completed the examination of the operations of a large electrical construction company. The item that they felt needed closer attention was the budget control of new construction work.

The audit showed that most electrical designs for new construction were carried out at the headquarters of the company by a project manager. In preparing a budget for a new project, he checked the expenses for similar jobs in the past, then simply multiplied them by various factors.

The auditors found that during the past 2 years, most budgets had been greatly overestimated. Incidentally, it was about 2 years ago that the project manager had been given the primary responsibility for budgeting. In this role, he would submit his budget to the Expenditure Control Committee, consisting of higher-level managers who had only a limited interest in budgeting. It was to this committee that the project manager submitted requests for additional money whenever needed. Most of the requests were approved.

The chief auditor felt that the project team tended to "expand" the time needed to complete the task whenever the members thought the budget made it possible. In other words, they "adjusted" their productivity to match the money allocated to the project.

The auditors noted that other contractors could do similar jobs for 20 percent less money. They concluded that a new control procedure was needed.

1. What do you think of the budgeting process?
2. What kind of control procedure should the auditors recommend?

CASE 21-2
THE WHOLESALE DRUG COMPANY

The Wholesale Drug Company grew rapidly to become one of the largest firms of its kind. The success was due primarily to the leadership of the president, Ms. Johnson. Since many similar, but smaller, enterprises used the computer for recordkeeping and data processing, Ms. Johnson was under great pressure to install a computerized control system to keep track of twenty distributions centers scattered throughout the nation.

Up to that time, expenses and income were recorded by a relatively simple ledger sheet and a journal showing the data for the twenty centers. This kind of recordkeeping, which was done by hand, allowed for easy comparison of the centers. Payrolls were done in a similar manner, and checks were usually processed within 24 hours. At that time five people and two supervisors were employed in the accounting department.

Several computer companies looked at the system but their analysis showed that cost savings were hardly possible. However, one firm made a rather convincing case for a new data-processing system. The consulting firm predicted the following benefits: (1) faster processing of information, (2) more detailed information on the operation, and (3) a reduction in costs.

After 2 years of using the new system, Ms. Johnson, who had reluctantly agreed to computerize the system, related the following story: "Before the use of the computer, we had seven people in the accounting department. Now we have nine plus seven people in the data-processing center. It is true that it takes only a few minutes to get the output from the computer, but we cannot run the program until the last distribution center provides the data. Unfortunately, this means delays, because we depend on the slowest operational unit for their input. It is true that we can get more detailed information, but I do not know if anybody ever looks at it. It is just too time-consuming to find the relevant information in the stacks of computer printouts and to interpret the data. I just wish we could go back to the old ledger system. But we invested so much money and have reached a point of no return."

1. Why did the computerized system not live up to its expectations?

2. What should Ms. Johnson do now?

3. How would you design a computerized system? What factors would you consider?

REFERENCES

1. Primarily because of the negative implications of budgeting in the past, the more positive phrase "profit planning" is sometimes used and the budget is then known as the "profit plan."

2. But also separately developed as the Critical Path Method by engineers at the Du Pont Company at virtually the same time. Only PERT is discussed here because the Critical Path Method, although different in some respects, utilizes the same principles.

3. Siegfried Hoehn, "How Information Technology is Transforming Corporate Planning," _Long Range Planning_ (August 1986), pp. 18–30.

4. See also John C. Papageorgiou, "Decision Making in the Year 2000," _Interfaces_ (April 1983), pp. 77–86.

5. For organizational issues in establishing an MIS unit see Mark Klein, "Information Politics," _Datamation_ (Aug. 1, 1985), pp. 87–92.

6. Clark Holloway thinks that in the 1990s supercomputers may share many functions of top executives. See his article "Strategic Management and Artificial Intelligence," _Long Range Planning_ (October 1983), pp. 89–93. The use of information technology for formulating a strategy is discussed by Sid L. Huff, "Information Technology and Corporate Strategy," _Business Quarterly_ (Summer 1985), pp. 18 ff.

7. While some argue that senior managers can keep better control of the operation as well as of subordinates, others consider the impact on top management minimal. For discussions of this topic see John Dearden, "SMR Forum: Will the Computer Change the Job of Top Management?" _Sloan Management Review_ (Fall 1983), pp. 195–204; John C. Camillus and Albert L. Lederer, "Corporate Strategy and the Design of Computerized Information System," _Sloan Management Review_ (Spring 1985), p. 35 ff.

8. Lisa L. Spiegelman, "Top-Level Managers Not Using PCs, Survey Finds," _Infoworld_ (May 26, 1988), p. 24.

9. "Management Warms Up to Computer Graphics," _Business Week_ (Aug. 13, 1984), pp. 96–101.

10. Paul Duke, Jr., "Can We Talk?" _The Wall Street Journal, A Special Report: Technology in the Work Place_ (Nov. 10, 1986).

11. John Naisbitt, _Megatrends_ (New York: Warner Books, 1982), chap. 1.

12. David Needle, "Telecommuting: Off to a Slow Start," _Infoworld_ (May 19, 1986), pp. 43–46.

13. Margrethe H. Olson, "Do You Telecommute?" *Datamation* (Oct. 15, 1985), pp. 129–132.

14. For a discussion of Local Area Networks see Laurie Flynn, "LANs" *Infoworld* (Oct. 27, 1986), pp. 45–46.

FOR FURTHER INFORMATION

Anthony, Robert N., and John Dearden. *Management Control Systems,* 4th ed. (Homewood, Ill.: Richard D. Irwin, 1980).

Cash, James I., Jr., F. Warren McFarlan, and James L. McKenney. *Corporate Information Systems— Text and Cases* (Homewood, Ill.: Richard D. Irwin, 1983).

Churchill, Neil C. "Budget Choice: Planning vs. Control," *Harvard Business Review* (July–August 1984), pp. 150–164.

Davis, Gordon B., and Margrethe H. Olson. *Management Information Systems* (New York: McGraw-Hill Book Company, 1985).

Dickson, Gary W., and James C. Wetherbe. *The Management Information Systems* (New York: McGraw-Hill Book Company, 1985).

Holsapple, Clyde W., and Andrew B. Whinston. *Business Expert Systems* (Homewood, Ill.: Richard D. Irwin, 1987).

Karasik, Myron S. "Selecting a Small Business Computer," *Harvard Business Review* (January–February 1984), pp. 26–30.

Keen, Peter G. W., and Lynda A. Woodman. "What to Do With All Those Micros," *Harvard Business Review* (September–October 1984), pp. 142–150.

Kroeber, D. W. *Management Information Systems* (New York: The Free Press, 1982).

McFarlan, F. Warren. "Information Technology Changes the Way You Compete," *Harvard Business Review* (May–June 1984), pp. 98–103.

Wetherbe, James C., and John R. Montanari. "Zero Based Budgeting in the Planning Process," *Strategic Management Journal* (January–March 1981), pp. 1–14.

Productivity and Operations Management*

CHAPTER OBJECTIVES

After reading this chapter, you should be able to:

1. Identify the nature of productivity issues and suggest ways to improve effectiveness and efficiency.

2. Describe the nature of production and operations management as an applied case of managerial planning and control.

3. Discuss the managerial techniques found to be especially useful for operations planning and control as well as other areas of enterprise operation.

4. Describe techniques for improving productivity.

5. Suggest some probable future developments in operations planning and control.

---

*Additional topics in production and operations management are discussed in other parts of the book. See, for example, Chapter 6 for various aspects of decision making, including the topic of decision support systems, Chapter 13 for job design; and Chapter 21 for procedures planning and control, management information systems, and different kinds of control techniques.

*I*n a real sense, the whole book is about the improvement of productivity. But this important topic will receive special attention in this chapter, with an emphasis on the micro level of production and operations management.[1]

PRODUCTIVITY PROBLEMS AND MEASUREMENT

It is probably not too much to say that productivity will be one of the major concerns of managers not only for the remaining part of the 1980s but also for the 1990s, and probably beyond. But this concern extends beyond the boundaries of the United States into many parts of the world. Even Japan, which is admired for productivity improvements, is now concerned about remaining competitive in the world market.

Productivity Problems

Productivity implies measurement, which, in turn, is an essential step in the control process. Although there is general agreement about the need for improving productivity, there is little consensus about the fundamental causes of the problem and what to do about them.[2] The blame has been attributed to various factors. Some people place it on the greater proportion of less-skilled workers in respect to the total labor force, but others disagree. There are those who see the cutback in research and the emphasis on immediate results as the main culprit. Another reason given for the productivity dilemma is the growing affluence of people, which makes them less ambitious. Still others cite the breakdown in family structure, the workers' attitudes, and government policies and regulations. Increasingly, the attention shifts to management as the cause of the problem—as well as the solution, which will be our focus.

Measuring Productivity of Knowledge Workers

You might recall that we defined **productivity** in Chapter 1 as *the input-output ratio within a time period with due consideration for quality.* This definition can be applied to the productivity of organizations, managers, staff personnel, and workers. Measurement of skills work is relatively easy, but it becomes more difficult for knowledge work. The difference between the two kinds of work is the relative use of knowledge and skills. Thus, a person on the production line would be considered a skill worker while the assistant to the manager with planning as his or her main function would be a knowledge worker. Managers, engineers, and programmers are knowledge workers because the relative amount of their work does not consist of utilizing skills, as would be the case for bricklayers, mechanics, and butchers. But the job title cannot be the sole guide for making distinctions. The owner of a gas station may schedule the day's tasks, determine priorities, and direct subordinates, but the owner may also change brakes, adjust the carburetor, or realign the front wheels on a car.

It is clear that, in general, the productivity of the knowledge worker is more difficult to measure than that of the skill worker (note also that worker productivity measurement is somewhat artificial because it often ignores the cost of capital). One difficulty in measuring the productivity of knowledge workers is that some outputs are really activities that help to achieve end results. Thus, the engineer contributes indirectly to the final product. Another difficulty is that knowledge workers often assist other organizational units. The advertising manager's efforts should improve sales. But it is hard to say for sure what the exact contribution is. Still another difficulty is that the quality of the knowledge workers' outputs are often difficult to measure. The effects of a strategic decision, for example, may not be evident for several years, and even then the success or failure of the new strategic direction may depend on many external forces beyond the control of the manager.

Several Approaches to Productivity Improvement

There is not one best approach to productivity improvement, but there are many.[3] Here are some examples:

- Kaiser Aluminum and Chemical Corporation emphasized the formulation of improvement objectives, the measurement of performance against these objectives, an effective reporting system, and frequent reinforcement of good performance.

- Hughes Aircraft Company, with a very large portion of their employees being knowledge workers, provided principles and guidelines for productivity improvement covering areas such as recognition of good performance, use of work modules, design of meaningful work, emphasis on goals, and development of the ability to work with people.

It is evident, then, that productivity improvement is achieved by good management practices advocated throughout the book. But we will now turn to the specific area of production and operations management where measurement is relatively easy and consequently has been the focus of productivity improvement programs in the past.

PRODUCTION AND OPERATIONS MANAGEMENT[4]

One of the major areas in any kind of enterprise, whether business, government, or others, is production and operations management. It is also the area where managing as a scientifically based art got its start. As we recall the contributions of such pioneers in management as Taylor, Gantt, and Frank Gilbreth, to mention only a few, we note that their interest was largely to improve productivity and to manufacture products most efficiently while still recognizing, as they did, the importance of the human factor as an indispensable input.

In the past, **production management** was the term used to refer to those activities necessary to manufacture products. However, in recent years, the area has been generally expanded to include such activities as purchasing, warehousing, transportation, and other operations from the procurement of raw materials through various activities until a product is available to the buyer. In addition, the term **operations management** refers to activities necessary to produce and deliver a service as well as a physical product.

There are, of course, other essential activities undertaken by a typical enterprise. These enterprise functions often include, in addition to production, research and development, engineering, marketing and sales, accounting, and financing. We have chosen in this chapter to deal only with what has come to be called "operations management" or "production management," and often "production and operations management" (POM). It should be pointed out that this is not, of course, the same thing as "operational"-management theory. You should recall, as explained earlier, that operational-management theory is a study of the practice (managing) that theory or science is designed to underpin.

OPERATIONS MANAGEMENT SYSTEMS

Operations management has to be seen as a system. Figure 22-1 gives an overview of the operations function. In the operations management model the **inputs** include needs of customers, information, technology, labor and manage-

FIGURE 22-1

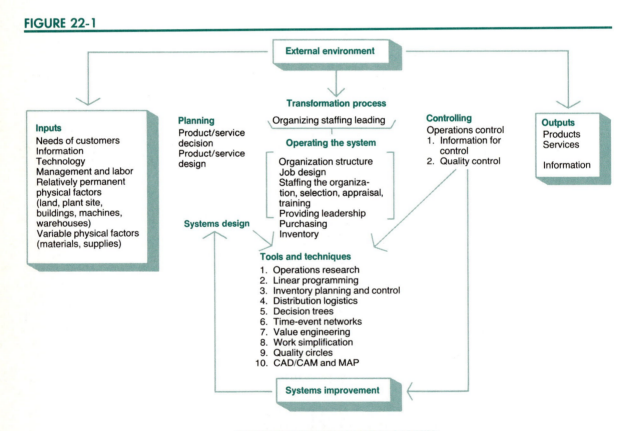

OPERATIONS MANAGEMENT SYSTEM.

ment, fixed assets, and variable assets that are relevant to the transformation process. Managers and workers use the information and physical factors to produce outputs. Some physical elements, such as land, plant site, buildings, machines, and warehouses, are relatively permanent. Other physical elements, such as materials and supplies, are consumed in the process of producing outputs. The **transformation process** incorporates planning, operating, and controlling the system. There are many tools and techniques available to facilitate the transformation process. The model also reflects a constant concern for improving the system. **Outputs** consist of products and services and may even be information, such as may be provided by a consulting organization.

The last part of the model shows that operations are influenced by many **external factors**, such as safety regulations or fair labor practices. Since the external environment is discussed elsewhere in this book, we will not expand on it here, but simply point out that operations management must be an open system interacting with its surroundings.

The operations management model (Figure 22-1) serves as a framework for the discussions that follow. Illustrations of operations systems[5] with inputs, transformation (sometimes also called "process"), and outputs are shown in Table 22-1. As you can see, there is a close relationship between this model and the one introduced in Chapter 1, since this operations model may be regarded as a subsystem of a total management system.

Planning Operations

Objectives, premises, and strategies of an enterprise (discussed in Part 2 of this book) determine the search for, and the selection of, the product or service. In this discussion, production of physical products is emphasized, but the concepts can also be applied to providing services. After an end product has been selected, the specifications are determined and the technological feasibility of producing it is considered. The design of an operations requires decisions concerning the location of facilities, the process to be used, the quantity to be produced, and the quality of the product.

Special interests in a product decision.   One of the basic decisions an enterprise makes is to *select* a product or products it intends to produce and market. This

TABLE 22-1   Examples of Operations Systems

Inputs	Transformation	Outputs
1. Plant, factory machines, people, materials	Assembling bicycles	Completed bicycles
2. Students with limited knowledge, skills, and attitudes	Lectures, cases, experiential exercises, term papers	Students with enhanced knowledge, skills, and attitudes
3. Client problem	Consulting: data-collection analysis, evaluation of alternatives, selection of alternative, recommendation	Consulting report recommending course of action

requires gathering product ideas that will satisfy the needs of customers and contribute to the goals of an enterprise while being consistent with the strategy of the firm.[6] In a product decision, the various interests of functional managers must be considered. For example, a production manager may want a product that can be produced without difficulty, at a reasonable cost, and with long production runs. Engineers may share many of these aims, but they are often looking for engineering sophistication and not how the product can actually be produced at a reasonable cost.

The sales or marketing manager's interest is likely to be the needs of customers, and his or her aim is to increase the sales of products with ready availability and competitive prices. Moreover, sales managers may want to offer a broad product line without considering the engineering, production, transportation, and warehousing costs and problems involved. The finance managers concerns are likely to be in costs and profits, high return on investment, and low financial risks. The divergent interests of these functionally oriented managers and professionals influence what products will be produced and marketed, but it is the general manager who has to integrate the various interests and balance revenues with costs, profits with risks, long-term with short-term growth.

Product and production design.   The design of a product and its production require a number of activities. The following steps have often been suggested:

1. Create product ideas by searching for consumer needs and screening the various alternatives.

2. Select the product on the basis of various considerations, including data from market and economic analyses, and make a general feasibility study.

3. Prepare a preliminary design by evaluating various alternatives, taking into consideration reliability, quality, and maintenance requirements.

4. Reach a final decision by developing, testing, and simulating the processes to see if they work.

5. Decide whether the enterprise's current facilities are adequate or if new or modified facilities are required.

6. Select the process for producing the product; consider the technology and the methods available.

7. After the product is designed, prepare the layout[7] of the facilities to be used, plan the system of production, and schedule the various things that must be done.

Systems design.   In producing a product, several basic kinds of production layouts can be considered.[8] One alternative is to arrange the layouts in the order in which the product is *produced* or *assembled*. For example, a truck assembly line may be arranged so that the preassembled front and rear axles are attached to the frame, followed by the installation of the steering, the engine, and the transmission. Then the brake lines and electrical cables are connected and other parts are assembled and painted, before the truck is road-tested.

A second alternative may be to lay out the production system according to the *process* employed. In a hospital, for example, specific steps are likely to be followed, beginning with the admission of the patient, the treatment of the patient—which usually involves specific subprocesses—billing for service, and dismissal. This may be followed up by posthospitalization treatment.

A third kind of layout can be selected in which the product stays in one place for assembly (sometimes called *fixed-position* layout). This layout is used for the assembly of extremely large and bulky items, such as printing presses, large strip-mining machines, or ships.

The fourth kind of layout is arranged according to the nature of the *project*. Building a bridge or tunnel is normally a one-time project and designed to fit specific geographic requirements.

The fifth kind of layout we find is to arrange the production process to facilitate the *sale* of products. In a supermarket, basic food items, such as dairy products, are normally located away from the checkout counter. This requires customers to walk through the long aisles and, it is hoped, select other items on the way to the dairy section.

A sixth basic approach to a production layout is to design the process so as to facilitate *storage or movement* of products. Storage space is costly and an effective and efficient design can keep the storage costs low. Also, in order to reach an item it should not be necessary to move many other items.

Operating the System

After the products have been selected and the systems for producing them have been designed and built, the next major step is to operate the system. This requires setting up an organization structure, staffing the positions, and training people. Managers are needed who can provide the supervision and leadership to carry out activities necessary to produce desired products or provide services. Other activities, such as purchasing and maintaining the inventory, are also required in operating the system. The aim is to obtain the best productivity ratio within a time period with due consideration to quality.

Controlling Operations with Emphasis on Information Systems

Controlling operations, as in any case of managerial control, requires the setting of performance criteria, measuring performance against them, and taking actions to correct undesirable deviations. Thus, one can control production, product quality and reliability levels, inventory levels, and work-force performance. A number of tools and techniques have been developed to do this. They, having wider application than operations or production, have been discussed previously, but some are also important to operations. Our concern here is with the role of information systems in operations control.

One type of planning and control system, and one which has been available for several years, integrates information on virtually an instantaneous basis, thereby reducing considerably the delays that usually impede effective control. With the development of computer hardware and software, it is now possible for virtually any measurable data to be reported as events occur. Systems are available to provide for fast and systematic collection of data bearing on total operation, for keeping these data readily available, and for reporting without delay the status of any of a large number of projects at any instant. They are thus primarily information systems designed to provide effective planning and control.[9]

These and other systems which use the technology of fast computation clearly promise to hasten the day when planning all the areas of production can

---

PERSPECTIVE:
HOW AN INFORMATION SYSTEM WORKS

Applied widely now to purchasing, storing, manufacturing, and shipping, those systems may operate through dispatch stations throughout a plant and through input centers, also located throughout a plant. At the dispatch centers, events are recorded as they occur and the information is dispatched immediately to a computer. For example, when a worker finishes an assigned task on the assembly of a product, the work-order time card is put into a transactor, which electrically transmits to a computer the information that item x has passed through a certain process, has accumulated y hours of labor, may or may not be on schedule, and other pertinent data. The input centers are equipped to originate information needed for a production plan automatically from programmed instructions, purchase orders, shop orders, and other authorization. These data are fed into a computer and compared against plans which are used as standards against which actual operations can be compared.

In addition to fast entry, comparison, and retrieval of information, such an integrated operations control system furnishes needed information for planning programs in such areas as purchasing, production, and inventory control. Moreover, it permits almost instantaneous comparison of results with plans, pinpointing where they differ, and providing a regular (daily or more often, if needed) system of reports on deviations from plans on items that may be behind schedule or costs that are running above budget.

Other planning, control, and information systems have been developed to reflect quickly the interaction between production and distribution operations and such key financial measures as costs, profit, and cash flow. Companies with real-time computer models can give operating managers virtually instant analysis of such "what-if" questions as the effects of reducing or increasing output or of reduction in demand, and the sensitivity of the system to labor cost increases, price changes, and new equipment additions. To be sure, system models, simulating actual operations and their impact on financial factors, are primarily planning tools. But so are most control techniques. However, by making possible exceptionally quick responses to the many "what-if" questions of operating managers, the time elapsed in correcting for deviations from plans can be greatly reduced and control materially improved.

be more precise and control more effective. The drawback is not cost, but rather the failure of managers to spend the time and mental effort to conceptualize the system and its relationships or to see that someone in the organization does so. But because of the time delays in any feedback system, as pointed out in Chapter 21, fast information availability can never make for true real-time controls of the time delays in any feedback system. Only a feedforward approach can overcome these delays.

OPERATIONS RESEARCH FOR PLANNING, CONTROLLING, AND IMPROVING PRODUCTIVITY

A number of techniques employed in many kinds of planning and controlling are especially useful in managing operations. This is understandable since most of the special techniques that have been developed are based on mathematical models and the use of quantitative data. Conceptual models and fairly exact quantitative data are available in many areas for production and operations management.

We have found it advantageous to discuss some of these techniques in the chapters on decision making and control techniques. Of special interest to managers of production and operations are the tools of operations research. Later in this chapter we will also discuss other techniques.

The Concept of Operations Research

Operations research is a product of World War II, although its forerunners in scientific methods, higher mathematics, and such tools as probability theory go back far beyond that period. The accelerated growth of operations research in recent years has followed the trend of applying the methods of the physical scientists and the engineers to economic and political problems. It has also been made possible by the development of rapid computing machines, particularly those using electronics, since much of the advantage of operations research depends upon our being able to apply, at low cost, involved mathematical formulas and to use data with complex relationships. There are almost as many definitions of operations research as there are writers on the subject. For our purposes, the most acceptable definition is that **operations research** is *the applications of scientific methods to the study of alternatives in a problem situation, with a view to obtaining a quantitative basis for arriving at a best solution.* Thus, the emphasis is on scientific method, on the use of quantitative data, on goals, and on the determination of the best means of reaching the goals. In other words, operations research might be called quantitative common sense.

The Essentials of Operations Research

Managers have long attempted to solve management problems scientifically, but operations researchers have supplied an element of novelty in the orderliness and completeness of their approach. They have emphasized defining the problem and goals, carefully collecting and evaluating data, developing and testing hypotheses, determining relationships among data, developing and checking predictions based on hypotheses, and devising measures to evaluate the effectiveness of a course of action.

Thus, the essential characteristics of operations research as applied to decision making can be summarized as follows:

1. It emphasizes *models*—the logical physical representation of a reality or problem. Models can, of course, be simple or complex. For example, the accounting formula "Assets minus liabilities equals proprietorship" is a model, since it represents an idea and, within the limits of the terms used, symbolizes the relationship among the variables involved.

2. It emphasizes *goals* in a problem area and the development of measures of effectiveness in determining whether a given solution shows promise of achieving these goals. For example, if the goal is profit, the measure of effectiveness may be the rate of return on investment, and every proposed solution will arrange the variables so that the end result can be weighed against this measure.

3. It incorporates in a model the *variables* in a problem, or at least those that appear to be important to its solution. Managers can control some variables; others may be uncontrollable factors in the problem.

4. It puts the model, and its variables, constraints, and goals, in *mathematical terms* so that they may be clearly identified, subjected to mathematical simplification, and readily utilized for calculation by substitution of quantities for symbols.

5. It *quantifies* the variables in a problem to the extent possible, since only quantifiable data can be inserted into a model to yield a measurable result.

6. It supplements much unavailable data with such usable mathematical and statistical devices as the *probabilities* in a situation, thus often making the mathematical and computing problem workable within a small margin of error despite gaps in accurate quantifiable data.

Of all these characteristics, perhaps the basic tool—and the major contribution—of operations research is the construction and use of conceptual models. There are many types of models. Some assert logical relationships among variables. These may be referred to as "simulative" or "descriptive" if they are designed only to describe the relationship of elements in a situation. The models useful for planning are referred to as "decision" or "optimizing" models, designed to lead to the selection of a best course of action among available alternatives.

Operations Research Procedure

Applying operations research generally involves the following six steps:

1. Formulate the problem.   As in any planning problem, the operations researcher must analyze the goals and the system in which the solution must operate. That complex of interrelated components in a problem area, referred to by operations researchers as a "system," is the environment of a decision and it represents planning premises. It may take in an entire business operation or be limited to planning production for presses and lathes. It is still, however, an interconnected complex of related human or material components. Obviously, unless managers can greatly simplify the problem by applying the principle of the limiting factor (that is, unless they eliminate alternatives that don't resolve the immediate problem), the more comprehensive the system, the more complex the problem.

2. Construct a mathematical model.   The next step is to restate the problem as a system of relationships in a mathematical model. For a single goal where at least some variables are subject to control, the general form of the operations research model is

$$E = f(x_i, y_j)$$

where E = measure of effectiveness of system
x_i = controllable variables
y_j = variables beyond control

This model may be classified as either a decision model or a simulation model. When it is being used as a decision model, values inserted for the uncontrollable variables (y_j) and the controllable variables (x_i) are manipulated to yield the greatest measure of effectiveness (E). For example, suppose that marketing managers wish to find out what actions on their part would yield the most total sales dollars. The model might include such uncontrollable variables as competitors' prices, gross national product, or price-level changes, and such controllable variables as number of salespeople, commissions allowed, product prices, and advertising expenditures.

Although all models are intended to represent reality, "simulation models" are those where users put in the model a set of factual values for the controllable variables and assume a set of values for the uncontrollable variables. By using one or more sets of values for the uncontrollable variables (because often they cannot be known), we can compute various E's until we find one we believe to be satisfactory. In this event, of course, there is no way of knowing whether an optimal solution has been found. There is something to be gained by restating a problem in concrete (visible) terms. Often a decision model cannot be used because we lack input data and cannot accurately simulate reality (at least the important elements of reality), and because it may be very complex and difficult to build.

3. Derive a solution from the model.   There are two basic procedures for arriving at a solution from a model. In the analytical procedure, we use mathematical deduction in order to reach, as nearly as possible, a mathematical solution before inserting quantities to get a numerical solution. This can be an important contribution to complex decision making. Variables can be reduced or restated in terms of common variables. Certain variables (for example, sales) can appear in a number of places in a model and we can factor some out or reduce them. In other cases, we can consolidate and simplify a series of mathematical equations. The result of this analytical procedure is that we have placed a complex series of relationships into as simple a mathematical form as possible. In addition, this analysis may disclose, mathematically, that certain variables are unimportant to a reasonable solution and may be dropped from consideration.

The second procedure is referred to as "numerical." In this, the analyst simply tries different values for the controllable variables to see what the results will be, and from this develops a set of values which seems to give the best solution. The numerical procedure varies from pure trial and error to complex iteration. In iteration, we undertake successive trial runs to approach an optimal solution. In some complex cases, such as the iterative procedures used in linear programming, rules have been developed to help analysts more quickly undertake trials and identify the optimum solution when it is reached.

4. Test the model. Because a model, by its very nature, is only a representation of reality and because it is seldom possible to include all the variables, models should usually be tested. We can do so by using the model to solve a problem and comparing the results with what actually happens. These tests can be carried out by using past data or by trying the model out in practice to see how it measures up to reality.

5. Provide controls for the model and the solution. Because a once-accurate model may cease to represent reality, because the variables that are beyond our control may change, or because the relationships of variables may shift, provision must be made for control of the model and the solution. This is done in the same way any control is undertaken, by providing means for feedback so that significant deviations can be detected and changes made. In many complex models, such as those used for production or distribution planning, the effect of the deviations must be weighed against the cost of feeding in the correction or against the usually greater cost of revising the entire program. As a result, we may sometimes decide not to correct the model or the inputs.

6. Put the solution into effect. The final step is to put the model and the inputs into operation. In anything but the simplest programs, this will involve revising and clarifying procedures so that the inputs (including control feedback information) become available in an orderly fashion, and this, in turn, often requires reorganization of an enterprise's available information. What many users of operations research have found a major stumbling block is that no one is willing to undertake the hard work of developing better information to use with the models. Accounting and other data normally available in a company are often not adequate to the requirements of successful operations research. Many managers, intrigued with the possibilities of operations research, wish that some of the research effort of experts, now so widely employed in constructing elegant models, could be channeled toward reorganizing information.

Other problems in making operations research useful for managers involve getting people to understand, appreciate, and use the techniques of operations research, and deciding such questions as what computing facilities to use, and how, and how the information outputs are to be made useful and understandable to those responsible for decisions. In this connection, operations researchers would do managers a real favor by frankly admitting the nature and margin of uncertainty in their solution.

All this is to say that operations researchers are not nearly done with their task when their model is reduced to paper and tested. Mathematical gymnastics may be interesting to the pure philosopher, but managers must make responsible decisions and the operations researcher who would be useful to managers must be more than a mathematical gymnast.

Linear Programming

A technique for determining the optimum combination of limited resources to obtain a desired goal, linear programming is one of the most successful applications of operations research. It is based upon the assumption that a linear, or straight-line, relationship exists between variables and that the limits of variations can be determined. For example, in a production shop, the variables may be units of output per machine in a given time, direct-labor costs or material costs per unit of output, number of operations per unit, and so forth. Most or all of these may have linear relationships, within certain limits, and by solving linear equations, the optimum in terms of cost, time, machine utilization, or other objectives can be established. Thus, this technique is especially useful where input data can be quantified and objectives are subject to definite measurement.

As one might expect, the technique has had its most promising use in such problem areas as production planning, shipping rates and routes, and the utilization of production and warehouse facilities to achieve lowest overall costs, including transportation costs. Because it depends on linear relationships and many decisions do not involve these or cannot be simulated accurately enough, newer and more complex systems of nonlinear programming have come into use.

Inventory Planning and Control

Perhaps in the history of operations research more attention has been directed to inventory control than to any other practical area of operations. If we wished to see the essential systems relationships as a little "black box," we could depict them as is done in Figure 22-2.

If these conceptual relationships were placed into a mathematical form, it might look something like this:

$$Q_e = \sqrt{\frac{2DS}{H}}$$

where Q_e = economic order quantity (EOQ)
D = demand per year
S = setup costs
H = inventory holding (carrying) cost per item, per year

The model in Figure 22-2 illustrates several things. It forces consideration of the goals desired and of the need for placing values on outputs and inputs. It also furnishes a manager with the basis for plans and with standards by which to measure performance.[10] However, with all its advantages, this is a subsystem and does not incorporate other subsystems, such as production planning, distribution planning, and sales planning.

The economic order quantity (EOQ) approach to determine inventory levels has been used by firms for many years. It works reasonably well for finding order quantities when demand is predictable and fairly constant throughout the year (i.e., no seasonal patterns). However, for determining inventory levels of parts and materials used for some production processes, the EOQ approach does not work well. For example, poor quality of parts may increase the demand for these production inputs. Thus, demand is likely to be intermittent, resulting in inventory shortages at some times and excesses at other times. Firms determining inventory levels in these manufacturing settings have

FIGURE 22-2

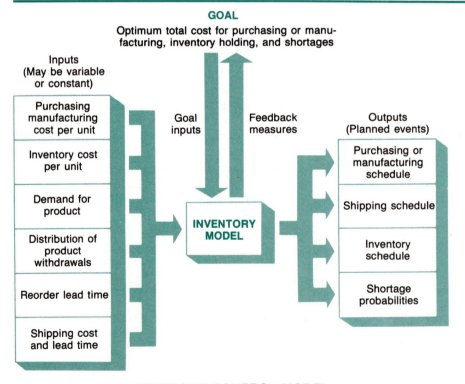

INVENTORY CONTROL MODEL.

found that inventory control approaches such as material requirement planning (MRP) and Kanban (Just-in-time) systems perform better than EOQ.[11]

The Just-in-Time Inventory System

One reason for Japan's high manufacturing productivity is the cost reductions it achieves through its **just-in-time** (JIT) inventory method. This means that the supplier delivers the components and parts to the production line "just in time" to be assembled. Other names for this or very similar methods are **zero inventory** and **stockless production**.[12]

The just-in-time method was successfully used after World War II by the Toyota automobile company. In the United States, General Motors, Ford, Chrysler, and American Motors have some of the more advanced systems. But other companies also have used JIT with favorable results. Consider Black & Decker, which, among other things, produces small appliances such as coffeemakers and irons: When the plant in North Carolina switched to JIT, inventory was reduced by 40 percent, and 30 percent fewer forklift trucks were required. Moreover, quality losses were reduced 60 percent and labor productivity increased by 15 percent.[13]

For the JIT method to work, a number of requirements must be fulfilled: (1) The quality of the parts must be very high; a defective part could hold up the assembly line. (2) There must be dependable relationships and smooth cooperation with suppliers.[14] (3) Ideally, the suppliers should be located near the company, with dependable transportation available.

Distribution Logistics

An exciting and profit-promising way of using systems logistics in planning and control is in the expansion of inventory control to include other factors, referred to here as "distribution logistics." In its advanced form, this treats the entire logistics of a business—from sales forecast through purchase and processing of material and inventorying to shipping finished goods—as a single system. The goal is usually to optimize the total costs of the system in operation, while furnishing a desired level of customer service and meeting certain constraints, such as financially limited inventory levels. This gathers into one system a large mass of relationships and information so as to optimize the whole. It is entirely possible that transportation, manufacturing, or any other single area of cost will not be optimized, but the total cost of material management will be.

Schematically, a distribution logistics system might appear as shown in Figure 22-3. This model, represented by a black box, would be expressed mathematically as an operating system. The figure shows the relationships between the goal desired, the input variables and limits, and the expected outputs. By optimizing *total* costs in a broad area of operation, the system might show that it would be cheaper to use more expensive transportation on occasion rather than to carry high inventories. Or it might show that production at less-than-economic order quantities would be justified in order to get better transportation or warehousing utilization or to meet customer service standards with limited inventories.

FIGURE 22-3

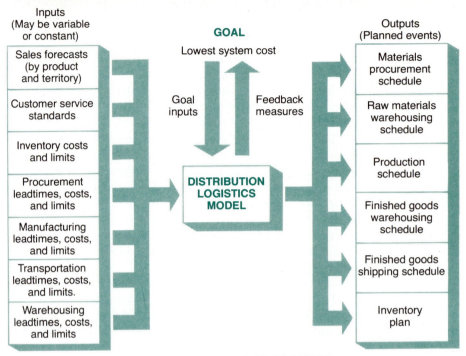

DISTRIBUTION LOGISTICS MODEL.

Limitations of Operations Research

So far, operations research has been used to solve only a fairly limited number of managerial problems. We should not overlook its limitations.

In the first place, there is the sheer magnitude of the mathematical and computing aspects. The number of variables and interrelationships in many managerial problems, plus the complexities of human relationships and reactions, calls for a higher order of mathematics than nuclear physics does. The late mathematical genius John von Neumann found, in his development of the theory of games, that his mathematical abilities soon reached their limit in a relatively simple strategic problem. Managers are, however, a long way from fully using the mathematics now available.

In the second place, although probabilities and approximations are being substituted for unknown quantities, and although scientific method can assign values to factors we could never measure before, a major portion of important managerial decisions still involves qualitative factors. Until these can be measured, operations research will have limited usefulness in these areas, and decisions will continue to be based on nonquantitative judgments.

Related to the fact that many management decisions involve unmeasurable factors is the lack of information needed to make operations research useful in practice. When we conceptualize a problem area and construct a mathematical model to represent it, we discover variables about which we need information not now available. What we need is far more emphasis on the part of those interested in the practical applications of operations research on developing this required information.

Still another limitation is the gap between practicing managers and trained operations researchers. Managers in general lack a knowledge and appreciation of mathematics, just as mathematicians lack understanding of managerial problems. This gap is being dealt with, to an increasing extent, by the business schools and, more often, by business firms that team up managers with operations researchers. But it is still the major reason why firms are slow to use operations research.

A final drawback of operations research—at least in its application to complex problems—is that analyses and programming are expensive, and many problems are not important enough to justify this cost. However, in practice this has not really been a major limitation.

OTHER TOOLS AND TECHNIQUES FOR IMPROVING PRODUCTIVITY

Besides operations research there are other techniques. We will discuss the application of time-event networks, value engineering, work simplification, quality circles, computer-aided design, computer-aided manufacturing, and the manufacturing automation protocol.

Time-Event Networks

In Chapter 21, we discussed time-event network analysis and saw how it is a logical extension of the famous Gantt chart. Often referred to as Program Evaluation and Review Technique (PERT) and in its essentials as Critical Path Method (CPM), this technique of planning and control has wide potential use in many applications. But PERT and its various refinements, like PERT/COST, have considerable potential for use in many aspects of planning and control of operations.

Perhaps the most useful application of time-event networks is in the planning and control of production. For example, the design of a typical assembly line, where parts and subassemblies must be fitted in at the right time and place, is a perfect example of such a network. It would be the rare assembly line where all activities were linear, that is, where an end product is assembled purely by a succession of sequential operations. One can hardly imagine an automobile assembly line, for example, where the assembly started with a frame, followed by assembly of the wheels, followed by assembly of the engine, and then the transmission. Indeed, assembly lines, in order to be at all efficient, must be based on a network of planned activities, many of them done simultaneously.

Much the same can be said for most other areas of production or operations. It is difficult to conceive of a warehousing and shipping operation where plans need not represent a network of events. Even warehousing finished goods and stacking them by model or style requires network planning if it is to be efficient. Loading a truck for delivery of various items to a number of customers in various locations is also likely to require a network of planned activities.

Students preparing term papers will clearly find it to their advantage to engage in network planning. It is hard to think of a student sitting down to write such a paper unless paper and a typewriter or word processor are available, the needed data have been gathered and analyzed, and an outline of the paper has been conceptualized.

By using network planning and control, those managing any phase of operations are forced to plan. In addition, if they do a fairly thorough job, they have a tool whereby critical paths may be identified, thus making possible pinpointing where corrective action can best be taken if deviations from plans become apparent.

Value Engineering

A product can be improved and its cost lowered through **value engineering**, which consists of analyzing the operation of the product or service, estimating the value of each operation, and attempting to improve that operation by trying to keep costs low at each step or part. The following specific steps are suggested:

1. Divide the product into parts and operations.
2. Identify the costs for each part and operation.
3. Identify the relative value of contribution of each part to the final part.
4. Find a new approach for those items which appear to have a high cost and low value.

Work Simplification

Work methods can also be improved through work simplification. The purpose is to obtain the participation of workers in simplifying their work. Training sessions are conducted to teach concepts and principles of techniques such as time and motion studies, work-flow analyses, and the layout of the work situation.

Quality Circles

Quality control circles, or simply **quality circles** (QC), are groups of people, usually between six and twelve, from the same organizational area, who meet regularly to solve problems they experience at work.[15] Members are trained in solving problems, in statistical quality control, and in working in groups. Usually a facilitator works with the group. The QCs may meet 4 hours a month. Although QC members may receive recognition, they usually do not receive monetary rewards.

Quality circles evolved from suggestion programs. In both approaches, workers participate in solving work-related problems. Although in suggestion programs the problems are usually quite specific, those dealt with by quality

PERSPECTIVE:
QUALITY CIRCLES IN JAPAN

For some time now, Japanese companies have been successful in marketing products. To a great extent this has been due to the quality of their products, but this has not always been the case. In fact, in the 1950s and 1960s many products made in Japan had the image of poor quality.

In order to compete in the world market, Japanese firms had to improve the quality of their products.[16] The drive for improved quality of Japanese products was due first to regulatory action by the Japanese government. Shortly after World War II ended, the Japanese, realizing that their economic situation depended on increasing exports, encouraged their government to set up a system of regulations requiring all exporters to submit to a government agency a sample of a product to be exported and to meet demanding requirements for quality before a permit to export was issued.

The legislative drive for quality was supported by various management techniques encouraging or requiring product quality. One of the interesting techniques is the quality control circle, now in widespread use in Japan. At first, employees were trained in the analysis of quality problems. But now other problems are also dealt with, such as cost reduction, workshop facilities improvement, safety problems, employee morale, pollution control, and the education of employees.

control circles are often more complex and require the involvement of several team members. The team consists primarily of rank-and-file workers and sometimes also includes supervisors. So-called efficiency experts are usually excluded from the team.

It is interesting to note that while the concept of quality control originated in the United States, the Japanese appear to have perfected it. More recently, American firms have "rediscovered" the importance of quality, as stressed, for example, in the advertisements for Chrysler and Ford automobiles. At any rate, there is no reason to doubt that quality circles can be used by American companies who are now faced with a competitive situation in a world market that demands quality products.

CAD/CAM and MAP

Product design and manufacturing have been changing greatly in recent years, largely because of the application of computer technology. Computer-aided design (CAD), computer-aided manufacturing (CAM), and the manufacturing automation protocol (MAP) are some of the cornerstones of the factory of the future.

CAD/CAMs help engineers to design products much more quickly than with the traditional paper-and-pencil approach. This will become increasingly important since the product life cycles are getting shorter. Capturing the market quickly is crucial in the very competitive environment. Moreover, firms can

> **PERSPECTIVE:**
> **IBM's PC CONVERTIBLE**
>
> The IBM laptop PC Convertible is the first computer built in the United States completely by robots.[17] It is manufactured on an automated assembly line with modular workstations that put together, check, and package the computers without people turning even a screw. What is special about this assembly line is that it not only can produce the Convertible but it also can assemble other personal computers, printers, and even household appliances. This kind of production line is probably the first one in the world and may help IBM to stay competitive with its Asian rivals.

respond more rapidly to the requests of customers with specific requirements. The ultimate aim of many companies is "computer-integrated manufacturing."[18]

Automobile companies, but also firms such as Deere, Boeing, and Eastman Kodak, developed what is called "manufacturing automation protocol" (MAP), which is a network of machines and various office devices hooked together. MAP is a sophisticated extension of local area networks (LANs). One of the most committed supporters of MAP is General Motors (GM) chairman Roger Smith, who sees it as a key to the factory of the future. At General Motors, for example, MAP is used to link robots with numerically controlled machine tools. To illustrate the advantage of MAP, consider the savings gained by using the new method to change the production line for introducing a different kind of front axle for an automobile. What previously took 3 days now takes only 10 minutes. With the new technology, General Motors and other U.S. manufacturers hope to overtake Japanese firms, which now are quite advanced in automation.[19]

THE FUTURE OF OPERATIONS MANAGEMENT

What factors show signs of influencing future developments in this field? Several major trends can be expected in operations management.[20]

1. The increased complexity of technology will be reflected in the products themselves as well as in the processes used to produce them.[21] Fifteen years ago few people would have expected that sophisticated home computers could be produced at a price affordable by the usual consumers.

2. Automation is becoming increasingly more important in the production process.[22] General Motors, which pioneered the application of robots, is importing a new generation of robots from Japan. New machine tools, microprocessors, sensory technology, and computer controls now make it possible to reduce machine setup time and costs.[23] This means a greater variety of products at a lower cost. In the past, lower costs tended to be achieved through high-volume production of a particular model. Now, through high technology, setup times are reduced dramatically. This means a better use of machines with lower direct-labor costs. Moreover, work-in-process inventories can thereby be reduced. Finally, maintenance costs are reduced by simplifying processes, controls, and machines. These simplification technologies were pioneered by Toyota when it doubled its automobile model range without incurring the high costs traditionally associated with a variety of models.

3. The service industry in the United States is providing an increasingly important portion of the gross national product. This means that the concepts and principles of "production" have been advantageously adapted to such non-manufacturing activities as banking, health care, and tourism.

4. The production function will become increasingly a global challenge.[24] As we have recently seen, car engines produced in Japan and Germany are now installed in American cars. Moreover, major car manufacturers in the United States made arrangements to produce cars in Japan and market them under their own names in the United States and elsewhere.

In summary, then, productivity, and the concern for measuring it, will continue to be a challenge for managers operating in an increasingly competitive global market. Operations management systems are expected to become more productive through the application of operations research, a variety of other tools, and information technology.

FOR DISCUSSION

1. How would you measure the productivity of managers and other knowledge workers? Explain in detail.

2. Why is the field of production and operations management such a good one to use as a case example of planning and control techniques? Why do you believe that this was a favored area for analysis and productivity improvement by the pioneers in the field of management?

3. Distinguish between planning and control techniques that are usually found only in production and operations management and those found to be useful in all areas for managing. Why is this so?

4. Explain the nature of and reasons for each step usually found in the development of a production and operations management program.

5. There are many typical layouts used in the design of a production program. Which one is ordinarily used for the manufacture of automobiles, and why? Which one do you believe was used for construction of the trans-Alaska pipeline, and why?

6. Real-time information can be widely used in the area of production, but this does not solve the problem of control. Why?

7. What tools generally found in operations research have been widely used in production and operations management? Do they have anything in common? If so, what is it?

8. What makes distribution logistics a more useful and complex tool of planning and control than an inventory model?

9. Why do you believe that quality control circles have been used so much in Japan?

10. Can you suggest any element that tends to be common in the summary of major trends expected in the future of production and operations planning and control?

EXERCISES/ACTION STEPS

1. After the class has been divided into groups of four or five students, take Case 22-1 and try to answer the six questions raised by Lampert's business colleague. For question No. 2, each group should display the drawing of their lamp on the blackboard with its main specifications (e.g., voltage) and usages (show several). One member of each group should try to "sell" the lamp to the class. If the class size is large enough, one group should act as an independent panel, evaluating each lamp proposal in terms of creativity, esthetics, feasibility and other criteria developed by the group.

2. Draw the layout of your apartment or your house and the pathways you walk while doing your typical daily chores. Indicate what rearrangements you could make to render you more effective and to increase your personal productivity.

CASES

CASE 22-1
LAMPERT & SONS COMPANY

John Lampert, president of Lampert & Sons Company, a small manufacturing firm producing electrical appliances, was an entrepreneur with a technical background. He recently moved into a new house, and his wife asked him to install some spotlights to accent various areas in the house, such as bookshelves, a sculpture, and certain items in a wall unit.

A trip to the local lighting stores showed that the lamps that might fit the purpose cost far more than he was willing to pay. He felt that there was a real need for a low-cost, attractive spotlight or clamp-on lamp. He discussed his idea with a business colleague, who raised a number of questions such as these:

1. Is there really a need for such a product?

2. What should such a lamp look like?

3. How or where should it be produced (e.g., in his plant in the Midwest or abroad, such as in Korea, Hong Kong, or Taiwan)?

4. What arrangements would have to be made if the lamp were to be produced by Lampert & Sons?

5. What kind of distribution channel(s) should be used to sell the product?

6. How would he maintain the quality if the price of the lamp was to be kept low?

After this discussion, Mr. Lampert realized that he really had not thought through his idea and could not satisfactorily answer several of the questions.

1. If you were a small-business consultant, how would you answer the questions Mr. Lampert's colleague raised?

2. What other actions would you recommend to make the product decision to design the product, to set up a production system, and to control the operation, especially the quality?

3. What decision-making tools and techniques could assist in making these decisions?

CASE 22-2
MANUFACTURING REQUIREMENTS PLANNING (MRP)

Proctor & Company, a high-technology supplier to the aerospace industry, had found itself in the enviable position of supplying some critical microwave components for the space shuttle. The business, which had started out in a garage, was founded and developed by two entrepreneurial partners, and had grown over a period of 10 years from $250,000 to $12 million in sales per year.

Along with the success of the operation had come some problems, and one of the most visible manifestations of the problems was the conflict between the partners, one of whom thought that the company should sell stock to the public, while the other thought that the company should remain privately owned. The former borrowed money from one of the principal banks in California, bought the other partner out, and proceeded to sell stock to the public.

The public offering was a great success, provided the company with all of the working capital it needed, and made the entrepreneur founder a millionaire in the process. However, while he was fulfilling his dreams, a lot of the basics in designing and producing the products had been overlooked or neglected, with the result that the operations of the company were running out of control.

Engineering changes proliferated and were always behind time in being documented and entered into document control records. Also, new products, which had been developed so easily in the early days and quickly brought to fruition, were now hopelessly bogged down in design and concept.

The president, who by instinct sensed that the flexibility and drive of the early days were no longer present, decided that he would have to move to impose some order upon the organization, much as an assembly line brings order to manufacturing operations. Since the firm was heavily engineering- and research-oriented, the "order" for the program was at first perceived as something which could be readily purchased from specialists and which by its nature would ask the right questions and provide the essential elements in order to provide data necessary for planning and control.

The task of implementing the program was given to Jim Martin, the master scheduler. At the onset of program development, it was discovered that the parts master list—a complete listing of all parts used in manufacturing assemblies—was neither correct nor complete. Nor were engineering drawings or manufacturing bills of material in order. A general feeling of dismay set in as it became obvious why production schedules were so often overrun and deliveries late, and why parts seemed always to be in short supply: No one knew what component parts were really needed to make subassemblies and what end items were required in order to deliver products on time.

As a result, a single task such as compiling the data on parts contained in the storeroom, which should have taken 1 week to complete, ended up taking over 2 months. Each step uncovered problems of a similar magnitude: Bills of material and assembly structures were wrong. Part numbers were incorrect. Material and parts counts were off by a wide margin. Issues of parts to the plant and purchasing receipts were not recorded properly. Shop floor loading was done only for final assembly. Purchasing and material files were incorrect. Order quantities, lead times, and costs were out of date—and so on throughout the system.

The master scheduler was in a quandary. The estimated few months' task of implementing an orderly control program was turning into a year-long nightmare. Worse still was the difficulty he was having discussing the scope of the problem with top management, since he knew that top management's policies had caused or contributed to the mess. On the one hand, he needed a large allocation of funds and labor-hours if the task was to be completed. On the other hand, he was paralyzed because of the limits of authority in the job's assignment and because of the fact that he was potentially bearing bad news to an optimistic president.

1. What do you think the key management issues were in the above situation?

2. What, if any, techniques or principles should have been effected?

3. What recommendations could you offer the master scheduler?

REFERENCES

1. Certain sections of the discussion of productivity in this chapter are based on Heinz Weihrich, *Management Excellence* (New York: McGraw-Hill Book Company, 1985).

2. See, for example, Vernon M. Buehler and Y. Krishna Shetty (eds.), *Productivity Improvement* (New York: AMACOM, 1981), reporting on the experiences of companies in improving their productivity. See also Bernard J. Reilly and Joseph P. Fuhr, Jr., "Productivity: An Economic and Management Analysis with a Direction Towards a New Synthesis," *Academy of Management Review* (January 1983), pp. 108–117.

3. Buehler and Shetty, *Productivity Improvement* (1981).

4. In the preparation of this chapter, the authors have received considerable assistance from Richard B. Chase and Nicholas J. Aquilano, *Production and Operations Management* (Homewood, Ill.: Richard D. Irwin, 1981).

5. The input-transformation-output model is widely used in the discussion of operations management. See, for example, Chase and Aquilano, *Production* (1981); Harold Fearon, William A. Ruch, Patrick G. Decker, Ross R. Reck, Vincent G. Reuter, and C. David Wieters, *Fundamentals of Production/Operations Management* (St. Paul: West Publishing Company, 1979); Elwood S. Buffa and James S. Dyer, *Management Science/Operations Research* (New York: John Wiley & Sons, 1981).

6. For a discussion of the relationship between strategy and operations management, see Wickham Skinner, *Manufacturing in the Corporate Strategy* (New York: John Wiley & Sons, 1978); Stephen C. Wheelwright, "Operations as Strategy Lessons from Japan," *Stanford GSB* (Fall 1981–1982), pp. 3–7.

7. For some interesting ideas about office layout see Philip J. Stone and Robert Luchetti, "Your Office Is Where You Are," *Harvard Business Review* (March–April 1985), pp. 102–117.

8. See Chase and Aquilano, *Production* (1981), sec. 2; see also Arthur C. Laufer, *Operations Management* (Cincinnati: South Western Publishing Company, 1979), chap. 16.

9. For a detailed discussion of information and control see Edward E. Lawler and John G. Rhode, *Information and Control in Organizations* (Santa Monica, Calif.: Goodyear Publishing Company, 1976).

10. For the application of analytical techniques and the use of graphics see David J. Armstrong, "Sharpening Inventory Management," *Harvard Business Review* (November–December 1985), pp. 42–58. For a variety of graphics software for the microcomputer see David Needle, "Presentation Graphics Software," *Infoworld* (Sept. 22, 1986).

11. Discussion with Professor Robert N. Mefford. His paper "The Productivity Nexus of New Inventory and Quality Control Techniques" has been submitted for review and publication. See also Richard B. Chase and Nicholas J. Aquilano, *Production and Operations Management*, 4th ed. (Homewood, Ill.: Richard D. Irwin, 1985), chap. 18.

12. Alan L. Saipe and Richard J. Schonberger, "Don't Ignore Just-in-Time Production," *Business Quarterly* (Spring 1984), pp. 60–66.

13. Saipe and Schonberger, "Don't Ignore Just-in-Time Production" (1984).

14. Richard C. Walleigh, "What's Your Excuse for Not Using JIT?" *Harvard Business Review* (March–April 1986), pp. 38–54.

15. Edward E. Lawler III and Susan A. Mohrman, "Quality Circles after the Fad," *Harvard Business Review* (January–February 1985), pp. 65–71. See also S. G. Goldstein, "Organizational Dualism and Quality Circles," *Academy of Management Review* (July 1985), pp. 504–517.

16. For a discussion of quality circles in Japan and in the United States see Tai K. Oh, "The Fate of QC Circles in the U.S.: A Case Study Testing the Cultural, Convergence, and Tradition-Modernity Theories," in Ryine T. Hsieh and Steven A. Scherling, eds., *Proceedings of the Academy of International Business, Southeast Asia Regional Conference, Taipei,* vol. 1 (June 26–28, 1986), pp. 749–759.

17. Bill Saporito, "IBM's No-Hands Assembly Line," *Fortune* (Sept. 15, 1986), pp. 105–104.

18. Gene Bylinsky, "GM's Road Map to Automated Plants," *Fortune* (Oct. 28, 1985), pp. 89–102. For another discussion of computer-integrated manufacturing (CIM) see Robert S. Kaplan, "Must CIM Be Justified by Faith Alone?" *Harvard Business Review* (March–April 1986), pp. 87–95.

19. Bylinsky, "GM's Road Map" (1985). For difficulties with the new technology, especially at General Motors' Hamtramck plant in Michigan, which was supposed to be the showcase of high technology, see Amal Nag, "Auto Makers Discover 'Factory of the Future' Is Headache Just Now," *The Wall Street Journal* (May 13, 1986).

20. Fearon et al., *Fundamentals* (1979). See also Joseph Finkelstein and David Newman, "The Third Industrial Revolution: A Special Challenge to Managers," *Organizational Dynamics* (Summer 1984), pp. 53–65; Vincent G. Reuter, "Trends in Production Management Education and Training," *Industrial Management* (May–June 1983), pp. 1–3.

21. For a discussion of flexible automation see Ramchandran Jaikumar, "Postindustrial Manufacturing," *Harvard Business Review* (November–December 1986), pp. 69–76. A holistic approach to developing new products has been suggested by Hirotaka Takeuchi and Ikujiro Nonaka, "The New Product Development Game," *Harvard Business Review* (January–February 1986), pp. 137–146.

22. For a discussion of how robotics are changing organizations and manufacturing tasks see Daniel E. Whitney, "Real Robots Do Need Jigs," *Harvard Business Review* (May–June 1986), pp. 110–116.

23. "The Big Revolution on the Factory Floor," *The Wall Street Journal* (July 12, 1982).

24. For futuristic ideas about floating factories see Alonzo L. McDonald, "Of Floating Factories and Mating Dinosaurs," *Harvard Business Review* (November–December 1986), pp. 82–86.

FOR FURTHER INFORMATION

Adam, Everett E., Jr., and Ronald J. Ebert. *Production and Operations Management: Concepts, Models, and Behavior,* 2d ed. (Englewood Cliffs, N.J.: Prentice-Hall, 1982).

Buffa, Elwood S. *Elements of Productions/Operations Management* (New York: John Wiley & Sons, 1981).

Eastman Kodak Company. *Information Age Technology* (Reading, Mass.: Addison-Wesley Publishing Co., 1985, 1986).

Hyer, Nancy L., and Urbam Wemmerloev. "Group Technology and Productivity," *Harvard Business Review* (July–August 1984), pp. 140–149.

Reuter, Vincent G. "What Good Are Value Analysis Programs?" *Business Horizons* (March–April 1986), pp. 73–79.

Reuter, Vincent G. "Work Study as a Tool for Increased Productivity and Profits," *Industrial Management* (March–April 1986), pp. 28–31.

Schonberger, Richard J. *Japanese Manufacturing Techniques: Nine Hidden Lessons in Simplicity* (New York: The Free Press, 1982).

Schonberger, Richard J. "The Transfer of Japanese Manufacturing Management Approaches to U. S. Industry," *Academy of Management Review* (July 1982), pp. 479–487.

Sharman, Graham. "The Rediscovery of Logistics," *Harvard Business Review* (September–October 1984), pp. 71–79.

Weiss, Andrew. "Simple Truths of Japanese Manufacturing," *Harvard Business Review* (July–August 1984), pp. 119–125.

Wheelwright, Steven C., and Robert B. Hayes. "Competing Through Manufacturing," *Harvard Business Review* (January–February 1985), pp. 99–109.

23

Overall and Preventive Control

CHAPTER OBJECTIVES

After reading this chapter, you should be able to:

1. Discuss the concept of overall control.

2. Describe the most widely used techniques of overall control of an enterprise.

3. Present the principle of preventive control and distinguish its nature and application from those of the many direct controls.

4. Explain the nature and potential of the management audit and the enterprise self-audit.

5. Summarize the major challenges facing management and explain what needs to be done to develop excellent managers.

6. Present, as a summary of the chapters on controlling, some major principles, or guides, in this area.

Most controls are designed for specific things: policies, wages and salaries, employee selection and training, research and development, product quality, costs, pricing, capital expenditures, cash, and other areas where we wish performance to conform to plans. Such controls are partial in the sense that they apply to a part of an enterprise and do not measure total accomplishments against total goals. There clearly is a need for some overall measures, and, not surprisingly, many are expressed in financial terms.

Many of the controls are based on feedback by measuring deviations from plans. Also, the traditional approach is to find out who is responsible for the undesirable deviation and to get that person to correct it. This is direct control. But, as you will learn later in this chapter, this kind of control is based on some questionable assumptions. Would it not be better to prevent undesirable deviations from occurring in the first place? Most would answer, "Of course." We will therefore recommend what is called "preventive control," which means that a highly qualified manager will make fewer mistakes, thus reducing (but certainly not eliminating) the need for direct control. But let us first discuss the more traditional—and important—overall controls of budget summaries and other financial controls.

CONTROL OF OVERALL PERFORMANCE

Planning and control are increasingly being treated as an interrelated system. Along with techniques for partial control, control devices have been developed to measure the overall performance of an enterprise—or an integrated[1] division or project within it—against total goals.

There are many reasons for control of overall performance. In the first place, as overall planning must apply to enterprise or major division goals, so must overall controls be applied. In the second place, decentralization of authority—especially in product or territorial divisions—creates semi-independent units, and these must be subjected to overall controls to avoid the chaos of complete independence. In the third place, overall controls permit measuring an integrated area manager's *total* effort, rather than parts of it.

Many overall controls in business are, as one might expect, financial. Business owes its continued existence to profit making; its capital resources are a scarce, life-giving element. Since finance is the binding force of business, financial controls are certainly an important objective gauge of the success of plans.[2]

Financial measurements also summarize, as a common denominator, the operation of a number of plans. Further, they accurately indicate total expenditures of resources in reaching goals. This is true in all forms of enterprise. Although the purpose of an educational or government enterprise is not to make monetary profits, any responsible manager must have some way of knowing what goal achievement has cost in terms of resources. Proper accounting is important not only for business but for government as well. Professor Anthony at Harvard points out that in government, accounting often hides important facts. Otherwise, how could it happen that several cities, including New York, were nearly bankrupt before their financial conditions became clear?[3]

Financial controls, like any other control, have to be tailored to the specific needs of the enterprise or the position. Doctors, lawyers, and managers at different organizational levels do have different needs for controlling their area of operation.[4] Financial analyses also furnish an excellent "window" through which accomplishment in nonfinancial areas can be seen. A deviation from planned costs, for example, may lead a manager to find the causes in poor planning, inadequate training of employees, or other nonfinancial factors.

BUDGET SUMMARIES AND REPORTS

A widely used control of overall performance takes the form of a summary of budgets. A **budget summary**, being a resume of all the individual budgets, reflects company plans so that sales volume, costs, profits, utilization of capital, and return on investment may be seen in their proper relationship. In these terms it shows top management how the company as a whole is succeeding in meeting its objectives.

For the best control through a budget summary, a manager must first be satisfied that total budgets are an accurate and reasonably complete portrayal of the company's plans. The manager should study the budget reports and any material accompanying them to determine whether the comparison of budget and actual costs shows the real nature of any deviations. As an example, a company head criticized his factory manager for being considerably over his labor budget in a month when the labor force had been materially reduced and the temporary increase in expenses was due to severance pay.

Minor discrepancies should receive appropriately little attention. The purpose of a control system is to draw attention to important variations, and both the budget reports and the attention paid to them should reflect this. Above all, a manager should never forget that a budget summary is no substitute for profitable operation. Budgeting is never more perfect than the planning behind it, and plans—especially long-range plans—are subject to the imperfections caused by change and uncertainty. There may even be times when a manager must forget the budget and take special action to meet unexpected events. Budgets are meant to be tools, and not masters, of managers.

On the other hand, managers should not underestimate the value of budget summaries in providing an effective means for overall control where there is decentralization of authority. Budget summaries furnish a means whereby enterprise objectives can be clearly and specifically defined, and departmental plans can be made to contribute toward such objectives. Should the budget summary and the reports of actual events indicate that the enterprise as a whole is not tending toward its objectives, top managers have a convenient and positive means of finding out where the deviations are occurring. The summaries thus furnish a useful guide for corrective action.

PROFIT AND LOSS CONTROL

The income statement for an enterprise as a whole serves important control purposes, largely because it is useful for determining the immediate revenue or cost factors that have accounted for success or failure. Obviously, if it is first put in the form of a forecast, it is even a better control device in that it gives managers a chance, before things happen, to influence revenues, expenses, and, consequently, profits.

The Nature and Purpose of Profit and Loss Controls

Since the survival of a business usually depends on profits and since profits are a definite standard against which to measure success, many companies use the income statement for divisional or departmental control. Because this is a statement of all revenues and expenses for a given time, it is a true summary of the results of business operations. Profit and loss control, when applied to divisions or departments, is based on the premise that if it is the purpose of the entire business to make a profit, each part of the enterprise should contribute to this purpose.[5] Thus, the ability of a part to make an expected profit becomes a standard for measuring its performance.

In profit and loss control, each major department or division details its revenues and expenses—normally including a proportionate share of company overhead—and calculates periodically its profit or loss. Some units have their own accounting group, whereas in others, the statement is prepared by the central accounting department. In either case, the organizational unit, in being expected to turn in a separate record of profitable operation, is considered by headquarters in much the same way that a holding company considers its subsidiary companies.

Profit and loss control usually is practicable only for major segments of a company since the paperwork involved in building up profit and loss statements for smaller departments tends to be too heavy. Also, profit and loss control usually implies that managers of a division or a department have a fairly wide authority to run their part of the business as they see fit, with profit the primary standard of success. However, many companies that do not so decentralize authority have nonetheless found profit and loss control valuable. The focus on profit and the sensitivity of the organizational unit to it are worthwhile even when managers have limited independence to seek profit as they wish.

The more integrated and complete the organization unit, the more accurate a measuring stick profit and loss control can be. For this reason, it works best in product or territorial divisions, where both sales and production functions for a product or service are under one general manager. For example, it is much easier to use the standard of profit for measuring the operations of the general manager of the Buick division of General Motors than it would be to use it for the supervisor of the motor-block-boring section of the manufacturing department of this division.

At the same time, companies organized on a functional basis do occasionally employ profit and loss control. The heat-treating department may produce and

PERSPECTIVE:
KODAK'S PROFIT PICTURE IN FULL COLOR AGAIN[6]

For a long time, Eastman Kodak Company, with headquarters in Rochester, New York, was considered one of the excellent companies. However, in the middle of the 1980s, the company encountered difficulties, partly because of the strong U.S. dollar and the tough competition from Fuji Films in Japan, Kodak's main rival. The profit picture changed for the better, with an increase of about 14 percent in earnings in 1986.

What, then, accounted for the turnaround? Among the various reasons for the change are the following:

1. The decline of the value of the U.S. dollar had a positive effect on profits. It also made Kodak more competitive with Fuji.

2. Cost was reduced by a reduction in the work force of almost 25,000.

3. In 1986 Kodak introduced 100 new products, including new films (e.g., the VR-G films with vibrant colors) and a new 35-mm camera.

4. Kodak is also selling minilabs for developing films that use great amounts of chemicals and paper made by Kodak.

5. The company diversified into areas such as optical-disk data storage, long-life batteries, and electronic publishing.

6. The reorganization resulted in seventeen fairly autonomous business units which enable the company to respond more quickly to changes in the market.

Kodak is also preparing for the more distant future, realizing that it has to expand its domain beyond photography. Thus, the company is venturing into health care, drugs (e.g., to fight cancer), electronic imaging, and data storage (it acquired the floppy disk maker Verbatim in 1985). While the future is not without problems and challenges, for now a combination of factors such as changes in the external environment, some clever strategic choices, cost cutting, and the reorganization hint at a colorful future for Kodak.

"sell" its service to the machining department, which in turn "sells" its product to the assembly department, which in turn "sells" a complete product to the sales department. This can be done, although the paperwork required is often not worth the effort, and the problem of determining the right transfer price may occasion much negotiation or many difficult executive decisions. If the transfer is made at cost, clearly only the sales department would show a profit or a loss. If it is made at a figure above cost, the question of what price to charge arises.

In most instances, profit and loss control is not applied to central staff and service departments. Although these departments could "sell" their services, the most satisfactory practice is to place them under some other form of control, such as the variable expense budget.

Limitations

Profit and loss control suffers its greatest limitations from the cost of accounting and paper transactions involving intracompany transfer of costs and revenues. Duplication of accounting records, efforts involved in allocating the many overhead costs, and time and effort required to calculate intracompany sales can make this control too costly if it is carried too far.

Profit and loss control also may be inadequate for overall performance. Top managers may not wish to yield so much authority to division managers as to make their division completely integrated, and they may desire the additional assurances of good budgetary control. In addition, profit and loss control in and of itself does not provide a standard of desirable profits or policy controls in the area of product line development or in other matters of long-term overall company concern.

Another limitation of profit and loss control, especially if it is carried very far in the organization, is that departments may come to compete with an aggressive detachment not helpful to enterprise coordination. On the other hand, in many companies there is not enough feeling of departmental responsibility for company profit, and departments may develop the smugness of a monopolist with an assured market. The parts fabrication department that knows its products must be "bought" by the assembly department, the manufacturing or the service department that can force its output on the sales department, and the engineering group that has a monopolistic hold on both production and sales are dangerous monopolists indeed. Profit and loss control can break down these islands of monopoly. So, in spite of limitations—and especially if accompanied by an intracompany pricing policy requiring departments to meet competitive prices of suppliers outside the enterprise rather than being based on cost—profit and loss control can give top managers an extraordinary measure of overall control.

CONTROL THROUGH RETURN ON INVESTMENT (ROI)

One of the most successfully used control techniques is that of measuring both the absolute and the relative success of a company or a company unit by the ratio of earnings to investment of capital. The return-on-investment approach, often referred to as simply ROI, has been the core of the control system of the Du Pont Company since 1919. A large number of companies have adopted it as their key measure of overall performance. This yardstick is the rate of return that a company or a division can earn on the capital allocated to it. This tool, therefore, regards profit not as an absolute but as a return on capital employed in the business. The goal of a business is seen, accordingly, not necessarily as optimizing profits but as optimizing returns from capital devoted to business purposes. This standard recognizes the fundamental fact that capital is a critical factor in almost any enterprise and, through its scarcity, limits progress. It also emphasizes the fact that the job of managers is to make the best possible use of assets entrusted to them.

The Return-on-Investment System in Action

As the system has been used by the Du Pont Company, return on investment involves consideration of several factors. Return is computed on the basis of capital turnover (that is, total sales divided by capital, or total investment) multiplied by earnings as a percentage of sales. This formula recognizes that a division with a high capital turnover and low percentage of earnings to sales may be more profitable in terms of return on investment than another with a high percentage of profits to sales but with low capital turnover. As can be seen, the system measures effectiveness in the use of capital. Investment includes not only the permanent plant facilities but also the working capital of the unit. In the Du Pont system, investment and working capital represent amounts invested without reduction for liabilities or reserves, on the ground that such a reduction would result in a fluctuation in operating investments as reserves or liabilities change, which would distort the rate of return and render it less meaningful. Earnings are, however, calculated after normal depreciation charges, on the basis that true profits are not earned until allowance is made for the write-off of depreciable assets.

Return-on-investment control is perhaps best summarized in chart form, as in Figure 23-1. Here, analysis of variations in rate of return leads into every financial aspect of the business. Rate of return is the common denominator used in comparing divisions, and differences can easily be traced to their causes.

However, other companies have taken the position that the return on investment should be calculated on fixed assets less depreciation. Such companies hold that the depreciation reserve represents a write-off of the initial investment and that funds made available through such charges are reinvested in other fixed assets or used as working capital. Such a treatment appears more realistic to operating people, partly because it places a heavier rate-of-return burden on new fixed assets than on worn or obsolete ones.

In any control through return on investment, the number of ratios and comparisons behind the yardstick figure cannot be overlooked. Although improvement in rate of return can come from a higher percentage of profit to sales, improvement may also come from increasing the rate of turnover by lowering price and reducing return on sales. Moreover, the ratio of return on investment might be improved by getting more products (and sales) out of a given plant investment or by reducing the cost of sales for a given product.

Application to Product Lines

Functional-line organizations without integrated product divisions have applied return-on-investment control to their various product lines. By grouping its many products into a number of major classifications, a typical company follows through with the allocation of sales, costs, and investment in fixed assets and working capital to arrive at the same kind of rate-of-return analysis used by multidivision companies. A simplified example of these results is shown in Table 23-1.

To use the rate-of-return yardstick (as return on assets employed) for product lines, the company has allocated certain expenses and assets, but these

FIGURE 23-1

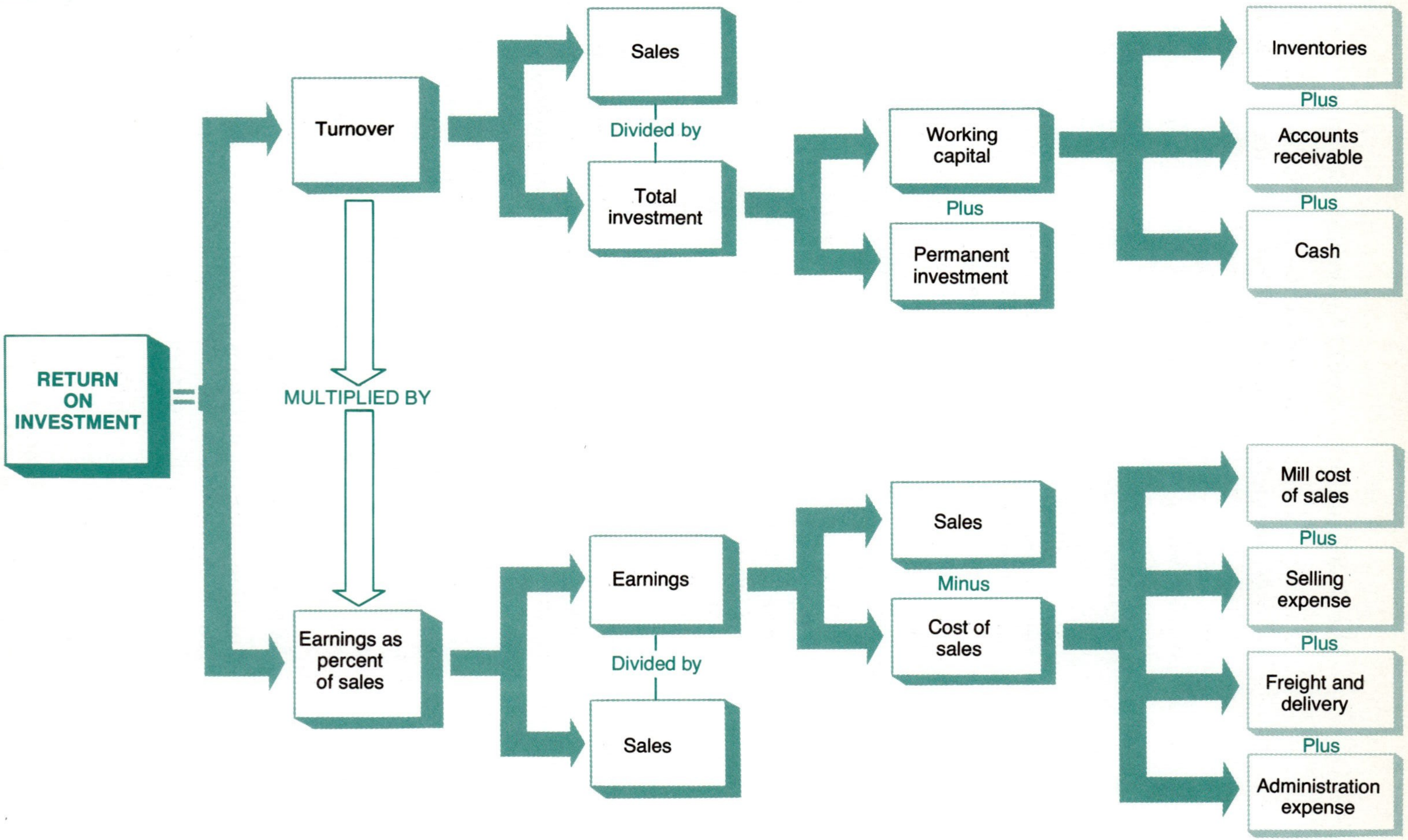

THE RELATIONSHIP OF FACTORS AFFECTING RETURN ON INVESTMENT.

TABLE 23-1 Comparative Rates of Return on Assets Employed: Multiproduct Company
(In Thousands of Dollars)

	Total sales		Assets employed		Operating income*		
	Amount	Percent of total	Amount	Per dollar of sales	Amount	Percent return on sales	Percent return on assets
Base year:							
Product A	$ 39,300	40	$ 20,700	52.9%	$ 4,800	12.2	23.1
Product B	29,500	30	16,900	57.3	2,800	9.4	16.4
Product C	19,600	20	8,900	45.1	2,100	10.8	23.9
Product D	9,800	10	2,700	27.5	500	5.1	18.5
Total	$ 98,200	100	$ 49,200	50.1%	$10,200	10.4	20.8
Current year:							
Product A	$ 48,100	25	$ 28,400	59.0%	$ 5,600	11.6	19.7
Product B	96,200	50	75,300	78.3	8,500	8.8	11.2
Product C	38,500	20	19,500	50.7	3,900	10.2	20.1
Product D	9,600	5	2,900	29.9	500	5.2	17.2
Total	$192,400	100	$126,100	65.5%	$18,500	9.6	14.6

* Before interest on borrowed money and federal income taxes.

allocations apparently have not caused much difficulty. Most production costs are maintained by product, and common costs, such as sales branch expenses, are allocated by volume of sales. More difficulty is incurred in determining asset usage by product lines, but cash, accounts receivable, and administrative and sales facilities are allocated in accordance with sales, while inventories and factory and plant equipment are prorated to the various products on the basis of special analyses.

In addition to comparing rates of return on assets of products, as indicated in Table 23-1, this company compared actual experience with trends for the various products (identified for purposes of simplicity as the "base year" in the table). An advantage of these comparisons is that the company is able to keep a sharp eye on its product lines, with a view to determining where capital is being most efficiently employed and as a guide toward obtaining a balanced use of capital for greatest overall profit. Thus, the company has been able to identify products that are either strong and established, new and improved, or past their peak growth and profitability.

Advantages

One of the principal advantages of using return on investment to control overall performance is that it, like profit and loss control, focuses managerial attention on the central objective of the business—to make the best profit possible on the capital available. It measures the efficiency of the company as a whole and of its major divisions or departments, its products, and its planning. It takes attention away from mere increase in sales volume or asset size or even from the level of costs, and draws attention to the combination of factors making for successful operation.

Another advantage of control by return on investment is that it is effective where authority is decentralized. It not only is an absolute guide to capital efficiency but also offers the possibility of comparing efficiency in the use of capital within the company and with other enterprises. By holding departmental managers responsible for performance in terms of the dollars invested in their parts of the business, it forces them to look at their operations from the point of view of top management. Managers often insist on heavy capital investments for new equipment or drive for lower prices to increase sales without taking into account the possible effect of their requests on the company as a whole. They also often feel isolated, particularly in large businesses, with respect to their performance. If managers are furnished a guide to efficiency that applies to a business as a whole, they develop a keener sense of responsibility for their department or division and top managers can more easily hold subordinate managers responsible.

A further advantage of return-on-investment control, if it is complete and shows all the factors bearing upon the return, is that it enables managers to locate weaknesses. If inventories are rising, the rate of return will be affected, or if other factors camouflage inventory variations and leave the rate looking good, tracing back influences will disclose any weakness of the inventory situation and open the way for consideration of a remedy.

Limitations

With all its advantages and with widespread use by well-managed and successful companies, this method of control is not foolproof. Difficulties involve availability of information on sales, costs, and assets and proper allocation of investment and return for commonly sold or produced items. Does the present accounting system give the needed information? If not, how much will it cost to get it, through either changes in the system or special analyses? Where assets are jointly used or costs are common, what method of allocation between divisions or departments shall be used? Should a manager be charged with assets at their original costs, their replacement costs, or their depreciated values? Setting up a return-on-investment control system is no simple task.

Another question is: What constitutes a reasonable return? Comparisons of rates of return are hardly enough, because they do not tell the top manager what the rate of return should be. Perhaps as good a standard as any is one that meets or surpasses the level of competing firms, since, in a practical sense, the best tends to be measured not by an absolute level but, rather, by the level of the competition for capital.

One of the dangers of overemphasis on the rate of return is that it may lead to undesirable inflexibility in investing capital for new ventures. Many companies using this important measuring tool have set minimum rates which a division, new product program, or investment must meet before the allocation of additional capital would be approved. It is said that even Du Pont, for many years, would not approve a new product program which would not promise a minimum of 20 percent return on investment. According to one executive of the company, this rigid minimum caused it to pass up such great product opportunities as xerography and the Land (Polaroid) camera. More recently, the company has used a more flexible minimum rate of return, requiring a higher rate when risks are greater and a lower rate when results are very promising or more certain, or when an investment supplements an established business.

Perhaps the greatest danger in return-on-investment control, as with any system of control based on financial data, is that it can lead to excessive preoccupation with financial factors within a firm or an industry. Undue attention to ratios and financial data can cause a firm to overlook environmental factors such as social and technical developments. It might also lead a company to overlook the fact that capital is not the only scarce resource from which a business can grow, prosper, and endure. Every bit as scarce are competent managers, good employee morale, and good customer and public relations. A well-managed company would never regard any financially based control as the sole gauge of overall performance.

DIRECT CONTROL VERSUS PREVENTIVE CONTROL

The preceding analysis of controls stresses the variety of approaches that managers follow to make results conform to plans. At the basis of control is the fact that the outcome of plans is dependent on the people who carry them out. For instance, a poor educational system cannot be controlled by criticizing its product, the unfortunate graduate; a factory turning out inferior products cannot be controlled by consigning products to the scrap heap; and a firm plagued with customer complaints cannot be controlled by ignoring the complainers. Responsibility for controllable deviations lies with whoever has made unfortunate decisions. Any hope of abolishing unsatisfactory results lies in changing the future actions of the responsible person, through additional training, modification of procedures, or new policy. This is the crux of controlling the quality of management.

There are two ways of seeing to it that the responsible people modify future action. The normal procedure is to trace the cause of an unsatisfactory result back to the persons responsible for it and get them to correct their practices. This may be called **direct control**. The alternative in the area of management is to develop better managers who will skillfully apply concepts, techniques, and principles and who will look at managing and managerial problems from a systems point of view, thus eliminating undesirable results caused by poor management. This will be referred to as **preventive control**.[7]

DIRECT CONTROL

In every enterprise, hundreds, and even thousands, of standards are developed to compare the actual output of goods or services—in terms of quantity, quality, time, and cost—with plans. A negative deviation indicates—in terms of goal

PERSPECTIVE:
CONTROL AT APPLE COMPUTER[8]

Apple Computer, Inc., enjoyed a phenomenal early success after it was founded in 1977 by Steve Wozniak, the technical expert, and Steve Jobs, the marketing genius.

However, success did not last for very long, partly owing to the introduction of the IBM Personal Computer. In the early 1980s, in the view of some observers, Apple needed tighter control and a more professional approach to managing. John Sculley was lured from Pepsi-Cola Company to give Apple a new direction.

To bring the company under control, Sculley employed cost-cutting measures to improve its profitability. At the same time, however, research and development expenditures were increased so that the company could remain a technological leader in the field. The firm was also reorganized to reduce duplication of efforts, to lower the break-even point, and to reduce friction among the departments. To improve its effectiveness and efficiency, Apple introduced new reporting procedures. Furthermore, considerable efforts were made to control the inventory level, which is a serious problem in the personal computer industry. These measures, combined with a successful strategy (Apple's Macintosh computer is making inroads into business corporations which are dominated by IBM), helped by the popularity of desktop publishing, has resulted in an increase of over 150 percent in earnings in the 1986 fiscal year.

achievement, cost, price, personnel, labor-hours, or machine-hours—that performance is less than good or normal or standard and that results are not conforming to plans.

Causes of Negative Deviations from Standards

The causes of negative deviations will often determine whether control measures are possible. Although an incorrect standard may cause deviations, if the standard is correct, plans may fail because of (1) uncertainty and (2) lack of knowledge, experience, or judgment by those who make the decisions or take actions.

Uncertainty.   Elements affecting a given plan may be grouped into facts, risks, and uncertainty. Facts, such as number of employees, costs, or machine capacity, are known. Considerably less is known about the element of risk. Insurable risks are readily converted to factual status through the payment of a known premium, and costs of certain noninsurable risks may be included in a business decision on the basis of probability. But most risks arise from uncertainty. The total of facts and risks is small, compared with the element of uncertainty, which includes everything about which nothing is certain. For instance, the success of a plan to manufacture aluminum pistons will depend not only on known facts and risks but also on such uncertainties as future world conditions, competition of known and yet unknown metals, and power technology that may eliminate all piston prime movers. Not even probability can be estimated for all the uncertain factors, and yet they can wreck a plan.

Managerial errors caused by unforeseeable events cannot be avoided. The fixing of personal responsibility by direct control techniques is of little avail in such situations.

Lack of knowledge, experience, or judgment. Plans may misfire and negative deviations occur when people appointed to managerial posts lack the necessary background. The higher in the organizational structure managers are placed, the broader the knowledge and experience they need. Long years as an engineer, a sales manager, a production executive, or a controller may be inadequate qualifications for a top manager.

If the cause of error is poor judgment, whether due to inadequate training, to experience, or to failure to use appropriate information in decision making, corrections can be made. Managers can improve their education, be transferred to acquire broader experience, or be cautioned to take better stock of the situation before making decisions.

Questionable Assumptions Underlying Direct Control

In addition to its cost, the shortcomings of direct control may also be the results of questionable assumptions: (1) that performance can be measured,[9] (2) that personal responsibility exists, (3) that the time expenditure is warranted, (4) that mistakes can be discovered in time, and (5) that the person responsible will take corrective steps.

1. That performance can be measured. At first glance, almost any enterprise appears to be a maze of controls. Input, output, cost, price, time, complaints, and quality are subject to numerous standards, and the standards may be expressed in terms of goal achievement, time, weight, tolerances, averages, ratios, dollars, and indexes. In terms of usefulness, the standards may be correct, acceptable, or merely better than nothing. Close analysis will often reveal shortcomings of two types. In the first place, the ability of a manager to develop potential managers, the effectiveness of research, and the amount of creativity, foresight, and judgment in decision making can seldom be measured accurately.

The second shortcoming concerns the location of the control. Managers know that critical stages exist in acquiring input factors, manipulating them to produce a finished product, and selling and delivering the product. In a factory operation, for example, critical stages would include receiving inspection, inspection for each assembly process, shipping, and billing. These are critical because effective control here will minimize costs. No amounts of control at other points can make up for lack of control at these stages.

2. That personal responsibility exists. Sometimes no manager is responsible for poor results. Increase in interest rates or inflation may cause the costs of many activities to rise precipitously. Scarcity of a particular fuel may necessitate use of less economical sources of power. And markets may shrink for reasons unconnected with the firm.

3. *That the time expenditure is warranted.* Whether managers undertake the inquiry themselves or assign it to others, executive time must be spent in ferreting out causes of poor results. Large scrap losses, for example, may call for meetings attended by persons representing quality control, production planning, engineering, purchasing, and manufacturing. Passage of time may make the recall of facts quite different. These drawbacks may convince managers that the cost of investigation exceeds any benefit they may derive. This often precludes investigation of clear violations of standards.

4. *That mistakes can be discovered in time.* Discovery of deviations from plans often comes too late for effective action. Although true control can be applied only to future action, most controls depend on historical data—all that most managers have available. Managers should, of course, interpret such data in terms of their implications for the future.

The cost of errors in major areas—such as cash or inventories—have led to the use of feedforward techniques as the basis for control. Since these are often difficult to use, the natural tendency to rely on historical reports seriously blocks adequate controls. Feedforward control techniques offer hope, but as yet they have not been widely developed or utilized. No manager really has control unless he or she can correct mistakes. And the best way to correct mistakes is to avoid them.

5. *That the person responsible will take corrective steps.* Fixing the responsibility may not lead to correction. High production costs, for example, might be traced back to a marketing manager who insists that "slight" product modification will make selling easier and that this involves "really" no change in a production run. If the marketing manager is a member of top management, a subordinate investigator may be intimidated. Although great effort may be made to correct subordinate managers, it is sometimes very difficult to correct an executive to whom one reports.

THE PRINCIPLE OF PREVENTIVE CONTROL

The principle of preventive control embraces the idea that most of the responsibility for negative deviations from standards can be fixed by applying fundamentals of management. It draws a sharp distinction between performance reports, essential in any case, and determining whether managers act in accordance with established principles in carrying out their functions. The **principle of preventive control**, then, can be stated as follows: *The higher the quality of managers and their subordinates, the less will be the need for direct controls.*

The extensive adoption of preventive control must await a wider understanding of managerial principles, functions, and techniques as well as management philosophy. While such an understanding is not achieved easily, it can be gained through university training, through on-the-job experience, through coaching by a knowledgeable superior, and by means of constant self-education.

Moreover, as progress is made in appraising managers as managers, we can expect preventive control to have more practical meaning and effectiveness.

Assumptions of the Principle of Preventive Control

The desirability of preventive control rests upon three assumptions: (1) that qualified managers make a minimum of errors, (2) that managerial performance can be measured and that management concepts, principles, and techniques are useful diagnostic standards in measuring managerial performance, and (3) that the application of management fundamentals can be evaluated.

1. That qualified managers make a minimum of errors.   J. P. Morgan has often been quoted as saying that the decisions of good managers are right two-thirds of the time. However, an accurate analysis of the quality of decision making should not rely upon quantity of errors but should be concerned with the nature of the error. As J. Paul Getty once told one of the authors, his concern in his worldwide empire was not the percentage of decisions in which an executive was right or wrong—he could be wrong on only 2 percent of them and seriously endanger a company if the errors were critical. Managers can logically be held strictly accountable for the performance of their functions because these functions should be undertaken in conformance with the fundamentals of management.[10] However, accountability cannot be exacted for errors attributable to factors beyond managers' authority or their ability to forecast the future with a reasonable degree of accuracy.

2. That management fundamentals can be used to measure performance.   The chief purpose of this book has been to draw together concepts, principles, theory, and basic techniques or approaches of management and relate them to a system of managerial functions. As we stated in previous chapters, the completeness and certitude of these vary considerably, depending largely upon the state of knowledge concerning managing. There is, for instance, greater general acceptance of some of the principles of organizing than there is of the principles relating to other functions. Nevertheless, we are convinced that the fundamentals set forth here are useful in measuring managerial performance, even though our statement will undoubtedly be refined and better verified by future specialists.

3. That the application of management fundamentals can be evaluated. Evaluation can provide for periodic measurement of the skill with which managers apply management fundamentals. This can be done not only by judging performance against these but also by casting them into a series of fairly objective questions. An approach to the proper evaluation of managers as managers was set forth in Chapter 14. The ability to set and achieve verifiable objectives is one measure of a manager's performance. But much depends on being able to evaluate the performance of a manager as a manager. As crude as these standards of measurement may be at the present state of the art of managing, they can still highlight the extent to which an individual has the knowledge and ability required to fill the managerial role.

Advantages

Controlling the quality of managers and thus minimizing errors has several advantages. In the first place, greater accuracy is achieved in assigning personal responsibility. The ongoing evaluation of managers is practically certain to uncover deficiencies and should provide a basis for specific training to eliminate them.

In the second place, preventive control should hasten corrective action and make it more effective. It encourages control by self-control. Knowing that errors will be uncovered in an evaluation, managers will themselves try to determine their responsibility and make voluntary corrections. For example, a report of excessive scrap will probably cause the department supervisor to determine quickly whether the excess was due to poor direction of subordinates or to other factors. The same report will cause the chief inspector to look into whether inspections employees acted properly, the purchasing agent to check the material purchased with engineering specifications, and the engineers to determine whether appropriate material was specified. All this action can be immediate and voluntary. Managers who conclude privately that they were in error are likely to do their best to prevent recurrence, for they realize their responsibility.

The third advantage of preventive control is the potential for lightening the burden now caused by direct controls. This is a net gain, since the evaluation of managers is already part of staffing. The amount of potential savings is as yet unknown, although it must be considerable.

Last, the psychological advantage of preventive control is impressive. The feeling of subordinates that superiors do not rate fairly, rely on hunch and personality, and use improper measuring standards is almost universal, but preventive control of the kind suggested in Chapter 14 can go far in removing this feeling. Subordinate managers know what is expected of them, understand the nature of managing, and feel a close relationship between performance and measurement.

THE MANAGEMENT AUDIT AND THE ENTERPRISE SELF-AUDIT

A question might be raised as to how a management audit may be distinguished from an enterprise self-audit. The latter emphasizes where a company is and where it is probably going in the face of present and future economic, political, and social developments. The **enterprise self-audit**, then, is really an audit of an organization's operations and only indirectly an audit of its managerial system.

The **management audit**, on the other hand, is not nearly as broad as the enterprise self-audit in that it aims only at evaluating the quality of managing and the quality of managing as a system. It will be discussed first.

The Management Audit

Application of the principle of preventive control has led to action in several directions. One of the most promising and effective has been the improvement of programs in recent years to appraise individual managers. Primarily, this has taken the form of appraising performance against the standard of setting and achieving verifiable goals. However, much must still be done to make even this widely accepted approach effective. A second essential aspect of this process, still done only on a limited and experimental basis, is the appraisal of managers in their role as *managers*. Both these approaches were discussed in Chapter 14.

Another direction in which the principle of preventive control has led is in a developing interest in management audits. Compared with the practice of other forms of management evaluations, these do not aim at evaluating managers as individuals but rather at looking at the entire system of managing an enterprise. While little progress has been made in such management audits, some pioneering programs have been undertaken.

Management audits and accounting firms.   Although many management consulting firms have undertaken various kinds of appraisal of management systems, usually as a part of an organization study, the greatest interest in pursuing management audits has been demonstrated by accounting audit firms. One of the significant developments of recent years has been their entry into the field of management services of a broad consultancy nature. While this has been an attractive field of expansion for these auditing companies, since they are already inside an organization and financial information furnishes a ready window on problems of managing, it does open some question of conflict of interest. In other words, the question is often raised whether the same firm can be in the position of a management consultant furnishing both advice and services and still be completely objective as an accounting auditor. To be sure, accounting firms have attempted to avoid this problem by organizationally separating these two activities.

Regardless of whether auditing firms should be in management services, the fact is that they are. Since many are experienced in both auditing and management services, it is only a short step to management auditing. If it is possible for these firms to set up a completely detached and objective management auditing operation and if this can be staffed by individuals with truly professional knowledge and ability in management, it is very possible that this may result in acceleration in the practice of management auditing. At least, as long as the various professional and academic associations with a specific interest in management seem to be doing little in this field, perhaps accounting firms will show the way.

The certified management audit.   Another possibility for the future is the development of a **certified management audit**, an independent appraisal of a company's management by an outside firm. For years investors and others have relied on an independent certified accounting audit designed to make certain that the company's records and reports reflect sound accounting principles. From the standpoint of investors and even from that of managers and those desiring to work for a company, an independent audit of management quality would be extremely important. It is probably not too much to say that an investor would get more value from a certified management audit than from a certified accounting audit, since the future of a company is likely to depend more on the quality of its managers than on any other single factor.

To ensure objectivity, the certified management audit should be the responsibility of a recognized outside firm, staffed with individuals qualified to appraise a company's managerial system and the quality of its managers. Although this would require considerable study from the inside and a set of reasonably objective standards, it probably would take little more time than a thorough accounting audit. Moreover, except for the audit of top-level managers, and the preparation of a final analysis of the company's management as a total system, much work on the management audit could be done, as in the case of accounting audits, with the help of suitable inside managerial and staff personnel. Furthermore, as with the accounting audit, when a group of special auditors once becomes familiar with a company, subsequent audits take less time than the first. In order to ensure real objectivity, a management audit should be made by a recognized and qualified group of management appraisers with a reporting responsibility, like that of most accounting auditors, to the board of directors or another responsible top management group.

It is quite obvious that any management audit report must go far beyond the typical accounting auditor's statements. It must do more than say that a management group has followed "generally accepted standards of management." To be meaningful it would require that the quality of managers and the system within which they manage be assessed objectively in fairly specific terms. This, as one can see, gives rise to problems. How many accounting or management consulting firms can really be expected to be objective where, as so often occurs, managerial deficiencies exist at the top and when the firms are retained by, and report to, these same top managers? This is not an easy hurdle to overcome, at least until almost completely objective standards can be agreed upon by true professionals, and applied impartially. One cannot help but wonder whether this might not necessitate a specially licensed group independent of present accounting and management consulting firms and reporting, as professionals, to some agency independent of the organization being audited.

The Enterprise Self-Audit

J. O. McKinsey, who achieved an outstanding position in the realm of management several decades ago, came to the conclusion that a business enterprise should periodically make a "management audit," an appraisal of the enterprise in all its aspects, in the light of its present and probable future environment. Although McKinsey called this a management audit, it is actually an audit of the entire enterprise.

The **enterprise self-audit** appraises the company's position to determine where it is, where it is heading under present programs, what its objectives should be, and whether revised plans are needed to meet those objectives. In most enterprises, objectives and policies become obsolete. If the enterprise does not change course to suit the changing social, technical, and political environment, it loses markets, personnel, and other requirements for continued existence. The enterprise self-audit is designed to force managers to meet this situation.

Procedure.   The self-audit may be made annually or, more likely, once every 3 or 5 years. The first step is to study the outlook of the firm's industry. What are recent trends and prospects? What is the outlook for the product? Where are the markets? What technical developments are affecting the industry? How may demand be changed? What political or social factors may affect the industry?

A second step in the self-audit is to appraise the position of the firm in the industry, both current and prospective. Has the company maintained its position? Has it expanded its influence and markets? Or has competition reduced its position? What is the competitive outlook? To answer such questions, the company may undertake studies on competitor standing, development of competition, customer reactions, and other factors bearing on its position within the industry.

On the basis of such studies, the next logical step for the company would be to reexamine its basic objectives and major policies to decide where the company wishes to be in, say, 5 or 10 years. After this reexamination, the company may audit its organization, policies, procedures, programs, facilities, financial position, personnel, and management. This examination should identify any deviations from objectives and facilitate the revision of many major and minor plans.

Contribution of the self-audit.   Most top managers do not think in terms of an enterprise's future or evaluate overall performance in relation to long-range objectives. The enterprise self-audit has the distinct advantage of forcing them to appraise overall performance in terms not only of current goals but also of future ones. Top managers who expend mental effort for this kind of audit will almost certainly be well repaid and will be surprised at how many day-to-day decisions will be simplified by a clear picture of where the business is attempting to go.

This is often done when a company evaluates a firm it wishes to acquire. Without in any way detracting from the major importance of financial performance, it is realized that a firm's value depends upon its future rather than its past. For this evaluation to be made, financial factors need to be supplemented by such consideration of such factors as product lines and basic competition, marketing strengths, research and development record, personnel and public relations, and the quality of management. If this is of importance to a buyer of a company, one cannot help but wonder why it should not be significant on a regular and continuing basis to a firm.

DEVELOPING EXCELLENT MANAGERS

Although the introductory analyses of the task of the manager are presented in this book as a start toward understanding the science underlying managerial practice, more is required. Among the more important considerations in ensuring the development of excellent managers, we would like to offer the following. Surely effective future managerial practice will depend at least on these.

A Willingness to Learn

If managers are to avoid the stultifying effect of basing too much of their learning on experience, they must be aware of the dangers of experience.[11] Undistilled experience can lead an individual toward assuming that events or programs of the past will or will not work in a different future. But managers need more than this. They need to be willing to learn and to take advantage of new knowledge and new techniques. This necessitates a humble approach to their successes and limitations. It demands a recognition that there is no finishing school or terminal degree for management.

Acceleration of Management Development

The preceding discussion underlines the urgent importance of accelerated programs of management development. This implies not only more pertinent management seminars and conferences but also other means of transmitting to practicing managers in as simple and useful a way as possible the new knowledge and tools in the field of management.

One of the major challenges in this connection is that of compressing and transmitting the available knowledge. Every field of art based on a burgeoning science has the same problem. No field has completely solved it, although certain areas, such as specialized aspects of medicine and dentistry, have made considerable progress.

We have no adequate answer for this problem. It does appear that those on the management faculties of our universities have an obligation to practicing managers to do much of the task of compressing and transmitting this knowledge as easily and quickly as possible. There is still inadequate evidence that many university professors see the social importance of this role. Also, one might expect a greater contribution from various management associations, as well as from management consultants, who can certainly greatly improve their value to clients by doing this. Perhaps more can be done through intelligent digesting of articles and books. Also, it is entirely possible that there might be regularly established a series of special management clinics in which managers at all levels in alert companies would spend a day every few weeks being brought up to date on a specific area of new knowledge and techniques.

The Importance of Planning for Innovation

As competition becomes sharper, as problem solving grows in complexity, and as knowledge expands, one expects that the managers of the future will have to place greater importance on planning for innovation. Even now it is widely recognized that a business enterprise, at least, must "innovate or die," that new products just do not happen, and that new marketing ideas do not often occur by luck. The manager of the future must place more emphasis than ever before on developing an environment for effective planning. This means, even more than at present, planning goals which call for stretch, creating policy guidelines to channel thinking toward them without stifling imagination, designing roles where people can be creative and yet constructive, keeping abreast of the entire external environment (discussed in greater detail in Chapters 24 and 25), which affects every kind of organization, and recognizing the urgency of channeling research toward desired ends.

Measuring and Rewarding Management

One of the significant areas of concern to the manager of the future will be the importance both of objectively measuring managerial performance and of rewarding good performance, imposing sanctions on a poor operation, and providing corrective action where it is indicated. Managers must be willing to work toward establishing objective measures of performance through both a verifiable results approach and the measurement of abilities of individuals as managers.

Tailoring Information

Another important area for the manager of the future will be to obtain the right information in the right form and at the right time. Tailoring information, as outlined in this book, requires a high order of intelligence and design. Until more managers realize that very little of their operation can be planned and controlled through "handbook" approaches, and until more managers recognize that they themselves must become involved in tailoring the information they require, progress will continue to be slow in this area. As long as information design is confused with the clerical work of information gathering and summarizing, managers will understandably continue to fret about the inadequacy of the data on which they are forced to act.

The Need for Research and Development in Tools and Techniques

All these areas mentioned should command greater managerial attention. In addition, a great need exists for more real research and development in management tools and techniques themselves. The level of research effort and support in the field of management is woefully low. It is also not particularly great in the disciplines underlying management or, for that matter, in the entire area of social science. Nevertheless, it is probable that research in underlying disciplines far outpaces that in the central area of management.

There are many reasons for this. General management research is difficult, exceedingly complex, and dynamic. It is an area where facts and proved relationships are hard to come by and where the controlled experiment of the laboratory is difficult to use without dangerous oversimplification. Likewise, management research is expensive, and the funds that have gone into it are abysmally inadequate.

Still another reason for the low state of management research is that there are few clinical analyses, despite a considerable volume of clinical experience. Consulting efforts of both professional consultants and individual academics, extensive management case collections, and studies and analyses made internally in business, government, and other enterprise almost certainly encompass a huge mass of undigested, largely unsummarized, and relatively useless information. If this clinical experience could be given the analytical and summarizing work so common in the health sciences, there might now be considerable evidence of what is workable in practice and where deficiencies exist.

In undertaking this research, patience and understanding are needed. Perfection of analysis to include all kinds of variables is a laudable goal for a researcher. But, particularly in the field of management, a little light can be a massive beam in a hitherto dark area. We must often settle for small advances so that cumulatively, and over time, we may gain larger ones.

The Need for Managerial Inventions

But research without development is insufficient. One of the major challenges for the manager of the future is the need for developing more managerial inventions. It is interesting that so much creative talent has been channeled into the invention of physical designs and chemical compositions and how little into social inventions. The Gantt chart has sometimes been regarded as the most important social invention of the first half of the twentieth century. Other management inventions include the variable budget, rate-of-return-on-investment analysis, and PERT. Mere reference to these inventions underscores the fact that they are creative tools developed from a base of principles on the one hand and needs on the other. Reference to them indicates also that they are useful devices in improving the art of managing.

Inventions tend to reflect the cultural level of an art. There are few of them in management. Surely even the present inadequate cultural level can be coupled with urgent needs to give rise to many more management innovations, particularly if those concerned are willing to spend some time and money to direct their energies toward these inventions. It is very easy to see that one significant management invention, such as those mentioned in the previous paragraph, can make important contributions to management effectiveness and economy of operations. Applied research and development in this field surely justify a considerable expenditure of time and money.

The Need for Strong Intellectual Leadership

That intellectual leadership in management is urgently needed can hardly be denied. Managing can no longer be only a practical art requiring merely native intelligence and experience. The rapid growth of underlying knowledge and the obvious need for even more, particularly that knowledge which is organized and useful for improvement of practice, are requirements which have tremendous significance.

For people in every type of enterprise, at any part of the globe, the challenge to create a highly productive society is great. History teaches us that when needs exist and are recognized, leadership usually arises to inspired solutions. The challenging needs are here waiting the application of knowledge discussed in this book, which is aimed to make you more effective as a person and as a manager so that you can lead a productive organization.

FOR DISCUSSION

1. Why do most controls of overall performance tend to be financial? Should they be? What else would you suggest?

2. "Profit and loss control is defective in that it does not emphasize return on investment; the latter is defective in that it places too great an emphasis on present results, possibly endangering future results." Discuss.

3. In applying rate of return on investment as a control tool, would you favor using an undepreciated or a depreciated asset base?

4. If preventive control were completely effective, would a company need any direct controls?

5. What distinction would you draw between management appraisal, as dealt with in Chapter 14, and the management audit discussed in this chapter?

6. How would you proceed to make a management audit? Are there any similarities between it and an accounting audit or an enterprise audit?

7. Taking any major area of management theory and principles, discuss how it can be applied to reality.

8. In reference to specific management problem areas, such as new product development, organization structure, or budgets, what are the ways managers can introduce flexibility, and what are the inflexibilities usually encountered in each?

9. How would you anticipate that the computer will affect the manager's role at the top-management level? The middle-management level? First-level supervision?

10. What can be done about the problem of top-level executive malnutrition?

EXERCISES/ACTION STEPS

1. Interview two managers in business firms and ask them about the kinds of controls used to measure overall performance. What are the similarities and differences of the responses of the two managers?

2. Take any federal, state, or local government agency you wish, and check whether or not it has some kind of overall control. If not, could you develop a system or program for evaluating overall performance?

CASES

CASE 23-1
HOSPITAL SERVICES, INC.

In past decades, considerable interest was generated in hospital care. The aged and the poor were heavily subsidized by government programs aimed, among other things, at helping those in need to get adequate hospital care. During the same time, the cost of hospital services doubled, and still there were not enough beds for patients. Federal and state governments saw the need to distinguish among the most suitable types of care. It was clear that not everyone needed the full-service care of general hospitals. The law contemplated that once discharged from such a facility, patients would be sent to a convalescent hospital for a limited time, where the service level and costs were much lower. And, theoretically, having completed the allowed time, or as much of it as was needed, in this institution, patients would be returned to their homes, where they could receive needed services.

Jules McDonald was among several people who had the idea of building or buying a chain of convalescent hospitals to fill the growing need for beds. He thought that a chain could probably achieve some economies of operation that a single hospital would not find possible. He intended to broaden his business by purchasing land, securing a mortgage to take care of the hospitals, and selling the whole package to investors. He would place his own optical stores and drugstores within each hospital, have his own wholesalers in drugs and hospital equipment, and create his own construction companies.

McDonald needed money to do these things. He knew that the shares of convalescent hospital chains were being traded in multiples from 60 to 200 times earnings, and so he determined to tap the investment market for capital. He got together a few scattered assets, packaged them attractively, and took his business public. It could not be said that he could show any earnings, but he stressed his prospective earnings per share. Amazingly, the idea sold, and he raised about $25 million.

With cash in the bank and an attractive vision in his head, McDonald was ready to go with his Hospital Services, Inc. Plush offices came first. Then a group of lawyers and tax accountants was added. A salesman sold him a computer. Convalescent hospitals were purchased at high prices; land was bought across the country and construction was begun; and acquisitions were eagerly sought. McDonald did not do this all by himself. He was specially gifted in his public relations, government relations, and negotiations skills and tended to specialize in them. Managers were hired to take care of construction, hospital management, and finance.

As the months passed, the cash raised from the public issue was fast used. On paper, the cash flow from operations seemed to be adequate, but it did not actually materialize. No one, it seemed, was able to get a reading on hospital finances. In some cases, there were no profits; in other cases, the individual institution kept its own cash balance; and in others, there was a heavy drain of funds to cover expenses. The government did not help, either. Its agencies were new at this activity; new interpretations of the law were being made so frequently that no one knew what practice to follow.

Throughout this period of operation there was no slowdown in activity. McDonald was in his element, but his controller failed to warn him of imminent bankruptcy. There did come a day when he ran out of money. This occurred at a time when bankers were tightening up credit and the stock market was falling fast.

As he looked over his wreck, he inquired, "What control system should I have had?"

1. How did Hospital Services, Inc., get out of control?

2. Exactly what controls should have been used, and how?

3. To assess the success of the company, what other things should have been done?

CASE 23-2
BANKAMERICA CORPORATION[12]

BankAmerica, once the largest bank in the United States, ranked 299th among the 300 most admired companies. In other words, it ranked almost last in this group identified by *Fortune* magazine.[13] In this group BankAmerica was among the least admired groups in terms of quality of management, innovativeness, and other characteristics.

In the early 1980s, the bank was one of the most profitable banks in the nation. At that time, it had over 87,000 employees and more than 2000 offices in about 100 countries. But over a period of 5 years, over $4 billion of loans were written off, many of them to home builders, shipping firms, farmers, and foreign customers. But in 1986 Samuel Armacost stated that the situation was under control.[14] Yet the stock price dropped sharply in 1986. The headquarters building in San Francisco was sold; then followed the sale of Charles Schwab & Co., BankAmerica's brokerage subsidiary, in 1987.

The bank expanded its mortgage business in 1979 and 1980 with the expectation that the interest rates would fall. Instead, they skyrocketed in the early 1980s. Being stuck with low mortgages, but paying high interest rates on deposits, put a great burden on the institution. Deregulation resulted in an easing of interest rate ceilings and

created a dynamic environment for which most financial institutions were not prepared. Savings and loan associations became more like banks in their operations; greater competition resulted in lower margins; lower margins, in turn, led some inefficient organizations to fail or to become acquired.

Competition came not only from other banks but also from many other institutions. General Motors, for example, became one of the top consumer lenders. Other firms were Sears, Ford Motor Company, National Steel, General Electric, and American Express, just to mention a few.

BankAmerica, like many other banks, also made loans to less-developed countries. One of the reasons was to spread the risks for savers and investors. But some of the loans were not collectible.

In 1986 Armacost was replaced by A. W. Clausen, who was also his predecessor.

1. Did BankAmerica get out of control? If your answer is "yes," how did it happen?

2. What safeguards would you recommend so that it does not happen again? What, for example, would you recommend so that loan officers do not make risky loans?

REFERENCES

1. "Integrated" here is used as meaning that an operation includes the functions necessary to gain an overall objective. Thus, a product division of a company would normally include engineering, manufacturing, and marketing, and these functions represent enough of a total operation for the division manager—even though subject to some direction and control from headquarters—to be held basically responsible for a profit. To

a lesser degree, an engineering design operation might be regarded as integrated: If its head supervises all the engineering functions and specialties necessary for complete product design, he or she can then be held responsible for the efficient accomplishment of the project.

2. For a discussion of different kinds of measurement, see Joseph W. Wilkinson, "The Meanings of Measurement," in Max D. Richards (ed.), *Readings in Management*, 7th ed. (Cincinnati: South-Western Publishing Co., 1986), pp. 318–324.

3. Robert N. Anthony, "Games Government Accountants Play," *Harvard Business Review* (September–October 1985), pp. 161–170.

4. Michael J. Sandretto, "What Kind of Cost System Do You Need?" *Harvard Business Review* (January–February 1986), pp. 110–118.

5. Frances Gaither Tucker and Seymour M. Zivan, "A Xerox Cost Center Imitates a Profit Center," *Harvard Business Review* (May–June 1985), pp. 168–174.

6. Leslie Helm, "Why Kodak Is Starting to Click Again," *Business Week* (Feb. 23, 1987), pp. 134–138; Leslie Helm and Barbara Buell, "Kodak Fights Fuji with 'Me-Too' Tactics," *Business Week* (Feb. 13, 1987), p. 138; Alex Taylor III, "Kodak Scrambles to Refocus," *Fortune* (Mar. 3, 1986), pp. 34–39.

7. In previous editions we used a different terminology. Following the recommendations of our colleagues, we now use "preventive" and "direct" control.

8. Deborah C. Wise, "Can John Sculley Clean Up the Mess at Apple?" *Business Week* (July 29, 1985), pp. 70–71; Deborah C. Wise, "Apple, Part 2: The No-Nonsense Era of John Sculley," *Business Week* (Jan. 27, 1986), pp. 96–98; Katherine M. Hafner and Geoff Lewis, "Apple's Comeback," *Business Week* (Jan. 19, 1987), pp. 84–89.

9. See also Geert Hofstede, "The Poverty of Management Control Philosophy," in Max D. Richards (ed.), *Readings in Management,* 7th ed. (Cincinnati: South-Western Publishing Co., 1986), pp. 302–315.

10. See also Derek F. du Toit, "Confessions of a So-So Controller," *Harvard Business Review* (July–August 1985), pp. 50–56.

11. On the other hand, the contributions of managers in their forties and fifties are often underestimated. They are often the ones who keep the organization going and should be involved in important decisions. See Jay W. Lorsch and Haruo Takagi, "Keeping Managers Off the Shelf," *Harvard Business Review* (July–August 1986), pp. 60–65.

12. The information for this case has been drawn from a variety of sources, including Harvey Rosenblum and Diane Siegel, *Competition in Financial Services: The Impact of Nonbank Entry* (Federal Reserve Bank of Chicago, Staff Study #83-11, p. 17); Teresa Carson, "Who Needs BankAmerica? Not Joe Pinola," *Business Week* (Feb. 23, 1987), p. 46; Jonathan B. Levine, "1985 Won't Be Any Better for BofA," *Business Week* (June 24, 1985), p. 46; "Banks Give Farmers Loans and Pray for Bailout," *The Wall Street Journal* (June 6, 1985).

13. Edward C. Baig, "America's Most Admired Corporations," *Fortune* (Jan. 19, 1987), pp. 18–31.

14. Gary Hector, "The Most Beleaguered Banker," *Fortune* (Jan. 5, 1987), p. 86.

FOR FURTHER INFORMATION

Behrman, Jack N., and Richard I. Levin. "Are Business Schools Doing Their Job?" *Harvard Business Review* (January–February 1984), pp. 140–147.

Donnell, Susan M., and Jay Hall. "Men and Women as Managers: A Significant Case of No Significant Difference," in James H. Donnelly, Jr., James L. Gibson, and John M. Ivancevich (eds.), *Perspectives on Management,* 5th ed. (Plano, Tex.: Business Publications, 1984), pp. 377–396.

Ernst, Harry D. "New Balance Sheet for Managing Liquidity and Growth," *Harvard Business Review* (March–April 1984), pp. 122–136.

Kaplan, Robert S. "Yesterday's Accounting Undermines Production," *Harvard Business Review* (July–August 1984), pp. 95–101.

Ouchi, William. *The M-Form Society* (Reading, Mass.: Addison-Wesley Publishing Company, 1984).

Posner, Barry Z., James L. Hall, and Joseph W. Harder. " 'People Are Our Most Important Resource, But': Encouraging Employee Development," *Business Horizons* (September–October 1986), pp. 52–54.

Reuter, Vincent G. "Selected Management Controls: Audits, Budgets and Capital Funds Justification," *Journal of Systems Management* (August 1985), pp. 14–21.

Rhode, John G., Edward E. Lawler III, and G. L. Sundem. "Human Resource Accounting: A Critical Assessment," *Industrial Relations* (February 1976), pp. 13–25.

Schmidt, Warren H., and Barry Z. Posner. *Management Values and Expectations* (New York: American Management Association, 1982).

Weihrich, Heinz. *Management Excellence—Productivity Through MBO* (New York: McGraw-Hill Book Company, 1985).

Weston, J. Fred, and Eugene F. Brigham. *Managerial Finance* (Hinsdale, Ill.: Dryden Press, 1981).

A SUMMARY OF MAJOR PRINCIPLES, OR GUIDES, OF CONTROLLING

From the discussions in the previous chapters on management control, there have emerged certain essentials, or basic truths. These, which are referred to as "principles," are designed to highlight aspects of control that are regarded as especially important. In view of the fact that control, even though representing a system itself, is a subsystem of the larger area of management, certain of these principles are understandably similar to those identified in discussing the other managerial functions. Principles of control can be grouped into three categories, reflecting their purpose and nature, structure, and process.

The Purpose and Nature of Control

The purpose and nature of control may be summarized by the following principles:

Principle of the purpose of control. The task of control is to ensure that plans succeed by detecting deviations from plans and furnishing a basis for taking action to correct potential or actual undesired deviations.

Principle of future-directed controls. Because of time lags in the total system of control, the more a control system is based on feedforward rather than simple feedback of information, the more managers have the opportunity to perceive undesirable deviations from plans before they occur and to take action in time to prevent them.

These two principles emphasize the purpose of control in any system of managerial action as one of ensuring that objectives are achieved through detecting deviations and taking corrective action designed to attain them. Moreover, control, like planning, should ideally be forward-looking. This principle is often disregarded in practice, largely because the present state of the art in managing has not regularly provided for systems of feedforward control. Managers have generally been dependent on historical data, which may be adequate for tax collecting and determination of stockholders' earnings but are not good enough for the most effective control. Lacking means of looking forward, reference to history, on the questionable assumption that "what is past is prologue," is better than not looking at all. But time lags in the system of management control make it imperative that greater efforts be undertaken to make future-directed control a reality.

Principle of control responsibility. The primary responsibility for the exercise of control rests in the manager charged with the performance of the particular plans involved.

Since delegation of authority, assignment of tasks, and responsibility for certain objectives rest in individual managers, it follows that control over this work should be exercised by each of these managers. An individual manager's responsibility cannot be waived or rescinded without changes in the organization structure.

Principle of efficiency of controls. Control techniques and approaches are efficient if they detect and illuminate the nature and causes of deviations from plans with a minimum of costs or other unsought consequences.

Control techniques have a way of becoming costly, complex, and burdensome. Managers may become so engrossed in control that they spend more than it is worth to detect a deviation. Detailed budget controls that hamstring a subordinate, complex mathematical controls that thwart innovation, and purchasing controls that delay deliveries and cost more than the item purchased are instances of inefficient controls.

Principle of preventive control. The higher the quality of managers in a managerial system, the less will be the need for direct controls.

Most controls are based in large part on the fact that human beings make mistakes and often do not react to problems by undertaking their correction adequately and promptly. The more qualified managers are, the more they will perceive deviations from plans and take timely action to prevent them.

The Structure of Control

The principles that follow are aimed at pointing out how control systems and techniques can be designed to improve the quality of managerial control.

Principle of reflection of plans. The more that plans are clear, complete, and integrated, and the more that controls are designed to reflect such plans, the more effectively controls will serve the needs of managers.

It is not possible for a system of controls to be devised without plans since the task of control is to ensure that plans work out as intended. There can be no doubt that the more clear, complete, and integrated these plans are, and the more that control techniques are designed to follow the progress of these plans, the more effective they will be.

Principle of organizational suitability. The more that an organizational structure is clear, complete, and integrated, and the more that controls are designed to reflect the place in the organization structure where responsibility for action lies, the more they will facilitate correction of deviations from plans.

Plans are implemented by people. Deviations from plans must be the responsibility primarily of managers who are entrusted with the task of executing planning programs. Since it is the function of an organization structure to define a system of roles, it follows that controls must be designed to affect the role where responsibility for performance of a plan lies.

Principle of individuality of controls. The more that control techniques and information are understandable to individual managers who must utilize them, the more they will actually be used and the more they will result in effective control.

Although some control techniques and information can be utilized in the same form by various kinds of enterprises and managers, as a general rule controls should be tailored to meet the individual needs of managers. Some of this individuality is related to position in the organization structure, as noted in the previous principle. Another aspect of individuality is the tailoring of controls to the kind and level of understanding of managers. We have seen both company presidents and supervisors throw up their hands in dismay (often for quite different reasons) at the unintelligibility and inappropriate form of control information that was a delight to the figure- and table-minded controller. Control information which a manager cannot or will not use has little practical value.

The Process of Control

Control, often being so much a matter of technique, rests heavily on the art of managing, on know-how in given instances. However, there are certain propositions or principles which experience has shown have wide applicability.

Principle of standards.   Effective control requires objective, accurate, and suitable standards.

There should be a simple, specific, and verifiable way to measure whether a planning program is being accomplished. Control is accomplished through people. Even the best manager cannot help being influenced by personal factors, and actual performance is sometimes camouflaged by a dull or a sparkling personality or by a subordinate's ability to "sell" a deficient performance. By the same token, good standards of performance, objectively applied, will more likely be accepted by subordinates as fair and reasonable.

Principle of critical-point control.   Effective control requires special attention to those factors critical to evaluating performance against plans.

It would ordinarily be wasteful and unnecessary for managers to follow every detail of plan execution. What they must know is that plans are being implemented. Therefore, they concentrate attention on salient factors of performance that will indicate, without watching everything, any important deviations from plans. Perhaps all managers can ask themselves what things in their operations will best show them whether the plans for which they are responsible are being accomplished.

The exception principle.   The more that managers concentrate control efforts on significant exceptions, the more efficient will be the results of their control.

This principle holds that managers should concern themselves with significant deviations, the especially good or the especially bad situations. It is often confused with the principle of critical-point control, and they do have some kinship. However, critical-point control has to do with recognizing the points to be watched, while the exception principle has to do with watching the size of deviations at these points.

Principle of flexibility of controls.   If controls are to remain effective despite failure or unforeseen changes of plans, flexibility is required in their design.

According to this principle, controls must not be so inflexibly tied in with a plan as to be useless if the entire plan fails or is suddenly changed. Note that this principle applies to failures of plans, not failures of people operating under plans.

Principle of action.   Control is justified only if indicated or experienced deviations from plans are corrected through appropriate planning, organizing, staffing, and leading.

There are instances in practice where this simple truth is forgotten. Control is a wasteful use of managerial and staff time unless it is followed by action. If deviations are found in experienced or projected performance, action is indicated, in the form of either redrawing plans or making additional plans to get back on course. It may call for reorganization. It may require replacement of subordinates or training them to do the task desired. Or there may be no other fault than a lack of direction and leadership in getting a subordinate to understand the plans or to be motivated to accomplish them. But, in any case, action is implied.

Challenges in the Domestic and International Environment

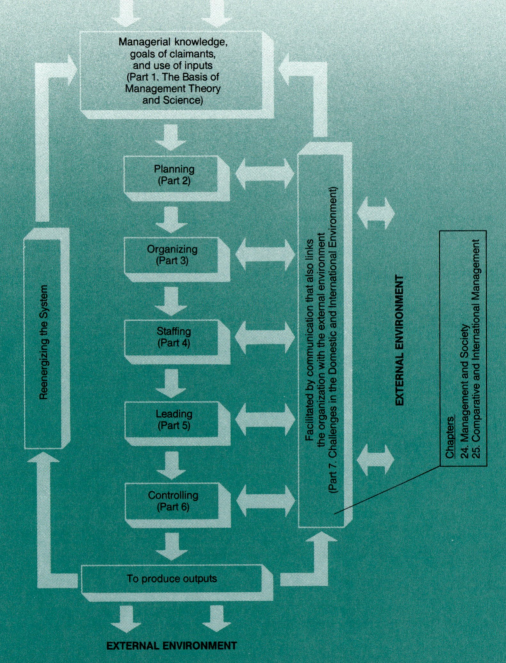

EXTERNAL ENVIRONMENT

Managerial knowledge,
goals of claimants,
and use of inputs
(Part 1. The Basis of
Management Theory
and Science)

Planning
(Part 2)

Organizing
(Part 3)

Staffing
(Part 4)

Leading
(Part 5)

Controlling
(Part 6)

Reenergizing the System

Facilitated by communication that also links
the organization with the external environment
(Part 7. Challenges in the Domestic and International Environment)

EXTERNAL ENVIRONMENT

Chapters
24. Management and Society
25. Comparative and International Management

To produce outputs

EXTERNAL ENVIRONMENT

SYSTEMS APPROACH TO MANAGEMENT.

Management and Society:
The External Environment, Social Responsibility, and Ethics

CHAPTER OBJECTIVES

After studying this chapter, you should be able to:

1. Describe the nature of the pluralistic society.

2. Discuss the economic, technological, social, political, and legal environments in which managers operate.

3. Explain the social responsibility of managers and the arguments for and against the social involvement of business.

4. Understand the nature and importance of ethics in managing and ways to institutionalize and raise ethical standards.

5. Recognize differing ethical standards in various societies.

Much of this book deals with interaction of managers and their subordinates with the environment inside the enterprise, but in most instances the effective manager must also deal with the outside environment. Every time managers plan, they take into account the wants and desires of members of society outside the organization, as well as needs for material and human resources, technology, and other requirements in the external environment. They do likewise to some degree with almost every other kind of managerial activity.

All managers, whether they operate in a business, a government agency, a church, a charitable foundation, or a university, must, in varying degrees, take into account the elements and forces of their external environment. While they may be able to do little or nothing to change these forces, they have no alternative but to respond to them. They must identify, evaluate, and react to the forces outside the enterprise that may affect its operations. The impact of the external environment on the organization is illustrated in Figure 24-1. The constraining influences of external factors on the enterprise are even more crucial in international management, as we will show especially in Chapter 25.

This chapter deals with the impact of the external environment on the organization and the relationships between business and the society in which it operates. First, the focus is on various factors in the domestic environment. Then the discussion extends to the topics of social responsibility and ethical behavior. Let us begin by appreciating what it means to manage in a pluralistic environment.

OPERATING IN A PLURALISTIC SOCIETY

Managers in the United States operate in a pluralistic society, with many organized groups representing various interests. Each group has an impact on other groups but no one group exerts an inordinate amount of power. Many groups exert some power over business. As we have seen in Chapter 1, there are many claimants on the organization, with divergent goals, and it is the task of the manager to integrate those aims.

Working within a pluralistic society has several implications for business.[1] First, business power is kept in balance by various groups, such as environmental groups. Second, business interests can be expressed by joining groups such as the Chamber of Commerce. Third, business participates in projects with other responsible groups for bettering society; an example might be working toward the renewal of inner cities. Fourth, in a pluralistic society there can be conflict or agreement among groups. Finally, in such a society one group is quite aware of what other groups are doing.

THE EXTERNAL ENVIRONMENT: ECONOMIC

It is sometimes thought that the economic environment is of concern only to businesses whose socially approved mission is the production and distribution of

FIGURE 24-1

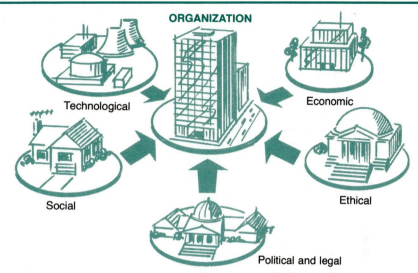

An organization must operate in, and be responsive to, a number of different external environments.

goods and services that people want and can pay for. But it is also of the greatest importance to other types of organized enterprises. A government agency takes resources, usually from taxpayers, and provides services desired by the public. A church takes contributions from members and serves their religious and social needs. A university takes resource inputs from taxpayers, students, and contributors of various kinds and transforms these into educational and research services.

Capital

Almost every kind of organization needs capital—machinery, buildings, inventories of goods, office equipment, tools of all kinds, and cash. Some of this may be produced by the organization itself, as happens when a business builds its own machinery or a church group prepares a church supper. Cash resources may also be generated within an organization to buy capital items outside, as happens when business profits are used for this purpose or when a university collects parking fees to build parking structures. But organized enterprises are usually dependent for capital requirements on various suppliers, whose job it is to produce the many materials and other items of capital that an organization requires for its operation.

This means that all kinds of operations are dependent on the availability and prices of needed capital items. Societies vary considerably in this availability. Railroad facilities may be in short supply in Brazil but in plentiful supply in the United States and countries of Western Europe. Capital, by way of fertilizers and advanced farm machines, may be scarce and hamper farm productivity in rural Russia but may be plentiful in rural America.

Labor

Another important input from the economic environment is the availability, quality, and price of labor. In some societies, untrained common labor may be plentiful, while highly trained labor may be in short supply. Engineers may be scarce at one time and plentiful at another, as has occurred in the ups and downs of the defense and space operations of the United States.

The price of labor is also an extremely important economic input to an enterprise. The relatively high wages in the United States and many European countries often create cost problems for producers in these countries. Many items can be produced at a lower cost in countries such as Mexico, Korea, and Taiwan. It is not surprising that many products requiring high labor input are often made outside the United States.

Price Levels

The input side of an enterprise is clearly affected by price-level changes. If the prices go up fairly rapidly, as happened in most parts of the world in the 1970s and early 1980s, the turbulence created in the economic environment on both the input and output sides can be severe. Inflation not only upsets businesses but also has highly disturbing influences on every kind of organization through its effects on costs of labor, material, and other items.

Government Fiscal and Tax Policy

Another important input to the enterprise is the nature of governmental fiscal and tax policies. Although these are, strictly speaking, aspects of the political environment, their economic impact on all enterprises is tremendous. Government control of the availability of credit through fiscal policy has considerable impact not only on business but also on most nonbusiness operations. Similarly, government tax policy affects every segment of our society. The way taxes are levied is also important, not only to business but to people generally. For example, if taxes on business profits are too high, the incentive to go into business or stay in it tends to drop, and investors will look elsewhere to invest their capital. If taxes are levied on sales, prices will rise and people will tend to buy less. If heavy taxes are placed on real estate, people may find it too expensive to own a house and may go to cheaper and less comfortable living quarters.

Customers

One of the most important factors for success of the enterprise is customers. Without them, a business cannot exist. But to capture customers, a business must try to find out what people want and will buy. Nonbusiness enterprises have "customers" also. Universities and colleges have students and alumni to satisfy. Similarly, police, fire, and government health departments must serve the public.

To be sure, the expectations and demands of the various publics served by organized enterprises are influenced by noneconomic as well as economic factors in the environment. The principal ones are the attitudes, desires, and expectations of people, many of which arise from cultural patterns in the social environment. Nevertheless, economic factors still play a major role. People want as much as possible for the money, whether it goes to businesses, government, or charitable organizations.

Another factor in the market is the appearance of substitute products. For example, publishers of magazines saw their market eroded when advertisers shifted to television. Also, people like different products. Some want a power boat, others want a sailboat, and still others do not want a boat at all. The needs of industrial buyers change as their products change, as new processes are developed, and as different equipment and materials come on the market. In the long run, any enterprise (at least in free economies) has to serve the different and changing needs of customers. To do otherwise is a sure road to enterprise failure.

THE EXTERNAL ENVIRONMENT: TECHNOLOGICAL

One of the most pervasive factors in the environment is technology. It is science that provides the knowledge and it is technology that uses it. The term **technology** refers to the sum total of knowledge we have of ways to do things. It includes inventions, it includes techniques, and it includes the vast store of organized knowledge about everything from aerodynamics to zoology. But its main influence is on ways of doing things, on how we design, produce, distribute, and sell goods as well as services.

The Impact of Technology: Benefits and Problems

The impact of technology is seen in new products, new machines, new tools, new materials, and new services.[2] A few of the *benefits* from technology are greater productivity, higher living standards, more leisure time, and a greater variety of products. Consider, for example, the great variety of cars available: subcompacts, compacts, intermediates, full-size, sports, and specialty cars. Consider also the many body styles, the various colors, and the many options in engines (sizes), transmissions (manual, automatic), and brakes (mechanical, power). In addition, one may select tinted glass, power windows, power steering, automatic speed control, air-conditioning, special mirrors, vinyl roof, sun roof, and the various interior and exterior trim strips.

But the benefits of technology must be weighed against the *problems* associated with technological developments, such as traffic jams, polluted air and water, shortage of energy, and the loss of privacy through the application of computer technology. What is needed is a balanced approach that takes advantage of technology and at the same time minimizes some of the undesirable side effects.

Categories of Technological Change

In a general way, we know that technology has had a wide and pervasive impact, so much so that we refer to various developments as "revolutions," such as the industrial revolution of the eighteenth century or the computer revolution of the latter half of the twentieth century. But we do not always appreciate the precise developments that make up these revolutions. To better comprehend the wide scope of technological change, the following categories and examples are helpful:

1. Increased ability to master time and distance for the movement of freight and passengers: railroads, automobiles and trucks, airplanes, space vehicles (to some extent)

2. Increased ability to generate, store, transport, and distribute energy: electricity, nuclear power, the laser

3. Increased ability to design new materials and change the properties of others so that they better serve needs: steel alloys, synthetic fibers, plastics, and new drugs

4. Mechanization or automation of physical processes: the large number of labor-saving devices, from Hargreaves's spinning jenny in 1770 to the largely automatic subway systems in San Francisco and Washington

5. Mechanization or automation of certain mental processes: the computer, which greatly expands our ability to store, manipulate, select, and supply data

6. Extension of human ability to sense things: radar, the electron microscope, night-vision instruments

7. Increased understanding of individual and group behavior and how to deal with it: psychological bases of motivation, group behavior patterns, improved managerial techniques

8. Increased understanding of diseases and their treatment: inoculations for polio, kidney transplants, antibiotic treatment of infections

THE EXTERNAL ENVIRONMENT: SOCIAL

In any classification of environmental elements having impact on a manager, it is extremely difficult to separate the social, political, and ethical environments. Conceptually, however, it is possible. The *social* environment is made up of the attitudes, desires, expectations, degrees of intelligence and education, beliefs, and customs of people in a given group or society. The *political* and *legal* environment is primarily that complex of laws, regulations, and government agencies and their actions which affects all kinds of enterprises, often to a varying degree. The concept of *social responsibility* requires organizations to consider the impact of their actions on society. The *ethical* environment—which could well be included as an element in the social environment—includes sets of generally accepted and practiced standards of personal conduct. These standards may or may not be codified by law, but for any group to which they are meant to apply, they sometimes have virtually the force of law.

The Complexity of Environmental Forces

The interweaving complexity of these environmental elements makes their study and comprehension exceptionally difficult. To forecast them so that a manager can anticipate and prepare for changes is even more difficult. Social desires, expectations, and pressures give rise to laws and standards of ethics. Social forces, including ethics, normally arise before laws are passed, since the legislative process is notably reactive in the sense it acts when a crisis is at hand, but seldom before. Furthermore, existing laws and regulations, which are so numerous and complex that even the best-trained lawyers cannot know all of them (though they would probably know where to find them), often are brought to our attention in surprising and unusual ways.

Social Attitudes, Beliefs, and Values

Managers of various enterprises have been criticized for not being responsive to the social attitudes, beliefs, and values of particular individuals, groups, or societies. But attitudes and values are different for workers and employers, rich and poor people, college students and alumni, accountants and engineers, Californians and New Yorkers. This variety of values makes it difficult for managers to design an environment conducive to performance and satisfaction. It is even more difficult to respond to these forces when they are outside the enterprise. Yet managers have no choice but to take them into account in their decision making.

Over the centuries of American social development, a number of social beliefs have evolved that are of significance to the manager. Among the most important of these are the following:

1. The belief that there are opportunities for people who are willing and able to work to take advantage of them

2. A faith in business and a respect for business owners and leaders

3. A belief in competition and competitiveness in all aspects of life, but particularly in business

4. A respect for the individual, regardless of race, religion, or creed

5. A respect for authority arising from ownership of property, expert knowledge, and elected or appointed political position

6. A belief in, and respect for, education

7. A faith in logical processes, science, and technology

8. A belief in the importance of change and experimentation to find better ways of doing things

It is true that these and other major beliefs have tended to erode as the country has become more populous and as social problems have forced more government involvement in everyone's life. It is also true, as usually happens in all cultures, that when people's standard of living improves, their expectations for a better life tend to increase even faster. Nonetheless, the long-held American beliefs are still strong, supported as they are by the American work ethic developed by early settlers and immigrants, by a long tradition of individual rights and freedoms, and by our remarkable Constitution.

THE EXTERNAL ENVIRONMENT: POLITICAL AND LEGAL

As was pointed out earlier, the political and legal environment of managers is closely intertwined with the social environment. Laws are ordinarily passed as the result of social pressures and problems. But what is bothersome is that once passed, laws often stay on the books after the socially perceived need for them has disappeared.

The Political Environment

Political environments—the attitudes and actions of political and government leaders and legislators—do change with the ebb and flow of social demands and beliefs. The effect of the patriotic fervor of World War II on virtually every segment of American society, and even the world society, may be contrasted with the effect on government and other organizations of the disillusionment concerning the unpopular conflict in Vietnam. Many legislators who strongly supported going into Vietnam did a complete turnabout when people became disenchanted with the conflict. In many communities, strong sentiments about air and water pollution control subsided when plants that were unable to meet new standards had to be shut down.

Government affects virtually every enterprise and every aspect of life. In respect to business, it acts in two main roles: It promotes and constrains business. For example, it promotes business by stimulating economic expansion and development, by providing assistance through the Small Business Administration, by subsidizing selected industries, by giving tax advantages in certain situations, by supporting research and development, and even by protecting some businesses through special tariffs. Finally, government is also the biggest customer, purchasing goods and services.

The Legal Environment

The other role of the government is to constrain and regulate business. Every manager is encircled by a web of laws, regulations, and court decisions. Some are designed to protect workers, consumers, and communities. Others are designed to make contracts enforceable and to protect property rights. Many are designed to regulate the behavior of managers and their subordinates in business and other enterprises. There is relatively little that a manager can do in any organization that is not in some way concerned with, and often specifically controlled by, a law or regulation.

Many of our laws and regulations are necessary, even though many become obsolete. But they do present a complex environment for all managers. Managers are expected to know the legal restrictions and requirements applicable to their actions. Thus, it is understandable that managers in all kinds of organizations, and in business and government especially, usually have a legal expert close at hand as they make their decisions.

In many areas laws are too slow to develop. For example, if one of the many businesses that contributed to the pollution of Lake Erie had gone to the great expense of eliminating the dumping of wastes into the lake, the costs would have put it at the mercy of competitors who did not go to this expense. If the city fathers of a single municipality that was polluting the lake had gone to similar expense, they would probably have had to answer to the taxpayers. Likewise, if one automobile manufacturer had produced a nonpolluting car 40 years ago and had offered it at a price a few hundred dollars higher than the prices of its competitors' models, there can hardly be a question that this company would have been at a competitive disadvantage. It took strong legislation to approach the solution of pollution problems.

Thus, not only must perceptive managers respond to social pressures but they also have the problem of foreseeing and dealing with political pressures, as well as laws that might be passed.[3] As can be readily understood, this is not an easy matter.

THE SOCIAL RESPONSIBILITY OF MANAGERS

In the early 1900s the mission of business firms was exclusively economic. Today, partly due to the interdependencies of the many groups in our society, the social involvement of business has increased. There is indeed a question as to what the social responsibility of business really is. Moreover, this same question, originally asked of business, is now being addressed with increasing frequency to the people in government, universities, nonprofit foundations, charitable organizations, and even churches. Thus, we talk about the social responsibility and social responsiveness of all organizations, although the focus of our discussion is on business. Society, awakened and vocal with respect to the urgency of social problems, is asking managers, particularly those at the top, what they are doing to discharge their social responsibilities and why they are not doing more.

Social Responsibility and Social Responsiveness

The concept of social responsibility is not new. Although the idea was already considered in the early part of the twentieth century, the modern discussion of social responsibility got a major impetus with the book *Social Responsibilities of the Businessman* by Howard R. Bowen, who suggested that businesses should consider the social implications of their decisions.[4] As might be expected, there is no complete agreement on the definition. In a survey of 439 executives, 68 percent of the responding managers agreed with the following definition: "*Corporate social responsibility* is seriously considering the impact of the company's actions on society."[5]

A newer concept, but still very similar to social responsibility, is *social responsiveness*, which in simple terms means "the ability of a corporation to relate its operations and policies to the social environment in ways that are mutually beneficial to the company and to society."[6] Both definitions focus on corporations, but we would like to expand these concepts (1) to include also enterprises other than businesses, and (2) to encompass relationships within the enterprise. The main difference between social responsibility and social responsiveness is that the latter implies actions and the "how" of enterprise responses. For our discussion, we will use the terms interchangeably.[7]

Arguments for and against Business Involvement in Social Actions

Although there are arguments for business involvement in social activities, there are also arguments against it, as shown in Table 24-1.

Today many businesses are involved in social action. A decision as to whether companies should extend their social involvement requires a careful examination of the arguments for and against such actions. Certainly society's expectations are changing and the trend seems to be toward greater social responsiveness. In fact, most respondents in a study of *Harvard Business Review* readers consider social responsibility a legitimate and achievable aim for business.[8] Still, the mission of the organization must be taken into account.

The Mission of the Enterprise

Various kinds of organized enterprises have different missions, entrusted to them by society. The mission of business is the production and distribution of goods and services. The mission of a police department is protection of safety and welfare of the people. The mission of a state highway department is the design and construction of highways. The mission of a university is teaching and research. And so on.

We should not hold business managers, for example, responsible for solving all social problems. There can hardly be any sense in making it the job of business to furnish public school education or the many other things, like police and fire protection, that the government provides. But business, like any other type of organized enterprise, must interact with, and live in, its environment.

Whether managers achieve their missions, and how they do so, are matters of great social importance. A society expects and deserves the accomplishment of the missions of approved enterprises. This also requires that managers must take into account elements in their surroundings that are important to their success and important to others who may be affected by the actions they take. In other words, managers respond to their environment and become active participants in the community to improve the quality of life. This is what they must do, since the survival of their enterprise depends upon successful interaction with all environmental elements.

Reaction or Proaction?

But to live within an environment and be responsive to it does not mean that managers should merely react in the face of stress. Since no enterprise can be

TABLE 24-1 Arguments for and against Social Involvement of Business

Arguments for social involvement of business

1. Public needs have changed, leading to changed expectations. Business, it is suggested, received its charter from society and consequently has to respond to the needs of society.

2. The creation of a better social environment benefits both society and business. Society gains through better neighborhoods and employment opportunities; business benefits from a better community, since the community is the source of its work force and the consumer of its products and services.

3. Social involvement discourages additional government regulation and intervention. The result is greater freedom and more flexibility in decision making for business.

4. Business has a great deal of power which, it is reasoned, should be accompanied by an equal amount of responsibility.

5. Modern society is an interdependent system, and the internal activities of the enterprise have an impact on the external environment.

6. Social involvement may be in the interest of stockholders.

7. Problems can become profits. Items that may once have been considered waste (for example, empty soft drink cans) can be profitably used again.

8. Social involvement creates a favorable public image. Thus, a firm may attract customers, employees, and investors.

9. Business should try to solve the problems which other institutions have not been able to solve. After all, business has a history of coming up with novel ideas.

10. Business has the resources. Specifically, business should use its talented managers and specialists, as well as its capital resources, to solve some of society's problems.

11. It is better to prevent social problems through business involvement than to cure them. It may be easier to help the hard-core unemployed than to cope with social unrest.

Arguments against social involvement of business

1. The primary task of business is to maximize profit by focusing strictly on economic activities. Social involvement could reduce economic efficiency.

2. In the final analysis, society must pay for the social involvement of business through higher prices. Social involvement would create excessive costs for business, which cannot commit its resources to social action.

3. Social involvement can create a weakened international balance of payments situation. The cost of social programs, the reasoning goes, would have to be added to the price of the product. Thus, American companies selling in international markets would be at a disadvantage when competing with companies in other countries which do not have these social costs to bear.

4. Business has enough power, and additional social involvement would further increase its power and influence.

5. Business people lack the social skills to deal with the problems of society. Their training and experience is with economic matters and their skills may not be pertinent to social problems.

6. There is a lack of accountability of business to society. Unless accountability can be established, business should not get involved.

7. There is not complete support for involvement in social actions. Consequently, disagreements among groups with different viewpoints will cause friction.

Source: Based on Keith Davis and William C. Frederick, *Business and Society*, 5th ed. (New York: McGraw-Hill Book Company, 1984), chap. 2.

expected to react very quickly to unforeseen developments, an enterprise must practice ways of anticipating developments through forecasts. An alert company, for example, does not wait until its product is obsolete and sales have fallen off before coming out with a new or improved product. A government agency should not wait until its regulations are obsolete and discredited before looking for another way to achieve its objectives. No enterprise should wait for problems to develop before preparing to face them. Proaction, as we saw in Part 2 on planning, is an essential part of the planning process.

The Role of the Government

There are many instances where social changes can be implemented only by the enactment of legislation. However, many managers in business and elsewhere have found it to their advantage to do something about pressing social problems. For example, many businesses have profited by filtering smokestack pollutants and selling or utilizing these recovered wastes. Some companies have made a profit by building low-cost apartment buildings in ghetto areas. The Internal Revenue Service learned that it increased tax collection efficiency and effectiveness by simplifying or eliminating certain burdensome reports and forms. In other words, contributing to the solution of social problems does not always involve net expense. But we may need the bludgeoning force of legislation to get improvements under way.

The Influence of Values and Performance Criteria on Behavior

Even if individual managers have full freedom to act in accordance with the currently conceived social responsibilities, they may not do so because of standards applied in evaluating their performance. Managers, like everyone else, want their performance positively appraised—they seek approval. Therefore, if their success is measured in terms of profit, living within a budget, tax collection as a percentage of income, the volume of blood contributed to a blood bank, or the number of communicants in a church, managers will tend to strive to achieve excellence in these regards. If success is measured in terms of pollution control, the number of convicts returned successfully to society, the dollar support for employees seeking university degrees, the ratio of "disadvantaged" to total number of employees, achievements in raising the productivity of subordinates, or combinations of these and similar goals, then managers will strive to achieve them.

In other words, managers will respond to socially approved values and will give priority to those held in highest esteem. If we want to make sure that organizations respond to social forces, we must clarify social values and then reward managers for their success in responding to them, recognizing, of course, that different organizations have a variety of missions.

The Social Audit

The discussion of social responsibility raises the question of how social performance should be evaluated. This led to the concept of the "social audit," which was first proposed in the 1950s by Howard R. Bowen.[9] But it is only more recently that corporations have seriously concerned themselves with this idea.[10] The **social audit** has been defined as "a commitment to systematic assessment of and reporting on some meaningful, definable domain of the company's activities that have social impact."[11]

One may distinguish between two types of audits. One is *required* by the government and involves, for example pollution control, product performance requirements, and adhering to equal employment standards. The other kind of social audit concerns a great variety of *voluntary* social programs.[12]

One survey of the *Fortune 500* firms indicated that 456 companies (91.2 percent) have made social responsibility disclosures in their annual reports.[13] Although these disclosures may not be equated with a social audit, the large number of firms making such disclosures shows a general concern of major corporations about their social responsibility.

It is rather difficult to determine what areas the social audit should encompass. Often the items include pollution and the hiring, training, and promotion of minorities, but there are many other areas. For example, General Electric developed a matrix which facilitates the analysis of the expectations of customers, investors, employees, communities, and other claimants in the following areas: product and technical performance, economic performance, employment performance, environment and natural resources, community welfare and development, government-business relations, as well as international trade and development.[14]

Another difficulty is to determine the amount of money an enterprise spends in selected areas. But cost alone is an inadequate measure. It does not necessarily indicate the results of social involvement. Other problems are the collection of the data and their presentation in a way that accurately reflects the social involvement of an enterprise. There is no doubt that many difficulties are associated with a social audit, but there is evidence that many companies and other organizations in the United States honestly attempt to address themselves to this challenge.

ETHICS IN MANAGING

All persons, whether in business, government, a university, or any other enterprise are concerned with ethics. In *Webster's Ninth New Collegiate Dictionary*, **ethics** is defined as "the discipline dealing with what is good and bad and with moral duty and obligation." Thus, *personal ethics* has been referred to as "the rules by which an individual lives his or her personal life," and *accounting ethics* pertains to "the code that guides the professional conduct of accountants."[15] *Business ethics* is concerned with truth and justice and has a variety of aspects such as expectations of society, fair competition, advertising, public relations, social responsibilities, consumer autonomy, and corporate behavior in the home country as well as abroad.[16]

Ethical Theories and a Model for Political Behavior Decisions

In organizations, managers compete for information, influence, and resources. The potential for conflicts in selecting the ends as well as the means to the ends is easy to understand, and the question of what criteria should guide ethical behavior becomes acute.

Three basic types of moral theories in the field of normative ethics have been developed. First, the *utilitarian theory* suggests that plans and actions should be evaluated by their consequences. The underlying idea is that plans or actions should produce the greatest good for the greatest number of people. The second theory is based on *rights* and holds that all people have basic rights such as the right to freedom of conscience, free speech, due process, and so on. A number of those rights can be found in the Constitutional Bill of Rights of the United States. Third, the *theory of justice* demands that decision makers be guided by fairness and equity, as well as impartiality.

Gerald Cavanagh, Dennis Moberg, and Manuel Velasquez point out the strengths and weaknesses of each theory and integrate them into a decision tree, shown in Figure 24-2, which can guide managers in making ethical decisions.[17] The theory is best illustrated by the following example:

Sam and Bob are highly motivated research scientists who work in the new-product development lab at General Rubber. Sam is by far the most technically competent scientist in the lab, and he has been responsible for several patents that have netted the company nearly $6 million in the past decade. He is quiet, serious, and socially reserved. In contrast, Bob is outgoing and demonstrative. While Bob lacks the technical track record Sam has, his work has been solid though unimaginative. Rumor has it that Bob will be moved into an administrative position in the lab in the next few years.

According to the lab policy, a $300,000 fund is available every year for the best new-product development idea proposed by a lab scientist in the form of a competitive bid. Accordingly, Sam and Bob both prepare proposals. Each proposal is carefully constructed to detail the benefits to the company and to society if the proposal is accepted, and it is the consensus of other scientists from blind reviews that both proposals are equally meritorious. Both proposals require the entire $300,000 to realize any significant results. Moreover, the proposed line of research in each require significant mastery of the technical issues involved and minimal need to supervise the work of others.

After submitting his proposal, Sam takes no further action aside from periodically inquiring about the outcome of the bidding process. In contrast, Bob begins to wage what might be termed an open campaign in support of his proposal. After freely admitting his intentions to Sam and others, Bob seizes every opportunity he can to point out the relative advantages of his proposal to individuals who might have some influence over the decision. So effective is this open campaign that considerable informal pressure is placed on those authorized to make the decision on behalf of Bob's proposal. Bob's proposal is funded and Sam's is not.

An ethical analysis of Bob's action in this case could begin by using the decision tree shown in Figure 24-2. The first question in the sequence requires a utilitarian analysis. Clearly, Bob's interests are better served than Sam's. However, the nature of the two proposals seems to require one of the two to be disappointed. Moreover, the outcome in terms of broader interests (i.e., company, society) appears not to be suboptimal, since both proposals were judged equivalent in the blind reviews. Consequently, it is appropriate to answer the first question affirmatively. The second

FIGURE 24-2

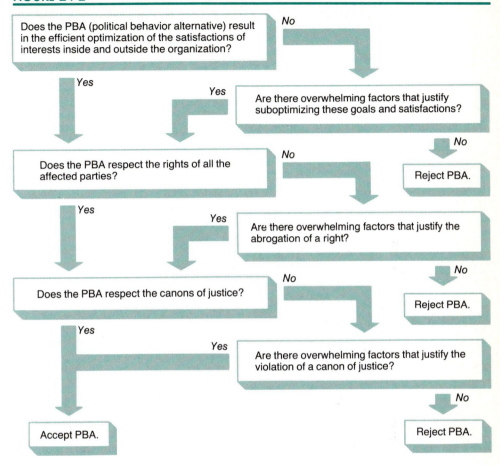

A DECISION TREE FOR INCORPORATING ETHICS INTO POLITICAL BEHAVIOR DECISIONS.

question inquires into the rights respected by Bob's behavior. Here again, the evidence seems persuasive that no one's rights were violated. Sam did not have (did not create) the same opportunity to point out the advantages of his proposal to those at whom Bob directed his lobbying campaign, but Bob's open campaign involved no deceit, and Sam's inaction may be taken as implied consent.

It is in light of the third question that Bob's actions are most suspect. Justice would have best been served in this case if there had been a clear situation-relevant difference between the two proposals. The blind reviews found them equivalent, so some other basis for differentiating between the proposals presumably had to be found. Bob's efforts served to create irrelevant differences between them. If anything, Sam's superior technical track record would have been a more relevant factor than Bob's initiative and social skills in determining who should be favored to perform a technical task. Bob's actions in this regard were therefore unjust. Interestingly, had the proposals required supervision of others or the ability to persuade others, Bob's approach would have been justified.[18]

PERSPECTIVE:
CODE OF ETHICS FOR GOVERNMENT SERVICE

The federal government has established the following code.[19] Any person in Government service should:

I. Put loyalty to the highest moral principles and to country above loyalty to persons, party, or Government department.

II. Uphold the Constitution, laws, and regulations of the United States and of all governments therein and never be a party to their evasion.

III. Give a full day's labor for a full day's pay; giving earnest effort and best thought to the performance of duties.

IV. Seek to find and employ more efficient and economical ways of getting tasks accomplished.

V. Never discriminate unfairly by the dispensing of special favors or privileges to anyone, whether for remuneration or not; and never accept, for himself or herself or for family members, favors or benefits under circumstances which might be construed by reasonable persons as influencing the performance of governmental duties.

VI. Make no private promises of any kind binding upon the duties of office, since a Government employee has no private word which can be binding on public duty.

VII. Engage in no business with the Government, either directly or indirectly, which is inconsistent with the conscientious performance of governmental duties.

VIII. Never use any information gained confidentially in the performance of governmental duties as a means of making private profit.

IX. Expose corruption wherever discovered.

X. Uphold these principles, ever conscious that public office is a public trust.

Managers are facing many situations that require ethical judgments and often there are no easy answers. The model shown in Figure 24-2 provides a conceptual framework that helps managers analyze and evaluate their decisions, as illustrated by the case.

Institutionalizing Ethics

Managers, and especially top managers, do have a responsibility to create an organizational environment that fosters ethical decision making by institutionalizing ethics. By this we mean applying and integrating ethical concepts into daily action. Theodore Purcell and James Weber suggest that this can be accomplished in three ways: through (1) company policy or a code of ethics, (2) a formally appointed ethics committee, and (3) the teaching of ethics in management development programs.[20] The most common way to institutionalize ethics is to establish a code of ethics; much less common is the use of ethics board committees. Management development programs dealing with ethical issues are very seldom used, although companies such as Allied Chemical, International Business Machines, and General Electric have instituted such programs.

Code of Ethics and Its Implementation through Formal Committees

A **code** is a statement of policies, principles, or rules that guide behavior. Certainly, codes of ethics do not apply only to business enterprises; they should guide the behavior of persons in all organizations and in everyday life.

Simply stating a code of ethics is not enough, and the appointment of an ethics committee, consisting of internal and external directors, is considered essential for institutionalizing ethical behavior.[21] The functions of such a committee may include (1) holding regular meetings to discuss ethical issues, (2) dealing with "gray areas," (3) communicating the code to all members of the organization, (4) checking for possible violations of the code, (5) enforcing the code, (6) rewarding compliance and punishing violations, (7) reviewing and updating the code, and (8) reporting activities of the committee to the board of directors.

Factors That Raise Ethical Standards

In the study cited earlier, the two factors that raise ethical standards the most, according to the respondents, are (1) public disclosure and publicity and (2) the increased concern of a well-informed public. These factors are followed by government regulations and by education to increase the professionalism of business managers.[22]

To make ethical codes effective, provisions must be made for their enforcement. Unethical managers should be held responsible for their actions. This means that privileges and benefits have to be withdrawn and sanctions have to be applied. Although the enforcement of ethical codes may not be easy, the mere existence of such codes can increase ethical behavior by clarifying expectations. On the other hand, one should not expect ethical codes to solve all problems. In fact, they can create a false sense of security. To enforce codes effectively requires consistent ethical behavior and support from top management.

Another factor that could raise ethical standards is the teaching of ethics and values in business and other schools and universities. The Harvard Business School has come under severe criticism by its own president Derek Bok for the lack of teaching of human values.[23] With the help of business executives, the school hired Dean John McArthur and faculty members trained to teach ethics to give a new direction to the school. While financial aspects received less attention in the revised curriculum, more emphasis was placed on people skills and ethical behavior. With Harvard having among the most B-school graduates who often hold top managerial positions, a somewhat greater awareness of the ethical dimension in managing may be expected.

The need for improvement of ethical behavior has become evident by way of some widely publicized cases. Saul Gellerman examined three in greater detail: the Manville Corporation, which apparently hid the real danger of asbestos; Continental Illinois Bank, in which some managers misinterpreted the overall interest of the enterprise; and E. F. Hutton and Company, which pleaded guilty to mail and wire fraud.[24]

In light of his analysis, the author made several suggestions, such as the following:

1. Provide clear guidelines for ethical behavior

2. Teach ethical guidelines and their importance

3. In gray areas where there are questions about the ethics of an action, refrain from it

4. Set up controls (e.g., establish an auditing agency reporting to outside directors) that check on illegal or unethical deeds

5. Conduct frequent and unpredictable audits

6. Punish trespassers in a meaningful way and make it public so that it may deter others

7. Emphasize regularly that loyalty to the company does not excuse improper behavior or actions

Differing Ethical Standards of Various Societies

Any person in business, government, a university, or some other organization is aware that ethical, as well as legal, standards do differ, particularly among nations and societies. This has long been true. For example, many nations with privately owned companies permit corporations to make contributions to political parties, campaigns, and candidates. (The United States does not.) In some countries, payments to government officials and other persons with political influence to assure expedited or favorable handling of a business transaction are not regarded as unethical bribes but as proper payment for services rendered. In many cases, payments made to assure the landing of a contract are even looked upon as a normal and acceptable way of doing business. Or consider the Quaker Oats Company, which was faced with a situation in which foreign officials threatened to close the operation if the demand for "payouts" was not met. Or what should a company do when the plant manager's safety is in question in case payoffs are not made?[25]

The question facing responsible American business managers is: What ethical standards should they follow? There is no question of what to do in the United States, and American executives have had to refuse the suggestion of putting money in a "paper bag." In a country where such practices are expected and common, American executives are faced with a difficult problem. With the passage of laws by the United States Congress and the adoption of regulations by the Securities and Exchange Commission, not only must American firms report anything that could be called a payoff but anything else that can be construed as a bribe is now unlawful. Thus, we have attempted to export our standards for doing business to other countries, which can improve ethical standards abroad.

In summary, managers operate in a complex environment. They are affected by—and to some extent influence—the economic, technological, social, political, legal, and ethical environment. The concept of social responsibility is still evolving. To determine the appropriate relationships between various organizations and society is not an easy task.[26] Nevertheless, many corporations and organizations are making serious efforts to establish an environment beneficial to individuals, business, and society.

FOR DISCUSSION

1. Why is the environment external to an enterprise so important to all managers? Can any manager avoid being influenced by the external environment?

2. Identify the elements of the external environment that are likely to be the most important to each of the following: a company president, a sales manager, a production manager, a controller, and a personnel manager.

3. What effects do the external social, political, and legal environments have on the enterprise? How do managers respond to these influences?

4. What are the major social responsibilities of business managers? Of government managers? Have these responsibilities changed over the years? How?

5. Briefly explain the major moral theories in the field of normative ethics. How do they relate to the decision tree for incorporating ethics into political behavior decisions?

6. Assume you were the chief executive officer of a large corporation; how would you "institutionalize" ethics in the organization?

7. List and discuss benefits and limitations of some codes of ethics.

8. What ethical codes would you recommend for your university, your class, your family? How should these codes be enforced?

EXERCISES/ACTION STEPS

1. The class should select and read an article published in a recent issue of *The Wall Street Journal, Business Week,* or *Fortune* that involves some ethical issues. Divide the class into groups and analyze the situation using the decision tree shown in this chapter. Each group, through its spokesperson, should present its analysis.

2. Interview one business manager and one administrator in the local government and ask how they perceive their social responsibilities. Do these responsibilities relate primarily to the environment external to the organization, or do they also include internal aspects?

CASES

CASE 24-1
TO STAY OR NOT TO STAY IN SOUTH AFRICA[27]

Many executives of large multinational corporations face a dilemma involving economic, social, political, and ethical issues. One question many firms face is whether or not to divest the companies' holdings in South Africa because of that country's apartheid policies. Arguments are advanced on both sides of the issue.

The arguments *for staying* in South Africa are as follows:

1. Foreign companies are a positive force for peaceful change and will benefit blacks.

2. Foreign firms should not get involved in social disputes. Their primary objective is to make a reasonable profit within a framework of fair policies.

3. The progress blacks have made is to a great extent due to a growing economy to which foreign firms have contributed.

4. Higher unemployment of blacks will result from the withdrawal of U.S. companies.

5. Foreign divestments will not induce the government to change its policies a great deal, if at all.

The arguments *against staying* in South Africa are as follows:

1. So far, companies have had only limited success in changing the poor conditions of blacks.

2. Businesses have a responsibility not only toward stockholders but also toward society in general. Consequently, they should not be doing business in a country that pursues a policy of apartheid.

3. The turmoil and the economic conditions (recession, falling gold prices, double-digit inflation, and other factors) suggest that it may be in the long-term economic interest of the stockholders to withdraw from South Africa.

4. Responsible black leaders realize the potential hardships associated with divestments in the short run, yet many blacks are willing to endure them with the hope of a better future.

5. In the long run, South Africa cannot afford being isolated from most of the world that opposes apartheid, and will have to change its policies.

While the debate continues, top executives of major multinational corporations are faced with the decision whether to stay or not to stay in that country.

1. If you were the CEO of a major multinational corporation with substantial investments in South Africa, how would you decide? What are your reasons for your decision?

2. What do you think is the morally right decision? Why?

CASE 24-2
BISHOPS' PASTORAL[28]

In 1984 the Catholic bishops issued statements about Catholic social teaching and the U.S. economy. The first draft was debated and criticized as being too negative about the free-market economy in the United States. A second draft was then issued which softened the tone, but the message was the same. Some of the key points are the following:

1. Economic decisions must be made with due consideration as to whether they help all people.

2. Government, corporations, and individuals must help to reduce the inequities created by the free-market system.

3. More resources should be allocated to help the poor and the jobless instead of for military uses.

The purpose of the document is to influence governmental and individual decisions in bringing about a more humane society. The poor, the letter suggests, have not adequately shared the economic resources, and the government has a role to play to bring this about.

Some of the recommendations in the draft are:

1. Pursue fiscal and monetary policies that result in full employment.

2. Support job-creating programs.

3. Remove employment barriers for women and minorities through affirmative action and job training.

4. Reform the welfare system to provide minimum levels of benefit for the poor.

5. Support international agencies to reduce poverty in Third World countries.

1. What are the implications for managers?

2. How does the letter relate to the various managerial functions?

REFERENCES

1. George A. Steiner, *Business and Society* (New York: Random House, 1975), chap. 5.

2. Periodically, *Business Week* publishes a list of new products and scientific innovations. See, for example, "The Best—Outstanding Achievements of 1986," *Business Week* (Jan. 12, 1987), pp. 123–131.

3. See also Gerald D. Keim and Carl P. Zeithaml, "Corporate Political Strategy and Legislative Decision Making: A Review and Contingency Approach," *Academy of Management Review* (October 1986), pp. 828–843.

4. Howard R. Bowen, *Social Responsibilities of the Businessman* (New York: Harper, 1953).

5. John L. Paluszek, *Business and Society: 1976–2000* (New York: AMACOM, 1976), in George A. Steiner, John B. Miner, and Edmund R. Gray, *Management Policy and Strategy,* 3d ed. (New York: Macmillan Publishing Company, 1986), pp. 38–39.

6. Keith Davis and William C. Frederick, *Business and Society,* 5th ed. (New York: McGraw-Hill Book Company, 1984), p. 564.

7. Edwin Epstein, realizing the differences, but also a great deal of overlap involving business ethics, corporate social responsibility, and corporate social responsiveness, combines the three in his new concept "Corporate Social Policy Process." For a detailed discussion see Edwin M. Epstein, *Beyond Business Ethics, Corporate Social Responsibility, and Corporate Social Responsiveness: An Introduction to the Corporate Social Policy Process,* Business and Public Policy Working Paper No. BPP-17 (University of California Berkeley Business School, July 1986).

8. Steven N. Brenner and Earl A. Molander, "Is the Ethics of Business Changing?" *Harvard Business Review* (January–February 1977), pp. 57–71.

9. Bowen, *Social Responsibilities of the Businessman* (1953), pp. 155–156.

10. See also Meinolf Dierkes and Ariane Berthoin Antal, "Whither Corporate Social

Reporting: Is It Time to Legislate?" *California Management Review* (Spring 1986), pp. 106–121.

11. Raymond A. Bauer and Dan H. Fenn, Jr., "What Is a Corporate Social Audit?" *Harvard Business Review* (January–February, 1973), p. 38.

12. Steiner et al., *Management Policy and Strategy* (1986), p. 47.

13. Social Responsibility Disclosure—1977 Survey of *Fortune 500* Annual Reports (Cleveland, Ohio: Ernst & Ernst, 1977).

14. Steiner, *Business and Society* (1975), pp. 202–203.

15. Manuel G. Velasquez, *Business Ethics* (Englewood Cliffs, N.J.: Prentice-Hall, 1982), p. 7.

16. Clarence D. Walton (ed.), *The Ethics of Corporate Conduct* (Englewood Cliffs, N.J.: Prentice-Hall, 1977), p. 6. See also La Rue Tone Hosmer, *The Ethics of Management* (Homewood, Ill.: Richard D. Irwin, 1987).

17. The discussion of this section is based on Gerald F. Cavanagh, Dennis J. Moberg, and Manuel Velasquez, "The Ethics of Organizational Politics," *Academy of Management Review* (July 1981), pp. 363–374, and has been used with their permission. See also Manuel Velasquez, Dennis J. Moberg, and Gerald F. Cavanagh, "Organizational Statesmanship and Dirty Politics: Ethical Guidelines for the Organizational Politician," *Organizational Dynamics* (Autumn 1983), pp. 65–80.

18. Cavanagh, Moberg, and Velasquez, "The Ethics" (1981), p. 369.

19. Source: Public Law 96-303, July 3, 1980.

20. Much of this discussion is based on James Weber, "Institutionalizing Ethics into the Corporation," *MSU Business Topics* (Spring 1981), pp. 47–52; Theodore V. Purcell, S.J., and James Weber, *Institutionalizing Corporate Ethics: A Case History* (New York: The Presidents Association, The Chief Executive Officers' Division of American Management Association, 1979), Special Study No. 71.

21. Weber, "Institutionalizing Ethics" (1981).

22. Brenner and Molander, "Is the Ethics" (1977), p. 63.

23. Gerald F. Cavanagh, *American Business Values,* 2d ed. (Englewood Cliffs, N.J.: Prentice Hall, 1984), chap. 5; Bruce Nussbaum and Alex Beam, "Remaking the Harvard B-School," *Business Week* (Mar. 24, 1986), pp. 54–58.

24. Saul W. Gellerman, "Why 'Good' Managers Make Bad Ethical Choices," *Harvard Business Review* (July–August, 1986), pp. 85–90.

25. Walton, *The Ethics of Corporate Conduct* (1977), chap. 7.

26. See Douglas R. Austrom and Lawrence J. Lad, "Problem-Solving Networks: Towards a Synthesis of Innovative Approaches to Social Issues Management," in John A. Pearce II and Richard B. Robinson, Jr. (eds.), *Academy of Management Best Papers—Proceedings 1986,* Forty-Sixth Annual Meeting of the Academy of Management, Chicago, Illinois, August 13–16, 1986, pp. 311–315.

27. John Nielsen, "Time to Quit South Africa?" *Fortune* (Sept. 30, 1985), pp. 18–23; Jonathan Kapstein, John Hoerr, and Elizabeth Weiner, "Leaving South Africa," *Business Week* (Sept. 23, 1985), pp. 104–112; Julian Redfearn, "The Sullivan Principles and U.S. Firms in South Africa," in Steiner, Miner, and Gray, *Management Policy* (1986), pp. 921–931; David T. Beaty and Oren Harari, "South Africa: White Managers, Black Voices," Harvard Business Review (July-August 1987), pp. 98–105.

28. Laurie McGinley, "Roman Catholic Bishops Soften Tone of Letter Calling for Action on Poverty," *The Wall Street Journal* (Oct. 7, 1985); "Catholic Social Teaching and the U.S. Economy: First Draft—Bishops' Pastoral," *Origins* (Nov. 15, 1984), pp. 337–383. See also

Second Draft—Pastoral Letter on Catholic Social Teaching and the U.S. Economy (Oct. 7, 1985). After lengthy discussions, the 115-page letter *Economic Justice for All: Catholic Social Teaching and the U.S. Economy* was approved in November 1986.

FOR FURTHER INFORMATION

Davis, Keith, and William C. Frederick. *Business and Society,* 5th ed. (New York: McGraw-Hill Book Company, 1984).

Diebold, John. *The Role of Business in Society* (New York: AMACOM, 1982).

Jones, Thomas M. "An Integrating Framework for Research in Business and Society: A Step toward the Elusive Paradigm?" *Academy of Management Review* (October 1983), pp. 559–564.

Magaziner, Ira C., and Robert B. Reich. *Minding America's Business* (New York: Harcourt Brace Jovanovich, 1982).

McCoy, Bowen H. "The Parable of the Sadhu," *Harvard Business Review* (September–October 1983), pp. 103–108.

McFarland, Dalton E. *Management and Society: An Institutional Framework* (Englewood Cliffs, N.J.: Prentice-Hall, 1982).

Murray, Keith B., and John R. Montanari, "Strategic Management of the Socially Responsible Firm: Integrating Management and Marketing Theory," *Academy of Management Review* (October 1986), pp. 815–827.

O'Toole, James. *Vanguard Management: Redesigning the Corporate Future* (Garden City, N.Y.: Doubleday & Company, 1985).

Comparative and International Management

CHAPTER OBJECTIVES

After reading this chapter, you should be able to:

1. Appreciate the importance of effective managing for economic growth.

2. Understand the Koontz model of comparative management, which separates environmental factors and enterprise functions from management fundamentals.

3. Recognize differences in managing in selected countries.

4. Describe and compare managerial practices in Japan and the United States, as well Theory Z.

5. Discuss the nature and purpose of international business and multinational corporations.

6. Explain how managerial functions are carried out in the international environment.

7. Identify trends toward a unified global theory of management.

*I*n Chapter 24 we focused on the external factors in the domestic environment. The constraining factors on managing are likely to be more severe for international firms. Executives operating in a foreign country need to learn a great deal about the country's educational, economic, legal, and political systems, and especially its sociological-cultural environment.

The first section in this chapter deals with comparative management and the question of whether or not management is culture-bound. We introduce a model for the study of comparative management. Then we will look more closely at the environmental impact on managing in selected countries. We will then compare and contrast more extensively Japanese and American managerial practices and we will discuss Theory Z. Then our discussion shifts to international management and the role of multinational corporations. Finally, we identify some trends that lead toward a unified global theory of management.

COMPARATIVE MANAGEMENT

Comparative management is defined as the study and analysis of management in different environments and the reasons that enterprises show different results in various countries.[1] We view management as an important element in economic growth and in the improvement of productivity.

Management as a Critical Element in Economic Growth

In light of the increasing concern for economic growth, it is natural for social scientists to look for underlying causes of that growth.[2] Why does one country have a higher per capita national income than another? Or why do productivity increases differ in various countries?

Concern for productivity and economic growth. Because of the disparity in national incomes and the problems caused in much of the world by incomes that do not allow for adequate subsistence, let alone the raising of cultural standards, attention of world leaders and development economists has naturally turned to the need for increasing productivity.[3]

The necessities of economic development were thought to be the transfer of technology, education, and capital. But as important as these are, it is now recognized that advanced managerial know-how is essential and often overlooked as an element responsible for growth and improved productivity.

Although one must grant that pure technical knowledge is necessary for economic growth, such knowledge is fairly easy to transfer between countries, and no nation holds a monopoly on it for very long. Even a technological development as sophisticated as that of the atomic bomb, whose secrecy was closely protected by the United States, became known in Russia, France, China, and elsewhere in less than two decades. Most advances in technology are neither as complex nor as well guarded, so that their transfer is not likely to be difficult, particularly when one realizes that in any country only a few people need to have this knowledge to make it available for use.

On the other hand, cultural factors such as the level of education and, particularly, knowledge of skills have an important impact on economic progress. Also, cultural variables such as the desire for the products and services can be significant. Similarly constraining on economic progress are a large number of political factors, such as fiscal policy, labor regulations, business restrictions, and foreign policy. But even with these and other constraints which may limit managerial effectiveness, qualified managers can do much to bring economic progress to a society by identifying constraints and by designing a managerial approach or technique to take them into account.

The need for management theory and practice.   The United States has generally been recognized as the world leader in the development of management know-how. Although American managers now look increasingly to Japan for improving productivity, the Japanese still send many of their managers to business schools in the United States.[4] American management is widely regarded as the standard of the world, and most scholars regard the issue of comparative management as one of transferring American management knowledge and practice to developed and less-developed countries. It is interesting to note that European managers do not look toward Japan for managerial leadership; rather, they adopt traditional American practices such as strategic planning, decentralization of decision making, and incentive systems.[5] What is needed for economic progress and improved productivity is a way of coordinating human resources for the achievement of the mission of the enterprise. And this demands sound management theory and practice.

PERSPECTIVE:
IS MANAGEMENT CATCHING ON IN THE SOVIET UNION?

The importance of managing is even recognized by Soviet leader Mikhail Gorbachev, who is relying on the new managerial elite to modernize industry.

In the past, important decisions were largely made by central planners. However, the need for decentralization has become evident. Interviewed by *Fortune* magazine, a Soviet manager indicated that his own expectations are stated in profit and revenues, but the decisions of resource allocation and salary increases for his employees are left to his discretion.[6] Managerial power even extends to the decision of firing an employee. But this authority may be more theoretical than real because the state guarantees employment. Thus, the dismissal may amount to a transfer of the employee to another organization. While, in the past, much of the decision authority was vested in governmental officials, the new authority relationships may cause a great deal of uncertainty among the managers themselves.

While raising the status of the managerial elite is a new phenomenon in Russia, management education lags far behind most Western nations. There are only two new management schools in the Soviet Union.

A New Management Frontier?

In the past, many countries looked to the United States for answers for their economic and managerial development. Increasingly, however, a number of Asian countries turn their attention to the Japanese model.[7] The French writer Jean-Jacques Servan-Schreiber, who at one time had high praise for American managerial approaches, now thinks that some of the Asian nations, through the use of microtechnology, will play an increasingly important role in business. While there is still the search for economic solutions to development,[8] the need for managerial know-how becomes evident. The rapid economic developments in places such as Hong Kong, Singapore, South Korea, and Taiwan need to be accompanied by more systematic approaches to managing. Although relatively little empirical research on management in these countries exists today,[9] the well-attended business and management conferences in Pacific Basin countries may give an indication of researches in the future.

Is Management Culture-Bound?

As the study of management has increasingly commanded worldwide interest and recognition, the question of whether management is a science with universal application has concerned many scholars and practitioners. A real science should explain phenomena regardless of national or cultural environments. Thus, the science of mechanics knows no boundaries, providing it applies to the reality being considered. Principles of the building sciences are no different whether they are applied to a small house or a large building and whether these structures are built in the tropics or in the arctic.

Unless basic management science can be useful for practitioners in varying circumstances, it is certainly suspect, for the task of an "operational" science is to organize pertinent knowledge so as to make it applicable, and thereby useful, to those who would achieve intended results.

Although views differ, we have taken the position that management fundamentals—concepts, theory, and principles—have universal application in every kind of enterprise and at every level of an enterprise. Yet we have constantly acknowledged that the specific problems with which managers deal, the individuals and groups with which they interact, and the elements of the external environment will differ. One expects, therefore, that given techniques and approaches, even though based upon the same fundamentals, will vary in their applications because of these differences, just as engineering design will vary if a mechanical engineer is planning a bridge rather than a precise pressure-measuring instrument.

We have attempted to give the concepts of management theory, principles, and science careful definition. In essence, **science** is organized knowledge, **theory** is a structure of fundamental concepts and principles around which knowledge in a field is organized, and **principles** are regarded as fundamental truths—or what are thought to be truths at a particular time—which can be used to describe and predict the results of certain variables in given situations. Management **know-how**, on the other hand, refers to the effective applications of knowledge; it includes knowledge of the underlying science and the artful ability to apply it in a particular situation. Unfortunately, the discussion of comparative management is often unnecessarily confused by the failure to distinguish between management fundamentals and management practice.

The Koontz Model of Comparative Management

In comparing management in various countries, Professors Richard N. Farmer and Barry M. Richman—two pioneers in comparative management—emphasized that environments external to the firm do affect management practices.[10] These authors were first to identify the critical elements in the management process and to evaluate their operation in firms in different cultures. They also described the environmental factors they considered to have a significant impact on the management process and managerial effectiveness. These factors, viewed as constraints, are classified as (1) educational variables, (2) sociological-cultural variables, (3) political and legal variables, and (4) economic variables.

Some problems with the traditional model.   There are some difficulties with the Farmer-Richman approach. The problem of separating the art and science of management has been noted. Also the effectiveness of an enterprise's operation depends not only on management but also on other factors. Management knowledge does not by any means encompass all the knowledge that is utilized in an enterprise. The specialized knowledge, or science, in such basic areas of enterprise operation as engineering, production, marketing, and finance is essential to enterprise operation. Many enterprises have been successful, despite poor management, because of brilliant marketing, strong engineering, well-designed and well-operated production, or astute financing.[11] Even though it is our judgment, based on an analysis of the histories of many companies, that effectiveness of management will ultimately make the difference between continued success and decline, at least in a competitive economy, it is still true that enterprises have for a time succeeded entirely through nonmanagerial factors.

A new approach to comparative management.   Enterprise activities fall into two broad categories: managerial and nonmanagerial. Either or both can be the causal factors for at least some degree of enterprise effectiveness. Also, nonmanagerial activities will be affected by relevant underlying science or knowledge, just as managerial activities will be affected by underlying management science. Both types of activities will be affected by the availability of human and material resources and by the constraints and influences of the external environment, whether these are educational, political-legal, economic, technological, or sociological-ethical.

If the factors affecting enterprise effectiveness and the role of underlying management science are to be brought to light more clearly than has been done, it would appear that we need a model of the kind shown in Figure 25-1.

This model is far more complex than those used by previous researchers in the field of comparative management. It is also believed to be far more accurate

FIGURE 25-1

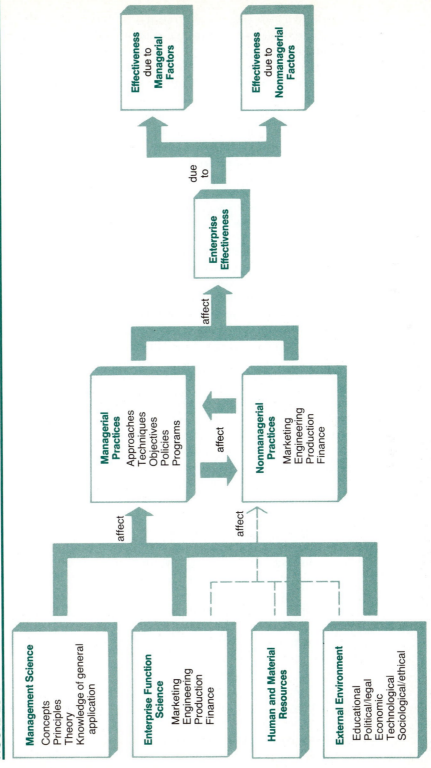

KOONTZ MODEL FOR ANALYZING COMPARATIVE MANAGEMENT.

From Harold Koontz, "A Model for Analyzing the Universality and Transferability of Management," *Academy of Management Journal* (December 1969), pp. 415–429.

and realistic. If the purpose is to study comparative management, something like this must be done in order to understand and see the elements of universality in management.

Rather than viewing factors in the environment simply as "constraints"—a term which has a negative connotation—it is preferable to consider them as environmental "factors," which may constitute constraints or opportunities. For example, in the economic category of factor endowments, a country may be short on capital but rich in natural resources. Similarly, some laws may be restrictive for conducting business, but others may be favorable. Therefore, environmental restraints could become opportunities in certain situations.

DIFFERENCES IN MANAGING IN SELECTED COUNTRIES

You may find it interesting to know some of the differences in managerial practices in selected countries. But note that the discussion is illustrative rather than comprehensive. Also, this discussion is based on generalizations. There are, for example, great differences among U.S. managers. The same holds true for managers in other countries. Furthermore, a society is not static and changes do occur over time. For instance, the traditional authoritarian style of German managers is slowly giving way to a more participative approach.

France: Le Plan

In France, government planning on a national scale (legal-political environment factor) helps coordinate plans of individual industries and companies (managerial function of planning). The government's aim is to utilize most effectively the country's resources and to avoid expansion in uneconomic areas. Although governmental planning—which is also extended to regional areas—is carried out by relatively few, but competent, people, cooperation and assistance are provided by other governmental departments, employers' organizations, unions, and consumers.

The plan, which is generally revised every 5 years, attempts to obtain economic growth, price stability, a balance in foreign payments, and a favorable employment situation. Managers, then, are not only constrained by "Le Plan" but also aided by having a great deal of information available for preparing plans for their own enterprises.

At times, the plan becomes a global strategy helping specific industries.[12] For example, the French government attempts to integrate the electronics industry into a whole so that it can overcome its weaknesses in information processing, consumer electronics, microelectronics, and automation. To implement the strategy, the government plans to support several national projects, such as speech synthesis, mini- and microcomputers, and large mainframe computers. Consider also the close relationship between the government and the auto maker Renault, with all shares owned by the government.[13] Despite the continuing investment by the government in the company, the chief executive officer maintains that the government does not interfere with its management. The relationship is limited to monthly meetings of the administrative council and the yearly agreement on corporate objectives. At the same time, the company is aided by restricting Japanese car imports to a certain percentage of the market share. Clearly, there is a close relationship between government planning and firms, especially those that are owned and directly aided by the government.

Germany: Authority and Codetermination

In the past, and to a lesser extent today, the German cultural environment favored reliance on authority in directing the work force, although it was often benevolent authoritarianism (managerial function of leading). Even today, while managers may show concern for subordinates, they also expect obedience.

It is almost a paradox that, on the one hand, the managerial style is characterized by considerable use of authority, while, on the other hand, labor, by law, is represented and actively involved in managing large corporations (legal-political environment). In 1951 a law was passed that provided for co-determination, which requires labor membership in the supervisory board and the executive committee of certain large corporations. Furthermore, a labor director is elected as a member of the executive committee.[14] This position is a difficult one. Labor directors supposedly must represent the interests of the employees and, at the same time, must make managerial decisions that are in the best interest of the enterprise.

Selected Factors Influencing Managing in Other Countries[15]

Managing in *Australia* is influenced by this country's moralistic stance and its emphasis on political and social value, achievement, and risk taking.

Italian managers are operating in an environment of low tolerance for risks. Italians are very competitive, but at the same time they like group decision making.

Management in *Austria* (and *Germany*) is characterized by self-realization and leadership. Independence and competitiveness are valued. The tolerance for risk taking is rather low.

In *Britain,* security is important, and so are resourcefulness, adaptability, and logic. Similarly, individualism is also highly valued.

Preparing Foreign Managers for Work in the United States

With the increasing investment of foreign firms in the United States, more attention must be given to the integration of managers and workers from other countries into American society.[16] To illustrate the need, consider that the number of intercompany transferees has more than tripled from the late 1970s to the mid 1980s. Japanese, for example, often find it difficult to be outspoken and direct in their interaction with their colleagues, and especially with their superior. People from Arabian countries usually find American teaching methods too impersonal.

Various approaches have been used to reduce culture shock. These include special programs about corporate life in the United States, as well as instruction in English, books, and movies; even tax advice is given to the newcomers. Some companies have found the buddy system useful for making the foreigner feel comfortable in the new environment. In this approach an American looks after the needs of the newcomer. Other firms use role playing to demonstrate alternative ways of managerial behavior. Because of the cultural background, Japanese managers usually find it rather difficult to conduct an American-style performance review that focuses on results.

In the past, training and development focused on preparing U.S. managers and workers for overseas assignments. Increasingly, firms are becoming aware of the need for helping foreigners coming to America to reduce the culture shock they may experience.

JAPANESE MANAGEMENT AND THEORY Z

Japan, one of the leading industrial nations in the world, has adopted managerial practices that are quite different from those of other economically advanced countries in the Western world. We will first discuss two common Japanese practices: lifetime employment and consensus decision making. Then we will compare and contrast Japanese and U.S. managerial practices and discuss Theory Z.

Lifetime Employment

Important features of Japanese management practice are lifelong employment (related to the staffing function), great concern for the individual employee, and emphasis on seniority. Typically, employees spend their working life with a single enterprise, which in turn provides employees with security and a feeling of belonging. This practice brings the culturally induced concept of "wa" (harmony) to the enterprise, resulting in employee loyalty and close identification with the aims of the company.

However, it also adds to business costs because employees are kept on the payroll even though there may be insufficient work. Consequently, firms are beginning to question the practice of lifelong employment. Indeed, changes appear to be in the making, but they are slow—very slow. What is often overlooked, however, is that this permanent employment practice, known as "nenko," is used only by large firms. In fact, it is estimated that the job security system applies to only about one-third of the labor force.[17]

Closely related to lifelong employment is the seniority system, which has provided privileges for older employees who have been with the enterprise a long time. But there are indications that the seniority system may be superseded by a more open approach that provides opportunities for advancement for young people. For example, the relatively new Sony Corporation has team leaders (a point is made of not calling them supervisors) who are often young women 18 or 19 years of age. There is practically no age difference between these leaders and the operators they lead.

Decision Making

The managerial practice of decision making is also considerably different from that in the United States. It is built on the concept that change and new ideas should come primarily from below. Thus, lower-level employees prepare proposals for higher-level personnel. Supervisors, rather than simply accepting or rejecting suggestions, tactfully question proposals, make suggestions, and encourage subordinates. If necessary, proposals are sent back to the initiator for more information.

Japanese management, then, uses decision making by consensus; lower-level employees initiate the idea and submit it to the next higher level until it reaches the desk of the top executive. If the proposal is approved, it is returned to the initiator for implementation. Although the decision-making process is time-consuming, the implementation of the decision—because of the general consensus at various levels of management—is swift and does not require additional "selling."

An important characteristic of Japanese decision making is the large amount of effort that goes into defining the question or problem; there is a great deal of communication *before* a decision is actually made. American managers are often accused of making decisions before defining the problem. In contrast, Japanese management makes a decision only after long discussions of the issue.

In summary, Japanese managerial practice still emphasizes (although changes are occurring) lifetime employment, concern for the individual, seniority, and a sense of loyalty to the firm. Furthermore, in decision making there is open communication among people at different levels of the organizational hierarchy, a great deal of collaboration, and a recognition of mutual dependence.

Japanese versus U.S. Management Practices and Theory Z

Of great concern is the declining growth rate in productivity in the United States. Thus, we increasingly examine Japanese management—rightly or wrongly—to find answers to our productivity crisis. In the preceding discussion we focused on two characteristics of Japanese management: lifetime employment and consensus decision making. But there are other characteristics that distinguish Japanese from American management practices; these are summarized in Table 25-1.[18] A word of caution must be added as to the interpretation of this table. It is obvious that not all American firms are managed the same way; the same is true of Japanese firms. We also must realize that few empirical studies exist on the subject and most of the available literature is descriptive. Therefore, the contrasting managerial approaches are suggestive and need to be substantiated by additional research.

In **Theory Z**, selected Japanese managerial practices are adapted to the environment of the United States and practiced by companies such as IBM, Hewlett-Packard, and the diversified retail company Dayton-Hudson.[19] One of the characteristics of Type Z organization is an emphasis on the interpersonal skills that are needed for group interaction. Yet, despite the emphasis on group decision making, responsibility remains with the individual (which is quite differ-

TABLE 25-1 Japanese and United States Management Approaches

Japanese management	U.S. management
Planning	

Japanese management	U.S. management
1. Long-term orientation	1. Primarily short-term orientation
2. Collective decision making (*ringi*) with consensus	2. Individual decision making
3. Involvement of many people in preparing and making the decision	3. Involvement of a few people in making and "selling" the decision to persons with divergent values
4. Decision flow from bottom to top and back	4. Decisions initiated at the top, flowing down
5. Slow decision making; fast implementation of the decision	5. Fast decision making; slow implementation requiring compromise, often resulting in suboptimal decisions

Organizing

Japanese management	U.S. management
1. Collective responsibility and accountability	1. Individual responsibility and accountability
2. Ambiguity of decision responsibility	2. Clear and specific decision responsibility
3. Informal organization structure	3. Formal, bureaucratic organization structure
4. Well-known common organization culture and philosophy; competitive spirit toward other enterprises	4. Lack of common organization culture; identification with profession rather than with company

Staffing

Japanese management	U.S. management
1. Young people hired out of school; hardly any mobility of people among companies	1. People hired out of schools and from other companies; frequent company changes
2. Slow promotion through the ranks	2. Rapid advancement desired and demanded
3. Loyalty to the company	3. Loyalty to the profession
4. Very infrequent performance evaluation for new (young) employees	4. Frequent performance evaluation for new employees
5. Appraisal of long-term performance	5. Appraisal of short-term results
6. Promotions based on multiple criteria	6. Promotions based primarily on individual performance
7. Training and development considered a long-term investment	7. Training and development undertaken with hesitation (for fear of turnover)
8. Lifetime employment common in large companies	8. Job insecurity prevailing

Leading

Japanese management	U.S. management
1. Leader acting as a social facilitator and group member	1. Leader acting as decision maker and head of the group
2. Paternalistic style	2. Directive style (strong, firm, determined)
3. Common values facilitating cooperation	3. Often divergent values; individualism sometimes hindering cooperation
4. Avoidance of confrontation, sometimes leading to ambiguities; emphasis on harmony	4. Face-to-face confrontation common; emphasis on clarity
5. Bottom-up communication	5. Communication primarily top-down

Controlling

Japanese management	U.S. management
1. Control by peers	1. Control by superior
2. Control focus on group performance	2. Control focus on individual performance
3. Saving face	3. Fixing blame
4. Extensive use of quality control circles	4. Limited use of quality control circles

ent from the Japanese practice, which emphasizes collective responsibility). There is also an emphasis on informal and democratic relationships based on trust. Yet, the hierarchical structure still remains intact, as illustrated by IBM, where not only goals but also authority, rules, and discipline guide corporate behavior.[20]

Participative management facilitates the free flow of information needed to reach consensus. Formal planning and objectives are important but numerical measures are not overly emphasized. Instead, a corporate philosophy and corporate values guide managerial actions. People are seen as whole human beings, not simply as factors in production. However, the Japanese practice of very infrequent performance evaluations and promotions is not emphasized by Theory Z-type companies. In short, these companies selectively use some Japanese managerial practices but make adjustments for the environment prevailing in the United States.

Japanese Companies Operating in the United States

In an attempt to demonstrate the effectiveness of Japanese managerial approaches, success stories of Japanese companies operating in the United States are often cited. Workers at Sony's television plant in San Diego are said to produce as well as workers in Japan. But other experiences are not quite as convincing. YKK, Inc., a manufacturer of zippers, has experienced labor-management confrontations similar to those experienced by U.S. companies. Let us look at a positive example.

The trend of Japanese firms investing in manufacturing facilities in the United States is probably going to continue. In 1983, 31 Japanese firms were established here, bringing the total of Japanese-owned companies to 309 in

PERSPECTIVE:
BRIDGESTONE TIRE COMPANY

The Bridgestone Corporation, a Japanese tire firm that took over the Firestone Tire & Rubber Company plant in Tennessee, was able not only to smooth the stormy labor relations that had plagued the company for years but also to improve both productivity and quality.[21] Some of the methods used to achieve these results were indeed rather traditional. They included investing in new equipment, setting high quality standards, and using a disciplined managerial approach that required employees to work harder and to give up some seniority provisions, thus allowing the company to fill key positions with the most suitable employees. Moreover, employees were also asked to participate in decisions that affected them and their jobs. For example, workers, not just inspectors, now have responsibility for the quality of the products. And this was done with the cooperation of the union. Bridgestone also used a management-by-objectives approach which is built on the concept of self-control and self-direction.

1984, employing 73,000 workers.[22] These firms often demand less costly labor contracts. Although Japanese firms generally resist unions, 23 percent of the 163 companies responding to a 1982 survey were unionized.

INTERNATIONAL MANAGEMENT AND MULTINATIONAL CORPORATIONS

The study of **international management** focuses on the operation of international firms in host countries. It is concerned with managerial issues related to the flow of people, goods, and money, with the ultimate aim being to manage better in situations that involve crossing national boundaries.

The environmental factors that affect domestic firms usually are more critical for international corporations operating in foreign countries. As illustrated in Table 25-2, managers involved in international business are faced with many factors that are different from those of the domestically oriented firm. Managers have to interact with employees who have different educational and cultural backgrounds and value systems; they also must cope with different legal, political, and economic factors. Thus, these environments understandably influence the way managerial and enterprise functions are carried out.

The Nature and Purpose of International Business

Although business has been conducted on an international scale for many years, international business has gained greater visibility and importance in recent

TABLE 25-2 Domestic and International Enterprises: Characteristics and Practices

The environment	Domestic enterprise (industrialized country)	International enterprise
Educational environment:		
1. Language (spoken, written, official	One	Multiple
2. Education system (quality, level, extent)	No or little constraint	Great constraint
Sociological-cultural environment:		
1. Values, attitudes (toward achievement, risk taking, scientific method, work)	Homogeneous	Heterogeneous
2. Social organization (authority, status, roles, institutions, mobility, social systems)	Similar	Different
Political-legal environment:		
1. Political orientation (power, ideologies)	Country-centered	Transnational
2. Legal environment (laws, codes, regulations)	Fairly uniform	Different
3. National sovereignties	One	Many
4. Government policies, regulations	Same	Different
Economic environment:		
1. Economic development (underdeveloped, industrialized)	At similar stages	At different stages
2. Economic system (capitalistic, mixed, Marxist)	Similar	Different

years because of the growth of large multinational corporations. **International businesses** engage in transactions across national boundaries. These transactions include the transfer of goods, services, technology, managerial knowledge, and capital to other countries.

The interaction of a firm with the host country can take many forms, as illustrated in Figure 25-2. One is the **exportation** of goods and services. Another is a **licensing** agreement for producing goods in another country. The parent company may also engage in **management contracts** that provide for operating foreign companies. Still another form of interaction is the **joint venture** with a firm in the host country. Finally, multinationals may set up wholly owned **subsidiaries** or **branches** with production facilities in the host country. Thus, in developing a global strategy, an international firm has many options.[23]

The contact between the parent firm and the host country is affected by several factors; some are unifying, others can cause conflicts.

Unifying effects.   Unifying influences occur when the parent company provides and shares technical and managerial know-how, thus assisting the host company in the development of human and material resources. Moreover, the parent corporation and the firm in the host country may find it advantageous to be integrated into a global organization structure. Whatever the interaction, policies must provide for equity and result in benefits for both the parent firm and the host company. Only then can one expect a long-lasting relationship.

Potentials for conflict.   Many factors can cause conflicts between the parent firm and the host country. Nationalistic self-interest may overshadow the benefits obtained through cooperation. Similarly, sociological-cultural differences can lead to breakdowns in communication and subsequent misunderstandings. Also, a large multinational firm may have such overpowering economic effects on a small country that the host country feels overwhelmed. Some international corporations have been charged with making excessive profits, hiring the best local people away from local firms, and operating contrary to social customs. The international corporation must develop social and diplomatic skills in its managers in order to prevent such conflicts and to resolve those that unavoidably occur.

Multinational Corporations

Multinational corporations (MNCs) have their headquarters in one country, but their operations in many countries. Of the ten largest industrial corporations, ranked by 1985 sales, eight are American.[24] They are (1) General Motors, (2) Exxon, (3) Royal Dutch/Shell Group (Dutch-English), (4) Mobil, (5) British Petroleum (English), (6) Ford Motor Company, (7) International Business Machines (IBM), (8) Texaco, (9) Chevron, and (10) American Telephone and Telegraph (AT&T).

From ethnocentric to geocentric orientation.   In its early stages, international business was conducted with an **ethnocentric** outlook; that is, the orientation

FIGURE 25-2

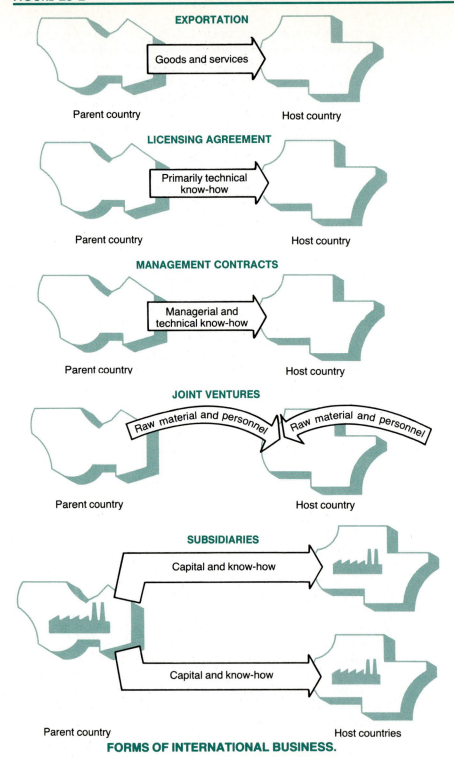

EXPORTATION

Goods and services

Parent country   Host country

LICENSING AGREEMENT

Primarily technical
know-how

Parent country   Host country

MANAGEMENT CONTRACTS

Managerial and
technical know-how

Parent country   Host country

JOINT VENTURES

Raw material and personnel   Raw material and personnel

Parent country   Host country

SUBSIDIARIES

Capital and know-how

Capital and know-how

Parent country   Host countries

FORMS OF INTERNATIONAL BUSINESS.

and type of operation was based on that of the parent company.[25] The **polycentric** attitude, on the other hand, is based on the notion that it is best to give the foreign subsidiaries, staffed by local nationals, a great deal of freedom to manage. It is assumed that nationals have the best understanding of the local environment. **Regiocentric** orientation favors the staffing of foreign operations on a regional basis. Thus, a European view may be composed of British, French, German, and Italian influences. The modern multinational corporation has a **geocentric** orientation. This means that the total organization is viewed as an interdependent system operating in many countries. The relationships between headquarters and subsidiaries are collaborative, with communication flowing in both directions. Furthermore, key positions are filled by managers of different nationalities. In short, the orientation of the multinational corporation is truly international and goes beyond a narrow nationalistic viewpoint.

Advantages of multinationals.   Multinational corporations have several advantages over firms that have a domestic orientation. Obviously, the MNC can take advantage of business opportunities in many different countries. It can also raise money for its operations throughout the world. Moreover, multinational firms benefit by being able to establish production facilities in countries where their products can be produced most effectively and efficiently. Companies with worldwide operations sometimes have better access to natural resources and materials that may not be available to domestic firms. Finally, the large MNCs can recruit management and other personnel from a worldwide labor pool.

Successful U.S. multinationals.   Despite the increasing competition and the cost advantages of some foreign corporations, a number of U.S. companies have done very well in the international environment.

PERSPECTIVE:
WOMAN CEO MANAGES BY THE TEXTBOOK

To illustrate the demand for managers with an international background, let us consider Marisa Bellisario, one of the most sought-after executives in Europe in 1984.[26] She was the first woman to head a major industrial firm in Italy, the state-controlled ITALTEL Società Italiana, the biggest Italian firm making telecommunications equipment. Her background, however, is international. After receiving her degree in economics and business administration from Turin University, she worked at Olivetti in the electronics division. When Olivetti sold its data-processing unit to General Electric, she spent time in Miami working on GE's worldwide marketing strategy for computers. She left GE to head corporate planning at Olivetti. As the CEO at ITALTEL, she turned the company around, showing a small profit. (The firm had experienced huge losses in the past.) Her managerial approach has been characterized as "straight out of the textbook," and companies such as GTE Corporation, IBM, AT&T, and other European and Japanese firms are interested in recruiting her.

Fortune studied a number of large companies that earn more than 20 percent of their revenues from overseas operations.[27] The reasons for the success of these firms differ greatly. IBM's size makes it possible to dominate the market. Coca-Cola is very adept at opening up new markets rather rapidly. McDonald's, on the other hand, does not rush into the market but carefully assesses the potential for success. Hewlett-Packard and Boeing bring foreign managers to the United States to expose them to their organizational culture.

The MNCs that were studied structure their organization very carefully to suit the needs of each individual country. In addition, these firms are flexible in their product design and marketing. It should also be noted that the operations abroad were largely management by foreign nationals.

Challenges for the multinationals.   The advantages of multinational operation must be weighed against the challenges and risks associated with operating in foreign environments. One problem is the increasing nationalism in many countries. Years ago, developing countries lacked managerial, marketing, and technical skills. Consequently, they welcomed the multinationals. But the situation is changing, with people in developing countries acquiring those skills. In addition, countries not only become aware of the value of their natural resources but also become more skilled in international negotiations. Finally, multinationals must maintain good relations with the host country, a task that may prove difficult because governments frequently change, and corporations must deal with, and adapt to, these changes.

THE MANAGERIAL FUNCTIONS IN INTERNATIONAL BUSINESS

There is evidence that shows that management fundamentals are applicable in different countries. However, the practice of carrying out the managerial functions of planning, organizing, staffing, leading, and controlling differs considerably in domestic and international enterprises, as shown in Table 25-3.

Planning in the Multinational Corporation

Planning requires setting objectives and then selecting strategies, policies, programs, and procedures for achieving them. A critically important activity for the MNC is the assessment of opportunities and threats in the external environment. This is a complex task even for a domestic enterprise, but it becomes much more intricate when many different, ever-changing world markets must be scanned.

External threats and opportunities must be matched with the internal strengths and weaknesses of the firm. For example, a poor educational system makes it difficult to find qualified personnel. Similarly, cultural orientation toward time will affect planning. Specifically, cultural attitudes that emphasize a short-time perspective will not be conducive to long-range planning. Finally, political and economic instability in a country makes it difficult to forecast and will discourage long-term commitment of resources.

TABLE 25-3 Managing Domestic and International Enterprises

Managerial functions	Domestic enterprise (industrialized country)	International enterprise
Planning:		
Scanning the environment for threats and opportunities	National market	Worldwide market
Organizing:		
1. Organization structure	Structure for domestic operations	Global structure
2. View of authority	Similar	Different
Staffing:		
1. Sources of managerial talent	National labor pool	Worldwide labor pool
2. Manager orientation	Often ethnocentric	Geocentric
Leading:		
1. Leadership and motivation	Influenced by similar culture	Influenced by many different cultures
2. Communication lines	Relatively short	Network with long distances
Controlling:		
Reporting system	Similar requirements	Many different requirements

Even large multinational companies may find it difficult to compete in the world market. Therefore, they form global strategic partnerships (GSPs).[28] General Motors formed a joint venture with Toyota to produce cars at the Fremont plant in California.[29] American Telephone and Telegraph Company shares technology with Olivetti and Philips,[30] both large multinational corporations in Europe. Kodak works with a Japanese company to produce some of its cameras. Clearly, success of the GSPs will depend on balancing cooperation with competitiveness among the firms.

Organizing the Multinational Corporation

Organization structures are established to achieve corporate objectives. The company can select from a great variety of structures.[31] An enterprise may, for example, establish a vice-presidential position at corporate headquarters with responsibility for the international division. An alternative is to organize according to geographical areas. For example, managers may be put in charge of regions such as North America, Latin America, Europe, Africa, and the Far East. Still another way of grouping organizational activities is according to product lines. For instance, at corporate headquarters, managers may be put in charge of a product line which is marketed worldwide. The truly multinational firm may integrate domestic and international business into a global structure which gives similar importance to domestic and foreign business activities.

Each structure has advantages and limitations, as we discussed in Chapter 8. It is important to realize that for the large multinational corporation any one structure may be insufficient. Consequently, different organizational designs may have to be mixed, depending on the environmental and task demands.

Staffing in the Multinational Corporation

The positions identified in the organization structure must be filled by qualified persons. This involves staffing.

Sources for managerial talent.   Managers of the MNC can be classified in three ways. First, managers may be nationals selected from the country in which the headquarters is located. These expatriates (with *home-country nationality*) are chosen to represent and manage the enterprise abroad. These managers, because of their experience, are usually familiar with the parent company's policies and operations.

Second, a firm may select managers who are *nationals of the host country*. These managers are familiar with the country's environment, its education system, its culture, its legal and political processes, and its economic environment. They usually also know local customers, suppliers, government officials, behavioral characteristics of employees, and the public in general.

The third source for managerial personnel consists of *third-country nationals*. These are managers who have a nationality that is different from either the country of the parent company or the host country. Such managers may have gained experience by working at the company headquarters as well as in different countries. Thus, they would have developed behavioral flexibility that eases their adaptation to different cultures. These managers may be truly transcultural.

Trends in staffing multinational corporations.   Each of the three sources for managers has advantages and disadvantages, and a firm may use a variety of combinations. But a few factors that influence the trend in staffing MNCs are worth noting. First, the cost of sending United States managers abroad has increased, partly owing to the declining value of the U.S. dollar in the 1970s and in 1986. Second, people in the host countries are now better prepared to assume responsible managerial positions. While conducting management development programs in Singapore, Hong Kong, and Taipei, one of the authors found the quality of middle managers measuring up to those in the United States. Finally, employing nationals of the host country can improve relations with that country. Therefore, as far as American firms are concerned, the trend is toward employing more host-country nationals than managers from the parent company.

Leading in the Multinational Corporation

Leading involves motivating and communicating. It requires exerting leadership by inducing employees to contribute to enterprise objectives.

Motivating and leading demand an understanding of employees and their cultural environment. For instance, participative management may work well in one country but may cause confusion among employees in another country with a tradition of autocratic rule.

**PERSPECTIVE:
LEADERSHIP AT LUFTHANSA[32]**

Leadership depends not only on the leader but also on the followers, and on the situation. Let us focus on the internal as well as external environment in which Heinz Ruhnau, Lufthansa's (German Airline) chief executive officer, (CEO) is operating.

1. The government owns about 77 percent of Lufthansa. This means that the leader has to be familiar with interrelationships between the government and Lufthansa.

2. A need for change is usually recognized by the work force when a company is in severe difficulties. But how do you change an enterprise when it has been relatively successful and employees do not see the urgent need for change? Ruhnau did this by reorganizing, which, in turn, set off a storm. Specifically, through organizational rearrangements, management has been given more decision power, with fewer requirements for consultation of workers. These actions by Ruhnau, a former labor leader, shocked some employees and surprised others, winning him few popularity contests. Yet increasing competition in the airline market demands fast responses to the changing environment.

3. Over the years, an elaborate and inefficient bureaucracy was established at Lufthansa. How do you cope with such a situation? According to Ruhnau, "you can't cure a bureaucracy. You have to kill it."

4. While, on the one hand, reorganization resulted in less consultation in certain areas, Ruhnau wants to stay close to the work force, as illustrated by his behavior. When he flies, for example, he talks to all flight attendants and serves coffee to the crew.

   To better understand Ruhnau's leadership behavior, let us look at his background. As a young man, he was an apprentice as an electrical tool and die maker. After graduating in business administration, he became a union official. Later he served in the senate in Hamburg. The federal government called him to be the state secretary in the Department of Transportation. In this role, he also was a member of the board of directors of Lufthansa. In 1982 he took over as the chief executive officer of the airline.

   His technical background, his union activities, his political experience, and his connections (networking) all served him well to assume a leadership role in an environment that requires intensive interactions between the company and its various claimants.

Communication is often a problem in multinational firms with subsidiaries and affiliates in countries where different languages are spoken. Even a firm with operations in a country where English is the primary language may encounter communication problems because of the distance between headquarters and the subsidiary. But new communication technology has greatly improved the transmission of information. Still, a telephone call is not quite the same as a visit and a person-to-person discussion.

Controlling in the Multinational Corporation

Controlling—the measurement and correction of performance to assure that events conform to plans—is an essential managerial function that is influenced by several environmental factors unique to international enterprises. First, revenues, costs, and profits are measured in different currencies. Second, the ratios between currencies are subject to considerable fluctuations. Third, accounting practices and financial reporting often differ from country to country. For example, accounting procedures may have to satisfy the demands of tax authorities of the host country as well as the government of the parent firm. The procedures should also satisfy stockholders in various countries, agencies in charge of regulating securities, and banks. Procedures must also be suitable to meet the internal requirements of the firm. To develop a procedure that meets all these demands at the same time is extremely difficult. Finally, and partly owing to the complex nature of measurement, there is a time lag in the measurement of performance which may delay detecting deviations from standards and the initiation of corrective action. Computers, however, have done much to speed up the process. In all, then, these few examples indicate that controlling the international corporation is considerably more difficult than monitoring a domestic operation.

TOWARD A UNIFIED GLOBAL THEORY OF MANAGEMENT

Today, the framework of planning, organizing, staffing, leading, and controlling (with some slight variations at times) has become the most popular way of structuring managerial knowledge.[33] Textbooks on management using this framework are widely used around the world. Still, there are challenging tasks ahead for integrating the body of managerial knowledge into a unified theory.

The Need for Untangling the Management Theory Jungle

In Chapter 2 of this book you learned about the many schools of, or approaches to, management. There is evidence that the management theory jungle not only continues to flourish but gets more dense, with nearly twice as many schools or approaches as were found over 20 years ago.

At the same time, there are signs that the various schools of thought are converging. Realizing that these are only signs along the road to a more unified and operational theory of management, and that there is more of this road to travel, let us briefly examine some of these tendencies toward convergence.

The Empirical Approach: Distilling Basics

In reviewing the many programs that use cases as a means of educating managers, one finds that there appears to be much greater emphasis on distilling fundamentals than there was two or three decades ago. Likewise, in the field of business policy, by which term these case approaches have tended to be known, there has been increased emphasis in teaching and research that goes beyond recounting what happened in a given situation to analyzing the underlying causes.[34] One major result of all this has been a new emphasis on strategic management. Furthermore, many textbooks on policy and strategy now have many international cases and considerable text material of distilled knowledge.[35]

Systems Thinking—Not a Separate Approach

Practicing managers as well as the operational theorists increasingly use the basics of systems theory in analyzing managerial jobs. On the macro level, managers, especially those of multinational corporations, are viewing their operations as a global interdependent system. Japanese managers, for example, are in charge of their manufacturing plants in the United States, and U.S. managers direct their firms in Europe and other countries.

Situational and Contingency Approaches— Not New or Separate

It is now clear that the concepts of situational, or contingency, management are merely a way of distinguishing between science and art, knowledge and practice. As pointed out at the beginning of this book, science and art are two different but complementary things. Those writers and scholars who have emphasized situational, or contingency, approaches have done the field of management theory and practice a great service by stressing that what the intelligent manager actually does depends on the realities of a situation, whether it is in the United States or abroad.

The Confluence of Motivation and Leadership Theory

Another interesting sign that we may be moving toward a unified operational theory of management is the way that research and analysis have tended to merge motivation and leadership theory.[36] As we have seen in Chapters 17 and 18, leadership research and theory have found that people tend to follow those who offer them a means of satisfying their own desires. Thus, explanations of leadership have been increasingly related to motivation.

Implied by most recent research and theory is the clear message that effective leaders design a system that takes into account the expectations of subordinates, the variability of motives between individuals, the factors specific to a situation, the need for clarity of role definition, interpersonal relations, and types of rewards.

The New, Managerially Oriented "Organization Development"

Both "organization development" and the field ordinarily referred to as "organization behavior" have grown out of the interpersonal and group behavior approaches to management. Many specialists in these areas are now beginning to see that basic management theory and techniques fit well into their programs of behavioral intervention.

Fortunately, a review of the latest organization behavior books indicates that many authors in this field are beginning to understand that the study of behavioral elements in group operations must be more closely integrated with study of organization structure design, staffing, planning, and control. This is a hopeful sign. It is a recognition that analysis of individual and group behavior, at least in managed situations, easily and logically falls into place in the scheme of operational-management theory.

The Impact of Technology: Researching an Old Problem

That technology has an important impact on organizational structure, behavior patterns, and other aspects of managing has been recognized by practitioners for many years. Fortunately, academic researchers in recent years have directed their attention to the impact of technology on managerial effectiveness.

The Merger of Theory and Practice

For some time now, scholars and practitioners looked to the total job of managing. As pointed out in Chapter 2, the 7-S framework for management analysis proposed by the respected management consulting firm is indeed close to the operational, or management process, model.

PERSPECTIVE:
RECENT RESEARCH SUPPORTING THE OPERATIONAL APPROACH

Some recent research studies have focused on the total managerial job. An example of this research was presented in the presidential speech at the Academy of Management in August 1986 by Fred Luthans. His findings are, in general, congruent with the operational approach to managing as used in this book. In his 4-year study of over 300 managers at different levels and in various kinds of organizations, he found that "real" managers carry out the following activities: (1) routine communication (see Part 5 in this book), (2) traditional managerial activities such as planning, decision making, and controlling (Parts 2 and 6 in this book), (3) human resource management activities (Parts 4 and 5), and (4) networking, by which is meant socializing, politicking, and interacting with outsiders (some of these concepts relate to the discussion of informal organization, coordination, and power discussed in Part 3). Luthans found a significant relationship between networking activities and managerial success (measured by a promotion index). The next level of analysis focused on managers' effectiveness (consisting of perceived work unit performance in terms of quantity and quality, and subordinate commitment and satisfaction). The findings showed the strongest relationships between effectiveness with routine communication, followed by human resource management, and traditional management. Although the research does not address all the key managerial activities (such as structuring the organization or the clarification of authority-responsibility relationships), it takes a comprehensive look at what successful and effective managers really do.

Clarification of Semantics: Some Hopeful Signs

One of the greatest obstacles to disentangling the jungle has been the problem of semantics. Those writing and lecturing on management and related fields have tended to use the same terms in different ways (or used different terms for the same concept). This is exemplified by the variety of meanings given to such terms as "organization," "line and staff," "authority," "responsibility," and "policies," to mention a few. While this semantics swamp still exists and we are a long way from general acceptance of meanings of key terms and concepts, there are some hopeful signs on the horizon.

It has become rather common now for leading management texts to include a glossary of key terms and concepts, and an increasing number of textbooks are beginning to use terms in a similar way. Furthermore, the Fellows of the International Academy of Management, a select group comprising management scholars and managerial leaders from over thirty countries, have responded to the demands of members and have undertaken to develop a glossary of management concepts and terms in a number of languages. It is necessary to agree not only on the translation of terms (although some terms such as "operations research" or "management" are used without translations in different languages) but on the precise meaning, understandable to all.

The Internationalization of Management

The term "global village" may appropriately describe the world we live in today. Advances in technology in aerospace, communication, fiber optics, and computers link people from around the globe.

While Japan sends its young people to the United States to study management techniques (and Japanese managers are eager readers of U.S. best-sellers on management), managers in the United States often look to Japan for implementing some of these techniques and theories more effectively. Recently, Korean managers have come with their style—which in many ways is similar to that of the Japanese—to lead their subsidiaries in the United States.[37] Samsung, Lucky Goldstar, Daewoo, and Hyundai are just a few of the Korean companies establishing themselves (quite successfully) in the United States. One Japanese manager admits that the Koreans, lacking the homogeneous culture of the Japanese, may be more flexible in adapting to the U.S. environment.

The point here is not that one approach is better than another, but rather that many countries can contribute to both managerial theory and practice. A special commission presented a sobering report on industrial competitiveness to the President of the United States.[38] In an environment of global competition, only the best companies will succeed and management, we suggest, will be an important factor for this success.

A perceptive observer will note that the role of managers is expanding. To avoid managerial obsolescence and to improve managerial productivity, we need more effective planning, flexible approaches to organizing, better managing of human resources, an environment favorable for motivation, and methods for effective and efficient control, using the new information technology. Above all, we urgently require in the field of management intellectual and inspirational leadership in the United States and around the world to make organizations more productive for the benefit of mankind.

FOR DISCUSSION

1. Do you think managerial concepts and practices we know and apply in the United States can be transferred to England, France, or West Germany?

2. What are some typical management practices in Japan and how do they compare to those in the United States?

3. What are likely to be the differences between the operation of a domestic firm and that of a multinational corporation? Select five differences and discuss their importance.

4. What advantages do multinational corporations have? What challenges must they meet? Give examples.

EXERCISES/ACTION STEPS

1. Contact a foreign firm operating in the United States and interview one or more managers. How do the managerial practices differ in the United States from the firm's home country?

2. From your knowledge of any foreign country, outline the major elements of its culture that would, in your judgment, influence managerial practices in that country.

CASES

CASE 25-1
CONSOLIDATED COMPUTERS, INC.

James Pruitt was ushered into the president's office. Three months ago he had been appointed manager of the first foreign plant of Consolidated Computers, Inc. A division manager of many proven talents, he appeared to be the ideal person for this assignment. He was an innovator and very much interested in a foreign appointment. Now he was calling on his superior just before catching a plane for Riyadh.

"I wanted to talk to you," the president began, "about some issues you will be facing when you reach Saudi Arabia. I guess you might call what I want to say a matter of my search for a business philosophy. We have not had to experi-

ence here the new issues that you will face, and we simply do not have a set of policies and procedures to cover such matters. Perhaps out of your experience we can move in that direction in case we later establish operations in other countries.

"I am not concerned about your encountering new principles of management. They are universal, you have developed great skill in applying them to domestic operations, and I have no doubt about your skills in applying them in a foreign environment. You will soon discover, however, that managing is different abroad because the cultural environment is so different.

"I think our best position is to realize that we

are going into Saudi Arabia as a guest. We each need the other at this time, but there may come a time when their political forces will require us to give up ownership of our plant. It is up to you to develop the rapport with all interested parties which will most benefit our long-run interests.

"Since all of your employees will be, or soon will be, Saudis, it is vital to learn as quickly as possible something about their culture. Perhaps your best move is to perfect your skill in the use of their language and really learn to think and act as a native. I am not sure anyone from the United States can do this. You and I were raised in the folds of Western civilization, which has very different institutions and behavior patterns from those you will encounter in the Near East. For instance, does one adhere to the ethical principles of the Saudis or to our own? Do they have the same trust and reliance on people that we do? Will they always react as we here are accustomed to do? Is social responsibility thought of in the same terms? What intentions and actions on your part will be well received by your suppliers, your customers, your competitors, and public figures?

"You know, I suppose that what is really on my mind is that we don't really know at what point there may be a conflict between our two cultures, or when it occurs, what choice you will make."

1. If you were James Pruitt, how would you go about finding out what the local business customs in Saudi Arabia are? What other environmental factors would you look for? How would you respond to them?

2. Suppose you found that it is customary not to lay off employees when work slackens. What would you do?

3. Suppose you found that it is normal business practice to give government employees a small amount of money when they help your people to get something through a department or clear up some paperwork jams. Would you do the same thing? Why or why not?

CASE 25-2
HONDA MOVES TO THE UNITED STATES[39]

Honda has debunked the auto industry's claim that "nobody can make an economy car in the United States at a profit." Not only is Honda's plant in Marysville, Ohio, profitable, it is said, but its cars are also as well built as those made in Japan.

Since Honda holds only a relatively small share of the Japanese car market, it needed an outlet to grow. In the early 1970s, when gas became scarce and expensive, Honda introduced its fuel-efficient cars in the United States. Strong demand and growing trade friction convinced Honda that it needed to repeat the strategy that worked for its motorcycles: Build a U.S. operation. The first cars rolled out in 1983—the year quotas became effective. In 1985, Honda outsold both Nissan and Toyota and became the fourth largest car manufacturer in the United States.

The Marysville plant is not demonstrably more automated than American factories, but it works differently. All employees are treated as equals. Workers are chosen for their team skills as well as their expertise. A quarter of the first employees spent up to 3 months in Honda's plant in Japan. When they returned, they taught their coworkers how to assemble cars in teams.

New workers spend several weeks practicing on training cars before they are assigned to a team. Team members trade jobs and learn as many tasks as they can. Team leaders check the workmanship and help the team in any way they can (solving problems, replacing an absent member, and so on).

Honda attributes its success to workers who are willing to work hard for the company. The "equal partnership" gives employees a stake in the company. Mr. Honda believes that all employees are equally important. Everyone, including the plant manager, wears coveralls and shares the facilities (same lunchroom, washrooms, parking). All employees can help making decisions. Initially, workers were surprised that their supervisors asked them for advice.

The workers are very proud of their work. They like working at Honda even though they earn roughly 20 percent less than other U.S. auto workers. Honda's labor costs are about 60 percent lower than the industry average because it has a lower overhead per worker.

Honda expects suppliers to establish the same quality standards it uses. It was willing to help U.S. parts suppliers that did not meet them. Those who insisted that Honda could simply return defective parts were replaced by Japanese suppliers. Some of them have built plants near Marysville, which, in turn, has helped Honda minimize inventory.

Although most U.S. manufacturers barely break even on compacts, Honda earns a handsome profit on each car, and it sells every car it makes. And while this is only half the profit Honda earns on the cars it imports from Japan, it expects the difference to narrow as the workers in the U.S. plant learn to be more efficient.

Now that the company is well established in the U.S. car market, Honda plans to double its U.S. capacity and build luxury cars, which should be more profitable than the less expensive cars. Honda attempts to avoid problems from its low-cost image by selling luxury cars under another name—Acura—through different dealerships. Far from importing the large, old-fashioned Japanese luxury cars, Honda is developing "European-style" models specifically for the U.S. market. European styling has two advantages: It appeals to the growing number of young professionals, and the cars are small enough that they can be built on Honda's existing compact car production lines.

1. Why did Honda build a plant in the United States (what were the objectives)? How is the plan of building a plant in the United States affecting the company in Japan? What problems or advantages might the U.S. operation give Honda in the future?

2. Why is Honda able to build economy cars in the United States when American car manufacturers could not? What advantages does Honda have over the American companies?

3. How much of Honda's success is due to its policies? How much is due to nonmanagerial factors?

4. Apply the steps in planning to the case.

REFERENCES

1. Richard N. Farmer, in Joseph W. McGuire (ed.), *Contemporary Management—Issues and Viewpoints* (Englewood Cliffs, N.J.: Prentice-Hall, 1974), p. 302.

2. For a discussion of the Economic Development Model see Karen Paul and Robert Barbato, "The Multinational Corporation in the Less Developed Country: The Economic Development Model versus the North–South Model," *Academy of Management Review* (January 1985), pp. 8–14.

3. The concern for productivity is shown by the many books on this subject. Rusty S. Byrne reviews eleven such books in the *Harvard Business Review* (September–October, 1981), pp. 36–42. In addition, the author discusses newsletters and articles dealing with productivity. Robert N. Mefford found that in a multinational firm operating thirty plants in Europe, Australia, Canada, Latin America, and Asia the most important factors influencing productivity were managerial performance, skills of workers, and the aspect of learning by doing. See his article "Determinants of Productivity Differences in International Manufacturing," *Journal of International Business Studies* (Spring 1986), pp. 63–82.

4. We will discuss Japanese management practices later in this chapter.

5. "Europe's New Managers—Going Global with a U.S. Style," *Business Week* (May 24, 1982), pp. 116–122.

6. Thomas Moore, "Managers: Russia's New Elite," *Fortune* (Nov. 25, 1985). John Pearson, "How a Soviet Manager Can Start Thinking for Himself," *Business Week* (Nov. 11, 1985), p. 93. Another indication of Soviet interest in management is the effort of translating a previous edition of this book into the Russian language.

7. David A. Heenan, *The Re-United States of America* (Reading, Mass.: Addison-Wesley Publishing Company, 1983).

8. Sam C. Hsieh, "A Sequential and Integrated Approach to Economic Development," *Academy of International Business Southeast Asia Regional Conference,* Taipei, 1986.

9. Dexter C. Dunphy, "The Comparative Study of Managerial Behavior in Eastasia and the West," in Ryine T. Hsieh and Steven A. Scherling (eds.), *Proceedings of the Academy of International Business Southeast Asia Regional Conference,* Taipei, 1986.

10. Richard N. Farmer and Barry M. Richman, *Comparative Management and Economic Progress* (Homewood, Ill.: Richard D. Irwin, 1965); Barry M. Richman, "Empirical Testing of a Comparative and International Management Research Model," *Proceedings of the 27th Annual Meeting of the Academy of Management* (Dec. 27–29, 1967), pp. 34–65. Another pioneer and major contributor is Professor Negandhi. See Anant R. Negandhi and B. D. Estafen, "A Research Model to Determine the Applicability of American Know–How in Differing Cultures and/or Environments," *Academy of Management Journal* (December 1967), pp. 309–318.

11. See, for example, Thomas F. O'Boyle, "German Technology Gains on U.S., Japan," *The Wall Street Journal* (Dec. 15, 1986); Peter F. Drucker, "What We Can Learn from the Germans," *The Wall Street Journal* (Mar. 6, 1986).

12. "France—An Electronics Plan with Global Ambitions," *Business Week* (May 31, 1982), p. 39.

13. "France Makes Renault Its Model," *Business Week* (May 31, 1982), pp. 48–57. More recently, however, the French government is considering withdrawing support for Renault and other business firms. See Shawn Tully, "Alain Madelin—Giving French Business a New Message: Sink or Swim," *Fortune* (Jan. 5, 1987), pp. 39–40.

14. See also Simcha Ronen, *Comparative and Multinational Management* (New York: John Wiley & Sons, 1986), chap. 9; David Heenan, *The Re-United States of America* (1983), chap. 1.

15. See Simcha Ronen, *Comparative and Multinational Management* (1986). See also the extensive studies by Geert Hofstede, such as "The Cultural Relativity of Organizational Practices and Theories," *Journal of International Business Studies,* vol. 14, no. 2 (1983), pp. 75–90; "Motivation, Leadership and Organization: Do American Theories Apply Abroad?" *Organization Dynamics,* no. 9 (1983), pp. 42–63; *Culture's Consequences: International Differences in Work Related Values* (Beverly Hills: Sage, 1980).

16. "American Culture Is Often a Puzzle for Foreign Managers in the U.S.," *The Wall Street Journal* (Feb. 12, 1986).

17. Tai K. Oh, "Japanese-Management—A Critical Review," *Academy of Management Review* (January 1976), pp. 14–25.

18. The information for Table 25-1 is based on a variety of sources:
Miscellaneous aspects of managing in Japan and the United States: Japanese managerial practices have been widely discussed in the literature and at professional meetings such as the Japanese-United States Business Conference held in Tokyo, Japan, April 4–8, 1983; the Pan-Pacific Conference held in Honolulu, Hawaii, March 26–28, 1984, in Seoul Korea, May 13–15, 1985, and in Taipei, Taiwan, May 17–20, 1987. See also Fred Luthans, Harriette S. McCaul, and Nancy G. Dodd, "Organizational Commitment: A Comparison of American, Japanese, and Korean Employees," *Academy of Management*

Journal (March 1985), pp. 213–219; Ikujiro Nonaka and Johny K. Johansson, "Japanese Management: What About the 'Hard' Skills?" *Academy of Management Review* (April 1985), pp. 181–191; "Remaking Japan," Special Report *Business Week* (July 13, 1987), pp. 48–64; Tai K. Oh, "Japanese Management—A Critical Review," *Academy of Management Review* (January 1976), pp. 14–25.

Planning aspects have been discussed by Ichiro Hattori, "A Proposition on Efficient Decision-Making in the Japanese Corporation," *Columbia Journal of World Business* (Summer 1978), pp. 7–15; Richard Tanner Johnson and William G. Ouchi, "Made in America (Under Japanese Management)," *Harvard Business Review* (September–October 1974), pp. 61–69; William G. Ouchi and Alfred M. Jaeger, "Type Z Organization: Stability in the Midst of Mobility," *Academy of Management Review* (April 1978), pp. 305–314; Steven C. Wheelwright, "Operations as Strategy Lessons From Japan," *Stanford GSB* (Fall 1981–82), pp. 3–7.

Aspects of **organizing** have been discussed as follows: Johnson and Ouchi, "Made in America" (1974); William G. Ouchi and Raymond L. Price, "Hierarchies, Clans, and Theory Z: A New Perspective on Organization Development," *Organizational Dynamics* (Autumn 1978), pp. 25–44; Michael Y. Yoshino, "Emerging Japanese Multinational Enterprises," in E. F. Vogel (ed.), *Modern Japanese Organization and Decision Making* (Berkeley: University of California Press, 1975), pp. 146–166.

Staffing aspects have been discussed by Terutomo Ozawa, "Japanese World of Work: An Interpretive Survey," *MSU Business Topics* (Spring 1980); Arthur M. Whitehill and Shin-ichi Takezawa, "Workplace Harmony: Another Japanese 'Miracle'?" *Columbia Journal of World Business* (Fall 1978), pp. 25–39.

Leading has been discussed by Peter F. Drucker, "Behind Japan's Success," *Harvard Business Review* (January–February 1981); Lee Smith, "Japan's Autocratic Managers," *Fortune* (Jan. 7, 1985), pp. 56–65; Hirotake Takeuchi, "Productivity: Learning from the Japanese," *California Management Review* (Summer 1981), pp. 5–20.

Controlling has been discussed as follows: Joel Dreyfuss, "Networking: Japan's Latest Computer Craze," *Fortune* (July 7, 1986), pp. 94–96; Dexter Hutchins, "Having a Hard Time with Just-in-Time," *Fortune* (June 9, 1986), pp. 64–66; Kazuo Koike, "Will America Regain Its Competitiveness?" *Economic Eye* (March 1981), pp. 26–32.

19. This discussion is based on William G. Ouchi, *Theory Z* (Reading, Mass.: Addison-Wesley Publishing Company, 1981).

20. "Life at IBM—Rules and Discipline and Praise Shape IBMer's Taut World," *The Wall Street Journal* (Apr. 8, 1982), pp. 1, 14.

21. "The Japanese Manager Meets the American Worker," *Business Week* (Aug. 20, 1984), pp. 128–129.

22. "The Japanese Manager" (1984).

23. An increasing number of overseas ventures combine direct investment, licensing, and trade. Farok J. Contractor, "A Generalized Theorem for Joint-Venture and Licensing Negotiations," *Journal of International Business Studies* (Summer 1985), pp. 23–50.

24. Alan Farnham and Carrie Gottlieb, "The World's Largest Industrial Corporations," *Fortune* (Aug. 4, 1986), p. 171.

25. David A. Heenan and Howard V. Perlmutter, *Multinational Organization Development* (Reading, Mass.: Addison-Wesley Publishing Company, 1979), chap. 2.

26. "ITALTEL's New Chief Gets What She Wants," *Business Week* (Apr. 30, 1984), p. 51; Robert Ball, "Italy's Most Talked-About Executive," *Fortune* (Apr. 2, 1984), pp. 99–102; Marisa Bellisario, "The Turnaround at ITALTEL," *Long Range Planning*, vol. 18, no. 6 (1985), pp. 21–24.

27. Kenneth Labich, "America's International Winners," *Fortune* (Apr. 14, 1986), pp. 34–46.

28. Howard V. Perlmutter and David A. Heenan, "Cooperate to Compete Globally,"

Harvard Business Review (March–April 1986), pp. 136–152; Jonathan B. Levine and John A. Byrne, "Corporate Odd Couples," *Business Week* (July 21, 1986), pp. 100–105.

29. Doron P. Levin, "GM-Toyota Venture Will Test Ability Of Workers in U.S. to Match Japanese," *The Wall Street Journal* (Apr. 5, 1985); William J. Holstein, "Japan, U.S.A.," *Business Week* (July 14, 1986), pp. 45–46.

30. For additional strategies of Philips, see Jonathan Kapstein, "The Big Two of Consumer Electronics: Squeezed—but Fighting Back," *Business Week* (Dec. 30, 1985), pp. 62–64.

31. See also Simcha Ronen, *Comparative and Multinational Management* (1986), chap. 8.

32. The information has been drawn from a variety of sources, including a speech by Heinz Ruhnau, the *Lufthansa Jahrbuch '85* (Cologne, West Germany: Deutsche Lufthansa Aktiengesellschaft, 1985/86); Susan Carey, "Lufthansa Jettisons Bureaucratic Baggage," *The Wall Street Journal* (Sept. 30, 1986).

33. See also Stephen J. Carroll and Dennis J. Gillen, "Are the Classical Management Functions Useful in Describing Managerial Work?" *Academy of Management Review* (January 1987), pp. 38–51.

34. See, for example, Michael E. Porter, *Competitive Advantage* (New York: The Free Press, 1985).

35. One example of a book with extensive text material, readings, and cases is George A. Steiner, John B. Miner, and Edmund R. Gray, *Management Policy and Strategy*, 3d ed. (New York: Macmillan Publishing Company, 1986); another book with extensive text material is Fred R. David, *Fundamentals of Strategic Management* (Columbus: Merrill Publishing Company, 1986); an example of a book with many international cases is Thomas J. McNichols, *Policymaking and Executive Action*, 6th ed. (New York: McGraw-Hill Book Company, 1983).

36. A high degree of motivation can also be obtained through self-leadership. See, for example, Charles C. Manz, "Self-Leadership: Toward an Expanded Theory of Self-Influence Processes in Organizations," *Academy of Management Review* (July 1986), pp. 585–600.

37. Laurie Baum, "Korea's Newest Import: Management Style," *Business Week* (Jan. 19, 1987), p. 66.

38. *Global Competition—The New Reality*, The Report of the President's Commission on Industrial Competitiveness, vol. 1 (January 1985), Washington, D.C.

39. This case has been drawn from several sources, including: Drexel Burnham Lambert auto analyst David B. Healy, quoted in "AMC's U.S. Car Plant May Go on the Scrap Heap," *Business Week* (June 3, 1985), p. 42; "Meanwhile Back in Marysville," *Forbes* (Mar. 12, 1984), p. 127; W. J. Hampton, "Detroit Beware: Japan Is Ready to Sell Luxury," *Business Week* (Dec. 9, 1985), p. 118; "Here Comes Honda" (interview with Tetsuo Chino), *Barron's* (Dec. 2, 1985), p. 13; Thomas Hout, Michael E. Porter, and Eileen Rudden, "How Global Companies Win Out," *Harvard Business Review* (September–October 1982), pp. 98–108; Faye Rice, "America's New No. 4 Automaker—Honda," *Fortune* (Oct. 28, 1985), p. 30.

FOR FURTHER INFORMATION

Abegglen, James C., and George Stalk, Jr. "The Japanese Corporations as Competitor," *California Management Review* (Spring 1986), pp. 9–27.

Dickson, Douglas N. "Self-Help from Japan" (review of books on Japan), *Harvard Business Review* (January–February 1986), pp. 8–20.

Fanning, W. R., and C. B. Gilmore. "Developing a Strategy for International Business," *Long Range Planning* (June 1986), pp. 81–85.

Farmer, Richard N. (ed.). *Advances in International Comparative Management,* vol. 1 (Greenwich, Ct.: JAI Press, 1984).

Gladwin, Thomas N., and Ingo Walter. *Multinationals under Fire: Lessons in the Management of Conflict* (New York: John Wiley & Sons, 1980).

Grosse, Robert, and Gerald W. Perritt (eds.). *International Business Curricula—A Global Survey* (Cleveland: Academy of International Business, 1980).

Koontz, Harold. "A Model for Analyzing the Universality and Transferability of Management," in Harold Koontz, Cyril O'Donnell, and Heinz Weihrich (eds.), *Management: A Book of Readings,* 5th ed. (New York: McGraw-Hill Book Company, 1980), pp. 88–97.

Kujawa, Duane. "Technology Strategy and Industrial Relations: Case Studies of Japanese Multinationals in the United States," *Journal of International Business Studies* (Winter 1983), pp. 9–22.

Main, Jeremy. "The Trouble with Managing Japanese-Style," *Fortune* (Apr., 1984), pp. 50–56.

Negandhi, Anant R. *International Management* (Newton, Mass.: Allyn and Bacon, 1987).

Porter, Michael E. "Changing Patterns of International Competition," *California Management Review* (Winter 1985), pp. 9–40.

Schonberger, Richard J. *Japanese Manufacturing Techniques: Nine Hidden Lessons in Simplicity* (New York: The Free Press, 1982).

Sullivan, Jeremiah J. "A Critique of Theory Z," *Academy of Management Review* (January 1983), pp. 132–142.

Yang, Charles Y. "Management Styles: American Vis-à-Vis Japanese," in Harold Koontz, Cyril O'Donnell, and Heinz Weihrich (eds.), *Management* (1980), pp. 98–104.

Yang, Charles Y. "Demystifying Japanese Management Practices," *Harvard Business Review* (November–December 1984), pp. 172–182.

Glossary

Glossary

Absoluteness of responsibility See *Responsibility, absoluteness of*.

Administrators See *Managers*.

Approach to management, contingency or situational An analysis of management that emphasizes the fact that what managers do in practice depends upon a given set of circumstances or the "situation" and that there is no single "best way" to manage.

Approach to management, cooperative social system An analysis of management as a study of human relationships in a cooperative social system.

Approach to management, decision theory An analysis of management that concentrates on rational decision making as the core of the managerial task.

Approach to management, empirical or case An analysis of management as a study of experience from instances of managing.

Approach to management, group behavior An analysis of management as a study in group behavior patterns.

Approach to management, interpersonal behavior An analysis of management as a study of interpersonal relations.

Approach to management, managerial roles A means of analyzing management by observing what managers actually do and from such observations come to conclusions as to what managerial activities (or roles) are.

Approach to management, mathematical, or "management science" An analysis of management primarily as a matter of developing mathematical models of managerial decision areas.

Approach to management, McKinsey's 7-S framework An analysis of management which organizes managerial knowledge around the following categories: strategy, structure, systems, style, staff, shared values, and skills.

Approach to management, operational An analysis of management which draws together knowledge that is unique to managing and knowledge from other fields pertinent to managing, and relates it to the task of managing in a way most useful to the managerial practitioner; it is thus in part eclectic and in part a summary of the central core of knowledge which exists in management situations.

Approach to management, systems approach An analysis of management which emphasizes looking at managerial knowledge from the point of view of systems.

Approaches to management, sociotechnical systems An analysis of management viewing managerial situations as involving a combination of interacting social and technical systems.

Art Practice; skill acquired by experience.

Assessment center A technique to aid in the selection and evaluation of potential managers whereby candidates are subjected to various tests and exercises and their performance is observed and evaluated by assessors.

Authority, organizational See *Organizational authority*.

Authority, parity with responsibility The principle that responsibility for action should not be greater than authority delegated, nor should it be less. Authority is the discretionary power to carry out assignments and responsibility is the obligation owed a delegant to accomplish these activities.

Board of directors A plural executive, that is, a committee, with power to exercise authority and make decisions, which normally stands at the top of a corporation and is charged by law with the responsibility of "managing" the corporation.

Boundaries See *Systems, boundaries*.

Bounded rationality Rational action limited because of lack of information, lack of time, or ability to analyze alternatives in the light of a goal sought, unclear goals, or the human tendency not to take risks in making a decision, to "play it safe." See also *Satisficing*.

Brainstorming An approach to improve problem

discovery and solving by encouraging unfettered suggestions and ideas, usually from a group of individuals.

Break-even point analysis   Charting and analyzing relationships, usually between sales and expenses, to determine at what size or volume point an operation breaks even between a loss and a profit; it can be used in any problem area where marginal effects can be pinpointed.

Budget   A statement of plans and expected results expressed in numerical terms: a "numberized" program.

Budget, program   See *Program budgeting.*

Budget summary   A master summary of operating and capital budgets, usually with a forecast income statement and balance sheet.

Budgets, variable or flexible   See *Variable budgets.*

Budgets, Zero-base   See *Zero-base budgeting.*

Business units   See *Strategic business units.*

Centralization of authority   The tendency to restrict delegation of decision making in an organization structure, usually by holding authority at or near the top of the organization structure.

Chart of approval authorizations   A technique by which the various authority delegations of an enterprise are charted in a matrix form showing the nature of the subjects over which authority exists and the organizational positions where decision-making authority rests.

Commitment principle   All logical planning should cover a period of time in the future necessary to foresee, through a series of actions, the fulfillment of commitments involved in a current decision.

Committee   A group of persons to whom, as a group, some matter is committed for purposes of information, advice, interchange of ideas, or decision.

Communication   The transfer of information from one person to another with the information being understood by both the sender and the receiver.

Comparative management   The study and analysis of management in different environments and in various countries.

Completed staff work   Implies presentation of a clear recommendation to a superior based upon full consideration of a problem, clearance with persons importantly affected, suggestions about avoiding any difficulties involved, and, often, the preparation of necessary paperwork for implementing recommendations so that the receiving person can accept or reject the proposal without further study, long conferences, or unnecessary work.

Composite strategies   A group of strategies in various related areas that a company or other enterprises may have.

Computer-aided design (CAD)   The application of computer technology to design products much more quickly than with the traditional paper-and-pencil approach.

Computer-aided manufacturing (CAM)   The application of computer technology to the manufacturing process. The ultimate goal for some companies is "computer-integrated manufacturing," which computerizes the total manufacturing process.

Concepts   Mental images of anything formed by generalization from particulars; for example, a word or term.

Contingency approach to leadership   A theory that leadership depends upon the group task situation and the degree to which the leader's style, personality, and approach fit the group.

Contingency management   Managing which recognizes differences or contingencies in people, at various times and in actual situations; also referred to as "situational management"; an approach that emphasizes that there can be no "one best way" in all situations.

Contingency model of leadership effectiveness   A leadership model developed by Fred Fiedler that postulates that a leader's effectiveness depends on three variables: (1) how well a leader is accepted by subordinates, (2) the degree to which subordinates' positions are routine and clearly spelled out in contrast to being vague and undefined, and (3) the formal authority in the position occupied by a leader.

Contingency planning   Planning for possible future environments which are not expected to occur but which may occur; if this possible future is widely different from that premised, alternative premises and plans are required.

Contingency strategies   Strategies developed to be used when unforeseen events or circumstances may make a selected strategy obsolete or unsuitable.

Control of overall performance   Control designed to measure the total performance of an enterprise, an integrated division of it, or a major program or project.

Control process   In managing, the basic process involves (1) establishing standards, (2) measuring performance against standards, and (3) correcting for undesirable deviations.

Controlling   The managerial function of measuring and correcting performance of activities of subordinates in order to assure that enterprise objectives and plans are being accomplished.

Cooperative system A system, as perceived by Chester Barnard, as one whose purpose is cooperation and which comprises physical, biological, social, and psychological elements.

Coordination Achieving harmony of individual and group efforts toward the accomplishment of group purposes and objectives.

Corporate social responsibility There is no complete agreement about the definition of this term. In a broad context it means that corporations consider seriously the impact of the enterprise's actions on society.

Cost effectiveness analysis Seeking the best ratio of benefits and costs; this means, for example, finding the least costly way of reaching an objective, or getting the greatest value for given expenditures.

Creativity The ability to develop new concepts, ideas, and problem solutions.

Decentralization of authority The tendency to disperse decision-making authority in an organization structure.

Decentralization of performance The geographic dispersal of operations in an enterprise.

Decision making The selection from among alternatives of a course of action; a rational selection of a course of action.

Decision support systems (DSS) The application of computers to facilitate the decision-making process of semistructured tasks.

Decision trees An approach toward seeing risks and probabilities in a problem situation involving uncertainty, or chance events, by sketching in the form of a "tree" decision points, chance events, and the probabilities involved in various courses that might be undertaken.

Delegation of authority The vesting of decision-making discretion in a subordinate.

Delegation of authority, process of The determination of results expected from a subordinate, the assignment of tasks, the delegation of authority for accomplishing these tasks, and the holding of people responsible for the accomplishment of such tasks.

Delphi technique A technique normally used for forecasting such future events and conditions as technological developments by obtaining estimates of experts in a field and feeding back summaries of these estimates for additional estimates by those experts, until a reasonable degree of convergence in estimates is obtained.

Department A distinct area, division, or branch of an enterprise over which a manager has authority for the performance of specified activities and results.

Departmentation by customer The grouping of activities around customers.

Departmentation by function The grouping of activities in departments in accordance with the characteristic functions an enterprise undertakes; for example, in a manufacturing company—marketing, production, engineering, and finance.

Departmentation by process or equipment The grouping of activities around a process or type of equipment used, such as electronic data-processing or painting departments.

Departmentation by product The grouping of activities around a product or product line.

Departmentation by territory The grouping of activities by territorial segments; geographic departmentation.

Differentiation A characteristic of an open system, and a social system in particular, by which it tends to become more specialized in its structure and behavior patterns.

Direct control Control techniques designed to identify and correct for deviations in plans.

Distribution logistics An operations research optimizing model that treats the entire materials flow system of an enterprise—from sales forecasting through purchasing and processing of materials, inventorying them, to shipping of finished goods to sales warehouses—as a single system.

Effectiveness The achievement of objectives; the achievement of desired effects.

Efficiency The achievement of the ends with the least amount of resources; the accomplishment of objectives at the least cost or other unsought consequences.

Elaboration The tendency of an open system, and a social system in particular, to enlarge its boundaries or create a new suprasystem with wider boundaries.

Enterprise self-audit The making by an enterprise of an audit, or appraisal, of its position, where it is heading under present programs, what its objectives should be, and whether revised plans are needed to meet these objectives.

Entrepreneurs People with the ability to see an opportunity, to obtain the necessary capital, labor, and other inputs, and to know how to put together an operation successfully, and with the willingness to take the personal risk of success or failure.

Environment, economic That environment of managers which has to do with such elements as capital, materials, labor availability, quality, and price; price levels, productivity, availability of high-quality entrepreneurs and managers, government fiscal and tax policy, customers, and demands for goods and services.

Environment, ethical   That environment of managers which has to do with generally accepted sets of standards of personal conduct. See also *Ethics*.

Environment, political   That environment of managers which has to do with the complex of laws, regulations, and government agencies and their actions.

Environment, social   That environment of managers which has to do with the attitudes, desires, expectations, degrees of intelligence, beliefs, and customs of people in any given group or society; social forces.

Environment, technological   That environment of managers which has to do with such elements as knowledge of ways of doing things; inventions; and techniques in the areas of processes, machines, and tools.

Environmental forecasting   Forecasting the future environment—economic, technological, social, ethical, and political—as it may affect the enterprise.

Equity theory   Refers to the individuals' subjective judgments about the equity or fairness of the reward they receive in relation to their inputs (which include factors such as effort, experience, and education) in comparison with others.

Ethics   A system of moral principles or values dealing with moral judgment, duty, and obligation; the discipline concerned with what is good or bad, right or wrong. See also *Environment, ethical*.

Executives   See *Managers*.

Expectancy theory of motivation   The theory that people will be motivated by their expectancy that a particular action on their part will lead to a desired outcome.

Feedback   An informational input in a system transmitting messages of system operation to indicate whether the system is operating as planned; information concerning any type of planned operation relayed to the responsible person for evaluation.

Feedforward control   A control system that attempts to identify future deviations from plans, early enough to take action before the deviations occur, by developing a model of system or process inputs, monitoring these inputs, and taking action in time to prevent undesired or unplanned system outputs.

Field theory of motivation   Psychologist Lewin's theory that motivations depend on organizational climate and must be looked upon as an element in a larger field of restraining and driving forces.

Flexibility principle   The more that flexibility (the ability to change direction without undue cost, embarrassment, or friction) can be built into plans, the less the danger of losses incurred by unexpected events.

Functional authority   The right or power inherent in a position to issue instructions or approve actions of persons in positions not reporting directly to the person holding such authority; normally it is a limited line-type of authority applicable only to specialized areas and representing a delegation to a specialist by a superior manager with authority over both the position given functional authority and the position subjected to this authority. For example, a company controller is ordinarily given functional authority to prescribe the system of accounting throughout the company, but this specialized authority is really a delegation from the chief executive.

Functions of managers   See *Managers, functions of; Managers, task of*.

Gantt chart   A technique for planning and control developed by Henry L. Gantt showing by bars on a chart the time requirements for the various tasks, or "events," of a production or other program.

Goal of managers   See *Managers, goal of*.

Goals   See *Objectives*.

Grapevine   A kind of informal organization network over which information tends to flow, usually regularly, between persons who know and trust each other.

Hierarchy of needs   Psychologist Abraham Maslow's theory that basic human needs exist in an ascending order of importance (physiological, security or safety, affiliation or acceptance, esteem, and self-actualization) and that once a lower-level need is satisfied, actions appealing to it cease to motivate.

Homeostasis, dynamic   The characteristic of a system whereby it is constantly in motion, with a tendency to seek equilibrium at various changing levels.

Human asset accounting   Programs attempting to measure the value, and its changes, of investment in human assets of an enterprise.

Hygiene factors in motivation   Psychologist Herzberg's theory that certain human needs motivate and others merely cause dissatisfaction if they are not met; in other words, the meeting of this latter class of needs is a "maintenance" or "hygiene" factor; these are such factors in a work situation as salary, company policy and administration, quality of supervision, working conditions, interpersonal relations, status, and job security.

Informal organization Generally, patterns of human behavior and relationships coexisting with, or lying outside, the formal organization structure. According to Professor Keith Davis it is "a network of personal and social relations not established or required by the formal organization but arising spontaneously as people associate with one another."

Job design The structuring of a job in terms of content, function, and relationships. It may focus on individual positions or on work groups.

Job enrichment Programs of building into jobs a high sense of meaning, challenge, and potential for accomplishment.

Just-in-time inventory system (JIT) The supplier delivers the components and parts to the production line "just in time" to be assembled. Other names for this or similar methods are "zero inventory" and "stockless production."

Leadership continuum The concept advanced by Tannenbaum and Schmidt in which leadership is seen as involving a variety of styles ranging from highly boss-centered to highly subordinate-centered, depending on situations and personalities.

Leadership, definition of Influence, or the art or process of influencing people so that they strive willingly and enthusiastically toward the accomplishment of group goals.

Leading The function of managers involving the process of influencing people so that they will contribute to organization and group goals.

Limiting factor, principle of In choosing from among alternatives, the more individuals can recognize and solve for those factors which are limiting or critical to the attainment of the desired goal, the more clearly, accurately, and easily they can select the most favorable alternative.

Line An authority relationship in organizational positions where one person (a manager) has responsibility for the activities of another person (the subordinate). It is commonly, but erroneously, thought of as a department or a person, and not a relationship; it is also commonly, but inaccurately, thought of as the major departments of an enterprise believed to be most closely contributing to the achieving of enterprise objectives, such as marketing and production in a manufacturing company.

Linear programming A technique for determining the optimum combination of limited re-

sources to obtain a desired goal; it is based on the assumption that a linear relationship exists between variables and that the limits of variables can be determined.

Mainframe computer A full-scale computer that is capable of handling huge amounts of data. Some of these "supercomputers" are used for engineering, simulation, and the manipulation of large data bases.

Management The process of designing and maintaining an environment in which individuals work together in groups accomplish efficiently selected aims.

Management as an art The use of underlying knowledge (science) and application of it to realities in a situation, usually with blend or compromise, to obtain practical results; managing is an art but management is more properly used to refer to the body of knowledge—science—underlying this art.

Management as a science Organized knowledge—concepts, theory, principles, and techniques—underlying the practice of managing; science systematically explains phenomena in managing, as it does in any field.

Management auditing Auditing the quality of managers through appraising them as individual managers and appraising the quality of the total system of managing in an enterprise.

Management information system A formal system to gather, integrate, compare, analyze, and disperse information internal and external to the enterprise in a timely, effective, and efficient manner.

Management inventory A technique, usually by use of a chart, whereby managers in an enterprise are designated as promotable now, promotable in one year, have potential for future promotion, are satisfactory but not promotable, or should be terminated. Another term for "inventory chart" is "management replacement chart."

Management techniques Ways of doing things in managing.

Management theory jungle The term applied by Harold Koontz in 1961 to identify the existence of a variety of schools of, or approaches to, management theory and knowledge. He found just six such schools or approaches in 1961, but in 1979 identified eleven. He found that the schools or approaches tended to vary in their semantics and their view of management, and approached the theory of management from different specialists' points of view.

Management training The provision of opportunities through various approaches and programs to improve a person's knowledge of, and proficiency in, the managerial task.

Manager development The progress a person makes in learning how to manage effectively.

Managerial appraisal Evaluating the performance of managers in their positions, ideally evaluating performance in setting and achieving verifiable objectives and performance as a manager.

Managerial environment See *Environment, economic; Environment, ethical; Environment, political; Environment, social; Environment, technological.*

Managerial grid A way of analyzing leadership styles, developed by Blake and Mouton, whereby leaders are classified on a grid with the two dimensions of concern for people and concern for production.

Managerial know-how Managerial knowledge applied effectively in practice; it includes both knowledge of the science underlying managing and the artful ability to apply it to realities.

Managers Those who undertake the tasks and functions of managing, at any level in any kind of enterprise.

Managers, functions of Planning, organizing, staffing, leading, and controlling.

Managers, goal of To so establish and maintain an environment for performance that individuals will contribute to group objectives with the least cost—whether money, time, effort, materials, discomfort, or dissatisfaction—to create a surplus value, or "profit."

Managers, task of The design and maintenance of an environment for the effective and efficient performance of individuals working together in groups toward the accomplishment of preselected missions and objectives.

Managing by objectives Programs of basing much of managerial planning, operation, and appraisal on having each manager set objectives in verifiable terms (with the superior's approval) and assessing his or her performance against the achievement of these objectives. Sometimes called management by objectives or "MBO." More recently, MBO is seen as a system of managing that includes key managerial activities in planning, organizing, staffing, leading, and controlling.

Manufacturing automation protocol (MAP) A network of machines and various office devices hooked together. General Motors, for example, has been very active in linking robots with numerically controlled machine tools.

Matrix organization A form of organization in which two or more basic types of departmentation are combined; in engineering and marketing this is likely to be a combination of project (or product) and functional departments with one overlay-

ing the other; often referred to as "grid" organization structures, "project," or "product" management.

Microcomputer Smaller than the minicomputer; may be a desk computer, home computer, personal computer, portable computer, or a computer for a small business system.

Milestone budgeting Budgeting by breaking down a program or project into identifiable and controllable pieces, or "milestones."

Minicomputer Smaller than the mainframe computer but more powerful than the microcomputer. This kind of computer is often connected with peripheral equipment.

Missions, or purposes The basic function or task of an enterprise or agency or any department of it.

Motivators Forces that induce individuals to act or perform; forces that influence human behavior.

Motives The drives, desires, needs, wishes, and similar forces that channel human behavior toward goals. See *Equity theory, Expectancy theory of motivation, Field theory of motivation, Hierarchy of needs, Hygiene factors in motivation, Job enrichment. Job enrichment.*

Multinational corporations Corporations headquartered usually in one country, but having operations (usually at least manufacturing and marketing) in other countries.

Navigational change, principle of The more planning decisions commit for the future, the more important it is that managers periodically check on events and expectations and redraw plans as necessary to maintain a course of action toward a desired goal; this implies a willingness to change plans.

Objectives, or goals The ends toward which activity is aimed—the end points of planning.

Objectives, verifiable An objective is verifiable if, at some target date in the future, a person can look back with certainty and determine whether or not it has been accomplished; goals or objectives may be verifiable either if expressed quantitatively (i.e., in numbers) or qualitatively (a program with certain specific characteristics to be put into effect by a certain date).

Operational audit The regular and independent appraisal by a staff of internal auditors of the accounting, financial, and other operations of an enterprise.

Operational-management theory and science See *Approach to management, operational.*

Operations management Activities necessary to

produce and deliver a product or service; see also *Production management.*

Operations research The use of mathematical models to reflect the variables and constraints in a situation and their effect on a selected goal, ordinarily thought of as using optimizing models; the application of scientific method in a problem situation with a view to providing a quantitative basis for arriving at an optimum solution in terms of goals sought.

Organization A concept used in a variety of ways such as (1) a system or pattern of any set of relationships in any kind of undertaking, (2) an enterprise itself, (3) cooperation of two or more persons, (4) all behavior of all participants in a group, and (5) the intentional structure of roles in a formally organized enterprise.

Organization culture The general pattern of behavior, shared beliefs, and values that members of an organization have in common.

Organization development (OD) A systematic, integrated, and planned approach to improving the effectiveness of groups of people and of the whole organization; OD uses various techniques for identifying and solving problems.

Organizational authority The degree of discretion in organizational positions conferring on persons occupying these positions the right to use their judgment in decision making.

Organizational role An organizational position designed for individuals to fill; to be meaningful to people, it should incorporate (1) verifiable objectives, (2) a clear concept of the major duties or activities involved, (3) an understood area of discretion, or authority, (4) the availability of information and resources necessary to accomplish a task.

Organizing Establishing an intentional structure of roles for people to fill in an organization.

Parity of authority and responsibility See *Authority, parity with responsibility.*

Partial controls Controls designed to measure performance in a specific activity, such as quality, cash, production, or sales.

Path-goal approach to leadership effectiveness An approach that sees as the main function of the leader clarifying and setting goals with subordinates, helping them to find the best path for achieving the goals, and removing obstacles.

Peer rating Appraising of managers by other managers at the same or similar organizational level.

PERT (Program Evaluation and Review Technique) A time-event network analysis system in which the various events in a program or project are identified, with the planned time for each, and are placed in a network showing the relationships of each event to other events: from the sequence of interrelated events, the path of those events in which there is zero (or the least) slack time in terms of planned completion is the "critical path"; PERT/TIME systems deal only with time; PERT/COST systems introduce costs of each event and are usually combined with elapsed time of each event or series of events.

Peter Principle Principle enunciated by Laurence J. Peter and Raymond Hall that managers tend to be promoted until they reach the level of their incompetence.

Planning Selecting missions and objectives—and the strategies, policies, programs, and procedures for achieving them; decision making; the selection of a course of action from among alternatives.

Planning premises The planning assumptions—the expected environment in which plans will operate; they may be forecasts of the planning environment or basic policies and existing plans which will influence any given plan.

Planning premises, types of Premises may be internal or external to an enterprise, quantitative or qualitative, or controllable, uncontrollable, or semicontrollable.

Planning process A rational approach to setting and accomplishing an objective and evaluating alternatives in light of goals sought and against the environment of planning premises.

Plans, types of Purpose or missions, objectives, strategies, policies, procedures, rules, programs, and budgets.

Plural executive A committee, or group, which has the authority to execute, as a group, managerial functions.

Pluralistic society A society in which many organized groups present various interests. Each group has an impact on other groups, but no one group has an inordinate amount of power.

Policies General statements or understandings which guide thinking in decision making; the essence of policies is the existence of discretion, within certain limits, in guiding decision making.

Positive reinforcement Psychologist Skinner's theory that people are best motivated by properly designing their work environment, giving them prompt feedback on performance, and finding ways to help them and praise them for the good things they do.

Power The ability of individuals or groups to induce or influence the beliefs or actions of other persons or groups. Several kinds of power may be identified such as legitimate power, expertness, referent power, reward power, and coercive power.

Preference, or utility, theory The theory that individual attitudes toward risk will vary from statistical probabilities, with some individuals being willing only to take lower risks than indicated by probabilities ("risk averters") and others taking greater risks ("gamblers").

Principles Fundamental truths, or what are believed to be truths at a given time, explaining relationships between two or more sets of variables, usually an independent variable and a dependent variable; may be descriptive, explaining what will happen, or prescriptive (or normative), indicating what a person should do: in the latter case, principles reflect some scale of values, such as efficiency, and therefore imply value judgments.

Procedures Plans that establish a required method of handling future activities. They are guides to action; they detail the exact manner in which certain activities must be accomplished.

Production management Those activities necessary to manufacture products or create services. It includes activities such as purchasing, warehousing, transportation, and other operations to procure raw materials until the product or service is bought by the customer.

Productivity The output-input ratio within a time period with due consideration for quality.

Profit The surplus of sales dollars over expense dollars.

Profit and loss control A control technique designed to measure a division or other part of a business enterprise by calculating the total profit (or loss) performance of that entity.

Program budgeting A budgeting approach, used primarily by government agencies, emphasizing goals, the programs to achieve them, and budgetary allocations designed to support such programs.

Programs A complex of goals, policies, procedures, rules, task assignments, steps to be taken, resources to be employed, and other elements necessary to carry out a given course of action and normally supported by capital and operating budgets.

Promotion A change within the organization to a higher position with greater responsibilities and usually requiring more advanced skills and knowledge than the previous position. Promotion normally brings greater status and an increase in pay.

Promotion based on open competition The policy of filling positions or making promotions from the most qualified people available whether from inside or outside a given enterprise.

Promotion from within The practice of making all promotions in an enterprise from people within it if it is possible to do so.

Quality control circles (or quality circles) Participation of workers in solving work-related problems. Often several people, usually rank and file workers, are involved in solving the problems.

Quality of working life (QWL) Programs representing a systems approach to job design and job enrichment which will make jobs more interesting and challenging. QWL programs are closely associated with the sociotechnical systems approach.

Rationality Analysis requiring a clear goal, a clear understanding of alternatives by which a goal can be reached, an analysis and evaluation of alternatives in terms of the goal sought, needed information, and a desire to optimize.

Real-time information Information on events as they occur.

Recentralization of authority The recall of some or all authority previously delegated.

Recruitment of managers Attracting candidates for managerial positions in order to meet the objectives of the enterprise.

Responsibility The obligation owed by subordinates to their superiors for exercising authority delegated to them in a way to accomplish results expected.

Responsibility, absoluteness of The concept that, since responsibility is an obligation owed, it cannot be delegated.

Return-on-investment control A control technique designed to measure a division or other part of a business enterprise by looking on the profit made as a percentage of the investment in assets in that entity.

Risk analysis An approach to problem analysis which weighs risk in a situation by introducing probabilities to give a more accurate assessment of the risks involved.

Rules Required action or nonaction, allowing no discretion, e.g., "positively no smoking."

Sales forecast A prediction of expected sales, by product or service and price, for a period of time in the future; sales forecasts are both derived from plans and are major planning premises.

Satisficing A term used by Herbert A. Simon to denote the tendencies of managers, normally in instances of bounded rationality, in making decisions to pick a course of action that is deemed "good enough" under the circumstances. See *Bounded rationality*.

Scalar relationships Authority relationships are

said to be scalar when subordinates report to their immediate superiors and when their superiors report directly, as subordinates, to their superiors (i.e., in "scales"). In other words, the chain of command that runs from the top of an organization to its lowest ranks.

Science   Organized knowledge of pertinence to an area, usually an area of practice.

Scientific management   A term originally used as denoting the work and approach of F. W. Taylor and his associates in analyzing management. It implies that the methods of scientific inquiry, analysis, and summary can be applied to the activities of managers. It later implied time study and similar methods used by Taylor and his followers to analyze activities of people in organizations. Basically, it sought to develop (1) ways of increasing productivity by making work easier to perform and (2) methods for motivating people to take advantage of labor-saving techniques it developed. It may be summarized as (1) replacing rules of thumb with rules of science, (2) obtaining harmony rather than discord, (3) achieving cooperation rather than chaotic individualism, (4) working for maximum rather than restricted output, (5) developing workers to the fullest extent possible.

Sensitivity training   A form of training based on behavior of persons in groups and, through undirected group interchange, designed to make these persons more aware of their feelings and the feelings of others toward them.

Situational approach to leadership   The approach that studies leadership on the premise that it is strongly influenced by the situation from which the leader emerges and in which he or she operates.

Situational management   See *Contingency management*.

Social audit   An audit of the performance of an enterprise in those areas which have a significant social impact and importance.

Social responsibility of managers   The responsibility of managers, in carrying out their socially approved missions, to be responsive, to be congruent with, and to interact and live with the forces and elements of their social environment.

Social responsiveness   The ability of an enterprise to relate policies and operations to the environment that are beneficial to both the organization and the society.

Sociotechnical system   A system viewed as an interconnection of physical (technical) and social elements in an organization.

Span of control   See *Span of management*.

Span of management   The phenomenon that there is a limit to the number of persons a manager can supervise, even though this limit varies depending on situations and the competence of a manager.

Splintered authority   The situation where the total authority to accomplish a given result rests in more than one position and must be pooled, or combined, to make the required decision.

Staff   A relationship in an organizational position where an incumbent's task is to give some other person advice or counsel.

Staffing   Filling, and keeping filled, the positions in the organization structure with competent people. This is done through (1) defining work-force requirements, (2) inventorying the people available, (3) recruiting, (4) selecting candidates for positions, (5) placing candidates, (6) promoting, (7) appraising, (8) planning the career of, (9) compensating, and (10) training or otherwise developing people.

Strategic business units (SBUs)   A distinct form of organization, usually employed within a larger company, constructed around a product or service, so that it will receive the attention normally given a complete product or project organization structure. These units are expected to be handled as though they were independent businesses.

Strategies   General programs of action and deployment of resources to attain comprehensive objectives; the program of objectives of an organization and their changes, resources used to attain these objectives, and policies governing the acquisition, use, and disposition of these resources; the determination of the basic long-term objectives of an enterprise and the adoption of courses of action and allocation of resources necessary to achieve these goals.

Strategies, composite   See *Composite strategies*.

Strategies, contingency   See *Contingency strategies*.

Supervisors   Same as managers, but ordinarily used to apply to managers at the lowest level, or first line, of managing.

System, definition of   A set or assemblage of things connected, or interdependent and interacting so as to form a complex unity; a whole composed of parts in orderly arrangement according to some scheme or plan. For any system there must be boundaries that separate it from its environment. See *Cooperative system; Differentiation; Elaboration; Feedback; Homeostasis, dynamic; Sociotechnical system.*

Systems, boundaries   The demarcation lines or area definition separating a given system from its environment.

Systems, closed   Not having interactions with the system's environment.

Systems, open Having interaction with the system's environment and exchanging information, energy, or material with that environment.

Tactics Action plans by which strategies are implemented.

Task of the manager See *Managers, task of*.

Technology The sum total of knowledge of ways of doing things; it includes inventions, techniques, and the vast store of organized knowledge of how to do things.

Telecommuting A situation where a person can work at home at the computer terminal instead of commuting to work by car, public transportation, or other means.

Teleconference A group of people interacting with each other using audio and video media with moving or still pictures.

Theory The systematic grouping of interdependent concepts and principles which give a framework to, or tie together, significant knowledge.

Theory X and Theory Y Assumption about the nature of people as suggested by Douglas McGregor. For example, Theory X suggests that people dislike work and will avoid it if they can. On the other hand, Theory Y suggests, for instance, that the expenditure of physical and mental effort in work is as natural as play or rest.

Theory Z Several authors proposed theories using the letter "Z." In general, Theory Z refers to selected Japanese managerial practices adapted to the environment of the United States as suggested by William Ouchi. For example, one of the characteristics of Type Z organizations is the emphasis on interpersonal skills needed for group decision making.

Trait appraisals Appraising people, whether managers or nonmanagers, on the basis of personality traits and work-oriented characteristics.

Unity of command Having each subordinate report to only one superior. The principle of unity of command implies only that the more an individual reports to a single superior, the less the problem of conflict in instructions and the greater the feeling of personal responsibility for results.

Universality of management The concept that essential, or basic, management science, theory, principles, and concepts are applicable in any culture even though applications in practice may vary depending on cultural differences, contingencies, or situations.

Value engineering The analysis of the operation of a product or service, estimating the value of each operation, and attempting to improve the operation by trying to keep costs low at each step or part.

Variable budgets Budgets constructed by distinguishing between period costs (costs that vary only with time or remain fixed over time) and variable costs (costs that vary to some extent with the volume of enterprise output) and showing budgeted expenses of an organizational unit as they vary with volume.

Verifiable objectives See *Objectives, verifiable*.

Zero-base budgeting Budgeting in which enterprise programs are divided into "packages" comprising goals, activities, and needed resources, and costs are calculated for each package from the ground up.

Indexes

Name Index

Abegglen, James C., 652
Aburdene, Patricia, 180
Adam, Everett E., Jr., 564
Adams, J. Stacy, 421
Alderfer, Clayton P., 264
Altman, Steven, 385
Ansoff, H. Igor, 133
Anthony, Robert N., 538, 566
Argyris, Chris, 384, 478, 484
Armacost, Samuel, 589
Armstrong, J. Scott, 133
Asch, S. E., 259
Athos, A. G., 48
Austin, Larry M., 53
Austin, Nancy, 37
Avery, Sewell, 77
Axley, Stephen R., 484

Badawy, M. K., 384
Baker, Kenneth R., 53
Baker, Michael, 484
Banks, Robert L., 508
Barnard, Chester I., 23, 26, 33, 36,
    42, 155, 163, 180, 461
Bartlett, Christopher A., 180
Bartolomé, Fernando, 316
Bass, Bernard M., 155, 459
Beam, Alex, 54
Beam, R. D., 180

Bedeian, Arthur G., 180, 490
Behrman, Jack N., 384, 591
Bellisario, Marisa, 6, 447, 637
Bergerac, Michel C., 298
Birnbaum, Philip H., 180, 240
Blake, Robert R., 379, 445, 446
Blanchard, Kenneth H., 459
Boesky, Ivan S., 425
Bok, Derek, 615
Bolles, Richard N., 361
Bolt, James F., 316
Bowen, Donald D., 180
Bowen, Howard R., 607, 611
Boyatzis, Richard E., 459
Bradshaw, Thornton, 60
Brigham, Eugene F., 591
Brousseau, Kenneth, 361
Brown, Donaldson, 401–402
Brown, Rex V., 155
Buchanan, Peter T., 298
Buehler, Vernon M., 23
Buffa, Elwood S., 564
Burns, James R., 53
Burns, Tom, 282–283
Burr, Donald, 21
Bylinsky, G., 435

Carroll, Stephen J., 5
Cash, James I., Jr., 538

Cavanagh, Gerald F., 288, 612
Chaffee, Ellen E., 79
Chandler, Alfred D., 106, 180
Christensen, H. Kurt, 361
Churchill, Neil C., 538
Clausen, A. W., 589
Comte, Thomas E., 361
Condon, Thomas J., 316
Cordiner, Ralph, 255
Cunningham, Mary, 316

Dale, Ernest, 240
Dalton, Dan R., 205
David, Fred R., 180
Davis, Gordon B., 538
Davis, Keith, 164, 288, 307, 316,
    394, 397, 400, 409, 477, 609,
    621
Dearden, John, 538
Decker, Richard C., 264
Dickson, Douglas N., 652
Dickson, Gary W., 538
Diebold, John, 621
Dietrich, Noah, 325
Dipboye, Robert L., 337
Donaldson, Gordon, 85
Donaldson, Lex, 288
Donnell, Susan M., 591
Donnelly, James H., Jr., 23

Dowd, Ann Reilly, 79
Driver, Michael J., 361
Drucker, Peter F., 8, 87, 116, 180, 298
Dublin, Robert, 23
Dubose, Lori, 21
Duncan, Jack W., 155
Durant, W. C., 106

Ebert, Ronald J., 563
Eisenhower, Dwight D., 170
Ernst, Harry D., 591

Fanning, W. R., 652
Farmer, Richard N., 626, 652
Fauber, Chairman, 60
Fayol, Henri, 26, 30–34, 54, 240
Ference, Thomas P., 361
Fiedler, Fred E., 337, 450–453
Fielden, John, 477, 485
Fielding, Gordon J., 205
Fiol, C. Marlene, 385
Fitch, H. Gordon, 435
Flamholtz, Eric, 508
Flax, Steven, 240
Flesch, Rudolf, 484
Ford, Henry, Sr., 227
Ford, Henry, II, 325
Fottler, Myron D., 508
Frazer, Douglas A., 253
Frederick, William C., 609, 621
Frederickson, James W., 133, 205
French, Wendell L., 385
Frost, Peter J., 288
Fry, Art, 173

Gabarro, John J., 240
Gantt, Henry L., 26, 28–29, 521, 541
Gellerman, Saul, 616
George, Claude S., Jr., 26
Getty, J. Paul, 579
Ghiselli, Edwin, 440
Giglioni, Giovanni B., 490
Gilbreth, Frank, 26, 28–30, 541
Gilbreth, Lillian, 26, 28–30, 34
Gilmore, C. B., 652
Given, William P., 310
Gladwin, Thomas N., 652
Goggin, William C., 205
Gorbachev, Mikhail, 624
Gordon, William J., 403

Graeff, Claude L., 459
Gray, Edmund R., 79
Green, Charles H., 264
Greenbaum, H. H., 475
Greer, Charles R., 337
Greer, Sarah, 30
Grosse, Robert, 652
Guest, Robert H., 435
Gulick, L., 30
Gutteridge, Thomas G., 361

Hackman, J. Richard, 409
Hagan, Ward, 108
Hall, Douglas T., 361, 417
Hall, James L., 591
Hall, Jay, 591
Hall, Raymond, 329
Hamermesh, Richard G., 79
Harder, Joseph W., 591
Hayes, Robert B., 564
Haynes, Robert S., 435
Heenan, David A., 309
Helmer, Olaf, 121
Herbert, Theodore T., 205
Hersey, Paul, 459
Herzberg, Frederick, 417, 419, 427
Hisrich, Robert D., 180
Hoehn, Siegfried, 530
Hofstede, Geert, 435
Holsapple, Clyde W., 538
Homans, G. C., 9
House, Robert, 452
Huber, George P., 155
Hughes, Howard, 325
Humble, John W., 102, 367
Hunt, Raymond F., 435
Hurst, David K., 23, 459
Hyer, Nancy L., 564

Iacocca, Lee A., 298, 412
Isenberg, Daniel J., 409
Ivancevich, John M., 316

Jackson, John H., 180, 205
Jaeger, Alfred M., 385
James, William, 34
Jauch, Lawrence R., 133
Jenkins, Roger L., 385
Jerdee, Thomas H., 5
Jobs, Steven, 173, 404, 576
Johnson, Ross H., 264
Jones, Thomas M., 621

Kahn, Robert L., 180
Kallman, Ernest A., 150
Kaplan, Robert S., 591
Karasik, Myron S., 538
Katz, Daniel, 180
Katz, Robert L., 322
Keen, Peter G. W., 150, 538
Kelleher, Herbert, 438
Kendall, Donald M., 325
Kepner, Charles H., 155
Kiechel, Walter, III, 240
King, Martin Luther, 208
Klein, Janice A., 435
Kolb, David A., 264
Koontz, Harold, 90, 102, 180, 235, 627, 652
Kotter, John P., 240, 385
Krein, T. J., 240
Kroc, Ray, 130, 437
Kroeber, D. W., 538
Kroop, Dean H., 53
Kuhn, A., 180
Kujawa, Duane, 652

Land, Edwin H., 281, 324
Latham, Gary P., 361, 385
Law, Warren A., 316
Lawler, Edward E., III, 409, 416, 419–421, 435, 591
Lawrence, Paul R., 23, 180, 283
Leontiades, Milton, 133, 337
Levin, Richard I., 384, 591
Lewin, Kurt, 374
Likert, J. G., 444
Likert, Rensis, 296, 440, 442–445
London, Manuel, 361
Lorange, Peter, 79, 133
Lorsch, Jay W., 23, 180, 283, 396
Luthans, Fred, 644
Luther, Martin, 418–419
Lyles, Marjorie A., 385

McArthur, John, 615
McClelland, David C., 422–424
McConkey, Dale D., 459
McCoy, Bowen H., 621
McCreary, Edward A., 155
McFarlan, F. Warren, 508, 538
McFarland, Dalton E., 621
McFarlin, Dean B., 435
McFillen, James M., 409
McGlade, Randy, 79
McGregor, Douglas, 87, 394–396, 398, 400, 409

McIntyre, James M., 264
McKenney, James L., 508, 538
McKinsey, J. O., 582
McMurry, Robert M., 337
Magaziner, Ira C., 621
Mahoney, Thomas A., 5
Main, Jeremy, 652
Malek, Fredric V., 93, 326
March, James G., 23, 180, 240
Mark, M. A., 102
Maslow, Abraham, 415–417, 419
Matteson, Michael T., 23, 54, 316
Matthews, Glenn H., 288
Mayo, Elton, 26, 35, 36
Meyer, Alan D., 151, 155
Michael, Steven R., 508
Mihal, William L., 361
Miles, Raymond E., 394, 398–400
Mills, Peter K., 508
Mills, Quinn D., 316
Miner, John B., 79, 180, 409, 435
Mintzberg, Henry, 45–47, 180, 206, 240, 297, 442
Mitchell, Terence R., 180, 240, 435
Moberg, Dennis J., 288, 612
Montanari, John R., 538, 621
Morgan, Cyril P., 180, 205
Morse, John J., 396
Moses, 166
Mouton, Jane S., 379, 445, 446
Münsterberg, Hugo, 26, 33–34
Murray, Keith B., 621

Naisbitt, John, 72, 180, 533
Near, Janet P., 435
Negandhi, Anant R., 652
Newstrom, John W., 288, 307, 397, 409, 477
Nichols, Ralph G., 484
Nordhoff, Heinz, 324
Nougaim, Khalil, 417
Nussbaum, Bruce, 54

Odiorne, George, 88, 102, 412
Olson, Margrethe H., 538
Osborn, Alex F., 402
O'Toole, James, 288, 621
Ouchi, William, 26, 37, 591
Oxenfelt, Alfred R., 155

Pareto, Vilfredo, 26, 34–36
Parety, Harold, 21
Pascale, Richard T., 48, 337

Pearce, John A., II, 79, 133, 180
Pericles, 280
Perlmutter, Howard V., 309
Perot, Ross, 282, 404
Perritt, Gerald W., 652
Peter, Laurence J., 26, 37, 329
Peters, Thomas J., 7, 26, 37, 280, 442
Pickens, T. Boone, Jr., 298
Pinchot, Gifford, 11, 172
Pine, Randall C., 435
Porter, Lyman W., 205, 394, 400, 409, 419–421
Porter, Michael E., 116, 652
Posner, Barry Z., 591
Posner, Victor, 298
Prince, J. Bruce, 361
Procter, William Cooper, 281
Purcell, Philip, 311
Purcell, Theodore, 614
Pyburn, Philip, 508

Quinn, James Brian, 133, 405

Raia, Anthony P., 102
Reagan, Ronald, 469
Reich, Robert B., 621
Reinharth, Leon, 150
Reizenstein, Richard C., 385
Reuter, Vincent G., 564, 591
Rhode, John G., 591
Rice, Robert W., 435
Richards, Edward P., III, 316
Richards, Max D., 54, 435
Richman, Barry M., 626
Robey, Daniel, 385
Robinson, Richard B., Jr., 79, 133
Rodgers, F. G., 385
Roethlisberger, F. J., 26, 35, 477
Rogers, Carl R., 477
Rowe, Mary P., 484
Rowland, Kendrith M., 316
Rubin, Irwin M., 264
Ruhnau, Heinz, 641
Rush, H. M. F., 378

Saxberg, Borje O., 508
Schein, Edgar H., 316, 394, 484
Schlesinger, Leonard A., 385
Schmidt, Warren H., 447–449, 591
Schonberger, Richard J., 564, 652
Scott, Walter Dill, 26, 34
Scott, William G., 54, 180, 240

Scott Morton, Michael S., 150
Sculley, John, 576
Selye, Hans, 298–299
Seyna, Eugene J., 385
Shafitz, Jay M., 54
Sharman, Graham, 564
Shim, Jae K., 79
Simon, Herbert A., 23, 42, 136, 155, 180, 240
Skinner, B. F., 422
Sloan, Alfred, 401–402
Smith, David E., 385
Smith, Howard L., 508
Smith, Rober B., 60, 108, 282, 558
Sorce, Patricia A., 361
Spendolini, Michael J., 205
Spicer, Michael W., 435
Stalk, George, Jr., 652
Stalker, G. M., 282–283
Stanton, Erwin S., 435
Staw, Barry M., 155
Steiner, George A., 79
Stevens, Leonard A., 484
Stieglitz, Harold, 206
Stodgill, Ralph M., 440
Stoneman, Alan, 324
Stoner, James A. F., 361
Strunk, William, Jr., 484
Stumpf, Stephen A., 361
Sullivan, Jeremiah H., 652
Sundem, G. L., 591
Suttle, J., 416
Sutton, Charlotte Decker, 316

Tannenbaum, Robert, 447–449
Taylor, Frederick Winslow, 25–30, 33, 34, 541
Thierauf, Robert J., 54
Thomson, A. A., Jr., 48
Tichy, Noel M., 385
Todor, William D., 205
Toffler, Alvin, 298–299, 533
Tregoe, Benjamin B., 155
Treybig, Jim, 281
Trist, E. L., 42
Turner, Fred, 437

Ulvila, Jacob W., 155
Umstot, D. D., 381
Urwick, Lyndall, 30, 164–165, 271

Vail, Theodore, 281, 405
Vallee, Jacques, 484

Vancil, Richard F., 264
Van Fleet, David D., 180
Velasquez, Manuel, 288, 612
Von Glinow, Mary Ann, 361
Vrom, Victor H., 418

Walker, James W., 361
Walter, Ingo, 652
Wanous, J. P., 337
Warren, E. Kirby, 361
Waterman, Robert H., Jr., 7, 26, 37, 48, 280, 442

Watson, Charles E., 385
Weber, James, 614
Weber, Max, 26, 34
Weihrich, Heinz, 102, 346, 361, 409, 591
Weiss, Andrew, 564
Wemmerloev, Urbam, 564
Werther, William B., Jr., 316
Weston, J. Fred, 591
Wetherbe, James C., 538
Wexley, Kenneth N., 361, 385
Wheelwright, Steven C., 508, 564
Whinston, Andrew B., 538

White, E. B., 484
White, Louis P., 385
Wolff, Richard H., 316
Wood, Ronald R., 150
Woodman, Lynda A., 538
Woodward, Joan, 283
Wooten, Kevin C., 385
Wozniak, Steve, 173, 576
Wright, John W., 361

Yang, Charles Y., 652
Ylvisaker, William, 108

Product and Organization Index

Acura, 648
Air Force, U.S., 380
Allied Chemical, 615
American Aluminum (ALCOA), 427
American Brake Shoe Company, 310
American Express, 589
American Management Association, 165, 254, 484
American Motors, 11, 109, 553
American Optical, 108
American Telephone and Telegraph (AT&T), 6, 11, 281, 332, 405, 427, 467, 635, 637, 639
Anheuser-Busch, 467
Apple Computer, Inc., 109, 173, 404, 576
Army, U.S., 215, 380

Bank of America, 468, 479
BankAmerica Corporation, 589
Bay Banks, 308
Bell System, 405
Black & Decker, 553
Boeing Aircraft Company, 7, 558, 638

Boston Consulting Group (BCG), 111–113
Bridgestone Tire Company, 633
British Petroleum, 635
Buick, 380, 568
Businessland, Inc., 534

California, University of, 263, 399
Caterpillar Tractor, 116, 281
Charles Schwab & Company, 589
Chevrolet, 380
Chevron, 635
Chrysler Corporation, 253, 298, 412, 553
Citicorp, 7
Coca-Cola Corporation, 7, 638
Compaq, 136
Conference Board, 339
Congress, U.S., 246, 298, 616
Continental Illinois Bank, 616
Control Data Corporation, 467
Corporate Ombudsman Association, 467

Daewoo, 645
Daimler Benz, 242
Dayton-Hudson, 631

Deere Corporation, 558
Defense, U.S. Department of, 68
Delta Airlines, 281
Deskpro 386 computer, 136
Dow Jones, 7
Du Pont Company, 61, 106, 229, 281, 311, 570, 571, 574
DWG, 298

E. F. Hutton, 468, 616
Eastman Kodak Company, 7, 558, 564, 569, 639
Electronic Data Processing, 404
Electronic Data Systems Corporation, 63, 282
Emery Air Freight Corporation, 422
Entenmann bakery firm, 108
Equal Employment Opportunity Commission, 339
Export-Import Bank, 243
Exxon, 7, 471, 635

Fanuc Ltd., 63
Federal Deposit Insurance Corporation, 243
Federal Express, 308

Federal Reserve Board, 186, 243
Firestone Tire & Rubber Company, 633
First Boston, 298
Ford Motor Company, 68, 227, 298, 325, 412, 553, 589, 635
Fuji Films, 569

General Dynamics, 68, 467
General Electric Company, 87, 199, 255, 281, 308, 340, 404, 427, 467, 589, 611, 615, 637
General Foods, 427
General Motors, 11, 60, 63, 106, 108, 109, 192, 229, 252, 274, 282, 311, 322, 380, 401, 404, 428, 429, 553, 558, 568, 589, 635, 639
Gould Inc., 108
GTE Corporation, 6, 637

Hallmark, 62
Harvard Business School, 210, 373, 615
Health, Education, and Welfare, U.S. Department of, 93, 428
Hewlett Packard, 173, 442, 468, 631, 638
Honda, 647–648
Honeywell, 96
Hughes Aircraft Company, 282, 479, 541
Hyundai, 645

Intel, 136
Internal Revenue Service (IRS), 186, 201, 610
International Academy of Management, 644, 645
International Business Machines (IBM), 6, 7, 105, 108, 109, 136, 149, 173, 281, 285–286, 309, 326, 479, 558, 576, 615, 631, 635, 637, 638
International Harvester, 227
Isuzu Motors Ltd., 63
ITALTEL, 447, 637

K mart, 60
Kaiser Aluminum and Chemical Corporation, 541
Kimberly-Clark, 61

Kleenex, 61
Koppers Company, 252

Lever Brothers, 75
Libby, McNeil & Libby, 197
Lincoln Electric, 116
Lockheed Aircraft Corporation, 252
Lucky Goldstar, 645
Lufthansa, 641

McDonald's, 130–131, 437, 638
McDonnell Douglas, 467
Macintosh computer, 109, 150, 576
McKinsey & Company, 37, 38, 47–48, 108, 311
Manville Corporation, 616
Marshall Field and Company, 227
Maryland, University of, 88
Maytag, 281
Mercedes Benz, 242
Merck, 7
Merrill Lynch Relocation Management Inc., 328
Mesa Petroleum, 298
Midvale Steel Company, 25, 28
Mobil Oil Company, 310, 635
Montgomery Ward, 77
Morgan Bank, 7

National Aeronautics and Space Administration (NASA), 62, 468
National Research Council, 35
National Steel, 589
Navy, U.S., 343, 380, 521
New Jersey Bell Telephone Company, 36
Nynex Business Information, 105

Occidental Chemical Company, 199
Office of Federal Contract Compliance, 339
Office of Strategic Services, 332
Oldsmobile, 380
Olivetti, 11, 637, 639

Pacific Bell Telephone Company, 534
PC Convertible, 558
People Express, 21

Pepsico, Inc., 325, 480, 533
Pepsi-Cola Company, 576
Philips, 639
Polaris Weapon System, 521
Polaroid, 281, 324
Porsche, 116
Postal Service, U.S., 186
Post-it notes, 173
Presidential Airways, Inc., 21
Procter & Gamble, 7, 197, 281, 308, 310, 427
Purex Corporation, 324

Quaker Oats Company, 616

Radio Corporation of America (RCA), 60
RAND Corporation, 121
Renault, 11
Revlon, 298
Robert H. Hayes & Associates, Inc., 244
Rolm Corporation, 108
Roman Catholic Church, 170, 246, 618–619
Royal Dutch/Shell Group, 635
Rubbermaid, 7

Saab, 428
Samsung, 645
Sears, Roebuck & Company, 109, 229, 232, 281, 310, 311, 589
Securities and Exchange Commission (SEC), 616
Sibson & Company, 298
Sloan School of Management, 373
Small Business Administration (SBA), 606
Sony Corporation, 630, 633
Southwest Airlines, 438
Stanford Executive Program, 373
Stanford University, 399
Sun Chemical Company, 252
Supreme Court, U.S., 246
Suzuki Motors Company, 63

Tandom, 281
Tavistock Institute, 42
Tennessee Valley Authority (TVA), 243
Texaco, 635
Texas Instruments, 427

3M Corporation, 7, 173
Toyota Motor Corporation, 11, 63,
    109, 253, 639

United Airlines, 442
United Automobile Workers
    (UAW), 253

United States Rubber Company,
    252

Verbatim Company, 569
Volkswagen, 15, 324, 471, 529
Volvo, 322, 428

Warner-Lambert, 108
Western Electric Company, 26, 35

YKK, Inc., 633

Subject Index

Acceptance needs, 416
Accounting firms, management audits by, 581
Achievement, need for, 423
Achievement-oriented leadership, 452
"Acting" managers, 369
Action, principle of, 595
Action plans, 119
Affiliation needs, 416, 423
Age factor in manager selection, 327–328
Aims (*see* Objectives)
Alliance, strategic, 11
Alternative budgets, 516
Alternatives:
  determination of, 72
  development of, 136–138
  evaluation of, 72–73, 138–140
Analytical ability, 324
Appraisal, 339–353
  criteria for, 341–342
  in management by objectives, 87–88
  of managers as managers, 342, 347–352
    common responsibilities, 350–351
    simple questions for, 348–349

Appraisal (*Cont.*):
  principle of, 386–387
  problem of, 340–341
  purposes and uses of, 339–340
  team approach to, 352–353
  trait, 342–344
  against verifiable objectives, 344–347
Approval authorization, chart of, 232–235, 278
Aptitude tests, 331
Assessment centers, 332–333
"Assistant-to" positions, 369
Assumptions, unclarified, 470
Attitudes:
  as communication barriers, 474
  social, 605–606
Audits:
  communication, 474–475
  enterprise self-, 580, 582–583
  management, 580–582
  operational, 520
  social, 610–611
Australia, 629
Austria, 629
Authority, 289–290
  consolidation of, 248
  decentralization of, 218–220

Authority (*Cont.*):
  delegation of, 169, 220–231
    availability of managers, 228
    business dynamics and, 229–230
    clarity of, 221
    to committees, 246–247, 256–257
    control techniques, 228–229
    costliness of decision and, 225
    decentralized performance, 229
    environmental influences on, 230–231
    failure to balance, 267
    functional, 212, 213
    history and culture of enterprise and, 227
    lack of, 267
    management philosophy and, 227–228
    personal attitudes toward, 223–224
    process of, 220–221
    recovery of, 222
    by results expected, 290
    size and character of organization and, 226–227
    uniformity of policy and, 226

Authority delegation
  of (*Cont.*):
    weak, guides for overcoming,
      224–225
    functional, 212–215
      misuse of, 269
    in international environment, 629
    leadership based on, 440–442
    line (*see* Line and staff
      relationships)
    lines of, confusion of lines of in-
      formation with, 267–268
    in operational-management the-
      ory, 31
    parity of responsibility and, 290
    of plural executive, 251–252
    power and, 208–209
    recentralization of, 231
    relationships of, understanding,
      273–274
    without responsibility, 268
    splintered, 221–222
Autocratic leadership, 440, 442
Autocratic model of behavior, 397
Autocratic task management, 446
Avoidance of conflict, 275–278, 377

Balance, principle of, 290–291
Bases of power, 208
Behavioral models, 393–401
  assumptions in, 394
  contrasting, 394–395
  dual-model theory and, 398–400
  eclectic view of, 400–401
  in historical perspective, 397–398
  Theory X and Theory Y,
    395–397
Behavioral sciences, 26, 33–36
Behaviorism, 395
Beliefs, social, 605–606
Benevolent-authoritative management, 443
Bible, 166
Bill of Rights, 612
Board of directors, 251–253
  composition of, 253
Brainstorming, 402–403
Branches of multinationals, 635
Budgets, 61, 69, 73, 510–518
  alternative, 516
  dangers of, 512–513
  effective, 517–518
  milestone, 521
  purpose of, 510
  summary of, 567

Budgets (*Cont.*):
  supplementary, 516
  types of, 511–512
  variable, 69, 513–516
  zero-based, 69, 516–517
Business ethics (*see* Ethics)
Business Portfolio Matrix, 111,
  112–114
Business Week, 7, 11, 72, 298

CAD/CAM (Computer-aided de-
  sign/Computer-aided
  management), 557–558
Capital, 601
Capital expenditure budgets, 512
Capital standards, 493
Career goals, 210
Career strategies, 353–357
Carrot and stick view of motivation,
  414–415
Case approach to management
  analysis, 37, 38, 40
Cash budgets, 512
Centralization, 32, 219–220
CEOs (*see* Chief executive officers)
Certainty, decision making under,
  143–144
Certified management audit,
  581–582
Chairpersons, committee, 258
Change:
  adjustment to, insufficient period
    for, 473
  affecting manager and organiza-
    tion development, 374
  need for, 273
  rate of, 169–170
    delegation and, 229–230
  resistance to, 376
  strategy for, 379
  techniques for initiating, 374–376
  technological, 603–604
Chief executive officers (CEOs):
  financial rewards of, 298
  in international management,
    637
Civil Rights Act (1964), 339
Claimants, 12, 14
Clarification, avoiding conflict by,
  275–278
Coaching, 370
Codetermination, 629
Coercive power, 209
Collegial model of behavior,
  397–398

Colorful writing style, 477
Command, unity of, 32, 290
Commitment principle, 75–76, 157
Committees, 242–261
  avoidance of action by, 249
  compromise as least common de-
    nominator in, 249–250
  consolidation of authority in, 248
  coordination by, 247
  cost of, 249
  delegation of authority to,
    246–247
  deliberation and judgment in,
    244–246
  as developmental technique,
    369–370
  formality of, 243
  functions of, 242–243
  group processes in, 242
  indecision in, 250
  misuse of, 255–256
  motivation through participation
    in, 248
  representation of interest groups
    on, 247
  self-destructiveness of, 250
  splitting of responsibility in,
    250–251
  successful operation of, 256–258
  transmission and sharing of in-
    formation in, 247
  tyranny of minority in, 251
Communication, 461–480
  barriers and breakdowns in,
    470–474
  clarity of, 485
  in committees, 247
  delegation of authority and, 224
  double-loop learning and, 478
  electronic media in, 478–480
  flow of, 466–469
  in groups, 260
  guidelines for improving,
    475–476
  impersonal, 472
  importance of, 461
  integrity of, 485
  in international environment, 471
  listening as key to, 476–477
  manager's need to know and,
    465–466
  in multinational corporations,
    641–642
  noise and feedback in, 464–465
  nonverbal, 470
  oral, 469

Communication (*Cont.*):
  organizational levels and, 167
  of premises, 118–119, 128–129
  process of, 462–464
  purpose of, 461–462
  situational and organizational factors in, 465
  skills in, 324–325
  span of management and, 170
  of strategies, 118
  system of, 14
  written, 469
    improving, 477–478
Communication audit, 474–475
Comparative management, 622–628
  cultural factors and, 625–626
  economic growth and, 623–624
  models of, 626–628
Complex assumptions, 394
Comprehensive appraisal, 345
Compromises:
  in committees, 249–250
  managing conflict by, 377
Computer-aided design (CAD), 557–558
Computer-aided manufacturing (CAM), 557–558
Computers, 480, 531–532
  in decision making, 149–150
  graphics produced by, 371
  networks of, 535
  resistance to application of, 533
Concepts, scientific, 9
Conceptual skill, 323
Conference programs, training in, 371
Conflict:
  avoidance of, 275–278, 377
  managing, 377
  sources of, 376–377
Conformity, pressure toward, 259
Consistency, 111
Constitution, U.S., 606, 612
Consultive management, 443
Contingency approach:
  to international management, 643
  to leadership, 449–455
  to management analysis, 37, 39, 45
Contingency plans, 111
  alternative premises for, 127
  development of, 119
  principle of, 387

Continuous monitoring of performance, 345–346
Control, 17–18, 490–505
  basic process of, 490–492
  budgetary (*see* Budgets)
  critical points of, 492–494, 504, 594
  delegation of authority and, 224, 228–229
  direct, 575–578
  economy of, 505
  efficiency of, 593
  fads in, 11
  as feedback system, 494–495
  feedforward, 497–502
  flexibility of, 504–505, 595
  future-directed, 592
  individuality of, 594
  inventory, 551–553
  leading to corrective action, 505
  in management by objectives, 96–97
  in multinational corporations, 642
  nonbudgetary devices for, 518–520
  objectivity of, 504
  of operations, 545–547
  organizational climate and, 505
  organizational levels and, 167
  of overall performance, 566–567
  planning and, 59, 60, 494, 502–503, 529, 593
    procedures, 526–528
  preventive, 575, 593
    enterprise self-audit, 582–583
    management audit, 581–582
    principle of, 578–580
  principles of, 592–595
  profit and loss, 568–570
  real-time information and, 496
  responsibility for, 592–593
  through return-on-investment approach, 570–575
  strategies and, 109
  tailored to individual managers, 503
  time-event network analysis for, 520–526
Cooperative social systems approach to management analysis, 37, 38, 42
Coordination, 18
Corporate culture (*see* Organization culture)

Correlation analysis, 125
Cost:
  of committees, 248, 258
  of controls, 505
  of organizational levels, 167
Cost benefit analysis, 139
Cost effectiveness analysis, 139–140
Cost leadership strategy, 116
Cost standards, 493
Country club management, 445
CPM (Critical Path Method), 10
Creativity, 401–404
  in decision making, 149
Critical Path Method (CPM), 10
Critical-point control, 492–494, 504, 594
Crosswise communication, 467–468
Custodial model of behavior, 397
Customers, 602–603
  departmentation by, 188–189
Cycles, analysis of, 124

Decentralization, 218–220
  advantages of, 236
  balance as key to, 233, 236
  clarifying, 232–233
  limitations of, 236
  obtaining desired degree of, 231–232
Decision making, 135–152, 297
  under certainty, 143–144
  communication of strategies and, 118
  delegation of authority and, 225
  development of alternatives in, 136–138
  evaluation in, 138–140
    cost effectiveness analysis, 139–140
    marginal analysis, 139
    quantitative and qualitative factors, 138
  experience and, 140–141
  experimentation and, 141–142
  group (*see* Committees)
  importance of, 148
  in international environment, 631
  nonprogrammed, 143
  on products, 543–544
  programmed, 143
  rationality in, 135–136
    "bounded," 136
  research and analysis in, 142–143
  systems approach to, 152

Decision making (*Cont.*):
  under uncertainty, 143–148
    decision trees, 144–145
    preference theory, 145–148
    risk analysis, 144
Decision roles, 46
Decision Support Systems (DSS),
  149–150
Decision theory approach, 37, 38,
  43–44
Decision trees, 144–145
Deductive forecasting method, 123,
  125
Delegation (*see* Authority, delegation of)
Delphi technique of forecasting,
  121
Demassing, 11
Democratic leadership, 440
Departmentation, 164, 182, 290
  centralization and, 220
  choosing patterns of, 199–202
  committees and, 247
  customer, 188–189
  equipment, 189–190
  functional, 183–184
  line and staff relationships ver-
    sus, 210–212
  mixed, 201–202
  objectives and, 201
  by process, 189–190
  by product, 190–192
  by simple numbers, 182
  by territory or geography,
    186–188
  by time, 183
  (*See also* Matrix organization)
Derivative plans, 73
Descriptive principles, 10
Design:
  of production systems, 544
  of products, 544
  skill in, 323
Development (*see* Manager development; Organization
  development; Research and
  development)
Deviation from standards:
  causes of, 576–577
  correction of, 491–492
Diagonal flow of information, 467
Differentiation, 283
  strategy of, 116
Direct control, 575–578
Direction, unity of, 32

Directors (*see* Board of directors)
Discipline, 31
Dissatisfiers, 417
Distribution logistics, 553–554
Distrust as communication barrier,
  472–473
Division of work, 31
Double-loop learning, 478
Downward communication,
  466–467
DSS (Decision Support Systems),
  149–150
Dual-career couples, 328–329
Dual-model theory, 398–400

Economic environment, 600–603
Economic growth, 623–624
Economic order quantity (EOQ),
  552, 553
Economic view of behavior, 394,
  395
Effectiveness, 8
Efficiency, 8
  of controls, 593
  organizational, 289
  of plans, 60–61, 156
Electronic data processing, 480
  procedures analysis and, 528
Electronic media, 478–480
Emotional view of behavior, 394
Empathy, 324–325
Empirical approach:
  to international management,
    642–643
  to management analysis, 37, 38,
    40
Encounter groups, 370–372
Engineering:
  feedforward control in, 497–498
  matrix organization in, 194–197
  value, 556
Enterprise profile, 106
Enterprise self-audit, 580, 582–583
Entertainment, policy on, 65
Entrepreneurs, 172–173
  innovation by, 404–405
  managers as, 297
Environment (*see* External environ-
  ment; International
  environment)
EOQ (economy order quantity),
  552, 553
Equal employment opportunity,
  307–308

Equipment departmentation,
  189–190
Equity, 32
Equity theory, 421–422
Esprit de corps, 32
Esteem needs, 416
Ethics, 611–617
  code of, 615
    for government service, 614
  institutionalizing, 614–615
  standards of, factors raising,
    615–616
  theories of, 612–614
Ethnocentricity, 635, 637
Evaluation:
  in decision making, 138–140
  premature, 471–472
Exception principle, 594
Executive:
  individual, 253–255
  plural, 243, 251–255
  (*See also* Chief executive officers)
Expectancy theory, 418–421
Experience, decision making based
  on, 140–141
Experimentation, decision making
  based on, 141–142
Expertness, 208
Exploitive-authoritative management, 443
Exportation, 635
External environment, 7, 14–15, 19
  career strategy and, 355
  delegation of authority and,
    230–231
  economic, 600–603
  ethics and, 611–617
  legal, 606–607
  political, 606
  rules and procedures imposed
    by, 68
  social, 604–606
  social responsibility and, 607–611
  staffing and, 306–309
  strategies and, 108–109
  technological, 603–604
  (*See also* International
    environment)

Face-to-face meetings, 170–171
Fads, management, 11
Fear:
  as communication barrier, 473
  motivation through, 414–415

Feedback, 109, 378
  in communication, 465
  control as, 494–495
  feedforward versus, 498–499
Feedforward control, 497–502
Field force theory, 374
Financial rewards, 298
  motivation through, 424–425
Financial strategies, 115
Fiscal policy, 602
Fitness programs, 11
Fixed-position production layout, 545
Flexibility:
  of budgets, 69
  of control, 504–505, 595
  of plans, 157
  principle of, 291
Focused strategy, 116–117
Forceful writing style, 477
Forcing, managing conflict by, 377
Forecasting, 71–72
  with Delphi technique, 121
  premising and, 120–121
  sales (see Sales forecasting)
  values and areas of, 121
Formal organization, 162, 163
Fortune 500 companies, 6, 298, 308, 325, 442, 533, 611
Fortune magazine, 7, 110, 297, 308, 589, 624, 638
France, 11, 30, 447, 628–629
Free-rein leadership, 440
Functional authority, 212–215
Functional definition, principle of, 290
Future-directed controls, 592

Gantt charts, 521, 522, 555, 586
Geocentricity, 637
Geographic departmentation, 186–188
Germany, 332
Gifts from suppliers, policy on, 65
Global village, 645
Goals (see Objectives)
Government:
  code of ethics in, 614
  committees in, 243, 246, 247
  fiscal and tax policy of, 602
  problems of program budgeting in, 526
  setting objectives in, 93–94
  social responsibility and role of, 610

Grapevine, 279
Great Britain, 30, 332, 426, 447, 629
Great man school (theory) of leadership, 296, 439
Grid organization development, 379
Group behavior approach to management analysis, 37, 38, 41–42
Groups, 258–261
  advantages of, 261
  characteristics of, 259
  creativity in, 402–403
  decision making in, 149
  disadvantages of, 261
  encounter, 370–372
  functions of, 260–261
  (See also Committees)
Growth strategies, 114

Harmony of objectives, 405–406, 485
Harvard Business Review, 6, 87, 244, 608
Hawthorne studies, 35–36
Hidden agenda, 250
Hierarchy:
  of needs, 415–417
  of objectives, 81–83
  organizational (see Organizational hierarchy)
Honesty of prospective managers, 325
Hong Kong, 625, 640
Horizontal flow of information, 467
Human factors in managing, 392–393
  modification for, 271–272
Human relations managerial model, 398, 399
Human resource management, 381, 398, 399
  (See also Staffing)
Human skill, 323
Human systems, feedforward in, 498

Ideal, the, planning for, 271
Impersonal communication, 472
Impersonal writing style, 477
Impoverished management, 445
Indecisiveness of committees, 250
Industrial activities, 30–31

Industrial psychology, 33–34
Inflexibility, 272–273
Influence, 297
Informal organization, 162–164, 277, 279
  supplemental use of, 485
Information:
  budgets and, 518
  exchange of, in selection of managers, 326–327
  lines of, 267–268
  in operations management, 545–547
  overload of, 473
  real-time, 496
  sources of, 304–305
  for staff, 274
  tailoring, 585
Information technology, 528–535
  challenges created by, 532–535
  computers and, 531–532
Informational roles, 46
INFOWORLD, 149
Initiative, 32
Innovation, 404–405
  in decision making, 149
  planning for, 584
Inputs, 12, 14, 106
  ratio of outputs and, 8
Insight, 402
Instrumental leadership, 452
Intangible standards, 493–494
Integration, organizational, 283
Integrity:
  of communication, 485
  of potential managers, 325
Intellectual leadership, 586–587
Intelligence services, 531
Intelligence tests, 331
Interest groups, 247
International environment, 628–635, 642–646
  authority and codetermination in, 629
  communication in, 471
  contingency approach in, 643
  empirical approach in, 642–643
  ethical standards in, 615–617
  leadership in, 643
  motivation in, 643
  organization development in, 643–644
  planning and, 628–629
  situational approach in, 643
  staffing in, 309

International environment (*Cont.*):
  strategies in, 63
  systems approach in, 643
  technology and, 644
  Theory Z in, 630–634
  (*See also* Comparative management; Multinational corporations)
Interpersonal behavior approach to management analysis, 37, 38, 40–41
Interpersonal roles, 46
Interpersonal skills, 371
Interviews with potential managers, 330–331
Intrapreneurs, 11, 172–173
Intuition, 401–402
Inventions, managerial, 586
Inventory planning and control, 551–553
Investment decisions, 150, 151
  for new products, 145
Italy, 447, 629

Japan, 328, 558–559, 569, 623–625, 629–634, 643, 645
  automobile industry in, 60, 63
  innovation in, 405
  productivity in, 8, 298, 553
  quality circles in, 11, 557
Job content, 417
Job definition, principle of, 386
Job design, 318, 321–322
  managerial skills required by, 320–321
Job enlargement, 427
Job enrichment, 427–429
Job requirements (*see* Position requirements)
Job rotation, 369
Joint ventures, 635
Junior boards, 369–370
Jury of executive opinion sales forecasting method, 123
Just-in-time inventory system, 553
Justice, theory of, 612

Kanban systems, 553
Key managers, selection of, 311–312
Key result areas, 81
Korea, 60, 602, 625, 645

Labor, 602
LANs (local area networks), 558
Leadership, 17, 18, 297, 392, 437–455
  based on authority, 440–442
  as continuum, 447–448
  definition of, 437–438
  facilitation of, 291
  fads in, 11
  group, 260
  harmonizing objectives as key to, 405–406
  ingredients of, 438–439
  intellectual, 586–587
  in international management, 643
  managerial grid and, 445–447
  motivation and, 430
  in multinational corporations, 640–642
  organization culture and, 281–282
  principles of, 485
  situational approach to, 449–455
    contingency model, 450–452
    path-goal approach, 452–455
  systems of management and, 442–445
  trait approaches to, 439–440
Learning, double-loop, 478
Legal environment, 606–607
Legitimate power, 208
Licensing agreements, international, 635
Lifetime employment, 630
Limiting factor, 137–138
Line and staff relationships, 209–212
  benefits of using staff in, 215–217
  careless application of, 268–269
  departmentation versus, 210–212
  effective staff work in, 273–275
  limitations on staff in, 217–218
  nature of, 209–210
Line committees, 243
Linear programming, 551
Listening, 476–477
  poor, 471–472
Lively writing style, 477
Local area networks (LANs), 558
Logical formulation, 402
Logistics of distribution, 553–554
Long-range plans, 76–77
  in management by objectives, 88

Management:
  definition of, 4–8
  span of (*see* Span of management)
Management analysis, 37–50
  case approach to, 37, 38, 40
  contingency approach to, 37, 39, 45
  decision theory approach to, 37, 38, 43–44
  empirical approach to, 37, 38, 40
  group behavior approach to, 37, 38, 41–42
  interpersonal behavior approach to, 37, 38, 40–41
  management science approach to, 44–45
  managerial roles approach to, 37, 39, 45–47
  mathematical approach to, 37, 39, 44–45
  operational approach to, 37, 39, 48–50
  7-S approach to, 37, 39, 47–48
  situational approach to, 37, 39, 45
  systems approach to, 44
    cooperative, 42
    sociotechnical, 42–43
Management audit, 580–582
Management by objectives (MBO), 87–92, 94–98
  benefits of, 96–97
  in government, 93, 94
  long-range planning in, 88
  performance appraisal in, 87–88
  process of, 89–92
  short-term goals and motivation in, 88
  systems approach to, 88–89
  weaknesses of, 97–98
Management by Walking Around (MBWA), 442
Management contracts, international, 635
Management Information System (MIS), 149, 150, 528, 529
Management inventory, 301–304
Management science, 8–9, 37, 39, 44–45
  cultural differences and, 625
  elements of, 9–12
Management techniques, 10–12
  fads versus, 11
Management theory, 9, 25–50

Management theory (*Cont.*):
  behavioral sciences and, 26, 33–36
  cultural differences and, 625
  operational, 26, 30–33
  patterns of analysis in (*see* Management analysis)
  recent contributions to, 37
  role of, 10
  scientific management in, 25–30
  unified global, 642–646
Manager development, 363, 387
  acceleration of, 584
  changes affecting, 374
  failures of, 363–364
  internal and external training in, 370–374
  on-the-job training in, 368–370
  operational approach to, 364–366
  process of, 366–368
Managerial appraisal (*see* Appraisal)
Managerial grid, 445–447
Managerial roles approach to management analysis, 37, 39, 45–47
Managerial skills:
  job design and, 321–322
  organizational hierarchy and, 322–324
Managerial training, 363
Managing:
  defining job of, 296–297
  rewards of, 297–298
  stress in, 298–299
Manpower Report of the President, 305
Manufacturing automation protocol (MAP), 557–558
Marginal analysis, 139
Marketing strategies, 115–116
Material, budgeting of, 511–512
Material order, 32
Material requirement planning, 553
Mathematical approach to management analysis, 37, 39, 44–45
Mathematical models, 125
  in operations research, 548–550
Matrix organization, 193–198
  in engineering, 194–197
  guidelines for, 198
  problems with, 198
  in product management, 197
  in research and development, 196–197
  variations in practice of, 196
MBO (*see* Management by objectives)

MBWA (Management by Walking Around), 442
Mechanistic management system, 282
Membership on committees, 257
Mexico, 602
Microcomputers, 532
Milestone budgeting, 521
Minority, tyranny of, 251
Minutes, committee, 258
MIS (*see* Management Information System)
Missions of enterprise, 61–62, 608
Money as motivator, 424–425
Monthly Labor Review, 305
Motivation, 411–430
  carrot and stick view of, 414–415
  complexity of, 413–414
  definition of, 411
  differences between satisfaction and, 414
  equity theory of, 421–422
  expectancy theory of, 418–421
  in groups, 260
  hierarchy of needs theory of, 415–417
  in international environment, 643
  job enrichment and, 427–429
  in management by objectives, 88
  motivation-hygiene approach to, 417
  need-want-satisfaction chain in, 411–413
  needs theory of, 422–424
  through participation on committees, 248
  principle of, 485
  systems approach to, 430
  techniques of, 424–427
    money, 424–425
    participation, 425–426
    quality of working life, 426–427
Motivators, 413–414, 417
Multinational corporations, 635–642
  advantages of, 637
  challenges for, 638
  control in, 642
  examples of, 635
  leadership in, 640–642
  organization in, 639–640
  planning in, 638–639
  staffing in, 640
  successful, 637–638

Multiple management, 369

Navigational change, principle of, 157
Need-want-satisfaction chain, 411–413
Needs, hierarchy of, 415–417
Needs theory of motivation, 422–424
Networks:
  computer, 535
  local area, 558
  of objectives, 83–86
  time-event (*see* Time-event network analysis)
New products, investment in, 145
Noise, 464
Nonprogrammed decisions, 143
Nonverbal communication, 470

Objective standards, span of management and, 169
Objectives, 48, 61–63, 81
  action plans and, 119
  appraisal of performance in accomplishing, 341–342, 344–347
  conflict over, 377
  contribution of plans to, 156
  departmentation and, 201
  establishment of, 71
  failure of development efforts to support, 363–364
  harmonizing, 405–406, 485
  hierarchy of, 81–83
  management by (*see* Management by objectives)
  multiplicity of, 86–87
  network of, 83–86
  principle of, 156
  rational approach to achievement of, 73–77
  recycling, 92
  setting, 83, 92–94
    difficulty of, 97
    in government, 93–94
    guidelines for, 94
    preliminary, by top management, 89–91
    quantitative and qualitative, 92–93
    for subordinates, 91–92

Objectives (*Cont.*):
  short-term, 88
    emphasis on, 97–98
  of staffing, 386
  as standards, 494
  strategies and, 108
  of training, 387
  unity of, 289
Ombudsperson, 467
On-the-job training, 368–370
Open competition, policy of, 311, 387
Operational audits, 520
Operational management, 37, 39, 48–50
  functional authority in, 213–214
  premises in, 364–366
  systems approach to, 12–15
  theory of, 26, 30–33
  (*See also* Production and operations management)
Operations research, 547–555, 644
  concept of, 547
  distribution logistics and, 553–554
  essentials of, 547–548
  inventory planning and control in, 551–553
  limitations of, 554–555
  linear programming in, 551
  procedure of, 548–551
Opportunities, awareness of, 71
Oral communication, 470
Organic management system, 283
Organization, 16–18, 162
  climate of (*see* Organizational climate)
  conflict and structure of, 377
  contingencies in, 282–283
  culture of (*see* Organization culture)
  departmental (*see* Departmentation)
  ensuring understanding of, 278–279
  fads in, 11
  formal, 162, 163, 277
  function of communication in, 462
  inflexibility of, 272–273
  informal, 162–164, 277, 279
    supplemental use of, 485
  intrapreneurs in, 172–173
  levels of (*see* Organizational levels)

Organization (*Cont.*):
  logic of, 174
  management as essential for, 5
  matrix (*see* Matrix organization)
  misconceptions about, 174
  mistakes in, 266–271
  in multinational corporations, 639–640
  planning of, 272
  principles of, 289–291
  size and character of, 226–227
  span of management and (*see* Span of management)
  structure and process of, 173–174, 289–290
  suitability of structure of, 593
  use of committees in, 243–244
Organization charts, 275–277
Organization culture, 11, 280–282
  decision making and, 149
  delegation and, 227
Organization development (OD), 306, 363, 377–381
  in action, 380–381
  changes affecting, 374
  in internationl environment, 643–644
  methods of, 379–380
  process of, 378–379
Organizational climate:
  control and, 505
  dependence of motivation on, 430
Organizational conflict, 376–377
Organizational diagnosis, 378
Organizational hierarchy:
  managerial skills and, 322–324
  setting objectives and, 83
Organizational levels, 164–168, 171
  communication and, 474
  delegation of authority and, 290
  impact of computers on, 531–532
  problems with, 166–167
Organizational roles, 162
  clarification of, 91, 96
Organizational socialization, 334
Organizational strategies, 114
Orientation of new employees, 334
Outputs, 15
  ratio of inputs and, 8
Outside employment, policy on, 65
Overorganization, 270–271

Parkinson's Law, 10

Participation:
  in budgeting, 517–518
  motivation through, 248, 425–426
Participative-group management, 443
Participative leadership, 440, 442, 452
Passive writing style, 477
Past performance of managers, 325
Path-goal approach to leadership, 452–455
Paying for performance, 11
Perception, selective, 473–474
Peformance:
  appraisal of (*see* Appraisal)
  measurement of, 491
    direct control and, 577
    management fundamentals for, 579
    rewards and, 585
  paying for, 11
  periodic reviews of, 345
Personal commitment, 96
Personal computers, 532
Personal dignity, importance of, 393
Personal goals, long-range, 353–355
Personal observation, control through, 520
Personal profile, preparation of, 353
Personal risk, 147–148
Personal values, 149
Personal writing style, 477
Personality tests, 332
Personnel strategies, 114–115
PERT (*see* Program Evaluation and Review Technique)
Peter Principle, 329
Phenomenological view of behavior, 395
Physical standards, 493
Physical stress, 299
Placement of staff, 305–306, 327
Planned progression training technique, 368
Planning, 16, 18, 58–77, 156–157
  clarity of, 169
  by committees, 247
  of communication, 470
  contingency (*see* Contingency plans)

Planning (*Cont.*):
  contribution to purpose and objectives of, 58
  control and, 59, 60, 494, 502–503, 526–529, 593
  efficiency and, 60–61, 156
  fads in, 11
  failure of, 266–267
  flexible, 157
  framework for, 105–106, 156
  for ideal, 271
  for innovation, 584
  in international environment, 628–629
  inventory, 551–553
  in management by objectives, 88
  modification for human factor in, 271–272
  in multinational corporations, 638–639
  operational, 106, 543–545
  of organization structure, 272
  organizational levels and, 167
  pervasiveness of, 59–60
  primacy of, 58–59, 156
  of procedures, 526–528
  process of, 73–77, 156–157
  short-range: long-range coordination with, 76–77
    strategies and, 109
  steps in, 70–73
  strategic (*see* Strategies)
  structure of, 156
  types of, 61–69
    budgets, 69
    objectives, 62–63
    policies, 64–66
    procedures, 66–67
    programs, 68–69
    purposes or missions, 61–62
    rules, 67, 68
    strategies, 63
Plural executive, 243, 251–253
  individual executive versus, 253–255
Pluralistic society, 600
Policies, 61, 64–66, 105
  committees and, 247
  framework of, 156
  plural executive and, 252–253
  uniformity of, 226
Political environment, 606
Polycentricity, 637
Portfolio Matrix (*see* Business Portfolio Matrix)
Position descriptions, 277–278

Position requirements, 318–321
  matching qualifications with, 325–329
Power, 297
  authority and, 208–209
  communication and, 474
  need for, 423
Predictive principles, 10
Preference theory, 145–148
Premature evaluation, 471–472
Premises:
  development of, 71–72
    communication and, 118–119
  effective, 126–128
  forecasting and, 120–121, 122
  principle of, 156
Preventive control (*see* Control, preventive)
Price levels, 602
Pricing, policies on, 65
Principles:
  of management, 10
  scientific, 9
Privacy Act (1974), 331
Problem recognition, 378
Problem-solving ability, 324
Problem-solving approach to conflict, 377
Procedures, 61, 66–67
  control of, 526–528
Process consultation, 379
Process departmentation, 189–190
Process production layout, 545
Product lines, application of return on investment to, 571–573
Product management, 197
Product strategies, 115
Production and operations management, 541–547
  future of, 558–559
  information system for, 545–547
  planning in, 543–545
Productivity, 8, 540–541
  CAD/CAM and MAP and, 557–558
  international differences in, 623–624
  quality circles and, 556–557
  time-event networks and, 555–556
  value engineering and, 556
  work simplification and, 556
  (*See also* Operations research)
Products:
  budgets for, 511–512
  decision making on, 543–544

Products (*Cont.*):
  departmentation by, 190–192
  design of, 544
  new, investment in, 145
Professional goals, long-range, 353–355
Proficiency tests, 331
Profit and loss controls, 568–570
Program budgeting, 69, 525–526
Program Evaluation and Review Technique (PERT), 10, 497, 520–525, 555, 586
Program standards, 493
Programmed decisions, 143
Programs, 61, 68–69
Progress reviews, 345
Project-based production layout, 545
Promotion, 305–306, 327
  from within, 309–311
Psychological needs, 415–416
Psychological stress, 299
Psychology, industrial, 33–34
Public relations strategies, 115
Punishments, rewards and, 414–415
Purpose of enterprise, 58, 61–62
  strategies and, 108

Qualifications, matching position requirements with, 325–329
Qualitative objectives, 92–93
Quality circles, 11, 556–557
Quality of working life (QWL) programs, 426–427
Quantitative factors, 138
Quantitative objectives, 92–93

Rational-economic assumptions, 394
Rationality, 135–136
  "bounded," 136
Reading in training programs, 372
Real-time information, 496
Recruitment, 305–306, 326
Referent power, 208
Regiocentricity, 637
Remuneration, 32
Reports, 519–520
Research and analysis approach to decision making, 142–143
Research and development, 585–586
  matrix organization in, 196–197

Responsibility:
  absoluteness of, 290
  without authority, 268
  common, of managers, 350–351
  for control, 592–593
  direct control and, 577
  in operational-management the-
    ory, 31
  parity of authority and, 290
  social, 607–611
  splitting of, 250–251
  for staffing, 312, 329
Responsiveness, social, 607–608
Retention of information, poor,
  471
Return on investment (ROI),
  570–575
Revenue and expense budgets, 511
Revenue standards, 493
Reward power, 208
Rewards:
  of effective delegation, 225
  financial, 298, 424–425
  of managing, 297–298
  performance measurement and,
    585
  punishments and, 414–415
Rights, ethical theory based on, 612
Risk:
  analysis of, 144
  in preference theory, 146–148
ROI (return on investment),
  570–575
Roles:
  multiplicity of, 392
  (See also Organizational roles)
Rules, 61, 67–68

Safety needs, 416
Sales, production layout to facili-
  tate, 545
Sales budgets, 511
Sales force composite sales forecast-
  ing method, 123–124
Sales forecasting, 122–127
  methods of, 123–126
  nature and use of, 122
  in practice, 126–127
Satisfaction, differences between
  motivation and, 414
Satisficing, 136
Satisfiers, 417
Scalar chain, 32
Scalar principle, 209, 289
Scientific management, 25–30

Scientific method, 9
Security needs, 416
Selection of managers (see Staffing,
  selection process in)
Selective perception, 473–474
Self-actualization, 394, 395
  need for, 416
Self-destructiveness of committees,
  250
Self-motivation, 412
Semantics:
  clarification of, 645
  distortions in, 470–471
Sensitivity training, 370–372
Service departments, misunder-
  standing function of, 269–270
Service strategies, 115
7-S approach to management anal-
  ysis, 37, 39, 47–48
Short-range plans (see Planning,
  short-range)
Singapore, 625, 640
Situational approach:
  to international management,
    643
  to leadership, 449–455
  to management analysis, 37, 39,
    45
Size:
  of committees, 257
  of organization, 226
Smoothing, managing conflict by,
  377
Social audit, 610–611
Social environment, 604–606
Social needs, 394
Social order, 32
Social responsibility, 607–611
Social responsiveness, 607–608
Social systems theory, 36
Socialization of new employees, 334
Sociological approach to manage-
  ment analysis, 34–35
Sociotechnical systems approach to
  management analysis, 37, 38,
  42–43
South Africa, 618
Soviet Union, 624
Space, budgeting of, 511–512
Span of management, 164–172
  choice of, 164–166
  factors influencing, 168–172
  narrow, 165
  principle of, 167, 289
  wide, 165
Spanish-American War, 215

Speech recognition devices, 533
Splintered authority, 221–222
Staff (see Line and staff
  relationships)
Staff committees, 243
Staffing, 17, 18, 296–312
  definition of, 296
  fads in, 11
  in multinational corporations,
    640
  principles of, 386–387
  responsibility for, 312, 329
  selection process in, 305–306,
    318–334
    assessment centers, 332–333
    interviews, 330–331
    job design, 318, 320–322
    limitations of, 333–334
    matching qualifications with
      position requirements,
      325–329
    orienting and socializing new
      employees, 334
    position requirements, 318–321
    skills and personal charac-
      teristics, 322–325
    tests, 331–332
  situational factors affecting,
    306–312
    external environment, 306–309
    open competition policy, 311
    promotion from within,
      309–311
    selection of key managers from
      outside, 311–312
  systems approach to, 299–306
    career planning, 306
    external and internal informa-
      tion sources, 304–305
    factors affecting requirements,
      301
    management inventory,
      301–304
    managerial appraisal, 306
    promotion, 305–306
    recruitment, 305–306
    training and development, 306
  top management support of, 312
Standards:
  budgetary, 518
  deviations from, 491–492
    causes of, 576–577
  establishment of, 490–491
  ethical, 615–617
  principle of, 594
  types of, 492–494

Statistical data, 518–519
Statistical forecasting methods, 123, 124–125
Status, communication and, 474
Stockless production, 553
Storage, production layout to facilitate, 545
Strategic alliance, 11
Strategic business units (SBUs), 199
Strategic control, 494
Strategies, 61, 63, 104
  in Business Portfolio Matrix, 112–114
  cost leadership, 116
  in declining industries, 110
  differentiation, 116
  financial, 114
  focused, 116–117
  framework of, 156
  growth, 114
  implementation of, 117–120
    failure of, 117–118
    successful, 118–120
  international, 63
  marketing, 115–116
  organizational, 114
  personnel, 114–115
  process for formulating, 106–111
  product or service, 115
  public relations, 115
  in TOWS Matrix, 111–113
Stress, 298–299
  management of, 11, 371
Subordinates:
  behavioral models for, 398–400
  setting objectives for, 91–92
  training of, 168–169
  willingness to trust, 224
Subordination:
  of individual to general interest, 32
  multiply, 269
Subsidiaries of multinational corporations, 635
Supplemental monthly budget, 516
Suppliers, gifts from, policy on, 65
Supportive leadership, 452
Supportive model of behavior, 397
Survey feedback method of organization development, 379
Sweden, 322, 428
Synectics, 403
Systems approach, 12–15, 18–19, 26, 36, 37, 39, 44
  cooperative, 37, 38, 42

Systems approach (*Cont.*):
  decision making and, 152
  to international management, 643
  to management by objectives, 88–89
  to motivation, 430
  to procedures, 528
  sociotechnical, 37, 38, 42–43
  to staffing, 299–306

T-Groups, 370–372
Tactics, 106
Taipei, 640
Taiwan, 602, 625
Tax policy, 602
Team approach to performance appraisal, 352–353
Team building, 379
Team management, 445
Technical skill, 323
Technological environment, 603–604
  international, 644
Telecommunications, 479, 533–534
Teleconferencing, 479–480
Temporary positions, training in, 369
Tenure, stability of, 32
Territorial departmentation, 186–188
Tests in manager selection process, 331–332
Thailand, 471
Theory X, 395–397
Theory Y, 395–397
Theory Z, 37, 630–634
Threat:
  as communication barrier, 472–473
  motivation through, 414–415
Time:
  budgeting of, 511–512
  costs in, of committees, 249
  departmentation by, 183
  management of, 371
  TOWS Matrix and, 113
  unwarranted expenditure of, 578
Time-event network analysis, 521
  productivity and, 555–556
Top management:
  budgets and, 517
  computers and, 532, 533
  effective staffing and, 312

Top management (*Cont.*):
  manager development and, 365
  strategy formulation by, 106, 108
  (*See also* Chief executive officers)
TOWS Matrix, 111–113
Training, 306, 387
  in conference programs, 371
  evaluation of, 373–374
  managerial, 363
    at all levels, 365
    methods determined by needs for, 365
  on-the-job, 368–370
  sensitivity, 370–372
  special, 372–373
  of subordinates, 168–169
  transfer of, 372–373
  in university management programs, 372, 373
  variety of needs for, 365
Trait appraisal, 342–344
Transmission of information, loss by, 471
Trends, analysis of, 124

Uncertainty:
  decision making under, 143–148
  deviations from standards due to, 576–577
Unconscious scanning, 401
Underorganization, 270–271
Unity:
  of command, 32, 290
  of objective, 289
University management programs, 372, 373
Upward communication, 467
  lack of, 468
Users' expectation sales forecasting method, 123, 124
Utilitarian theory, 612

Value engineering, 556
Values:
  personal, 149
  social, 605–606, 610
Variable budgets, 69, 513–516
Verification of insight, 402
Vietnam War, 606
Vocational tests, 332

Wellness programs, 11

West Germany, 447, 628, 629
Whole person, consideration of,
    393
Willingness to learn, 584
Women:
    career opportunities for, 308
    in international environment, 637
    married, in work force, 328–329

Women (*Cont.*):
    in organizational hierarchy, 6
Work, division of, 31
Work activities of managers, 297
Work simplification, 556
Work teams, job design for, 321,
    322
World War II, 170, 332, 606

Written communication, 470
    improving, 477–478

Zero-base budgeting, 69, 516–517
Zero inventory, 553